We the People

An Introduction to American Politics

ESSENTIALS
★ edition ★
13

We the People

An Introduction to American Politics

★ **BENJAMIN GINSBERG**
THE JOHNS HOPKINS UNIVERSITY

★ **THEODORE J. LOWI**
LATE OF CORNELL UNIVERSITY

★ **MARGARET WEIR**
BROWN UNIVERSITY

★ **CAROLINE J. TOLBERT**
UNIVERSITY OF IOWA

★ **ANDREA L. CAMPBELL**
MASSACHUSETTS INSTITUTE OF TECHNOLOGY

★ **ROBERT J. SPITZER**
SUNY CORTLAND

W. W. NORTON & COMPANY
Independent Publishers Since 1923

W. W. Norton & Company has been independent since its founding in 1923, when William Warder Norton and Mary D. Herter Norton first published lectures delivered at the People's Institute, the adult education division of New York City's Cooper Union. The firm soon expanded its program beyond the Institute, publishing books by celebrated academics from America and abroad. By midcentury, the two major pillars of Norton's publishing program—trade books and college texts—were firmly established. In the 1950s, the Norton family transferred control of the company to its employees, and today—with a staff of five hundred and hundreds of trade, college, and professional titles published each year—W. W. Norton & Company stands as the largest and oldest publishing house owned wholly by its employees.

Editor: Peter Lesser
Project Editor: Laura Dragonette
Associate Editor: Anna Olcott
Developmental Editor: John Elliott
Manuscript Editor: Sarah Johnson
Managing Editor, College: Marian Johnson
Managing Editor, College Digital Media: Kim Yi
Production Manager, College: Elizabeth Marotta
Media Editor: Spencer Richardson-Jones
Media Editorial Assistant: Lena Nowak-Laird
Media Project Editor: Marcus Van Harpen

Marketing Manager, Political Science: Ashley Sherwood
Art Director: Lissi Sigillo
Text Design: Jen Montgomery
Photo Editor: Thomas Persano
Photo Researcher: Donna Ranieri
Director of College Permissions: Megan Schindel
Permissions Consultant: Elizabeth Trammell
Information Graphics: Kiss Me I'm Polish LLC, New York
Composition: Graphic World, Inc.
Manufacturing: Transcontinental

Permission to use copyrighted material is included in the credits section of this book, which begins on page A89.

Library of Congress Cataloging-in-Publication Data

Names: Ginsberg, Benjamin, author. | Lowi, Theodore J., author. |
   Weir, Margaret, author. | Tolbert, Caroline J., author. | Campbell,
   Andrea Louise, 1966- author.
Title: We the people : an introduction to American politics / Benjamin
   Ginsberg, The Johns Hopkins University, Theodore J. Lowi, late of
   Cornell University, Margaret Weir, Brown University, Caroline J.
   Tolbert, University of Iowa, Andrea L. Campbell, Massachusetts Insitute
   of Technology.
Description: Thirteenth edition. | New York : W.W. Norton & Company, [2021] |
   Includes bibliographical references and index.
Identifiers: LCCN 2020051064 | ISBN 9780393427035 (hardcover)
Subjects: LCSH: United States—Politics and government—Textbooks.
Classification: LCC JK276.G55 2021 | DDC 320.473—dc23
LC record available at https://lccn.loc.gov/2020051064

ISBN: 978-0-393-42702-8

W. W. Norton & Company, Inc., 500 Fifth Avenue, New York, N.Y. 10110
www.wwnorton.com

W. W. Norton & Company Ltd., 15 Carlisle Street, London W1D 3BS

1 2 3 4 5 6 7 8 9 0

To:

Teresa Spitzer

Sandy, Cindy, and Alex Ginsberg

David, Jackie, Eveline, and Ed Dowling

Dave, Marcella, Logan, and Kennah Campbell

Contents

2 ★ The Founding and the Constitution 28

4 ★ Civil Liberties 88

5 ★ Civil Rights 118

PART II POLITICS

6 ★ Public Opinion   148

7 ★ The Media   180

8 ★ Political Parties and Interest Groups   212

9 ★ Participation, Campaigns, and Elections 250

PART III INSTITUTIONS

10 ★ Congress 290

13 ★ The Federal Courts 394

PART IV POLICY

14 ★ Domestic Policy 428

15 ★ Foreign Policy   462

Appendix

Preface

he coronavirus pandemic and the racial injustice protests raging across the nation vividly display the relevance of government to the lives of ordinary Americans—even to those normally absorbed by school, work, and family. These profound events also reaffirm the commitment of this book to exploring the fundamental democratic question: Why should we be engaged with government and politics? Through the first 12 editions, we sought to answer this question by making the text directly relevant to the lives of the students who would be reading it. We tried to make politics interesting by demonstrating that students' concerns are at stake and that they therefore need to take a personal, even selfish, interest in the outcomes of government. With many students newly attentive and energized, we realize that they need guidance in how to become politically engaged. Beyond providing students with a core of political knowledge, we show them how they can apply that knowledge as participants in the political process. The (**NEW**) How To sections in Chapters 1, 3, 6, 7, 8, 9, 10, and 12 help achieve that goal.

As events from the past several years have reminded us, "what government does" inevitably raises questions about political participation and political equality. The size and composition of the electorate, for example, affect who is elected to public office and what policy directions the government will pursue. Challenges to election administration, from the reliability of voting machines, to the ability of local officials to handle the many complications of running a voting operation during a global pandemic, became important in the 2020 election. Many questions arose about the integrity of the voting process, from fears of foreign attacks to concerns that there was not enough mail-in voting—or too much. Fierce debates about the policies of the Trump administration have heightened students' interest in politics. Other recent events have underscored how Americans from different backgrounds experience politics. Arguments about immigration became contentious as the nation once again debated the question of who is entitled to be an American and have a voice in determining what the government does. Debates about who benefited from pandemic relief legislation—and who slipped through the cracks—raised questions about which interests have effective voices in government policy. And charges that the police often use excessive violence against members of minority groups have raised questions about whether the government treats all Americans equally. Reflecting all of these trends, this new Thirteenth Edition shows more than any other book on the market (1) how students are connected to government, (2) why students should think critically about government and politics, and (3) how Americans from different backgrounds experience and shape politics.

To help us explore these themes, Professor Andrea Campbell has joined us as the most recent in a group of distinguished coauthors. Professor Campbell's scholarly work focuses on the ways in which government and politics affect the lives of ordinary citizens. Among her contributions are new chapter introductions that focus on stories of individuals and how government has affected them. Many Americans, particularly the young, can have difficulty seeing the role of government in their everyday lives. Indeed, that's a chief explanation of low voter participation among younger citizens. The new chapter openers profile various individuals and illustrate their interactions with government, from residents of Seattle who used an experimental government voucher program to run for city council (Chapter 9), to a small business owner receiving relief payments during the coronavirus pandemic (Chapter 10), to a convict-turned-lawyer fighting to restore former felons' voting rights (Chapter 5). Several chapters highlight the racial injustice protests following the killing of George Floyd in May 2020, and many show how the pandemic affects ordinary Americans and their interactions with government.

Several other elements of the book also help show students why politics and government should matter to them. These include:

- **(NEW) How To guides** feature interviews with political experts to provide students with concrete advice about how to participate in politics. These guides offer easy-to-follow instructions about getting involved in politics in effective ways.

- **Who Participates? infographics** show students how different groups of Americans participate in key aspects of politics and government, using engaging graphics and thought-provoking questions. The InQuizitive course includes accompanying exercises that encourage students to engage with these features.

- **America Side by Side boxes** in every chapter use data figures and tables to provide a comparative perspective. By comparing political institutions and behavior across countries, students gain a better understanding of how specific features of the American system shape politics.

- **Up-to-date coverage**, with more than 15 pages and numerous graphics on the 2020 elections, including a 7-page section devoted to analysis of these momentous elections in Chapter 9, as well as updated data, examples, and other information throughout the book.

- **What Do You Think? chapter conclusions** ask students to relate the chapter content and the personal profiles that begin each chapter to fundamental questions about the American political system and to reflect on the significance of government to the lives of individuals.

- **(NEW) Weekly News Quiz feature** engages students with contemporary political news stories (in print, video, or podcast form) and the key concepts of the course. The Weekly News Quiz is supported by assessment and suggestions for classroom use.

- **This Thirteenth Edition is accompanied by InQuizitive**, Norton's award-winning formative, adaptive online quizzing program. The InQuizitive course for *We the People* guides students through questions organized around the text's chapter learning objectives to ensure mastery of the core information and to help with assessment. More information and a demonstration are available at digital.wwnorton.com/wethepeople13ess.

We note with regret the passing of Theodore Lowi as well as Margaret Weir's decision to step down from the book. We miss them but continue to hear their voices and to benefit from their wisdom in the pages of our book. We also continue to hope that our book will itself be accepted as a form of enlightened political action. This Thirteenth Edition is another chance. It is an advancement toward our goal. We promise to keep trying.

Acknowledgments

We are pleased to acknowledge the many colleagues who had an active role in criticism and preparation of the manuscript. Our thanks go to:

Amy Acord, Lone Star College–CyFair

Janet Adamski, University of Mary Hardin-Baylor

Craig Albert, Augusta University

Maria J. Albo, University of North Georgia

Andrea Aleman, University of Texas at San Antonio

Stephen P. Amberg, University of Texas at San Antonio

Molly Andolina, DePaul University

Lydia Andrade, University of the Incarnate Word

Milan Andrejevich, Ivy Tech Community College

Greg Andrews, St. Petersburg College

Steve Anthony, Georgia State University

Brian Arbour, John Jay College, CUNY

Phillip Ardoin, Appalachian State University

Gregory Arey, Cape Fear Community College

Juan F. Arzola, College of the Sequoias

Joan Babcock, Northwest Vista College

Ellen Baik, University of Texas–Pan American

Ross K. Baker, Rutgers University

Thomas J. Baldino, Wilkes University

Evelyn Ballard, Houston Community College

Robert Ballinger, South Texas College

Alexa Bankert, University of Georgia

M. E. Banks, Virginia Commonwealth University

Mary Barnes-Tilley, Blinn College

Nathan Barrick, University of South Florida

Robert Bartels, Evangel University

Nancy Bednar, Antelope Valley College

Christina Bejarano, University of Kansas

Paul T. Bellinger, Jr., Stephen F. Austin State University

Annie Benifield, Lone Star College–Tomball

Donna Bennett, Trinity Valley Community College

Sarah Binder, Brookings Institution

David Birch, Lone Star College–Tomball

Daniel Birdsong, University of Dayton

Jeff Birdsong, Northeastern Oklahoma A&M College

Paul Blakelock, Lone Star College–Kingwood

Melanie J. Blumberg, California University of Pennsylvania

Louis Bolce, Baruch College

Matthew T. Bradley, Indiana University–Kokomo

Amy Brandon, El Paso Community College

Phil Branyon, University of North Georgia

Mark Brewer, University of Maine

Lynn Brink, Dallas College–North Lake

Gary Brown, Lone Star College–Montgomery

Sara Butler, College of the Desert

Joe Campbell, Johnson County Community College

Bill Carroll, Sam Houston State University

Jim Cauthen, John Jay College, CUNY

Ed Chervenak, University of New Orleans

Jeffrey W. Christiansen, Seminole State College

Gary Church, Dallas College–Mountain View

Mark Cichock, University of Texas at Arlington

Adrian Stefan Clark, Del Mar College

Dewey Clayton, University of Louisville

Jeff Colbert, Elon University

Cory Colby, Lone Star College–Tomball

Annie Cole, Los Angeles City College

John Coleman, University of Wisconsin–Madison

Darin Combs, Tulsa Community College

Greg Combs, University of Texas at Dallas

Sean Conroy, University of New Orleans

Amanda Cook Fesperman, Illinois Valley Community College

Paul Cooke, Lone Star College–CyFair

Cassandra Cookson, Lee College

Kevin Corder, Western Michigan University

McKinzie Craig, Marietta College

Brian Cravens, Blinn College

Christopher Cronin, Methodist University

John Crosby, California State University–Chico
Anthony Daniels, University of Toledo
Courtenay Daum, Colorado State University
Kevin Davis, North Central Texas College
Paul Davis, Truckee Meadows Community College
Terri Davis, Lamar University
Vida Davoudi, Lone Star College–Kingwood
Jennifer De Maio, California State University–Northridge
Louis DeSipio, University of California–Irvine
Robert DiClerico, West Virginia University
Corey Ditslear, University of North Texas
Peter Doas, University of Texas–Pan American
Kathy Dolan, University of Wisconsin–Milwaukee
John Domino, Sam Houston State University
Doug Dow, University of Texas at Dallas
Jeremy Duff, Midwestern State University
Jenna Duke, Lehigh Carbon Community College
Francisco Durand, University of Texas at San Antonio
Christopher D'Urso, Valencia College
Bruce R. Drury, Lamar University
Denise Dutton, University of Tulsa
Daphne Eastman, Odessa College
Carrie Eaves, Elon University
Sheryl Edwards, University of Michigan–Dearborn
Lauren Elliott-Dorans, Ohio University
Ryan Emenaker, College of the Redwoods
Heather Evans, Sam Houston State University
Andrew I. E. Ewoh, Texas Southern University
Hyacinth Ezeamii, Albany State University
Dennis Falcon, Cerritos College
William Feagin, Jr., Wharton County Junior College
Otto Feinstein, Wayne State University
Leslie Feldman, Hofstra University
Kathleen Ferraiolo, James Madison University
Del Fields, St. Petersburg College
Glen Findley, Odessa College
Bob Fitrakis, Columbus State Community College
Brian Fletcher, Truckee Meadows Community College
Paul M. Flor, El Camino College Compton Center
Elizabeth Flores, Del Mar College
Paul Foote, Eastern Kentucky University
Brandon Franke, Blinn College
Heather Frederick, Slippery Rock University
Adam Fuller, Youngstown State University
Frank Garrahan, Austin Community College
Steve Garrison, Midwestern State University

Michael Gattis, Gulf Coast State College
Jason Ghibesi, Ocean County College
Patrick Gilbert, Lone Star College–Tomball
Kathleen Gille, Office of Representative David Bonior
James Gimpel, University of Maryland at College Park
Jill Glaathar, Southwest Missouri State University
Randy Glean, Midwestern State University
Jimmy Gleason, Purdue University
Donna Godwin, Trinity Valley Community College
Christi Gramling, Charleston Southern University
Matthew Green, Catholic University of America
Steven Greene, North Carolina State University
Jeannie Grussendorf, Georgia State University
Matt Guardino, Providence College
Precious Hall, Truckee Meadows Community College
Sally Hansen, Daytona State College
Tiffany Harper, Collin College
Todd Hartman, Appalachian State University
Mary Jane Hatton, Hawaii Pacific University
M. Ahad Hayaud-Din, Brookhaven College
Virginia Haysley, Lone Star College–Tomball
David Head, John Tyler Community College
Barbara Headrick, Minnesota State University, Moorhead
David Helpap, University of Wisconsin–Green Bay
Rick Henderson, Texas State University–San Marcos
Shaun Herness, George Washington University
Rodney Hero, University of California–Berkeley
Richard Herrera, Arizona State University
Thaddaus Hill, Blinn College
Alexander Hogan, Lone Star College–CyFair
Justin Hoggard, Three Rivers Community College
Steven Holmes, Bakersfield College
Kevin Holton, South Texas College
Steven Horn, Everett Community College
Joseph Howard, University of Central Arkansas
Glen Hunt, Austin Community College
Teresa L. Hutchins, Georgia Highlands College
John Patrick Ifedi, Howard University
Cryshanna A. Jackson Leftwich, Youngstown State University
Robin Jacobson, University of Puget Sound
Amy Jasperson, Rhodes College
Mark Jendrysik, University of North Dakota

Krista Jenkins, Fairleigh Dickinson University

Loch Johnson, University of Georgia

Joseph Jozwiak, Texas A&M University–Corpus Christi

Carlos Juárez, Hawaii Pacific University

Mark Kann, University of Southern California

Demetra Kasimis, California State University–Long Beach

Eric T. Kasper, University of Wisconsin–Eau Claire

Robert Katzmann, Brookings Institution

Nancy Kinney, Washtenaw Community College

William Klein, St. Petersburg College

Casey Klofstad, University of Miami

Aaron Knight, Houston Community College

Kathleen Knight, University of Houston

Robin Kolodny, Temple University

Melinda Kovacs, Missouri Western State University

Nancy Kral, Lone Star College–Tomball

Douglas Kriner, Boston University

Thom Kuehls, Weber State University

Ashlyn Kuersten, Western Michigan University

Rick Kurtz, Central Michigan University

Paul Labedz, Valencia College

Elise Langan, John Jay College of Criminal Justice

Boyd Lanier, Lamar University

Jennifer L. Lawless, American University

Jeff Lazarus, Georgia State University

Jeffrey Lee, Blinn College

Alan Lehmann, Blinn College

Julie Lester, Middle Georgia State University

LaDella Levy, College of Southern Nevada

Steven Lichtman, Shippensburg University

Robert C. Lieberman, Columbia University

Timothy Lim, California State University–Los Angeles

Kara Lindaman, Winona State University

Mary Linder, Grayson College

Samuel Lingrosso, Los Angeles Valley College

Mark Logas, Valencia Community College

Fred Lokken, Truckee Meadows Community College

Timothy Lynch, University of Wisconsin–Milwaukee

William Lyons, University of Tennessee at Knoxville

Scott MacDougall, Diablo Valley College

Shari MacLachlan, Palm Beach State College

David Mann, College of Charleston

David A. Marcum, Laramie County Community College

Christopher Marshall, South Texas College

Guy Martin, Winston-Salem State University

Laura R. Winsky Mattei, State University of New York at Buffalo

Mandy May, College of Southern Maryland

Phil McCall, Portland State University

Kelly McDaniel, Three Rivers Community College

Larry McElvain, South Texas College

Corinna R. McKoy, Ventura College

Elizabeth McLane, Wharton County Junior College

Eddie L. Meaders, University of North Texas

Rob Mellen, Mississippi State University

Marilyn S. Mertens, Midwestern State University

Suzanne Mettler, Cornell University

Eric Miller, Blinn College

Michael Miller, Barnard College

Don D. Mirjanian, College of Southern Nevada

R. Shea Mize, Georgia Highlands College

Fred Monardi, College of Southern Nevada

Dana Morales, Montgomery College

Nicholas Morgan, Collin College

Vincent Moscardelli, University of Connecticut

Matthew Murray, Dutchess Community College

Christopher Muste, University of Montana

Jason Mycoff, University of Delaware

Carolyn Myers, Southwestern Illinois College–Belleville

Sugumaran Narayanan, Midwestern State University

Jalal Nejad, Northwest Vista College

Adam Newmark, Appalachian State University

Stephen Nicholson, University of California–Merced

Joseph Njoroge, Abraham Baldwin Agricultural College

Larry Norris, South Plains College

Anthony Nownes, University of Tennessee at Knoxville

Elizabeth Oldmixon, University of North Texas

Anthony O'Regan, Los Angeles Valley College

Harold "Trey" Orndorff III, Daytona State College

John Osterman, San Jacinto College–Central

Cissie Owen, Lamar University

Richard Pacelle, University of Tennessee at Knoxville

Randall Parish, University of North Georgia

Michelle Pautz, University of Dayton

Mark Peplowski, College of Southern Nevada

Maria Victoria Perez-Rios, John Jay College, CUNY

Robert L. Perry, University of Texas of the Permian Basin
Gerhard Peters, Citrus College
Michael Petri, Santa Ana College
Michael Pickering, Tulane University
Eric Plutzer, Pennsylvania State University
Sarah Poggione, Florida International University
Andrew Polsky, Hunter College, CUNY
Christopher Poulios, Nassau Community College
Michael A. Powell, Frederick Community College
Suzanne Preston, St. Petersburg College
Wayne Pryor, Brazosport College
David Putz, Lone Star College–Kingwood
Donald Ranish, Antelope Valley College
David Rankin, State University of New York at Fredonia
Grant Reeher, Syracuse University
Elizabeth A. Rexford, Wharton County Junior College
Richard Rich, Virginia Polytechnic
Glenn W. Richardson, Jr., Kutztown University of Pennsylvania
Sara Rinfret, University of Wisconsin–Green Bay
Andre Robinson, Pulaski Technical College
Jason Robles, Colorado State University
Paul Roesler, St. Charles Community College
J. Philip Rogers, San Antonio College
Susan Roomberg, University of Texas at San Antonio
Auksuole Rubavichute, Dallas College–Mountain View
Andrew Rudalevige, Bowdoin College
Ionas Aurelian Rus, University of Cincinnati–Blue Ash
Ryan Rynbrandt, Collin College
Robert Sahr, Oregon State University
Mario Salas, Northwest Vista College
Michael Sanchez, San Antonio College
Amanda Sanford, Louisiana Tech University
Elizabeth Saunders, Georgetown University
Mary Schander, Pasadena City College
Thomas Schmeling, Rhode Island College
Laura Schneider, Grand Valley State University
Ronnee Schreiber, San Diego State University
Ronald Schurin, University of Connecticut
Kathleen Searles, Louisiana State University
Jason Seitz, Georgia Perimeter College
Jennifer Seitz, Georgia Perimeter College
Allen K. Settle, California Polytechnic State University

Subash Shah, Winston-Salem State University
Greg Shaw, Illinois Wesleyan University
Kelly B. Shaw, Iowa State University
Mark Shomaker, Blinn College
John Sides, Vanderbilt University
Andrea Simpson, University of Richmond
Shannon Sinegal, University of New Orleans
Tracy Skopek, Stephen F. Austin State University
Roy Slater, St. Petersburg College
Captain Michael Slattery, Campbell University
Brian Smentkowski, Southeast Missouri State University
Daniel Smith, Northwest Missouri State University
Don Smith, University of North Texas
Michael Smith, Sam Houston State University
Matthew Snyder, Delgado Community College
Chris Soper, Pepperdine University
Thomas Sowers, Lamar University
Bartholomew Sparrow, University of Texas at Austin
Scott Spitzer, California State University–Fullerton
Laurie Sprankle, Community College of Allegheny County
Jim Startin, University of Texas at San Antonio
Robert Sterken, University of Texas at Tyler
Maryam T. Stevenson, University of Indianapolis
Debra St. John, Collin College
Dara Strolovitch, University of Minnesota
Barbara Suhay, Henry Ford Community College
Bobby Summers, Harper College
Steven Sylvester, Utah Valley University
Ryan Lee Teten, University of Louisiana at Lafayette
John Theis, Lone Star College–Kingwood
John Todd, University of North Texas
Dennis Toombs, San Jacinto College–North
Delaina Toothman, University of Maine
Linda Trautman, Ohio University–Lancaster
Elizabeth Trentanelli, Gulf Coast State College
David Trussell, Cisco College
Stacy Ulbig, Southwest Missouri State University
Ronald W. Vardy, University of Houston
Justin Vaughn, Boise State University
Linda Veazey, Midwestern State University
John Vento, Antelope Valley College
Kevin Wagner, Florida Atlantic University
Timothy Weaver, State University of New York at Albany
Aaron Weinschenk, University of Wisconsin–Green Bay
Eric Whitaker, Western Washington University

Clay Wiegand, Cisco College
Nelson Wikstrom, Virginia Commonwealth
University
Clif Wilkinson, Georgia College
Donald Williams, Western New England University
Walter Wilson, University of Texas at San Antonio
Christina Wolbrecht, University of Notre Dame
Carolyn Wong, Stanford University
John Wood, Rose State College
Laura Wood, Tarrant County College
Robert Wood, University of North Dakota
Terri Wright, California State University–Fullerton
Peter Yacobucci, Buffalo State College
Kevan Yenerall, Clarion University
Michael Young, Trinity Valley Community College
Tyler Young, Collin College
Rogerio Zapata, South Texas College
Julian Zelizer, Princeton University

For this Thirteenth Edition:

Andrea Benjamin, University of Missouri–
Columbia
David Birch, Lone Star College–Tomball

Melissa Buehler, Miami Dade College
Jeffrey W. Christiansen, Seminole State College
Andrew Clayton, McLennan Community College
Brian Cravens, Blinn College
Darin DeWitt, California State University–
Long Beach
Maria Gabryszewska, Lone Star College–CyFair
Patrick Gilbert, Lone Star College
Virginia Haysley, Lone Star College–Tomball
Anika Jackson, Los Angeles City College
Anthony Jordan, Central Texas College
Milosz Kucharski, Lone Star College–CyFair
Paul Labedz, Valencia College
Prakash K. Mansinghani, Laredo College
Katie Marchetti, Dickinson College
Mandy May, College of Southern Maryland
Justin Moeller, West Texas A&M University
Patrick Novotny, Georgia Southern University
Jennifer Selin, University of Missouri
John Theis, Lone Star College–Kingwood
Herschel Thomas, University of Texas at Arlington
Austin Trantham, Jacksonville University
Corena White, Tarrant County College–
Trinity River

We are also grateful to Daniel Fuerstman of State College of Florida Manatee-Sarasota, who contributed to the America Side by Side boxes.

Perhaps above all, we thank those at W. W. Norton. For the book's first five editions, editor Steve Dunn helped us shape it in countless ways. Ann Shin carried on the Norton tradition of splendid editorial work on the Sixth through Ninth Editions and on the Eleventh Edition. Lisa McKay contributed smart ideas and a keen editorial eye to the Tenth Edition. Peter Lesser brought intelligence, dedication, and keen insight to the development of the Twelfth and Thirteenth Editions. For our InQuizitive course, digital resources for learning management systems, and other instructor support, Spencer Richardson-Jones has been an energetic and visionary editor. Elizabeth Marotta, Lena Nowak-Laird, and Anna Olcott also kept the production of the Thirteenth Edition and its accompanying resources coherent and in focus. John Elliott helped streamline and sharpen our ideas. Sarah Johnson copy-edited the manuscript, and our superb project editor Laura Dragonette and media project editor Marcus Van Harpen devoted countless hours to keeping on top of myriad details. We thank Donna Ranieri for finding new photos and our photo editor Thomas Persano for managing the image program. Finally, we thank the former head of Norton's college department, Roby Harrington, who provided guidance and support through these many editions.

Benjamin Ginsberg
Caroline J. Tolbert
Andrea L. Campbell
Robert Spitzer

October 2020

ESSENTIALS
★ *edition* ★
13

We the People

An Introduction to American Politics

Introduction: The Citizen and Government

WHAT GOVERNMENT DOES AND WHY IT MATTERS

When Kimberly Green-Yates, chief operating officer of a group of nursing homes in Oklahoma, heard about the coronavirus deaths in Washington State nursing homes in early 2020, she ordered a large supply of PPE, personal protective equipment such as masks and gloves, and locked it away. "The people we take care of are the most vulnerable. Without PPE, we can't keep them safe," she said. But Green-Yates worried; some of the equipment was used up during the flu season and it wasn't clear whether new equipment would be available. Her state's department of emergency management had requested additional supplies from the Strategic National Stockpile, which is managed by the federal Department of Health and Human Services (HHS) for use during crises that overwhelm local resources. Usually such emergencies—think of hurricanes or chemical plant explosions—are geographically concentrated. But the nationwide coronavirus outbreak forced HHS to make decisions about how to allocate its stockpile around the country. It chose to allot medical masks, gloves, and gowns by a formula using outbreak severity and state population, rather

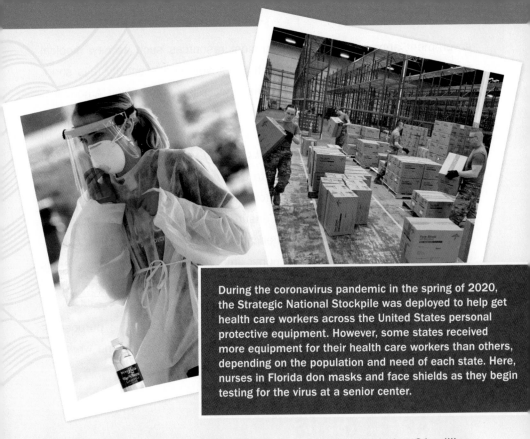

During the coronavirus pandemic in the spring of 2020, the Strategic National Stockpile was deployed to help get health care workers across the United States personal protective equipment. However, some states received more equipment for their health care workers than others, depending on the population and need of each state. Here, nurses in Florida don masks and face shields as they begin testing for the virus at a senior center.

than outbreak severity alone. That meant that Florida, population 21 million, received all of the 180,000 masks it requested, while Oklahoma, population 4 million, received only 10 percent of its 500,000-mask request.

Moreover, nearly all of the supplies in the national stockpile were expired. Most had been purchased in 2007 when extra funding for pandemic flu preparation had been included in the federal budget. But by 2020 they had "exceeded their shelf life," according to an HHS letter. "Public health emergency preparedness . . . has been chronically underfunded for years," said Michael Lanza, spokesman for the New York City Health Department, which had requested 2.2 million masks and received 78,000, all expired.[1]

Every day, government affects our lives and those of our family members, friends, and community. Sometimes those efforts are difficult to recognize, like when we eat a hamburger that because of government meat inspection doesn't make us sick. Sometimes government's activity is very visible, like when the governors of New York and Washington State, in response to the coronavirus pandemic, requested major disaster declarations, which the federal government approved, freeing government resources such as new medical stations for those states. And sometimes government's activity falls short, like the beleaguered Strategic National Stockpile, undermining Americans' security and well-being.

Americans have a variety of different views about the appropriate role of government. Some saw the work-from-home orders put in place by some local and state governments in response to the coronavirus pandemic as threats to their liberty and a classic case of government overreach. Yet others thought such mandates came too late to ensure Americans' health and security. Moreover, the pandemic affected Americans very differently, as both the coronavirus's health effects and its economic implications varied by age, gender, race, and class. Government's success in offsetting the virus's health and economic effects varied across different groups as well.

Thus government affects us all in ways big and small. The purpose of this book is to show what government does, how, and why—and what you can do about it.

CHAPTER GOALS

★ **Differentiate between forms of government (pp. 5–9)**

★ **Describe the rights and responsibilities that citizens have in a democracy (pp. 9–10)**

★ **Describe the social composition of the American population and how it has changed over time (pp. 10–17)**

★ **Describe how cultural values of liberty, equality, and democracy influence the U.S. system of government (pp. 17–21)**

★ **Summarize Americans' attitudes toward government (pp. 21–24)**

Government Is How We Are Ruled

Differentiate between forms of government

Government is the term generally used to describe the formal institutions through which a territory and its people are ruled. A government may be as simple as a town meeting in which community members make policy or as complex as the vast establishments found in many large countries today, with extensive procedures, laws, and bureaucracies. In the history of civilization, thousands of governments have been established. The hard part is establishing one that lasts.

Even more difficult is developing a stable government that is true to the core American political values of liberty, equality, and democracy. Though in principle these three values are endorsed by most Americans, in practice each of them means different things to different people, and they often seem to conflict with one another. This is where politics comes in. **Politics** refers to conflicts and struggles over the leadership, structure, and policies of governments.

IS GOVERNMENT NEEDED?

Government is needed to provide basic services, sometimes called "public goods," that citizens all need but probably cannot individually provide adequately for themselves. These include defense against foreign aggression, maintenance of public order, a stable currency, enforcement of contractual obligations and property rights, and some measure of economic security. Government, with its powers to tax and regulate, is viewed as the best way to provide public goods. However, there is often disagreement about which public goods are essential and how they should be provided.

Much of what citizens have come to depend on and take for granted as part of their everyday environment is in fact created by government. Throughout the day, for example, a typical college student relies on a host of services and activities organized by national, state, and local government agencies. The extent of this dependence is illustrated in Table 1.1 on p. 6.

DIFFERENT FORMS OF GOVERNMENT ARE DEFINED BY FREEDOM AND POWER

Two questions are of special importance in determining how governments differ: Who governs? And how much government control is permitted?

Some nations are governed by a single individual—a king or dictator, for example. This system is called **autocracy**. Where a small group—perhaps landowners, military officers, or the wealthy—controls most of the governing decisions, that government is said to

government institutions and procedures through which a territory and its people are ruled

politics conflict over the leadership, structure, and policies of governments

autocracy a form of government in which a single individual—a king, queen, or dictator—rules

TABLE 1.1

The Presence of Government in the Daily Life of a Student at "State University"

TIME	SCHEDULE
7:00 A.M.	Wake up. Standard time set by the national government.
7:10 A.M.	Shower. Water courtesy of local government, and supplied by either a public entity or a regulated private company.
7:30 A.M.	Have a bowl of cereal with milk for breakfast. "Nutrition Facts" on food labels are a federal requirement.
8:30 A.M.	Drive or take public transportation to campus. Airbags and seat belts required by federal and state laws. Roads and bridges paid for by state and local governments.
8:45 A.M.	Arrive on campus of large public university. Buildings are 70 percent financed by state taxpayers.
9:00 A.M.	First class: Chemistry 101. Tuition partially paid by a federal loan (more than half the cost of university instruction is paid for by taxpayers), chemistry lab paid for with grants from the National Science Foundation (a federal agency) and smaller grants from business corporations made possible by federal income tax deductions for charitable contributions.
Noon	Eat lunch. College cafeteria financed by state dormitory authority on land grant from federal Department of Agriculture.
2:00 P.M.	Second class: American Government 101 (your favorite class!). You may be taking this class because it is required by the state legislature or because it fulfills a university requirement.
4:00 P.M.	Third class: Computer Science 101. Free computers, software, and internet access courtesy of state subsidies plus grants and discounts from Apple and Microsoft, the costs of which are deducted from their corporate income taxes; internet built in part by federal government. Duplication of software prohibited by federal copyright laws.
6:00 P.M.	Eat dinner: hamburger and french fries. Meat inspected for bacteria by federal agencies.
7:00 P.M.	Work at part-time job at the campus library. Minimum wage set by federal, state, or local government.
8:15 P.M.	Go online to check the status of your application for a federal student loan (FAFSA) on the Department of Education's website at studentaid.gov.
10:15 P.M.	Watch TV. Networks regulated by federal government, cable public-access channels required by city law. Weather forecast provided to broadcasters by a federal agency.
Midnight	Put out the trash before going to bed. Trash collected by city sanitation department, financed by user charges.

be an **oligarchy**. If citizens or the general adult population have the power to rule themselves, that government is a **democracy**.

Governments also vary considerably in terms of how they govern. In the United States and a number of other nations, constitutions and other laws limit what governments can do and how they go about it. Governments limited in this way are called liberal or **constitutional governments**.

In other nations, including some in Latin America, Asia, and Africa, the government recognizes no formal limits, but is nevertheless kept in check by other political and social institutions that it cannot control—such as self-governing territories, an organized religion, business organizations, or labor unions. Such governments are generally called **authoritarian**.

In a third group of nations, including the Soviet Union under Joseph Stalin, Nazi Germany, and North Korea today, governments not only lack legal limits but also try to eliminate institutions that might challenge their authority. These governments typically attempt to control all of a nation's political, economic, and social life and, as a result, are called **totalitarian**.

Americans have the good fortune to live in a nation in which limits are placed on what governments can do and how they can do it. By one measure, 52 percent of the global population lives in democracies, but only 14 percent enjoy true liberal democracy with free and fair elections, the rule of law, and constraints on the executive (president or prime minister); 38 percent live in more limited democracies.[2]

oligarchy a form of government in which a small group—landowners, military officers, or wealthy merchants—controls most of the governing decisions

democracy a system of rule that permits citizens to play a significant part in the governmental process, usually through the election of key public officials

constitutional government a system of rule in which formal and effective limits are placed on the powers of the government

authoritarian government a system of rule in which the government recognizes no formal limits but may nevertheless be restrained by the power of other social institutions

totalitarian government a system of rule in which the government recognizes no formal limits on its power and seeks to absorb or eliminate other social institutions that might challenge it

LIMITS ON GOVERNMENT ENCOURAGED FREEDOM

The founding generation of the young United States established many of the principles that would come to define individual liberty for all citizens—freedom of speech, of assembly, and of conscience, as well as freedom from arbitrary search and seizure. Yet the Founders generally did not favor democracy as we know it. They supported property requirements and other restrictions for voting and for holding office so as to limit political participation to the White middle and upper classes. Once these institutions and the right to engage in politics were established, however, it was difficult to limit them to the economic elite.

THE EXPANSION OF PARTICIPATION SHIFTED POLITICAL POWER

America's Founders were influenced by the English thinker John Locke (1632–1704). Locke argued that governments need the consent of the people.

Pressure to expand voting rights came both from below (the excluded groups themselves agitating for the vote) and from above (by others who hoped to gain political advantage by expanding the franchise to groups they viewed as potential allies). After the Civil War, a chief reason that Republicans gave the vote to formerly enslaved people was to use their support to maintain Republican control in the defeated southern states. Similarly, in the early twentieth century, the Progressive movement advocated women's suffrage at least partly because they believed women were more likely than men to support Progressive reforms.

PARTICIPATION IN GOVERNMENT IS HOW PEOPLE HAVE A SAY IN WHAT HAPPENS

As Harold Lasswell, a famous political scientist, once put it, politics is the struggle over "who gets what, when, how."[3] In this book *politics* will refer to conflicts over who the government's leadership is, how the government is organized, or what its policies are. Having a share or a say in these issues is called having **political power** or influence.

Participation in politics can take many forms, including voting, donating money, signing petitions, attending political meetings, tweeting and commenting online, sending emails to officials, lobbying legislators, working on a campaign, and participating in protest marches and even violent demonstrations. A system of government that gives citizens a regular opportunity to elect top government officials is usually called a **representative democracy**, or a **republic**. A system that permits citizens to vote directly on laws and policies is called a **direct democracy**.

political power influence over a government's leadership, organization, or policies

representative democracy (republic) a system of government in which the populace selects representatives, who play a significant role in governmental decision-making

direct democracy a system of rule that permits citizens to vote directly on laws and policies

At the national level, the United States is a representative democracy in which citizens select government officials but do not vote on legislation. Some states and cities, however, do provide for direct legislation through initiatives and referenda. These procedures allow citizens to collect petitions, or legislators to pass bills, requiring a direct popular vote on an issue. In 2020, 128 referenda appeared on state ballots, often dealing with hot-button issues, including measures in 6 states legalizing medical or recreational marijuana, in 12 states affecting taxes, in 2 states regarding abortion access and funding, and in 14 states regarding elections policies such as redistricting, voting requirements, and campaign finance.[4]

Groups and organized interests also participate in politics. Their political activities include providing funds for candidates, lobbying, and trying to influence public opinion. The pattern of struggles among interests is called group politics, or **pluralism**. Americans have always had mixed feelings about pluralist politics. On the one hand, the right of groups to support their views and compete for influence in the government is the essence of liberty. On the other hand, groups may sometimes exert too much influence, advancing their own interests at the expense of larger public interests. (We return to this problem in Chapter 9.)

Citizenship Is Based on Participation, Knowledge, and Efficacy

> **Describe the rights and responsibilities that citizens have in a democracy**

Citizenship in the United States comes with many rights but also with important responsibilities. Civil liberties such as freedom of speech, freedom of worship, and trial by jury are found in the Constitution, particularly in the Bill of Rights, as Chapter 4 discusses. Citizens also have responsibilities, such as upholding the Constitution; obeying federal, state, and local laws; paying taxes; serving on juries when called; and being informed about issues.[5]

One key ingredient for political participation is **political knowledge** and information. Democracy functions best when citizens are informed and have the knowledge needed to participate in political debate. Indeed, our definition of **citizenship** derives from the ideal put forth by the ancient Greeks: *enlightened* political engagement.[6] It is also important to know the rules and strategies that govern political institutions and the principles on which they are based, *and* to know them in ways that relate to your own interests.

Without political knowledge, citizens cannot be aware of their stakes in political disputes. For example, during the debate in 2017 about whether to repeal the health care reform enacted in 2010, one-third of Americans did not know that "Obamacare" and the "Affordable Care Act" are the same thing.[7] That meant that some of those enrolled in "Obamacare" did not realize their access to health insurance would be affected if the ACA were repealed.

Surveys show that large majorities of Americans get political information online, although inequalities in internet access by income, education, race, and age remain. While the internet has made it easier than ever to learn about politics, political knowledge in the United States remains spotty. Most Americans know little about current issues or debates, or even the basics of how government works. For example, in 2019 only 39 percent of those surveyed

pluralism the theory that all interests are and should be free to compete for influence in the government; the outcome of this competition is compromise and moderation

political knowledge information about the formal institutions of government, political actors, and political issues

citizenship informed and active membership in a political community

Protests are a form of direct action citizens can take to influence policy outcomes. Many citizens, including students and children, have used peaceful protests and marches to convey concerns about global climate change and demand government action.

could identify all three branches of the federal government and only 53 percent knew the size of the majority in Congress needed to override a presidential veto (two-thirds).[8]

Another ingredient in participation is **political efficacy**, the belief that ordinary citizens can affect what government does. The feeling that you can't affect government decisions can lead to apathy, declining political participation, and withdrawal from political life. Americans' sense of political efficacy has declined over time. In 1960, only 25 percent felt shut out of government.

In 2019, 71 percent of Americans said that elected officials don't care what people like them think.[9] Accompanying this sense that ordinary people are not heard is a growing belief that government is not run for the benefit of all. In 2019, 52 percent of the public disagreed with the idea that the "government is really run for the benefit of all the people."[10] Research shows that efficacy and participation are related: a feeling that one can make a difference leads to higher participation, and joining in can increase one's efficacy.

political efficacy the belief that one can influence government and politics

Who Are Americans?

Describe the social composition of the American population and how it has changed over time

While American democracy aims to give the people a voice in government, the meaning of "we the people" has changed over time. Who are Americans? Throughout American history, Americans have puzzled and fought over the answer to this fundamental question.

IMMIGRATION HAS CHANGED AMERICAN IDENTITY

The U.S. population has grown from 3.9 million in 1790, the year of the first official census, to 330 million in 2020.[11] At the same time, it has become more diverse on nearly every dimension imaginable.[12]

In 1790, when the United States consisted of 13 states along the Eastern Seaboard, 81 percent of Americans traced their roots to Europe, mostly Britain and elsewhere in northern Europe; and nearly 20 percent were of African origin, the vast majority of whom were enslaved people.[13] Only 1.5 percent of the Black population were free. There were also an unknown number of Native Americans, the original inhabitants of the land, not counted by the census because the government did not consider them Americans. The first estimates of Native Americans and Latinos in the mid-1800s showed that each group made up less than 1 percent of the total population.[14]

Fast-forward to 1900. The country now stretched across the continent, and waves of immigrants, mainly from Europe, had boosted the population to 76 million. The population was still predominantly composed of people of European ancestry, but now included many from southern and eastern as well as northwestern Europe; the Black population stood at 12 percent. Residents who traced their origin to Latin America or Asia each accounted for less than 1 percent of the population.[15] The large number of new immigrants was reflected in the high proportion of foreign-born people in the population; this figure reached its height at 14.7 percent in 1910.[16] As

In the 1900s many immigrants entered the United States through New York's Ellis Island, where they were checked for disease before being admitted.

growing numbers of immigrants from southern and eastern Europe crowded into American cities, anxiety mounted among those of British and other northwestern European ancestry, who feared their group could lose its long-dominant position in American society and politics.

After World War I, Congress responded to the fears swirling around immigrants with new laws that sharply limited how many could enter the country each year. It also established a new National Origins quota system, based on the nation's population in 1890, before the wave of immigrants from eastern and southern Europe arrived.[17] Supporters of these measures hoped to turn back the clock to an earlier America in which northern Europeans dominated. The new system set up a hierarchy of admissions: northern European countries received generous quotas for new immigrants, whereas eastern and southern European countries were granted very small quotas. By 1970, these guidelines had reduced the foreign-born population in the United States to an all-time low of 5 percent.

The use of ethnic and racial criteria to restrict the country's population and to draw boundaries around "American" identity began long before the National Origins quota system, however. Most people of African descent were not deemed citizens until 1868, when the Fourteenth Amendment to the Constitution granted citizenship to the formerly enslaved people (see Chapter 2). Native Americans were not officially citizens until 1924. Efforts to limit nonwhite immigration and citizenship dated back to a 1790 law stating that only free Whites could become naturalized citizens, a ban not lifted until 1870. Even then, different restrictions applied to Asians: the Chinese Exclusion Act of 1882 outlawed the entry of Chinese laborers to the United States, a limit lifted only in 1943, when China became America's ally during World War II. Additional barriers enacted after World War I meant that virtually no Asians entered the country as immigrants until the 1940s.

With laws about citizenship linked to "Whiteness," questions arose about how to classify people of Latino origin. In 1930, for example, the census counted people of Mexican origin as nonwhite, but a decade later reversed this decision—after protests by those affected and by the Mexican government. Only in 1970 did the census officially begin counting persons of Hispanic origin, noting that they could be any race.[18] (Note that the census uses the term *Hispanic*, but we will generally use the terms *Latino* and *Latina* to refer to people of Spanish or Latin American descent.)

WHO ARE AMERICANS IN THE TWENTY-FIRST CENTURY?

Race and Ethnicity Recent immigration patterns have profoundly shaped the nation's current racial and ethnic profile. The primary cause was Congress's decision in 1965 to lift the tight restrictions of the 1920s, allowing for much-expanded immigration from Asia and Latin America (see Figure 1.1). Census figures for 2018 show that Latinos, who can be of any race, constitute 18.3 percent of the total population, and Asians make up 5.6 percent. The Black, or African American, population is 12.7 percent of the total, while non-Latino Whites account for 60.2 percent—their lowest share ever. Moreover, 3.4 percent of the population now identifies itself as of "two or more races," a new category that the census added in 2000.[19]

FIGURE 1.1

Immigration by Continent of Origin

Where did most immigrants come from at the start of the twentieth century? How does that compare with immigration in the twenty-first century?

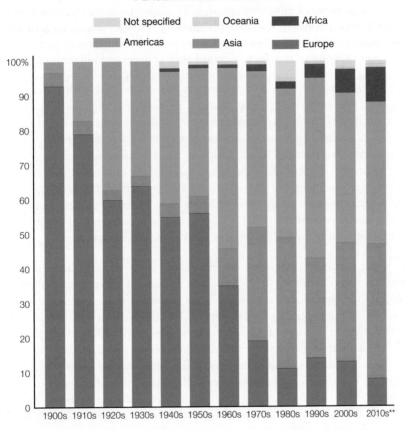

PERCENTAGE OF IMMIGRANTS*

Legend: Not specified | Oceania | Africa | Americas | Asia | Europe

*Less than 1 percent not shown.
**Through 2018.
Note: Figure shows those who have obtained "lawful permanent resident status" by continent of origin.
SOURCE: Department of Homeland Security, www.dhs.gov (accessed 1/19/20).

Large-scale immigration means that many more residents are foreign-born. In 2018, 13.7 percent of the population was born outside the United States, a figure comparable to that in 1900.[20] About half of the foreign-born population came from Latin America and the Caribbean—almost 1 in 10 from the Caribbean, just over one-third from Central America (including Mexico), and 1 in 15 from South America.[21] Those born in Asia made up 31 percent of foreign-born residents.[22] In sharp contrast to the immigration patterns of a century earlier, just 10.9 percent came from Europe.[23]

Estimates are that 12 million immigrants live in the country without legal authorization. The majority of these people are from Mexico and Central America.[24] This unauthorized population has become a flashpoint for controversy as states and cities have passed a variety of conflicting laws regarding their access to public services. Several decades ago, some states tried to exclude undocumented immigrants from public services such as education and emergency medical care, but the Supreme Court ensured access to K-12 education in its 1982 *Plyler v. Doe* ruling, and Congress guaranteed access to emergency medical care in a 1986 law.[25] Today, undocumented immigrants remain ineligible for most federal public benefits, but some states offer them driver's licenses or in-state tuition at public colleges and universities.[26]

Religion The new patterns of immigration have combined with differences in birth rates and underlying social changes to alter the religious affiliations of Americans. By 2019, only 35 percent of Americans identified themselves as Protestant, Catholics 22 percent, 10 percent Christian (nonspecific), 2 percent Jewish, 1 percent Mormon, and 6 percent "Other," which includes Muslim identifiers, who have grown to nearly 1 percent of the population. A growing number of people identify with no organized religion: 21 percent of the population in 2019.[27] Although many Americans think of the United States as a "Judeo-Christian" nation—and indeed it was 95 percent Protestant, Catholic, or Jewish as recently as 50 years ago—by 2019 this number had fallen to 70 percent of the adult population.[28]

Age As the American population has expanded and diversified, the country's age profile has shifted with it. In 1900 only 4 percent of the population was over age 65. As life expectancy increased, so did the number of older Americans: by 2018, 16 percent of the population was over 65. Over the same period, the percentage of children under the age of 18 fell, from 44 percent in 1900 to 25 percent in 2018.[29] As a group, Americans are still younger than the populations of many other industrialized countries, mainly because of the large number of immigrants. The share of the population aged 65 and over is 20 percent in the European Union and 27 percent in Japan.[30] But an aging population poses challenges to the United States as well. As the elderly population grows relative to those of working age, funding programs such as Social Security becomes more difficult.

Geography Over the nation's history, Americans have mostly moved from rural areas and small towns to large cities and suburbs. Before 1920 less than half the population lived in urban areas; today 82 percent of Americans do.[31] As a result, the national political system created when the population was still largely rural underrepresents urban Americans. Providing each state with two senators, for example, overrepresents sparsely populated rural states and underrepresents those with large urban populations (see Chapter 2). In addition, the American population has shifted regionally. During the past 50 years especially, many Americans have left the Northeast and Midwest and moved to the South and Southwest, with congressional seats reapportioned to reflect the population shift.

Forms of Government

The question of whether a country is democratic or authoritarian is complex. Every year, countries are rated on a scale from "Full Democracies" to "Authoritarian" systems based on expert evaluations of electoral processes, political culture, respect for civil liberties, political participation, and other indicators. In 2016, for the first time, the United States was classified as a "Flawed Democracy" in response to declines in public confidence in governance and a rise in polarization.

1. Is there a geographic pattern to which countries are labeled "Full" or "Flawed Democracies" and which are labeled "Hybrid" or "Authoritarian" systems? What factors, historical, economic, geographic, or otherwise, might help explain this pattern?

2. What do you think separates a "Full Democracy" from a "Flawed Democracy"? The United States' categorization as a "Flawed Democracy" happened during the Obama administration and persisted during the Trump administration. What changes have you seen in the past five years that might explain this shift? How concerned should Americans be by this categorization?

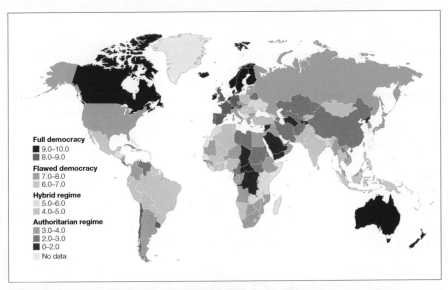

Full democracy
- 9.0–10.0
- 8.0–9.0

Flawed democracy
- 7.0–8.0
- 6.0–7.0

Hybrid regime
- 5.0–6.0
- 4.0–5.0

Authoritarian regime
- 3.0–4.0
- 2.0–3.0
- 0–2.0
- No data

SOURCE: "Democracy Index 2019," The Economist Intelligence Unit.

Socioeconomic Status For much of U.S. history, most Americans were relatively poor working people, many of them farmers. A new, extremely wealthy elite emerged in the late 1800s, a period called "the gilded age," and by 1928 nearly one-quarter of the total annual national income went to the top 1 percent of earners; the top 10 percent took home 46 percent of the total. In the middle of the twentieth century, the distribution of income and wealth shifted away from the top. A large middle class grew after New Deal programs helped counteract the Great Depression of the 1930s, and grew further with the postwar economic boom of the 1950s and '60s. The share of national income going to the top 1 percent dropped sharply, to just 9 percent by 1976.

Since then, however, economic inequality has once again widened in what some call a "new gilded age."[32] By 2018 the top 1 percent earned 21.8 percent of annual income and the top 10 percent took home 50.5 percent of it.[33] At the same time, the incomes of the broad middle class have largely stagnated,[34] and the numbers of the poor and near poor have swelled to nearly one-third of the population.[35] (See Figure 1.2, which shows similar data for household income.)

FIGURE 1.2
. . . .

Income in the United States

The graph shows that while the income of most Americans has risen only slightly since 1975, the income of the richest Americans (the top 5 percent) has increased dramatically. What are some of the ways that this shift might matter for American politics? Does the growing economic gap between the richest groups and most other Americans conflict with the political value of equality?

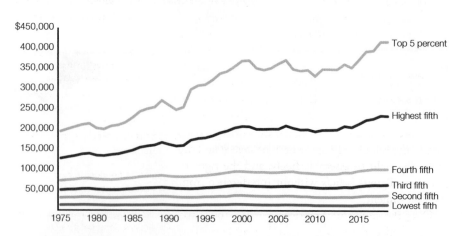

HOUSEHOLD INCOME*

*Dollar values are given in constant 2018 dollars, which are adjusted for inflation so that we can compare a person's income in 1975 with a person's income today.
SOURCE: U.S. Census Bureau, www.census.gov/data/tables/2019/demo/income-poverty/p60-266.html (accessed 1/19/20).

Population and Politics Population growth and shifts have spurred politically charged debates about how the population should be apportioned among congressional districts and how those districts should be drawn. These conflicts have major implications for the balance of representation among different regions of the country and between urban and rural areas. The representation of various other demographic and political groups may also be affected, as substantial evidence shows that Americans are increasingly divided from one another geographically according to their education, income, marriage rates, and party voting.[36] In addition, immigration and the cultural and religious changes that result spark passionate debate today, just as they did 100 years ago.

American Political Culture Is Built on Liberty, Equality, and Democracy

Describe how cultural values of liberty, equality, and democracy influence the U.S. system of government

The essential documents of the American Founding—the Declaration of Independence and the Constitution—proclaimed a set of principles about the purposes of the new republic: liberty, equality, and democracy. (See these documents in the Appendix.) Most Americans continue to affirm these values, which form our **political culture**.

LIBERTY MEANS FREEDOM

No ideal is more central to American values than liberty. The Declaration of Independence defined three "unalienable" rights: "Life, Liberty and the pursuit of Happiness." The Constitution likewise identified the need "to secure the Blessings of Liberty" as one of the key reasons for drawing up the document. For Americans, **liberty** means both personal freedom and economic freedom. Both are closely linked to the idea of **limited government**.

The Constitution's first 10 amendments, known collectively as the Bill of Rights, delineate individual personal liberties and rights. In fact, the word *liberty* has come to mean many of the freedoms guaranteed in the Bill of Rights: freedom of speech and the press, the right to assemble freely, and the right to practice religious beliefs without interference from the government.

Over the course of American history, the scope of personal liberties has expanded as laws have become more tolerant and as individuals have successfully used the courts to challenge restrictions on their individual freedoms. Far fewer restrictions

political culture broadly shared values, beliefs, and attitudes about how the government should function; American political culture emphasizes the values of liberty, equality, and democracy

liberty freedom from governmental control

limited government a principle of constitutional government; a government whose powers are defined and limited by a constitution

exist today on the press, political speech, and individual behavior than in the early years of the nation. Even so, conflicts emerge when personal liberties violate a community's accepted standards of behavior. For example, a number of cities have passed "sit-lie" ordinances, which limit the freedom of individuals to sit or lie down on sidewalks. Designed to limit the presence of the homeless and make city streets more attractive to pedestrians, the ordinances have also been denounced as restrictions on individual liberties.

The central historical conflict regarding liberty in the United States, the enslavement of Africans and their descendants, has cast a long shadow over all of American history. In fact, scholars today note that the American definition of freedom has been formed in relation to the concept of slavery. The rights to control one's labor and to be rewarded for it have been central elements of this definition precisely because these rights were denied to enslaved people.[37]

In addition to personal freedom related to one's labor, the American concept of economic freedom supports capitalism, free markets (including open competition and unrestricted movement of goods), and the protection of private property.[38] In the first century of the Republic, support for capitalism often meant support for the principle of *laissez-faire* (French for "allow to do"). **Laissez-faire capitalism** allowed the national government very little power to regulate commerce or restrict the use of private property. Today, however, federal and state governments impose many regulations to protect the public in such areas as health and safety, the environment, and the workplace. Government regulations to slow the spread of the coronavirus in 2020 included school closures, stay-at-home orders, and cancellations of entertainment and sporting events.

laissez-faire capitalism an economic system in which the means of production and distribution are privately owned and operated for profit with minimal or no government interference

equality of opportunity a widely shared American ideal that all people should have the freedom to use whatever talents and wealth they have to reach their fullest potential

EQUALITY MEANS TREATING PEOPLE FAIRLY

The Declaration of Independence declares as its first "self-evident" truth that "all men are created equal." As central as it is to the American political creed, however, equality has been an even less well-defined ideal than liberty, because people interpret it in such different ways. Few Americans have wholeheartedly embraced the ideal of full equality of results (that everyone deserves equal wealth and power), but most share the ideal of **equality of opportunity** (that everyone deserves a fair chance to go as

FOR CRITICAL ANALYSIS ▶

1. Which states had the largest increase in youth voting in 2018? Which states saw youth turnout decline?

2. What factors do you think led to increased youth participation? Characteristics of the candidates running? The importance of key issues to young people? Something else?

Can Young People Make a Difference in Politics?

Young people are less likely to participate in politics than older people. Only 46 percent of young people (age 18–29) voted in the 2016 presidential election, compared to 71 percent of those over age 65. The 2018 election was historic, with the highest voter turnout for a midterm election in four decades, and youth voter turnout broke records in many states.

Change in Voter Turnout, 2014–2018

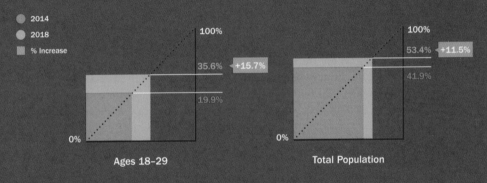

- 2014
- 2018
- % Increase

Ages 18–29
- 100%
- 35.6% +15.7%
- 19.9%
- 0%

Total Population
- 100%
- 53.4% +11.5%
- 41.9%
- 0%

Change in Voter Turnout by State, 2018

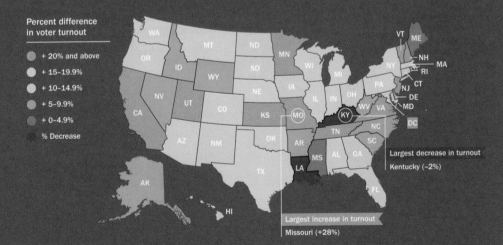

Percent difference in voter turnout

- + 20% and above
- + 15–19.9%
- + 10–14.9%
- + 5–9.9%
- + 0–4.9%
- % Decrease

Largest decrease in turnout
Kentucky (−2%)

Largest increase in turnout
Missouri (+28%)

SOURCE: William H. Frey, "Analysis of U.S. Census Bureau Current Population Survey Voting and Registration Supplement micro-files," www.brookings.edu; U.S. Census Bureau, "2018 Voting and Elections Supplement, Current Population Survey," www.census.gov (accessed 5/23/19).

political equality the right to participate in politics equally, based on the principle of "one person, one vote"

far as his or her talents will allow). Yet it is hard to agree on what constitutes equality of opportunity. Furthermore, in contrast to liberty, which requires limits on the role of government, equality implies an *obligation* of the government to the people.[39] But how far does this obligation extend? Must a group's past inequalities be redressed to ensure equal opportunity in the present? Should legal, political, and economic inequalities all be given the same weight?

Americans do make clear distinctions between social or economic equality and **political equality**, the right of a community's members to participate in politics on equal terms. Beginning from a very restricted definition of political community, which originally included only White men who owned a certain amount of property, the United States has moved much closer to an ideal of political equality that can be summed up as "one person, one vote." Most Americans agree that all citizens should have an equal right to participate and that government should enforce that right.

Many Americans see economic inequality as largely due to individual choices, virtues, or failures, and so they tend to be more skeptical of government action to reduce it (compared to government action to reduce political inequality). Income inequality rose on the political agenda during the coronavirus pandemic of 2020, when the economic slowdown most affected lower-income workers without employee benefits, including those in the restaurant, retail, and gig economy sectors. As Congress deliberated economic stimulus measures and policy changes, perennial debates about the role of government reemerged. Would

The Fight for $15—a nationwide effort to increase the minimum wage to $15 an hour—first gained traction in 2013, increasing public awareness of income inequality in the United States. By 2020 many states had increased their minimum wage above the federal minimum wage, but few had reached the $15 threshold that workers had protested for.

increased unemployment benefits to workers breed dependence and undermine Americans' work ethic? Would a temporary new federal paid-leave policy "crowd out" the existing paid-leave policies of larger corporations and substitute taxpayer-provided benefits? Such debates appear even under the toughest economic circumstances.[40]

DEMOCRACY MEANS THAT WHAT THE PEOPLE WANT MATTERS

The essence of democracy is the participation of the people in choosing their rulers and the ability of the people to influence what those rulers do. The idea of placing power in the hands of the people is known as **popular sovereignty**, and together with political equality, it makes politicians accountable to the people.

American democracy rests on the principle of **majority rule** with **minority rights**. Majority rule means that the wishes of the majority determine what government does. The House of Representatives—a large body elected directly by the people—was designed in particular to ensure majority rule. But the Founders feared that popular majorities could turn government into a "tyranny of the majority"; thus, concern for individual rights and liberties has been a part of American democracy from the beginning. The rights enumerated in the Bill of Rights and enforced through the courts provide an important check on the power of the majority.

popular sovereignty a principle of democracy in which political authority rests ultimately in the hands of the people

majority rule, minority rights the democratic principle that a government follows the preferences of the majority of voters but protects the interests of the minority

What Americans Think about Government

Summarize Americans' attitudes toward government

Since the United States was established as a nation, Americans have been reluctant to grant government too much power, and they have often been suspicious of politicians. But they have also turned to government for assistance in times of need and have strongly supported it in periods of war. In 1933 the power of the government began to expand to meet the crises created by the stock market crash of 1929, the massive business failures and unemployment of the Great Depression, and the threatened failure of the banking system. Congress passed legislation that brought the government into the businesses of home mortgages, farm mortgages, credit, and relief of personal financial distress. More recently, when the economy fell into a deep recession in 2008 and 2009, the federal government took action to stabilize the financial system, oversee the restructuring of the failing auto manufacturers, and provide hundreds of billions of dollars in economic stimulation.

Debate Respectfully

APRIL LAWSON, the director of debates for Better Angels

Government by the people functions best when individuals discuss ideas, share their preferences, and talk about what government is doing. But political discussion and debate can be uncomfortable, particularly among people who disagree or when politics is polarized, as it is in the current era.

To learn how to engage others and to debate respectfully, we spoke with April Lawson, the director of debates for Better Angels, a national organization that works with individuals from across the political spectrum to "combat polarization and restore civil dialogue across America." She offers these tips for successful and civil political conversations:

1 The most important thing is the presumption of good faith. If someone says something you can't stand, know that the other person is trying, just like you are, to address hard questions. Assume that the other person is smart and that they are moral.

2 Say what you actually believe. Genuineness and sincerity are crucial. You could debate either by making a case no one could disagree with or by sharing what you really feel about the issue. The latter will make for a more productive exchange of ideas.

3 How can you launch such a conversation and set the tone? A good technique is to start with a question of genuine curiosity for the other person, which reassures them that you

want to know what they believe. Another tip is to paraphrase what they have said before you respond, to make sure the other person feels heard.

4 When you respond, it helps if you express some doubt or nuance in your own argument, or mention that you agree with some aspect of the other person's position. You do not need to agree with everything they have said, but you can pick something reasonable the other person said and affirm, "You said X, which makes sense because of Y."

5 Know that you may need to be the bigger person in the conversation. In order to be an "ambassador of civility," you may need the patience to ask several genuine questions of curiosity before the other person believes that you are actually interested in what they have to say. And you need to control your own emotions and triggers, to manage your activation, since you know these rules for civil engagement, and they may not.

6 **Finally, realize that you have agency.** Prepare yourself for these tough conversations by telling yourself, "I will probably have feelings about this. But I can be patient and manage them." Remember, you're not trapped. You can take a break. You can change topics. Or you may want to have a conversational exit in mind. If it's Thanksgiving and you're speaking with your crazy uncle, you might pivot to the football game.

Debating respectfully requires coming to the table with a "posture of openness" and helping the other person feel heard. In America, at the talking point level, which is a surface level, we don't agree at all. But if you can go down even one level to political values, or even one more level to moral values, then there's a lot of common ground. With these conversations, we're not trying to change how you see the issue, we're trying to change how you see the other person.

April Lawson conducts trainings to encourage more respectful political dialogues.

While levels of participation in politics are relatively low for young Americans, presidential primary campaigns often draw many young people to volunteer and to vote. What factors might energize young people to become involved in campaigns?

TRUST IN GOVERNMENT HAS DECLINED

A key characteristic of contemporary political culture is low *trust* in government. In the early 1960s three-quarters of Americans said they trusted government most of the time or always. By 2020 only 20 percent did.[41] Trust in government declined again during the early stages of the coronavirus pandemic, particularly trust in the federal government, which many Americans felt reacted more slowly to the crisis than their local and state governments.[42]

Does it matter if Americans trust their government? For the most part, the answer is yes. As we have seen, most Americans rely on government for a wide range of services and protections that they simply take for granted. But long-term distrust in government can result in opposition to the taxes necessary to support such programs and also make it difficult to attract talented workers to public service.[43] Likewise, a weak government can do little to help citizens weather periods of tumultuous economic or technological change. Declining trust is important because public confidence in government is vital for the health of a democracy.

The Citizen and Government: What Do You Think?

In this chapter we examined various components of American political culture. Nearly every American supports the political values of liberty, equality, and democracy. How we put them into practice, however, sparks many of the debates that shape American political life. In addition, the makeup of the American people deeply influences American politics. Race, gender, and class divisions foster disagreement and debate and, as we will see throughout this book, influence how government and politics function.

At the start of this chapter, we introduced Kimberly Green-Yates, who was struggling to get protective medical equipment for the nursing homes she runs in Oklahoma.

Given what you learned in this chapter about American political culture, take a closer look at the account of the coronavirus pandemic on pp. 2–4 and consider the following questions:

★ Given your political values—your beliefs about liberty, equality, and democracy—what do you think of government efforts to address the coronavirus pandemic? If you were to contact an elected official about these efforts, which American values would you emphasize?

★ In what ways does the diversity of the American people represent a strength for American democracy? In what ways is it a challenge for democracy?

★ How important do you think participation, knowledge, and efficacy are for the functioning of American democracy? What would make you more engaged in government? Are your friends, family, or fellow students engaged in politics? How do you imagine Kimberly Green-Yates would answer these questions?

★ STUDY GUIDE ★

Practice Quiz

1. What is the difference between a totalitarian government and an authoritarian government? *(p. 7)*
   a) Authoritarian governments require popular participation, while totalitarian governments do not.
   b) Totalitarian governments are generally based on religion, while authoritarian governments are not.
   c) Authoritarian governments are often kept in check by other institutions, while totalitarian governments are not.
   d) Totalitarian governments acknowledge strict limits on their power, while authoritarian governments do not.
   e) There is no difference between these two kinds of government.

2. In all constitutional governments *(p. 7)*
   a) the government recognizes no formal limits on its power.
   b) presidential elections are held every four years.
   c) governmental power is held by a single individual.
   d) laws limit what governments can do and how they go about doing it.
   e) the government follows the wishes of the majority.

3. A state that permits its citizens to vote directly on laws and policies is practicing a form of *(p. 8)*
   a) representative democracy.
   b) direct democracy.
   c) pluralism.
   d) laissez-faire capitalism.
   e) republicanism.

4. How has the internet affected Americans' relationship with politics? *(p. 9)*
   a) Thanks to the internet, Americans' sense of political efficacy has increased in recent years.
   b) The internet has equalized access to political knowledge for people of different incomes, education levels, races, and ages.
   c) The internet now allows Americans to vote online.
   d) Large majorities of Americans now get political information from the internet.
   e) The internet has driven a decrease in rates of political participation among Americans.

5. *Political efficacy* is the belief that *(p. 10)*
   a) government operates efficiently.
   b) government has grown too large.
   c) government cannot be trusted.
   d) ordinary citizens can affect what government does.
   e) government is wasteful and corrupt.

6. The percentage of foreign-born individuals living in the United States *(p. 12)*
   a) has increased significantly since reaching its low point in 1970.
   b) has decreased significantly since reaching its high point in 1970.
   c) has remained the same since 1970.
   d) has never been less than the percentage of native-born individuals living in the United States.
   e) has not been studied since 1970.

7. In 2018, Latinos composed approximately what percentage of the American public? *(p. 12)*
   a) 67 percent
   b) 52 percent
   c) 31 percent
   d) 18 percent
   e) 6 percent

8. Which of the following statements best describes the shift in America's age profile since 1900? *(p. 14)*
   a) The percentage of adults over the age of 65 has declined dramatically.
   b) The percentage of adults over the age of 65 has increased dramatically.
   c) The percentage of adults over the age of 65 has remained constant.
   d) The percentage of children under the age of 18 has increased dramatically.
   e) The percentage of children under the age of 18 has remained constant.

9. What percentage of Americans live in urban areas today? *(p. 14)*
   a) less than 10 percent
   b) about 20 percent
   c) about 40 percent
   d) about 60 percent
   e) about 80 percent

10. Which of the following statements best describes the history of income inequality in the United States? *(p. 16)*
    a) The top 1 percent has never earned more than 10 percent of the nation's annual income.
    b) The top 1 percent has never earned less than 10 percent of the nation's annual income.
    c) Income inequality has remained fairly constant since the late 1970s.
    d) Income inequality has increased considerably since the late 1970s.
    e) Income inequality has decreased considerably since the late 1970s.

11. The phrase "Life, Liberty and the pursuit of Happiness" appears in *(p. 17)*
    a) the preamble to the Constitution.
    b) the Bill of Rights.
    c) the Declaration of Independence.
    d) the Magna Carta.
    e) the Gettysburg Address.

12. An economic system that allows the government very little power to regulate commerce or restrict the use of private property is called *(p. 18)*
    a) socialism.
    b) communism.
    c) laissez-faire capitalism.
    d) corporatism.
    e) feudalism.

13. The principle of political equality can be best summed up as *(p. 20)*
    a) "equality of results."
    b) "equality of opportunity."
    c) "one person, one vote."
    d) "equality between the sexes."
    e) "leave everyone alone."

14. Why are minority rights important for American democracy? *(p. 21)*
    a) The wishes of the minority determine what government does.
    b) The House of Representatives was designed to ensure minority rights.
    c) Minority interests are the backbone of popular sovereignty.
    d) Protecting minority interests ensures that government does not become a "tyranny of the majority."
    e) Minority rights are not important for American democracy.

15. Americans' trust in their government *(p. 24)*
    a) is at an all-time high.
    b) has risen steadily since the early 1960s.
    c) has remained relatively constant since the early 1960s.
    d) has declined since the early 1960s.
    e) has modestly increased since the early 1960s.

Key Terms

government *(p. 5)*

politics *(p. 5)*

autocracy *(p. 5)*

oligarchy *(p. 7)*

democracy *(p. 7)*

constitutional government *(p. 7)*

authoritarian government *(p. 7)*

totalitarian government *(p. 7)*

political power *(p. 8)*

representative democracy (republic) *(p. 8)*

direct democracy *(p. 8)*

pluralism *(p. 9)*

political knowledge *(p. 9)*

citizenship *(p. 9)*

political efficacy *(p. 10)*

political culture *(p. 17)*

liberty *(p. 17)*

limited government *(p. 17)*

laissez-faire capitalism *(p. 18)*

equality of opportunity *(p. 18)*

political equality *(p. 20)*

popular sovereignty *(p. 21)*

majority rule, minority rights *(p. 21)*

The Founding and the Constitution

WHAT GOVERNMENT DOES AND WHY IT MATTERS
Sometimes a concrete way the U.S. Constitution affects average Americans comes vividly to life, highlighting the framers' views about the nature of government. Because they feared that centralizing governmental powers might endanger individual liberties, they divided executive, legislative, and judicial powers across separate institutions, each of which restrains the others. Power was further divided across two levels in the federal system, between the national and state governments.

This constitutional system dramatically shaped the life of Jim Obergefell, a real estate agent and IT consultant in Cincinnati who in 1992 met and fell in love with John Arthur.[1] Although the couple wanted to marry, they could not. In 1996, Congress passed and President Bill Clinton signed the Defense of Marriage Act (DOMA), a federal law defining marriage as between one man and one woman. States could still permit same-sex marriage, but the marriages would not be recognized for federal purposes such as filing taxes or earning Social Security survivor benefits. The law also

From America's founding to today, debates over the role of the government in citizens' lives have persisted. After the historic decision to rule same-sex marriage a right guaranteed by the Constitution, Jim Obergefell holds a photo of his late husband on the steps of the Supreme Court to celebrate his bittersweet victory.

permitted states to refuse to recognize same-sex marriages performed in other states.

Thus Obergefell and Arthur were barred from marriage by the actions of two branches of the federal government—the executive and legislative—and their state, Ohio. The issue became more acute when Arthur was diagnosed with ALS, or Lou Gehrig's disease—a progressive debilitating disease. Obergefell served as Arthur's primary caregiver, and in 2013 the couple flew to Maryland, where same-sex marriage was permitted, and wed on the airport tarmac. Then they sued Ohio to have Obergefell be recognized as the surviving spouse on Arthur's imminent death certificate. "We decided to stand up for our marriage and to no longer accept being treated as second-class citizens,"[2] Obergefell explained. Arthur passed away three months later.

The case, *Obergefell v. Hodges*, made it to the Supreme Court, the top of the judicial branch of government, which in 2015 ruled that the due process and equal protection clauses of the Fourteenth Amendment to the Constitution guarantee to same-sex couples nationwide the fundamental right to marry.[3]

Thus the Court secured a civil right that the executive and legislative branches and a number of states had denied.

The U.S. Constitution lays out the purposes of government: to promote justice, to maintain peace at home, to defend the nation from foreign foes, to provide for the "general welfare" of Americans, and, above all, to secure the "blessings of liberty" for them. It also spells out a plan for achieving these objectives, including institutions to exercise legislative, executive, and judicial powers and a division of powers among the federal government's branches and between the national and state governments. Jim Obergefell's quest to marry the love of his life intersected with all three branches and both levels of government.

His story also shows that although many Americans believe strongly in the values of liberty, equality, and democracy, the ways those values are defined and implemented by the institutions that the Constitution created lead to considerable controversy. The framers believed that a good constitution created a government with the capacity to act forcefully. But they also believed that government should be compelled to take a variety of interests and viewpoints into account when it formulates policies. Sometimes the deliberation and compromise encouraged by the constitutional arrangements of "separated institutions sharing powers" can result in policy making that is slow or even gridlocked.[4] As this chapter will show, the Constitution reflects high principle as well as political self-interest.

CHAPTER GOALS

★ Explain the conflicts and coalitions that led to the Declaration of Independence and the Articles of Confederation (pp. 31–34)

★ Describe the political context of the Constitutional Convention and the compromises achieved there (pp. 34–39)

★ Describe the principles of governance and the powers of the national government defined by the Constitution (pp. 39–46)

★ Differentiate between the Federalists' and Antifederalists' stances on the ratification of the Constitution (pp. 47–51)

★ Explain how, and how often, the Constitution has been changed (pp. 51–55)

The First Founding: Interests and Conflicts

Explain the conflicts and coalitions that led to the Declaration of Independence and the Articles of Confederation

The American Revolution and the American Constitution were outgrowths of a struggle among economic and political forces within the colonies. Five sectors of society were important in colonial politics: (1) New England merchants; (2) southern planters; (3) "royalists"—holders of royal lands, offices, and patents (licenses to engage in a profession or business activity); (4) the "middling stratum" of shopkeepers, artisans, and town workers; and (5) small farmers.

Throughout the eighteenth century, these groups differed over issues of taxation, trade, and commerce. The merchants, planters, and royalists—that is, the colonial elite—maintained a political alliance that held in check the more radical forces representing the other two groups. After 1760, however, British tax and trade policies split the elite, enhancing the radicals' political influence and setting off a chain of events that culminated in the American Revolution.

BRITISH TAXES AND COLONIAL INTERESTS

During the first half of the eighteenth century, Britain ruled its American colonies with a light hand. British rule was hardly evident outside the largest towns, and colonists avoided most taxes levied in London. Beginning in the 1760s, however, debts and other financial problems forced the British government to search for new revenue sources. This search quickly led to the North American colonies.

The British government reasoned that much of its debt was due to defense of the colonies during the French and Indian War, which ended in 1763, and continuing British protection from Indian attacks and for colonial shipping. Thus, during the 1760s, Britain tried to impose new, though relatively modest, taxes on the colonists.

The Stamp Act of 1765 and other taxes on commerce, such as the Sugar Act of 1764, which taxed sugar, molasses, and other commodities, most heavily affected the two groups in colonial society with the most extensive commercial interests and activities—the New England merchants and the southern planters. United under the slogan "No taxation without representation," these members of the elite broke with their royalist allies and turned to their former adversaries—the shopkeepers, small farmers, laborers, and artisans—for help in opposing the tax measures. With their assistance, the merchants and planters organized demonstrations and a boycott of British goods that ultimately forced the Crown to rescind most of its hated new taxes.

In contrast to their new allies, the merchants and planters were now anxious to end the unrest they had helped arouse. Indeed, most respectable Bostonians supported the actions of the British soldiers involved in the Boston Massacre—the 1770 killing of five colonists by British soldiers who were attempting to repel an angry mob gathered outside the Town House, the seat of the colonial government. In their subsequent trial, the soldiers were defended by John Adams, a pillar of Boston society and a future president of the United States. Adams asserted that the soldiers' actions were entirely justified, provoked by "a motley rabble of saucy boys, negroes and mulattoes, Irish teagues and outlandish Jack tars." All but two of the soldiers were acquitted.[5]

Despite the efforts of the British government and the colonial elite, however, it proved difficult to end the political strife. Under leadership that included Samuel Adams, a cousin of John Adams, the more radical forces asserted that British power supported an unjust political and social structure within the colonies and soon advocated an end to British rule.[6]

POLITICAL STRIFE RADICALIZED THE COLONISTS

Growing colonial strife was the background for the events of 1773–74. With the Tea Act of 1773, the British government granted the politically powerful East India Company a monopoly on the export of tea from Britain, eliminating a lucrative trade for colonial business interests. Worse, the company planned to sell the tea directly in the colonies instead of working through the colonial merchants. Tea was an extremely important commodity during the 1770s, and these British actions posed a serious threat to New England business interests.

The British helped radicalize colonists through bad policy decisions in the years before the Revolution. For example, Britain gave the ailing East India Company a monopoly on the tea trade in the American colonies. Colonists feared that the monopoly would hurt colonial merchants' business and protested by throwing East India Company tea into Boston Harbor in 1773.

Together with their southern allies, the merchants once again called for support from the radicals, whose own grievances against the British and the colonial government included the Tea Act's continuation of an earlier tea tax. The most dramatic result was the Boston Tea Party. In three other colonies, antitax Americans blocked the unloading of taxed tea, resulting in its return to Britain. The royal governor of Massachusetts, however, refused to allow three shiploads of unsold tea to leave Boston Harbor. The radicals seized this opportunity: on the night of December 16, 1773, a group led by Samuel Adams, some of them "disguised" as Mohawk Indians, boarded the three vessels and threw all 342 chests of tea into the harbor.

Although the merchants had hoped to force the British to rescind the Tea Act, they did not seek independence from Britain. Through the Boston Tea Party, however, Adams and the other radicals hoped to provoke the British into actions that would alienate their colonial supporters and pave the way for a rebellion. Their plan succeeded, as Parliament enacted a number of harsh reprisals that included closing the port of Boston to commerce, changing the colonial government of Massachusetts, removing accused persons to Britain for trial, and, most important, restricting colonists' movement to the west—further alienating the southern planters, who depended on access to new western lands.

These acts of repression further radicalized Americans, and set in motion a cycle of provocation and retaliation that in 1774 resulted in the convening of the First Continental Congress. An assembly of delegates from 12 colonies, the Congress called for a total boycott of British goods and, under the prodding of the radicals, began to consider the possibility of ending British rule. The eventual result was the Declaration of Independence.

THE DECLARATION OF INDEPENDENCE EXPLAINED WHY THE COLONISTS WANTED TO BREAK WITH GREAT BRITAIN

In 1776, more than a year after open warfare had commenced in Massachusetts, the Second Continental Congress appointed a committee consisting of Thomas Jefferson of Virginia, Benjamin Franklin of Pennsylvania, Roger Sherman of Connecticut, John Adams of Massachusetts, and Robert Livingston of New York to draft a statement of American independence from British rule. The Declaration of Independence, written by Jefferson and adopted by the Congress, was an extraordinary document both philosophically and politically. Philosophically, it was remarkable for its assertion that government could not deprive people of certain "unalienable rights" that include "Life, Liberty, and the pursuit of Happiness." In the world of 1776, in which some kings still claimed a God-given right to rule, this was a dramatic statement. Politically, the Declaration was remarkable because, despite the differences among the colonists along economic, regional, and philosophical lines, it focused on grievances, goals, and principles that might unify the various groups. The Declaration was an attempt to identify and put into words a set of principles to forge national unity.[7]

THE ARTICLES OF CONFEDERATION CREATED AMERICA'S FIRST NATIONAL GOVERNMENT

Having declared independence, the colonies needed to establish a government. In November 1777 the Continental Congress adopted the **Articles of Confederation**—the United States' first written constitution. Eventually ratified by all the states in 1781, it functioned as the country's constitution until the final months of 1788.

The first goal of the Articles was to limit the powers of the central government; as provided under Article II, "each state retains its sovereignty, freedom, and independence." (These attributes define a **confederation**.) Given that there was no president or other presiding officer, the entire national government consisted of a Congress with very little power. Its members were little more than messengers from the state legislatures: their salaries were paid out of the state treasuries; they were subject to immediate recall by state authorities; and each state, regardless of its population, had only one vote. All 13 states had to agree to any amendments to the Articles of Confederation after it was ratified.

Articles of Confederation America's first written constitution; served as the basis for America's national government until 1789

confederation a system of government in which states retain sovereign authority except for the powers expressly delegated to the national government

Congress was given the power to declare war and make peace, to make treaties and alliances, to issue currency, to borrow money, and to regulate trade with the Native Americans. Any laws it passed, however, could be carried out only by state governments. It could also appoint the senior officers of the U.S. Army, but there was no such army because the nation's armed forces consisted only of the state militias. These extreme limits on the power of the national government made the Articles of Confederation hopelessly impractical.[8]

The Failure of the Articles of Confederation Made the "Second Founding" Necessary

Describe the political context of the Constitutional Convention and the compromises achieved there

A series of developments following the armistice with Britain in 1783 highlighted the shortcomings of the Articles of Confederation in holding the former colonies together as an independent and effective nation-state.

First, the United States had great difficulty conducting its foreign affairs successfully, as there was no national military and competition among the states for foreign commerce allowed the European powers to play them off against one another. At one point, John Adams, who had become a leader in the independence struggle, was sent to negotiate a new treaty with Britain, one that would cover disputes left over from the war. The British responded that since the United States under the Articles was unable to enforce existing treaties, it would negotiate with each of the 13 states separately.

Second, the power that states retained under the Articles of Confederation began to alarm well-to-do Americans, in particular New England merchants and southern planters, when radical forces gained power in a number of state governments. As a result of the Revolution, one key segment of the colonial elite—the royal land, office, and patent holders—was stripped of its economic and political privileges. While the elite was weakened, the radicals had gained strength and now controlled states including Pennsylvania and Rhode Island, where they pursued policies that struck terror in the hearts of business and property owners throughout the country. The central government under the Articles was powerless to intervene.

The Congress of the Confederation did, however, agree on two laws that helped to shape American history: the Land Ordinance of 1785 and the Northwest Ordinance of 1787. The Land Ordinance established the principles of land surveying and ownership that governed America's westward expansion. Under the Northwest Ordinance, the individual states agreed to surrender their claims to incorporate land on their western frontiers, opening the way for the admission of new states to the Union.

THE ANNAPOLIS CONVENTION WAS KEY TO CALLING A NATIONAL CONVENTION

Continued international weakness and domestic economic turmoil led many Americans to consider revising their newly adopted form of government. In the fall of 1786, the Virginia legislature invited representatives of all the states to a convention in Annapolis, Maryland. Delegates from only five states actually attended, so nothing substantive could be accomplished. The only concrete result of the Annapolis Convention was a carefully worded resolution calling on the Congress to send commissioners to Philadelphia at a later time "to devise such further provisions as shall appear to them necessary to render the Constitution of the Federal Government adequate to the exigencies of the Union."[9] But the resolution did not necessarily imply any desire to do more than improve the Articles of Confederation.

SHAYS'S REBELLION

It is quite possible that the Constitutional Convention of 1787 in Philadelphia would never have taken place at all except for Shays's Rebellion. In the winter following the Annapolis Convention, Daniel Shays, a former army captain, led a mob of debt-ridden farmers in an effort to prevent foreclosures on their land by keeping the county courts of western Massachusetts from sitting until after the next election. A militia organized by the state governor and funded by a group of prominent merchants dispersed the mob, but Shays and his followers then attempted to capture the federal arsenal at Springfield. Within a few days, the state government regained control and captured 14 of the rebels. Later that year, a newly elected

Daniel Shays's rebellion proved the Articles of Confederation were too weak to protect the fledgling nation.

Massachusetts legislature granted some of the farmers' demands.

George Washington summed up the effects of the incident on the leaders of the new nation: "I am mortified beyond expression that in the moment of our acknowledged independence we should by our conduct verify the predictions of our transatlantic foe, and render ourselves ridiculous and contemptible in the eyes of all Europe."[10] The Congress under the Confederation had shown itself unable to act decisively in a time of crisis, providing critics of the Articles with precisely the evidence they needed to push the Annapolis resolution through the Congress. Thus, the states were asked to send representatives to Philadelphia to discuss constitutional revision. Delegates were eventually sent by every state except Rhode Island.

THE CONSTITUTIONAL CONVENTION DIDN'T START OUT TO WRITE A NEW CONSTITUTION

The delegates who convened in Philadelphia in May 1787 had political strife, international embarrassment, national weakness, and local rebellion fixed in their minds. Recognizing that these issues were symptoms of fundamental flaws in the Articles of Confederation, the delegates soon abandoned the plan to revise the Articles and committed themselves to a second founding—a second, and ultimately successful, attempt to create a legitimate and effective national system of government. This effort would occupy the convention for the next five months.

A Marriage of Interest and Principle For years, scholars have disagreed about the motives of the Founders in Philadelphia. Among the most controversial views is the "economic interpretation" by the historian Charles Beard and his disciples,[11] in which the Founders were a group of securities speculators and property owners motivated only by money. From this perspective, the Constitution's lofty principles were little more than sophisticated masks behind which its sponsors aimed to enrich themselves.

The opposite view is that the framers of the Constitution *were* concerned with philosophical and ethical principles—that they aimed to create a system of government consistent with the dominant philosophical and moral principles of the day, including limited government, separation of powers, and individual liberty. But in fact these two views belong together: the Founders' interests were reinforced by their principles. The convention that drafted the Constitution was chiefly organized by the New England merchants and southern planters. Although the delegates representing these groups did not all hope to profit personally from an increase in the value of their securities, as Beard would have it, they did hope to benefit in the broadest sense by breaking the power of their radical foes and establishing a system of government more compatible with their long-term economic and political interests. A new government, they believed, should be capable of promoting commerce and protecting property from radical state legislatures and populist forces hostile to the commercial and propertied classes.

The Great Compromise Supporters of a new government fired their opening shot on May 29, 1787, when Edmund Randolph of Virginia offered a resolution that proposed sweeping corrections and additions to the Articles of Confederation. The proposal, which showed the strong influence of James Madison, provided for virtually every aspect of a new government.

The portion of Randolph's motion that became most controversial was called the **Virginia Plan**. This plan provided for representation in the national legislature to be based on the population of each state or the proportion of each state's revenue contribution to the national government, or both. (Randolph also proposed a second chamber of the legislature, to be elected by the members of the first chamber.) Since the states varied enormously in population and wealth, the Virginia Plan was heavily biased in favor of the large states.

While the convention was debating the Virginia Plan, opposition to it began to mount as more delegates arrived in Philadelphia. William Paterson of New Jersey introduced a resolution known as the **New Jersey Plan**. Its main proponents were delegates from the less populous states, including Delaware, New Jersey, Connecticut, and New York, who asserted that the more populous states—Virginia, Pennsylvania, North Carolina, Massachusetts, and Georgia—would dominate the new government if representation were determined by population. The smaller states argued that each state should be equally represented regardless of its population.

The issue of representation threatened to wreck the entire constitutional enterprise. As factions maneuvered and tempers flared, the Union, as Luther Martin of Maryland put it, was "on the verge of dissolution, scarcely held together by the strength of a hair."[12] Finally, the debate was settled by the Connecticut Compromise, also known as the **Great Compromise**. Under its terms, in one chamber of Congress—the House of Representatives—seats would be apportioned according to population, as delegates from the large states had wished. But in a second chamber—the Senate—each state would have equal representation, as small states preferred.

Virginia Plan a framework for the Constitution, introduced by Edmund Randolph, that called for representation in the national legislature based on the population of each state

New Jersey Plan a framework for the Constitution, introduced by William Paterson, that called for equal state representation in the national legislature regardless of population

Great Compromise the agreement reached at the Constitutional Convention of 1787 that gave each state an equal number of senators regardless of its population but linked representation in the House of Representatives to population

The Question of Slavery: The Three-Fifths Compromise Many of the conflicts that emerged during the Constitutional Convention reflected the fundamental differences between the southern and northern states related to slavery. These disputes pitted the southern planters against the New England merchants at the convention and would almost destroy the Republic in later years. Even in the midst of debate about other issues, James Madison observed that "the great danger" lay in the opposition of "southern and northern interests."[13]

More than 90 percent of the country's enslaved people lived in five states—Georgia, Maryland, North Carolina, South Carolina, and Virginia—where they accounted for 30 percent of the total population. Were they to be counted as part of a state's population even though they were not citizens, thereby giving southern states increased representation in the House? If the Constitution was to incorporate the principle of the national government's supremacy over the states, decisions were required about slavery.

Most delegates from northern states opposed counting the population of enslaved people in the apportionment of congressional seats, although this did not necessarily mean they opposed slavery itself. James Wilson of Pennsylvania, for example, argued that if enslaved people were counted for this purpose, other forms of property should be as well. But southern delegates made it clear that they would

Despite the Founders' emphasis on liberty, the new Constitution allowed slavery, counting three-fifths of all enslaved people in apportioning seats in the House of Representatives. In this 1792 painting, *Liberty Displaying the Arts and Sciences*, the books, instruments, and classical columns at the left contrast with the kneeling enslaved people at the right—illustrating the divide between America's rhetoric of liberty and equality and the reality of slavery.

never agree to the new government if the northerners refused to give in. Northerners and southerners eventually reached agreement through the **Three-Fifths Compromise**: congressional seats would be apportioned according to a "population" in which three-fifths of enslaved people would be counted.

Slavery was the most difficult issue the framers faced, and it nearly destroyed the Union. Although some delegates saw it as an evil institution that made a mockery of the ideals expressed in the Constitution, morality was not what caused individual framers to support or oppose the Three-Fifths Compromise. Indeed, to keep the South in the Union, northerners even allowed the slave trade to continue. But in due course, the incompatible interests of the North and the South could no longer be reconciled, and a bloody civil war was the result.

The Constitution Created Both Bold Powers and Sharp Limits on Power

> **Describe the principles of governance and the powers of the national government defined by the Constitution**

The Great Compromise and the Three-Fifths Compromise reinforced the unity of the merchant and planter forces aiming to create a new government. The Great Compromise reassured those in both groups who feared the new framework would reduce their own local or regional influence, and the Three-Fifths Compromise temporarily defused the rivalry between the groups. Their unity secured, members of the alliance moved to fashion a constitution consistent with their economic and political interests.

In particular, the framers wanted a new government that, first, would be strong enough to promote commerce and protect property from radical state legislatures such as Rhode Island's. This goal led to the constitutional provisions for national control over commerce and finance, for national judicial supremacy over state courts, and for a strong presidency. (See Table 2.1 for a comparison of the Articles of Confederation with the Constitution.)

Second, the framers wanted to prevent what they saw as the threat posed by the "excessive democracy" of both state and national governments under the Articles of Confederation. This desire led to such constitutional principles as a **bicameral**, or two-chambered, legislature; **checks and balances** among the branches of government; staggered terms in office; and indirect election (selection of the president

Three-Fifths Compromise the agreement reached at the Constitutional Convention of 1787 that stipulated that for purposes of the apportionment of congressional seats only three-fifths of enslaved people would be counted

bicameral having a legislative assembly composed of two chambers or houses; distinguished from *unicameral*

checks and balances mechanisms through which each branch of government is able to participate in and influence the activities of the other branches; major examples include the presidential veto power over congressional legislation, the power of the Senate to approve presidential appointments, and judicial review of congressional enactments

TABLE 2.1
. . . .

Comparing the Articles of Confederation and the Constitution

MAJOR PROVISIONS	ARTICLES OF CONFEDERATION	CONSTITUTION
Executive branch	None	President of the United States
Judiciary	No federal court system. Judiciary exists only at state level.	Federal judiciary headed by Supreme Court.
Legislature	Unicameral legislature with equal representation for each state. Delegates to the Congress of the Confederation were appointed by the states.	Bicameral legislature consisting of Senate and House of Representatives. Each state is represented by two senators, while apportionment in the House is based on each state's population. Senators are chosen by the state legislatures (changed to direct popular election in 1913) for six-year terms and members of the House by popular election for two-year terms.
Fiscal and economic powers	The national government is dependent upon the states to collect taxes. The states are free to coin their own money and print paper money. The states are free to sign commercial treaties with foreign governments.	Congress given the power to levy taxes, coin money, and regulate international and interstate commerce. States prohibited from coining money or entering into treaties with other nations.
Military	The national government is dependent upon state militias and cannot form an army during peacetime.	The national government is authorized to maintain an army and navy.
Legal supremacy	State constitutions and state law are supreme.	National Constitution and national law are supreme.
Constitutional amendment	Must be agreed upon by all states.	Must be agreed upon by three-fourths of the states.

by an electoral college and of senators by state legislatures, rather than directly by voters).

Third, lacking the power to force the states or the public to accept the new form of government, the framers wanted to identify principles that would help gain support for it. This goal became the basis of the constitutional provision for direct popular election of representatives and, later, of the addition of the **Bill of Rights** to the Constitution.

Finally, the framers wanted to ensure that the government they created did not pose an even greater threat to its citizens' liberties and property rights than did the radical state legislatures they despised. To prevent abuses of power, they incorporated principles such as the **separation of powers** and **federalism** into the Constitution. In Table 2.1, we assess the major provisions of the Constitution's seven articles to see how each relates to these objectives.

Bill of Rights the first 10 amendments to the U.S. Constitution, ratified in 1791; they ensure certain rights and liberties to the people

separation of powers the division of governmental power among several institutions that must cooperate in decision-making

federalism a system of government in which power is divided, by a constitution, between a central government and regional governments

THE LEGISLATIVE BRANCH WAS DESIGNED TO BE THE MOST POWERFUL

In Article I, Sections 1–7, the Constitution provides for a Congress consisting of two chambers: a House of Representatives and a Senate. Members of the House of Representatives were given two-year terms in office and were to be elected directly by the people. Members of the Senate were to be appointed by the state legislatures (a provision changed in 1913 by the Seventeenth Amendment, which instituted direct election of senators) for six-year terms. These terms were staggered so that the terms of one-third of the senators would expire every two years.

The Constitution assigned somewhat different tasks to the House and Senate. Though the enactment of a law requires the approval of both, the Senate alone is given the power to ratify treaties and approve presidential appointments. The House, on the other hand, is given the sole power to originate revenue bills.

The character of the legislative branch was related to the framers' major goals. The House was designed to be directly responsible to the people, with all members serving two-year terms, to encourage popular support for the new Constitution and thus enhance the power of the new government. At the same time, to guard against "excessive democracy," the power of the House was checked by that of the Senate, whose members were to be appointed by the states for long terms rather than elected directly by the people for short ones. The purpose of this provision, according to Alexander Hamilton, was to avoid "an unqualified complaisance to every sudden breeze of passion, or to every transient impulse which the people may receive."[14] Staggered terms in the Senate were intended to make that body even more resistant to popular pressure. Since only one-third of the senators would be selected every two years, the institution would be protected from changes in public opinion transmitted by the state legislatures.

The issues of governmental power and popular consent are important throughout the Constitution. Section 8 of Article I specifically lists the powers of Congress, which include the authority to collect taxes, borrow money, regulate commerce, declare war, and maintain an army and navy. By granting Congress these powers, the framers indicated clearly that they intended the new government to be far more

expressed powers specific powers granted by the Constitution to Congress (Article I, Section 8) and to the president (Article II)

elastic clause the concluding paragraph of Article I, Section 8, of the Constitution (also known as the "necessary and proper clause"), which provides Congress with the authority to make all laws "necessary and proper" to carry out its enumerated powers

powerful than its predecessor under the Articles of Confederation. At the same time, by assigning its most important powers to Congress, they promoted popular acceptance of this critical change by reassuring citizens that their views would be fully represented whenever these powers were used.

As a further guarantee that the new government would pose no threat to the people, the Constitution implies that any powers not listed were not granted at all. This is what Chief Justice John Marshall named the doctrine of **expressed powers**: the Constitution grants only those powers specifically expressed in its text. But the framers intended to create an active and powerful government, so they also included the necessary and proper clause, also called the **elastic clause**, which declares that Congress can write laws needed to carry out its expressed powers. This clause indicates that expressed powers could be broadly interpreted and were meant to be a source of strength to the national government, not a limitation on it. In response to the charge that they intended to give it too much power, the framers included language in the Tenth Amendment stipulating that powers not specifically granted by the Constitution to the federal government were reserved to the states or to the people. As we will see in Chapter 3, the resulting tension between the elastic clause and the Tenth Amendment has been at the heart of constitutional struggles between federal and state powers.

THE EXECUTIVE BRANCH CREATED A BRAND-NEW OFFICE

The Articles of Confederation had not provided for an executive branch. The president under the Articles was the official chosen by the Congress to preside over its sessions, not the chief executive of the national government. The framers viewed the absence of an executive as a source of weakness. Accordingly, the Constitution provides for the presidency in Article II. As Hamilton commented, the article aims toward "energy in the Executive."[15] It does so in an effort to overcome the natural tendency toward stalemate that was built into the separation of the legislature into two chambers and of governmental powers among the three branches. The Constitution affords the president a measure of independence from both the people and the other branches of government—particularly the Congress.

In line with the framers' goal of increased power to the national government, the president is granted the power to accept ambassadors from other countries—to "recognize" other governments—as well as the power to negotiate treaties, although their acceptance requires the approval of the Senate by a two-thirds vote. The president also has the power to grant reprieves and pardons, except in cases of impeachment, appoint major departmental personnel, convene Congress in a special session, and veto bills it passes. The veto power is not absolute, since Congress can override it by a two-thirds vote, reflecting the framers' concern with checks and balances.

The framers hoped to create a presidency that would make the federal government rather than the states the agency capable of timely and decisive action to deal with national issues and problems. At the same time, however, they tried to help the presidency withstand excessively democratic pressures by establishing an electoral college through which to elect the president.

THE JUDICIAL BRANCH WAS A CHECK ON TOO MUCH DEMOCRACY

Article III created a single court intended to be the supreme judicial authority of the United States, not merely the highest court of the national government. The most important expression of this intention is granting the Supreme Court the power to resolve any conflicts between federal and state laws. In particular, it can determine whether a power is exclusive to the national government, exclusive to the states, or shared between the two.

In addition, the Supreme Court is assigned jurisdiction over controversies between citizens of different states. As the country developed a national economy, it came to rely increasingly on the federal judiciary, rather than state courts, to resolve disputes.

Federal judges are given lifetime appointments to protect them from political or public pressure and from interference by the other branches. The judiciary is not totally free of political considerations or the other branches, however, for the president appoints the judges and the Senate must approve the appointments. Congress also has the power to create inferior (lower) courts, change the jurisdiction of the federal courts (the geographic area or types of cases they have authority over), add or subtract federal judges, remove judges through impeachment, and even change the size of the Supreme Court.

The Constitution does not explicitly mention **judicial review**—the power of a court to determine whether the actions of the Congress or the executive are consistent with law and the Constitution. The Supreme Court eventually assumed the power of judicial review. Its assumption of this power, as we shall see in Chapter 13, was based not on the Constitution itself but on the politics of later decades and the membership of the Court.

judicial review the power of the courts to review actions of the legislative and executive branches and, if necessary, declare them invalid or unconstitutional; the Supreme Court asserted this power in *Marbury v. Madison* (1803)

NATIONAL UNITY AND POWER SET THE NEW CONSTITUTION APART FROM THE OLD ARTICLES

The Constitution addressed the framers' concern with national unity and power in the comity clause of Article IV, which provides for reciprocity among all states and their citizens. That is, each state is prohibited from discriminating against the citizens of or goods from other states in favor of its own citizens or goods, with the Supreme Court charged with deciding cases where such discrimination is alleged. The Constitution thus restricts the power of the states so as to give the national

supremacy clause Article VI
of the Constitution, which
states that laws passed by the
national government and all
treaties are the supreme law
of the land and superior to all
laws adopted by any state or
any subdivision

government enough power to ensure a free-flowing national economy.

The framers' concern with national supremacy was also expressed in Article VI, whose "**supremacy clause**" provides that national laws and treaties "shall be the supreme Law of the Land." This means that laws made under the "Authority of the United States" are superior to those adopted by any state or other sub-division and that the states must respect all treaties made under that authority. The supremacy clause also binds all state and local as well as federal officials to take an oath to support the national Constitution. Therefore, they must enforce national law over state law if the two conflict.

THE CONSTITUTION ESTABLISHES THE PROCESS FOR AMENDMENT

The Constitution establishes procedures for its own amendment in Article V. The requirements are so difficult that, as we shall see later in the chapter, the amending process has succeeded only 17 times since 1791, when the first 10 amendments were adopted.

THE CONSTITUTION SETS FORTH RULES FOR ITS OWN RATIFICATION

The rules for ratification, or adoption, of the Constitution are set forth in Article VII. Of the 13 states, 9 would have to ratify it in order for it to go into effect.

CONSTITUTIONAL LIMITS ON THE NATIONAL GOVERNMENT'S POWER

Although the framers wanted a powerful national government, they also wanted to guard against possible misuse of that power. Thus they incorporated two key principles into the Constitution—federalism and the separation of powers. A third set of limitations, the Bill of Rights, was added to the Constitution in the form of 10 amendments proposed by the first Congress and ratified by the states. Most of the framers had thought a Bill of Rights unnecessary but accepted the idea during the ratification debates after the new Constitution was submitted to the states for approval.

The Separation of Powers No principle of politics was more widely shared at the time of the 1787 Founding than that power must be used to balance power. Although the principle of the separation of powers is not explicitly stated in the Constitution, the entire structure of the national government was built precisely on Article I, the legislature; Article II, the executive; and Article III, the judiciary (see Figure 2.1).

FIGURE 2.1

The Separation of Powers

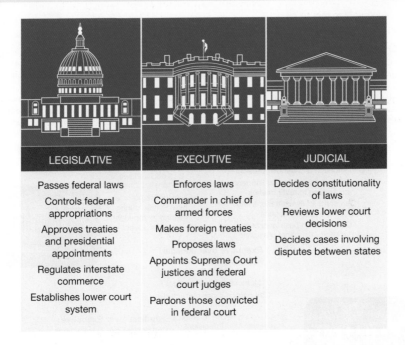

LEGISLATIVE	EXECUTIVE	JUDICIAL
Passes federal laws	Enforces laws	Decides constitutionality of laws
Controls federal appropriations	Commander in chief of armed forces	Reviews lower court decisions
Approves treaties and presidential appointments	Makes foreign treaties	Decides cases involving disputes between states
Regulates interstate commerce	Proposes laws	
Establishes lower court system	Appoints Supreme Court justices and federal court judges	
	Pardons those convicted in federal court	

The method adopted to maintain that separation became known by the popular label "checks and balances" (see Figure 2.2). Each branch is given not only its own powers but also some power over the other two branches. Among the most familiar checks and balances are the president's veto power over Congress and Congress's power over the president through its control of appointments to high executive posts and to the judiciary. Congress also has power over the president with its control of appropriations (the spending of government money) and the requirement that the Senate ratify treaties. The judiciary has the power of judicial review over the other two branches.

Another important principle of the separation of powers is giving each branch a distinctly different constituency—with the president chosen, indirectly, by electors; the House, by popular vote; the Senate (originally), by state legislatures; and the judiciary, by presidential appointment. By these means, the occupants of each branch would tend to develop very different outlooks on how to govern, different definitions of the public interest, and different alliances with private interests.

Federalism Compared with the decentralizing principle of the Articles of Confederation, federalism was a step toward greater concentration of power. The delegates

FIGURE 2.2

Checks and Balances

Executive over Legislative
Can veto acts of Congress
Can call Congress into a special session
Carries out, and thereby interprets, laws passed by Congress
Vice president casts tie-breaking vote in the Senate

LEGISLATIVE

Legislative over Judicial
Can change size of federal court system and the number of Supreme Court justices
Can propose constitutional amendments
Can reject Supreme Court nominees
Can impeach and remove federal judges

Legislative over Executive
Can override presidential veto
Can impeach and remove president
Can reject president's appointments and refuse to ratify treaties
Can conduct investigations into president's actions
Can refuse to pass laws or to provide funding that president requests

Judicial over Legislative
Can declare laws unconstitutional
Chief justice presides over Senate during hearing to impeach the president

JUDICIAL

Executive over Judicial
Nominates Supreme Court justices
Nominates federal judges
Can pardon those convicted in federal court
Can refuse to enforce Court decisions

Judicial over Executive
Can declare executive actions unconstitutional
Power to issue warrants
Chief justice presides over impeachment of president

EXECUTIVE

to the Constitutional Convention agreed that they needed to place more power at the national level without completely undermining the power of the state governments. Thus, they devised a system of two sovereigns, or supreme powers—the states and the nation—with the hope that competition between them would effectively limit the power of each.

The Bill of Rights Late in the convention, a motion to include a list of citizens' rights in the Constitution was almost unanimously turned down. Most delegates sincerely believed that since the federal government was already limited to its expressed powers, further protection of citizens was not needed. These delegates argued that it was states that should adopt bills of rights because their greater powers needed greater limitations. But almost immediately after the Constitution was ratified, a movement arose to adopt a national bill of rights. This is why the Bill of Rights, adopted in 1791, comprises the first 10 amendments to the Constitution rather than being part of the body of it. (We will have more to say about the Bill of Rights in Chapter 4.)

Ratification of the Constitution Was Difficult

Differentiate between the Federalists' and Antifederalists' stances on the ratification of the Constitution

The first hurdle faced by the proposed Constitution was ratification by state conventions of delegates elected by White, property-owning male voters. This struggle for ratification included 13 separate state campaigns, each influenced by local as well as national considerations.

Two sides faced off in all the states, calling themselves **Federalists** and **Antifederalists** (see Table 2.2). The Federalists (who more accurately could have called themselves "Nationalists") supported the Constitution and preferred a strong national government. The Antifederalists opposed the Constitution and preferred a more decentralized federal system. The Federalists were united in their support of the Constitution, whereas the Antifederalists were divided over possible alternatives.

FEDERALISTS AND ANTIFEDERALISTS FOUGHT BITTERLY OVER THE WISDOM OF THE NEW CONSTITUTION

Thousands of essays, speeches, pamphlets, and letters were presented for and against ratification of the proposed Constitution. The best-known pieces in support were the 85 articles published in New York City newspapers by Alexander Hamilton, James Madison, and John Jay. These *Federalist Papers*, as they are known today, defended the principles of the Constitution and sought to dispel fears of a strong national government. Meanwhile, the Antifederalists, including Patrick Henry and Richard Henry Lee, argued in their speeches and writings that the new Constitution betrayed the Revolution and was a step toward monarchy.

Federalists those who favored a strong national government and supported the Constitution proposed at the American Constitutional Convention of 1787

Representation One major area of contention between the two sides was the nature of political representation. The Antifederalists asserted that representatives must be "a true picture of the people . . . [possessing] the knowledge of their circumstances and their wants."[16] This could be achieved, they argued, only in small republics such as each of the existing states, whose people were relatively similar to one another. In their view, the size and diverse population of the entire nation made a truly representative form of government impossible.

Federalists saw no reason that representatives should be precisely like those they represented. In

Antifederalists those who favored strong state governments and a weak national government and who were opponents of the Constitution proposed at the American Constitutional Convention of 1787

Federalist Papers a series of essays written by Alexander Hamilton, James Madison, and John Jay supporting ratification of the Constitution

TABLE 2.2

Federalists versus Antifederalists

	FEDERALISTS	ANTIFEDERALISTS
Who were they?	Property owners, creditors, merchants	Small farmers, frontiersmen, debtors, shopkeepers, some state government officials
What did they believe?	Believed that elites were most fit to govern; feared "excessive democracy"	Believed that government should be closer to the people; feared concentration of power in hands of the elites
What system of government did they favor?	Favored strong national government; believed in "filtration" so that only elites would obtain governmental power	Favored retention of power by state governments and protection of individual rights
Who were their leaders?	Alexander Hamilton, James Madison, George Washington	Patrick Henry, George Mason, Elbridge Gerry, George Clinton

their view, one of the great advantages of representative government over direct democracy was precisely the possibility that the people would choose individuals with experience and talent greater than their own to represent them. In Madison's words, rather than mirroring society, representatives must be "[those] who possess [the] most wisdom to discern, and [the] most virtue to pursue, the common good of the society."[17]

Tyranny A second important issue dividing Federalists and Antifederalists was the threat of **tyranny**—unjust rule by the group in power. The two sides, however, had different views of the most likely source of tyranny, and thus they had different ideas about how to keep it from emerging.

For the Antifederalists, the great danger was the tendency of republican governments to become gradually more and more "aristocratic," with members of the small group in authority using their positions to gain more and more power over other citizens. In essence, Antifederalists feared, the few would tyrannize the many. For this reason, they sharply criticized those features of the Constitution that created governmental institutions without direct responsibility to the people—such as the Senate, the presidency, and particularly the federal judiciary, with its lifetime appointments.

The Federalists, on the other hand, viewed the danger particularly associated with republican governments not as aristocracy but as tyranny over the few by the many. They feared that a popular majority, "united and actuated by some common impulse of passion, or of interest, adverse to the rights of other citizens," would "trample on the rules of justice."[18] From their perspective, those features of the Constitution that the Antifederalists attacked as potential sources of tyranny actually

tyranny oppressive government that employs cruel and unjust use of power and authority

Democratic Systems

Executive authority is vested in different positions in different countries. In parliamentary systems the prime minister is both the chief executive and the head of the legislature. In presidential systems, such as in the United States, the executive and legislative branches are separate. Some countries use a semi-presidential system in which there is a president who heads the executive branch and has limited authority, and a prime minister who heads the legislative branch. Parliamentary systems can be more efficient, as the prime minister can wield a lot of authority, but only if his or her party has a sizable and stable majority in Parliament. Presidential and semi-presidential systems can lead to more gridlock, as there are multiple seats of power.

1. Does one system seem more common than another? Why might one country have a parliamentary system while its neighbor has a presidential system?
2. What do you think would be the advantages to having executive and legislative authority vested in the same individual? What are the advantages to a system such as that of the United States, where powers are separated in independent branches? Do you think the advantages of one system over another are different today than they were 250 years ago at the founding of the United States?

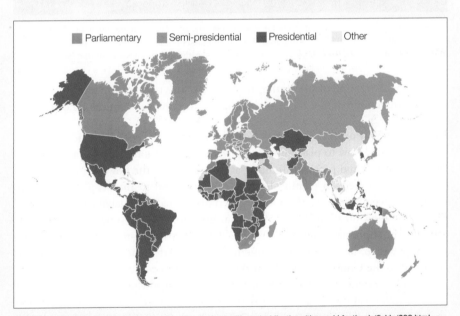

Legend: ■ Parliamentary ■ Semi-presidential ■ Presidential ■ Other

SOURCE: CIA World Factbook, "Government Type," www.cia.gov/library/publications/the-world-factbook/fields/299.html (accessed 12/5/19).

Debates over how much power the national government should have continue today. After the San Bernardino shooting in 2015, the FBI demanded Apple unlock the perpetrator's iPhone for details into his criminal activity. Here, a group protests the FBI's infringement on the right to privacy.

offered the best hope of preventing it. They saw the nation's size and diversity as further protection because these made it harder to unite a tyrannical majority.

Governmental Power A third major difference between Federalists and Antifederalists concerned how to place limits on governmental action. Antifederalists favored **limited government** and proposed limiting and spelling out the powers granted to the national government in relation both to the states and to the people at large. To them, its powers ought to be "confined to certain defined national objects"[19] so that it did not "swallow up all the power of the state governments."[20] Antifederalists bitterly attacked the supremacy and elastic clauses of the Constitution as dangerous surrenders of power to the national government.[21] They also demanded that a bill of rights be added to the Constitution to limit the government's power over the people.

In reply, Federalists such as Hamilton acknowledged the possibility that every power could be abused, but argued that the risk was worth taking in order to give the government the powers needed to achieve essential national goals. In addition, the risk of abuse would be minimized by the various checks and controls on power incorporated into the Constitution. As Madison put it, "the power surrendered by the people is first divided between two distinct governments (state and national), and then the portion allotted to each subdivided among

limited government a principle of constitutional government; a government whose powers are defined and limited by a constitution

distinct and separate departments. Hence, a double security arises to the rights of the people. The different governments will control each other, at the same time that each will be controlled by itself."[22] The Federalists' concern with avoiding unwarranted limits on governmental power led them to oppose a bill of rights as unnecessary, although this Antifederalist demand was eventually embraced by Federalists, including Madison.

BOTH FEDERALISTS AND ANTIFEDERALISTS CONTRIBUTED TO THE SUCCESS OF THE NEW SYSTEM

Antifederalist criticisms did force the addition of a bill of rights, but it was the Federalist vision of America that triumphed. The Constitution adopted in 1789 created the framework for a powerful national government that for more than 200 years has defended the nation's interests, promoted its commerce, and maintained national unity. In one notable instance, the government fought and won a bloody war to prevent the nation from breaking apart. And at the same time, the system of checks and balances has functioned reasonably well, as the Federalists predicted, to prevent the government from tyrannizing its citizens.

The Citizen's Role and the Changing Constitution

> Explain how, and how often, the Constitution has been changed

The Constitution has endured for more than two centuries as the framework of government because it has changed over time.

AMENDMENTS: MANY ARE CALLED; FEW ARE CHOSEN

The inevitable need for change was recognized by the framers of the Constitution, and provisions for **amendment** were incorporated into Article V. Four methods of amendment are described:

1. Passage in House and Senate by two-thirds vote, then ratification by majority vote of the legislatures of three-fourths (now 38) of the states; in nine cases Congress mandated a time limit for state ratification

2. Passage in House and Senate by two-thirds vote, then ratification by conventions called for the purpose in three-fourths of the states

3. Passage in a national convention called for by Congress in response to petitions by two-thirds of the states, then ratification by majority vote of the legislatures of three-fourths of the states

4. Passage in a national convention (as in method 3), then ratification by conventions called for the purpose in three-fourths of the states

> **amendment** a change added to a bill, law, or constitution

FIGURE 2.3
· ·

Four Ways the Constitution Can Be Amended

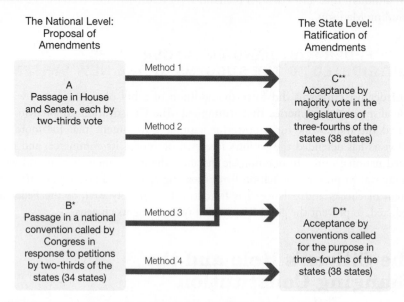

The National Level:
Proposal of
Amendments

The State Level:
Ratification of
Amendments

Method 1

A
Passage in House
and Senate, each by
two-thirds vote

Method 2

C**
Acceptance by
majority vote in the
legislatures of
three-fourths of the
states (38 states)

B*
Passage in a national
convention called by
Congress in
response to petitions
by two-thirds of the
states (34 states)

Method 3

Method 4

D**
Acceptance by
conventions called
for the purpose in
three-fourths of the
states (38 states)

*This method of proposal has never been employed. Thus, amendment routes 3 and 4 have never been attempted.
**For each amendment proposal, Congress has the power to choose the method of ratification, the time limit for consideration by the states, and other conditions of ratification. The movement to repeal Prohibition in the Twenty-First Amendment was the only occasion in which route 2 was used successfully.

Figure 2.3 illustrates each of these possible methods. Since no amendment has ever been proposed by national convention, however, methods 3 and 4 have never been employed. And method 2 has been employed only once (the Twenty-First Amendment, which repealed the Eighteenth Amendment, or Prohibition). Method 1 has been used for all the others.

The Constitution has proved extremely difficult to amend. Since 1789, more than 11,000 amendments have been formally introduced in Congress. Of these, Congress officially proposed only 29, and 27 of these were eventually ratified by the states. Two of these—Prohibition and its repeal—cancel each other out, so for all practical purposes, only 25 amendments have been added to the Constitution since 1791.

FOR CRITICAL ANALYSIS ▶

1. Which amendment had the greatest effect in increasing the percentage of the population allowed to vote?

2. Roughly how many voters today would have been denied the chance to vote if not for the ratification of the Twenty-Sixth Amendment? Do you think the voting age should be decreased even further?

Who Gained the Right to Vote through Amendments?

The right to vote is seen as a cornerstone of American democracy, but not all Americans have had that right. Three constitutional amendments, ratified over roughly a 100-year span, have had a profound effect on who can vote in U.S. elections.

Adult Citizens Eligible to Vote in National Elections*

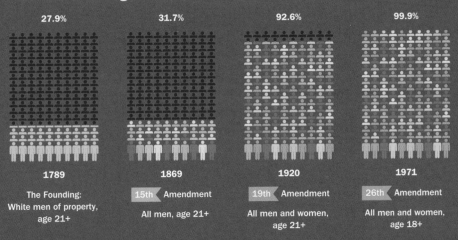

27.9%	31.7%	92.6%	99.9%
1789	**1869**	**1920**	**1971**
The Founding: White men of property, age 21+	15th Amendment — All men, age 21+	19th Amendment — All men and women, age 21+	26th Amendment — All men and women, age 18+

Proportion of 2018 Electorate by Amendment

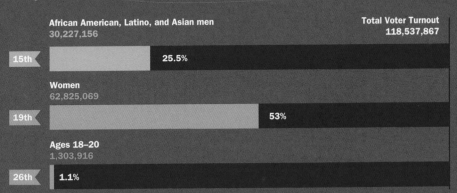

African American, Latino, and Asian men
30,227,156

Total Voter Turnout
118,537,867

15th — 25.5%

Women
62,825,069

19th — 53%

Ages 18–20
1,303,916

26th — 1.1%

* Percentages are of the adult (18+) population. These figures are approximate for 1789 and 1869. The voting rights of convicted felons are restricted in some states, and of noncitizens in all states.

SOURCE: Data from U.S. House of Representatives, U.S. Census Bureau, Pew Research Center, United States Election Project, and Catalist Data (accessed 6/12/19).

THE AMENDMENT PROCESS REFLECTS "HIGHER LAW"

Most amendment efforts have failed because they simply attempted to use the Constitution instead of ordinary legislation to deal with a specific public problem. The 25 successful amendments, on the other hand, are concerned with the structure or composition of government (see Table 2.3). This pattern is consistent with the dictionary, which defines *constitution* as the makeup or composition of something. And it is consistent with the concept of a constitution as "higher law," whose purpose is to establish a framework within which the processes of governing and making ordinary law can take place.

TABLE 2.3

Amendments to the Constitution

AMENDMENT	PURPOSE
I	Congress is not to make any law establishing a religion or abridging free exercise of religion, speech, press, assembly, or petitioning the government for redress of grievances.
II, III, IV	No branch of government may infringe on the right of people to keep arms (II), is not arbitrarily to occupy homes for a militia (III), and is not to engage in the search or seizure of evidence without a court warrant swearing to belief in the probable existence of a crime (IV).
V, VI, VII, VIII	The courts* are not to hold trials for serious offenses without provision for a grand jury (V), a petit (trial) jury (VII), a speedy trial (VI), presentation of charges (VI), confrontation of hostile witnesses (VI), immunity from testimony against oneself (V), and immunity from more than one trial for the same offense (V). Neither bail nor punishment can be excessive (VIII), and no property can be taken without just compensation (V).
IX, X	*Limits on national government:* All rights and powers not enumerated are reserved to the states or the people.
XI	Limited jurisdiction of federal courts over suits involving the states.
XII	Provided separate ballot for vice president in the electoral college.
XIII	Eliminated slavery and eliminated the right of states to allow property in persons.**
XIV	Asserted the principle of national citizenship and prohibited the states from infringing upon the rights of citizens of the nation, no matter that they happened to live in that state. Also prohibited states from denying voting rights to male citizens over the age of 21.†
XV	Extended voting rights to all races.
XVI	Established national power to tax incomes.

TABLE 2.3
Amendments to the Constitution—cont'd

AMENDMENT	PURPOSE
XVII††	Provided direct election of senators.
XIX	Extended voting rights to women.
XX	Eliminated "lame-duck" session of Congress.
XXII	Limited presidential term.
XXIII	Extended voting rights to residents of the District of Columbia.
XXIV	Extended voting rights to all classes by abolition of poll taxes.
XXV	Provided presidential succession in case of disability.
XXVI	Extended voting rights to citizens aged 18 and over.†
XXVII	Limited Congress's power to raise its own salary.

* These amendments also impose limits on the law-enforcement powers of federal and (especially) state and local executive branches.

** The Thirteenth Amendment was proposed January 31, 1865, and adopted less than a year later, December 18, 1865.

† In defining *citizenship*, the Fourteenth Amendment actually provided the constitutional basis for expanding the electorate to include all races, women, and residents of the District of Columbia. Only the "18-year-olds' amendment" should have been necessary, since it changed the definition of citizenship. The fact that additional amendments were required following the Fourteenth suggests that voting is not considered an inherent right of U.S. citizenship. Instead, it is viewed as a privilege.

†† The Eighteenth Amendment, ratified in 1919, outlawed the sale and transportation of liquor. It was repealed by the Twenty-First Amendment, ratified in 1933.

‡ The Twenty-Sixth Amendment holds the record for speed of adoption. It was proposed on March 23, 1971, and adopted on July 5, 1971.

Even those who would have preferred more changes to the Constitution must admit the great wisdom in this principle. A constitution ought to make laws and policies possible, but not determine what they ought to be. For example, property is one of the most fundamental and well-established rights in the United States not because it is recognized as such in the Constitution, but because legislatures and courts, working within an agreed-upon constitutional framework, have made it a crime for anyone, including the government, to trespass or to take away property without compensation. A constitution is good if it leads to good legislation, courts that protect citizens' liberties and rights, and appropriate police behavior. Its principles can be a citizen's dependable defense against the abuse of power.

Despite the Constitution's promises, a blight marred America's founding—the institution of slavery. The new nation's population included several hundred thousand enslaved Black persons—individuals who had been transported to America from Africa and their native-born descendants. Indeed, as Thomas Jefferson sat writing the Declaration of Independence, boldly declaring that all men are created equal, he was reportedly attended by an enslaved teenage boy who happened to be his wife's half brother. The Civil War brought an end to slavery, but in the decades following the war and Reconstruction, African Americans were subject to persecution and vilification. As a result of two centuries of resistance and protest from enslaved Africans and their descendants, America was gradually forced to recognize and act in accordance with its declared principles. Black struggles, moreover, paved the way for other groups, including women, LGBTQ people, immigrants, and others, to assert their own rights. In this way, the descendants of enslaved people helped to build American democracy.

The Constitution: What Do You Think?

Jim Obergefell's fight to secure marriage equality for same-sex couples illustrates the ways in which the Constitution's structure shapes politics to this day. The framers placed individual liberty ahead of all other political values. They feared that democracy could degenerate into a tyranny of the majority. They feared that economic or social equality would inspire the have-nots to interfere with the liberty of the haves. As a result, they designed many of the Constitution's key provisions, such as separated powers, internal checks and balances, and federalism, to safeguard liberty, and designed others, such as indirect election of senators and the president and the appointment of judges for life, to limit democracy and the threat of majority tyranny.

By championing liberty, however, the framers virtually guaranteed that democracy and even a measure of equality would eventually come to the United States. Liberty promotes political activity and participation, encouraging people and groups to fight for their rights and interests. In so doing, they may achieve greater equality, as did Jim Obergefell (featured at the beginning of this chapter).

★ What do you think about the values of liberty, equality, and democracy? Which is most important to you? Which do you think is most important to Jim Obergefell? How might your life be different if you lived in a country with different commitments to these values?

★ Advocates arguing for a particular policy position often invoke cherished values such as liberty, equality, and democracy to support their positions. What kinds of arguments could both supporters and opponents of same-sex marriage make using these three values?

★ Are there policy areas where you were frustrated by the slow policy-making process created by the separation of powers and the system of checks and balances? Or policy areas where you were relieved that changes that you opposed were slowed or halted? How do you think Jim Obergefell would answer these questions?

★ STUDY GUIDE ★

Practice Quiz

1. The British attempted to raise revenue in the North American colonies by *(p. 31)*
   a) imposing income taxes.
   b) imposing taxes on commerce.
   c) expropriating and selling Native American lands.
   d) levying licensing fees for the mining of natural resources.
   e) requesting voluntary donations.

2. In their fight against British taxes, such as the Stamp Act and the Sugar Act of 1764, New England merchants and southern planters allied with which of the following groups? *(p. 31)*
   a) shopkeepers, small farmers, laborers, and artisans
   b) shopkeepers only
   c) laborers only
   d) artisans only
   e) shopkeepers and laborers only

3. The first governing document in the United States was *(p. 34)*
   a) the Declaration of Independence.
   b) the Articles of Confederation.
   c) the Constitution.
   d) the Bill of Rights.
   e) the Virginia Plan.

4. Who was responsible for carrying out laws passed by the national Congress under the Articles of Confederation? *(p. 34)*
   a) the presidency
   b) the Congress
   c) the states
   d) the federal judiciary
   e) the federal bureaucracy

5. Which event led directly to the Constitutional Convention by providing evidence that the government created under the Articles of Confederation was unable to act decisively in times of national crisis? *(pp. 35–36)*
   a) the Boston Massacre
   b) the Boston Tea Party
   c) Shays's Rebellion
   d) the Annapolis Convention
   e) the War of 1812

6. Which proposal argued that states should be represented in the national legislature according to their size and wealth? *(p. 37)*
   a) the Connecticut plan
   b) the Maryland plan
   c) the New Jersey plan
   d) the Rhode Island plan
   e) the Virginia plan

7. The agreement reached at the Constitutional Convention that determined how enslaved people would be counted for the purposes of taxation and congressional representation was called the *(p. 39)*
   a) Virginia Plan.
   b) New Jersey Plan.
   c) Connecticut Compromise.
   d) Three-Fifths Compromise.
   e) Great Compromise.

8. What are expressed powers? *(p. 42)*
   a) powers granted to the federal government by Supreme Court decisions
   b) powers specifically expressed in the text of the Constitution
   c) powers expressed in legislation passed by Congress

d) powers granted to the federal government by the Tenth Amendment
   e) powers exercised according to the necessary and proper clause

9. The framers hoped to create a presidency that would be *(p. 43)*
   a) unconditionally powerful.
   b) easily influenced by popular democratic pressures.
   c) constrained by congressional stalemates.
   d) capable of timely and decisive action.
   e) completely dependent on Congress.

10. Which of the following best describes the Supreme Court as understood by the Founders? *(p. 43)*
   a) the body that would choose the president
   b) the principal check on presidential power
   c) an arbiter of disputes within the Congress
   d) a figurehead commission of elders
   e) the highest court of both the national government and the states

11. During the debate over ratification, the Federalists were *(p. 47)*
   a) those who opposed the new Constitution because it created a stronger national government than existed under the Articles of Confederation.
   b) those who opposed the new Constitution because it created a weaker national government than existed under the Articles of Confederation.
   c) those who opposed the new Constitution because it did not end slavery.
   d) those who supported the new Constitution because it created a stronger national government than existed under the Articles of Confederation.
   e) those who supported the new Constitution because it ended slavery.

12. Which feature of the Constitution did Antifederalists fear would lead to the emergence of tyranny? *(p. 48)*
   a) the Three-Fifths Compromise
   b) the provisions that created government institutions without direct responsibility to the people
   c) the provisions that lent power to a popular majority of citizens
   d) the checks that the Constitution placed on the legislative branch of government
   e) the supremacy clause

13. Which of the following best describes the process of amending the Constitution? *(p. 52)*
   a) It is difficult and has rarely been used successfully to address specific public problems.
   b) It is difficult and has frequently been used successfully to address specific public problems.
   c) It is easy and has rarely been used successfully to address specific public problems.
   d) It is easy and has frequently been used successfully to address specific public problems.
   e) It is easy, but it has never been used for any purpose.

Key Terms

Federalism

WHAT GOVERNMENT DOES AND WHY IT MATTERS

As the coronavirus pandemic swept through the nation in early 2020, people looked to government for answers. But who had the responsibility, and the power, to help—the states, the federal government, or both? And how should they work together to provide the testing and support needed to battle the virus's spread?

Early on, federal and state officials assured Americans that they could get tested to see if they had contracted the virus. During a March 2020 visit to the Centers for Disease Control and Prevention in Atlanta, President Trump said, "Anybody that wants a test can get a test. That's what the bottom line is."[1] Unfortunately, this proved not to be true when the president said it. So how was that promise being addressed by the state and local workers who needed to provide testing and care? Bill Whitmar, director of the Missouri state public-health laboratory, worried that statements such as Trump's resulted in far more people requesting testing than local medical communities could handle, creating supply shortages. "When that happens, then

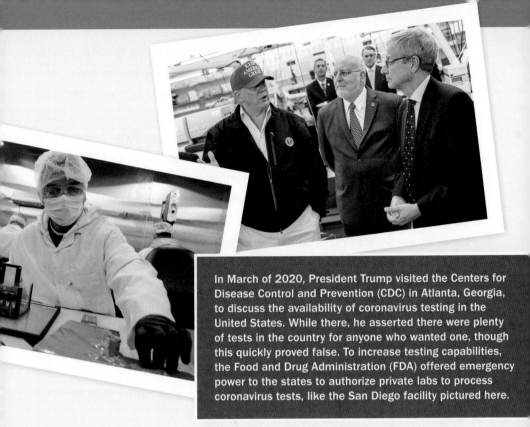

In March of 2020, President Trump visited the Centers for Disease Control and Prevention (CDC) in Atlanta, Georgia, to discuss the availability of coronavirus testing in the United States. While there, he asserted there were plenty of tests in the country for anyone who wanted one, though this quickly proved false. To increase testing capabilities, the Food and Drug Administration (FDA) offered emergency power to the states to authorize private labs to process coronavirus tests, like the San Diego facility pictured here.

the supply chain on the front end—which is the swabs, the viral transport media, the collection tubes—started to evaporate from suppliers." He said that before promising widespread testing, "you have to look at your supply chain and analyze it closely. Not just make a promise, but look at your ability to provide a test for everybody. If you think you can, you may be surprised."

Under pressure from states, the federal government tried to address the testing shortfall. President Trump signed a memorandum allowing state public-health laboratories to authorize other labs in their states to develop and run coronavirus tests, a regulatory power normally reserved for the Food and Drug Administration (FDA), a federal agency.

Although granting this power to the states was intended to expand much-needed testing capacity, state lab directors worried about their new authority. Joanne Bartkus, director of the Minnesota state public-health laboratory, said, "There is pressure to get these tests out: from the public, from the laboratories, from the politicians. It is a challenge to do that in a scientific and equitable way when you have no expertise in authorizing other labs to do testing." When other lab directors saw the headline on the FDA memo, "States Are Now in Charge of Testing," they "thought it was a hoax," she added. "It's almost like the FDA has thrown in the towel and said, 'Hey, you know, do whatever.'"[2]

The struggle over coronavirus-testing authority engages some of the oldest questions in American government: What is the responsibility of the federal government, and what is the responsibility of the states? Throughout American history, politicians and citizens have wrestled with balancing federal and state powers and responsibilities. Some responsibilities, such as international relations, clearly lie with the federal government. Others, such as divorce laws, are controlled by state governments. In fact, most of the rules and regulations that Americans face in their daily lives are set by state and local governments. In response to the coronavirus pandemic, President Trump could only issue guidelines suggesting social distancing; it was mayors and governors who had the legal authority to ban large gatherings and issue work-from-home orders.

Some mayors and governors did so, while others did not. Should there be uniformity across the states and within states on a matter such as this? What about on other issues?

Given overlapping responsibilities and policy variation across subnational units like cities and states, the American form of federalism inevitably brings conflict. The debate about "who should do what" remains one of the most important discussions in American politics.

CHAPTER GOALS

★ Describe how the Constitution structures the relationships among the national, state, and local governments (pp. 63–70)

★ Explain how the relationship between the federal and state governments has evolved over time (pp. 70–76)

★ Analyze what difference federalism makes for politics and government (pp. 76–83)

Federalism Is Established by the Constitution

Describe how the Constitution structures the relationships among the national, state, and local governments

The Constitution shapes American life through **federalism**, the division of powers and functions between a national government and lower levels of government, such as regions or states. Federalism contrasts with a **unitary system**, in which lower levels of government have little independent power and primarily just implement decisions made by the central government.

The United States was the first nation to adopt federalism as its governing framework. By granting "expressed powers" to the national government and reserving the rest to the states, the original Constitution recognized two authorities: state governments and the federal government.

The nations most likely to have federalism are those with diverse ethnic, linguistic, or sectional groupings, such as Switzerland and Canada and certainly the United States. The multiple governments at the national, state, and local levels present many opportunities for citizens to express their preferences, promising to maximize democratic participation. Because states and even localities have their own taxing, spending, and policy-making powers (especially in the United States), policy experimentation and innovation is another feature, as is the tailoring of policy to local preferences. And competition among states and localities to attract individuals and businesses promises to maximize the efficiency of government services.[3]

The question is how well federalism delivers on these promises. In the American version of federalism, state and local governments have even more policy-making responsibilities than in most federal systems. The result is wide variation in policies and a centuries-long tug-of-war between the national and state governments, and between state and local governments. The federal structure's division of labor across the levels of government makes **intergovernmental relations**—the processes by which those levels of government negotiate and compromise over policy responsibility—one of the most characteristic aspects of American government.

federalism a system of government in which power is divided, by a constitution, between a central government and regional governments

unitary system a centralized government system in which lower levels of government have little power independent of the national government

intergovernmental relations the processes by which the three levels of American government (national, state, local) negotiate and compromise over policy responsibility

THE POWERS OF THE NATIONAL GOVERNMENT

expressed powers specific powers granted by the Constitution to Congress (Article I, Section 8) and to the president (Article II)

implied powers powers derived from the necessary and proper clause of Article I, Section 8, of the Constitution; such powers are not specifically expressed but are implied through the expansive interpretation of delegated powers

necessary and proper clause Article I, Section 8, of the Constitution, which provides Congress with the authority to make all laws "necessary and proper" to carry out its expressed powers

reserved powers powers, derived from the Tenth Amendment to the Constitution, that are not specifically delegated to the national government or denied to the states

police power power reserved to the state government to regulate the health, safety, and morals of its citizens

As we saw in Chapter 2, the **expressed powers** granted to the national government are found in Article I, Section 8, of the Constitution. These 17 powers include the power to collect taxes, coin money, declare war, and regulate commerce. Article I, Section 8, also contains another important source of power for the national government: the **implied powers** that enable Congress "to make all Laws which shall be necessary and proper for carrying into Execution the foregoing Powers." Not until several decades after the Founding did the Supreme Court allow Congress to exercise the power implied in this **necessary and proper clause**. But as we shall see later in this chapter, this power allowed the national government to expand considerably—if slowly—the scope of its authority. In addition to these expressed and implied powers, the Constitution affirmed the power of the national government in the supremacy clause (Article VI), which made all national laws and treaties "the supreme Law of the Land."

THE POWERS OF STATE GOVERNMENT

One way in which the framers preserved a strong role for the states in the federal system was through the Tenth Amendment to the Constitution, which says that the powers the Constitution does not delegate to the national government or prohibit to the states are "reserved to the States respectively, or to the people." The Antifederalists, who feared that a strong central government would encroach on individual liberty, repeatedly pressed for such a "**reserved powers** amendment."

The most fundamental power that the states retain is that of coercion—the power to develop and enforce criminal codes, to administer health and safety rules, and to regulate the family through marriage and divorce laws. States also have the power to regulate individuals' livelihoods; if you're a doctor or a lawyer or a plumber or a barber, you must be licensed by the state. Even more fundamentally, the states have the power to define private property—which exists only because state laws against trespass define who is and is not entitled to use it. Owning a car isn't worth much unless government makes it a crime for someone else to drive your car without your consent.

A state's authority to regulate these fundamental matters of the health, safety, welfare, and morals of its citizens is much greater than the powers of the national government and is commonly referred to as the **police power**. Policing is what states

Federal and Unitary Systems

Worldwide, unitary systems of government are much more common than federal systems. Geographically they may appear to be roughly even on this map, but that is because larger countries such as the United States and Russia often use federal systems. In fact, fewer than 15 percent of the world's countries use federal systems. Each type of system brings its own strengths and drawbacks: unitary systems can be more efficient, but federal systems can allow for more regional autonomy and policy innovation.

1. What explains why a country might use a federal or a unitary system? Why would a country with a large amount of territory to govern, such as Canada or Brazil, prefer a federal arrangement? Are there any geographic or regional patterns that you see? What might lead to countries on a continent being more likely to have similar government arrangements?

2. What are some of the other advantages to having a unitary system? In what ways might a federal system be more responsive? If you were designing your own country, which would you prefer and why?

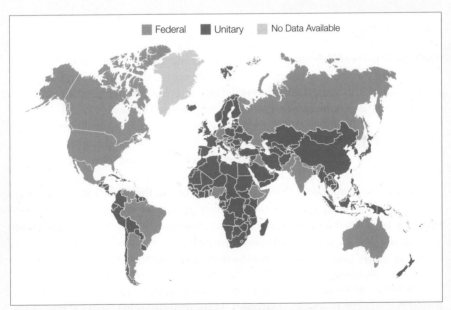

SOURCE: CIA World Factbook, cia.gov (accessed 3/31/2020).

As businesses like this bakery in Arizona pushed the limits of stay-at-home orders during the coronavirus pandemic, police officers stepped in to enforce the state's authority to regulate the public health and safety of citizens.

do—they coerce you in the name of the community and, for example, order you to self-isolate during the coronavirus pandemic, in the interest of maintaining public order and safety. This was exactly the type of power that the Founders intended the states, not the federal government, to exercise.

States also share with the national government **concurrent powers** to regulate commerce and the economy—for example, they can charter banks, grant or deny charters for corporations, grant or deny licenses to engage in a business or practice a trade, regulate the quality of products or the conditions of labor, and levy taxes. Wherever there is a direct conflict of laws between the federal and state levels, the issue will most likely be resolved in favor of national supremacy.

STATES' OBLIGATIONS TO ONE ANOTHER

The Constitution also creates obligations among the states, spelled out in Article IV. By requiring the states to recognize or uphold governmental actions and decisions in other states, the framers aimed to make the states less like independent countries and more like components of a unified nation. Article IV, Section 1, calls for "Full Faith and Credit" among states, meaning that each state is normally expected to honor the "Public Acts, Records, and Judicial Proceedings" of the other states. So, for example, if a restraining order is placed on a stalker in one state, other states are required to enforce that order as if they had issued it.

Nevertheless, some courts have found exceptions to the **full faith and credit clause**: if one state's law is against the "strong public policy" of another state, that state may not be obligated to recognize it.[4] The history of interracial marriage policy shows how much leeway states have had about recognizing marriages performed in other states. In 1952, 30 states prohibited interracial marriage, and many of these also refused to recognize such marriages performed in other states.[5] For example, in the 1967 Supreme Court case of *Loving v. Virginia*, which successfully challenged state bans on interracial marriage, Mildred and Richard Loving, a Black woman and a White man, were married in the District of Columbia. However, when they returned to their home state of Virginia, it refused to recognize them as a married couple.[6]

concurrent powers authority possessed by *both* state and national governments, such as the power to levy taxes

full faith and credit clause provision from Article IV, Section 1, of the Constitution requiring that the states normally honor the public acts and judicial decisions that take place in another state

Until recently, same-sex marriage was in a similar position to interracial marriage. Thirty-five states had passed "Defense of Marriage Acts," defining marriage as a union between one man and one woman, or had adopted constitutional amendments to this effect. In 1996 Congress passed a federal Defense of Marriage Act, which declared that states were not required to recognize a same-sex marriage from another state and that the federal government did not recognize same-sex marriage even if it was legal under state law.

In 2015, however, the Supreme Court ruled that the Fourteenth Amendment guaranteed a fundamental right to same-sex marriage. The case, *Obergefell v. Hodges*, challenged four home states' refusals to grant same-sex marriage licenses or recognize same-sex marriages performed out of state.[7] The Court's 5–4 decision meant that all states must now offer marriage licenses to two people of the same sex and recognize same-sex marriages licensed by other states. In one stroke, same-sex marriage turned from a state-level policy choice to a nationally recognized right.

Article IV, Section 2, known as the "comity clause," also seeks to promote national unity, by providing that citizens enjoying the "**privileges and immunities**" of one state should be entitled to similar treatment in other states. This has come to mean that a state cannot discriminate against someone from another state or give special privileges to its own residents. For example, in the 1970s, the Supreme Court struck down as unconstitutional an Alaska law that gave Alaska residents preference over nonresidents for jobs on the state's oil and gas pipelines.[8] The comity clause also regulates criminal justice among the states by requiring states to return fugitives to the states from which they have fled.

privileges and immunities clause provision, from Article IV, Section 2, of the Constitution, that a state cannot discriminate against someone from another state or give its own residents special privileges

home rule power delegated by the state to a local unit of government to manage its own affairs

LOCAL GOVERNMENT AND THE CONSTITUTION

Local government occupies a peculiar but very important place in the American system (see Table 3.1). It has no status in the U.S. Constitution. Instead, state constitutions define local government structures and responsibilities. Thus local goernments are subject to ultimate control by the states.

This imbalance of power means that state governments could legally dissolve local governments or force multiple local governments to consolidate into one. Most states have amended their constitutions to give their larger cities **home rule**—a guarantee

TABLE 3.1

90,126 Governments in the United States

TYPE	NUMBER
National	1
State	50
County	3,031
Municipal	19,495
Townships	16,253
School districts	12,754
Other special districts	38,542

SOURCE: U.S. Census Bureau, 2017 Census of Governments. Table 2, www.census.gov/data/tables/2017/econ/gus /2017-governments.html (accessed 1/21/2020).

Make Your Voice Heard at a Local Meeting

DOMINGO MOREL, cofounder of the Rhode Island Latino Policy Institute and assistant professor at Rutgers University–Newark

How can you change policy in your community? There are over 90,000 local governments in the United States, including school boards, city councils, county boards, and special districts for public transportation, utilities, libraries, parks, police, fire, water, and more. Domingo shared his advice for making your voice heard in local government:

1 **Figure out which governmental entity has jurisdiction over your issue and get on its agenda.** Most school boards, city councils, and other local government entities have an online sign-up to speak at their meetings.

2 **Do research on your issue.** Local governments often do not have staffs to do research. Many local officeholders have day jobs. You can be an effective advocate and partner by supplying the research they can't do. Young people would be surprised to learn how far that can get them.

3 **Prepare your statement.** Your time will be limited, so lay out your issue concern and suggested solution succinctly. The most effective statements don't just articulate an argument but also attach a personal narrative about why this issue is important and convey that to the people who are in power.

4 **Follow up.** Email the members of the board or council. Broadcast your issue concern and proposals on social media. Monitor the agenda and attend subsequent meetings. Build relationships with local officials.

5 **Consider that collective action may be even more powerful.** I recall a mother who attended Newark school board meetings for four months, urging, without success, that Muslim holidays be added to the school calendar. In the fifth month she said, "Today I brought my community. Can all of the Muslims in attendance please stand up?" Seeing an auditorium full, the school board changed the policy. I advise bringing friends, finding out what groups may already work on your concerns, or creating your own group if needed (see How to Start an Advocacy Group on p. 236).

6 **Work across the generations.** Seek the advice of elders and community leaders who worked on such issues in the past. In turn, recruit younger people to keep the effort going, giving them information so they don't have to start over. It's not easy getting engaged, it's not easy to go out there and be an activist on the individual or collective level, but once you get to that place, it's important to ensure you're recruiting others.

7 **Work the federal system.** Many issues are addressed at multiple levels of government. Strategize about the best level for addressing your particular concern. And if you make no headway at one level, target another. Federalism brings its challenges but also has its advantages.

of noninterference in various areas of local affairs.[9] In recent years, however, as discussed below, some local governments have passed laws making policy on matters from minimum wage to public broadband, only to have state legislatures preempt, or remove, that authority.

National and State Powers Have Shifted over Time

> **Explain how the relationship between the federal and state governments has evolved over time**

Federalism has determined which level of government does what and, through that, the political development of the country. As we shall see, important aspects of federalism have changed, but the framework has survived two centuries and a devastating civil war.

At the time of the Founding, the states far surpassed the federal government in their power to influence the lives of ordinary Americans. In the system of shared powers, they played a much more active role in economic and social regulation than the federal government, which tended toward a hands-off approach. Although Supreme Court decisions gradually expanded its authority in this area, not until the New Deal of the 1930s did the national government gain vast new powers. Since then, the states have asserted themselves at certain times and in certain policy areas, sometimes aided by the courts. But at other moments a crisis shifts power toward the national government again, as during the September 11, 2001, terror attacks, the fiscal crisis that began in 2008, and the coronavirus-induced economic crisis in 2020.

RESTRAINING NATIONAL POWER WITH DUAL FEDERALISM

Historically, **dual federalism** has meant that states have done most of the fundamental governing. We call this state-centered federalism the "traditional system" because it prevailed for much of American history. Under this system, the national government was quite small and very narrowly specialized in the functions it performed (see Table 3.2).

What do the functions of the national government reveal? First, virtually all of them were aimed at assisting commerce, such as building roads or protecting domestic industries with tariffs on imported goods. Second, virtually none of them directly coerced citizens. The emphasis was on promotion and encouragement— providing land or capital needed for economic development.

dual federalism the system of government that prevailed in the United States from 1789 to 1937 in which most fundamental governmental powers were shared between the federal and state governments

State legislatures were also actively involved in economic regulation during the nineteenth century. American capitalism took its form from state property and trespass laws and from state laws and court decisions regarding contracts, markets, credit, banking, incorporation, and insurance. Until the Thirteenth Amendment abolished slavery, property law

TABLE 3.2

The Federal System: Governmental Functions in the Traditional System, 1789–1937

NATIONAL GOVERNMENT POLICIES (DOMESTIC)	STATE GOVERNMENT POLICIES	LOCAL GOVERNMENT POLICIES
Internal improvements	Property laws (including slavery)	Adaptation of state laws to local conditions
Subsidies	Estate and inheritance laws	
Tariffs	Commerce laws	Public works
Public land disposal	Banking and credit laws	Contracts for public works
Patents	Corporate laws	
Currency	Insurance laws	Licensing of public accommodation
	Family laws	
	Morality laws	Zoning and other land-use regulation
	Public health laws	Basic public services
	Education laws	
	General penal laws	
	Eminent domain laws	
	Construction codes	
	Land-use laws	
	Water and mineral laws	
	Criminal procedure laws	
	Electoral and political party laws	
	Local government laws	
	Civil service laws	
	Occupations and professions laws	

extended to slavery, with the fugitive slave clause of the Constitution (Article IV, Section 2) requiring even "free states" without slavery to return freedom-seeking enslaved people to the states from which they had escaped.

THE SLOW GROWTH OF THE NATIONAL GOVERNMENT'S POWER

In the first several decades after the Founding, the Supreme Court decided several critical cases that expanded federal powers when there was a conflict between the states and the federal government, removed interstate barriers to trade, and laid the groundwork for a national economy. These early decisions to expand federal power rested on a pro-national interpretation of Article I, Section 8, of the Constitution.

commerce clause Article I, Section 8, of the Constitution, which delegates to Congress the power "to regulate Commerce with foreign Nations, and among the several States, and with the Indian Tribes"; this clause was interpreted by the Supreme Court in favor of national power over the economy

That article enumerates the powers of Congress, including the power to tax, raise an army, declare war, establish post offices, and "regulate commerce with foreign nations, and among the several States and with the Indian tribes." Though its scope initially was unclear, this **commerce clause** would later form the basis for expanding federal government control over the economy.

The first and most important such case was *McCulloch v. Maryland* (1819), which involved the question of whether Congress could charter a national bank—an explicit grant of power nowhere to be found in Article I, Section 8.[10] Chief Justice John Marshall answered that this power could be "implied" from other powers expressly delegated to Congress, such as the power to regulate commerce. His decision rested on the necessary and proper clause of Article I, Section 8, which gave Congress the power to enact laws "necessary and proper" for carrying out its delegated powers. Marshall also concluded in *McCulloch* that any state law conflicting with a federal law is invalid since the Constitution states that "the Laws of the United States...shall be the supreme Law of the Land."

Another major case, *Gibbons v. Ogden* (1824), reinforced this nationalistic interpretation of the Constitution. The issue was whether New York State could grant a monopoly to Robert Fulton's steamboat company to operate an exclusive service between New York and New Jersey. In arguing that the state lacked the power to do so, Chief Justice Marshall had to define what Article I, Section 8 meant by "commerce among the several states." He insisted that the definition was "comprehensive," extending to "every species of commercial intercourse." However, this comprehensiveness was limited "to that commerce which concerns more states than one." *Gibbons* is important because it established the supremacy of the national government in all matters affecting what later came to be called "interstate commerce."[11]

Later in the nineteenth century, though, any effort of the national government to *regulate* commerce in such areas as fraud, product quality, child labor, or working conditions or hours was declared unconstitutional by the Supreme Court. The Court said that with such legislation the federal government was entering workplaces—local areas—and attempting to regulate goods that had not yet passed into interstate commerce. To enter local workplaces was to exercise police power—a power reserved to the states.

No one questioned the power of the national government to regulate businesses that by their nature crossed state lines, such as railroads, gas pipelines, and waterway transportation. But well into the twentieth century the Supreme Court used the concept of interstate commerce as a barrier against most efforts by Congress to regulate local conditions. Thus, federalism, as interpreted by the Supreme Court for 70 years after the Civil War, enabled business to have its cake and eat it, too: entrepreneurs enjoyed the benefits of national policies promoting commerce and were shielded by the courts from policies regulating commerce by protecting consumers and workers.[12]

This barrier fell after 1937, however, when the Supreme Court issued a series of decisions that laid the groundwork for a much stronger federal government. Most significant was the Court's dramatic expansion of the commerce clause. By throwing out the old distinction between interstate and intrastate commerce, the Court converted the clause from a source of limitations to a source of power for the national government. The Court upheld acts of Congress that protected the rights of employees to organize and engage in collective bargaining, regulated the amount of farmland in cultivation, extended low-interest credit to small businesses and farmers, and restricted the activities of corporations dealing in the stock market.[13]

The Court also upheld many other laws that contributed to the construction of the modern safety net of social programs created in response to the Great Depression. With these rulings, the Court decisively signaled that the era of dual federalism was over. In the future, Congress would have very broad powers to regulate activity in the states.

THE NEW DEAL: NEW ROLES FOR GOVERNMENT

The economic crisis of the Great Depression and the nature of the government response signaled a new era of federalism in the United States. Before this national economic catastrophe, states and localities took responsibility for assisting the poor, usually channeling aid through private charity. But the extent of the depression quickly exhausted their capacities. By 1932, 25 percent of the workforce was unemployed, and many people had lost their homes. Elected in 1928, the year before the depression hit, President Herbert Hoover steadfastly maintained that the federal government could do little to alleviate the misery caused by the depression. It was a matter for state and local governments, he said.

When Franklin Delano Roosevelt took office in 1933, he energetically threw the federal government into the fight against the depression through a number of proposals known collectively as the New Deal. He proposed a variety of temporary relief and work programs, most of them to be financed by the federal government but administered by the states. In addition, Roosevelt presided over the creation of several important federal programs designed

The New Deal expanded the scope of the federal government. One of the largest and most effective New Deal programs, the Works Progress Administration (WPA) employed millions of Americans in projects such as constructing highways, bridges, and public parks.

to provide future economic security for Americans. The New Deal signaled the rise of a more active national government.

FROM LAYER CAKE TO MARBLE CAKE: COOPERATIVE FEDERALISM AND THE USE OF CATEGORICAL GRANTS

The Roosevelt administration programs typically offered states **grants-in-aid**, money provided on the condition that it be spent for a particular purpose defined by Congress, such as providing grants to the states for financial assistance to poor children. Congress added more grant programs after World War II to help states fund activities such as providing school lunches and building highways. Sometimes state or local governments were required to match the national contribution dollar for dollar, but in programs such as the development of the interstate highway system, the congressional grants provided 90 percent of the cost.

These types of federal grants-in-aid are called **categorical grants**, because the national government determines the purposes, or categories, for which the money can be used. One of the most important—and expensive—was the federal Medicaid program, which provides grants to pay for medical care for the poor, the disabled, and many nursing home residents. Over time the value of categorical grants has risen dramatically, increasing from $54.8 billion in 1960 to an estimated $598.2 billion in 2021 (see Figure 3.1).

grants-in-aid programs through which Congress provides money to state and local governments on the condition that the funds be employed for purposes defined by the federal government

categorical grants congressional grants given to states and localities on the condition that expenditures be limited to a problem or group specified by law

cooperative federalism a type of federalism existing since the New Deal era in which grants-in-aid have been used strategically to encourage states and localities (without commanding them) to pursue nationally defined goals; also known as *intergovernmental cooperation*

The growth of categorical grants created a new kind of federalism. If the traditional system of two sovereigns—the federal government and the states—performing highly different functions could be called dual federalism, historians of federalism suggest that the system since the New Deal could be called **cooperative federalism**. The political scientist Morton Grodzins characterized this as a move from "layer cake federalism" to "marble cake federalism,"[14] in which intergovernmental cooperation and sharing have blurred a once-clear distinguishing line, making it difficult to say where the national government ends and the state and local governments begin (see Figure 3.2).

As important as the states were in this new system of grants, some new federal grants, particularly during the War on Poverty of the 1960s, bypassed the states and instead sent money directly to local governments and even to local nonprofit organizations. One of the reasons for this shift was discriminatory treatment of African Americans in the South. As the civil rights movement gained momentum, the southern defense of segregation on the grounds of states' rights confirmed the belief in Washington that the states could not be trusted to carry out national purposes.

FIGURE 3.1

The Growth of Federal Grants-in-Aid*

Spending on federal grants-in-aid to the states and local governments has grown dramatically since 1990. These increases reflect the growing public expectations about what government should do. What has been the most important cause of the steady increase in these grants?

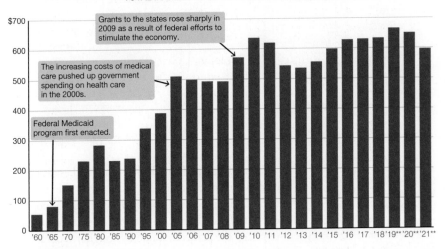

TOTAL IN BILLIONS OF CONSTANT 2012 DOLLARS

Grants to the states rose sharply in 2009 as a result of federal efforts to stimulate the economy.

The increasing costs of medical care pushed up government spending on health care in the 2000s.

Federal Medicaid program first enacted.

*Excludes outlays for national defense, international affairs, and net interest. Data in constant (fiscal year 2012) dollars.
**Estimate.
SOURCE: Office of Management and Budget, U.S. Budget for Fiscal Year 2020, "Historical Tables: Table 12.1," www.whitehouse.gov/omb/historical-tables/ (accessed 1/21/20).

REGULATED FEDERALISM AND THE RISE OF NATIONAL STANDARDS

Giving policy responsibilities to states raises questions about to what extent and in what areas it is acceptable for states to differ from one another. Supreme Court decisions have provided important answers to many of these questions, typically pushing for greater uniformity across the states. But in other policy areas, the national government has created greater uniformity by offering incentives or imposing rules.

As Congress in the 1970s began to enact legislation in new areas, such as environmental policy, it resorted to another tool: regulations on states and localities, called regulated federalism,[15] in which the national government began to set standards of conduct for the states. As a result, state and local policies in environmental protection, social services, and education are more uniform from coast to coast than are other nationally funded policies.

> **regulated federalism** a form of federalism in which Congress imposes legislation on states and localities, requiring them to meet national standards

FIGURE 3.2

Dual versus Cooperative Federalism

In layer-cake (dual) federalism, the responsibilities of the national government and state governments are clearly separated. In marble-cake (cooperative) federalism, national policies, state policies, and local policies overlap in many areas.

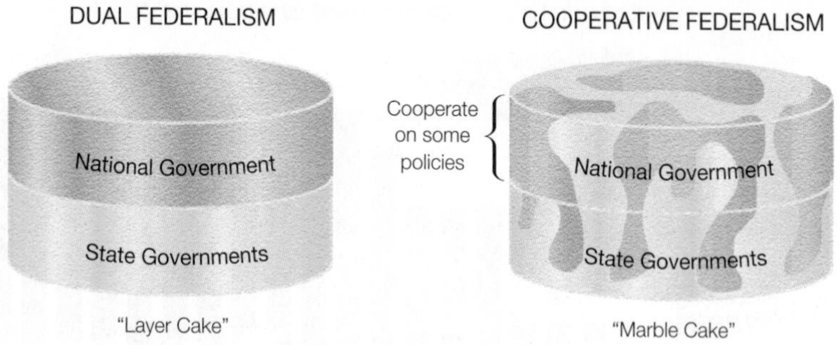

DUAL FEDERALISM

COOPERATIVE FEDERALISM

Cooperate on some policies

National Government

State Governments

"Layer Cake"

National Government

State Governments

"Marble Cake"

preemption the principle that allows the national government to override state or local actions in certain policy areas; in foreign policy, the willingness to strike first in order to prevent an enemy attack

Sometimes the federal government takes over areas of regulation from state or local governments when their standards are less strict or otherwise inconsistent with federal ones. In the 1970s, such **preemptions** required the states to abide by tougher federal rules in areas including air and water pollution, occupational health and safety, and access for the disabled. The regulated industries often opposed preemptions because they increased the cost of doing business. After 1994, however, when Republicans took control of Congress, the federal government used its preemption power to limit the ability of states to tax and regulate industry.

The Trump administration took actions much like the congressional Republicans of 1994. California has long had more stringent vehicle emissions and mileage targets than the federal government, but the administration moved to prohibit any state from setting standards different from federal ones.[16] In 2019, California and 22 other states sued to keep their ability to set stricter regulations in place.[17]

Federalism Today Is as Important as Ever

Analyze what difference federalism makes for politics and government

Debates about the appropriate role for each level of government—national, state, and local—continue. Intergovernmental tensions have shifted and even increased. The significant role for the states in particular raises important questions. Might states be sources of experimentation and innovation, the "laboratories of democracy," as Supreme Court Justice Louis Brandeis suggested?[18] Which responsibilities are states capable of managing and financing? Does interstate competition enhance or impede efficiency? Who prefers national rather than state control? And do multiple levels of government in fact promote citizen engagement?

STATES' RIGHTS

The Tenth Amendment, which reserves to the states the powers the Constitution does not specifically delegate to the national government, has been used over time to bolster the role of the states in the federal system. For much of the nineteenth century, when federal power remained limited, the Tenth Amendment was used to argue in favor of **states' rights**. The

> **states' rights** the principle that the states should oppose the increasing authority of the national government; this principle was most popular in the period before the Civil War

extreme version of this position, known as nullification, claimed that the states did not have to obey federal laws that they believed exceeded the national government's constitutional authority.

Prior to the Civil War, sharp differences between the North and the South over tariffs and slavery gave rise to nullification arguments that were most fully articulated by South Carolina senator John C. Calhoun. (Calhoun was a slaveowner and White supremacist, and his political positions were often informed by his support of the expansion of the institution of slavery.) Such arguments were voiced less often after the Civil War. But the Supreme Court continued to use the Tenth Amendment to strike down laws that it thought exceeded national power, including the Civil Rights Act passed in 1875, which would have eliminated discrimination against African Americans in public accommodations and transportation.

By the late 1930s, the Supreme Court had expanded federal power—so much so that the Tenth Amendment appeared irrelevant. Yet the idea that some powers should be reserved to the states did not go away.

For example, in the 1950s, southern opponents of the civil rights movement revived the idea in order to maintain racial segregation. In 1956, 96 southern members of Congress issued a "Southern manifesto" in which they declared that southern states were not constitutionally bound by Supreme Court decisions outlawing segregation. With the eventual triumph of the civil rights movement, the slogan of "states' rights" became tarnished by its association with racial inequality. The 1990s, however, saw a revival of interest in the Tenth Amendment and important Supreme Court decisions limiting federal power. Much of the interest stemmed from conservatives who believed that a strong federal government encroached on individual liberties. They favored returning more power to the states through the process of devolution, as we'll see later.[19]

For example, in *United States v. Lopez* (1995), the Court, stating that Congress had exceeded its authority under the commerce clause, struck down a federal law that barred handguns near schools. This was the first time since the New Deal that the Court had limited congressional powers in this way.

DEVOLUTION

Since the 1970s, the idea of **devolution**—transferring responsibility for policy from the federal government to states and localities—has become popular. Its proponents maintain that states are potential innovators and experimenters, whose good ideas might spread horizontally to other states and even vertically to the federal government. Devolution's supporters also assert that governments closer to the people can better tailor policies to local needs than can the federal government in "far-off" Washington, D.C.

An important tool of devolution is the **block grant**, federal funding that states have considerable leeway in spending. President Nixon led the first push for block grants in the early 1970s as part of his **New Federalism** initiative, when programs in the areas of job training, community development, and social services were consolidated into three large block grants. In addition, Congress provided an important new form of federal assistance to state and local governments, called **general revenue sharing**, which had no strings attached; recipients could spend the money as they wished.

In his version of the New Federalism in the 1980s, President Reagan also looked to block grants to reduce the national government's control and return power to the states. But unlike Nixon, he used them to cut federal spending as well. The 12 new block grants enacted between 1981 and 1990 cut federal spending in those areas by 12 percent.[20] Reagan's view was that states could spend their own funds to make up the difference if they chose to do so.

devolution a policy to remove a program from one level of government by delegating it or passing it down to a lower level of government, such as from the national government to the state and local governments

block grants federal grants-in-aid that allow states considerable discretion in how the funds are spent

New Federalism attempts by Presidents Nixon and Reagan to return power to the states through block grants

general revenue sharing the process by which one unit of government yields a portion of its tax income to another unit of government, according to an established formula; revenue sharing typically involves the national government providing money to state governments

The Republican Congress elected in 1994 took devolution even further through more block grants and spending cuts in federal programs. Their biggest success was the 1996 welfare reform law, which delegated to states important new responsibilities.[21]

Those who argue for state policy control note that states have often been important sources of policy innovations that have diffused to other states or to the federal government. For example, Minnesota first created charter schools in 1991; now 44 states and the District of Columbia permit them.[22] In 1990, San Luis

Obispo, California, became the first city to ban smoking in bars and restaurants. The state of California followed with a statewide ban on smoking in enclosed workplaces in 1995, and the federal government banned smoking on commercial flights in 1998. The Massachusetts health care reform of 2006 became the template for the federal Affordable Care Act of 2010 ("Obamacare").

States often complain about **unfunded mandates**—requirements on states imposed by the national government without accompanying funding. For example, a 1973 federal law prohibiting discrimination against the disabled required state and local governments to make public transit accessible. But the legislation provided no funding for the wheelchair lifts and elevators that would be necessary, leaving states to cover the multi-billion-dollar cost.[23]

Additional concerns with state responsibility are variation in policy outcomes and questions of who benefits or suffers from government action or inaction. For example, Congress enacted major welfare reform in 1996 that changed welfare from a combined federal–state program into a block grant, giving the states more responsibility for programs that serve the poor.

The federal government frequently passes laws that impose mandates on the states, such as the 1990 Americans with Disabilities Act, which protects against discrimination based on disability. States were required to pay for changes to meet federal standards for accessibility in public transportation and public facilities.

Supporters of the change hoped to reduce welfare spending and argued that states could experiment with many different approaches to find those that best met the needs of their citizens.

Minnesota adopted an incentive-based approach that offers extra assistance to families that take low-wage jobs, while six other states imposed very strict time limits on receiving benefits, allowing welfare recipients less than the five-year benefits limit in the federal legislation (the lifetime limit is shortest in Arizona: 12 months).[24] As of 2018, cash welfare benefits per month for a family of three are $714 in California, $462 in Colorado, and $290 in Texas.[25] After the passage of the 1996 law, welfare rolls declined dramatically—on average, by more than half from their peak in 1994. In 12 states the decline was 70 percent or higher.

unfunded mandate a law or regulation requiring a state or local government to perform certain actions without providing funding for fulfilling the requirement

FEDERAL–STATE TENSIONS IN TWO ISSUE AREAS

One source of federalism-based controversy concerns whether states and localities have to enforce federal immigration laws. For example, the Secure Communities program, launched in 2008 and expanded under President Obama, required state and local authorities to check the fingerprints of people being booked into jail against a Department of Homeland Security database. The program led to a record number of deportations in 2009 and 2010 and then to several states and localities pulling out of it on the grounds that too many of the undocumented immigrants being detained had not committed a crime. The Obama administration softened its deportation policy in 2011 and ended the Secure Communities program in 2014, replacing it in 2015 with one containing a more limited deportation policy.[26]

Having campaigned on promises for more rigorous immigration enforcement, President Trump signed an executive order days after his inauguration restarting Secure Communities and expanding the types of immigrants considered a priority for deportation, from those convicted of felonies or multiple misdemeanors (as under Obama) to those accused or convicted of minor crimes as well.[27] In response, a growing number of cities, counties, and states declared themselves "sanctuaries" that limit their cooperation with federal enforcement of immigration law. Trump pledged to withhold federal grants from these jurisdictions, but a federal judge's ruling blocked him from doing so.[28] In 2019, a federal appeals court ruled that the Trump administration did have authority to withhold Community Oriented Policing Services (COPS) grants from sanctuary cities.[29]

With regard to marijuana policy, federal authority has also been upheld by the courts. In 2005, the Supreme Court upheld the right of Congress to ban medical marijuana, even though 11 states had legalized its use. The Court found that the commerce clause gave the federal government the power to regulate marijuana use. Nonetheless, by 2020, 35 states and the District of Columbia had legalized medical marijuana (see Figure 3.3). Amid this legal confusion, a medical marijuana industry began to flourish, and a number of states went further by legalizing recreational marijuana. The mismatch between federal and state laws has precipitated federal raids on marijuana dispensaries and growers, even if their states have legalized the practice.[30]

STATE–LOCAL TENSIONS

Another notable development in the recent politics of federalism has been the willingness of state governments to preempt local policy. Just as states sometimes seize the policy initiative from the federal government, so too have cities made policy in areas where states have

> ### FOR CRITICAL ANALYSIS ▶
>
> 1. Why don't more people attend local government meetings and participate in local elections? Is this a problem for democracy? Why or why not?
>
> 2. Many local elections are off-cycle (held in odd-numbered years when no national elections take place). Should local elections be moved so they overlap with national elections? Why or why not?

Who Participates in Local Elections Compared to National Elections?

Local politics is critically important to the lives of Americans, but participation in local politics is low. Who does participate at the local level? And why don't more people participate in the politics closest to home?

Percent of U.S. Adults Who Say They ...

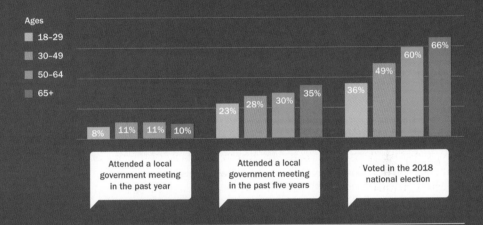

Ages
- 18–29
- 30–49
- 50–64
- 65+

Attended a local government meeting in the past year
8% · 11% · 11% · 10%

Attended a local government meeting in the past five years
23% · 28% · 30% · 35%

Voted in the 2018 national election
36% · 49% · 60% · 66%

Turnout in Most Recent Municipal Election

Percentage of voting-age population in selected cities*

Chicago	Seattle	Washington, D.C.	Detroit
33%	43%	38%	27%

Denver	Houston	San Antonio	New York City
24%	22%	10%	7%

* The voting-eligible population excludes noncitizens and people who are institutionalized or not allowed to vote in some states because they are ex-felons. The voting-age population includes everyone over 18.

SOURCE: Data from U.S. Vote Foundation and Pew Research Center (accessed 11/18/19).

FIGURE 3.3
Marijuana Laws across the States

While buying, selling, and possessing marijuana remain federal crimes, states have adopted policies that conflict with federal laws. Should this be allowed?

Medical marijuana broadly legalized
Marijuana legalized for recreational use
No broad laws legalizing marijuana

SOURCE: National Organization for the Reform of Marijuana Laws, "State Laws," https://norml
.org/laws (accessed 11/7/18); "33 Legal Medical Marijuana States and DC," November 7, 2018,
https://medicalmarijuana.procon.org/view.resource.php?resourceID=000881 (accessed
11/7/18); Marijuana Policy Project, 2020 Ballot Initiatives, www.mpp.org/policy/ballot-initiatives
(accessed 11/5/20).
CREDIT: State Marijuana Laws in 2018 Map, originally published by Governing.com, March 30,
2018. Reprinted by permission of Governing.

not or where policy preferences in the city differ from those in the state at large. In recent years some cities have set higher minimum wages than are in effect elsewhere in the state, required employers to provide paid sick leave, regulated the "sharing economy" of car- and home-sharing (such as Uber and Airbnb), prohibited gender-based discrimination in public facilities such as bathrooms, and attempted to establish public broadband services.

In each of these areas, however, some state legislatures have responded with laws preempting (limiting or prohibiting) municipal law or authority. As of 2019, 25 states preempt local minimum-wage ordinances, 23 prohibit local paid-leave ordinances, 44 limit local authority to regulate ride-sharing, and 10 ban local regulation of e-cigarettes. Michigan bans cities from banning plastic bags; Texas bans them from banning fracking. Twenty states prohibit localities from establishing municipal broadband service, and three—most famously North Carolina—preempt local antidiscrimination ordinances.[31]

POLITICAL RAMIFICATIONS OF FEDERALISM

American federalism has significant effects on policy outcomes. Because of the policy variation made possible by the sovereignty of state and local governments, where you live determines the age at which you can get a license to drive or get married, the amount you pay for public college tuition, the licensing requirements to work as a barber or accountant or athletic trainer, and, if you were out of work, whether you would get unemployment benefits and how much. But federalism has important effects on American politics as well.

Despite the Charlotte City Council's ordinance prohibiting sex discrimination in public facilities, state preemption allowed for the North Carolina legislature to pass the "Charlotte bathroom bill," which undid the provisions originally set out by the city council.

Political preferences arising from federalism are not set in stone. Although conservatives typically support a smaller federal government or a return of power to the states, once in power, they find at times that federal power can be used to advance conservative policy goals. For President George W. Bush, for example, the importance of a strong federal government became apparent after the terrorist attacks in 2001. Aware that the American public was looking to Washington for protection, Bush worked with Congress to pass the USA PATRIOT Act, which greatly increased the surveillance powers of the federal government. A year later he created the enormous new federal Department of Homeland Security. Bush also increased federal control and spending in policy areas far removed from security. The 2001 No Child Left Behind Act (NCLB) introduced unprecedented federal intervention in public education, traditionally a state and local responsibility, through detailed new requirements for states' testing of students and treatment of failing schools.

Democratic presidents, too, have sometimes made decisions about national–state responsibilities that defy the usual ideological expectations. As president, Obama released the states from the federal NCLB mandates, and in 2015 he sponsored a new law called Every Student Succeeds that returned power to the states to evaluate schools—a move that might have been expected more from a conservative president. A second important political implication of federalism concerns individuals' democratic participation and the accountability of government to the people. The multiple layers of government provide many opportunities for ordinary citizens to vote, contact elected officials, and engage in "venue shopping"—seeking policy change at a different level of government if stymied at first. But federalism can also demobilize individuals. The overlapping policy responsibilities facilitated by federalism make it difficult for individuals to figure out which government is responsible for the problem that concerns them, and they may give up; it is difficult for individuals to demand answers from government if they can't determine which government is in charge.[32]

Federalism: What Do You Think?

As described in the opening of this chapter, turning federal authority over to the states for certifying laboratories for coronavirus testing, and allowing some states and localities to issue stay-at-home orders while others do not, highlights the tensions inherent in a federal system of government. The United States' history of federalism shows that Americans generally accept the idea that states should have the freedom to enact policies that best serve their residents, within the bounds set by Congress and the courts. But variation across the states may not be desirable in some policy areas. These are perennial questions in American government.

★ Is the federal government endangering people by allowing states to certify coronavirus-testing labs? Or would it have harmed people by requiring all certifications to go through the FDA?

★ Are some of the issues on which the states differ matters of fundamental rights that should be uniform across the country? Or is it important to preserve state choice on most matters?

★ Is it fair that a transgender person in California can legally change the sex on their birth certificate, but a transgender person in Tennessee cannot? Is it reasonable that a gun owner can openly carry a handgun in Georgia but not in Florida? Why or why not?

★ How might your life be different if you lived in a different state? Imagine being a student in a state with very different state-college tuition levels. Or a state with a very different minimum-wage level. For example, in 2020 the minimum wage is $7.25 per hour in Texas and $13.00 in California.[33]

★ How do you think government response to the coronavirus pandemic would be the same or different in a unitary system in which the national government had all the power, compared to a federal system in which national, state, and local governments shared power?

Practice Quiz

1. Which term describes the division of powers and functions between the national government and lower levels of government? *(p. 63)*
   a) separation of powers
   b) federalism
   c) checks and balances
   d) expressed powers
   e) unitary system

2. Which amendment to the Constitution states that the powers the Constitution does not delegate to the national government or prohibit to the states are "reserved to the states"? *(p. 64)*
   a) First Amendment
   b) Fifth Amendment
   c) Tenth Amendment
   d) Fourteenth Amendment
   e) Twenty-Sixth Amendment

3. A state government's authority to regulate the health, safety, welfare, and morals of its citizens is frequently referred to as *(p. 64)*
   a) the reserved power.
   b) the expressed power.
   c) the police power.
   d) the concurrent power.
   e) the implied power.

4. Which constitutional clause requires that states normally honor the public acts and judicial decisions of other states? *(p. 66)*
   a) privileges and immunities clause
   b) necessary and proper clause
   c) interstate commerce clause
   d) preemption clause
   e) full faith and credit clause

5. Most states have amended their constitutions to guarantee that their larger cities will have the authority to manage local affairs without interference from state government. This power is called *(p. 67)*
   a) home rule.
   b) preemption.
   c) devolution.
   d) states' rights.
   e) New Federalism.

6. Under which system of federalism have states done most of the fundamental governing? *(p. 70)*
   a) dual federalism
   b) regulated federalism
   c) states' rights
   d) cooperative federalism
   e) New Federalism

7. In which case did the Supreme Court create the potential for increased national power by ruling that Congress could, based on the necessary and proper clause, exercise powers "implied" by its delegated powers? *(p. 72)*
   a) *United States v. Lopez*
   b) *Printz v. United States*
   c) *Loving v. Virginia*
   d) *McCulloch v. Maryland*
   e) *Gibbons v. Ogden*

8. In 1937 the Supreme Court laid the groundwork for a stronger federal government by issuing a number of decisions that *(p. 73)*
   a) dramatically narrowed the definition of the commerce clause.
   b) dramatically expanded the definition of the commerce clause.
   c) struck down the supremacy clause.
   d) struck down the privileges and immunities clause.
   e) struck down the full faith and credit clause.

9. Over time, the value of categorical grants has *(p. 74)*
   a) increased from $51.5 billion in 1960 to approximately $115 billion in 2019.
   b) increased from $51.5 billion in 1960 to approximately $630 billion in 2019.
   c) decreased from $31 billion in 1960 to approximately $2 billion in 2019.
   d) decreased from $667 billion in 1960 to approximately $2 billion in 2019.
   e) remained the same between 1960 and 2019.

10. The principle that allows the federal government to take over areas of regulation from states or local governments is called *(p. 76)*
   a) regulated federalism.
   b) devolution.
   c) preemption.
   d) "layer cake" federalism.
   e) exemption.

11. The process of transferring responsibility for policy from the national level to the state level is known as *(p. 78)*
   a) dual federalism.
   b) devolution.
   c) preemption.
   d) home rule.
   e) incorporation.

12. To what does the term *New Federalism* refer? *(p. 78)*
   a) the era of federalism initiated by President Roosevelt during the late 1930s
   b) the national government's regulation of state action through grants-in-aid
   c) the type of federalism that uses categorical grants to influence state action
   d) efforts to return more policy-making discretion to the states through the use of block grants
   e) the recent emergence of local governments as important political actors

13. When state and local governments conform to requirements imposed by the national government but do not receive funding for the expenditures required to fulfill them, they are complying with *(p. 79)*
   a) states' rights.
   b) block grants.
   c) general revenue sharing.
   d) unfunded mandates.
   e) redistributive programs.

14. One of the downsides of state control over policy is that *(p. 79)*
    a) states may come up with policy innovations that diffuse to other states or the federal government.
    b) states are not as in tune with the needs of their citizens as the federal government is, so state policy may be inadequate.
    c) citizens may benefit or suffer unevenly from government action or inaction depending on where they live.
    d) cities are unable to create and enforce local policies that differ from those at the state level.
    e) the laws and judicial decisions that take place in a given state may not be honored in other states.

15. From the perspective of democratic participation, the multiple layers of government in a federal system *(p. 83)*
    a) can make it difficult for individuals to figure out which government is responsible for the problem that concerns them.
    b) provide very limited opportunities for citizens to become involved in the political process.
    c) narrow the channels through which citizens can demand answers from their government.
    d) can clarify for citizens which levels of government are responsible for which policy issues.
    e) encourage citizens to vote for candidates of different parties at different levels of government.

Key Terms

federalism *(p. 63)*

unitary system *(p. 63)*

intergovernmental relations *(p. 63)*

expressed powers *(p. 64)*

implied powers *(p. 64)*

necessary and proper clause *(p. 64)*

reserved powers *(p. 64)*

police power *(p. 64)*

concurrent powers *(p. 66)*

full faith and credit clause *(p. 66)*

privileges and immunities clause *(p. 67)*

home rule *(p. 67)*

dual federalism *(p. 70)*

commerce clause *(p. 72)*

grants-in-aid *(p. 74)*

categorical grants *(p. 74)*

cooperative federalism *(p. 74)*

regulated federalism *(p. 75)*

preemption *(p. 76)*

states' rights *(p. 77)*

devolution *(p. 78)*

block grants *(p. 78)*

New Federalism *(p. 78)*

general revenue sharing *(p. 78)*

unfunded mandate *(p. 79)*

Civil Liberties

WHAT GOVERNMENT DOES AND WHY IT MATTERS In Portland in 2006, Simon Tam founded what *Oregon Music News* called the first and only all Asian American dance-rock band, or "Chinatown Dance Rock," as the band prefers. The various members of the band are of Chinese, Taiwanese, Vietnamese, and Filipino descent. In addition to playing at anime conventions and cultural festivals, they are known for their activity battling Asian stereotypes and supporting young Asian people.[1]

They are also known for a First Amendment case over the band's name, the Slants. The name had three sources. "We can share our personal experiences about what it's like being people of color—our own slant on life, if you will," Tam said. "It's also a musical reference. There are slant guitar chords that we use in our music." The legal case grew out of the third source: a "reclaiming" and repurposing of an old ethnic slur about Asian people. When the band members were growing up, Tam explained, "having slanted eyes was always considered a negative thing. Kids would pull their eyes back in a slant-eyed gesture to make fun of us. . . . I wanted to change it to something that was powerful, something that was considered beautiful or a point of pride instead."

The First Amendment protects Americans from government infringement on their right to free speech. In the case of the Slants, they used the First Amendment as grounds to re-appropriate a term deemed offensive for themselves and their cultures.

The U.S. Patent and Trademark Office had a different view. Tam's application for a trademark on the band's name was rejected as a violation of the "disparagement clause" of the Lanham Act of 1946, which prohibits trademarks that disparage a racial or ethnic group. The denial stated that although the "applicant, or even the entire band, may be willing to take on the disparaging term as a band name, in what may be considered an attempt . . . to wrest 'ownership' of the term," that "does not mean that all [Asian Americans] share the applicant's view." The case ultimately went to the Supreme Court, which in 2017 ruled unanimously that the disparagement clause violated the First Amendment's guarantee of free speech. The band could keep the name.

But in a further twist, the band's victory inadvertently undermined legal challenges to the name of the Washington Redskins football team. A group of Native Americans who found the "Redskins" name offensive had filed a petition to revoke the team's trademark, citing the Lanham Act's disparagement clause. Once the Court declared the clause unconstitutional, they lost the legal basis for their argument, so the team was able to keep the name. Thus the Slants' success in reclaiming what had been a term offensive to their group meant that one offensive to another group remains in use. The Slants' free speech was protected to their joy, but so was the Redskins' free speech to the disappointment of many Native Americans (in 2020, amid protests over racial justice, the Redskins changed their name to the Washington Football Team).

Free speech, along with the freedoms of assembly, religion, and privacy, is among the civil liberties contained in the Bill of Rights and elsewhere in the Constitution. Thomas Jefferson said that a bill of rights "is what people are entitled to against every government on earth." Note the wording: *against government*. Civil liberties are *protections from* improper government action.

Today in the United States, we often take for granted the liberties contained in the Constitution. But these freedoms raise difficult questions. Do the cases of the Slants and the Redskins strike you as different or the same? Under what circumstances can the government restrict Americans' liberties, especially in the realms of speech, assembly, and privacy? Do freedoms for some people, such as free speech, threaten other people? How should conflicting views be reconciled, or can they? And how should we think about possible trade-offs, as between the right of privacy from surveillance and the need for national security? Can freedom of assembly and even free exercise of religion be restricted by state governments that seek to slow the spread of a contagious disease?

CHAPTER GOALS

★ Outline the founding debate about civil liberties and explain how civil liberties apply to the federal government and the states (pp. 91–94)

★ Explain how the Supreme Court has interpreted freedom of religion through the establishment and free exercise clauses (pp. 94–97)

★ Explain how the Supreme Court has interpreted freedom of speech, assembly, petition, and the press (pp. 97–104)

★ Explain how the Supreme Court has interpreted the right to bear arms (pp. 104–7)

★ Explain how the Supreme Court has interpreted the right to due process (pp. 107–11)

★ Describe how the Supreme Court has identified and interpreted the right to privacy (pp. 112–15)

The Bill of Rights Originated with Opponents of the Constitution

Outline the founding debate about civil liberties and explain how civil liberties apply to the federal government and the states

Civil liberties are related to but different from civil rights, which we will discuss in Chapter 5. Civil liberties protect people from the government. Civil rights are protections of citizen equality *by* the government. The foundations of civil liberties and civil rights are to be found in the state and federal constitutions, which guarantee freedom of speech, freedom of the press, freedom of assembly, and so forth. The federal Constitution's Bill of Rights includes both liberties and rights.

When the first Congress under the newly ratified Constitution met in 1789, the most important item of business was the consideration of a proposal to add a bill of rights to the Constitution. Such a proposal had been turned down with little debate in the waning days of the Philadelphia Constitutional Convention in 1787 because, as the Federalists, led by Alexander Hamilton, later argued, it was "not only unnecessary in the proposed Constitution but would even be dangerous."[2]

civil liberties areas of personal freedom constitutionally protected from government interference

First, according to Hamilton, a bill of rights would be irrelevant to a national government that was given only delegated powers in the first place. To put restraints on "powers which are not granted" could provide a pretext for governments to claim such powers: "For why declare that things shall not be done which there is no power to do?"[3] Second, to Hamilton and the Federalists the Constitution as originally written amounted to a bill of rights (see Table 4.1). For example, Article I, Section 9,

TABLE 4.1

Rights in the Original Constitution (Not in the Bill of Rights)

CLAUSE	RIGHT ESTABLISHED
Article I, Section 9	Guarantee of habeas corpus
Article I, Section 9	Prohibition of bills of attainder
Article I, Section 9	Prohibition of ex post facto laws
Article I, Section 9	Prohibition against acceptance of titles of nobility, etc., from any foreign state
Article III	Guarantee of trial by jury in state where crime was committed
Article III	Treason defined and limited to the life of the person convicted, not to the person's heirs

included the right of **habeas corpus**, which prohibits the government from depriving a person of liberty without an open trial before a judge. Many of the framers, moreover, saw the very structure of the Constitution, including checks and balances, as protective of citizens' liberties.

Antifederalists, most of whom had not been delegates in Philadelphia, argued that the lack of a bill of rights was a major imperfection. The Federalists realized that to gain ratification they would have to add a bill of rights, including a confirmation (in what would become the Tenth Amendment) that all powers not expressly delegated to the national government or explicitly prohibited to the states were reserved to the states.[4]

The House of Representatives approved 17 amendments; of these, the Senate accepted 12. Ten of the amendments were ratified by the necessary three-fourths of the states on December 15, 1791; from the start, these 10 were called the **Bill of Rights** (see Table 4.2).[5]

TABLE 4.2

The Bill of Rights

Amendment I	Congress cannot make any law establishing a religion or abridging freedoms of religious exercise, speech, the press, assembly, or petition.
Amendments II, III, IV	No branch of government may infringe upon the right of the people to keep arms (II), cannot arbitrarily take houses for militia (III), and cannot search for or seize evidence without a court warrant swearing to the probable existence of a crime (IV).
Amendments V, VI, VII, VIII	The courts cannot hold trials for serious offenses without provision for a grand jury (V), a trial jury (VII), a speedy trial (VI), presentation of charges and confrontation by the accused of hostile witnesses (VI), and immunity from testimony against oneself and immunity from trial more than once for the same offense (V). Furthermore, neither bail nor punishment can be excessive (VIII), and no property can be taken without "just compensation" (V).
Amendments IX, X: Limits on the national government	Any rights not enumerated are reserved to the state or the people (X), and the enumeration of certain rights in the Constitution should not be interpreted to mean that those are the only rights the people have (IX).

THE FOURTEENTH AMENDMENT NATIONALIZED
THE BILL OF RIGHTS THROUGH INCORPORATION

The First Amendment provides that "Congress shall make no law. . . ." But this is the only amendment in the Bill of Rights that addresses itself exclusively to the national government. Thus a fundamental question inevitably arises: Do the provisions of the Bill of Rights other than the First Amendment put limits only on the national government, or do they limit the state governments as well?

The Supreme Court first answered this question in 1833 by ruling that the Bill of Rights limited only the national government.[6] This meant that the actions of state governments were restricted only by their own state constitutions as interpreted by their own courts. But the question arose again in 1868 with the adoption of the Fourteenth Amendment, which reads:

> No State shall make or enforce any law which shall abridge the privileges or immunities of citizens of the United States; nor shall any State deprive any person of life, liberty, or property, without due process of law; nor deny to any person within its jurisdiction the equal protection of the laws.

This language sounds like an effort to extend the entire Bill of Rights to all citizens, in whatever state they might reside.[7] Yet this was not the Supreme Court's interpretation for nearly 100 years. Within 5 years of ratification of the Fourteenth Amendment, the Court was making decisions as though the amendment had never been adopted.[8]

In 1897, the Supreme Court did hold that the amendment's due process clause prohibited states from taking property for a public use without just compensation, a form of deprivation of property that is specifically prohibited in the Fifth Amendment.[9] But even though in both amendments "due process" is required for the taking of life and liberty as well as property, only the provision protecting property was "incorporated" into the Fourteenth Amendment as a limitation on state power.

Civil liberties did not expand through the Fourteenth Amendment again until 1925, when the Supreme Court held that freedom of speech is "among the fundamental personal rights and 'liberties' protected by the due process clause of the Fourteenth Amendment from impairment by the states." In 1931 the Court added freedom of the press to that "fundamental" list;[10] from then to 1939[11] it added other First Amendment freedoms. Until the 1960s, that was as far as the Court was willing to go. Indeed, in the 1937 case of *Palko v. Connecticut*, the Court affirmed the states' existing power to determine their own laws on a number of fundamental civil liberties issues. In that case, a Connecticut court had found Frank Palko guilty of second-degree murder and sentenced him to life in prison. Unhappy with the verdict, Connecticut appealed it to the state's highest court, won the appeal, and succeeded in getting Palko convicted of first-degree murder in a new trial. Palko appealed to the Supreme Court on what seemed an open-and-shut case of double jeopardy, which is prohibited by the Fifth Amendment.

The majority of the Court, however, decided that protection against double jeopardy was *not* one of the provisions of the Bill of Rights incorporated into the

Fourteenth Amendment as a restriction on the powers of the states. Not until more than 30 years later did the Court reverse this ruling. Palko was eventually executed for the crime. The *Palko* case established the principle of **selective incorporation**, by which each provision of the Bill of Rights was to be considered separately as a possible limit on the states through the Fourteenth Amendment.

Table 4.3 shows the progress of this revolution in the interpretation of the Constitution. Today, only the Third and Seventh amendments remain unincorporated, though it should be noted that almost every state voluntarily complies with the Seventh Amendment's requirement of jury trials.

The First Amendment Guarantees Freedom of Religion

Explain how the Supreme Court has interpreted freedom of religion through the establishment and free exercise clauses

Congress shall make no law respecting an establishment of religion, or prohibiting the free exercise thereof; or abridging the freedom of speech, or of the press; or the right of the people peaceably to assemble, and to petition the Government for a redress of grievances.
—from the First Amendment

The Bill of Rights begins by guaranteeing freedom of religion, and the First Amendment provides for that freedom in two distinct clauses: "Congress shall make no law [1] respecting an establishment of religion, or [2] prohibiting the free exercise thereof." The first clause is called the "establishment clause," and the second is called the "free exercise clause."

SEPARATION BETWEEN CHURCH AND STATE

The **establishment clause** and the idea of "no law" regarding the establishment of religion could be interpreted in several ways. One interpretation is simply that the national government is prohibited from establishing an official church. Official "established" churches, such as the Church of England, were common in Europe in the eighteenth century as well as in some of the 13 colonies and were viewed by many Americans as inconsistent with a republican form of government. Indeed, many American colonists had fled Europe to escape persecution for having rejected established churches.

TABLE 4.3

Incorporation of the Bill of Rights into the Fourteenth Amendment

SELECTED PROVISIONS AND AMENDMENTS	INCORPORATED	KEY CASE
Eminent domain (V)	1897	*Chicago, Burlington and Quincy R.R. v. Chicago*
Freedom of speech (I)	1925	*Gitlow v. New York*
Freedom of press (I)	1931	*Near v. Minnesota*
Free exercise of religion (I)	1934	*Hamilton v. Regents of the University of California*
Freedom of assembly (I) and freedom to petition the government for redress of grievances (I)	1937	*DeJonge v. Oregon*
Free exercise of religion (I)	1940	*Cantwell v. Connecticut*
Nonestablishment of state religion (I)	1947	*Everson v. Board of Education*
Freedom from warrantless search and seizure (IV) ("exclusionary rule")	1961	*Mapp v. Ohio*
Freedom from cruel and unusual punishment (VIII)	1962	*Robinson v. California*
Right to counsel in any criminal trial (VI)	1963	*Gideon v. Wainwright*
Right against self-incrimination and forced confessions (V)	1964	*Malloy v. Hogan*
Right to counsel (VI)	1964	*Escobedo v. Illinois*
Right to remain silent (V)	1966	*Miranda v. Arizona*
Right against double jeopardy (V)	1969	*Benton v. Maryland*
Right to bear arms (II)	2010	*McDonald v. Chicago*
Excessive fines prohibited (VIII)	2019	*Timbs v. Indiana*
Jury trial (VI)	2020	*Ramos v. Louisiana*

A second possible interpretation is that the government may provide assistance to religious institutions or ideas as long as it does not take sides or show favoritism among them. The United States accommodates religious beliefs in a variety of ways, from the reference to God on currency to the prayer that begins every session of Congress. These forms of religious establishment have always been upheld by the courts.

The First Amendment affects everyday life in a multitude of ways. Because of the amendment's ban on state-sanctioned religion, the Supreme Court ruled in 2000 that school-sponsored prayer in public schools is illegal. Requiring pregame prayer at public schools violates the establishment clause of the First Amendment.

The third view regarding religious establishment, the most commonly held today, favors a "wall of separation"—Jefferson's formulation—between church and state. For two centuries, Jefferson's words have powerfully influenced Americans' understanding of the proper relationship between government and religion. Despite the seeming absoluteness of the phrase, however, there is ample room to disagree on how high the "wall of separation" should be.

One area of conflict over the appropriate boundary is public education. For example, the Court has consistently struck down such practices in public schools as Bible reading,[12] prayer,[13] a moment of silence for meditation, and pregame public prayer at sporting events.[14] In each of these cases, the Court reasoned that organized religious activities, even when apparently nondenominational, strongly suggest the school is sponsoring them and therefore violate the prohibition against establishment of religion.

Another area of ongoing dispute over the meaning of the establishment clause is in public displays of religious symbols, such as city-sponsored nativity scenes. In *Van Orden v. Perry*, the Court decided that a display of the Ten Commandments outside the Texas state capitol did not violate the Constitution.[15] However, in *McCreary County v. American Civil Liberties Union of Kentucky*, the Court determined that a display of the Ten Commandments inside two Kentucky courthouses was unconstitutional.[16] Justice Stephen Breyer, the deciding vote in both cases, said that the display in *Van Orden* had a secular purpose, whereas the displays in *McCreary* had a purely religious purpose.

FREE EXERCISE OF RELIGION

The **free exercise clause** protects the right to believe and to practice whatever religion one chooses (and also protects the right to be a nonbeliever). The precedent-setting case involving free exercise is *West Virginia State Board of Education v. Barnette* (1943), which involved the children in a family of Jehovah's

Witnesses who refused to salute and pledge allegiance to the American flag in their school on the grounds that their religious faith did not permit it.[17]

More recently, the principle of free exercise has been bolstered by legislation prohibiting religious discrimination by public and private entities in a variety of realms. In *Burwell v. Hobby Lobby Stores*,[18] the owners of a chain of craft stores claimed that a section of the Affordable Care Act (ACA, or Obamacare) requiring employers to provide their female employees with free contraceptive coverage violated the owners' religious beliefs as protected by the Religious Freedom Restoration Act. This law, enacted in 1993, requires the government to prove a "compelling interest" for requiring individuals to obey a law that violates their religious beliefs. The Supreme Court ruled in favor of Hobby Lobby. Despite these cases, free exercise of religion continues to have limits, though those limits are contested. During the coronavirus pandemic in 2020, a Louisiana minister was cited on a misdemeanor charge for ignoring the state's ban on gatherings of more than 50 people. He said he was being persecuted for his religion in violation of the Constitution. However, the power of the state to protect the public's health probably takes precedence over the minister's right to hold religious services.

The First Amendment's Freedom of Speech and of the Press Ensure the Free Exchange of Ideas

> **Explain how the Supreme Court has interpreted freedom of speech, assembly, petition, and the press**

Congress shall make no law . . . abridging the freedom of speech, or of the press.
—from the First Amendment

Freedom of speech and freedom of the press have a special place in American political thought. Democracy depends on the ability of individuals to talk to one another and to disseminate information. It is difficult to conceive how democratic politics could function without free and open debate.

Such debate, moreover, is seen as an essential way to evaluate competing ideas. As Justice Oliver Wendell Holmes said in 1919, "The best test of truth is the power of the thought to get itself accepted in the competition of the market. . . . That at any rate is the theory of our Constitution."[19] What is sometimes called the "marketplace of ideas" receives a good deal of protection from the courts. In 1938 the Supreme Court held that any legislation restricting speech "is to be subjected to a more exacting judicial scrutiny . . . than are most other types of legislation."[20]

This higher standard, which came to be called "strict scrutiny," places a heavy burden of proof on the government if it seeks to restrict speech. Americans are assumed to have the right to voice their ideas publicly unless a compelling reason can be identified to prevent them. But strict scrutiny does not mean that speech can never be regulated. Over the past 200 years, the courts have scrutinized many different forms of speech and constructed different principles and guidelines for each. According to the courts, although virtually all speech is protected by the Constitution, some forms are entitled to a greater degree of protection than others.

POLITICAL SPEECH

Political speech was the form of greatest concern to the framers of the Constitution, even though some found it the most difficult one to tolerate. Within seven years of the ratification of the Bill of Rights in 1791, Congress adopted the infamous Alien and Sedition Acts (long since repealed), which, among other things, made it a crime to say or publish anything that might tend to defame or bring into disrepute the government of the United States.

"clear and present danger" test used to determine whether speech is protected or unprotected, based on its capacity to present a "clear and present danger" to society

The first modern free speech case arose immediately after World War I and involved persons convicted under the federal Espionage Act of 1917 for opposing U.S. involvement in the war. The Supreme Court upheld the Espionage Act and refused to protect the speech rights of the defendants on the grounds that their activities—appeals to draftees to resist the draft—constituted a **"clear and present danger"** to national security.[21] This is the first and most famous "test" for when government intervention or censorship can be permitted, though it has since been discarded. Since the 1920s, political speech has been consistently protected by the courts even when judges acknowledged that the speech was "insulting" or "outrageous."

In the important and controversial 2010 case of *Citizens United v. Federal Election Commission*, the Court struck down a ban on corporate funding of political advertisements supporting or opposing particular candidates[22] on the grounds that this spending is political speech that the Constitution prohibits the government from regulating. In 2014 the Court again expanded its protection of campaign expenditures under the First Amendment by overturning limits on the total amount an individual may contribute.[23] As a result of this decision, wealthy donor contributions to presidential candidates skyrocketed in 2016.

Republicans hailed the recent decisions deregulating campaign spending, while Democrats denounced them. President Obama called *Citizens United* "a major victory for big oil, Wall Street banks, health insurance companies, and the other powerful interests that marshal their power every day in Washington to drown out the voices of everyday Americans."[24]

FIGHTING WORDS AND HATE SPEECH

Speech can lose its protected position only when it moves from the symbolic realm to the realm of actual conduct—for example, "expressive speech" that directly incites physical conflict with the use of

> **fighting words** speech that directly incites damaging conduct

so-called **fighting words.** In 1942 a man who had called a police officer a "goddamned racketeer" and "a damn Fascist" was arrested and convicted of violating a state law forbidding the use of offensive language in public. The Supreme Court upheld his arrest on the grounds that such words are not protected by the First Amendment because they "are no essential part of any exposition of ideas."[25] This decision was reaffirmed in 1951 in *Dennis v. United States,*[26] when the Court held that there is no substantial public interest in permitting certain kinds of speech, including "fighting words." Since that time, however, the Court has reversed almost every conviction based on arguments that the speaker had used "fighting words."

In recent years, the increased activism of minority and women's groups has prompted a movement against language considered to be racial or ethnic or gender slurs. Many universities have attempted to develop codes to suppress such "hate speech." Students and faculty on some campuses have also demanded that certain public figures (usually conservative and far-right ones) be banned from speaking, on the grounds that they promote hatred. There seems little doubt that the Constitution protects the right of individuals to share controversial views. The conflict arises when that right comes up against university policies to emphasize safety—a consideration that not so long ago led to bans on left-wing speakers. Perhaps people of all political

Are social media companies responsible for the proliferation of offensive and hateful speech on their sites? Here, Facebook CEO Mark Zuckerberg testifies before Congress on Facebook's role in allowing hateful content on the site.

persuasions should think about the words of Supreme Court Justice Oliver Wendell Holmes, who said, "If there is any principle of the Constitution that more imperatively calls for attachment than any other, it is the principle of free thought—not free thought for those who agree with us but freedom for the thought that we hate."[27]

Many of these cases have involved action by the federal or state governments, but what about private action to prohibit various forms of speech? Today, the ability to post messages on social media platforms like Facebook is critically important to those who want to disseminate their ideas. In 2019, Facebook announced a change in its terms-of-service agreement designed to prevent users from posting hateful commentary and claims. Facebook is, of course, a private organization so the constitutional restrictions on the government's actions may not apply.

STUDENT SPEECH

One category of speech with only limited protection is that of students in public high schools. In 1986 the Supreme Court backed away from a broad protection of student free speech rights by upholding the punishment of a high school student for making a sexually suggestive speech. The Court opinion held that such speech interfered with the school's goal of teaching students the limits of socially acceptable behavior.[28] Two years later the Court restricted students' freedom of speech and the press even further, defining their speech and journalism in school as part of their education and not protected with the same standard as adult speech in a public forum.[29]

A later case[30] dealt with the policies of a high school in Juneau, Alaska. In 2002 the Olympic torch relay passed through Juneau on its way to Salt Lake City for the opening of the Winter Olympics. As the torch passed Juneau-Douglas High, a student unfurled a banner reading "BONG HITS 4 JESUS." The school's principal promptly suspended the student, who then brought suit for reinstatement, alleging that his free speech rights had been violated. Like most of America's public schools, Juneau-Douglas High prohibits assemblies or expressions on school grounds that advocate illegal drug use. In the Supreme Court's majority decision in 2007, Chief Justice John Roberts said that the First Amendment did not require schools to permit students to advocate illegal drug use.

COMMERCIAL SPEECH

Commercial speech, such as newspaper or television advertisements, was initially considered to be entirely outside the protection of the First Amendment and is still subject to limited regulation. For example, the Federal Trade Commission's prohibition of false and misleading advertising is an old and well-established power of the federal government. The Supreme Court has upheld city ordinances prohibiting the posting of all commercial signs on publicly owned property (as long as the ban is total so that there is no hint of selective censorship).[31]

However, commercial speech has become more protected under the First Amendment. For example, in 1975 the Supreme Court struck down a state law making it a misdemeanor to sell or circulate newspapers encouraging abortions; the Court

The Supreme Court has ruled that high school students' speech can be restricted. In a 2007 case involving a student who displayed the banner above, the Court found that the school principal had not violated the student's right to free speech by suspending him.

ruled that the statute infringed both on constitutionally protected speech and on readers' right to make informed choices.[32]

SYMBOLIC SPEECH, SPEECH PLUS, AND THE RIGHTS OF ASSEMBLY AND PETITION

Because the First Amendment treats the freedoms of religion and political speech as equal to those of assembly and petition, the Supreme Court has always largely protected an individual's right to "symbolic speech": peaceful actions designed to send a political message. One example is the burning of the American flag as a protest.

Closer to the original intent of the assembly and petition clause is the category of **"speech plus"**—combining speech with physical activity such as picketing, distributing leaflets, and other forms of peaceful demonstration or assembly. In the 1939 case of *Hague v. Committee for Industrial Organization*, the Supreme Court declared that the government may not prohibit speech-related activities such as demonstrations or leafleting in public areas traditionally used for that purpose, though it may impose rules to protect the public safety at such events so long as they do not discriminate against particular viewpoints.[33] Such "public forum" assemblies have since been consistently protected by courts.

But the same kind of assembly on private property is quite another matter and can in many circumstances be regulated, such as at a shopping center. Even in public areas, assemblies or demonstrations can be restricted under some circumstances, especially when they jeopardize the health, safety, or rights of others.

"speech plus" speech accompanied by conduct such as sit-ins, picketing, and demonstrations; protection of this form of speech under the First Amendment is conditional, and restrictions imposed by state or local authorities are acceptable if properly balanced by considerations of public order

FREEDOM OF THE PRESS

With the exception of the broadcast media, which are subject to federal regulation, the press is protected against **prior restraint**. That is, beginning with the landmark 1931 case of *Near v. Minnesota*, the Supreme Court has held that, except under the most extraordinary circumstances, the First Amendment prohibits government agencies from preventing newspapers or magazines from publishing whatever they wish.[34] Indeed, in the 1971 case *New York Times Co. v. United States* (the so-called Pentagon Papers case), the Supreme Court ruled that the government could not block publication of secret Defense Department documents furnished to the *New York Times* by an opponent of the Vietnam War who had obtained the documents illegally.[35]

Another press freedom issue that the courts have often been asked to decide is whether journalists can be compelled to reveal their sources of information. Journalists assert that if they cannot ensure their sources' confidentiality, the flow of information will be reduced and press freedom effectively curtailed. Government agencies, however, argue that names of news sources may be relevant to criminal or even national security investigations. Nearly 40 states have "shield laws" that protect journalistic sources to varying degrees. There is, however, no federal shield law and no special constitutional protection for journalists.[36]

Libel and Slander Some speech is not protected at all. If a written statement is made in "reckless disregard of the truth" and is considered damaging to the victim because it is "malicious, scandalous, and defamatory," it can be punished as **libel**. If such a statement is made orally, it can be punished as **slander**.

prior restraint an effort by a governmental agency to block the publication of material it deems libelous or harmful in some other way; censorship; in the United States, the courts forbid prior restraint except under the most extraordinary circumstances

libel a written statement made in "reckless disregard of the truth" that is considered damaging to a victim because it is "malicious, scandalous, and defamatory"

slander an oral statement made in "reckless disregard of the truth" that is considered damaging to the victim because it is "malicious, scandalous, and defamatory"

Most libel suits today involve freedom of the press, but American courts have narrowed the meaning of libel to the point that it is extremely difficult for politicians or other public figures (as opposed to private individuals) to win a libel suit against a newspaper. In the important 1964 case of *New York Times Co. v. Sullivan*, the Supreme Court held that to be found libelous, a story about a public official not only had to be untrue but also had to result from "actual malice" or "reckless disregard" for the truth.[37] In other words, the newspaper had to print false and damaging material deliberately. Because in practice this charge is nearly impossible to prove, essentially the print media have become able to publish anything they want about a public figure. President Trump asserted that stricter libel laws were needed to prevent what he called "fake news," though no policies changed.

With the emergence of the internet as a communications medium, the courts have had to decide how traditional libel law applies to online content. In 1995

Global Freedom of the Press

While freedom of the press is a cornerstone of American civil liberties, in other countries it is neither as firmly enshrined in law nor as respected as a matter of practice. This map looks specifically at how "free and independent" the media are in each country.

1. Where is the press most free and independent? Where is it less so? Are there regions of the world that are better at respecting freedom of the press than others? How does the United States fare in comparison to other countries on this measure?

2. Why might a government want to impose constraints on media operating in its borders? On the other hand, what do governments gain by allowing, or even encouraging, the functioning of a free and independent press?

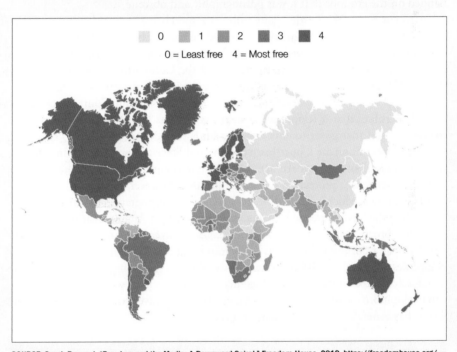

SOURCE: Sarah Repucci, "Freedom and the Media: A Downward Spiral," Freedom House, 2019, https://freedomhouse.org/report/freedom-media/freedom-media-2019 (accessed 2/24/20).

the New York courts held that an online bulletin board could be held responsible for the libelous content of material posted by a third party. To protect internet service providers, Congress subsequently enacted legislation absolving them of responsibility for third-party posts. The federal courts have generally upheld this law.[38]

Obscenity and Pornography Cases involving pornography and obscenity can be even trickier than libel and slander. Not until 1957 did the Supreme Court try to define obscenity, and its definition may have caused more confusion than it cleared up. The Court's opinion defined obscenity as speech or writing that appeals to the "prurient interest"—that is, whose purpose is to excite lust, as this appears "to the average person, applying contemporary community standards." Even so, the work should be judged obscene only when it is "utterly without redeeming social importance."[39] In 1964, Justice Potter Stewart confessed that, although he found pornography impossible to define, "I know it when I see it."[40] The vague and impractical standards that had been developed meant ultimately that almost nothing could be banned on the grounds that it was pornographic and obscene.

In recent years, the battle against obscene speech has targeted online pornography, whose opponents argue that it should be banned because of the easy access children have to the internet. In 1996, Congress passed the Telecommunications Act. Attached to it was an amendment, called the Communications Decency Act (CDA), designed to regulate the online transmission of obscene material. In the 1997 case of *Reno v. American Civil Liberties Union*, the Supreme Court struck down the CDA, ruling that it suppressed speech that "adults have a constitutional right to receive" and that governments may not limit the adult population to messages fit for children. Supreme Court Justice John Paul Stevens described the internet as the "town crier" of the modern age and said it was entitled to the greatest degree of First Amendment protection possible.[41] In 2008, however, the Court upheld the PROTECT Act, which outlawed efforts to sell child pornography via the internet.[42]

In 2000 the Court extended the highest degree of First Amendment protection to cable (not broadcast) television. In *United States v. Playboy Entertainment Group*,[43] it struck down a portion of the 1996 Telecommunications Act that required cable TV companies to limit the availability of sexually explicit programming to late-night hours.

Closely related to the issue of obscenity is the question of whether governments can prohibit broadcasts or publications considered excessively violent. Here, too, the Court has generally upheld freedom of speech.[44]

The Second Amendment Protects the Right to Bear Arms

Explain how the Supreme Court has interpreted the right to bear arms

A well regulated Militia, being necessary to the security of a free State, the right of the people to keep and bear Arms, shall not be infringed.
—from the Second Amendment

The Second Amendment was included in the Bill of Rights to provide for "well-regulated" militias, which were called up to maintain local public order and national defense and to enforce the "security of a free State." *Militias* were a military or police resource composed of part-time citizen-soldiers for the state and national governments and were distinguished from professional armies, which came within the sole constitutional jurisdiction of Congress. While the right of the people "to keep and bear Arms" was linked to citizen service in militias, many have argued that the Second Amendment also establishes an individual right to bear arms.

In 1939 the Supreme Court upheld a federal gun law in a case in which the Court concluded that the Second Amendment pertained to "the preservation or efficiency of a well regulated militia,"[45] but the Court made no further Second Amendment decisions for nearly 70 years. Thus, states and localities across the country have very different gun-ownership laws. For instance, in Wyoming, there is no ban on owning any type of gun, there is no waiting period to purchase a firearm, and individuals are not required to obtain a permit for carrying a concealed weapon. In California, in contrast, the possession of assault weapons is banned, there is a 10-day waiting period to purchase a firearm, and a permit is required to carry a concealed weapon. Figure 4.1 shows the background-check requirements to purchase a firearm across the country.

The Supreme Court's silence on the meaning of the Second Amendment ended in 2008 with the first of two rulings in favor of expansive gun rights. In *District*

A string of mass shootings in the United States, including one at a Walmart in El Paso, Texas, in which 22 people were killed and 24 injured, have prompted calls for legislation to limit the availability of guns.

FIGURE 4.1

Gun Rights by State

Although state gun laws must conform to the Second Amendment as interpreted by the U.S. Supreme Court, laws concerning gun sales and ownership vary widely from state to state. It is much more difficult to buy a gun in, say, New York or California than in Texas or Kentucky. While federal law requires background checks when purchasing a firearm from a licensed seller, only 21 states require them from unlicensed sellers as well. Should all states require unlicensed firearm sellers to perform background checks? Why or why not?

BACKGROUND CHECKS AT UNLICENSED GUNSELLERS
REQUIRED FOR THE PURCHASE OF . . .

■ All firearms   ■ Only handguns   None

SOURCE: Background Checks, Gun Law Navigator, www.everytownresearch.org/ (accessed 6/12/18).

of Columbia v. Heller, the Court struck down a strict Washington, D.C., law that banned handguns. It ruled 5–4 that the Second Amendment provides a constitutional right to keep a loaded handgun at home for self-defense. In the majority opinion, Justice Antonin Scalia stated that the decision was not intended to cast doubt on all laws limiting firearm possession, such as by felons or the mentally ill.[46] In his dissenting opinion, Justice Stevens asserted that the Second Amendment protects the rights of individuals to bear arms only as part of a militia force, not in an individual capacity.

Because the District of Columbia is an entity of the federal government, the Court's ruling did not apply to state firearms laws. However, in the 2010 case of *McDonald v. Chicago*, the Supreme Court applied the Second Amendment to the states, its first new incorporation decision in 40 years. The ruling effectively overturned a Chicago ordinance that made it extremely difficult to own a gun within city limits.[47]

Despite these rulings, the debate over gun control continues to loom large in American politics. The issue of gun laws has been kept firmly on the national agenda by a recent series of tragic shootings (including the killings of 50 people at a nightclub in Orlando, Florida; 59 individuals at a concert in Las Vegas, Nevada; 27 worshippers at a church in Sutherland Springs, Texas; 17 students and staff members at a high school in Parkland, Florida; 11 worshippers at a synagogue in Pittsburgh, Pennsylvania; and 22 people at a Walmart in El Paso, Texas). Proponents of gun control point to these shootings as evidence of the need for stricter gun laws; opponents say they demonstrate that Americans are not safe and should be free to carry arms for self-protection.

Rights of the Criminally Accused Are Based on Due Process of Law

> **Explain how the Supreme Court has interpreted the right to due process**

The Fourth, Fifth, Sixth, and Eighth amendments, pertaining to the rights of the accused, are the essence of the **due process of law**, even though these precise words for this fundamental concept do not appear until the end of the Fifth Amendment.

THE FOURTH AMENDMENT AND SEARCHES AND SEIZURES

The right of the people to be secure in their persons, houses, papers, and effects, against unreasonable searches and seizures, shall not be violated, and no Warrants shall issue, but upon probable cause, supported by Oath or affirmation, and particularly describing the place to be searched, and the persons or things to be seized.   —from the Fourth Amendment

The purpose of the Fourth Amendment is to guarantee the security of citizens against unreasonable (i.e., improper) searches and seizures. In 1990 the Supreme Court summarized its understanding of the Fourth Amendment: "A search compromises the individual interest in privacy; a seizure deprives the individual of dominion over his or her person or property."[48] But how are we to define what is reasonable and what is unreasonable?

The 1961 case of *Mapp v. Ohio* illustrates one of the most important principles to have grown out of the Fourth Amendment—the **exclusionary rule**, which prohibits evidence obtained during an illegal search from being introduced in a trial. Acting on a tip that Dollree (Dolly) Mapp was harboring a suspect in a bombing incident, several policemen forcibly entered Mapp's house, claiming they had a search warrant. They did not find the suspect but, in an old trunk in the basement, did find some

due process of law the right of every individual against arbitrary action by national or state governments

exclusionary rule the ability of courts to exclude evidence obtained in violation of the Fourth Amendment

materials they declared to be obscene. Although no warrant was ever produced, Mapp was convicted of possessing obscene materials.

The Supreme Court's opinion in the case affirmed the exclusionary rule: under the Fourth Amendment (applied to the states through the Fourteenth Amendment), "all evidence obtained by searches and seizures in violation of the Constitution . . . is inadmissible."[49] This means that even people who are clearly guilty of the crime of which they are accused cannot be convicted if the only evidence for their conviction was obtained illegally.

In recent years, however, the Supreme Court has softened the application of the exclusionary rule, allowing federal courts to use their discretion about it depending on the "nature and quality of the intrusion."[50]

The Fourth Amendment is also at issue in the controversy over mandatory drug testing. In 1989 the Supreme Court upheld the U.S. Customs Service's drug-testing program for its employees[51] and drug and alcohol tests for railroad workers if they were involved in serious accidents.[52] Since then, more than 40 federal agencies have initiated mandatory employee drug tests, giving rise to controversy about the general practice of "suspicionless testing" of employees.

The most recent cases suggest, however, that the Court is beginning to consider limits on the war against drugs. In 2013, for example, the Court held that the use of a drug-sniffing dog on the front porch of a home constituted a search that violated the Fourth Amendment in the absence of consent or a warrant.[53]

Changes in technology have also had an impact on Fourth Amendment jurisprudence. In the 2012 case of *United States v. Jones*, the Court held that prosecutors violated a defendant's rights when they attached a Global Positioning System (GPS) device to his Jeep and monitored his movements for 28 days.[54] On the other hand, in *Maryland v. King*,[55] the Court upheld DNA testing of arrestees without the need for individualized suspicion. In the 2014 case of *Riley v. California*, the Court held that the police were constitutionally prohibited from seizing a cell phone and searching its digital contents during an arrest.

THE FIFTH AMENDMENT

No person shall be held to answer for a capital, or otherwise infamous crime, unless on a presentment or indictment of a Grand Jury, except in cases arising in the land or naval forces, or in the Militia, when in actual service in time of War or public danger; nor shall any person be subject for the same offence to be twice put in jeopardy of life or limb; nor shall be compelled in any criminal case to be a witness against himself, nor be deprived of life, liberty, or property, without due process of law; nor shall private property be taken for public use, without just compensation. —from the Fifth Amendment

grand jury jury that determines whether sufficient evidence is available to justify a trial; grand juries do not rule on the accused's guilt or innocence

Grand Juries The first clause of the Fifth Amendment, the right to a **grand jury** to determine whether a trial is warranted, is considered "the oldest institution known to the Constitution."[56] A grand jury is a body of citizens that must agree that a prosecutor has sufficient evidence to bring criminal charges against a suspect. Although grand juries do play an important role in federal criminal cases, the provision for them is the one important civil liberties provision of the Bill of Rights that was not incorporated into the Fourteenth Amendment and applied to state criminal prosecutions. Thus, some states operate without grand juries. In such states, the prosecutor simply files a "bill of information" affirming that sufficient evidence is available to justify a trial. For the accused person to be held in custody, the prosecutor must persuade a judge that the evidence shows "probable cause" to justify further action.

Double Jeopardy "Nor shall any person be subject for the same offence to be twice put in jeopardy of life or limb" is the constitutional protection from **double jeopardy**, or being tried more than once for the same crime. The protection from double jeopardy was at the heart of the *Palko* case in 1937, which, as we saw earlier in this chapter, also established the principle of selective incorporation of the Bill of Rights. However, in the 1969 case of *Benton v. Maryland*, the Supreme Court expressly overruled *Palko* and declared that the double jeopardy clause did, in fact, apply to the states.[57]

Self-Incrimination Perhaps the most significant liberty found in the Fifth Amendment is the guarantee that no citizen "shall be compelled in any criminal case to be a witness against himself." The most famous case concerning self-incrimination is one of such importance that Chief Justice Earl Warren assessed its results as going "to the very root of our concepts of American criminal jurisprudence."[58]

In 1963, Ernesto Miranda was convicted and sentenced to between 20 and 30 years in prison for the kidnapping and rape of a woman in Arizona. The woman had identified him in a police lineup, and after two hours of questioning, Miranda confessed and subsequently signed a statement that his confession had been made voluntarily, without threats or promises of immunity. The statement was admitted into evidence and served as the basis for Miranda's conviction.

After his conviction, Miranda argued that his confession had not been truly voluntary and that he had not been informed of his right to remain silent or his right to consult an attorney. In a controversial ruling, the Supreme Court agreed and overturned the conviction. *Miranda v. Arizona* (1966) produced the rules the police must follow before questioning an arrested criminal suspect, and the reading of a person's "Miranda rights" became a standard scene in every police station and on virtually every television and film dramatization of police action.

Miranda expanded the Fifth Amendment's protection against coerced confessions and self-incrimination and also confirmed the right to counsel, as discussed below. Although the Supreme Court later considerably loosened the *Miranda* restrictions, the **Miranda rule** still stands as a protection against police abuses.

double jeopardy the Fifth Amendment right providing that a person cannot be tried twice for the same crime

Miranda rule the requirement, articulated by the Supreme Court in *Miranda v. Arizona*, that persons under arrest must be informed prior to police interrogation of their rights to remain silent and to have the benefit of legal counsel

```
DEFENDANT                          LOCATION

        SPECIFIC WARNING REGARDING INTERROGATIONS

  1. YOU HAVE THE RIGHT TO REMAIN SILENT.

  2. ANYTHING YOU SAY CAN AND WILL BE USED AGAINST YOU IN A COURT
     OF LAW.

  3. YOU HAVE THE RIGHT TO TALK TO A LAWYER AND HAVE HIM PRESENT
     WITH YOU WHILE YOU ARE BEING QUESTIONED.

  4. IF YOU CANNOT AFFORD TO HIRE A LAWYER ONE WILL BE APPOINTED
     TO REPRESENT YOU BEFORE ANY QUESTIONING, IF YOU WISH ONE.

  SIGNATURE OF DEFENDANT                        DATE


  WITNESS                                       TIME


  ☐ REFUSED SIGNATURE    SAN FRANCISCO POLICE DEPARTMENT      PR.9.1.4
```

The case of Ernesto Miranda resulted in the creation of Miranda rights, which must be read to those arrested to make them aware of their constitutional rights.

THE SIXTH AMENDMENT AND THE RIGHT TO COUNSEL

In all criminal prosecutions, the accused shall enjoy the right to a speedy and public trial, by an impartial jury of the State and district wherein the crime shall have been committed, which district shall have been previously ascertained by law, and to be informed of the nature and cause of the accusation; to be confronted with the witnesses against him; to have compulsory process for obtaining witnesses in his favor, and to have the Assistance of Counsel for his defence.

—from the Sixth Amendment

Some provisions of the Sixth Amendment, such as the right to a speedy trial and the right to confront witnesses before an impartial jury, are not very controversial. The "right to counsel" provision, however, like the exclusionary rule of the Fourth Amendment and the self-incrimination clause of the Fifth Amendment, is notable for sometimes freeing defendants who seem to be clearly guilty as charged.

Gideon v. Wainwright (1963) involved a disreputable person who had been in and out of jails for most of his 51 years. Clarence Earl Gideon received a five-year sentence for breaking into and entering a poolroom in Panama City, Florida. He was too poor to afford a lawyer, and Florida law provided for court-appointed counsel only for crimes carrying the death penalty. While serving time, however, Gideon made his own appeal on a handwritten petition, and eventually won the landmark ruling on the right to counsel in all felony cases.[59] The right to counsel has been expanded during the past few decades, even as the courts have become more conservative.

THE EIGHTH AMENDMENT AND CRUEL AND UNUSUAL PUNISHMENT

Excessive bail shall not be required, nor excessive fines imposed, nor cruel and unusual punishment inflicted.   —from the Eighth Amendment

Virtually all the debate over Eighth Amendment issues focuses on the last clause of the amendment, because what is considered "cruel and unusual" varies from culture to culture and from generation to generation. In 1972 the Supreme Court overturned several state death penalty laws, not because they were cruel and unusual but because they were being applied unevenly—that is, African Americans were much more likely than Whites to be sentenced to death, the poor more likely than the rich, and men more likely than women.[60] Very soon after that decision, a majority of states revised their capital punishment provisions to meet the Court's standards, and the Court reaffirmed that the death penalty could be used if certain standards were met.[61] Since 1976, the Court has consistently upheld state laws providing for capital punishment, although it also continues to review death penalty appeals each year.

Between 1976 and October 2020, states executed 1,524 people. Most of those executions occurred in southern states, with Texas leading the way at 570. As of October 2020, 28 states had statutes providing for capital punishment for specified offenses, a policy supported by a majority of Americans, according to polls.[62] On the other hand, 22 states bar the death penalty, and since the end of the 1990s, both the number of death sentences and the number of executions have declined annually.[63]

The Supreme Court has long struggled to establish principles to govern executions under the Eighth Amendment. In recent years, the Court has declared that death was too harsh a penalty for the crime of rape of a child,[64] prohibited the execution of a defendant with an IQ under 70 and of a youthful defendant, and invalidated a death sentence for an African American defendant after the prosecutor improperly excluded African Americans from the jury.[65] In 2015, however, the Court upheld lethal injection as a mode of execution despite arguments that this form of execution was likely to cause considerable pain.[66]

The Eighth Amendment also prohibits excessive fines. In the 2019 case of *Timbs v. Indiana*, the Supreme Court ruled that this prohibition applied to the states.[67] In the *Timbs* case, the state confiscated Timbs's car after he was convicted of drug possession. The car was worth much more than the maximum possible fine Timbs could have received. The Indiana Supreme Court agreed that the fine may have been excessive but said this did not matter because the Eighth Amendment had never been applied to the states. The U.S. Supreme Court reversed that decision and added excessive fines to the list of constitutional provisions the states were obligated to recognize.

The Right to Privacy Means the Right to Be Left Alone

> **Describe how the Supreme Court has identified and interpreted the right to privacy**

A **right to privacy** was not mentioned in the Bill of Rights. In a 1928 case, however, Supreme Court Justice Louis Brandeis argued in a dissent that the Fourth Amendment's provision for "the right of the people to be secure in their persons, houses, papers, and effects, against unreasonable searches and seizures" should be extended to a more general principle of "privacy in the home."[68]

EMINENT DOMAIN

One important element of privacy is the possession of private property—property belonging to individuals for their own peaceful enjoyment. The privacy of private property, however, is conditioned by the needs of the public at large. What if the government believes that the construction of a public road or other public project requires that a private home be torn down to make way for the public good? Where does privacy end and the public good begin? The power of any government to take private property for public use is called **eminent domain.**

right to privacy the right to be left alone, which has been interpreted by the Supreme Court to entail individual access to birth control and abortions

eminent domain the right of government to take private property for public use

The Fifth Amendment, through the "takings clause," regulates that power by requiring that the government show a public purpose and provide fair payment for the taking of someone's property. This provision is now observed by all governments within the United States.

BIRTH CONTROL

The sphere of privacy as a constitutional principle was formally recognized in 1965, when the Court ruled that a Connecticut law forbidding the use of contraceptives (and even information about contraception) by married couples violated the right of marital privacy. The Supreme Court declared the Connecticut law unconstitutional because it violated "a right of privacy older than the Bill of Rights."[69] Justice William O. Douglas, who wrote the majority opinion in the *Griswold v. Connecticut* case, argued that this right of privacy is also grounded in the Constitution because it fits into a "zone of privacy" created by a combination of the Third, Fourth, and Fifth amendments.

> **FOR CRITICAL ANALYSIS ▶**
>
> 1. Compare each state's restrictions on abortions and the number of facilities in that state that provide abortions. Which state offers the most access to abortion, and which the least?
>
> 2. Should civil liberties like the right to privacy vary from state to state?

Abortion and the Right to Privacy

Do Americans have a right to obtain an abortion? In its 1973 landmark case *Roe v. Wade*, the Supreme Court established a right to privacy enshrined in the Bill of Rights that included a person's right to receive an abortion. President Trump's appointment of two antiabortion justices has fueled opposition to *Roe*, and in 2019 nine states passed laws that effectively ban abortions statewide. These bans are not yet in effect and will likely face extended legal challenges, where the Supreme Court may ultimately decide whether Americans have this form of a right to privacy.

Access to Abortion, 2019

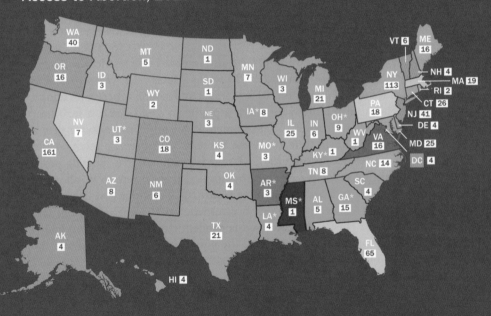

Abortion prohibited after...

● 15 Weeks　● 18 Weeks　● 22 Weeks　● 24 Weeks　● 25 Weeks　● Viability　● None

#　**Number of clinics, 2017**

* Several states, including Alabama, Georgia, Kentucky, Louisiana, Mississippi, and Missouri, have recently passed laws effectively banning abortion that have not yet gone into effect.

SOURCE: Data from R. K. Jones, E. Witwer, and J. Jerman, *Abortion Incidence and Service Availability in the United States, 2017* (New York: Guttmacher Institute, 2019), www.guttmacher.org/report/abortion-incidence-service-availability-us-2017 (accessed 11/18/19).

ABORTION

The right to privacy was confirmed and extended in 1973 in a revolutionary Supreme Court decision: *Roe v. Wade*, which established a woman's right to seek an abortion. The decision prohibited states from making abortion a criminal act prior to the point in pregnancy at which the fetus becomes viable, which in 1973 was the 27th week.[70]

In extending privacy rights to include the rights of women to control their own bodies, the Court was following both historical and recent precedents. The states did not begin regulating abortion until the 1840s, when 6 of the 26 states existing at the time outlawed the practice. By the twentieth century, many states had begun to ease their abortion restrictions well before the 1973 *Roe* decision.

By extending the umbrella of privacy, this sweeping ruling dramatically changed abortion practices in America. In addition, it galvanized and nationalized the abortion debate. Groups opposed to abortion, such as the National Right to Life Committee, organized to fight the liberal new standard, while abortion rights groups have fought to maintain that protection.

While the Supreme Court has continued to affirm a woman's right to seek an abortion, it has increasingly limited that right. For example, in the 1992 case of *Planned Parenthood of Southeastern Pennsylvania v. Casey*, another 5–4 majority upheld *Roe* but narrowed its scope, defining the right to an abortion as a "limited or qualified" right subject to regulation by the states as long as the regulation does not constitute an "undue burden."[71]

In recent years a number of states have also imposed new restrictions, including lowering the viability standard to 20 weeks (Texas), 12 weeks (Arkansas), and 6 weeks (North Dakota). In 2019, Georgia and several other states adopted "heartbeat" bills, prohibiting abortion if a physician could detect a fetal heartbeat, usually at about 6 weeks. Some women might not even be aware they are pregnant at this point. In June 2020, the Supreme Court struck down an effort by Louisiana to restrict abortion rights. A state law required that abortion providers have admitting privileges in a nearby hospital if they were to be allowed to perform abortions. In a 5–4 decision the Court ruled that this law, like a similar Texas statute that had been previously overturned, was an impermissible effort to restrict abortion rights.[72] The coronavirus pandemic of 2020 offered opponents of abortion a new opportunity to limit the practice. Texas banned all abortions for the duration of the crisis as a public-health measure. This ban was upheld by a federal appeals court.

SEXUAL ORIENTATION

In the last three decades, the right to be left alone began to include the privacy rights of people in the LGBTQ community. In the 1986 case of *Bowers v. Hardwick* the Court ruled in favor of a state anti-sodomy law on the grounds that "the federal Constitution confers [no] fundamental right upon homosexuals to engage in sodomy."[73]

Seventeen years later, to almost everyone's surprise, in *Lawrence v. Texas* (2003) the Court overturned *Bowers v. Hardwick* with a dramatic pronouncement that gay people are "entitled to respect for their private lives"[74] as a matter of constitutional due process and that "the State cannot demean their existence or control their destiny by making their private sexual conduct a crime."[75] In 2015 the Court took another important step in the protection of gay rights by declaring that state bans on same-sex marriage were unconstitutional because they violated the Fourteenth Amendment's equal protection and due process clauses.[76] See Chapter 5 for more on same-sex marriage.

In 2020, LGBTQ and transgender individuals won a significant victory in the Supreme Court. In a 6–3 decision written by Justice Neil Gorsuch, the Court ruled that the 1964 Civil Rights Act prohibited employment discrimination based on sexual orientation, just as it prohibited employment discrimination based on race and gender.[77] The fact that the decision was authored by one of the Court's most conservative justices suggests that LGBTQ and transgender individuals have won an increased measure of acceptance in the United States.

Civil Liberties: What Do You Think?

The prominent place of civil liberties is one of the hallmarks of American government. The freedoms enshrined in the Constitution and its amendments help define the relationship between government and citizens by limiting what government can do to individuals. But these freedoms also come with trade-offs, as the Slants and Native Americans experienced in the debate over legal protections from ethnicity- or race-based disparagement.

★ Have you had experiences where someone else's exercise of freedom interfered with yours? How do you think members of the Slants thought about the trade-offs between their freedom to choose their band name and the implications for others, such as Native American critics of the Redskins football team's name?

★ What do you think about questions concerning the right to bear arms, the use of the death penalty, and religious freedom? What are your rights to act upon your beliefs? What are the rights of people who disagree with you? How do you think the Slants would react to critics of their First Amendment claims?

★ How have new technologies affected the government's ability to monitor its citizens? What are your expectations of privacy in your email conversations, your plane tickets, your reading habits?

Practice Quiz

1. The process by which some of the liberties in the Bill of Rights were considered separately as a possible limit on the states is known as *(p. 94)*
   a) habeas corpus.
   b) ratification.
   c) selective incorporation.
   d) establishment.
   e) preemption.

2. Which of the following issues is commonly debated and considered in terms of the establishment clause? *(p. 96)*
   a) whether public schools can sponsor prayer sessions
   b) whether corporations can fund political advertisements
   c) whether hate speech can be restricted on social media platforms
   d) whether states can ban the possession of assault weapons
   e) whether states can place restrictions on abortion

3. Which piece of recent legislation was challenged in the Supreme Court on the grounds that some of its provisions violated the free exercise clause? *(p. 97)*
   a) the Affordable Care Act
   b) the Religious Freedom Restoration Act
   c) the Espionage Act
   d) the Bipartisan Campaign Reform Act
   e) the Higher Education Act

4. The judicial standard that places a heavy burden of proof on the government when it seeks to restrict speech is called *(p. 98)*
   a) judicial restraint.
   b) judicial activism.
   c) habeas corpus.
   d) prior restraint.
   e) strict scrutiny.

5. Which of the following describes a written statement made in "reckless disregard of the truth" that is considered damaging to a victim because it is "malicious, scandalous, and defamatory"? *(p. 102)*
   a) slander
   b) libel
   c) speech plus
   d) fighting words
   e) expressive speech

6. In *District of Columbia v. Heller*, the Supreme Court ruled that *(p. 106)*
   a) states can require citizens to own firearms.
   b) federal grants can be used to support the formation of state militias.
   c) felons cannot be prevented from purchasing assault rifles.
   d) the Second Amendment provides a constitutional right to keep a loaded handgun at home for self-defense.
   e) the Second Amendment applies only to the federal government and not to states.

7. The Fourth, Fifth, Sixth, and Eighth amendments, taken together, are the essence of *(p. 107)*
   a) due process of law.
   b) free speech.
   c) the right to bear arms.
   d) civil rights of minorities.
   e) freedom of religion.

8. In *Mapp v. Ohio*, the Supreme Court ruled that *(pp. 107–8)*
   a) evidence obtained from an illegal search cannot be introduced in a trial.
   b) the government must provide legal counsel for defendants who are too poor to provide for themselves.

c) persons under arrest must be informed prior to police interrogation of their rights to remain silent and to have the benefits of legal counsel.

d) the government has the right to take private property for public use if just compensation is provided.

e) a person cannot be tried twice for the same crime.

9. Which landmark ruling deals with the Sixth Amendment's guarantee of the right to counsel? *(p. 110)*
   a) *Roe v. Wade*
   b) *Mapp v. Ohio*
   c) *Gideon v. Wainwright*
   d) *McDonald v. Chicago*
   e) *Miranda v. Arizona*

10. The Eighth Amendment prohibits not only cruel and unusual punishment but also *(p. 111)*
    a) capital punishment.
    b) double jeopardy.
    c) slander and libel.
    d) excessive fines.
    e) unreasonable searches and seizures.

11. The power of government to take private property for public use is called *(p. 112)*
    a) habeas corpus.
    b) eminent domain.
    c) selective incorporation.
    d) the Miranda rule.
    e) double jeopardy.

12. In which case was a right to privacy related to the use of birth control first formally recognized by the Supreme Court? *(p. 112)*
    a) *Griswold v. Connecticut*
    b) *Roe v. Wade*
    c) *Lemon v. Kurtzman*
    d) *Planned Parenthood v. Casey*
    e) *Miranda v. Arizona*

13. In which case did the Supreme Court rule that state governments no longer had the authority to make private sexual conduct a crime? *(pp. 114–15)*
    a) *Webster v. Reproductive Health Services*
    b) *Gonzales v. Oregon*
    c) *Lawrence v. Texas*
    d) *Bowers v. Hardwick*
    e) *Texas v. Johnson*

Key Terms

civil liberties *(p. 91)*

habeas corpus *(p. 92)*

Bill of Rights *(p. 92)*

selective incorporation *(p. 94)*

establishment clause *(p. 94)*

free exercise clause *(p. 97)*

"clear and present danger" *(p. 98)*

fighting words *(p. 99)*

"speech plus" *(p. 101)*

prior restraint *(p. 102)*

libel *(p. 102)*

slander *(p. 102)*

due process of law *(p. 107)*

exclusionary rule *(p. 107)*

grand jury *(p. 108)*

double jeopardy *(p. 109)*

Miranda rule *(p. 109)*

right to privacy *(p. 112)*

eminent domain *(p. 112)*

★ chapter ★

05

Civil Rights

WHAT GOVERNMENT DOES AND WHY IT MATTERS In August 2005, Desmond Meade stood by a railroad track in South Florida, contemplating suicide. Out of prison but homeless and unemployed, he had difficulty getting a job due to his felony record, nor could he vote in Florida, where since 1868 the state's constitution had banned felons from voting. "I didn't see any light at the end of the tunnel. I didn't have any hope or any self-esteem and I was ready to end my life."[1] It was then that Meade vowed to change his life. He first attended community college and then earned a law degree from Florida International University.

Despite his degrees, his civil rights remained limited. He still couldn't vote, even when his wife was running for the state legislature.[2] Nor was he able to practice law, as the state's bar association prevented him from sitting for the bar exam. But he put his legal training to use to fight the ban on voting. As president of the Florida Rights Restoration Coalition (FRRC), he lobbied policy makers across the state and gathered more than 750,000 signatures to place an initiative on the November 2018 ballot to restore former felons' voting rights.

In 2018, Amendment 4, a ballot initiative to restore voting rights to former felons, passed in Florida thanks to the efforts of the Florida Rights Restoration Coalition and its executive director, Desmond Meade, pictured here.

Amendment 4 passed, with more than 64 percent of the vote. On January 8, 2019, Meade walked into the Orange County Supervisors of Elections office to register to vote. "The impact of Amendment 4 will be felt for decades to come and I believe that we have not yet even begun to see the impact that it will have," he said. He framed his voter registration card and hung it in his office above his law degree.

But Meade's fight isn't over yet. In 2019 Florida enacted a bill undercutting the amendment. The new law requires felons to pay back all of their court fees and fines before being eligible to vote. A recent study found that only about 20 percent of Floridians with criminal records had repaid these debts, thus disenfranchising hundreds of thousands of former felons.[3] Voting rights groups filed lawsuits over the new law, which they call a modern-day "poll tax," referring to the now-unconstitutional practice of requiring voting fees, which was historically used to limit African Americans' voting rights.[4] Meade's FRRC organization started a fund to help what it calls "returning citizens" pay off their financial penalties, although disenfranchisement continued because of the state's inability to inform many such citizens of how much they owed.[5]

As we saw in the previous chapter, civil liberties are phrased as negatives—what government must *not* do. Civil rights, on the other hand, are positives—what the government *must* do to guarantee equal citizenship and protect citizens from discrimination. Civil rights regulate *who* can participate in the political process and *how*: for example, who can vote, who can hold office, who can serve on juries, and when and how citizens can petition the government to take action. Civil rights also define how people are treated in employment, education, and other aspects of American society.

CHAPTER GOALS

★ Outline the legal developments and social movements that affected civil rights (pp. 121–32)

★ Explain how the courts have evaluated recent civil rights concerns (pp. 132–41)

★ Explain the key Supreme Court decisions on affirmative action (pp. 141–42)

Civil Rights Are Protections *by* the Government

Outline the legal developments
and social movements that
affected civil rights

In the United States the history of slavery and legalized racial **discrimination** against African Americans coexists uneasily with a strong tradition of individual liberty. With the adoption of the Fourteenth Amendment in 1868, **civil rights** became part of the Constitution, guaranteed to each citizen through "equal protection of the laws." This **equal protection clause** launched a century of political and legal movements to press for racial equality.

For African Americans, the central fact of political life for most of American history has been a denial of full citizenship rights. By accepting the institution of slavery, the Founders embraced a system fundamentally at odds with the "Blessings of Liberty" promised in the Constitution. Their decision set the stage for two centuries of African American struggles to achieve full citizenship.

For women, electoral politics was a decidedly masculine world. Until 1920, not only were most women barred from voting in national elections, but electoral politics was closely tied to such male social institutions as lodges, bars, and clubs. Yet the exclusion of women from this political world did not prevent them from engaging in public life. Instead, women carved out a "separate sphere" emphasizing female responsibility for moral issues, and they became important voices in social reform well before they won the right to vote.[6] Prior to the Civil War, for example, women played leading roles in the abolitionist movement.

discrimination the use of any unreasonable and unjust criterion of exclusion

civil rights obligation imposed on government to take positive action to protect citizens from any illegal action of government agencies and of other private citizens

equal protection clause provision of the Fourteenth Amendment guaranteeing citizens "the equal protection of the laws." This clause has been the basis for the civil rights of African Americans, women, and other groups

SLAVERY AND THE ABOLITIONIST MOVEMENT

No issue in the nation's history so deeply divided Americans as that of slavery. The importation and subjugation of Africans kidnapped from their native lands was a practice virtually as old as European colonial settlement: the first enslaved people brought to what became the United States arrived in Jamestown, Virginia, in 1619, a year before the Plymouth colony was established in Massachusetts. White southerners built their agricultural economy (especially cotton production) on a large slave-labor force. By 1840 nearly half of the populations of Alabama and Louisiana consisted of enslaved Black people. Even so, only about one-quarter of southern White families were slaveowners.

In 1857 the Supreme Court inflamed the slavery controversy with its infamous decision in *Dred Scott v. Sanford*. Dred Scott was an enslaved person who sued for his

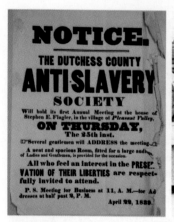

Slavery tore the nation apart and ultimately led to the Civil War. The abolition movement organized in the North and pushed to end slavery. Harriet Tubman (far left in photograph) was an abolitionist and formerly enslaved person who helped many enslaved people escape bondage through a system of safe houses called the "underground railroad."

freedom because his owner had taken him to Illinois and the territory of Wisconsin, both of which prohibited slavery. The Court, however, ruled that enslaved people—indeed, all Blacks—were not citizens of the United States and that Scott was his master's permanent property, regardless of where he lived.[7] This decision split the country deeply and helped to precipitate the Civil War. From the ashes of that conflict came the Thirteenth, Fourteenth, and Fifteenth amendments, which would redefine civil rights from that time on.

THE WOMEN'S RIGHTS MOVEMENT

Through the nineteenth century, American women were denied rights that most take for granted today. In most American states, women did not have the right to vote, and the doctrine of "coverture" gave the husband control over his wife's property. Lacking political and property rights, women in the United States were effectively second-class citizens.

Less than 10 years before the Dred Scott decision, in 1848, the quiet upstate New York town of Seneca Falls played host to a convention that began the modern women's movement. The centerpiece of the convention, organized by Elizabeth Cady Stanton and Lucretia Mott, was adoption of a Declaration of Sentiments and Resolutions patterned after the Declaration of Independence. The most controversial provision of the declaration, nearly rejected as too radical, was the call for the right to vote for women.

THE CIVIL WAR AMENDMENTS TO THE CONSTITUTION AND THEIR AFTERMATH

Thirteenth Amendment one of three Civil War amendments; it abolished slavery

African American hopes for achieving full citizenship seemed fulfilled when three constitutional amendments were adopted soon after the Civil War: the **Thirteenth Amendment** abolished slavery, the

Fourteenth Amendment guaranteed equal protection and due process under the law, and the **Fifteenth Amendment** guaranteed voting rights for Blacks. Protected by the federal troops occupying the former Confederate states to enforce their "Reconstruction," or reintegration into the Union, African American men in the South (where the overwhelming majority of them lived) began exercising their political rights. During Reconstruction, 16 Blacks were elected to the U.S. Congress and over 600 served in southern state legislatures. As voters and public officials, Black citizens found a home in the Republican Party, the party of President Lincoln, which had sponsored the constitutional amendments and legislation guaranteeing their rights.[8]

Fourteenth Amendment one of three Civil War amendments; it guaranteed equal protection and due process

Fifteenth Amendment one of three Civil War amendments; it guaranteed voting rights for African American men

Jim Crow laws laws enacted by southern states following Reconstruction that discriminated against African Americans

This political equality was short-lived, however. The national government withdrew its troops from the South and turned its back on African Americans in 1877. After that, southern states erected a "Jim Crow" system of social, political, and economic inequality that made a mockery of the promises in the Constitution. The first **Jim Crow laws** were adopted by the southern states beginning in the 1870s, to criminalize intermarriage of the races and establish segregation of railroad travel, all public accommodations, and public schools.

Even after formerly enslaved men won the right to vote, most politicians in both parties still rejected appeals for women's suffrage. In 1872, Susan B. Anthony and several other women were arrested in Rochester, New York, for illegally registering and voting in that year's national election. (The men who allowed them to do so were also indicted. Anthony paid their expenses and eventually won presidential pardons for them.)

At Anthony's trial, the judge ordered the jury to find her guilty without deliberation. Yet Anthony was allowed to address the court, saying, "Your denial of my citizen's right to vote is the denial of my right of consent as one of the governed, the denial of my right of representation as one of the taxed, the denial of my right to a trial of my peers as an offender against the law."[9] Anthony was fined $100 but was not sentenced to jail. She refused to pay the fine.

Suffrage organizations grew, and by the early 1900s they were staging mass meetings, parades, protests, and circulated petitions. Some protests were aimed at President Woodrow Wilson, who refused to support a constitutional amendment to guarantee women's suffrage. The Nineteenth Amendment granting women the right to vote was ratified in 1920. Yet it took sixty years for voter turnout among women to equal that of men.

CIVIL RIGHTS AND THE SUPREME COURT: "SEPARATE BUT EQUAL"

Jim Crow laws were enforced in the infamous Supreme Court case of *Plessy v. Ferguson* (1896). The Court upheld a Louisiana law that *required* segregation of the races on trolleys and other public transit (and, by implication, in all public facilities,

The 1896 Supreme Court case of *Plessy v. Ferguson* upheld legal segregation and created the "separate but equal" rule, which fostered national segregation. Overt discrimination in public accommodations was common.

"separate but equal" rule
doctrine that public accommodations could be segregated by race but still be considered equal

including schools). Homer Plessy, a man defined as "one-eighth Black," sat in a trolley car reserved for Whites and was found guilty of violating a law providing for "equal but separate accommodations" on trains. The Court held that the Fourteenth Amendment's equal protection clause was not violated by racial restrictions as long as the facilities were equal.

Plessy v. Ferguson legally authorized Whites' use of race to exclude nonwhites and established the **"separate but equal" rule** that prevailed through the mid-twentieth century. Judges in this period generally accepted the false pretense that accommodations for Blacks were equal to those for Whites.

LITIGATING FOR EQUALITY AFTER WORLD WAR II

Even before World War II, the Supreme Court had begun to enforce more strictly the requirement of equal facilities in the "separate but equal" rule. In 1938, for example, the Court rejected Missouri's policy of paying the tuition of Black students at out-of-state law schools rather than admitting them to the University of Missouri Law School.[10] In 1950, the Court rejected Texas's claim that its new "law school for Negroes" provided education equal to that of the all-White University of Texas Law School, a ruling that opened the question of whether any segregated facilities could be truly equal.[11] These and other cases strongly encouraged Black leaders, led by NAACP lawyers, to confront the "separate but equal" rule head-on.

Oliver Brown, the father of three girls, lived in a racially mixed neighborhood of Topeka, Kansas. Every school day, his daughter Linda took the school bus to the Monroe Elementary School, for Black children, about a mile away. In September 1950, Linda's father took her to the all-White Sumner School, closer to their home, and tried to enroll her in the third grade, in defiance of state law and local segregation rules. When they were refused, Brown went to the NAACP, and soon thereafter, the case *Brown v. Board of Education* was born.

In 1954, the Supreme Court ruled unanimously in one of the most important decisions in its history:

> Does segregation of children in public schools solely on the basis of race, even though the physical facilities and other "tangible" factors may be equal, deprive the children of the minority group of equal educational opportunities? We believe that it does. . . . We conclude that in the field of public education the doctrine of "separate but equal" has no place. Separate educational facilities are inherently unequal.[12]

The *Brown* decision not only altered the constitutional framework by striking down "separate but equal" as unconstitutional; it also signaled the Court's determination to use the **strict scrutiny** test in cases related to discrimination. That is, the burden of proof would fall on the government to show that the law in question *was* constitutional—not on the challengers to show the law's *un*constitutionality.[13]

CIVIL RIGHTS AFTER *BROWN V. BOARD OF EDUCATION*

Most states refused to obey the *Brown* decision until sued, and many ingenious schemes were created to delay obedience (such as paying the tuition for White students to attend newly created "private" academies). In addition, even as southern school boards began to eliminate their legally enforced (**de jure**) school segregation, extensive actual (**de facto**) school segregation remained, in the North as well as in the South, as a consequence of racially segregated housing. Also, discrimination in employment, public accommodations, juries, voting, and other areas of political, social, and economic activity was not directly affected by *Brown*.

Social Protest after *Brown* Ten years after *Brown*, fewer than 1 percent of Black school-age children in the Deep South were attending schools with Whites,[14] making it obvious that the goal of "equal protection" required not just court decisions but also positive, or affirmative, action by Congress and government

Brown v. Board of Education the 1954 Supreme Court decision that struck down the "separate but equal" doctrine as fundamentally unequal; this case eliminated state power to use race as a criterion of discrimination in law and provided the national government with the power to intervene by exercising strict regulatory policies against discriminatory actions

strict scrutiny a test used by the Supreme Court in racial discrimination cases and other cases involving civil liberties and civil rights that places the burden of proof on the government rather than on the challengers to show that the law in question is constitutional

de jure literally, "by law"; refers to legally enforced practices, such as school segregation in the South before the 1960s

de facto literally, "by fact"; refers to practices that occur even when there is no legal enforcement, such as school segregation in much of the United States today

"Massive resistance" among White southerners attempted to block the desegregation efforts of the national government. For example, at Little Rock Central High School in 1957, an angry mob of White students prevented Black students from entering the school.

agencies. And given massive southern resistance and only lukewarm northern support for racial integration, progress also required intense, well-organized support.

Organized demonstrations escalated after *Brown v. Board of Education*. Only a year later, African Americans in Montgomery, Alabama, challenged the city's segregated bus system with a yearlong boycott that began with the arrest of Rosa Parks, who refused to give up her seat to a White man. Parks eventually became a civil rights icon, as did one of the ministers leading the boycott, Martin Luther King, Jr. A year of private carpools and walking ended with Montgomery's bus system desegregated, but only after the Supreme Court ruled the system unconstitutional.

By the 1960s, the civil rights movement stretched across the South and used the media to attract nationwide attention and support. Images of protesters being beaten, attacked by police dogs, and set upon with fire hoses did much to win broad sympathy for the cause of Black civil rights and to discredit state and local governments in the South. In the massive March on Washington in 1963, the Reverend Martin Luther King, Jr., staked out the movement's moral claims in his famous "I Have a Dream" speech. Steadily, the movement created intense pressure for a reluctant federal government to take more assertive steps to defend Black civil rights.

Protests against discriminatory treatment of African Americans did not end in the 1960s. In recent years, a variety of protests coalesced under the banner Black Lives Matter to focus attention on allegations of police misconduct toward African Americans. The movement took off in Ferguson, Missouri, after the 2014 shooting of an unarmed Black man by a White police officer and spread across the nation, often via social media, which presented live photos and videos taken by cell phone cameras. This led many police departments to adopt new training methods and new rules governing police behavior.

In 2020, a graphic cell phone video of the killing of George Floyd, a Black man, by a Minneapolis, Minnesota, police officer touched off nationwide protests and a new debate on policing in America. Protesters charged that police in many cities commonly treated African Americans with disrespect and brutality. In New York, Seattle, Minneapolis, and elsewhere protesters demanded that police department funding be drastically restructured to provide more funding to social service agencies focused on fighting poverty and defusing conflict. Critics charged that the idea of reducing police budgets would simply lead to more crime and violence. Most Americans agreed that police departments should receive better training, that officers with records of abuse should be promptly fired, and that new approaches to public safety, including expanded social services in poor and minority communities, should be instituted.

THE CIVIL RIGHTS ACTS

Congress passed a landmark civil rights law in 1964, the Civil Rights Act. Its purpose was to strengthen voting rights provisions enacted earlier, and to attack discrimination in public accommodations, segregation in the schools, and discrimination by employers in hiring, promoting, and laying off employees. Protections from discrimination against women were also included.

Public Accommodations After the 1964 Civil Rights Act was passed, public accommodations quickly removed some of the most blatant forms of racial discrimination, such as signs labeling "colored" and "White" restrooms, water fountains, waiting rooms, and seating arrangements. In addition, the federal government filed more than 400 antidiscrimination suits in federal courts against hotels, restaurants, taverns, gas stations, and other establishments.

The issue of racial discrimination in public settings is by no means over. In 2014, for example, an African American customer at a Vancouver, Washington, restaurant noticed that he was being asked to pay for his food before it was served, while White customers were not. The case was settled out of court for an undisclosed amount.[15] But some forms of such discrimination, such as taxi drivers' refusing to pick up Black passengers,[16] are difficult to prove or prevent through laws.

School Desegregation, Phase Two The 1964 Civil Rights Act also declared discrimination by state governments and their agencies (such as school boards) illegal and created administrative agencies to help the courts implement laws against it. Title IV of the act, for example, authorized the Justice Department to implement federal court orders for school desegregation without waiting for individual parents to bring complaints. Title VI of the act provided that federal grants-in-aid for education must be withheld from any school system practicing racial segregation.

Title VI became the most effective weapon for desegregating schools outside the South, because segregation in northern school districts was subtler and more difficult to address. In the South, the problem was segregation by law coupled with open resistance to the national government's efforts to change the situation. Outside the South, the instruments of segregation were more subtle. These included such practices as "redlining," through which banks declined to offer mortgages in Black neighborhoods; school district boundaries seemingly neutral but actually conforming to segregated neighborhood patterns; and restrictive covenants written into private real estate deeds designed to prevent the sale of homes to nonwhite buyers. These practices often resulted in de facto segregation without a clear legal or "de jure" basis. To address this problem, the 1964 Civil Rights Act gave (1) the president, through the Justice Department's Office for Civil Rights, the power to withhold federal education

TABLE 5.1

Cause and Effect in the Civil Rights Movement

Political action and government action worked in tandem to produce dramatic changes in American civil rights policies.

JUDICIAL AND LEGAL ACTION	POLITICAL ACTION
1954 *Brown v. Board of Education*	**1955** Montgomery, Alabama, bus boycott
1956 Federal courts order school integration; of special note is one ordering that Autherine Lucy be admitted to the University of Alabama, with Governor Wallace officially protesting	
1957 Civil Rights Act creating Civil Rights Commission; President Eisenhower sends 101st Airborne Division paratroops to Little Rock, Arkansas, to enforce integration of Central High School	**1957** Southern Christian Leadership Conference formed, with Martin Luther King, Jr., as president
1960 First substantive Civil Rights Act, primarily voting rights	**1960** Student Nonviolent Coordinating Committee formed to organize protests, sit-ins, freedom rides
1961 Interstate Commerce Commission orders desegregation on all buses and trains and in terminals; President Kennedy (JFK) favors executive action over civil rights legislation	
1963 JFK shifts, supports strong civil rights law; JFK's assassination; President Johnson asserts strong support for civil rights	**1963** Nonviolent demonstrations in Birmingham, Alabama, lead to King's arrest and his "Letter from Birmingham Jail"; March on Washington
1964 Congress passes historic Civil Rights Act covering voting, employment, public accommodations, education	
1965 Voting Rights Act	**1965** King announces drive to register 3 million Blacks in the South
1966 War on Poverty in full swing	**Late 1960s** Movement diverges: part toward litigation, part toward community action programs, part toward war protest, part toward more militant "Black Power" actions

grants[17] and gave (2) the attorney general of the United States the power to initiate suits (rather than having to await complaints) wherever there was a "pattern or practice" of discrimination.[18]

In 1971 the Supreme Court held that state-imposed desegregation could be brought about by busing children across school districts.[19] Under certain circumstances, the Court said, even racial quotas could be used as the "starting point in shaping a remedy to correct past constitutional violations," and pairing or grouping schools and reorganizing attendance zones would also be acceptable. Three years later, however, this principle was severely restricted when the Court determined that only districts found guilty of deliberate and de jure racial segregation would have to desegregate their schools,[20] effectively exempting most northern states and cities from busing.

The prospects for further school integration diminished with a 1991 Supreme Court decision holding that lower federal courts could end supervision of local school districts that could show "good faith" compliance with court orders to desegregate and evidence that "vestiges of past discrimination" had been eliminated "to the extent practicable."[21]

In a 2007 ruling, the Court limited school-integration measures still further.[22] By making race one factor in assigning students to schools, the cities of Seattle, Washington, and Louisville, Kentucky, had hoped to achieve greater racial balance across their school systems. The Court ruled, however, that these plans were unconstitutional because there was no compelling government interest in using race as a criterion in assigning students to schools.

Outlawing Discrimination in Employment Progress in the right to participate in politics and government dramatized the relative lack of progress in the economic domain.

The federal courts and the Justice Department entered this area through Title VII of the Civil Rights Act of 1964, which outlawed job discrimination by all private and public employers, including governmental agencies (such as fire and police departments) that employed more than 15 workers. Title VII makes it unlawful to discriminate in employment on the basis of color, religion, sex, or national origin, as well as race.

Title VII also gave the federal government the power to revoke or prohibit federal contracts for goods and services with any private company that could not guarantee that its rules for hiring, promotion, and firing were nondiscriminatory. In 1972 the Equal Employment Opportunity Commission (EEOC) was strengthened when it was given authority to initiate suits rather than wait for grievances.

Voting Rights In the 1965 Voting Rights Act, Congress significantly strengthened voting rights protections by barring literacy and other tests as a condition for voting in six southern states,[23] by setting criminal penalties for interference with efforts to vote, and by providing for the replacement of local registrars with federally appointed ones in counties designated by the attorney general as significantly resistant to registering eligible Blacks to vote. The right to vote was further strengthened in 1964 with ratification of the Twenty-Fourth Amendment, which abolished the poll tax, and in 1975 with legislation permanently outlawing literacy tests in all 50 states and mandating bilingual ballots or oral assistance for Spanish, Chinese, Japanese, and Korean speakers and for Native Americans and Alaska natives.

TABLE 5.2

Registration by Race and State in Southern States Covered by the Voting Rights Act (VRA)

The VRA had a direct impact on the rate of Black voter registration in the southern states, as measured by the gap between White and Black voters in each state. Further insights can be gained by examining changes in White registration rates before and after passage of the VRA and by comparing the gaps between White and Black registration. Why do you think registration rates for Whites increased significantly in some states and dropped in others? What impact could the increase in Black registration have had on public policy?

	BEFORE THE ACT*			AFTER THE ACT* 1971–72		
	WHITE	BLACK	GAP**	WHITE	BLACK	GAP
Alabama	69.2%	19.3%	**49.9%**	80.7%	57.1%	**23.6%**
Georgia	62.6	27.4	**35.2**	70.6	67.8	**2.8**
Louisiana	80.5	31.6	**48.9**	80.0	59.1	**20.9**
Mississippi	69.9	6.7	**63.2**	71.6	62.2	**9.4**
North Carolina	96.8	46.8	**50.0**	62.2	46.3	**15.9**
South Carolina	75.7	37.3	**38.4**	51.2	48.0	**3.2**
Virginia	61.1	38.3	**22.8**	61.2	54.0	**7.2**
TOTAL	73.4	29.3	**44.1**	67.8	56.6	**11.2**

*Available registration data as of March 1965 and 1971–72.

**The gap is the percentage-point difference between White and Black registration rates.

SOURCE: U.S. Commission on Civil Rights, *Political Participation* (1968), Appendix VII; Voter Education Project, attachment to press release, October 3, 1972.

The progress in Black political participation produced by these acts has altered the shape of American politics. In 1965, in the seven states of the Old Confederacy covered by the Voting Rights Act, 29.3 percent of the eligible Black residents were registered to vote, compared with 73.4 percent of the White residents (see Table 5.2). By 1972 the racial gap in registration was only 11.2 points. And today, more African Americans hold public office in the states of the Deep South than in the North.

The 1965 Voting Rights Act had also required some state and local governments with a history of voting discrimination to obtain prior federal approval, or preclearance, for any changes to their voting laws or practices. In the 2013 case *Shelby County v. Holder*, however, the Supreme Court overturned the preclearance formula, saying it was based on data more than 40 years old.[24]

A more recent controversy over voting rights concerns so-called voter ID laws. Most states have enacted legislation requiring voters to show identification before they cast a ballot, and some require a specific type with a photograph. Republicans generally support such laws, arguing that they deter voter fraud. Democrats generally oppose them, saying they are designed to discourage poor and minority voters, who are less likely than others to possess such IDs. Cases challenging voter ID laws on equal protection grounds have met mixed success. In 2008 the Supreme Court upheld the constitutionality of Indiana's law, affirming the state's "valid interest" in improving election procedures and deterring fraud.[25] On the other hand, in 2013 the Court struck down an Arizona law requiring proof of U.S. citizenship in order to register to vote. Voter ID laws have been struck down or modified by courts in several states. In the 2020 primary and general elections, many states sought to expand voting by mail procedures. Historically, Republicans have benefited from mail-in voting since it appeals to older voters who prefer to avoid a trip to the polling station, but the GOP fears that expansion of mail-in voting would make it easier for Democratic campaign workers to mobilize young and minority voters who generally support Democrats but often do not go to the polls.

Housing In 1968 Congress passed the Fair Housing Act specifically to prohibit housing discrimination. It eventually covered the sale or rental of nearly all the nation's housing. Housing was among the most controversial discrimination issues because of entrenched patterns of residential segregation across the country. Besides the lingering effects of restrictive covenants, local authorities had deliberately segregated public housing, and federal guidelines had allowed discrimination in Federal Housing Administration mortgage lending, effectively preventing Blacks from joining the movement to the suburbs in the 1950s and '60s.

The procedures for proving discrimination remained quite challenging until Congress passed the Fair Housing Amendments Act in 1988. This law put more teeth in the enforcement mechanisms and allowed the Department of Housing and Urban Development (HUD) to initiate legal action in cases of discrimination.[26]

Marriage The Civil Rights Act of 1964 was also silent on interracial marriage, which 16 states continued to outlaw in 1967. In that year, the Supreme Court ruled in *Loving v. Virginia* that such state laws were unconstitutional. The case concerned a Virginia couple, a White man and a Black woman, who married in Washington, D.C., where such unions were legal. When they moved back to Virginia, they were charged with violating the state's law against interracial marriage. The Lovings challenged

The Supreme Court ruled in 1967 that state laws banning interracial marriage were unconstitutional. The case *Loving v. Virginia* was invoked numerous times in the Court's decision almost 50 years later that declared marriage a fundamental right for same-sex couples.

the Virginia law. In striking such laws down, the Court declared marriage "one of the 'basic civil rights of man,' fundamental to our very existence and survival."[27]

Mass Incarceration Some have argued that mass incarceration and the disenfranchisement of former convicts is a key civil rights issue. More than 2.2 million Americans are currently incarcerated, most in state prisons and local jails. African Americans account for about one-third of these inmates, though making up only about 12 percent of the U.S. population. About 20 percent of prison inmates, including many African Americans, are minor drug offenders who received harsh mandatory sentences stemming from the "war on drugs" begun in the 1970s and '80s.

Former prison inmates often lose their voting rights. Since many are poor and members of minority groups, the Democratic Party has pushed for restoration of voting rights to former inmates. For the same reason, the GOP has resisted the effort. As we saw with the story of Desmond Meade at the beginning of the chapter, Florida has recently restored voting rights to felons released from prison. Other states may follow suit.

Civil Rights Have Been Extended to Other Groups

> **Explain how the courts have evaluated recent civil rights concerns**

Title VII of the 1964 Civil Rights Act prohibited discrimination not only against African Americans but against other groups as well, prohibiting discrimination based upon such characteristics as gender, religion, and national origin. Eventually other groups also sought protection under Title VII.

WOMEN AND GENDER DISCRIMINATION

In many ways Title VII fostered the growth of the women's movement in the 1960s and '70s. Beginning in the 1970s the Supreme Court helped establish gender discrimination as a major and highly visible civil rights issue. While refusing to treat it as the equivalent of racial discrimination,[28] the Court did make it easier for plaintiffs to file and win gender-discrimination suits.[29]

In recent years, laws and court decisions designed to deal with discrimination

FOR CRITICAL ANALYSIS ▶

1. How much does each of these factors—education, political office, and income—say about gender equality in the United States?

2. While most Americans support the principle of equal opportunity for all groups, there is disagreement over how much the government should do to ensure equal outcomes. Discuss the difference between equal opportunity and equal outcomes in the context of women's rights.

Have Women Achieved Equal Rights?

Title VII of the 1964 Civil Rights Act prohibits gender discrimination, and the Supreme Court has consistently upheld the principle that women should have the same rights as men. Since 1960 the United States has made great strides toward gender equality in some areas but, as the data show, still has a long way to go in other areas.

Education

■ Percentage of college students who are women

Year	Percentage
1960	39%
1970	39%
1980	42%
1990	45%
2000	48%
2010	56%
2019	57%

Politics

■ Percentage of members of Congress who are women
■ Percentage of state legislators who are women

Year	Members of Congress	State legislators
1960	4%	
1970	2%	
1980	11%	2%
1990	17%	6%
2000	23%	13%
2010	25%	17%
2019	29%	25%

Median Weekly Earnings by Race and Gender

White women earned 80 percent as much as their male counterparts, compared with 91.8 percent for Black women, 78.3 percent for Asian women, and 86.7 percent for Latina women.

White		African American		Latino		Asian American	
Men	Women	Men	Women	Men	Women	Men	Women
$1,033	$826	$772	$709	$728	$631	$1,299	$1,017

SOURCE: Data from the Bureau of Labor Statistics, Congressional Research Service, and National Conference of State Legislatures (accessed 9/25/19).

against women have been used to press for equal rights for transgender people, especially in employment. For example, in 2015 President Obama issued an executive order prohibiting federal contractors from discriminating against workers based on their sexual orientation or gender identity, and the EEOC filed its first-ever lawsuits to protect transgender workers under Title VII.

Controversy arose after some states passed laws requiring transgender individuals to use public bathrooms that correspond to the gender designated on their birth certificates. In 2016, North Carolina enacted such a law, leading to boycotts and protests, with several corporations announcing plans to reduce their operations in the state. When the Department of Justice warned North Carolina that the law violated the Civil Rights Act, the state sued the federal government over the issue. In 2017, the law was repealed under pressure from the business community. More recently, President Trump banned transgender individuals from joining the military, though those already in the armed forces would generally be allowed to continue.

Equality in Education Title IX of the 1972 Education Act outlawed gender discrimination in education. It led to few lawsuits until the Supreme Court ruled in 1992, in *Franklin v. Gwinnett County Public Schools*, that monetary damages could be awarded for gender discrimination.[30] In the two years after the *Franklin* case, complaints to the Education Department's Office for Civil Rights about unequal treatment of women's athletic programs nearly tripled. In several high-profile legal cases, prominent universities were ordered to create more women's sports programs, prompting many other schools to follow suit to avoid potential litigation.[31]

In 1997 the Supreme Court refused to hear a petition by Brown University challenging a lower-court order that the university establish strict sex equity in its athletic programs. The decision meant a school's varsity athletic positions for men and women must reflect its overall enrollment numbers.[32] Though the ruling has had a major impact on college athletic programs, advocates for gender equality note that gender barriers continue in fields such as science, technology, engineering, and math, which female students are less likely to enter.[33]

Sexual Harassment During the 1970s, using Title VII of the 1964 Civil Rights Act, courts began to find sexual harassment to be a form of sex discrimination. In 1986 the Supreme Court recognized two forms of sexual harassment. One is "quid pro quo" harassment, an explicit or strongly implied threat that submission is a condition of continued employment. The second is harassment that creates offensive or intimidating working conditions amounting to a "hostile environment."[34]

In two 1998 cases, the Court strengthened the law when it said that whether or not harassment causes economic harm to the employee, the employer is financially liable if someone with authority over the employee committed it—a supervisor, for example. But the Court also said that an employer may defend itself by showing that it had a sexual harassment prevention and grievance policy in effect.[35]

In 2011 the Department of Education's Office of Civil Rights (OCR) issued a letter to the more than 7,000 colleges and universities receiving federal money, advising them, under the authority of Title IX, to adopt strict procedures to deal

Global Economic Gender Equality

There are many measures one could use when trying to determine whether there is parity between the genders in a country. Participation in the labor force, wage equality, and representation in the managerial and technical professions are used to measure economic equality: countries at the top of the list are ones where women are most likely to have the same participation and opportunities as men, regardless of the level of income or the skill level of the employment.

1. Does the United States' position, 19th out of 149 countries, surprise you? What do you think accounts for the country ranking in the top 25? What might explain why 18 other countries ranked higher? Cameroon ranks 8th while its neighbor, Nigeria, ranks 79th. What kinds of factors could explain why geographically close countries might differ on this kind of ranking?

2. The measurement used here prioritizes gender equality over attempting to measure the quality of the opportunities that women have. What do you think are the benefits to this approach? What might be gained if we looked instead at a ranking of countries by women's economic opportunities rather than their economic equality?

COUNTRY	RANK	INDEX RATING	COUNTRY	RANK	INDEX RATING
Lao PDR	1	0.915	Philippines	14	0.801
Barbados	2	0.871	Slovenia	15	0.795
Bahamas	3	0.863	Iceland	16	0.793
Benin	4	0.850	Finland	17	0.786
Burundi	5	0.839	Moldova	18	0.785
Belarus	6	0.838	**United States**	**19**	**0.782**
Guinea	7	0.820	Mongolia	20	0.780
Cameroon	8	0.816	Lithuania	21	0.765
Sweden	9	0.808	Thailand	22	0.763
Latvia	10	0.807	New Zealand	23	0.761
Norway	11	0.806	Singapore	24	0.761
Namibia	12	0.804	Ghana	25	0.753
Botswana	13	0.802			

SOURCE: World Economic Forum, "Economic Participation and Opportunity Subindex," *Global Gender Gap Report 2018*, www3.weforum.org/docs/WEF_GGGR_2018.pdf (accessed 7/26/19).

with charges of sexual assault and harassment on campus. OCR told colleges to shift the burden of proof from the accuser toward the accused in such cases, to allow accusers to appeal not-guilty findings (contrary to the Fifth Amendment's ban on double jeopardy), and to refrain from allowing accused persons to cross-examine their accusers (contrary to the Sixth Amendment). These procedures have led on many campuses to charges of false accusations and unfair proceedings.[36] In 2018, Education Secretary Betsy DeVos rescinded the Obama-era guidelines and announced new rules that strengthened protections for those accused of sexual misconduct on college campuses.

LATINOS

The labels *Latino* and *Hispanic* encompass a wide range of groups with diverse national origins, cultural identities, and experiences. As a result, civil rights issues for them have varied considerably by group and by place.

For example, the early political experiences of Mexican Americans were shaped by race and by region. In 1848, under the Treaty of Guadalupe Hidalgo, Mexico ceded to the United States the territory that now comprises Arizona, California, New Mexico, and parts of Colorado, Nevada, and Utah, as well as extended the Texas border to the Rio Grande. Although the treaty guaranteed full civil rights to the residents of these territories, Mexican Americans experienced ongoing discrimination. Even after the courts in 1898 reconfirmed their formal political rights, including the right to vote, they were prevented from voting through various means in many places, especially in Texas.[37] They also had to attend separate schools in Texas and much of southern California, and in many neighborhoods restrictive covenants banned them from buying or renting houses.

Mexican American civil rights organizations pursued a legal strategy like the NAACP's to eliminate the segregation of Mexican American students. In 1954, the League of United Latin American Citizens (LULAC) achieved a major victory in the case of *Hernandez v. Texas*.[38] In this case the Supreme Court affirmed that Mexican Americans and all other nationality groups were entitled to equal protection under the Fourteenth Amendment.

Latino political strategy has developed along two tracks. One is a traditional ethnic-group path of voter registration and voting along ethnic lines. This path was blazed by La Raza Unida, an organization that worked to register Mexican American voters in Texas and in other states. The other is a legal strategy using the various civil rights laws designed to ensure fair access to the political system.

Immigrants and Civil Rights Since the 1960s, rights for Latinos have been intertwined with immigrant rights. For much of American history, legal immigrants were treated much the same as citizens. But continuing immigration and growing economic insecurity have led many voters to support drawing a sharper line between immigrants and citizens.

The Supreme Court has ruled that unauthorized immigrants are eligible for education and emergency medical care but can be denied other government benefits.

In 2019 President Trump moved to penalize legal immigrants by denying green cards (a permit to live and work in the United States) if they receive, or are thought likely to receive, public welfare benefits.[39]

One priority for Latino advocacy groups has been the status of undocumented immigrants who were brought to the United States as young children and have no real ties to the nation in which they were born. Congress has never enacted protective legislation for these people, however.

Immigration is one of today's most controversial issues. Supporters of immigration advocate for the rights of undocumented people and believe they should have a path to American citizenship.

Absent legislation, the Department of Homeland Security instituted its own policy, Deferred Action for Childhood Arrivals (DACA), instructing immigration officials to take no action to deport law-abiding individuals who entered the United States illegally as children. In 2014, President Obama issued executive memoranda granting quasi-legal status and work permits to some 5 million people who entered the United States illegally as children or who have children who are American citizens. In 2017, President Trump announced that DACA would be discontinued. Trump's action was blocked by a federal court decision. In 2020, the Supreme Court ruled that the Trump administration did not follow the proper procedure for dismantling DACA, and therefore could not end the program. Though this decision does not ensure the program's future, it was touted as a win for immigrant rights.

Immigration was a very divisive topic during the 2016 presidential election. During his campaign, Donald Trump asserted that he would build a wall along the U.S. border with Mexico, institute a temporary ban on Muslims seeking to travel to the United States, and end the Obama administration's program to accept several thousand Syrian refugees every year. When Trump took office, he lost little time in seeking to implement these campaign promises, though not all came to fruition.

ASIAN AMERICANS

Like *Latino*, the label *Asian American* encompasses a wide range of people from very different national backgrounds who came to the United States, or whose ancestors came, at different points in history.

The early Asian experience in the United States was shaped by a series of naturalization laws dating back to 1790, the first of which declared that only White immigrants were eligible for citizenship. Chinese immigrants began arriving in California in the 1850s, drawn by the gold rush, but met with intense antagonism. In 1870,

During World War II, many Japanese Americans were forced into unsanitary internment camps on the grounds of "military necessity" after the Japanese government launched an attack on Pearl Harbor. Internees faced great losses both during and in the aftermath of internment.

Congress declared Chinese immigrants ineligible for citizenship; in 1882 the first Chinese Exclusion Act suspended the entry of Chinese laborers.

At the time of the Exclusion Act, most Chinese people in the United States were single male laborers, with few women and children. The few Chinese children in San Francisco were denied entry to the public schools until parents of those who were American-born pressed legal action, and even then they had to attend a separate Chinese school. American-born Chinese children could not be denied citizenship, however; in 1898, the Supreme Court ruled in *United States v. Wong Kim Ark* that anyone born in the United States was entitled to full citizenship.[40] Still, new Chinese immigrants were barred from the United States until 1943. After China had become a key World War II ally, Congress repealed the Chinese Exclusion Act and permitted Chinese immigrants to become citizens.

The earliest Japanese immigrants, who came to California in the 1880s, faced similar discrimination. Early in the twentieth century, California and several other western states passed laws denying them the right to own property. The denial of their civil rights culminated in President Franklin Roosevelt's decision to forcibly remove people of Japanese descent from their homes and confine them in internment camps during World War II, after Japan launched its attack on Pearl Harbor.

Suspected of disloyalty, 120,000 people of Japanese descent, including 90,000 American citizens, were forced to move to 10 internment camps located mostly in western states and characterized by overcrowding, insufficient food, and primitive sanitary facilities. The Supreme Court ruled that the internment was constitutional on the grounds of military necessity.[41] Although in 1944 Roosevelt closed the camps and ended internment, many of the internees would never recover from the property losses and health problems they had suffered from it. Not until the Civil Liberties Act of 1988 did the federal government formally acknowledge this denial of civil rights as a "grave injustice" that had been "motivated largely by racial prejudice, wartime hysteria, and a failure of political leadership."[42]

NATIVE AMERICANS

Although the political status of Native Americans was left unclear in the Constitution, in the early 1800s the courts defined each Indian tribe as a nation and thus declared Native Americans to be noncitizens of the United States. In fact, in the 1823 case of *Johnson v. McIntosh*,[43] the Supreme Court declared that Native Americans did not actually own the land upon which they lived. The 1830 Indian Removal Act forced many Native Americans to give up their lands east of the Mississippi River and forcibly removed them to tribal "reservations" on less desirable lands west of the Mississippi.

In 1924, Congress granted citizenship to all persons born in the United States, including Native Americans. Though Native Americans were now citizens, it was not clear whether the government viewed them as individuals or as members of tribes. Several pieces of legislation enacted in the nineteenth century, including the 1887 Dawes Act, sought to break up the various tribes by encouraging individuals to leave their tribal groups and strike out on their own. The 1934 Wheeler-Howard Law, however, renewed tribal rights and tribal self-government, though individuals were still free to leave their tribal lands.

Despite the problems associated with tribal reservations, strengthening of tribal sovereignty gave Native Americans a ready-made instrument through which to achieve a measure of political influence. In the 1960s, Native Americans used the tribes as vehicles for protest and litigation to improve their situation. The federal government responded with the Indian Self-Determination and Education Assistance Act, which gave Native Americans more control over their own land.[44]

As a language minority, Native Americans also benefited from the 1975 amendments to the Voting Rights Act, which established their right to be taught in their own languages. In boarding schools run by the federal Bureau of Indian Affairs, Native Americans had been forbidden to speak their own languages until reforms began in the 1930s.

Native Americans have also expanded their rights on the basis of their sovereign status. Most significant in economic terms was a 1987 Supreme Court decision that freed Native American tribes from most state regulations prohibiting gambling. The establishment of casino gambling on tribal lands has brought a substantial flow of new income to desperately poor reservations.

DISABLED AMERICANS

The concept of rights for disabled people emerged in the 1970s out of a little-noticed provision of the 1973 Rehabilitation Act, which outlawed discrimination against individuals on the basis of disabilities. As it did with many other groups, the law helped give rise to the movement demanding rights.[45] Inspired by the NAACP's use of a legal defense fund, the disability movement founded the Disability Rights Education and Defense Fund to press its legal claims.

The movement achieved its greatest success with the passage of the Americans with Disabilities Act (ADA) of 1990, which guarantees disabled people access to public spaces and prohibits discrimination in employment, housing, and health care. The impact of the law has been far-reaching, as businesses and public facilities have installed ramps, elevators, and other devices to meet its requirements.[46]

LGBTQ AMERICANS

Over the last 50 years, the lesbian, gay, bisexual, transgender, and queer (LGBTQ) movement has become one of the largest civil rights movements in contemporary America. For most of American history, any sexual orientation other than heterosexuality was considered "deviant," and many states criminalized sexual acts considered "unnatural." Gay people were usually afraid to reveal their sexual orientation for fear of the consequences, including being fired from their jobs, and the police in many cities raided bars and other establishments where they gathered. While their political participation was not formally restricted, they faced the likelihood of discrimination, prosecution, and even violence.[47]

The contemporary gay rights movement began in earnest in the 1960s. In 1962, Illinois became the first state to repeal its sodomy laws. The movement drew national attention in 1969 after patrons at the Stonewall Inn, a gay bar in New York City, rioted when police attempted to raid the establishment. The first march for gay rights was held in New York the following year to mark the anniversary of the Stonewall riots, and gay pride parades now take place in dozens of cities across the country.

No Supreme Court ruling or national legislation explicitly protected gay men and lesbians from discrimination until 1996. After losing the first gay rights case decided by the Court, *Bowers v. Hardwick* (see Chapter 4), the gay rights movement brought test cases challenging local ordinances restricting the right to marry and allowing discrimination in employment, adoption, and parental rights.

In 2015 the Supreme Court legalized same-sex marriage nationwide with its decision in *Obergefell v. Hodges*. Supporters outside the Supreme Court and across the country celebrated the landmark decision.

In 1996 the Supreme Court, in *Romer v. Evans*, explicitly extended civil rights protections to gay men and lesbians by declaring unconstitutional a 1992 amendment to the Colorado state constitution that prohibited local governments from passing ordinances to protect gay rights.[48] Then in 2003, in *Lawrence v. Texas*, the Court overturned *Bowers* and extended the right to privacy to sexual minorities. In 2015, the Supreme Court's decision in *Obergefell v. Hodges* guaranteed same-sex couples the right to marry in all states and required states to recognize same-sex marriages performed in other juris-dictions (see Chapter 2).[49] Gay rights advocates won a significant victory of a different kind in 2009, when new legislation extended the definition of hate crimes to include crimes motivated by hatred of gay and transgender people.

Affirmative Action Seeks to Right Past Wrongs

> **Explain the key Supreme Court decisions on affirmative action**

Beginning in the 1960s, the rela-tively narrow goal of equalizing educational and economic oppor-tunity by eliminating discrimina-tory barriers evolved into the broader goal of **affirmative action**, policies designed to compensate for disadvantages due to past discrimination and to encourage greater diversity. Such policies take race or some other status into account in order to provide greater opportunities to historically disadvantaged groups. For example, in 1965, President Lyndon Johnson issued executive orders promoting minor-ity employment in the federal civil service and in companies doing business with the government.

Affirmative action also took the form of efforts by the Department of Health, Education, and Welfare to shift the focus of "desegregation" efforts to "integration."[50] HEW agencies, sometimes using court orders, required school districts to present plans for busing children across district lines, for closing certain schools, and for redistrib-

affirmative action government policies or programs that seek to redress past injustices against specified groups by making special efforts to provide members of those groups with access to educational and employment opportunities

uting faculties as well as students. These efforts, enforced by threats of ending federal grants-in-aid, dramatically increased the number of children attending integrated classes.

THE SUPREME COURT AND THE BURDEN OF PROOF

Efforts by the government to shape the meaning of affirmative action today tend to center on one key issue: What is the appropriate level of judicial scrutiny in affir-mative action cases? That is, on whom should the burden of proof be placed: the person or organization seeking to show that discrimination has not occurred, or the individual attempting to show that discrimination has occurred?

The reason this question is difficult is that the cases in which the Court strictly scrutinized and struck down racially discriminatory laws—cases like *Brown* and *Loving*—all involved discrimination against historically disadvantaged racial minor-ity groups. The Court struck down those laws partly because it concluded they were motivated by racial hostility—which is not a valid government purpose—and partly because the disadvantaged groups were effectively unable to use the political process to challenge laws that harmed them.

Instead of being motivated by racial hostility, the new laws were enacted with the objective of assisting victims of past injustice. And instead of harming minority groups, they disadvantaged members of the dominant majority racial group. Yet critics argued that discriminating against *any* individual because of the person's race violated the equal protection clause.

This question was addressed directly by the Supreme Court in 1978 in the case of Allan Bakke. Bakke, a White male, brought suit against the medical school of the University of California at Davis on the grounds that, in denying him admission, the school had discriminated against him on the basis of his race. That year, the school had reserved 16 of 100 admission slots for minority applicants. Bakke argued that his grades and test scores ranked him well above many students who were accepted and that he had been rejected because he was White, whereas those others accepted were Black or Latino.

Although the Court ruled in Bakke's favor and ordered him admitted to the medical school, it stopped short of declaring affirmative action unconstitutional. It accepted the school's argument that achieving "a diverse student body" was a "compelling public purpose" but found that the method of a rigid quota of admission slots assigned on the basis of race violated the Fourteenth Amendment's equal protection clause. Thus, the Court permitted universities (and other schools and businesses) to continue to consider minority status but limited the use of quotas to situations in which (1) previous discrimination had been shown and (2) the quotas served more as a guideline than as a precisely defined ratio.[51]

The status of affirmative action remained ambiguous in 2003, when the Supreme Court decided two cases involving suits against the University of Michigan. The first alleged that by automatically adding 20 points (out of a maximum of 150) to the ratings of African American, Latino, and Native American applicants, the university's undergraduate admissions office discriminated unconstitutionally against White students. The Court agreed, saying that the admissions policy amounted to a quota because it lacked the necessary "individualized consideration" and instead used a "mechanical one," based too much on the extra minority points.[52]

In the second case, *Grutter v. Bollinger*, Michigan's law school was sued on the grounds that its admissions policy discriminated against White applicants with equal or superior grades and scores on law board exams. The Supreme Court sided with the law school; applying strict scrutiny to the policy, they found that it was tailored to a compelling state interest in diversity because it gave a "highly individualized, holistic review of each applicant's file" in which race counted but was not used in a "mechanical" way.[53] The Court's ruling that diversity in education is a compelling state interest and that racial categories can be used to serve that interest put affirmative action on stronger constitutional ground.[54]

Civil Rights:
What Do You Think?

The civil rights revolution, which began with African Americans, has broadened to include women and Latinos and to address such matters as sexual orientation, gender identification, and immigration status. As our nation becomes more and more diverse, equal protection of the laws will become more and more important if we are to succeed and prosper. The tumultuous history of civil rights in America demonstrates that exclusion is a recipe for national calamity. It also demonstrates that struggles for civil rights often take a long time, beginning with political action by a small group of committed individuals such as Desmond Meade and often ending with legislation and legal decisions from the highest court in the country.

★ Knowing what you know now, do you support the kinds of actions Desmond Meade took in trying to secure civil rights for himself and others? Do you feel that civil rights are absolute, or are there situations in which you think curtailing them is justified?

★ Have you—or people you know—experienced civil rights violations? What was the issue, and was there a remedy?

★ How does a country based on the democratic principle of majority rule ensure that the civil rights of minorities are protected? What can and should be done to remedy past wrongs that have current consequences, such as when discrimination has resulted in a racial or ethnic minority becoming an economic underclass? How do you think Desmond Meade would answer that question?

★ What civil rights battles now appear on the country's horizon? In 2017 the Department of Justice declared that it was planning to investigate discrimination against Whites. Some said it was high time for such an investigation, while others lamented what they saw as a step backward for the nation. What do you think?

★ STUDY GUIDE ★

Practice Quiz

1. When did civil rights first become part of the Constitution? *(p. 121)*
   a) in 1789 at the Founding
   b) with the adoption of the Fourteenth Amendment in 1868
   c) in 2008 when Barack Obama was elected president
   d) with the adoption of the Nineteenth Amendment in 1920
   e) in the 1954 *Brown v. Board of Education* decision

2. Which of the Civil War amendments abolished slavery? *(p. 122)*
   a) the Twelfth Amendment
   b) the Thirteenth Amendment
   c) the Fourteenth Amendment
   d) the Fifteenth Amendment
   e) the Sixteenth Amendment

3. Which of the following could be described as a Jim Crow law? *(p. 123)*
   a) a law forcing Black people and White people to ride in separate train cars
   b) a law criminalizing interracial marriage
   c) a law requiring Black students and White students to attend different schools
   d) a law segregating all public accommodations, such as hotels, restaurants, and theaters
   e) All of the above are examples of Jim Crow laws.

4. Which Supreme Court case established the "separate but equal" rule? *(p. 124)*
   a) *Plessy v. Ferguson*
   b) *Grutter v. Bollinger*
   c) *Brown v. Board of Education*
   d) *Regents of the University of California v. Bakke*
   e) *Loving v. Virginia*

5. What is the difference between de jure segregation and de facto segregation? *(p. 125)*
   a) De jure segregation is segregation in private housing, and de facto segregation is segregation in employment and public accommodations.
   b) De jure segregation is segregation in employment and public accommodations, and de facto segregation is segregation in private housing.
   c) De jure segregation is legally enforced segregation, and de facto segregation is segregation in practice that is not enforced by law.
   d) De jure segregation is segregation in practice that is not enforced by law, and de facto segregation is legally enforced segregation.
   e) De jure segregation is based on race, and de facto segregation is based on gender.

6. Which of the following outlawed discrimination by employers in hiring, promoting, and laying off their employees? *(p. 127)*
   a) the Fourteenth Amendment
   b) the Fifteenth Amendment
   c) *Brown v. Board of Education*
   d) the 1964 Civil Rights Act
   e) *Regents of the University of California v. Bakke*

7. The Voting Rights Act of 1965 significantly strengthened voting rights protections by *(p. 129)*
   a) barring literacy tests as a condition for voting in six southern states.
   b) requiring all voters to register two weeks before any federal election.
   c) eliminating all federal-level registration requirements.

d) allowing voters to sue election officials for monetary damages in civil court.

e) requiring that all voters show a valid government-issued photo ID.

8. What is "quid pro quo" workplace harassment? (p. 134)

a) harassment that involves a systemic gender pay gap between women and men

b) sexual harassment that involves an explicit or strongly implied threat that the employee's submission is a condition of continued employment

c) harassment in which an employer retaliates against an employee for reporting racial discrimination

d) harassment that does not cause financial harm to an employee

e) harassment in which employees are subjected to racial or gendered slurs

9. The Supreme Court's decision in *Hernandez v. Texas* was significant because it (p. 136)

a) affirmed all nationality groups were entitled to equal protection under the Fourteenth Amendment.

b) determined that anyone born in the United States was entitled to full citizenship.

c) allowed school districts to achieve racial integration through busing.

d) held that public accommodations could be segregated by race but still be equal.

e) eliminated the government's power to use race as a criterion for discrimination in law.

10. Unauthorized immigrants in the United States are all eligible to (p. 136)

a) vote.

b) receive an education.

c) receive government-funded health insurance.

d) receive a green card.

e) sponsor other members of their family who want to immigrate to the United States.

11. In *United States v. Wong Kim Ark*, the Supreme Court ruled that (p. 138)

a) school districts must provide bilingual education for students whose English is limited.

b) the internment of Japanese Americans during World War II was constitutional on the grounds of military necessity.

c) the 1882 Chinese Exclusion Act was an unconstitutional form of racial discrimination.

d) anyone born in the United States was entitled to full citizenship.

e) Chinese immigrants were ineligible for citizenship in the United States.

12. How did the 1975 amendments to the Voting Rights Act benefit Native Americans? (p. 139)

a) They granted citizenship to all Native Americans.

b) They renewed tribal rights and tribal self-government.

c) They established Native Americans' right to be taught in their own languages.

d) They established reservations for Native Americans.

e) They freed Native Americans from state regulations prohibiting gambling.

13. No Supreme Court ruling or national legislation explicitly protected gay men and lesbians from discrimination until (p. 140)

a) 1934.

b) 1964.

c) 1975.

d) 1996.

e) 2015.

14. In Allan Bakke's case against the medical school of the University of California at Davis, the Supreme Court ruled that *(p. 142)*

a) race can never be considered as a factor in university admissions, even to promote diversity.

b) achieving "a diverse student body" was a "compelling public purpose," and the method of a rigid quota of admission slots assigned on the basis of race was consistent with the Fourteenth Amendment's equal protection clause.

c) achieving "a diverse student body" was a "compelling public purpose," but the method of a rigid quota of admission slots assigned on the basis of race violated the Fourteenth Amendment's equal protection clause.

d) achieving "a diverse student body" was a "compelling public purpose," but affirmative action policies can only be used to give preferences to African Americans.

e) achieving "a diverse student body" was a "compelling public purpose," but affirmative action policies can only be used to give preferences to Asian Americans.

15. In which case did the Supreme Court rule that race may be considered in college admissions decisions as part of a "highly individualized, holistic review of each applicant's file"? *(p. 142)*

a) *Ledbetter v. Goodyear Tire and Rubber Co.*

b) *Mendez v. Westminster*

c) *Brown v. Board of Education*

d) *Grutter v. Bollinger*

e) *Fisher v. University of Texas*

Key Terms

discrimination *(p. 121)*

civil rights *(p. 121)*

equal protection clause *(p. 121)*

Thirteenth Amendment *(p. 122)*

Fourteenth Amendment *(p. 123)*

Fifteenth Amendment *(p. 123)*

Jim Crow laws *(p. 123)*

"separate but equal" rule *(p. 124)*

Brown v. Board of Education (p. 125)

strict scrutiny *(p. 125)*

de jure *(p. 125)*

de facto *(p. 125)*

affirmative action *(p. 141)*

★ *chapter* ★

06

Public Opinion

WHAT GOVERNMENT DOES AND WHY IT MATTERS In 1991, Suzanna Hupp was eating lunch in a Texas restaurant when a man drove his truck through the window and began shooting. The gunman killed 23 people, including her parents. Hupp had often carried a handgun in her purse, but had recently taken it out because at the time Texas did not allow carrying a concealed handgun, and she was afraid she would lose her license as a chiropractor if caught.

"Could I have hit the guy? He was fifteen feet from me. . . . Could I have missed? Yeah, it's possible. But the one thing nobody can argue with is that it would have changed the odds," Hupp maintains. She has since become a strong proponent of gun rights. "One of my bugaboos is gun laws. Anytime we list a place where you can't carry guns, to me, that's like a shopping list for a madman."[1]

Fifteen-year-old Justin Gruber also survived a mass shooting, in his case at the Marjory Stoneman Douglas High School in Parkland, Florida, in 2018. The incident left 17 students and teachers dead but led Gruber and many of his schoolmates

Suzanna Hupp (left) and Justin Gruber (right) were both present during episodes of gun violence. These events pushed Hupp to advocate for more gun rights, and Gruber to speak out for more restrictive gun laws. How do political opinions form? And how do government officials respond to shifts in public opinion?

to the opposite view from Suzanna Hupp's: support for stronger gun control measures such as assault weapon bans and increased age limits for purchase. Objecting to one suggestion raised after the shooting, Gruber said that arming teachers is a "terrible idea. . . . Adding guns to solve a gun problem will increase the possible negative outcomes."[2] Some students formed a group, Never Again MSD, known by the hashtag #NeverAgain, to advocate for tighter gun control.

After mass shootings, public support for stronger gun control measures tends to increase. The percentage of Americans telling the Gallup Organization that they wanted stricter gun-sale laws increased 5 points after the 2017 mass shooting in Las Vegas and 7 more points after the Parkland shooting five months later, to 67 percent overall.[3] At the same time, gun sales often increase after mass shootings as gun supporters fear tighter controls (although this pattern was more muted under President Trump than it was under President Obama).[4] Soon after an incident, however, public outcry tends to fade, and elected officials seem to take no action. In these cases, are politicians following public opinion, or are they ignoring it?

We expect government to pay attention to the people. But whose opinion gets represented in public policy, particularly on issues such as gun control, where there are strong divides among the public? How influential is public opinion relative to other political forces, such as organized interest groups? How well informed are people, and by what channels can individuals make their voices heard? As we will see in this chapter, research shows that public opinion does indeed have a significant impact on public policy. But scholars continue to debate whether the public is sufficiently informed about politics, as well as whether elected officials represent the interests of all Americans or only some.

CHAPTER GOALS

★ Describe Americans' core political values and ideologies (pp. 151–56)

★ Describe the major forces that shape public opinion (pp. 156–63)

★ Explain how Americans' level of political knowledge affects public opinion and democracy (pp. 165–67)

★ Explain the relationship between public opinion and government policy (pp. 167–68)

★ Explain how surveys and big data can accurately measure public opinion (pp. 169–76)

Public Opinion Is Defined by Basic Values and Beliefs

Describe Americans' core political values and ideologies

The term **public opinion** refers to the attitudes that people have about policy issues, political events, and elected officials. It is useful to distinguish between values and beliefs, on the one hand, and attitudes and opinions, on the other. **Values (or beliefs)** make up a person's basic orientation to politics and include guiding principles. Values are not limited to the political arena; they include deep-rooted morals, ethics, aspirations, and ideals that shape an individual's perceptions of society, government, and the economy. **Liberty** (freedom), democracy, and **equality of opportunity**, for example, are basic political values held by most Americans.

Another useful term for understanding public opinion is *ideology*. **Political ideology** refers to a set of beliefs and values that form a general philosophy about government. For example, many Americans believe that governmental solutions to problems are inherently inferior to solutions offered by the private sector and free markets. Such a philosophy may predispose them to view specific government programs negatively even before they know much about them.

Attitudes (or opinions) are views about particular issues, persons, or events. An individual may have an attitude about American trade policy toward China or Mexico or an opinion about President Trump or House Speaker Nancy Pelosi. The attitude may have emerged from a broad belief about free trade, the role of government in the economy, or the political ideology of conservatism or liberalism, but the opinion itself is very specific. Some attitudes may be short-lived and can change based on changing circumstances or new information; others may change over a few years, and still others may not change over a lifetime.

When we think of public opinion, we often think in terms of differences of opinion. The media are fond of reporting political differences between Republicans and Democrats, rural and urban residents, Blacks and Whites, women and men, the young and the old, more versus less educated, people of different religions, and so on.

POLITICAL VALUES

Most Americans share a common set of values, including a belief in the principles, if not always the actual practice, of liberty, equality, and democracy. The United States was founded on the principle of individual liberty, or freedom, and Americans have

public opinion citizens' attitudes about political issues, leaders, institutions, and events

values (or beliefs) basic principles that shape a person's opinions about political issues and events

liberty freedom from governmental control

equality of opportunity a widely shared American ideal that all people should have the freedom to use whatever talents and wealth they have to reach their fullest potential

political ideology a cohesive set of beliefs that forms a general philosophy about the role of government

attitude (or opinion) a specific preference on a particular issue

always voiced strong support for that principle and usually also for the idea that governmental interference with individuals' lives and property should be kept to a minimum.

Americans have stronger views about the importance of liberty and freedom of expression than do citizens in other democratic countries. One example is the growing concern about privacy and security of personal information online in an era of digital commerce and social media. Nevertheless, support for freedom of speech, a free internet, and a free press is higher in the United States than in most other countries: 71 percent of Americans believe it is very important that "people can say what they want without state or government censorship," compared to a global average of 56 percent.[5]

Similarly, equality of opportunity has always been an important value in American society. Most Americans believe that all individuals should be allowed to seek personal and economic success. Moreover, most believe that such success should be the result of individual effort and ability, rather than family connections or other forms of special privilege. Quality public education and a college degree are among the most important mechanisms for obtaining equality of opportunity in that they allow individuals, regardless of personal or family wealth, a chance to get ahead.

Most Americans also believe in democracy and the rule of law. They believe that all citizens should have the opportunity to take part in the nation's elections and policy-making processes.[6] (See Chapter 9.) Figure 6.1 shows there is consensus among Americans on fundamental democratic values: for instance, nearly 90 percent believe free and fair elections are essential to U.S. democracy, while 83 percent say checks and balances of power among the president, the Congress, and the courts are also very important. Eighty percent believe people should be able to criticize the government, including engaging in nonviolent protest, and 74 percent believe democracy requires protecting the rights of people with unpopular views. But there are emerging partisan divisions, even over core values. For example, only half (49 percent) of Republicans say a free press is very important to maintaining a strong democracy, compared to 76 percent of Democrats.[7]

Obviously, the political values that Americans espouse have not always been put into practice. For 200 years, Americans proclaimed the principles of equality of opportunity and individual liberty while denying them in practice to generations of African Americans. Ultimately, however, slavery and, later, segregation were defeated in the arena of public opinion because these practices differed so sharply from the fundamental principles accepted by most Americans.

POLITICAL IDEOLOGY

Americans share many fundamental political values, but the application of these values to specific policies and political candidates varies. As noted earlier, a set of underlying ideas and beliefs through which people understand and interpret politics is called a *political ideology*. In the United States the definitions of the two most common political ideologies—liberalism and conservatism—have changed over time. To some extent, contemporary liberalism and conservatism can be seen as

Americans Agree on Many Core Democratic Values

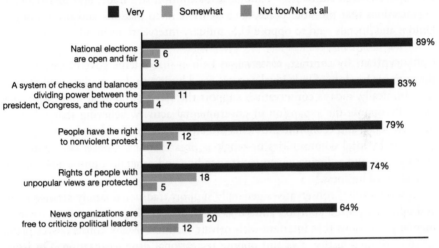

PERCENTAGE WHO SAY EACH IS VERY, SOMEWHAT, OR NOT TOO/NOT AT ALL
IMPORTANT TO MAINTAINING A STRONG DEMOCRACY IN THE UNITED STATES:

■ Very   ■ Somewhat   ■ Not too/Not at all

National elections are open and fair — 89% / 6 / 3

A system of checks and balances dividing power between the president, Congress, and the courts — 83% / 11 / 4

People have the right to nonviolent protest — 79% / 12 / 7

Rights of people with unpopular views are protected — 74% / 18 / 5

News organizations are free to criticize political leaders — 64% / 20 / 12

SOURCE: Pew Research Center, "Broad Public Agreement on Importance of Many Aspects of a
Strong Democracy," March 2, 2017, www.people-press.org (accessed 1/23/18).

differences in emphasis with regard to the fundamental American political values of liberty and equality.

Liberalism In classical political theory, a liberal was someone who favored individual entrepreneurship and was suspicious of government and its ability to manage economic and social affairs—a definition akin to that of today's libertarian. The proponents of a larger and more active government called themselves progressives. In the early twentieth century, however, many liberals and progressives united in support of "social liberalism," the belief that government action (laws and policies) are often needed to preserve individual liberty and promote equality. Today's liberals are social liberals rather than classical liberals. Many conservatives today are classical liberals.

In contemporary politics, being a **liberal** has come to mean supporting government policies to create a fairer economic system and opportunity for upward mobility, including more progressive taxation (taxing those with more income or wealth more heavily); the

liberal today this term refers to those who generally support social and political reform, governmental intervention in the economy, more economic equality, expansion of federal social services, and greater concern for consumers and the environment

expansion of federal social service and health care programs; government spending on education, on infrastructure, and on science and technology, including measures to fight climate change; efforts to protect people of color and women from discrimination; and vigorous protection of the environment. Liberals generally support reproductive rights for women and LGBTQ rights, and are concerned with protecting the rights of refugees, immigrants, and people accused of crimes. While they are in favor of legalizing marijuana, they seek more regulation of guns and assault weapons that have been linked to increased violence. In international affairs, liberals tend to support foreign aid to poor nations; arms control; free trade; and international organizations that promote peace, such as the United Nations and the European Union; and liberals tend to oppose U.S. military interventions in other countries.

Conservatism By contrast, **conservatives** believe that a large government poses a threat to the freedom of individual citizens, small businesses, free markets, and democracy. Ironically, today's conservatives support the views of classical liberalism: they generally oppose the expansion of governmental activity, believing that solutions to many social and economic problems can and should be developed in the private sector or by local communities or religious organizations. Conservatives support cutting taxes and reducing government spending and generally oppose government regulation of business.[8]

In social policy, conservatives generally support traditional family arrangements and oppose legalized abortion and same-sex marriage. They often oppose environmental protections that interfere with private business. Many conservatives prefer stricter criminal justice laws and oppose recreational drug legalization. On issues such as immigration, international trade, and the fairness of the U.S. economic system, conservatives today are deeply divided. For example, business-oriented conservatives often support a legal path to citizenship for immigrants, but social conservatives want to lower legal and illegal immigration and build a wall between the United States and Mexico. In international affairs, conservatism has come to mean support for military intervention abroad and the maintenance of American military power. Conservatives are also deeply divided on foreign trade. Business-oriented conservatives favor free trade while social conservatives prefer tariffs that reduce trade with foreign countries.

conservative today this term refers to those who generally support the social and economic status quo and are suspicious of efforts to introduce new political formulas and economic arrangements; conservatives believe that a large and powerful government poses a threat to citizens' freedom

libertarian someone who emphasizes freedom and believes in voluntary association with small government

Libertarianism Other political ideologies also influence American politics. **Libertarians**, for example, argue that government interferes with freedom of expression, free markets, and society, and so should be involved as little as possible in both the economy and society. Thus they oppose business- and environmental-regulation measures and support legalization of drugs and abortion. In 2016, Republican senator and libertarian Rand Paul ran for president based on his opposition to foreign wars and his commitment to civil liberties and smaller government.

Socialism and the Green Party While libertarians believe in less government across the board, **socialists** argue that more government is necessary to promote justice and to reduce economic and social inequality. In 2016 and 2020, Senator Bernie Sanders, who calls himself a "democratic socialist," gained widespread support from progressive and liberal Democrats, especially Millennials, in the party's presidential primaries. Like Social Democratic politicians in Europe, Sanders and House of Representatives member Alexandria Ocasio-Cortez support free markets and private enterprise but want government to ensure more equality of opportunity through such means as free public college, single-payer health care, higher taxes on the wealthy, and protection of workers' rights and unions.

> **socialist** someone who generally believes in social ownership, strong government, free markets, and a reduction in economic inequality

Americans' Ideologies Today Most Americans describe themselves as either liberals, conservatives, or moderates. Figure 6.2 shows that the percentages of Americans calling themselves moderates, liberals, or conservatives have remained relatively constant for the past 15 years, though liberals have recently been gaining. Gallup surveys indicate that as of 2019, 37 percent of Americans considered themselves

FIGURE 6.2

American Ideology

While slightly more Americans identify themselves as "conservatives" than "liberals," the majority identify as independent. During the period shown in this figure, however, Americans have had Democratic and Republican presidents. What might account for this apparent discrepancy? What role do moderates play in the electorate? How stable is Americans' ideology over time?

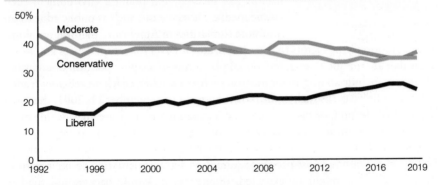

SOURCE: "The U.S. Remained Center-Right, Ideologically, in 2019," Gallup, January 9, 2020, https://news.gallup.com/poll/275792/remained-center-right-ideologically-2019.aspx (accessed 10/18/2020).

conservatives, 35 percent moderates, and 24 percent liberals. Among people aged 18 to 29, 26 percent identified as conservative, while 30 percent identified as liberals and 40 percent as moderates.[9] Some moderates tend to hold middle-ground opinions on issues across the board, while others are economically liberal but socially conservative or vice versa.

How We Form Political Opinions

> **Describe the major forces that shape public opinion**

As noted before, broad ideologies do not necessarily determine every political opinion a person holds. How are political opinions formed? When and how do political opinions change?

POLITICAL SOCIALIZATION

People's attitudes about political issues and elected officials tend to be shaped by their underlying political beliefs and values. For example, someone who dislikes government regulation of the economy would probably be predisposed to oppose the development of new health care programs. Similarly, someone who values environmental protection is probably likely to support the creation of a new national

political socialization the induction of individuals into the political culture; learning the underlying beliefs and values on which the political system is based

agents of socialization social institutions, including families and schools, that help to shape individuals' basic political beliefs and values

park, a ban on fracking, or tighter regulations on auto emissions. The processes through which these underlying political beliefs and values are formed are called **political socialization.**

Probably no nation, and certainly no democracy, could survive if its citizens did not share some fundamental beliefs. In contemporary America, the **agents of socialization** that promote differences in political opinions include family and friends, membership in social groups, religion, party affiliation, economic factors like income, and political environment such as the media. Other agents, such as public education, promote similarities in Americans' political opinions.

In addition to the factors that are important for everyone, experiences and influences that are unique to each individual play a role in shaping political orientation. These may include an important mentor, such as a teacher, coach, or religious leader. A major political event such as the terrorist attacks of September 11, 2001, the 2016 presidential election, or the 2020 coronavirus pandemic can leave an indelible mark on a person's political consciousness.

Family and Friends Most people acquire their initial orientation to politics from their families. As might be expected, differences in family background tend to produce divergent political perspectives. Although relatively few parents spend significant time directly teaching their children about politics, political conversations occur in many households, and children tend to absorb the political views of parents and other caregivers, often without realizing it. Studies find, for example, that party preferences are initially acquired at home, even in households that don't explicitly talk about politics. Children raised in households in which both primary caregivers are Democrats or Republicans tend to become Democrats or Republicans, respectively.[10] Of course, not all children absorb their parents' political views. Two of the four children of Republican president Ronald Reagan, for instance, rejected their father's conservative values and became active on behalf of Democratic candidates.

The family is one of the largest influences on a person's political views. Children raised in conservative or liberal families usually, but not always, hold those same views later in life.

In addition to family members, friends, coworkers, and neighbors are an important source of political orientation for nearly everyone. One study argues that individuals are "social citizens" whose political opinions and behavior are significantly influenced by their social networks.[11] When members of a social network express a particular opinion, others notice and conform, particularly if their conformity is likely to be highly visible. The conclusion is that political behavior is surprisingly subject to social pressures. Online social networks such as Facebook, Snapchat, Instagram, and Twitter may increase the role of peers in shaping public opinion as well.

Events in the world can change opinions too. Debates over the nation's gun laws have intensified following recent mass shootings. In 2019, mass shootings in El Paso, Texas, and Dayton, Ohio, brought renewed attention to gun violence. Mass shootings have increased support for stricter gun laws. Today 57 percent of U.S. adults say gun laws should be more strict. But there are big differences in opinion based on party. Nearly 80 percent of Democrats say gun laws should be stricter, while only 28 percent of Republicans do. Despite deep partisan divisions on guns, we also see some cross-party agreement. Ninety percent of Republicans and Democrats say people with mental illnesses should be prevented from buying guns, and more than 80 percent of both parties say people on federal no-fly or watch lists should be barred from purchasing firearms. And strong majorities of both Democrats (91 percent) and Republicans (79 percent) favor background checks for private gun sales and sales at gun shows.[12]

Education Governments use public education to try to teach all children a common set of civic values; it is mainly in school that Americans acquire their basic beliefs in liberty, equality, and democracy. At the same time, however, differences in formal education are strongly associated with differences in political opinions. In particular, those who attend college are often exposed to ways of thinking that will distinguish them from their friends and neighbors who do not attend. Education is one of the most important factors in predicting who engages in civic and political activities, such as regularly following the news, voting, and participating in politics, as well as in predicting how much an individual will earn over a lifetime—itself another important factor in political beliefs.[13]

SOCIAL GROUPS AND PUBLIC OPINION

The social groups to which individuals belong are another important source of political values. Social groups include those that individuals haven't chosen (national, gender, and racial groups, for example) and those they have (political parties, labor unions, the military, and religious, environmental, educational, and occupational groups).

Race Race plays an important role in shaping political attitudes and opinions, among both people of color and Whites. The experiences of African Americans, Whites, and Asian Americans, for example, can differ significantly. African Americans have been victims of persecution and discrimination throughout American history, and while many Asians are relatively recent immigrants to the United States, they, too, can face discrimination. African Americans and Whites also have different occupational opportunities and often live in separate communities and attend separate schools. Such differences tend to produce distinctive political views. Many Black Americans perceive other Blacks as members of a group with a common identity and a shared political interest in overcoming persistent racial and economic inequality. Political scientists refer to this phenomenon as "linked fate": African Americans see their fate as linked to that of other African Americans.[14] This linked fate acts as a sort of filter through which Black Americans evaluate information and determine their own opinions and policy preferences.

That Black and White Americans have different views is reflected in public perception of fair treatment across racial groups in the United States. Figure 6.3 shows that 84 percent of African Americans believe that Blacks in their community are treated less fairly than Whites in dealing with the police, compared to 63 percent of Whites. In a striking difference, 74 percent of Blacks but only 38 percent of Whites believe Blacks are treated unfairly in applying for a loan or home mortgage, while 82 percent of Blacks but just 44 percent of Whites believe Blacks are treated less fairly in hiring, pay, and promotions. Blacks are over 20 percentage points more likely to believe that Blacks face racial discrimination in voting in elections compared to Whites.[15]

Even with highly charged issues of race, events and circumstances can cause opinions to change. In 2009, 80 percent of African Americans said Blacks and other minorities did not get equal treatment under the law; the number of Whites giving this response was just 40 percent.[16] In recent years, however, widely publicized incidents of excessive use of police force against African

FOR CRITICAL ANALYSIS ▶

1. Who is more likely to talk about politics and express a political opinion online or at an event—those with less education or more?

2. Why do you think Democrats are more likely than Republicans to use social media to express their political opinions?

Who Talks about Politics?

If you turn on the TV or look at your social media feed, you might feel that everyone is expressing political opinions on an almost constant basis. Who expresses their opinions most often? And how do they do it?

Who Expresses Their Political Opinions?

Percentage of U.S. adults who say they express opinions about politics by discussing politics and government with others a few times a week or more

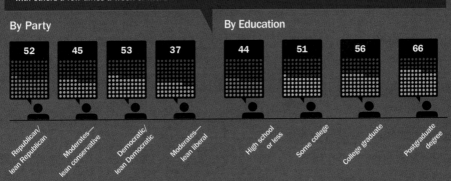

By Party

Republican/ lean Republican	Moderates— lean conservative	Democratic/ lean Democratic	Moderates— lean liberal
52	45	53	37

By Education

High school or less	Some college	College graduate	Postgraduate degree
44	51	56	66

How Do Americans Express Their Political Opinions?

Percentage of U.S. adults who say they have done the following activities on social media in the last year

By Party ■ Republican ■ Democratic

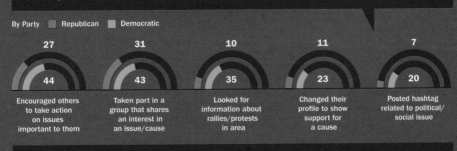

Encouraged others to take action on issues important to them	Taken part in a group that shares an interest in an issue/cause	Looked for information about rallies/protests in area	Changed their profile to show support for a cause	Posted hashtag related to political/ social issue
27	31	10	11	7
44	43	35	23	20

Percentage of U.S. adults who say they have done each of the following in the last year

By Education
■ High school or less
■ Some college
■ College graduate
■ Postgraduate degree

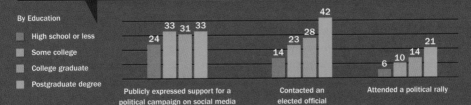

Publicly expressed support for a political campaign on social media: 24, 33, 31, 33

Contacted an elected official: 14, 23, 28, 42

Attended a political rally: 6, 10, 14, 21

SOURCE: Data from Pew Research Center (accessed 11/18/19).

FIGURE 6.3
· ·

Perception of Fair Treatment across Racial Groups

In the United States, racial groups may not perceive race relations in precisely the same way. According to the data in this figure, are Whites or Blacks more likely to think that race relations are good? What factors help to account for these differences in perception?

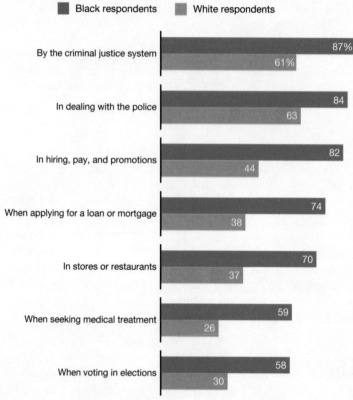

PERCENTAGE OF WHITES AND BLACKS SAYING BLACKS ARE TREATED LESS FAIRLY THAN WHITES IN EACH OF THE FOLLOWING SITUATIONS

Black respondents   White respondents

By the criminal justice system — 87% / 61%
In dealing with the police — 84 / 63
In hiring, pay, and promotions — 82 / 44
When applying for a loan or mortgage — 74 / 38
In stores or restaurants — 70 / 37
When seeking medical treatment — 59 / 26
When voting in elections — 58 / 30

SOURCE: Juliana Menasce Horowitz, Anna Brown, and Kiana Cox, "Race in America, 2019," Pew Research Center, pewresearch.org (accessed 7/15/20).

Americans and resulting protests by the Black Lives Matter movement have begun to cause a shift in public opinion on this issue (see Figure 6.3). Nationwide protests condemning police brutality erupted in May and June of 2020 when George Floyd, an unarmed African American man, was arrested and killed by police. The Black Lives Matter protests saw millions of people marching and demonstrating in the nation's cities to draw attention to the racial disparities not only in police treatment, but in American society at large. Two-thirds of U.S. adults supported the movement, with 38 percent saying they strongly supported it, though there was a 40 percent difference in strong support for the protests when comparing Whites to African Americans.[17] However, increased public support for the movement and the persistence of its organizers has galvanized police reforms across the country. As of October 2020, 653 police reform bills in 39 states had been introduced in state legislatures or passed.[18] Iowa, for example, restricted chokeholds and prevented the rehiring of officers fired for misconduct, while New York and New Jersey criminalized the use of chokeholds.

Ethnicity Ethnicity also affects political attitudes, separately from race. Latinos make up 17 percent of the total population and are the fastest-growing minority in the United States. While most Latinos and Latinas are racially White, their shared ethnic and, to a large extent, linguistic background contributes to a group consciousness that shapes opinions. The U.S. Latino population is diverse, comprising individuals of Mexican, Cuban, Central American, South American, and Caribbean descent whose backgrounds and circumstances are often quite different.[19] In spite of the differences, however, the Latino population has a growing sense of "linked fate."

There are 11.2 million first-generation immigrants from Mexico living in the United States today. Nationwide, foreign-born citizens account for 13.6 percent of the U.S. population, and Census estimates that about 23 percent are undocumented immigrants. Unsurprisingly, immigration is one of the most important policy issues among Latinos, with significant majorities of Latinos concerned about restrictive immigration policies and the threat of deportation to themselves, a family member, or a friend.[20]

While immigration has been at the forefront of a national political debate, a majority of Americans have positive views about immigrants. Just one in four Americans believe legal immigration to the United States should decrease.[21] Sixty-two percent say immigrants strengthen the country "because of their hard work and talents," while 28 percent say immigrants burden the country by taking jobs, housing, and health care.

Gender Men and women have important differences of opinion as well. Reflecting differences in social roles and occupational patterns, women tend to oppose military intervention more than men do and are more likely than men to favor gun control and government social programs. Perhaps because of these differences on issues, women are more likely than men to vote for Democratic candidates. In the 2020 presidential election, men were much more likely to favor Republican Donald Trump and women to favor Democrat Joe Biden. This tendency of men's and women's voting to differ is known as the **gender gap**.

gender gap a distinctive pattern of voting behavior reflecting the differences in views between women and men

In 2020, a majority of Americans believed the United States hasn't gone far enough when it comes to giving women equal rights with men. However, there were significant differences by gender—64 percent of women agreed with the statement, compared to 49 percent of men. Women are also more likely than men to believe there are major obstacles to gender equality, specifically in women's positions of political power.[22]

Religion Religious affiliation, frequency of church attendance, and the belief that religion and prayer are important in one's life are important predictors of opinion on a wide range of issues. White evangelical Protestants and weekly churchgoers are much more likely to hold conservative views and be Republican, while those without any religious affiliation (almost 25 percent of the population) are more likely to hold liberal views and favor the Democratic Party.[23] Just over 30 percent of evangelical Protestants believe abortion should always be permitted, compared to 75 percent of those without religious affiliation. Attitudes about LGBTQ rights show similarly sharp differences.[24] Religion also helps explain opinions on teaching evolution in the public schools, environmental policy, immigration, and other issues.

Party Affiliation Political party membership is one of the most important factors affecting political attitudes. We can think of partisanship as red (Republican)- or blue (Democratic)-tinted glasses that color opinion on how we "see" a vast array of issues. Self-identified partisans (individuals affiliating with the Republican or Democratic Party) tend to rely on party leaders and the media for cues on the appropriate positions to take on major political issues.[25]

In recent years, party polarization has become a defining feature of Congress, many state legislatures, and the mass public. As a result, the leadership of the Republican Party has become increasingly conservative, whereas that of the Democratic Party has become more liberal, a shift reflected in public opinion. Geographic sorting—with liberals choosing to live in neighborhoods, cities, counties, and states that are more liberal, while conservatives move to areas whose populations hold more conservative views—also contributes to mass polarization. Large cities have predominantly Democratic populations, while Republicans are more numerous in rural and suburban areas.

Economic Class and Group Self-Interest Another way that membership in groups can affect political beliefs is through economic class and self-interest. On many issues, for example, the interests of the rich and the poor differ significantly.

The framers of the Constitution thought that the inherent gulf between the rich and the poor would always be the most important source of conflict in political life. Today, 61 percent of Americans say there is too much income inequality in the United States, including 41 percent of Republicans and 78 percent of Democrats, and existing inequality has been magnified by the economic crisis from the coronavirus pandemic. But while there might be agreement on the problem, there are huge disagreements about the solution.

Natural group differences in interest also exist between generations. Millennials (born 1981–1996) and post-Millennials or Generation Z (born 1997 and later), for example, are much more accepting of legalization of marijuana and of LGBTQ rights than are older age cohorts, and they are more concerned about

Donald J. Trump ✓
@realDonaldTrump

I am SUBSTANTIALLY LOWERING MEDICARE
PREMIUMS. Have instituted Favored Nations Clause and
Rebates on Drug Companies. Never been done before.
Drug companies are hitting me with Fake Ads, just like
sleepy Joe. Be careful! Drug prices will be reduced
massively, and soon.

8:03 AM · Sep 17, 2020 · Twitter for iPhone

Presidents have used a variety of methods over the years to help shape public opinion in support
of their policies. President Franklin Delano Roosevelt held "fireside chats," or radio broadcasts that
highlighted his policy goals. President Trump frequently tweeted about policies and other politicians
to connect with citizens.

the high cost of a college education, climate change, criminal justice issues, and
privacy and security online (government surveillance). Older citizens, on the
other hand, are more concerned than the young with protecting Social Security
and Medicare benefits.

POLITICAL LEADERS

All governments try to influence, manipulate, or manage their citizens' beliefs.
But the extent to which public opinion is actually affected by government public
relations can be limited. Often, claims made by political leaders are disputed by the
media, by interest groups, and, increasingly, by the opposing political party.

These challenges haven't stopped modern presidents from focusing a great deal
of attention on shaping public opinion to support their policy agendas. Franklin
Delano Roosevelt did so through his famous "fireside chat" radio broadcasts. The
George W. Bush administration developed an extensive public-relations program to
bolster popular support for the president's policies, including the war against terrorism.[26] Barack Obama's White House was the first to use digital and social media
to promote the president's policy agenda, especially national health care reform.
Facebook posts served to personalize the president, and Obama was especially adept
at using Twitter, with 70 million followers on that network.

Though Obama was the first president to use Twitter, Donald Trump was the
nation's first Twitter president. Twitter and Facebook were key tools that helped
Trump win the presidency in 2016; as president he continued to use Twitter to
shape public opinion (with 80 million followers worldwide), though not always in a
purposeful way. Trump communicated his sentiments on politics like no other president in modern history, although his tweets often contradicted his own staff—and
sometimes even himself. He used Twitter for proposing policies, making announcements, attacking his enemies, defending himself, promoting his party and his policies, and just plain venting. Laced with emotion and frequent typos, his tweets
projected authenticity, even if they were not always factually correct.

Confidence in Democratic Institutions

Legislatures, political parties, and the press are three institutions that play an important role in making democracy work. While this is true of all democracies, we do notice that Americans tend to be much less confident in these institutions than are citizens in other democracies.

1. Is one of the three institutions more or less popular than the others across the globe? Are you surprised by any of the numbers on this chart? Why might some countries have a citizenry that has more trust in the press, while in others the legislature scores higher?

2. Why are the U.S. scores so low? What does it mean for politics when a large percentage of a population loses confidence in the institutions that keep its democracy functioning?

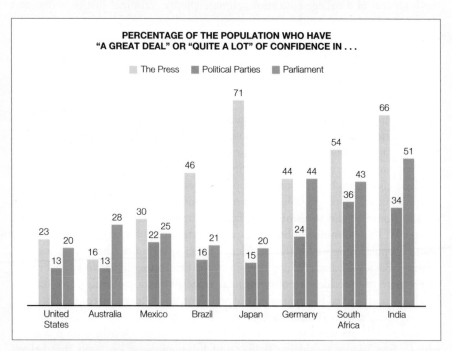

PERCENTAGE OF THE POPULATION WHO HAVE
"A GREAT DEAL" OR "QUITE A LOT" OF CONFIDENCE IN . . .

■ The Press ■ Political Parties ■ Parliament

	The Press	Political Parties	Parliament
United States	23	13	20
Australia	16	13	28
Mexico	30	22	25
Brazil	46	16	21
Japan	71	15	20
Germany	44	24	44
South Africa	54	36	43
India	66	34	51

Source: R. Inglehart et al., eds., "World Values Survey: Round Six—Country-Pooled Datafile Version," 2014, www.worldvaluessurvey.org (accessed 8/12/19).

Political Knowledge Is Important in Shaping Public Opinion

The underlying factors that shape individuals' political opinions remain relatively constant through time: one's level of education, for example, is generally set by early adulthood. However, individuals also encounter new information from political leaders and the media throughout their lives. What role does political knowledge and information play in forming opinions? What causes people's opinions to change?

POLITICAL KNOWLEDGE

What best explains whether citizens are generally consistent in their political views or are inconsistent and open to the influence of others? In general, knowledgeable citizens are better able to evaluate new information and determine whether it is relevant to and consistent with their beliefs and opinions; they are also more likely to be partisans and to have an ideology (such as liberal or conservative).[27] As a result, better-informed individuals can recognize their political interests and act consistently to further those interests.[28] Researchers found that the average American has little formal knowledge of policy debates or of political institutions, processes, or leaders. Many Americans cannot name their member of Congress and do not know that U.S. senators serve six-year terms.[29] Researchers also found that people who have more education and higher incomes and occupational status are more likely to know about and be active in politics. As a result, people with more income and education have a disproportionate influence in politics and are better able to get what they want from government.

Political knowledge may protect individuals from exposure to misinformation that can distort public opinion. While social media have created new platforms for organizing and voter mobilizing, discussing politics, and creating networks (see Chapter 7), they have also been associated with increased misinformation. Fake news on Facebook—with its billion users globally—was extensive in the 2016 election. In 2020, YouTube (owned by Google) became a primary platform for disinformation campaigns.

Russian "bot" accounts on Twitter were the source of many of the fake stories. Both Google and Facebook implemented new protocols to block content from deceptive outlets, and Twitter, Reddit, and Instagram deleted millions of fake accounts in response. During the 2020 presidential election and its aftermath, misinformation was spread largely by Americans and elected officials, including President Trump. In the days after the election, Twitter labeled 37 percent of Trump's tweets as false or misleading. Misinformation spread by elected officials and online news has encouraged more Americans to seek websites such as PolitiFact.com, FactCheck.org, and Snopes.com to verify the content of political information.

Shortcuts and Cues Because being informed politically requires a substantial investment of time and energy for reading the daily news, most Americans try to get political information and make political decisions "on the cheap" by using shortcuts. Researchers have found that individuals rely on cues from sources they trust—party elites, interest groups, and media outlets—to help them form their attitudes.[30] Today, tweets from trusted elected officials are an increasingly important source of information. Other "inexpensive" ways to become informed involve taking cues from trusted friends, social networks and social media, relatives, colleagues, and sometimes religious leaders.

The public's reliance on elite cues has taken on new significance in today's era of party polarization. As elected officials have become increasingly polarized, political scientists have found stark evidence that this new environment changes how citizens form opinions and make decisions. Notably, polarization means that party endorsements of an issue or candidate have a larger impact on public opinion than they used to.

Skim and Scan Another factor affecting political knowledge is the *form* in which people consume news and information. The transformation of media in the digital era has had a profound effect on the way the news is reported and how citizens learn about politics. Today more than three in four Americans read the news online or seek political information there.[31] Recent research also indicates a trend in journalism toward shorter articles and flashier headlines, and Twitter limits text to 280 characters. Americans today are likely to read the news by skimming and scanning multiple headlines online, in bits and bytes, rather than by reading long news articles.[32]

Costs to Democracy Low levels of political knowledge pose problems for democratic governments. People who lack political knowledge cannot effectively defend their political interests, rights, and freedoms and can easily become losers in political struggles and government policy. The presence of large numbers of politically ignorant citizens means that people can more easily be manipulated by political elites, the media, foreign governments, and wealthy special interests that seek to shape public opinion. If knowledge is power, then a lack of knowledge can contribute to growing political and economic inequality.

Take one of the most important areas of government policy: taxation. Although the United States has one of the largest gaps between the rich and the poor of any nation in the world, over the past several decades the rate of taxation on its wealthiest citizens has been substantially reduced. In 2001, President George W. Bush signed into law a bill providing a substantial tax break mainly benefiting the top 1 percent of the nation's wage earners. One study showed that the 2001 tax cuts were favored by millions of middle- and lower-middle-class citizens who did not stand to benefit from them, and that 40 percent of Americans had no opinion at all about the cuts.

The explanation for this odd state of affairs appears to be a lack of political knowledge. Millions of people who were unlikely to benefit from the cuts thought they would. Since most Americans think they pay too much in taxes, they favored the policy, even if the wealthy benefited much more than the middle class.

In 2017, President Trump and the Republican-controlled Congress adopted even larger tax cuts for the affluent and dramatically reduced corporate taxes. This time, however, polls showed a majority of Americans opposed the cuts. Did the opposition reflect increased political knowledge, or the low approval ratings for Trump and Congress at the time? The public response to the coronavirus outbreak in 2020 shows that lack of political knowledge can sometimes have dire consequences. Early in the outbreak, lack of knowledge of the seriousness of the pandemic hindered public health efforts encouraging social distancing and wearing face masks to prevent the spread of the disease. In turn, the public health crisis may deepen existing economic inequalities in the United States. Middle-class and lower-income Americans have taken the brunt of the economic fallout from the coronavirus outbreak in terms of lost jobs and reductions in salary. Half of lower-income Americans report household job or wage loss due to the coronavirus pandemic.[33]

Public Opinion Can Shape Government Policy

> **Explain the relationship between public opinion and government policy**

Given generally low levels of political knowledge among voters and the changing nature of public opinion, it's little wonder that politicians are sometimes unwilling to act solely on the basis of public opinion. But one could argue that consulting public opinion is a duty of elected officials in a democracy. Is government policy responsive to public opinion?

GOVERNMENT RESPONSIVENESS TO PUBLIC OPINION

Studies generally find that elected officials are influenced by the preferences of the public. Several studies have found that shifts in public opinion on particular issues do in fact tend to lead to changes in public policy.[34] This is especially true when

To what extent do political leaders listen to the opinions of their constituents? To what extent should they listen? Is Calvin's father right that leaders should do what they believe is right, not what the public wants?

there are wide swings in opinion on particularly high-profile issues that are relatively simple, such as requiring all Americans to have health insurance, and government aid for those unable to afford it.

However, there is reason to believe that the relationship between government policy and public opinion is more dynamic, with policy responding to opinion but also mass opinions shifting based on new government policies.[35] Recent studies have found government policy to have an effect on opinion in areas such as environmental protection, health care, welfare reform, the death penalty, and smoking bans. For example, in states that adopted smoking bans, public opinion then shifted to become more critical of cigarette smoking than in states without such bans.[36] This phenomenon is called policy feedback.

Of course, sometimes public opinion and policy do not align. For example, while a majority (53 percent) of Americans oppose building the wall between the United States and Mexico, it is being built. Sometimes public officials act on their own preferences if they believe doing so will benefit government, the private sector (businesses), or society, and lawmakers typically do use their own judgment when making policy choices.[37] When elected officials pursue policies not aligned with public opinion, it is often because they view particular groups of the electorate as more important than others. Groups or individuals that regularly vote for or contribute financially to a candidate have their interests more closely represented than the general public does.[38]

DOES EVERYONE'S OPINION COUNT EQUALLY?

In a democracy, where each person has one vote, it is assumed that elected representatives will implement the policies favored by the majority of the people, and in a general sense this happens in the United States. But when policy issues are more complicated (such as taxation or foreign policy regarding trade and tariffs), the public is likely to have less of a voice. Further, citizens who are more affluent and more educated have a disproportionate influence over politics and public policy decisions. Likewise, elected officials respond more strongly to voters than nonvoters, and to Whites more than people of color.

How do more affluent and educated citizens manage to exert outsize influence over policy makers? One way is obvious: they vote at higher rates and are more likely to express their political views and to contribute money to political campaigns. And a recent study of the roll-call votes of U.S. senators demonstrated that they are indeed responsive to the policy preferences of voters but not to those of nonvoters.[39]

In regard to income group, research has found that both Republican and Democratic senators are less likely to respond to the opinions of low-income constituents than higher-income ones.[40] Senate votes on such varied issues as the minimum wage, civil rights, and abortion are all more likely to reflect the opinions of the rich. Their influence may explain government policies such as failure to increase the federal minimum wage and the 2017 tax reform that significantly reduced corporate taxes and reduced taxes paid by the wealthiest citizens, policies that contribute to growing income inequality.[41]

Measuring Public Opinion Is Crucial to Understanding What It Is

> **Explain how surveys and big data can accurately measure public opinion**

Public officials and political campaigns make extensive use of data analytics and **public-opinion polls** to help them decide whether to run for office, what policies to support, how to vote on important legislation, and what types of appeals to make in their campaigns. Understanding how public opinion is measured can help us evaluate claims and arguments made by politicians and political commentators.

MEASURING PUBLIC OPINION FROM SURVEYS

It is not feasible to interview all 330 million–plus residents of the United States on their opinions of who should be the next president or how the government should improve the economy and create jobs. Instead, pollsters take a **sample** of the population and use it to make inferences (predictions and educated guesses) about the preferences of the population as a whole. For a political survey to be an accurate representation of the population, it must meet certain requirements, including an appropriate sampling method (choosing respondents randomly), a sufficiently large sample size, and the avoidance of selection bias.[42] Random sample surveys are used extensively in business and marketing as well as politics; they ensure that the samples are accurate and reliable predictions of the underlying population. Websites such as RealClearPolitics.com list the results of most political surveys released each day; during elections, this can be dozens of surveys daily.

Representative Samples One way to obtain a representative sample is what statisticians call a **simple random sample (or probability sample)**. To take such a sample, one would need a complete list of all the people in the United States, and individuals would be randomly selected from that list. Imagine that everyone's name was entered into a lottery, with names then drawn blindly from an enormous box. If everyone had an equal chance of selection, the result would be a random sample.

Since there is no complete list of all Americans, pollsters use census data, lists of telephone numbers, or national commercial voter-roll files (which, despite the name, include all U.S. adults—registered and nonregistered), to draw samples of people to interview. If respondents are chosen randomly and

public-opinion polls scientific instruments for measuring public opinion

sample a small group selected by researchers to represent the most important characteristics of an entire population

simple random sample (or probability sample) a method used by pollsters to select a representative sample in which every individual in the population has an equal probability of being selected as a respondent

everyone has an equal chance of being selected, then the results can be used to predict behavior for the overall population. If randomization is not used or some people are excluded from the chance to be selected, then the sample will be biased and cannot be used to generalize to the population accurately. The timing of surveys is important; surveys conducted two months before an election may produce very different results than those the week before an election, because public opinion may have changed during this time as one candidate gains momentum over the other.

Another method of drawing a random sample is a technique called **random digit dialing**. A computer random-number generator is used to produce a list of 10-digit telephone numbers. Given that 95 percent of Americans have telephones (cell phones or landlines), this technique usually results in a random national sample because almost every citizen has a chance of being selected for the survey. Telephone and text message surveys are fairly accurate, cost-effective, and flexible in the type of questions that can be asked; but many people refuse to answer political ones, and response rates—the percentage of those called who actually answer the survey—have been falling steadily, now averaging less than 10 percent.[43]

Sample Size A sample must be large enough to provide an accurate representation of the population. Surprisingly, the size of the population being measured doesn't matter, only the size of the sample. A survey of 1,000 people is almost as effective for measuring the opinions of all Texans (29.5 million residents) as the opinions of all Americans (over 330 million residents).

Flipping a coin shows how sample sizes work. After tossing a coin 10 times, the number of heads may not be close to 5. After 100 tosses of the coin, though, the number of heads should be close to 50 and, after 1,000 tosses, very close to 500. In fact, after 1,000 tosses, there is a 95 percent chance that the percentage of heads will be somewhere between 46.9 and 53.1.

This 3.1 percent variation from 50 percent is called the **sampling error (or margin of error)**: the chance that a sample used does not accurately represent the population from which it is drawn. In this case, 3.1 percent is the amount of uncertainty we can expect with a typical 1,000-person survey. If we conduct a national survey and find candidate A leads candidate B 52 to 47 percent with a margin of error of 3 percent, it means the likely support for candidate A is anywhere from 55 to 49 percent and the likely support for candidate B is anywhere from 50 to 44 percent. Thus, in this scenario, the margin of error tells us that despite seeming to trail by 5 percent, B could actually be leading the election (50 to 49 percent)!

Normally, samples of 1,000 people are considered sufficient for accurately measuring public opinion through the use of surveys. Larger sample sizes can yield even more accurate predictions, but there is a trade-off in terms of cost since it is

random digit dialing a polling method in which respondents are selected at random from a list of 10-digit telephone numbers, with every effort made to avoid bias in the construction of the sample

sampling error (or margin of error) polling error that arises based on the small size of the sample

more expensive to survey more people. Why is a sample size of only 1,000 generally accepted as adequately representative of much larger populations?

The answer is the "diminishing returns" of sampling more and more people. The sampling error from a sample of 500 people is 4.4 percent. With 1,000 respondents it drops to 3.1 percent, but with 1,500 only to 2.5 percent. That is, smaller and smaller gains in accuracy have to be weighed against the increasing costs of polling more people. The consensus among statisticians and pollsters is that the optimal trade-off point—the "gold standard"—is 1,000. But today many surveys conducted online include sometimes hundreds of thousands of respondents, making their predictions potentially even more accurate. But if the sample is biased or does not reflect the electorate, even very large surveys can be wrong.

Survey Design and Question Wording Even with a good sample design, surveys may fail to reflect the true distribution of opinion within a target population. One frequent source of measurement error is the wording of survey questions. The words used in a question can have an enormous impact on the answers it elicits. The reliability of survey results can be adversely affected by poor question wording (such as giving respondents only yes-or-no choices when many of them favor a third or middle-ground option), the ordering of questions (such as earlier questions encouraging certain responses to later ones), ambiguous questions, awkward questions, or questions with built-in biases (questions that prime answers in some way or another).

Differences in the wording of a question can convey vastly different meanings to respondents and thus produce quite different response patterns. For example, for many years the University of Chicago's National Opinion Research Center has asked respondents whether they think the federal government is spending too much, too little, or about the right amount of money on "assistance for the poor." Answering the question posed this way, about two-thirds of all respondents seem to believe that the government is spending too little. However, the same survey also asks whether the government spends too much, too little, or about the right amount for welfare. When the word *welfare* is substituted for "assistance for the poor," about half of all respondents indicate that too much is being spent.[44]

Online Surveys Today, pollsters are increasingly turning to the use of online surveys, often using similar techniques to those of telephone surveys. Online surveys can be more efficient, less costly, and more accurate than standard phone surveys, and they include much larger samples of young people and yield more accurate results within age cohorts. But many online surveys do not use probability random sampling and thus are not representative of the American population. Instead, they reflect only the opinions of those willing to take a quiz online.

Many surveys are now hybrid, sometimes using telephone for the first contact and online for a follow-up survey. Pollsters now often provide incentives, such as a $25 gift card, to respondents who complete a survey. Short text message surveys are now being used by political campaigns that hope to see higher response rates.

Evaluate a Poll

NEIL NEWHOUSE, partner and cofounder of Public Opinion Strategies, a leading Republican polling firm

One of the main ways in which elected officials, other policy makers, the media, and members of the public know what Americans think about government, politics, and policy is the public-opinion poll. How can you know which poll results are credible and worthy of your attention?

We spoke to Neil Newhouse, partner and cofounder of Public Opinion Strategies, a leading Republican polling firm. He gave us these tips for evaluating surveys:

1 Who did they interview? Did the pollsters interview adults? Registered voters? Likely voters? Different topics require different interviewees. If you are interested in which candidate is ahead in an electoral contest, for example, you want a poll of likely voters, because they're who are going to make that decision. A poll of adults would be misleading since only a subset of adults turn out to vote.

2 How did they interview their subjects? Surveys should strive for a random sample of the target population, meaning all members of the target population had an equal chance of being interviewed. Polls where people opt in to be interviewed do not have random samples and will be misleading.

3 How many did they interview? A random sample allows pollsters to draw accurate conclusions about the attitudes of the underlying population. Surveying just 800 people nationwide can provide an estimate of an attitude such

as presidential approval. It's just like the doctor's office. The doctor takes a sample of your blood rather than draining your entire body.

4 What confidence do we have in the results? Pollsters typically report a "point estimate," for example "43 percent of likely voters approve of the president's performance." Random sampling also allows calculation of the "confidence interval," how confident we are in the results; larger samples provide more certainty. A confidence interval of plus or minus 3 points means true presidential approval is probably between 40 and 46 percent. A smaller sample might have a confidence interval of plus or minus 5 points, meaning the true answer is probably between 38 and 48 percent.

5 Over what length of time? The ideal poll is a "snapshot in time," conducted over three to five days, particularly for outcomes like election preferences.

6 **What survey mode was used?** Was it a live phone call, an automated call ("press 1 for candidate Smith, 2 for candidate Jones"), or on the internet? Each survey mode has a bias. Online polls result in more male and younger respondents. Landline phone surveys yield more older individuals, while cell phone surveys yield more young people. Often it is better to have a live phone call than an automated call, but a live interviewer can introduce bias as well. For example, Donald Trump's support before the 2016 presidential election was 3 percentage points higher in automated polls than in live phone polls, since some people were reluctant to tell pollsters that they were planning to vote for him.

7 **In what order were questions asked, and with what question wording?** To assess trends, it is best to ask the same questions in the same order over time so that you can compare apples to apples. Question wording also matters; quality polls use appropriate wording that doesn't go begging for an answer.

8 **Who conducted the poll?** Look for a name brand, a pollster that surveys on an ongoing basis, not just occasionally. If you never heard of the outfit or it seems obscure, it may not be the most reliable source of poll data.

Go to the aggregators, such as RealClearPolitics.com or FiveThirtyEight. com. They have made some judgments about quality and only include credible polls. And even if some lower-quality polls are included, you can see many poll results at once and triangulate the overall picture.

UPDATED NOV. 5, 2019 AT 10:00 AM

FiveThirtyEight's Pollster Ratings

Based on the historical accuracy and methodology of each firm's polls.

Read more   Download the data   See the latest polls

Ratings	Definitions

Search for a pollster

POLLSTER	METHOD	LIVE CALLER WITH CELLPHONES	NCPP/ AAPOR/ ROPER	POLLS ANALYZED	SIMPLE AVERAGE ERROR	RACES CALLED CORRECTLY	ADVANCED +/-	PREDICTIVE +/-	538 GRADE	BANNED BY 538	MEAN-REVERTED BIAS
SurveyUSA	IVR/ online/ live	O	O	790	4.6	90%	-1.1	-0.8	A		D+0.1
Rasmussen Reports/ Pulse Opinion Research	IVR/ online			716	5.3	78%	+0.3	+0.8	C+		R+1.5
Zogby Interactive/JZ Analytics	Online			464	5.8	78%	+0.5	+1.0	C		R+0.8
Mason-Dixon Polling & Research Inc.	Live	O		428	5.2	86%	-0.5	-0.2	B+		R+0.7
Public Policy Polling	IVR/ online/ text			418	5.0	80%	-0.3	+0.2	B		D+0.3
YouGov	Online			395	5.0	89%	-0.1	+0.4	B-		D+0.4
Research 2000	Live*			278	5.5	88%	-0.1	+0.4	F		D+1.4

WHEN POLLS ARE WRONG

The history of polling and political data analytics over the past century contains many instances of getting results wrong and learning valuable lessons in the process. Opinion polls are best understood as best guesses of a political outcome but not as predictions of fact. The 2016 election provides a recent example. The vast majority of national public-opinion polls leading up to the election predicted that Hillary Clinton would win enough Electoral College votes to win the presidency, but in fact she lost. The failure of opinion polls was repeated in 2020, when they predicted Biden would win the presidency on average by 8.4 percentage points, but he ended up only winning by roughly 4 percent. In some states, like Wisconsin, the polls were off by nearly 10 percentage points.

Social Desirability Effects Survey results can sometimes be inaccurate because the surveys include questions about sensitive issues for which individuals do not wish to share their true preferences. For example, respondents tend to overreport their voting in elections and the frequency of their church attendance because these activities are considered socially appropriate. Political scientists call this the **social desirability effect**: respondents report what they expect the interviewer wishes to hear or what they think is socially acceptable, rather than what they actually believe or know to be true.[45] On other topics, such as their income or alcohol and drug use, respondents may feel self-conscious and choose not to answer the questions.

Social desirability makes it difficult to learn voters' true opinions about some subjects because respondents hide their preferences from the interviewer for fear of social retribution (against what might be deemed "politically incorrect" opinions). For example, researchers have found that respondents in surveys didn't want to admit that they opposed school integration or would not vote for a Black candidate and, therefore, abstained from answering questions about these topics. However, surveys using experiments can be designed to tap respondents' latent or hidden feelings about sensitive issues without directly asking them to express their opinions.

social desirability effect
the effect that results when respondents in a survey report what they expect the interviewer wishes to hear rather than what they believe

selection bias polling error that arises when the sample is not representative of the population being studied, which creates errors in overrepresenting or underrepresenting some opinions

Selection Bias Some polls prove to be inaccurate because of **selection bias**—when the sample chosen is not representative of the population being studied. Recently, selection bias came into play in preelection polls in the 2012 presidential election, when Gallup significantly overestimated Latino support for the Republican candidate, Mitt Romney, suggesting a close race between him and the Democratic candidate, Barack Obama. The Gallup numbers were incorrect because of selection bias.[46]

In the 2016 presidential election, although most polls predicted the direction of the popular vote correctly in Hillary Clinton's favor, they failed to predict the size of the vote margin and the election outcome.

Though public opinion is important, it is not always easy to interpret, and polls often fail to predict how Americans will vote. In 1948, election-night polls showed Thomas Dewey defeating Harry S. Truman for the presidency, which caused the *Chicago Daily Tribune* to print a banner incorrectly announcing Dewey's win. In 2016, most polls showed Hillary Clinton leading Donald Trump, causing many to doubt the possibility of Trump winning the election.

Possible explanations for the polling inaccuracies in 2016 and 2020 included the use of "likely voter models," which underrepresented some groups that ended up voting at higher-than-usual rates, such as rural, non-college-educated, blue-collar voters, who supported Trump in large numbers.

In 2016, an *LA Times*/USC survey accurately predicted a Trump win, relying on a different methodology than the others. It used rolling panel surveys, where the same individuals were interviewed repeatedly over time. This method detected a late surge in support for Trump. Panel surveys are now used increasingly for public-opinion polling because researchers can measure opinion change for the same sample of individuals.

In recent years, the issue of selection bias has been complicated by the growing number of individuals who refuse to answer pollsters' questions or who use voice mail or caller ID to screen unwanted callers. And certain demographic groups—young people, Latinos, and those who frequently move—are less likely to be found in national commercial voter-roll files that include information on most U.S. adults. Today most pollsters and political campaigns use these voter files from all 50 states to develop their samples.[47]

Push Polling Push polls are not scientific polls and are not intended to measure public opinion accurately. Instead, they involve asking respondents a loaded question designed to produce a particular response about a political candidate or issue and to simultaneously shape respondents' perception of that candidate or issue. One of the most notorious uses of push polling occurred in the 2000 South Carolina Republican presidential primary, in which George W. Bush defeated John McCain. Callers working for Bush supporters asked conservative White voters if they would be more or less likely to vote for McCain if they knew he had fathered an illegitimate Black child, a false statement.

push poll a polling technique in which the questions are designed to shape the respondent's opinion

The Bandwagon Effect Public-opinion polls can influence political realities and elections. In fact, sometimes polling can even create its own reality. The so-called

bandwagon effect a shift in electoral support to the candidate whom public-opinion polls report as the front-runner

bandwagon effect occurs when polling results convince people to support a candidate identified as the probable victor.

This effect is especially likely in the presidential nomination process, where multiple candidates are often vying to be a party's nominee. Researchers found that the change in the amount of national media coverage received by a candidate before and after the Iowa caucuses, the first nominating event, was a major predictor of how well the candidate would do in the New Hampshire primary (the second nominating event) and in later presidential primaries nationwide.[48] A candidate who has "momentum"—that is, one leading or rising in the polls—usually also finds it considerably easier to raise campaign funds than a candidate whose poll standing is poor. In 2020, Biden may have benefited from the national and statewide polls showing a wide advantage for the Democrats in a bandwagon effect.

Public Opinion: What Do You Think?

In theory, public opinion plays a major role in American politics. After all, a central purpose of democratic government, with its participatory procedures and representative institutions, is to ensure that political leaders will heed the public will.

★ It is not always clear what the public will is. How do you think Suzanna Hupp and Justin Gruber, featured at the start of this chapter, would characterize public preferences regarding gun policy?

★ Whose preferences should prevail when attitudes differ among groups? Or when they differ between the public and elites? Or between the affluent and the poor?

★ What are the methods elected politicians use to understand what the public wants? And what do they do when they hear conflicting messages?

★ The media are an important source of political information for the public, and the amount and diversity of that information has only grown as politics has migrated online. Do you think the greater availability of information increases the accuracy of public opinion?

STUDY GUIDE

Practice Quiz

1. The term *public opinion* is used to describe *(p. 151)*
   a) the collected speeches and writings made by a president during his or her term in office.
   b) political punditry and analysis broadcast on cable news channels.
   c) the attitudes that people have about policy issues, political events, and elected officials.
   d) decisions of the Supreme Court.
   e) any political statement that is made by a citizen outside of his or her private residence or place of employment.

2. Today, the term _____ refers to someone who believes that a large government poses a threat to the freedom of individual citizens and to free markets and democracy. *(p. 154)*
   a) libertarian
   b) liberal
   c) conservative
   d) democrat
   e) socialist

3. *Socialism* refers to a political ideology that *(p. 155)*
   a) argues that more government is necessary to promote justice and to reduce economic and social inequality.
   b) emphasizes freedom and voluntary association with small government.
   c) argues for the need to place strict limitations on voting rights and civil liberties.
   d) argues that a single ruler should have total control over every aspect of people's lives.
   e) argues that governments are inherently repressive and should be abolished entirely.

4. The process by which Americans form political beliefs and values is called *(p. 156)*
   a) brainwashing.
   b) propaganda.
   c) indoctrination.
   d) political socialization.
   e) political development.

5. Which of the following is *not* an agent of socialization? *(p. 156)*
   a) the family
   b) social groups
   c) education
   d) party affiliation
   e) All of the above are agents of socialization.

6. The fact that women tend to oppose military intervention more than men do is an example of *(p. 161)*
   a) the rally around the flag effect.
   b) partisan polarization.
   c) the peace paradox.
   d) the bandwagon effect.
   e) the gender gap.

7. Which of the following statements about political knowledge is *not* accurate? *(p. 165)*
   a) In general, citizens with high levels of political knowledge are more likely to be partisans (Democrats or Republicans).
   b) In general, citizens with high levels of political knowledge are more likely to have an ideology (such as liberal or conservative).
   c) In general, citizens with high levels of political knowledge are better able to evaluate new information and determine if it is consistent with their beliefs and opinions.

d) In general, citizens with high levels of political knowledge are less likely to belong to political organizations and to be active in politics.

e) In general, citizens with high levels of political knowledge are better able to recognize their political interests and act consistently to further those interests.

8. Most Americans try to get political information *(p. 166)*

a) by using shortcuts, such as taking cues from trusted friends and colleagues.

b) by consulting a range of nonpartisan news sources.

c) by reading long-form, in-depth political journalism.

d) by watching congressional proceedings on C-SPAN.

e) by attending their congressional representatives' town hall meetings.

9. Which statement best describes the relationship between public opinion and government policy? *(pp. 167–68)*

a) Public opinion almost never influences government policy.

b) Government policy almost never influences public opinion.

c) The relationship between government policy and public opinion is dynamic, with government policy responding to public opinion but mass opinions also shifting based on new government policies.

d) Public opinion always influences government policy because lawmakers are legally bound to enact the majority's preferences.

e) Government policy never influences public opinion because most Americans pay very little attention to politics.

10. What is policy feedback? *(p. 168)*

a) the process of submitting public comments on a proposed new policy

b) the tendency of lawmakers to focus only on one policy area for the length of a congressional term

c) the way in which government policy can work to shift public opinion

d) the effect that public policies have on citizens' voting decisions

e) the influence that interest groups and wealthy Americans have on policy formation

11. Which statement best describes citizens' influence over politics and public policy decisions in the United States? *(p. 168)*

a) All citizens exert an equal influence over politics and public policy decisions in the United States.

b) Citizens who are less affluent and less educated have a disproportionately large influence over politics and public policy decisions in the United States.

c) Citizens who are more affluent and more educated have a disproportionately large influence over politics and public policy decisions in the United States.

d) Less affluent and less educated citizens only exert an influence over politics and public policy decisions when the Democratic Party controls the U.S. Congress.

e) Less affluent and less educated citizens only exert an influence over politics and public policy decisions when the Republican Party controls the U.S. Congress.

12. The small group that pollsters use to make inferences about the opinions of the whole population is called *(p. 169)*

a) a control group.

b) a sample.

c) a micropopulation.

d) respondents.

e) median voters.

13. Surveys conducted with _____ people are generally considered sufficient for accurately measuring public opinion. *(p. 170)*

a) 100

b) 500

c) 1,000

d) 5,000

e) 10,000

14. A *push poll* is a poll in which *(p. 175)*

a) the questions are designed to shape the respondent's opinion rather than measure the respondent's opinion.

b) the questions are designed to measure the respondent's opinion rather than shape the respondent's opinion.

c) the questions are designed to reduce measurement error.

d) the sample is chosen to include only undecided or independent voters.

e) the sample is not representative of the population it is drawn from.

15. A familiar polling problem is the "bandwagon effect," which occurs when *(p. 176)*

a) the same results are used over and over again.

b) polling results influence people to support the candidate identified as the probable victor in a campaign.

c) polling results influence people to support the candidate who is trailing in a campaign.

d) background noise makes it difficult for a pollster and a respondent to communicate with each other.

e) a large number of people refuse to answer a pollster's questions.

Key Terms

public opinion *(p. 151)*

values (or beliefs) *(p. 151)*

liberty *(p. 151)*

equality of opportunity *(p. 151)*

political ideology *(p. 151)*

attitude (or opinion) *(p. 151)*

liberal *(p. 153)*

conservative *(p. 154)*

libertarian *(p. 154)*

socialist *(p. 155)*

political socialization *(p. 156)*

agents of socialization *(p. 156)*

gender gap *(p. 161)*

public-opinion polls *(p. 169)*

sample *(p. 169)*

simple random sample (or probability sample) *(p. 169)*

random digit dialing *(p. 170)*

sampling error (or margin of error) *(p. 170)*

social desirability effect *(p. 174)*

selection bias *(p. 174)*

push poll *(p. 175)*

bandwagon effect *(p. 176)*

★ *chapter* ★

07

The Media

WHAT GOVERNMENT DOES AND WHY IT MATTERS

For more than two decades, Christopher Blair of Maine worked in construction, but it was tough on his body and the jobs dried up during the Great Recession that began in 2007.[1] He had a way with words, though, and turned to political blogging as a creative outlet. The problem was that blogging didn't pay much. That changed a few years later when he realized that he could use Google's advertising platform to make money from the clicks on his sites. A new website he created on Facebook during the 2016 presidential campaign did particularly well.

Blair launched scores of stories that were entirely made up—the very definition of fake news. He made up stories that would outrage political conservatives, such as "BREAKING: Clinton Foundation Ship Seized at Port of Baltimore Carrying Drugs, Guns and Sex Slaves" or "BREAKING: New Orleans Saints Stranded on Runway in London after Pilot Takes a Knee and Walks Off." He meant it all as satire. Blair is a liberal Democrat who made up the headlines to lure in susceptible conservatives. Each story would close with

Christopher Blair turned to political satire after losing work in construction during the Great Recession. His posts now contribute to the growing presence of "fake news" on the internet—false news stories that are meant to inflame political divides. What effect does fake news have on how Americans perceive politics?

his kicker, that it was all made up to fool his readers: "Please don't use our page in conjunction with Google or the news, it will only serve to confuse you further." His goal was to "trick conservative Americans into sharing false news, in the hope of showing what he [called] their 'stupidity.'"[2] He would then trace and expose some of the more extreme fans, including Ku Klux Klan members, he claimed.

The only problem? His articles were widely shared, liked, and copied at other fake news sites. In fact, when a Belgian computer expert named Maarten Schenk began tracking and debunking stories that were trending on Facebook and other websites, he found that he could trace much of the content—which was often just cut and pasted from other fake news sites— back to one source: Christopher Blair.

So while Blair's goal had been to satirize and expose extremists, taken out of context his stories helped fuel the fake news explosion. In spring 2018, Congress held hearings about the spread of misinformation on social media, grilling Facebook CEO Mark Zuckerberg, among others. In response to the scrutiny, Facebook changed its algorithms in July 2018 to try to lessen "spam, clickbait, fake news and data misuse." That meant less traffic coming Christopher Blair's way.

The tussle over online content—from Christopher Blair's attempts to troll conservative readers to Congress's hearings on online content to Facebook's policy changes—underlines how important media of all types are to democracy. The fights would not be so fierce if the stakes were not so high. According to the Pew Research Center, 20 percent of adult Americans say they "often" get their news from social media and 33 percent from news websites (compared to 49 percent for television, 26 percent for radio, and 16 percent for print newspapers).[3] But, as the Blair story shows, it is increasingly difficult to tell real news from fake news, and the numbers of those who put out fake stories and those who try to debunk them are growing. As the nature of the media evolves, a full understanding of America's dynamic media landscape may be more important than ever.

CHAPTER GOALS

★ Describe the key roles the media play in American political life (pp. 183–87)

★ Describe how different types of media cover politics (pp. 187–200)

★ Analyze the ways the media can influence public opinion and politics (pp. 200–205)

★ Describe the relationship between politicians and journalists (pp. 205–7)

★ Describe the evolution of rules that govern broadcast media (pp. 207–8)

The Media Are Indispensable to American Democracy

Describe the key roles the media play in American political life

Freedom of the press is protected under the First Amendment along with the most cherished individual rights in American democracy, including freedom of speech and religion. Political speech is especially protected. In the United States, individuals, groups, private organizations, and companies have the right to publish newspapers, magazines, and digital media without government censorship and with few government restrictions. In many authoritarian countries there is no freedom of the press, and the government controls the news and political information through state-sponsored media.

Why would the Founders care so much about the rights of the media to report the news without interference from government? Under British rule, before the American Revolution, freedom of speech and the press did not exist in the American colonies. Criticizing the British king was a crime punishable, in some cases, by death.

When the colonists won their independence, they wanted to be able to express their political opinions freely without fear of retaliation. The first of 10 amendments to the U.S. Constitution adopted during the Founding period states, "Congress shall make no law respecting an establishment of religion, or prohibiting the free exercise thereof; or abridging the freedom of speech, or of the press; or the right of the people peaceably to assemble, and to petition the Government for a redress of grievances." Despite attacks from both Republicans and Democrats who claim that major media outlets are biased, most Americans believe that freedom of the press is very important for maintaining a strong democracy and that "news organizations are free to criticize political leaders."

The **media** serve three important roles in American democracy: informing the public about current political issues and events; providing a forum for candidates, politicians, and the public to debate policies and issues; and acting as a watchdog on the actions of politicians and government. Part of the media's role of informing the public involves providing a variety of perspectives and fact-checking sources to provide unbiased coverage of current events. The media serve as a type of public square where citizens become informed about their government, political leaders, societal problems, and possible solutions—a forum where information necessary for democracy is exchanged.

The information presented by the media about politics and current events, government policy, candidates, and political parties allows citizens to make informed decisions in elections and to form knowledgeable opinions about policy issues. American philosopher John Dewey believed the media served to educate the public. A strong democracy, he said, was based not only on voting rights, but also on ensuring

media print and digital forms of communication, including television, newspapers, radio, and the internet, intended to convey information to large audiences

The media's role as a watchdog includes investigating political scandals. In February 2019, a conservative website accused Virginia Governor Ralph Northam of appearing in a medical school yearbook photo in blackface. After initially denying the allegations, the governor eventually admitted to the incident and apologized to the public.

that public opinion on current issues is based on communication among citizens, experts, and elected officials. This communication ensures that elected officials adopt policies consistent, for the most part, with the preferences of the citizens and serves as a counterweight to communication among elites, the wealthy, and corporations.

In other words, the mass media help level the playing field between political elites and "the people," giving citizens a more potent voice in society. Without the news media, citizens would not know about the actions of political leaders, corporations, or foreign governments and would be powerless to challenge them in the face of corruption. Journalists (people trained to report the news) give ordinary citizens information, and this information is ultimately power.

Finally, the media serve as a watchdog for the public, scrutinizing the actions of elected officials on behalf of citizens—most of whom cannot closely follow the actions of politicians and government. Like an alarm system for a home, the media notify the public of government actions that may harm them. The media inform the public about what policy issues are at stake in terms of changes in laws and regulations. They reveal which individuals and groups are exerting power in politics and what their goals and strategies are, and shed light on the different arguments they are using (such as those for and against a national mask mandate during the coronavirus pandemic, escalating the trade war with China, or a law to create free public college). The media often expose scandalous behavior or ties between financial interests and political leaders and policy making. By reporting the news in the public interest, the media continuously monitor the actions of public officials and strive to protect the public from government overreach and corruption by serving as a check on political power.

JOURNALISM

Most journalists are trained in schools of journalism and mass communication. They are guided by standards in reporting the news in the public interest, known as the principles of journalism. Above all, they seek to report the truth, by fact-checking, verifying sources as legitimate and credible, and engaging in investigative journalism.

The traditional news media aim to balance coverage of current events by providing objective and factual reporting that avoids including personal views of reporters or editors. Objective journalism includes being as accurate as possible, relying on original sources whenever possible, being transparent about sources, and presenting multiple viewpoints. While complete objectivity—reporting the news without bias—is impossible because all individuals have biases that influence how they understand and describe events, it remains a journalistic ideal.

THE PROFIT MOTIVE

The media are sometimes referred to as the fourth branch of government, providing a check on the power of government and political leaders. But who checks or controls the media? In the United States the media are not part of government and not subject to checks and balances like Congress, the presidency, and the courts. Instead most media in the United States are privately owned for-profit companies, like Verizon, the New York Times Company, Amazon, Fox Corporation, or Apple.

Public broadcasting refers to television, radio, and digital media that receive partial funding from license fees and government subsidies. In most other democratic countries public broadcasting plays a major role in informing the public about politics and current events. In contrast, public broadcasting in the United States—such as National Public Radio (NPR) or the Public Broadcasting Service (PBS)—plays a relatively small role in the nation's media system. Public broadcasting in the United States has just 2 percent of market share, compared to 35 percent in France, 40 percent in Germany, and 65 percent in Denmark.[4] According to evidence from cross-national surveys, U.S. citizens have lower levels of political knowledge than those in European democracies, who consume more public broadcasting.[5]

U.S. media companies earn most of their revenue from advertising, although revenue from subscriptions has been increasing. They are, therefore, motivated by what audiences want, because higher ratings generate more advertising revenue. Because of the need to reach wide audiences to sell advertisements, the U.S. media are more focused on "soft news," such as entertainment, sports, and celebrity news, than are European media, which provide more "hard news" coverage of politics and government. This may help explain why political knowledge is higher in some European countries than in the United States.[6]

And when it comes to political news, American media tend to focus increasingly on more dramatic, highly conflictual events and issues. Sensational stories of scandals, corruption, or candidates' attacks often generate more interest—and thus revenue—than the stories of everyday governing and details of public policy. Nonetheless, objectivity is still the goal, and standard practice is that news, opinion, and ads should be separate and distinct; that is why the opinions of editors are reserved for opinion pages.

The profit motive of the news industry may have contributed to Donald Trump's unexpected victory in the 2016 election. Due to the novelty of a television celebrity running for president without previous political experience, Trump's campaign was a financial boon for the media industry. His candidacy received double the media coverage of his Democratic opponent, Hillary Clinton. The former head of CBS, Les Moonves, said the Trump phenomenon "may not be good for America, but it's damn good for CBS."[7] Throughout the election and Trump's first year in office, cable news channels profited from higher ratings because of the public's fascination with Trump; CNN, for example, earned about $100 million more in television and

Internet Freedom

AMERICA SIDE by SIDE

Digital communications are central to how the media function in the twenty-first century and how citizens stay informed about their government. Not every country allows for a free and largely uncensored internet, though. Every year selected countries are assessed on issues related to internet access, freedom of expression, and privacy, and placed on a scale from *free* to *not free*.

1. Which regions of the world appear to have more free access to information and privacy while viewing the internet? What factors might make a government more or less likely either to want to restrict access to information on the internet or to monitor its citizens' use of the internet? How might a country benefit from offering freer access to the internet?

2. Compare this map to the map in America Side by Side in Chapter 1 on types of governments. Do any patterns emerge? If so, why might there be a relationship between type of government and internet censorship?

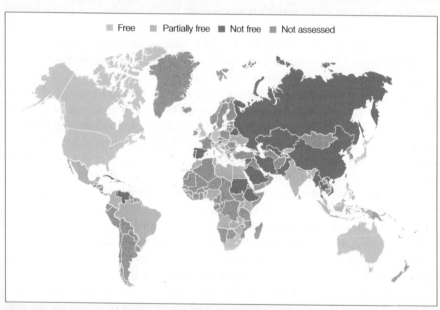

Free   Partially free   Not free   Not assessed

SOURCE: "Freedom on the Net: 2018," Freedom House (accessed 8/1/19).

advertising revenue than expected in 2016.[8] Newspapers and digital news outlets found that if the word *Trump* was mentioned in a headline, it was more likely to be read and shared online.

MASS MEDIA OWNERSHIP

One noteworthy feature of the traditional media in the United States is the concentration of their ownership. A small number of giant global corporations control a wide swath of media, including television networks, movie studios, record companies, cable channels and local cable providers, book publishers, magazines, newspapers, and online and digital media outlets.[9] **Media monopolies**, such as AT&T, Disney, Comcast, and Fox Corporation, have prompted questions about whether enough competition exists among traditional media to produce a truly diverse set of views on political matters.[10] As major newspapers, television stations, and radio networks fall into fewer hands, the risk increases that politicians and citizens who express less popular viewpoints will have difficulty finding a public forum.

media monopoly the ownership and control of the media by a few large corporations

Despite the appearance of substantial diversity overall, the number of traditional news-gathering sources operating nationally is actually quite small—several wire services, four broadcast networks, a few elite print newspapers, and a smattering of other sources, such as a few large local papers and several small, independent radio networks. More than three-fourths of the daily print newspapers in the United States are owned by large media conglomerates such as the Hearst Communications, McClatchy, and Gannett corporations. Much of the national news that is published by local newspapers is provided by one wire service, the Associated Press. More than 500 of the nation's 1,022 commercial television stations are affiliated with one of just four networks and carry that network's evening news programs.

The trend in concentration of traditional media ownership occurred in large part due to the relaxation of government regulations in the 1980s and '90s. The 1996 Telecommunications Act opened the way for additional consolidation; a wave of mergers has further reduced the field of independent media across the country (more on this below).

Modern Media Have Been Digitally Transformed

Describe how different types of media cover politics

The past three decades have resulted in a massive transformation of the U.S. news media, as competition from free digital sources has put pressure on traditional subscription-based news sources. Whether offline or online, today 47 percent of Americans prefer watching the news (television or streaming video) compared to reading it (34 percent) or listening to it on the radio (19 percent).[11] Of adults who prefer to read the news, 63 percent read the news online and 54 percent of U.S. adults regularly read news from social media.[12] Less than 20 years ago, most Americans said that after television, print newspapers were their main source for news, and under 20 percent read the news online.[13] As the media and news have migrated online, so has revenue generated from advertising. Today nearly half of all ad revenue in the United States is from digital advertising.[14]

Despite the digital transformation of the news media, much of what makes the media important in American politics remains the same. Major newspapers and TV networks—even if their content is increasingly delivered in digital form—remain popular and important sources of news. Political leaders are successful in making headline news and setting the news agenda. And journalists trained in professional schools create and develop much of what we consume as news, including original reporting.

But more and more, the media are online companies facing an environment where anyone with access to an internet connection can publish the news.[15] The number of organizations that have credibility and large audiences is still small; the leading newspapers in the United States, such as the *New York Times*, the *Wall Street Journal,* and the *Washington Post*, receive some of the highest traffic online. Nevertheless, the digital transformation of the media has created a reorganization of the industry that impacts how the news is made and how consumers learn about politics.

The news media are increasingly influenced by big technology companies. Before the internet, private, for-profit media companies largely controlled making the news, including original reporting, writing and production, packaging and delivery (think printed newspapers delivered to your front porch), and the selection of editors. In recent years, however, big technology companies like Apple, Amazon, Alphabet (owner of Google and YouTube), Microsoft, and Facebook (owner of Instagram and WhatsApp) have become major players in the business of journalism, creating media technology companies. This has changed many aspects of the production, packaging, and delivery of the news. Using advanced technology and market research, for example, they push specific news alerts to specific people based on those individuals' interests and preferences, often through social media. Editors choose stories and titles based on consumer interests. In 2018, half of all digital ad revenue for display ads went to just two tech companies: Facebook (40 percent) and Google (12 percent).[16]

The interdependence between technology and media companies continues to grow. In one of the latest trends, technology companies and their CEOs have been developing or buying major news media companies, such as eBay founder Pierre Omidyar creating the Intercept or Amazon CEO Jeff Bezos purchasing the *Washington Post*. Both the Intercept and the *Washington Post* have a reputation for forceful investigative journalism and original reporting. Facebook editors control trending topics in the news on the global platform, a key editorial role in what makes the headline news.

Beyond making some news outlets profitable again, these high-tech collaborations are changing how Americans learn about current events in the United States and globally.[17] This is evident in the growing number of Americans who read or watch the news using social network platforms such as YouTube, Twitter, or

Facebook. (In 2019, 54 percent of Americans regularly got their news on social media.)[18] One of the costs of the transformation of the media to digital and citizen journalism—news produced online by individuals and organizations other than professional journalists—has been less rigorous fact-checking and editorial standards for some news websites. Some digital-only news platforms, on both the ideological left and the ideological right, no longer follow the guiding principles of journalism.

Facebook's CEO Mark Zuckerberg came under fire for allowing politicians to lie in 2020 political campaign ads, highlighting how corporate decisions can shape the news and politics. While Facebook cracked down on made-up news flooding its platforms after the 2016 election, with fact-checking software to stop everyday users from sharing viral misinformation, politicians are exempt.

In contrast, Twitter announced that all political ads would be banned from its platform beginning in 2019. On all Google platforms and on YouTube, political advertisers are able to target only broad categories of individuals—by gender, age, or zip code—and cannot use more specific information such as voting records or political leaning. Advertisers are no longer able to target political ads based on users' interests learned from browsing or search history. To avoid misinformation about the 2020 election results, Facebook banned all political or issue ads after the polls closed on Election Day.

Despite more concentrated ownership of all types of media outlets, the American news media remain among the world's freest and most diverse. Americans get their news from (1) newspapers and magazines, (2) broadcast media (radio and television), and increasingly, (3) internet digital media (see Figure 7.1). Each of these three sources—newspapers, broadcast, and digital—has distinctive characteristics.

NEWSPAPERS

Newspapers are the oldest medium for the dissemination of the news, though today most Americans read digital rather than print versions. The leading newspapers have an especially influential audience because they help set the political agenda for the nation. Their audience of political elites and the mass public relies on the detailed coverage provided by professional journalists to inform their views about public matters and politics. In March 2019, for example, the *Washington Post* recorded 86.6 million unique visitors (or about one-third of U.S. adults).[19]

Beginning in the late nineteenth century, the emergence of newspapers (and later of radio and television networks) as mass-audience businesses operated primarily for profit significantly shaped politics in the United States. In fact, the development of standardized reporting and writing practices emphasizing objectivity in political news coverage was motivated largely by financial factors. The owners of large newspaper companies determined that the best way to make a profit was to appeal to as broad an audience as possible, which meant not alienating potential readers who held either liberal or conservative views. This goal, in turn, required training and "disciplining" reporters to produce a standardized, seemingly neutral news product. Today, in contrast, native digital news—that is, journalism in those media outlets that originated online—is less likely to emphasize neutrality than is journalism from older, predigital outlets.

FIGURE 7.1

Use of Online News Continues to Grow

The media landscape for news has seen remarkable shifts in a short period of time. Twenty years ago, more than 80 percent of Americans watched news on television and more than half read news in a newspaper. Today, fewer than half of Americans watch television news, while over one-third read the news online or in print. Since 2000, which media sources have gained rather than lost their audiences?

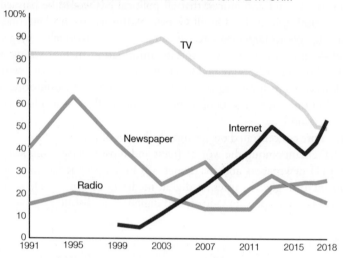

PERCENTAGE OF U.S. ADULTS WHO OFTEN GET THEIR NEWS ON EACH PLATFORM

SOURCE: Elisa Shearer, "Social Media Outpaces Print Newspapers in the U.S. as a News Source," Pew Research Center, December 10, 2018, pewresearch.org (accessed 7/21/20).

This approach proved successful in attracting readers, and for a long time most cities and towns in the country had their own newspaper, and often more than one. However, for most traditional newspapers, recent decades have been financially challenging. Competition from broadcast media and new online content sources has resulted in declines in advertising revenue and circulation levels, thus undermining the traditional business model of newspapers.[20] From 2008 to 2019, employment of newspaper journalists dropped 51 percent, from about 71,000 workers to 35,000.[21] Over the same time period, employment in digital-native newsrooms more than doubled.[22]

In the last four years, however, some major U.S. newspapers reported a sharp increase in digital subscriptions.[23] The *New York Times* added more than 500,000 digital subscriptions in 2016—a 47 percent increase from the previous year—while the *Wall Street Journal* and the *Chicago Tribune* also increased. Digital ad revenue continues to explode, accounting for 35 percent of all revenue to newspapers.

The *Washington Post* may be a model for making the news media profitable. While revenues for most newspapers have continued to decline or remain constant, the *Post* experienced double-digit revenue growth over multiple years. Along with providing a viable financial model, it has emerged as a leader in investigative reporting, data analytics, and marketing. New owner (and Amazon CEO) Jeff Bezos rebuilt the *Post* into a media technology company, producing over 1,200 articles, graphics, or videos per day, including staff-produced articles and wire stories written by others. The *Post* editorial staff produces about 500 stories per day, compared to 250 for the *New York Times*. The paper has an exploding digital readership and dynamic digital content. It distributes news content using social media and offers discounts to Amazon Prime members, and the *Post* app is preinstalled on Amazon's Fire tablets. The *Post* also tracks how different headlines and story framings affect readership of each story. For most newspapers and magazines today, non-ad revenue comes mainly from digital subscriptions rather than print circulation.

TELEVISION

Despite the rise of digital media, television news (local, national network, and cable) still commands much larger audiences than other kinds of news sources. Most Americans have a television, and tens of millions of people watch national and local news programs every day, though younger people are the least likely to get news from television, preferring to get news online. The major broadcasting television companies are NBC, CBS, ABC, Fox, and AT&T WarnerMedia (CNN).

Television news serves the important function of alerting viewers to issues and events—headline news—via brief quotes and short characterizations of the day's events. It generally covers relatively few topics, however, and provides little depth of coverage. Print and digital media, as (mostly) written text, can provide more detailed and complete information and context. Furthermore, **broadcast media** do very little of their own reporting, instead relying on leading newspapers or digital media to set their news agenda. Because they are aware of the character of television news coverage, politicians and others often seek to manipulate the news by providing sound bites that will dominate this coverage.

Twenty-four-hour cable news stations such as MSNBC, CNN, and Fox News offer more detail and commentary than the half-hour evening news shows on ABC, NBC, and CBS. But even these channels, especially during their prime-time broadcasts, are more focused on headlines and sound bites than newspapers are. In 2018, both viewership and revenue for the top three cable television news channels increased significantly, with viewership rising 8 percent and combined revenue growing over the previous year.

Politicians traditionally considered local broadcast news a friendlier venue than the national news. National reporters are often inclined to criticize and question, whereas local reporters are more likely to accept the pronouncements of national leaders at face value. Local TV continues to be a major source of news, especially for older Americans, African Americans, and people with lower formal education.[24] However,

> **broadcast media** television, radio, or other media that transmit audio and/or video content to the public

its importance is declining overall, especially among younger people.[25] Generally, however, Americans' reliance on television as a news source persists.[26]

RADIO

Radio has seen significant growth as a news source in recent years with the increasing popularity of online radio and podcasting. Listening to radio news while commuting is a primary way many Americans become informed about politics. Nationwide, one in five Americans prefers to get the news by listening to it on radio or from podcasts.[27]

In the 1990s, talk radio became an important source of political commentary as well as entertainment. Conservative radio hosts such as Rush Limbaugh and Sean Hannity have huge audiences and have helped to mobilize support for conservative political causes and candidates. In the political center or center left, National Public Radio (NPR) is a major source for in-depth political reporting. While public broadcasting, as noted earlier, has a much smaller share of the total media market in the United States than in many other countries, NPR remains a popular way for people to learn about politics each day.

While traditional AM/FM radio reaches almost all Americans and remains steady in its revenue, digital formats such as online radio and podcasting have expanded to the point that in 2018, 67 percent of Americans reported tuning in, up from just 20 percent in 2007.[28] And, on average, 28.5 million people tune in to NPR each week.[29]

DIGITAL MEDIA

The profound impact of the internet on mass communication has paralleled that of the steam-powered printing press in nineteenth-century America and the rise of the **penny press**, which allowed newspapers, books, and magazines to be widely read.[30] Today, even as the print newspaper business has consolidated, readership of online news increases. Digital media have become the medium of choice to consume entertainment, news, and information about politics for all age groups below 50.

This movement toward online news is more pronounced for younger people, 63 percent of whom often get news online, compared to just 36 percent of adults over age 65. Among older people, 8 in 10 frequently rely on television news, compared to just 16 percent for those age 18–29. Age differences are becoming more important in how people get news about politics, as young people are four times as likely to often get news from social media as those 65 and older.

Streaming video is a growing substitute for television for some viewers, fundamentally altering broadcast news, as dedicated channels provide political analysis, commentary, full-length features, and comedy. Presidential addresses are now regularly streamed live, and millions of people tune in to hear the president in this format.[31] As large gatherings were prohibited during the coronavirus pandemic in 2020, many

penny press cheap, tabloid-style newspaper produced in the nineteenth century, when mass production of inexpensive newspapers first became possible due to the steam-powered printing press; a penny press newspaper cost one cent compared with other papers, which cost more than five cents

political candidates streamed town halls and campaign speeches through live video to reach potential voters.

News aggregators such as Google News, Reddit, and RealClearPolitics generally compile and repackage stories that were created by other sources, and then deliver them online to consumers in convenient formats. They serve as a platform that allows users to share and comment on the news. The content producers include digital-only news organizations, mainstream media, social movement organizations, and ordinary users as well as political groups, governments, candidates, nonprofit organizations, corporations, and professional media organizations. Aggregators deliver thousands of news stories each day, as well as the latest public-opinion polls and their own synthesis of the headline news.

The term *digital citizenship* refers to the ability to participate in society and politics online. In 2019 73 percent of Americans were **digital citizens**, having home high-speed access and the skills to use it.[32] While less than half of the working poor (those earning less than $20,000 a year) have home broadband, 9 in 10 of those earning more than $100,000 a year do.[33] While broadband—wired or mobile access—is available to purchase in most places in the United States, affordability remains a barrier to access. These inequalities in access to digital information based on income are what is called the **digital divide**.[34] Because digital media are essential to participation in today's society, some argue that government and technology companies have a responsibility to provide affordable and universal access, as is provided by most other democratic countries. Smartphones, some argue, are helping to bridge the digital divide; as of 2016 more Americans owned a smartphone than a laptop computer.[35]

Social media, such as Facebook/Instagram, Reddit, and Twitter, tend to be a secondary source for politics and news for many Americans but are a primary source for young Americans. As the web becomes an increasingly important source for political news, young people may become more engaged.[36] Despite the high rate of exposure to political news via social media, young Americans overall are less engaged in politics than their older counterparts, though this may be changing. For example, among people 18–29 years old, voter turnout increased from 20 percent in 2014 to 36 percent in 2018, the largest percentage point increase for any group.[37]

In fact, use of social media for news is growing across all demographic groups, including older

news aggregator an application or feed that collects web content such as news headlines, blogs, podcasts, online videos, and more in one location for easy viewing

digital citizen a daily internet user with broadband (high-speed) home internet access and the technology and literacy skills to go online for employment, news, politics, entertainment, commerce, and other activities

digital divide the gap in access to the internet among demographic groups based on education, income, age, geographic location, and race/ethnicity

social media web- and mobile-based technologies that are used to turn communication into interactive dialogue among organizations, communities, and individuals; social media technologies take on many different forms, including text, blogs, podcasts, photographs, streaming video, Facebook, and Twitter

FIGURE 7.2
Social Media Users by Age, Race, Gender, and Education Level

People of different genders, ages, education levels, and races tend to use different social media sites to get news. What do you think causes this variation?

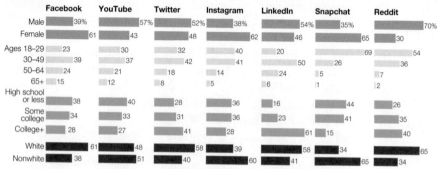

	Facebook	YouTube	Twitter	Instagram	LinkedIn	Snapchat	Reddit
Male	39%	57%	52%	38%	54%	35%	70%
Female	61	43	48	62	46	65	30
Ages 18–29	23	30	32	40	20	69	54
30–49	39	37	42	41	50	26	36
50–64	24	21	18	14	24	5	7
65+	15	12	8	5	6	1	2
High school or less	38	40	28	36	16	44	26
Some college	34	33	31	36	23	41	35
College+	28	27	41	28	61	15	40
White	61	48	58	39	58	34	65
Nonwhite	38	51	40	60	41	65	34

SOURCE: Elisa Shearer and Elizabeth Grieco, "Americans Are Wary of the Role Social Media Sites Play in Delivering the News," Pew Research Center, October 2, 2019 (accessed 6/4/2020).

people, both women and men, and groups defined by race, education, and income. Figure 7.2 shows the breakdown of each social media site's users across gender, age, education level, and race. As of 2019, 72 percent of Americans use social media, as do 90 percent of young people (age 18–29). Roughly 73 percent of Americans use YouTube, 69 percent use Facebook, 37 percent Instagram, and 22 percent Twitter, all of which feature political news.[38] With then-president Trump tweeting multiple times per day, and congressional leaders and other politicians using Twitter and Facebook, social media sites have become a news source in their own right, as well as forums to share news published in other media.

As discussed in Chapter 6, Obama was the first American president to use social media extensively in his campaign and during his administration. But Trump was the nation's first "Twitter President," communicating his opinions directly to the people, unmediated by the media or even his White House press staff. With over 81 million Twitter followers, Trump had an enormous audience. His unconventional political strategy involved using tweets and emotional speeches at live, televised rallies to communicate directly with the American people and set the media agenda (discussed later in this chapter), while attacking the credibility of other sources that provide information countering his statements.

On any given day, the president tweeted multiple times, often calling out his opponents in the famous celebrity take-down mode that he perfected during his years as a reality TV host. Among his core supporters, the truth was what Trump said it was on Twitter or in speeches before rally crowds. However, fact-checking websites such as PolitiFact have found that 70 percent of Trump's statements were false or misleading and another 15 percent were only half true.[39]

CITIZEN JOURNALISM

Digital news is creating a new generation of whistle-blowers, enhancing the media's traditional role as a watchdog against government corruption. **Citizen journalism** includes news reporting and political commentary by ordinary citizens and even crisis coverage from eyewitnesses on the scene, thus involving a wider range of voices in gathering news and interpreting political events. Cameras on cell phones give mil-lions of Americans the capacity to photograph or record events, thus providing eyewitness accounts. At the same time, social media permit users to upload videos that can be viewed by hundreds of thousands of subscribers or relayed by the main-stream media for even wider dissemination.

> **citizen journalism** news reported and distributed by citizens, rather than by professional journalists and for-profit news organizations

Citizen journalism supplements the work of professional journalists in many important ways. For one, new opinion leaders and voices have platforms to react to mainstream media, often improving the quality and accuracy of information reported. In recent years, for example, social media users have uncovered major factual errors in mainstream media reports and forced networks and newspapers to issue corrections. Furthermore, individuals and some online news outlets can post a story within minutes. This ability to scoop the mainstream media means digital media can frame stories about political candidates, for example, before those stories break in the mainstream media.[40]

By sharply lowering the technological and financial barriers that previously prevented all but a few individuals from reaching mass audiences, social media allow news created by ordinary people to be effective in political action. On the other hand, the freewheeling nature of social media often means that there is less of the traditional quality control provided by professional journalists and traditional institutional media. Because they do not face the burden of fact-checking required for the mainstream media or some digital-only news outlets, even well-meaning users can post false information.

BENEFITS OF ONLINE NEWS

The reasons Americans appear to prefer online news include (1) the convenience, (2) the up-to-the-minute currency of information, (3) the depth of information available, (4) the diversity of viewpoints, and (5) the low cost.[41]

Information online is always easily and rapidly available for those with access to the internet on a computer or through mobile devices. Pew surveys show that nearly half of those who access online news and political information cite its convenience.[42]

Online news can provide more information than the sound bites that dominate television and radio news. By blending more detailed and substantive treatment of topics with the emotive visual appeal of videos, digital media share the distinctive qualities of both print media (providing knowledge) and television (arousing inter-est and engagement).[43] Despite the multimedia capacities of digital media, most websites still rely heavily upon written text. Thus political "web surfing," which is based on reading, makes it easier for people to recall the information they encounter and, in turn, to acquire political knowledge.[44]

CONCERNS ABOUT ONLINE NEWS

The shift toward online media has also given rise to several major concerns. These include the quality of online news content, the increased presence of false information, and the negative effects of these factors on knowledge and tolerance.

Quality As already noted, the growing diversity of digital news sources has led to substantial variation in the quality of available information. Multiple perspectives create a livelier marketplace of ideas, but hate speech, unsubstantiated rumors, and factual errors can overwhelm thoughtful, original, and factually based voices, especially in anonymous online forums. This can influence public opinion, and it poses challenges for democratic government if people are misinformed.

Fake News and Misinformation Political candidates and leaders are particularly susceptible to online attacks because negative stories about them can easily "go viral," spreading quickly without fact-checking. **Fake news**—false stories circulated to benefit one candidate or party over another or just to generate ad revenue—is an increasing problem. In the 2016 presidential election, for example, circulation of the top 10 fake news stories on Facebook was more widespread than that of the top real news stories about the election. A study published by Stanford University found that fake news stories on social media about the election disproportionately favored Trump (the most widely publicized was the false story that the pope had endorsed him[45]). The Republican Senate Intelligence Committee and Special Counsel Robert Mueller both released reports that the Russian government was involved in generating many of the fake news stories to discredit Clinton and her campaign.[46]

Encountering misinformation online is a common problem; 38 percent of Americans say they often come across made-up news and information, and another 51 percent say they sometimes do. In response, people have changed their news and technology habits. Seventy-eight percent of Americans say they now regularly check the facts in news stories themselves, 63 percent have stopped getting news from a particular outlet, and 43 percent have reduced their overall news intake on social media.[47] (A number of websites, such as FactCheck.org, Snopes.com, the *Washington Post*'s Fact Checker, and PolitiFact.com, are devoted exclusively to checking the truthfulness of political claims.)

fake news false stories intended to be read as factual news that are circulated to benefit one candidate or party over another or to generate ad revenue

One example of fake news in the 2020 election surrounded the claim, which many people incorrectly believed, that Biden had voiced support for defunding the police, one of the reforms advocated for by the Black Lives Matter movement to end racial inequality in policing. Trump repeatedly made this claim about his opponent, and it was restated on conservative news channels. Sixty-six percent of Republicans who

Without traditional media's commitment to fact-checking, digital media sometimes spread inaccurate information and rumors. In 2008, the false claim that President Obama was not a natural-born citizen spread rapidly online and remained a top story even after Obama released his official long-form birth certificate.

frequently relied on Fox News or talk radio for political news believed that Biden supported defunding the police, versus 27 percent of people who use other news sources.

Despite frequent attacks on the mainstream media as fake news by conservatives and President Trump, only about a third of Americans blame journalists, the media, or a foreign government for the proliferation of fake news. Sixty percent of people say political leaders and their campaigns create a lot of made-up news, and about half say the same thing of political activist groups.[48] Two-thirds of Americans say that made-up news that is designed to mislead and video that is altered or made up causes "a great deal of confusion" about the basic facts of current events and politics. Nearly 8 in 10 Americans favor restrictions on this kind of content online.[49]

Effects on Tolerance and Knowledge Perhaps the greatest concern about politics in the digital age is that the very diversity of online news may actually *lower* tolerance for social, religious, and political diversity, leading to more partisan polarization and societal conflict. Fully 85 percent of Americans believe that the tone and nature of political debate in the United States has become more negative in recent years—as well as less respectful, less fact based, and less focused on policy issues.[50] Digital media often do not abide by traditional media's principle of objective journalism. Instead, the specialization of information online and on cable television means that liberals and conservatives alike can self-select media that are consistent with their existing beliefs and avoid exposure to information that might challenge these.[51] The natural tendency to select news that conforms with our own beliefs is strengthened by the way search engines cater to our individual preferences. This "filter bubble," or "self-selection bias," screens out information that might broaden our worldview.[52]

In addition, exposure to highly partisan news (for example, Fox News for conservatives, MSNBC for liberals) or to news on social media may actually lower political knowledge. Despite the dramatic rise in available political news and in

Evaluate a News Source

BILL ADAIR, the founder of the Pulitzer Prize–winning website PolitiFact and the Knight Professor of the Practice of Journalism and Public Policy at Duke University

 Every day we read news stories that we seek out, that friends and family send us, or that appear in our social media feed. How can we figure out which stories are credible and worthy of our attention?

Bill shared the techniques that fact checkers use to assess the content of stories in newspapers, on Facebook, and in other media sources. " Here are Bill's five tips for evaluating news sources:

1 **The most important step is to evaluate the web address.**
Established news sources will typically have a web address that ends in ".com," such as nbcnews.com or washingtonpost.com. Much good journalistic content is available at .org and .net addresses, but be suspicious and dig deeper when you see an ending other than .com. Of course all .coms are not reliable news sources—this is just step one.

2 **Check the labeling of the article to assess the type of content.** Is the article labeled as news or opinion or analysis? A lot of time we hear bad things about bias: "Bias! Bias is always bad!" But we read opinion because it is biased. But the best opinion publishers will label

the content as opinion, so you want to look for that label. The important point is to realize what you are reading: Is it a factual news article, or an opinion piece with a point of view?

3 **Check the attribution in the article—the sources cited.** Are there links to credible sources (government publications, research from prominent universities, and so on)? Do the links provide information that backs up the points in the article?

4 **Read the publication's "About" page (and be skeptical if it's missing).** Is the publisher a for-profit company or a nonprofit? If it is a nonprofit, does it list its funding sources?

Facebook posts

stated on March 20, 2020 in a text post:

Says the Coronavirus Aid, Relief, and Economic Security Act gives members of Congress a pay increase.

CONGRESS   FACEBOOK FACT-CHECKS   CORONAVIRUS   👤 FACEBOOK POSTS

This is a story from PolitiFact, showing a debunked Facebook post claiming the Coronavirus Aid Relief and Economic Security Act gives members of Congress a pay increase.

Is it transparent about any political leaning? If there is advertising, is it high quality ("Test Drive the Ford F-150 Today") or clickbait ("13 Potatoes That Look Like Channing Tatum")? Is the publisher transparent about its staff? Are they journalists? Or is it a business and the content essentially an infomercial?

5 **Figure out who's producing this content.** Is it written by the publication's staff or brought in from another source? If the content is copied or purchased from elsewhere, you need to check out that source as well.

All of these are clues that a smart reader can use to assess the credibility of what the reader is consuming. I also encourage people to engage with multiple points of view. One thing I recommend students do is try to get out of their filtered bubble by reading every day one person or post or publication that they disagree with. I think that's really important.

diversity of the media over the last few decades, average levels of political knowledge in the population have not increased, due to individuals "customizing" the political information they receive and therefore, as discussed earlier, being less likely to encounter new information that challenges their partisan viewpoints.[53] If the new digital media are to create a more informed democratic process, citizens must have "information literacy," the ability to find and evaluate information.[54] Education and critical thinking among citizens are more important than ever before.

DO AMERICANS TRUST THE MEDIA TODAY?

According to Pew, just one in five American adults has a lot of trust in "information from national news organizations," 49 percent have some trust, and 29 percent have not much/none at all.[55] (During the coronavirus pandemic, however, public trust in media seemed to rise, as most people believed the media was providing needed information.[56]) There are large partisan differences in trust of the news media; Democrats, for example, are 23 percentage points more likely than Republicans to think information from national news organizations is very trustworthy. Distrust in the mainstream media increased with the Trump presidency. In response to negative coverage of his campaign and administration, Trump waged an unprecedented war on the American media, frequently referring to major newspapers and broadcast media as "fake news" to discredit them (though these mainstream sources are generally not producing fabricated news). In a tweet shortly after his inauguration, he even called the press "the enemy of the American people."

Media Influence Shapes What We Think About

> **Analyze the ways the media can influence public opinion and politics**

The content and character of news programming—what the media choose to present and how they present it— can have far-reaching political consequences. The media can shape and modify, if not fully form, the public's perception of events, issues, and institutions. Media coverage can rally support for, or intensify opposition to, national policies on important matters such as health care, the economy, wars, or impeachment proceedings of a president. And as discussed earlier, it can enhance or damage the careers of political leaders.

At the same time, the media are influenced by the individuals or groups who are subjects of the news.

FOR CRITICAL ANALYSIS ▶

1. When they encounter fake news, what do highly politically aware people do compared to those who are less politically aware? Are there differences between the two groups in who spreads made-up news?

2. Young people are more likely to read news online than other age groups and are thus more likely to be exposed to misinformation online. What effect does this exposure have on young people's motivation to engage with politics?

Who Sees Fake News . . . and Who Does Something about It?

More and more Americans are getting their news via social media. Social media can be an effective and efficient way to share news and information, but it can also be used to spread fake news and misinformation. Who tends to encounter fake news, and what do those people do about it?

Who Sees, and Shares, Fake News?

Percentage of U.S. adults who . . . ▪ Highly politically aware* ▪ Less politically aware

46   29

Often come across made-up
news and information

5   14

Shared news and information
they knew at the time
was made up

46   51

Shared news and information
they later found out
was made up

What Do People Do about Fake News?

Percentage of U.S. adults who say the issue of made-up news and information has led them to . . .

▪ Highly politically aware*   ▪ Less politically aware

88
68

Check facts
of a news story
themselves

71
54

Stop getting
news from a
specific outlet

54   48

Change the
way they use
social media

34   28

Report or flag
a story they think
is made up

31   50

Reduce the amount
of news they
get overall

---

* Political awareness is measured by answers to three political knowledge questions and one question about
how closely respondents follow what is going on in government and public affairs.

SOURCE: Amy Mitchell et al, "Many Americans Say Made-Up News Is a Critical Problem That Needs to Be Fixed,"
Pew Research Center, June 5, 2019.

The president in particular has the power to set the news agenda through speeches, actions, and tweets. All politicians, for that matter, seek to shape their media images by cultivating good relations with reporters and by leaking news and staging news events.

In American political history, the media have played a central role in many major events. For example, in the civil rights movement of the 1950s and '60s, television images showing peaceful demonstrators attacked by club-swinging police helped to generate sympathy among northern Whites for the civil rights struggle and greatly increased the pressure on Congress to bring an end to segregation.[57] The media were also instrumental in compelling the Nixon administration to negotiate an end to American involvement in the Vietnam War by portraying the war as misguided and unwinnable.[58]

Conservatives have long charged that the liberal biases of journalists, and now media technology companies, result in distorted news coverage.[59] Though some professional journalists do lean Democratic, they generally defend their professionalism, insisting that their personal political leanings do not affect the way they perform their jobs.[60] Those who decry "the liberal media" seldom acknowledge the political leanings of media owners. Rupert Murdoch, for example, the chairman of the Fox Corporation, is a politically active conservative. Sheldon Adelson is another media mogul with a clear conservative partisan and ideological agenda, as is David D. Smith, who heads the Sinclair Broadcast Group. Sinclair owns more U.S. TV stations than any other media company.

Many news sources are perceived as distinctly left- or right-leaning, and people have a tendency to select ones that conform with their own ideology. With the exception of Fox News, there is not much credible evidence for the idea that any particular mainstream news source is, as a whole, explicitly ideologically biased in one direction or another, at least in terms of its news coverage. Most have been found to be centrist.[61]

HOW THE MEDIA INFLUENCE POLITICS

Traditional and digital media influence American politics in a number of important ways.[62] The power of all media collectively, offline and online, lies in their ability to shape what issues Americans think about (agenda setting and selection bias) and what opinions Americans hold about those issues (framing and priming).

agenda setting the power of the media to bring public attention to particular issues and problems

gatekeeping a process by which information and news are filtered to the public by the media; for example, a reporter choosing which sources to include in a story

Agenda Setting The first source of media power in politics is **agenda setting**, or gatekeeping: designating some issues, events, or people as important, and others not. The mass media act as a **gatekeeper** with the power to bring public attention to particular issues and problems. Groups or politicians that wish to generate support for policy proposals must secure media coverage. If the media are persuaded that an idea such as climate change is newsworthy, then they may declare it an "issue" that must be confronted or a "problem" to be solved, thus helping it clear the first hurdle in the policy-making process.

Some stories—such as those about wars, natural disasters, presidential impeachment, major health crises, and terrorist attacks—have such overwhelming significance that the main concern of political leaders is not whether a story will receive attention but whether they themselves will figure prominently and positively in media accounts. At the same time, many important issues don't often appear on the media's agenda, such as solar and wind power as alternative energy sources, homelessness, impacts of artificial intelligence on low-skill jobs, or election reform. When policy issues are not on the media's agenda they receive relatively little attention from politicians.

Political scientists have shown that the media have two "modes": an "alarm mode" for breaking stories and a "patrol mode" for covering them in greater depth.[63] The incentive to reach a wider audience (and generate ad revenue) often sets off the "alarm mode" around a story, after which news outlets go into "patrol mode" to monitor what effect (if any) the story has on government policy—until the next big story alarm goes off. This pattern results in skewed coverage of political issues, with a few issues receiving the majority of media attention while others receive none at all.

Political candidates also need the media's agenda-setting role to win elections. Candidates who receive positive news coverage gain momentum: they pick up political endorsements, attract campaign contributions, and win more support from voters.[64] In the 2020 Democratic primaries for president, Joe Biden exceeded the

During the 1960s, civil rights protesters learned a variety of techniques designed to elicit sympathetic media coverage. Television images of police brutality in Alabama led directly to the enactment of the 1965 Civil Rights Act.

media's expectations with his win in South Carolina and strong support among African Americans. Biden's victory earned him increased press attention and led him to win the Democratic nomination.[65]

Because most large media outlets are for-profit businesses looking for the largest possible audiences, they naturally tend to focus on stories with dramatic or entertainment value, such as crimes and scandals—especially those involving prominent people—and national emergencies. They also focus on who is ahead in elections (what is known as the horse race), instead of the policy issues.

What the mainstream media decide to report on or highlight and what they ignore or downplay have important implications. For example, the Bush tax cuts of 2001 and 2003, extended under Obama in 2010, dramatically increased the federal budget deficit and widened the income gap between the super-rich and most other Americans. But the media provided little coverage of these measures, the result being that 40 percent of Americans had no opinion on whether they favored the 2001 cuts.[66]

Framing Framing is the power of the media to influence how events, issues, and people's actions are interpreted and understood. Each issue or event has many different possible frames, each with a slightly different spin in describing the problem and possible solutions. Framing includes the media's power to include or exclude information. Frames, which political leaders and groups also help to develop, shape the meaning that individuals perceive from words or phrases, photographs, or video.[67]

In the lead-up to the 2016 election, for example, the mainstream media covered with zeal the controversy around Hillary Clinton's use of a private email server during her tenure as secretary of state with special focus on the risk of jeopardizing government secrets. The issue dominated the media agenda, especially in the 10 days before the election, when FBI director James Comey reopened the investigation into Clinton's email server. Clinton was framed by the media as possibly going to jail for her allegedly illegal use of a private email server (Trump even nicknamed her "crooked Hillary"). Clinton herself credits media coverage of the FBI investigation for changing public opinion and allowing Trump to win the 2016 presidential election.

Priming Another important way the media can shape political events is by **priming**, which involves calling attention to some issues, and not others, when evaluating political officials.[68] Priming is the power the media have to alter how voters make choices.

framing the power of the media to influence how events and issues are interpreted

priming the process of making some criteria more important than others when evaluating a politician, problem, or issue

While agenda setting is about gatekeeping and what issues the media are covering (such as presidential impeachment or the coronavirus pandemic), framing and priming involve the media filtering the news and providing cues to the public for how to interpret issues or events. As with agenda setting and framing, news media are not alone in priming; elected officials, interest groups, and other political players compete over all three in hopes of influencing public opinion.

Priming involves the public judging a politician according to the media's attention to one issue rather than others. In the lead-up to the 2020 elections, the coronavirus pandemic was in the national media spotlight. The continuing public health crisis coupled with the economic crisis became the most important lens through which the public evaluated the presidential candidates, benefiting Biden and hurting Trump.

Journalists Shape Political News

Describe the relationship between politicians and journalists

News coverage, or the content of the news, comes from numerous sources. Governments, politicians, corporations, interest groups, nonprofit organizations, and others produce press releases and hold press conferences to draw attention to issues and tell their side of the story. Journalists also gain information through investigative journalism and media leaks.

MEDIA LEAKS

Leaks, the disclosure of confidential government information to the news media, may originate from a variety of sources. These include "whistle-blowers," lower-level officials who hope to publicize what they view as their bosses' or the government's improper activities. In 1971, for example, Daniel Ellsberg, a minor Defense Department staffer, sought to discredit official justifications for America's military involvement in Vietnam by leaking top-secret documents to the press. The Pentagon Papers—the Defense Department's own secret history of the war—were published by the *New York Times* and the *Washington Post* after the U.S. Supreme Court ruled that the government could not block their release.[69] The Pentagon's credibility was severely damaged, hastening the erosion of public support for the war. Most leaks, though, originate not with low-level whistle-blowers but rather with senior government officials, prominent politicians, and political activists.

The mass media exposed possible misconduct by President Trump in a July 25, 2019, phone call between Trump and Ukrainian president Volodymyr Zelensky. A government whistle-blower alleged that Trump had pressured the Ukrainian president to open a corruption investigation against 2020 Democratic presidential candidate and former vice president Joe Biden—threatening to withhold $400 million in U.S. military aid if Zelensky didn't comply. The *Wall Street Journal* was one of the first to report that the military aid to Ukraine had been deliberately held up by the Trump administration in the weeks before the phone call. While Trump denied wrongdoing, the House of Representatives opened an impeachment inquiry of the president. The House voted to impeach Trump on December 18, 2019, on two articles of impeachment—abuse of power and obstruction of Congress; Trump was acquitted on both counts by the Republican-controlled Senate on February 5, 2020.

ADVERSARIAL JOURNALISM

The political power of the news media vis-à-vis the government has greatly increased in recent years through the growing prominence of **adversarial journalism**, a form of reporting in which the media adopt a skeptical or even hostile posture toward the government and public officials.

On the presidential level, the growth of adversarial journalism represented a reversal of the relationship between presidents and the media that had developed through much of the twentieth century. By communicating directly to the electorate through newspapers and magazines, Theodore Roosevelt and Woodrow Wilson established political constituencies for themselves, independent of party organizations, and thereby strengthened their own power relative to that of Congress. President Franklin Delano Roosevelt used the radio, most notably in his famous fireside chats, to reach out to voters throughout the nation and to make himself the center of American political life. Subsequent presidents all tried to use the media to enhance their popularity, and friendly relationships with journalists became a key strategy of presidential administrations.

The Vietnam War shattered this relationship between the press and the presidency. During the early stages of U.S. involvement, American officials in Vietnam who disapproved of the way the war was being conducted leaked to reporters information critical of administrative policy. Publication of this material infuriated the White House, which pressured publishers to block its release, but the national broadcast media and especially the two leading national newspapers, the *Washington Post* and the *New York Times*, refused to do so. As the war dragged on, adverse media coverage fanned antiwar sentiment among the public and in Congress. In turn, these shifts in opinion emboldened journalists and publishers to continue to present news reports critical of the war.

The media were also central figures in the Watergate affair, the cluster of scandals that ultimately forced President Nixon to resign from office in 1974. A series of investigations led by the *Washington Post* uncovered various crimes of which Nixon was guilty, leading to threats of impeachment and his subsequent resignation. Gradually, a generation of journalists developed a commitment to adversarial journalism.

Adversarial journalism intensified during Trump's administration as the president became embroiled in a federal investigation into possible collusion between Russia and Trump's 2016 campaign for president. The national news media revealed how Russia had used a sophisticated cyber campaign to interfere in the 2016 election to the benefit of the Trump campaign; they also closely followed the federal investigation led by Robert Mueller into whether anyone close to Trump had participated in the Russian interference.

adversarial journalism
a model of reporting in which the journalist's role involves adopting a stance of opposition and a combative style in order to expose perceived wrongdoings

Without rigorous investigative and adversarial journalism, citizens would not have the means (and information) necessary to hold their elected representatives accountable. It is easy to criticize the media for their aggressive tactics of investigation, publicity, and exposure, but without them, important questions about the conduct of American foreign and domestic policy, police violence, drone attacks, election interference by foreign governments, political corruption, and civil liberty violations may not ever be raised. Adversarial journalism is a critical part of what makes democratic governments work.

Regulation of the Media Is Limited

> **Describe the evolution of rules that govern broadcast media**

In many countries, such as China, the government exercises strict control over traditional media content. In others, the government owns some of the country's broadcast media (for example, the BBC in Britain) but does not tell the media what to say.

In the United States, the print and online media are essentially free from government interference. Broadcast radio and television, on the other hand, are regulated by the Federal Communications Commission (FCC). Radio and TV stations must have FCC licenses, which must be renewed every five years. Through regulations prohibiting obscenity, indecency, and profanity, the FCC has sought to prohibit radio and television stations from airing explicit sexual and excretory references between 6 A.M. and 10 P.M., the hours when the audience is most likely to include children. Generally speaking, FCC regulation applies only to the over-the-air broadcast media and not to cable television, the internet, or satellite radio.

In 1996, Congress passed the Telecommunications Act, a broad effort to end most regulations of business practices and mergers, allowing the formation of media

The debate over net neutrality highlights fundamental questions about democracy. If the media are intended to be a marketplace of ideas, what should the government do to regulate that marketplace? Should any single entity be allowed to exert more influence or control, or should everyone be allowed to participate equally?

tech giants and media conglomerates. The legislation loosened restrictions on media ownership and allowed telephone companies, cable television providers, and broadcasters to compete with one another to provide telecommunication services. Following the passage of this act, mergers between telephone and cable companies and different entertainment media produced a greater concentration of media ownership than had been possible since regulation of the industry began in 1934. In radio, for example, a 40-station ownership cap was lifted, leading to an unprecedented consolidation. ClearChannel Communications (rebranded as iHeartMedia in 2014) grew from 40 to 1,200 stations.

Although the government's ability to regulate the content of the internet is limited, the FCC has used its licensing power to impose several regulations that can affect the political content of radio and TV broadcasts. The first of these is the **equal time rule**, under which broadcasters must provide to candidates for the same political office equal opportunities to communicate their messages to the public. Under the terms of the Telecommunications Act, during the 45 days before an election, broadcasters are required to make time available to candidates at the lowest rate charged for that time slot. The second regulation affecting the content of broadcasts is the **right of rebuttal**, which requires that individuals be given the opportunity to respond to personal attacks.

For many years, a third important federal regulation was the *fairness doctrine*. Under this rule, broadcasters that aired programs on controversial issues were required to provide time for opposing views. In addition, the fairness doctrine included a requirement that TV and radio stations cover controversial issues of public and social importance in their communities. In 1985, however, the FCC stopped enforcing the fairness doctrine on the grounds that there were so many radio and television stations—to say nothing of newspapers and news magazines—that many different viewpoints were already being presented without each station being required to try to present all sides of every argument. In 1987 the FCC officially revoked the fairness doctrine. Critics charge that in many media markets the number of competing viewpoints is actually quite small.

equal time rule the requirement that broadcasters provide candidates for the same political office equal opportunities to communicate their messages to the public

right of rebuttal a Federal Communications Commission regulation giving individuals the right to have the opportunity to respond to personal attacks made on a radio or television broadcast

The Media and Democracy: What Do You Think?

The freedom of the press is essential to democratic government. Ordinary citizens depend on the media to investigate wrongdoing, publicize and explain governmental policy, evaluate politicians, and bring to light matters that might otherwise be known to only a handful of governmental insiders. Without free and active media, democratic government would be virtually impossible. Citizens would have few means through which to know or assess the government's actions—other than the claims or pronouncements of the government itself. Moreover, without active (indeed, aggressive) media, citizens would be hard-pressed to make informed choices among competing candidates at the polls. But the rise of digital media has fundamentally changed how political information is gathered and distributed. News today is participatory and involves citizens as well as professional journalists. New platforms raise new questions about who should decide what content is disseminated.

★ What do you think of investigations into online content and the debates over the responsibilities and liabilities of digital media companies such as Facebook and Twitter? Should they monitor and edit content and users? Should they be legally responsible for content that users post? What would Christopher Blair, featured at the beginning of this chapter, say?

★ How widely do your friends and family seek out information? Do they tend to rely on a small number of sources, or reach out more broadly? What about your media habits?

★ What media sources do you see playing the role of "watchdog" over government and politics? What kinds of stories do they publish? Do you see these sources as biased or unbiased?

Practice Quiz

1. Public broadcasting outlets that receive partial funding through license fees and government subsidies *(p. 185)*
   a) are prohibited by the Constitution from operating in the United States.
   b) account for less than 5 percent of media market share in the United States.
   c) account for nearly one-third of media market share in the United States.
   d) account for approximately half of media market share in the United States.
   e) account for more than two-thirds of media market share in the United States.

2. More than three-fourths of daily print newspapers are owned by *(p. 187)*
   a) large media conglomerates.
   b) the national government.
   c) small local companies.
   d) private individuals.
   e) the employees who run them.

3. Which of the following best describes the relationship that the news media have with big technology companies? *(p. 188)*
   a) Technology companies have largely stayed separate from the private, for-profit companies that drive news media.
   b) The news media and technology companies each promote news catered to completely different audiences.
   c) Traditional news media rely on ad revenue, while big technology companies are able to promote news without relying on ad revenue.
   d) Big technology companies place a higher value on fact-checking and editorial standards than traditional news media have in the past.
   e) Technology companies are increasingly developing or buying major news media companies.

4. Digital citizenship requires *(p. 193)*
   a) a subscription to one or more online newspapers.
   b) high-speed internet access and the skills to use it.
   c) a smartphone.
   d) a social media account, such as Facebook or Twitter.
   e) maintaining a political blog.

5. Which of the following is *not* a reason that many Americans appear to prefer online news? *(p. 195)*
   a) the depth of the information available online
   b) the diversity of online viewpoints
   c) the convenience of getting news online
   d) the accuracy and objectivity compared to traditional media outlets
   e) the up-to-the-minute currency of online information

6. Which of the following best describes Americans' level of trust in the media today? *(p. 200)*
   a) Nearly 90 percent of all Americans express high levels of trust in national news organizations.
   b) Just 10 percent of all Americans express high levels of trust in national news organizations.
   c) Republicans are more likely than Democrats to think that information from national news organizations is very trustworthy.
   d) Democrats are more likely than Republicans to think that information from national news organizations is very trustworthy.
   e) Republicans and Democrats are equally likely to think that information from national news organizations is very trustworthy.

7. Which of the following best describes the level of ideological bias in the news media overall? *(p. 202)*
   a) Most sources exhibit a clear liberal bias.
   b) Most sources exhibit a clear conservative bias.
   c) Most sources have been found to be centrist.
   d) Sources with conservative owners are likely to be conservative, and those with liberal owners are likely to be liberal.
   e) Sources tend to change from right-leaning to left-leaning, or vice versa, depending on which party has more power in government at the time.

8. *Framing* is the power the media has to *(p. 204)*
   a) deny coverage to certain politicians.
   b) bring public attention to particular issues and problems.
   c) designate some issues, events, or people as important, and others not.
   d) influence the issues that people consider when making judgments about public officials.
   e) influence how events, issues, and people's actions are interpreted and understood.

9. *Adversarial journalism* refers to *(p. 206)*
   a) the recent shift in American society away from general-purpose sources of information and toward narrowly focused niche sources.
   b) an era in American history when political parties provided all of the financing for newspapers.
   c) a form of reporting in which the media adopt a skeptical or even hostile posture toward the government and public officials.
   d) a form of reporting in which the media adopt an accepting and friendly posture toward the government and public officials.
   e) the process of preparing the public to take a particular view of an event or political actor.

10. In general, FCC regulations apply only to *(p. 207)*
   a) cable television.
   b) internet websites.
   c) over-the-air broadcast media.
   d) satellite radio.
   e) newspapers and magazines.

11. The now-defunct rule that required broadcasters to provide time for opposing views when they aired programs on controversial issues was called *(p. 208)*
   a) the equal time rule.
   b) the fairness doctrine.
   c) the right of rebuttal.
   d) the response rule.
   e) the free speech doctrine.

Key Terms

media *(p. 183)*
media monopoly *(p. 187)*
broadcast media *(p. 191)*
penny press *(p. 192)*
news aggregator *(p. 193)*
digital citizen *(p. 193)*
digital divide *(p. 193)*
social media *(p. 193)*
citizen journalism *(p. 195)*

fake news *(p. 196)*
agenda setting *(p. 202)*
gatekeeping *(p. 202)*
framing *(p. 204)*
priming *(p. 204)*
adversarial journalism *(p. 206)*
equal time rule *(p. 208)*
right of rebuttal *(p. 208)*

Political Parties and Interest Groups

WHAT GOVERNMENT DOES AND WHY IT MATTERS

Early in 2009, before the term *Tea Party* had been coined, Keli Carender was a conservative blogger in Seattle. She became concerned that the stimulus bill that Congress was considering to address the financial crisis and ensuing recession was simply more of "big government" trampling on her "freedom and liberty." After calls and emails to her congressional representative were ignored, she organized a "Porkulus Protest" in Seattle without support from any national organization. "I just got fed up and planned it. . . . I had 120 people show up, which is amazing . . . and on only four days' notice!! This was due to me spending the entire four days calling and emailing every person, think tank, policy center, university professors (that were sympathetic), etc. in town, and not stopping until the day came." She also contacted conservative author Michelle Malkin, who publicized the rally on her blog. At a second rally later that month, twice as many people showed up, in part because Carender had collected email addresses at the first rally.[1]

Individuals can have profound effects on political parties. Keli Carender took her belief in limited government and her anger over excessive government spending and started the Tea Party movement, which has strongly influenced the direction of the Republican Party.

Carender's protests were among the first events in what became known as the Tea Party movement, which gained steam when CNBC business analyst Rick Santelli called for a "tea party" protest of the Obama administration's plans for addressing the Great Recession. This conservative populist movement challenged not only Democratic policies but also the Republican Party establishment. As political candidates associated with the Tea Party ran for office starting in the 2010 midterm elections, they sometimes won Republican Party endorsement but often ran against the mainstream party. Donald Trump courted Tea Party supporters during his presidential campaign in 2016.

In many ways, Carender's activities in helping to form the Tea Party movement are similar to how interest groups organize and attempt to shape politics. Both link individuals and groups to government using democratic mechanisms, in order to change or shape government policy. In Carender's case, her efforts and those of the Tea Party directed their focus at both the government and the political parties, although the Tea Party movement grew and thrived within the Republican Party, which the movement succeeded in pushing in a more conservative direction.

Even though parties and interest groups are similar in that they exist to influence the direction of government, political parties are different from interest groups. Parties are broad coalitions while interest groups are typically more specific and numerous. Parties organize to nominate candidates and to win elected office; interest groups do not, although interest groups are increasingly engaged in political campaigns and help candidates and parties favorable to their policy goals win elections. In other words, parties tend to concern themselves with the *personnel* of government, while interest groups tend to focus on the *policies* of government. In this chapter we will examine the nature and consequences of political parties and interest groups in the United States.

CHAPTER GOALS

★ **Define political parties and their functions in politics (pp. 215–20)**

★ **Identify the reasons for and sources of party identification and increased party polarization (pp. 220–26)**

★ **Describe the history of U.S. party systems and the influence of third parties (pp. 226–32)**

★ **Describe the major types of interest groups and who they represent (pp. 232–39)**

★ **Explain how interest groups try to influence government and policy (pp. 240–46)**

What Are Political Parties?

Define political parties and their functions in politics

Political parties, like interest groups, are organizations that seek influence over government. They can generally be distinguished from interest groups on the basis of their mission. A party seeks to control the government by nominating candidates, electing them to public office, and winning elections. Interest groups do not seek to control the operation of government or win elections, but rather try to influence government policies, often through lobbying elected officials and contributing to campaigns.

Although the Founders did not envision the rise of political parties, these quickly became a core feature of the American political system. Parties and **partisanship** organize the political world and simplify complex policy debates for citizens and elected officials. Parties also play central roles in mobilizing citizens to vote, informing the public about government policies, and ensuring that the public voice is heard in policy debates.

THE UNITED STATES' TWO-PARTY SYSTEM

Over the past 200 years, Americans' conception of political parties has changed considerably. In the early Republic, parties were seen as threats to the social order and to the stability of the new democratic government and were referred to as "factions." In the *Federalist Papers*, both Alexander Hamilton and James Madison condemned factions that pursued narrow self-interest over the well-being of the nation as a whole.[2] In his 1796 Farewell Address, President George Washington warned his countrymen to shun partisan politics. Nonetheless, a **two-party system** emerged quickly. Beginning with the Federalists and the Jeffersonian Republicans in the late 1780s, two major parties have dominated national politics, although which two parties has changed with the times and issues.

Most other democratic countries use a proportional representation system for elections to their national legislature or parliament, in which some or all seats are allocated to political parties based on their share of the total votes cast in the election (if a party wins 40 percent of the votes in an election, it controls 40 percent of the seats in the legislature). In contrast, in most elections the United States uses geographic single-member districts combined with winner-take-all (or first-past-the-post) elections. For example, in a U.S. House district election, the candidate who wins the most votes (the plurality) wins the seat, no matter if that candidate won 40 percent, 51 percent, or 80 percent of the overall vote. That is why the system is winner-take-all: unlike in proportional

political parties organized groups that attempt to influence the government by electing their members to important government offices

partisanship identification with or support of a particular party or cause

two-party system a political system in which only two parties have a realistic opportunity to compete effectively for control

representation, no runners-up gain seats in government. Other countries require the winning candidate to win a majority (50 percent plus one), not just a simple plurality. This method of election exists because it is set out in the rules and laws that govern it. These laws encourage and support the American two-party system.

POLITICAL PARTIES ORGANIZE AND CHANNEL MANY VOICES

Political parties speak on behalf of citizens who individually have little voice but collectively, acting through the parties, can have a loud voice. Parties have been the chief points of contact between government officials, on the one side, and individual citizens and interest groups, on the other.

RECRUITING CANDIDATES

One of the most important party activities is the recruitment of candidates to run for office. Parties recruit candidates who are loyal to the party's philosophy and policy agenda, with the goal of controlling government and adopting laws that are consistent with the party's platform. Each election year, candidates run for thousands of state and local offices and congressional seats. For "open" seats, where no incumbent is running for re-election, party leaders attempt to identify strong candidates and encourage them to run. An ideal candidate has experience holding public office and the capacity to raise enough money to mount a serious campaign, especially if that candidate will face an incumbent or a well-funded opponent in the general election. Party leaders often have difficulty finding strong candidates and persuading them to run, especially at the state and local levels.[3]

PARTY ORGANIZATIONS DEFINE HOW PARTIES OPERATE

In the United States, **party organizations**, usually called committees, exist at every level of government (see Figure 8.1). State law and party rules dictate how such committees are created. Usually, committee members are elected at local party business meetings, called caucuses, or as part of primary elections. The best-known examples of these committees are at the national level: the Democratic National Committee (DNC) and the Republican National Committee (RNC).

NATIONAL COMMITTEES

The DNC and RNC are gatekeepers for their respective parties, influencing which candidates have a chance to win the primaries by giving candidates money for their campaigns. They also try to minimize disputes within the party, work to enhance its media image, and set the rules for primary elections and caucuses. Sometimes party rules cause disputes. The RNC was criticized for holding too many televised presidential debates in 2016, which some

party organization the formal structure of a political party, including its leadership, election committees, active members, and paid staff

Comparing Party Systems

While the American political system is dominated by two political parties, many countries have more than two parties. The number varies depending on the electoral rules in place. Here we compare the United States, which uses winner-take-all electoral rules, with the Netherlands, which uses a proportional representation system, and Mexico, which uses a mix of both systems in determining seats in its lower house.

1. Which system do you think would do a better job of reflecting the will of the voters? Do you see any evidence for your answer in the data?

2. We can see that 3 percent of Americans voted for third parties in Congressional elections but all the seats in the House are held by Democrats and Republicans. Why do you think third parties in America find it so difficult to win seats in the legislature?

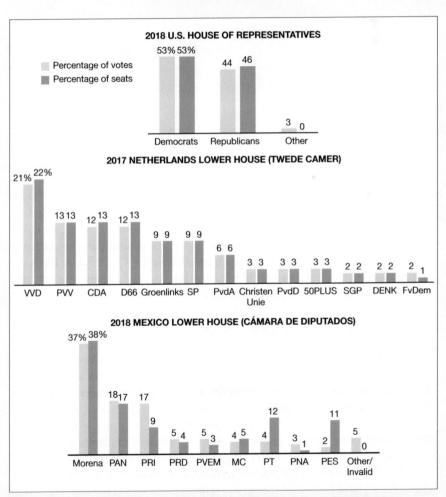

SOURCE: U.S. Clerk of the House of Representatives, https://history.house.gov/Institution/Election-Statistics/Election-Statistics/; www.kiesraad.nl; www.electionguide.org/elections/id/3064/; and https://computos2018.ine.mx/#/diputaciones/nacional/1/3/1/1 (accessed 8/8/19).

FIGURE 8.1

How American Parties Are Organized

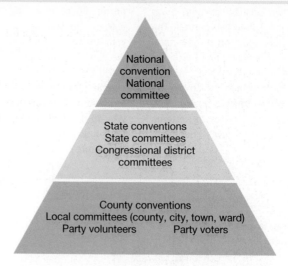

National
convention
National
committee

State conventions
State committees
Congressional district
committees

County conventions
Local committees (county, city, town, ward)
Party volunteers   Party voters

think helped Trump (a former television celebrity) win his party's nomination. In 2020, the DNC used performance in polls as a key criterion for candidates to qualify for the nationally televised presidential debates, which some candidates objected to.

Money for campaigns is critical to winning elections. The DNC and RNC have each established Super PACs (political action committees) as critical fundraising organizations. These Super PACs promote and publicize political issues, including by airing campaign ads. As nonprofit political advocacy groups, they can claim tax-exempt status under Section 527 of the Internal Revenue Code. Super PACs can raise and spend unlimited amounts of money as long as their activities are not coordinated with those of formal party organizations or candidates.

PARTIES SEEK TO CONTROL GOVERNMENT

When the bumps, bruises, and dust of the campaign and election have settled, does it matter which party has won? Yes. The party with the majority of seats in the House, Senate, or in the seat of the presidency controls party leadership positions and sets the policy-making agenda.

Parties and Policy For decades, one of the most familiar complaints about American politics was that the two major parties tried to be all things to all people and were therefore indistinguishable from each other. But since the 1980s fundamental differences have emerged between the positions of Democratic and Republican party leaders on many key issues.

For example, the national leadership of the Republican Party supports reducing spending on social and health care programs, cutting taxes on corporations and the wealthy, protecting rights of gun owners, reducing immigration to the United States, maintaining or increasing military spending, preserving traditional family structures, and opposing abortion. The Republican Party also opposes government regulation of businesses, including environmental laws.

The Democratic Party, on the other hand, supports expanded funding for public education and social services, a national health insurance system, increased regulation of business to address climate change, higher taxes on the wealthy and corporations to reduce economic inequality, restrictions on gun ownership, and consumer protection programs. Democrats also support legalized abortion and support protecting the rights of racial, ethnic, religious, and sexual minorities and undocumented immigrants.

Partisan conflict has intensified in recent years. Americans believe there are stronger conflicts in U.S. society today between Democrats and Republicans than between Blacks and White non-Hispanics, the rich and the poor, and other social groups. In 2020, 91 percent of Americans said conflicts between Democrats and Republicans are either strong or very strong.[4]

FACTIONS WITHIN THE PARTIES

While party polarization, or the depth of divisions between Republicans and Democrats, is at an all-time high, the divisions *within* each party may be nearly as important. Parties are coalitions of people and groups who agree on a broad common approach to issues but also represent many diverse interests competing for power and influence. For leaders in Congress and state legislatures, keeping these different groups working toward shared goals can be difficult.

The Republican Party today, for example, is divided in at least four major ways. Pro-business conservatives, or traditional Republicans, such as Nebraska senator Benjamin Sasse, are a generally affluent group that favors small government and lower corporate taxes along with global free trade. Far-right or alt-right conservatives, such as President Trump, are opposed to immigration and global free trade and to institutions like the United Nations. They favor tariffs on imports to the United States in order to protect American-made products and tend to be social conservatives, often with lower levels of education. Social and religious conservatives, such as Texas senator Ted Cruz, are primarily driven by their values on cultural and moral issues, such as opposition to abortion and gay marriage. Finally, libertarians, such as Kentucky senator Rand Paul, believe in small government, less government regulation, and more individual freedoms, and they oppose foreign wars. These divisions can present severe challenges for governing.

In 2020, Democrats in Congress staunchly opposed President Trump and his policies, but differences between the moderate and progressive wings of the party threatened to undermine Democratic Party unity. The super-progressives like members of "The Squad"—Representatives Alexandria Ocasio-Cortez (N.Y.), Ayanna Pressley (Mass.), Rashida Tlaib (Mich.), and Ilhan Omar (Minn.)—seek European

Union–type policies to create universal national health care and to eliminate private health insurance. Traditional Democrats support traditional liberal government policies, but seek more incremental rather than dramatic change. Such divisions may have contributed to the Democrats losing the White House and Congress in 2016, as many Sanders supporters refused to vote for Clinton in the general election and 10 percent voted for Trump. Democrats strongly favor expanded social safety nets, reducing student-loan debt, and addressing climate change.

Party Identification Guides Voters

> **Identify the reasons for and sources of party identification and increased party polarization**

One reason why parties are so important is that individuals tend to develop an identification with one of them at a young age. **Party identification** has been likened to wearing blue- or red-tinted glasses: they color voters' understanding of politics in general and are the most important cue in how to vote in elections. Party identification can create information bubbles and filters, where citizens follow news media or candidates on social media that are of the same partisan leaning. The vast majority of Republicans vote for Republican candidates, and the vast majority of Democrats vote for Democrats.

Although it is partly an emotional attachment, party identification also has a rational component. Voters generally form attachments to the party that reflects their views and interests. Once those attachments are formed, usually in youth, they are likely to persist and even be handed down to children, unless some very strong factors convince individuals that their party is no longer serving their interests.[5]

Yet 34 percent of Americans describe themselves as independents, while 33 percent call themselves Democrats and 29 percent Republicans. The number of people identifying as Democrats has outnumbered Republican identifiers for a long time, but independents are growing, especially among young people (see Figure 8.2). However, most independents lean toward one of the major parties, and political scientists often consider independents who lean as identifying with that party. Independent leaners have been called "hidden partisans" because even if they hold policy opinions similar to partisans they don't tend to voice these opinions publicly.[6] Just 7–10 percent of Americans are true political independents—they tend to avoid politics and are significantly less interested in politics.[7]

party identification an individual voter's psychological ties to one party or another

party activists partisans who contribute time, energy, and effort to support their party and its candidates

Party identification gives citizens a stake in election outcomes that goes beyond the particular race at hand. This is why strong party identifiers are more likely to vote, to be contacted by campaigns, and to become activists for their party. **Party activists** are those who not only vote but also actively contribute their time, money, and effort to party affairs, organizations, and elections, thus giving them an outsize role in the party. They also tend to be more ideologically extreme than the average person in the party.

FIGURE 8.2

Trends in Party Identification, 1970–2019

Over time, the Democrats have lost strength as more Americans identified themselves as Republicans and independents. Since 2004, however, the number of Democrats has held steady and the number of Republicans has declined, while the number of Americans identifying as independent of either party has increased to an all-time high. Why do you think this is?

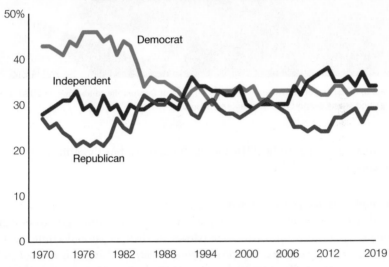

PERCENTAGE IDENTIFYING THEMSELVES AS . . .

SOURCE: Pew Research Center, "Democratic Edge in Party Identification Narrows Slightly," June 2, 2020, https://www.pewresearch.org/politics/2020/06/02/democratic-edge-in -party-identification-narrows-slightly/ (accessed 8/7/20).

WHO ARE REPUBLICANS AND DEMOCRATS?

The Democratic and Republican parties are currently the only truly national parties that draw substantial support from every region of the country. Each party draws support from different social groups, defined by race and ethnicity, gender, religion, ideology, region, and age.[8] These many different divides are becoming more important in defining partisanship.[9]

The Democratic Party at the national level seeks to unite organized labor, the poor, the working class, middle-class professionals, people with college degrees, nonwhite racial and ethnic groups, the young, the nonreligious, and civilian government workers. Most liberals identify with the Democrats. The Republicans, by contrast, appeal to business, non-Hispanic Whites, non-college-educated Whites, the very wealthy, the elderly, military families, and religious conservatives. Most conservatives identify with the Republicans. Women are more likely to affiliate with the Democrats than the Republicans. Rural areas tend to vote for Republicans, while urban areas are dominated by Democrats. The suburbs are a swing region, more evenly divided between Republicans and Democrats. Suburbs in larger metro

Members of racial and ethnic minority groups tend to favor Democratic candidates. In 2020, Joe Biden gained strong support from African Americans.

areas swung Democrat in the 2018 and 2020 elections, but those in smaller metros often remained Republican.

Race and Ethnicity The United States' growing racial and ethnic diversity is reflected both in changing partisanship among racial and ethnic groups and growing divisions between the two major parties in their racial and ethnic makeup. One group whose partisan allegiance remains largely unchanged is African Americans; approximately 90 percent describe themselves as Democrats and support Democratic candidates in national, state, and local elections. In 2020, between 87–89 percent of African Americans voted for Democrat Joe Biden for president.[10] In contrast, a small majority of non-Hispanic Whites regularly vote Republican; in 2018, 53 percent of non-Hispanic Whites overall and 56 percent of non-Hispanic Whites without a college degree supported Republican House candidates.[11]

Latinos and Latinas now make up over 18 percent of the population and as voters are less monolithic than African Americans. Cuban Americans, for example, generally vote Republican, whereas Mexican Americans have favored Democrats. Overall, however, a strong Democratic shift occurred in 2008, when 67 percent of Latinos supported Obama. This trend has continued, with 63–65 percent voting for Democrats in 2020.[12] Latino party affiliation is particularly important because it has the potential to alter the electoral map and change traditionally "red" states (states that reliably vote for the Republican presidential candidate) to "blue" states (states that reliably vote for the Democratic presidential candidate).[13]

Asian Americans were also politically divided until recent years but now solidly favor Democratic candidates. In 2018, 77 percent voted for Democratic House candidates, and in 2020 nearly two-thirds voted for Joe Biden. Like Latinos, they are extremely diverse, reflecting cultural differences and political influences from their home countries.

Gender Women are more likely to support Democrats than Republicans, and men are more likely to
support Republicans. This difference, known as the
gender gap, reflects the fact that women tend to prioritize health care, education, and social services, issues

emphasized by the Democratic Party, while men tend to prioritize budgetary and
economic issues and national security, issues emphasized by the Republican Party.
There are also more women lawmakers in the Democratic party. The gender gap
in voting has hovered at 10 percent since 1992 but is now wider than at any point
over the past two decades. In 2020, the gender gap was approximately 15 percent,
with women favoring Democrat Joe Biden (57 percent) to Republican Donald
Trump (42 percent). Men favored Trump over Biden 53 to 45 percent.

Religion Religious beliefs and preferences also affect partisanship. White Protestants are more likely to identify with the Republican Party. White evangelical
Protestants, in particular, have been drawn to the Republicans' conservative stances
on social issues, such as opposition to same-sex marriage and abortion. Jews are
among the Democratic Party's most loyal constituent groups, with nearly 90 percent
of Jewish Americans describing themselves as Democrats. Those unaffiliated with
a religion—a growing segment of the population, at roughly 25 percent—strongly
favor the Democratic Party.[14] Sixty-eight percent of people unaffiliated with a
religion supported Democrats in 2018.[15]

Class Rising income inequality has led to economic populism in the United States.
The patterns of class voting that emerged from the New Deal of the 1930s were
simple: upper-income Americans were considerably more likely to be Republican,
whereas lower-income Americans were far more likely to identify with the Democrats, and this pattern still generally holds, driven by differences between the two
parties on economic issues.[16] In general, Republicans support reductions in taxes,
in regulation of business, and in spending on social services—positions that often
reflect the interests of the wealthy. Democrats favor increasing government spending
and raising taxes on the wealthy—positions consistent with the interests of less
affluent Americans.

But beginning in the 1970s, many White working-class voters turned to the
Republican Party, and today a majority of White workers without a college degree
vote Republican, while working-class minorities tend to vote Democratic. In the
2016 election, non-college-educated voters favored Trump over Clinton by 8 percentage points (52 to 44 percent), but in 2020, that gap narrowed to 2 percent as
Democrats gained ground among this group. College-educated voters continued to
support Democrats in 2020, favoring Biden over Trump 55 to 43 percent.

Region Since the 2000 election, maps showing the regional distribution of the
vote have given rise to the idea of America being divided between "blue" and "red"
states and areas. Democrats, represented as blue, tend to be clustered on the coasts,
in the upper Midwest, across the northern states, and in urban areas nationwide.
Republicans, represented as red, tend to be concentrated in the Mountain West, the

Great Plains, and the South, and in suburbs and rural areas.[17] Some states that used to be solidly red or blue are now turning "purple" as Republicans and Democrats battle to win elections.

Age Today young people are much more likely to be Democrats and older voters are likely to be Republicans. Individuals from the same age cohort are likely to have experienced a similar set of events during the period when their party loyalties were formed. Millennials, for example, who came of age during the Great Recession and growing economic inequality, reacted sharply against the Republican Party as a result. In the 2020 elections, support for Republicans among the elderly decreased in part because older voters were concerned about the coronavirus pandemic.

There has been a striking uptick in the percentage of young people who identify as independent, which may be a reflection of increasing frustration with government. Nonetheless, in 2020, between 59–60 percent of people ages 18 to 29 voted for Joe Biden, compared to just 36 percent for Donald Trump.[18] As a group, young people have distinct policy preferences that overlap with the Democratic Party, including support for LGBTQ rights, legalization of marijuana, protection of the environment, and greater economic equality.

PARTY POLARIZATION IN SOCIETY

Since Trump's election in 2016, divides between people who affiliate with the Republican and Democratic parties have been growing. Negative feelings among partisans toward members of the opposing party have intensified too. A recent survey asked respondents to rate individuals or groups on a scale from 0 to 100, with 0 being very cold, 100 very warm, and 50 neutral. A cold rating is a number below 50. Overall about 8 in 10 Democrats and Republicans give the opposite party a cold rating. The share of Republicans who give Democrats a cold rating grew 14 percentage points from 2016 to 2019, and Democrats' negative views of Republicans grew at a similar rate.[19]

Political divisions have moved beyond disagreements about policy and become more personal. A majority of Republicans (63 percent) believe Democrats are more unpatriotic compared to other Americans. Just 23 percent of Democrats say the same about Republicans. Five in ten Republicans say Democrats are more immoral compared to other Americans; a similar number of Democrats say the same about Republicans. And three in four Democrats say Republicans are more "closed-minded" than other Americans.[20] Party polarization is so intense that a nationally representative survey finds that 20 percent of Republicans and 15 percent of Democrats say the country would be better off if large numbers of the other party died.[21]

Yet on many basic policy issues there is a fair amount of agreement. Significant majorities of Americans want to expand

FOR CRITICAL ANALYSIS ▶

1. Are participation rates higher, lower, or about the same for primaries versus caucuses? Why?

2. Determine which states have the highest voter turnout and look into voting laws in those states. Do these states' laws impact their high voter turnout?

Who Votes in Primaries and Caucuses?

During presidential primary elections, early primaries and caucuses have important impacts on who the parties' nominees will be. Despite this impact, voter turnout in primary elections remains low, even in states with early contests like Iowa and New Hampshire. In recent years, many states have turned away from caucuses, which require voters to attend events in person, and instituted primaries instead in an attempt to increase voter turnout.

Turnout in 2020 Primaries

Percentage of voting-eligible population

- 1–9.9%
- 10–19.9%
- 20–29.9%
- 30–39.9%
- 40–46%
- (1) Earliest primary

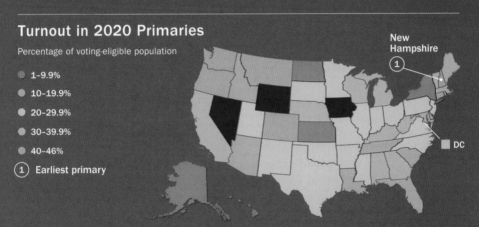

Turnout in 2020 Caucuses

Percentage of voting-eligible population

- 1–9.9%
- (1) Earliest caucus

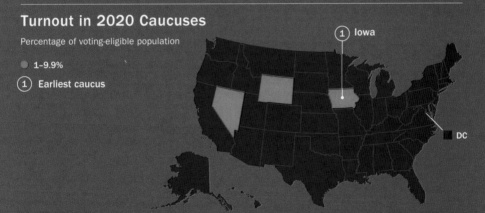

SOURCE: Michael P. McDonald, "2020 Presidential Nomination Contest Turnout Rates," United States Election Project, September 15, 2020, www.electproject.org/ (accessed 9/15/20).

NOTES:
Alaska, Hawaii, Kansas, South Carolina, Virginia: Data are for the Democratic primary only.
Nevada: Data are for the Democratic caucus only. No Republican caucus was held.
North Dakota: Data are for the Democratic primary only. The Republican presidential candidate was decided via convention.
Wyoming: Data are for the Democratic caucus only. The Republican presidential candidate was decided via convention.

Since there was no significant Republican challenger in the 2020 primary contests, data reflects mostly Democratic turnout measured over the total voting-eligible population.

national health care, want to rebuild the nation's economy following the pandemic, favor a tax on millionaires and billionaires to address growing economic inequality, support increased environmental regulations, and favor marijuana legalization and stronger gun laws.

Electoral Realignments Define Party Systems

> **Describe the history of U.S. party systems and the influence of third parties**

The term *party system* refers to the organization of the parties, the dominant form of campaigning, the main issues that divide the parties, the balance of power between and within party coalitions, and the parties' social bases over a long period of time (see Figure 8.3). Seen from this broader perspective, the character of a nation's party system can change even if the number of parties remains the same and even when the same two parties seem to be competing for power. Over the course of American history, changes in political alignments have produced six distinct party systems.

THE FIRST PARTY SYSTEM: FEDERALISTS AND JEFFERSONIAN REPUBLICANS

The first party system emerged in the 1790s and pitted the Federalists, who favored a strong national government and president, against the Jeffersonian Republicans, or Antifederalists, who favored a weaker national government, with the states retaining protections for individuals from government interference. The Federalists represented mainly New England merchants and supported protective tariffs to encourage manufacturing, forgiveness of states' Revolutionary War debts, creation of a national bank, commercial ties with Britain, and a strong national government. The Jeffersonians, led by southern agricultural interests, opposed these policies and instead favored free trade, promotion of agriculture, friendship with France, and states' rights.

In the election of 1800, Thomas Jefferson defeated the incumbent Federalist president, John Adams, and over the following years, the Federalists gradually weakened. The party disappeared after the pro-British sympathies of some Federalist leaders during the War of 1812 led to charges of treason against the party.

From the collapse of the Federalists until the 1830s, America had only one political party, the Jeffersonian Republicans, who gradually came to be known as the Democrats. Throughout this period, however, the party experienced intense internal conflict, particularly between the supporters and opponents of General Andrew Jackson, America's great hero of the War of 1812. Jackson was the first populist president and had a wide base of mass support; he sought to give rank-and-file members more say in party politics through national conventions. Although his opponents united to deny him the presidency in 1824, he won it in 1828 and 1832. Jackson's support was in the South and Midwest, and he generally favored policies that appealed to those regions, including free trade.

FIGURE 8.3

How the Party System Evolved

During the nineteenth century, the Democrats and Republicans emerged as the two dominant parties in American politics. As the American party system evolved, many third parties emerged, but few of them remained in existence for very long.

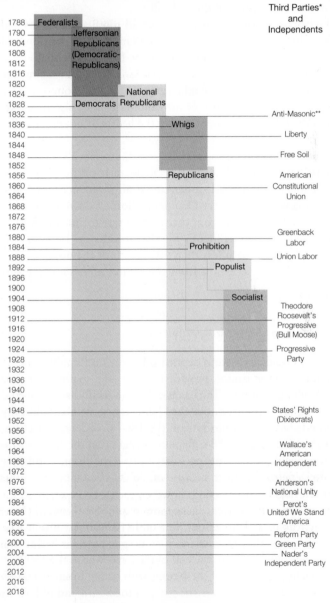

*Or, in some cases, fourth parties; most of these parties lasted through only one term.
**The Anti-Masonics had the distinction of being not only the first third party but also the first party to hold a national nominating convention and the first to announce a party platform.

THE SECOND PARTY SYSTEM: DEMOCRATS AND WHIGS

During the 1830s, groups opposing Jackson united to form a new political force, the Whig Party, giving rise to the second American party system. Both the Democrats and the Whigs built party organizations throughout the nation and tried to enlarge their bases of support by eliminating the requirement of property ownership for voting. Support for the Whigs was stronger in the Northeast than in the South and West and among merchants than among small farmers. Hence, in some measure, the Whigs were the successors of the Federalists.

Yet conflict between the two parties revolved more around personalities than policies. The Whigs were a diverse group united more by opposition to the Democrats than by policies. In 1840 they won their first presidential election, under the leadership of General William Henry Harrison. The Whig campaign carefully avoided issues—since the party could agree on almost none—and emphasized the personal qualities and heroism of the candidate. They also invested heavily in campaign rallies and entertainment to win the hearts, if not exactly the minds, of the voters.

During the late 1840s and early 1850s, conflicts over slavery produced sharp divisions within both the Whig and the Democratic parties. By 1856 the Whig Party had all but disintegrated under the strain, and many Whig politicians and voters, along with antislavery Democrats, joined the new Republican Party, which pledged to ban slavery from the western territories. In 1860 the Republicans nominated Abraham Lincoln for the presidency. Lincoln's victory in a four-way candidate race with less than 40 percent of the popular vote strengthened southern calls for secession from the Union and, soon thereafter, led to civil war.

THE CIVIL WAR PARTY SYSTEM

During the war, President Lincoln depended heavily on Republican governors and state legislatures to raise troops, provide funding, and maintain popular support for a long and bloody conflict. The secession of the South had stripped the Democratic Party of many supporters, but the Democrats remained politically competitive throughout the war and nearly won the 1864 presidential election. With the defeat of the Confederacy in 1865, Republicans granted the right to vote to newly freed enslaved people, thus creating a large pro-Republican voting bloc. Voting rights for Blacks failed, however, because of violent resistance by southern Whites via the Ku Klux Klan.

After the war, the former Confederate states regained full control of their internal affairs and party politics. Throughout the South, African Americans were deprived of political rights, including the right to vote, despite post–Civil War constitutional guarantees to the contrary. From the end of the Civil War to the 1890s, the Republican Party remained the party of the North, with strong business and middle-class support, while the Democrats were the party of the South and of farmers, with the support of northern working-class and immigrant groups.

Richard Nixon's "southern strategy" helped broaden the Republican Party's base in the late 1960s and the 1970s by appealing to White southerners. Here, Nixon meets supporters in Georgia in 1968.

THE SYSTEM OF 1896: POPULISM AND REPUBLICAN RESPONSES

During the 1890s, profound and rapid social and economic changes led to the emergence of a variety of protest third parties, including the Populist Party, which won support in the South and West. The Populists appealed mainly to small farmers but also attracted western miners and urban workers. In the 1892 elections, the Populist Party carried four states in the presidential race and elected governors in eight. In 1896 the Populists effectively merged with the Democrats, who nominated William Jennings Bryan for the presidency. The Republicans nominated the conservative senator William McKinley.

In the ensuing campaign, northern and midwestern business interests made an all-out effort to defeat what they saw as a radical threat from the Populist–Democratic alliance, and the Republicans won a resounding victory, advocating for low taxes and high tariffs on imports. They carried the more heavily populated North and confined the Democrats to their smaller bases of support in the South and far West. For the next 36 years, the Republicans remained the nation's majority party, winning seven of nine presidential elections and majorities in both houses of Congress in 15 of 18 contests.[22] The Republicans favored government regulation, expanded voting rights, and the creation of the national bureaucracy to professionalize the work of government.

THE NEW DEAL PARTY SYSTEM: GOVERNMENT HELPS THE WORKING CLASS

Soon after Republican Herbert Hoover won the 1928 presidential election, the nation's economy collapsed. The Great Depression stemmed from a variety of causes, including high tariffs on imports, but from the perspective of the majority of voters, the Republican Party did not do enough to promote economic recovery and relief when up to a fourth of American workers were without jobs and millions were actually starving.[23] In 1932, Americans elected Democrat Franklin Delano Roosevelt (FDR) as president and a solidly Democratic Congress. Roosevelt developed a program for economic recovery that he dubbed the New Deal. The New Deal increased the size of the national government substantially, as it took responsibility for economic management and social welfare to an extent unprecedented in American history. For the first time, government took an active role in the individual lives of Americans, providing unemployment benefits, jobs, food, and more.

Roosevelt expanded the political base of the Democratic Party. He rebuilt and revitalized the party around unionized workers, upper-middle-class intellectuals and professionals, southern White farmers, Jews, Catholics, and northern African Americans—the so-called New Deal coalition that made the Democrats the nation's majority party for the next 36 years. Groping for a response, Republicans often wound up supporting popular New Deal programs such as Social Security. Even the relatively conservative administration of Dwight D. Eisenhower in the 1950s left the principal New Deal programs intact.

The New Deal coalition was severely strained during the 1960s by conflicts over civil rights and the Vietnam War. The movement for equal rights for African Americans divided northern Democrats, who supported it, from White southern Democrats, who defended racial segregation. As the movement launched a northern campaign aimed at equal access to jobs, education, quality public schools, and housing, northern Democrats also split, often along income lines. The Vietnam War further divided the Democrats, with upper-income Democrats strongly opposing President Lyndon Johnson's decision to greatly expand the numbers of U.S. troops fighting in Southeast Asia. These divisions provided an opportunity for the Republican Party, which recaptured the White House in 1968 under the leadership of Richard Nixon.

THE CONTEMPORARY AMERICAN PARTY SYSTEM

The Republican Party widened its appeal in the second half of the twentieth century. In 1968, Richard Nixon appealed to southern Whites by sending subtle signals of support for their resistance to racial equality, sparking the shift that gave Republicans a strong position in all the states of the former Confederacy. The shift of White voters in the South from Democrats to Republicans in national elections was also spurred by Democratic presidents who supported the civil rights movement, including Presidents John F. Kennedy and Johnson.

During the 1980s, under President Ronald Reagan, Republicans added two additional important groups to their coalition. The first was religious conservatives, who were opposed to abortion and felt the Democrats were not protecting traditional family and religious values. The second was working-class Whites, who were drawn to Reagan's tough approach to foreign policy and opposition to affirmative action. Many Republicans consider Reagan's tenure in office as a "golden era" that saw deregulation of many industries (airlines, railroads, mail), reduced government intervention in the economy, and robust economic growth.

Meanwhile the Democratic Party maintained its support among a majority of unionized workers, the poor and working class, upper-middle-class professionals, and racial and ethnic minorities. The 1965 Voting Rights Act greatly increased Black voter participation in the South and helped the Democratic Party retain some southern congressional seats. The Democrats appealed to Americans concerned with economic fairness and inequality, women's rights, the environment, and other progressive social causes.

In 2000, George W. Bush united the Republican Party behind a program of tax cuts, education reform, military strength, and family values. However, Republicans fared poorly in the 2008 elections, held during the worst financial crisis since the 1930s (replaced by the economic crisis in 2020). Democrat Barack Obama, the nation's first African American president, was elected in 2008 and re-elected in 2012. He united racial and ethnic minorities, youth, and other liberals with older White moderates in a powerful national coalition, winning large popular majorities in the 2008 and 2012 elections. Obama helped the nation recover from global economic recession; reformed national health care, the financial sector, and immigration; and promoted clean energy and environmental protections, labor policies, and LGBTQ rights. However, he became deeply unpopular with Republicans, who objected to what they saw as overreach by the federal government. Republicans captured both houses of Congress in 2014, and in 2016 they also won the presidency in a tight race.

During the Obama administration the Tea Party movement emerged and became a powerful conservative force in the Republican Party.[24] It succeeded in pushing the Republican Party in a more conservative direction, and its ideological influence has continued, including lending key support to the surprising election of Donald Trump and his conservative agenda. Democrats organized effectively to recruit strong candidates, increase voter turnout, and win back control of the House of Representatives in 2018.

THIRD PARTIES

Although the United States has a political system dominated by two parties, it has always had more than two parties. Typically, **third parties** in the United States have represented social and economic interests that were not addressed by the two major parties.[25] The Populists, centered in the rural areas of the West and Midwest, and the Progressives, representing the urban middle class, are important examples in the late nineteenth and early twentieth centuries. The most successful recent third-party presidential candidate, H. Ross Perot, who ran in 1992 as an independent and in 1996 as the Reform Party's nominee, won the votes of almost one in five Americans in 1992.

Third parties exist mainly as protest movements against the two major parties or to promote specific policies. Third parties can be sources of new ideas, and they can profoundly affect elections, taking votes from one of the major parties and enabling the

third parties parties that organize to compete against the two major American political parties

TABLE 8.1

Parties and Candidates in 2016

CANDIDATE	PARTY	VOTE TOTAL	PERCENTAGE OF VOTES	ELECTORAL COLLEGE VOTES*
Hillary Clinton	Democratic	65,147,421	48%	227
Donald Trump	Republican	62,634,907	46%	304
Gary Johnson	Libertarian	4,454,855	3%	0
Jill Stein	Green	1,426,922	1%	0
Other candidates		1,047,140	0.8%	0

*As was their right, seven members of the electoral college voted for other candidates despite Trump or Clinton carrying the state.

SOURCE: U.S. Election Atlas, "2016 Presidential General Election Results," www.uselectionatlas.org/RESULTS /national.php?year=2016&minper=0&f=0&off=0&elect=0 (accessed 12/1/16).

other to win. In the extremely close 2000 presidential election, for example, third-party candidate Ralph Nader won just 3 percent of the popular vote, but that split the Democratic vote enough to swing the election to Republican George W. Bush. In the 2016 election, neither major-party candidate won a majority of the popular vote because third parties took 5 percent of it. Third-party candidates fared better in 2016 than in the previous three presidential elections (see Table 8.1), though the 2020 election had low third-party voting compared to 2016, and Joe Biden won a majority of the popular vote.

Third parties have at times enjoyed an influence far beyond their electoral size because large parts of their platform were adopted by one or both of the major parties, which wanted to appeal to the voters mobilized by the new party and thus expand their own electoral strength.

Interest Groups Are Composed of Many Types

Describe the major types of interest groups and who they represent

interest group individuals who organize to influence the government's programs and policies

An **interest group** is an organized group of people or institutions that lobbies government to change public policy. This definition includes membership organizations of ordinary individuals as well as business organizations and trade associations, labor unions, university associations, professional groups for particular occupations, and even government groups such as the National League of Cities or National Governors Association that lobby other levels of government. Individuals and other entities form groups to increase the chance that their views will be heard and their interests treated favorably by the government. Unlike political parties, which represent the people, interest groups represent narrow, often economic, interests.

Interest groups are sometimes referred to negatively as "lobbies," "special interests," or "pressure groups," or discussed positively as "advocacy organizations" or, in some cases, "citizen groups." They are also sometimes confused with political action committees (PACs), which are groups that raise and distribute money for use in election campaigns. Many interest groups do create PACs in their name to be the money-giving arm of the interest group. For example, the NRA Political Victory Fund donates money to political candidates and officeholders on behalf of the NRA, which represents the interests of gun owners.

Interest groups serve important functions in American democracy, interacting with nearly all of the players in the governmental system. Millions of Americans are members of one or more citizen interest groups, at least to the extent of paying dues, attending an occasional meeting, following a group on social media, reading its newsletter or website, or being on its email list. Organized groups use these means to educate their members on policy issues and mobilize them for elections. Interest groups of businesses, professionals, governments, and other entities similarly conduct research and provide information to the members about relevant policy matters. Both types of groups furnish information to and lobby members of Congress during the lawmaking process. They provide information to the executive branch and participate in administrative rule making and the design of regulations. They also monitor government programs and regulations to ensure these do not adversely affect their members. Additionally, they use the judicial system to engage in litigation. Through these means, organized interest groups represent their members' interests and help promote democratic politics. But as we will see, not all interests are represented equally in society, nor are all organized groups equally successful.

TYPES OF INTEREST GROUPS

Corporate Groups and Trade Associations One predominant set of interest groups is those with a direct economic interest in governmental policy: businesses. Corporations commonly form trade associations with other businesses in their economic sector, such as the American Beverage Association or the American Fuel and Petrochemical Manufacturers. They may join broader groups as well, such as the U.S. Chamber of Commerce, which represents many types of businesses, and the National Federation of Independent Business, which represents small businesses. As government regulation increased in the 1970s, many individual firms began hiring their own lobbyists to try to persuade government officials and influence policy outcomes.[26]

Groups working on behalf of businesses and industry far outweigh citizen groups and unions in the number of registered lobbyists in Washington, D.C., and state capitals, and in terms of money spent. Corporations and trade associations constitute nearly half of all entries in the *Washington Representatives* directory, the "phone book" of organizations with a lobbying presence in the nation's capital.[27] Their financial resources are even more disproportionate. In 2018, labor organizations spent $48 million on lobbying, and "ideology/single issue" groups—the label used by the Center for Responsive Politics for citizen groups—spent $148 million. But those amounts are eclipsed by lobbying expenditures by businesses and business and trade associations. The health sector alone spent $567 million.[28] Altogether, corporations, trade associations, and business associations spend $34 on lobbying to every $1 spent by citizen groups and labor unions combined.[29]

Labor Groups Labor organizations are also active in lobbying government. Unions such as the United Auto Workers, the United Mine Workers, and the Teamsters lobby on behalf of organized labor in the private sector, while the American Federation of State, County and Municipal Employees (AFSCME) and the American Federation of Teachers (AFT) are examples of public-sector unions that represent members who work in government and public education. Some labor unions, such as the Service Employees International Union (SEIU), organize workers in both the private and public sectors.

Unions constitute less than 1 percent of the organized interests in Washington.[30] Despite declining membership, especially in the private sector, where union membership fell from 35 percent of workers in the 1950s to 6.4 percent in 2018,[31] and despite having fewer resources than business groups, labor unions continue to exercise influence in Washington and state capitals. Union members vote at high rates and often work on campaigns.[32]

Although public school teachers are a minority of the total population, the unions that represent them are an influential interest group in many states because they are highly informed and act as a group in support of issues related to their profession, including teachers' salaries.

Professional Associations Professional associations represent the interests of individuals who work in specific occupations (as opposed to trade associations, which are composed of business firms in a given sector), and constitute 5.4 percent of the organized groups in Washington.[33] Physicians, lawyers, accountants, real estate agents, dentists, and even college faculty have professional associations. Many individuals may not think of themselves as participants in the interest group system but nonetheless have professional associations working on their behalf. Some professional lobbies such as the American Bar Association, the American Medical Association, and the National Realtors Association have been particularly successful. Professional associations are active at the state level as well, in part because states are responsible for licensing many occupations, from physicians to beauticians.

Citizen Groups Citizen groups are open to ordinary citizens and represent a wide variety of interests, with groups organized on issues from the environment to abortion, to gun policy, to disability rights. The largest citizen group is AARP (formerly the American Association for Retired People), which has around 40 million members—anyone age 50 and older can join—and represents the interests of older Americans. Other citizen groups include the National Rifle Association, the Sierra Club, and Mothers Against Drunk Driving (MADD). The wide variety of citizen groups makes for some confusing terminology. Some citizen groups are referred to as "public interest groups" if they purport to lobby for the general good rather than their own economic interests.[34] Some citizen groups are also referred to as "ideological groups," organized in support of a particular political or philosophical perspective. Examples include the Christian Coalition, the National Taxpayers Union, and NARAL Pro-Choice America. Citizen groups make up only 14 percent of the groups with lobbying offices in Washington.[35]

WHY DO INTEREST GROUPS FORM?

Suppose there is a community where polluted air threatens the health of thousands or even millions of residents. Each resident wants to breathe clean air. But no single individual has an incentive to join an environmental group—and pay membership dues or volunteer—as the group works to reduce pollution. Why join the group and spend your precious time and money on this when you are going to benefit from the **collective good** of reduced pollution anyway? Each of the inactive residents would be a **free rider** on the efforts of the residents who joined the group and worked to reduce pollution. The collective action problem is that if all individuals follow the same logic, then no one would join environmental groups, and pollution would continue.

The challenge for interest groups is to overcome the free-rider problem. To do so, groups offer "selective benefits," available only to group members, to induce

collective goods benefits sought by groups that are broadly available and cannot be denied to nonmembers

free riders those who enjoy the benefits of collective goods but did not participate in acquiring or providing them

Start an Advocacy Group

SHANNON WATTS, the founder of Moms Demand Action for Gun Sense in America

 Do you ever think, "Hey, that's not right. Somebody should do something about that"? That somebody could be you. Shannon Watts, was a stay-at-home mom of five who "wasn't political at all" when the shooting at Sandy Hook Elementary School in Newtown, Connecticut, occurred in December 2012. She decided to mobilize "mothers and others" around gun safety, and her grassroots network now has chapters in all 50 states. Here is Shannon's advice for starting an advocacy group:

1 Figure out what you're passionate about and get educated about the issue. Don't be afraid to call people for their wisdom. You don't have to take every piece of advice—some people may even advise you not to start an organization. But seek out any input and issue information that will help.

2 Decide on the scope and the goal and the objective that you are trying to accomplish. Are you trying to create change in your neighborhood, your community, your state, your region, even nationwide? What policy change do you seek?

3 Think about the people you need around you. Start with your personal networks to find volunteers willing to help out. Seek help from experts for website development or pro bono legal work or other organizing help. Recruit in person, online—use every mode that works. (Shannon notes that she started with just 75 Facebook friends.) I was able to tap into the power of perfect strangers because of social media.

4 Figure out your group's branding": the group's look and feel, including name, logo, font, and colors. A successful brand brings people together, empowers them, and bonds them. Moms Demand Action uses the color red, which makes the mom members feel like they have superhero capes.

5 Keep going even when you face defeats. Regroup, learn from the loss, and take advantage of the positives that emerge even from setbacks. It's important to emphasize to your volunteers that you may have created new relationships with lawmakers; you may have made relationships with the media; you may have grown your organization.

6 **Realize that change typically comes in small steps.** I think young people are particularly frustrated with incrementalism, but that's how our democracy is set up. Change doesn't happen overnight. I always say, "Incrementalism is what leads to revolution."

Each generation and each segment of the population has very specific levers of power that are available to them and they have to figure out what those are. Our members' special power is motherhood and love for their children. What's your group's special power?

TABLE 8.2

Selective Benefits of Interest Group Membership

CATEGORY	BENEFITS
Informational benefits	Conferences
	Professional contacts
	Publications
	Coordination among organizations
	Research
	Legal help
	Professional codes
	Collective bargaining
Material benefits	Travel packages
	Insurance
	Discounts on consumer goods
Solidary benefits	Friendship
	Networking opportunities
Purposive benefits	Advocacy
	Representation before government
	Participation in public affairs

SOURCE: Adapted from Jack Walker, Jr., *Mobilizing Interest Groups in America: Patrons, Professions, and Social Movements* (Ann Arbor: University of Michigan Press, 1991), 86.

informational benefits
special newsletters, periodicals, training programs, conferences, and other information provided to members of groups to entice others to join

material benefits special goods, services, or money provided to members of groups to entice others to join

people to join. These benefits can be informational, material, solidary, purposive, or a combination of these (see Table 8.2).

Informational benefits, the most widespread and important category of selective benefits, are provided through online communication such as email, conferences, training programs, and newsletters and other periodicals sent automatically to those who have paid membership dues.

Material benefits include anything that can be measured monetarily, such as gifts like tote bags and mugs; discounts on travel (provided by AARP), gun club memberships (offered by the National Rifle Association), and other purchases; and health and retirement insurance (offered by many professional associations).

solidary benefits selective benefits of group membership that emphasize friendship, networking, and consciousness-raising

Solidary benefits include the friendship and networking opportunities that membership provides as well as the satisfaction of working toward a common goal with like-minded individuals. The Sierra Club, for example, offers "Sierra Singles" programming by which single people can participate in hikes, picnics, and cultural outings with others interested in environmental issues and meet new friends or perhaps a life partner at the same time.[36] Members of associations based on ethnicity, race, or religion also derive solidary benefits from interacting with individuals they perceive as sharing their own backgrounds, values, and perspectives.

purposive benefits selective benefits of group membership that emphasize the purpose and accomplishments of the group

pluralism the theory that all interests are and should be free to compete for influence in the government; the outcome of this competition is compromise and moderation

A fourth type of benefit involves the appeal of the purpose of an interest group. An example of these **purposive benefits** is businesses joining trade associations to further their economic interests. Similarly, individuals join consumer, environmental, or other civic groups to pursue goals important to them. Many of the most successful interest groups of the past 30 years have been organized largely around shared ideological goals, including government reform, civil rights, economic equality, "family values," and even opposition to government itself.

WHAT INTERESTS ARE NOT REPRESENTED?

Pluralism, the theory that all interests are and should be free to compete for influence in the government, was long the dominant view of the U.S. political system. However, critics point out that not all interests are equally represented in debates over government and policy. Some of them speak with loud voices (major corporations, for example), while others can barely make themselves heard (the homeless). Pluralism does not guarantee political equality. Research indicates that, through group politics, economic elites have considerably more influence than mass-based forces.[37] This version of pluralism is called elite pluralism and more accurately describes American politics.

As the political scientist E. E. Schattschneider put it, "The flaw in the pluralist heaven is that the heavenly chorus sings with a strong upper-class accent."[38] His point was that interest group politics is heavily skewed in favor of corporate, business, and upper-class groups, leaving those with lower socioeconomic status less able to participate in and influence government. The central reason for this skew is that people with higher incomes, more education, and managerial or professional occupations are much more likely to have the time, money, and skills needed to play a role in a group or contribute financially to it.[39]

What Do Interest Groups Do?

Interest groups work to improve the likelihood that their policy interests will be heard and treated favorably by the government. The quest for political influence or power takes many forms. "Insider strategies" include gaining access to key decision makers, lobbying, and litigating cases in courts. "Outsider strategies" include using electoral politics and going public. These strategies do not exhaust all the possibilities, but they paint a broad picture of ways that groups use their resources in the competition for influence (see Figure 8.4).

FIGURE 8.4
....

How Interest Groups Influence Congress

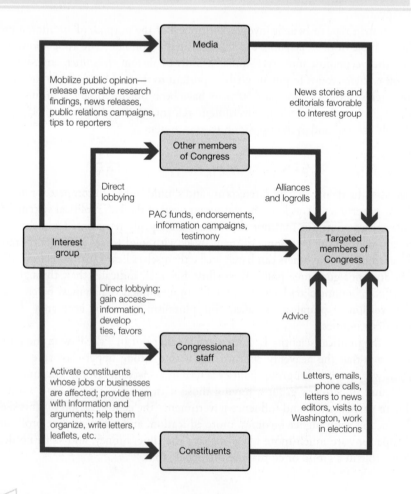

INTEREST GROUPS INFLUENCE CONGRESS THROUGH LOBBYING

Lobbying is an attempt by a group to influence the policy process through persuasion of government officials. Traditionally, the term *lobbyist* referred to those seeking to influence the passage of legislation in Congress. The First Amendment provides for the right to "petition the Government for a redress of grievances." As early as the 1870s, *lobbying* became the common term for petitioning: since petitioning cannot take place on the floor of the House or Senate, petitioners must confront members of Congress in the lobbies of the two chambers.

> **lobbying** a strategy by which organized interests seek to influence the passage of legislation by exerting direct pressure on government officials

The 1946 Federal Regulation of Lobbying Act defines a lobbyist as "any person who shall engage himself for pay or any consideration for the purpose of attempting to influence the passage or defeat of any legislation of the Congress of the United States." Some lobbyists are directly employed by a particular interest group or a specific business corporation, while others work for lobbying firms that can be hired by any group seeking representation and lobbying services. All organizations employing lobbyists are required to register with Congress and to disclose whom they represent, whom they lobby, what they are looking for, and how much they are paid.

Approximately 11,000 lobbyists are currently registered, down from a high of over 14,000 in 2007.[40] The large decline in the number of registered lobbyists may not be nearly as large as these numbers suggest.[41] Critics allege that recent changes in lobbyist registration requirements merely reduce the number of official lobbying registrations while the true amount of lobbying remains undiminished, and that disclosure laws have significant loopholes.[42]

Lobbyists attempt to influence the policy process in a variety of ways,[43] the most important being providing information to lawmakers, administrators, and committee staff about their interests and the legislation and regulations that they seek to promote, amend, or defeat. In addition, they often testify on behalf of their clients at congressional committee and agency hearings, talk to reporters, place ads in newspapers, and organize letter-writing, phone-call, email, and social media campaigns. Many lobbying efforts occur in private meetings with lawmakers and campaign leaders. Lobbyists also play an important role in fundraising, helping to direct clients' contributions to certain members of Congress and presidential candidates.

Congress has become more dependent on lobbyists. Over time, Congress has cut funding for its own research and support staff; the combined staffs of the Congressional Research Service, Government Accountability Office, and Congressional Budget Office fell by 45 percent between 1975 and 2015.[44] Also, the total number of congressional staff working directly for representatives and senators in Washington has fallen since the late 1970s, as lawmakers have sent more staff to home districts and states to help constituents. These D.C. staff members are stretched thin and work across many issue areas even as public policy has become more complex.[45] As a result, lobbyists have the ability to fill the information and expertise void to the benefit of those they lobby for.

Business owners are often able to gain special access to elected officials. Here, President Trump holds a roundtable discussion with small business owners from across the country.

Lobbying the President So many individuals and groups clamor for the president's time and attention that only the most skilled and best-connected members of the lobbying community can hope to influence presidential decisions. Typically, a president's key political advisers and fundraisers will include individuals with ties to the lobbying industry who can help their friends gain access to the White House. During the four years after President Donald Trump's January 2017 inauguration, more than 200 advocacy groups, companies, and foreign governments sought contact by booking events at Mar-a-Lago, his resort in Florida, and at various Trump golf courses and hotels. For example, the CEO of T-Mobile stayed at the Trump International Hotel in Washington, D.C., as his company sought federal government approval for a merger with Sprint.[46]

Lobbying the Executive Branch Even when an interest group is successful at getting its bill passed by Congress and signed by the president, full implementation of that law is up to executive branch agencies, and participation in their rule-making process is a key activity for many interest groups. Just like lawmakers and their staffs, executive branch bureaucrats engaged in rule making are in need of information and expertise, which lobbyists readily provide.

iron triangle the stable, cooperative relationship that often develops among a congressional committee, an administrative agency, and one or more supportive interest groups; not all of these relationships are triangular, but the iron triangle is the most typical

How Interest Groups Make Policy; Iron Triangles and Issue Networks Many government policies are the product of a so-called **iron triangle**, which has one

FIGURE 8.5
. . . .

The Iron Triangle in the Defense Sector

Defense contractors are powerful actors in shaping defense policy; they act in concert with defense committees and subcommittees in Congress and executive agencies concerned with defense.

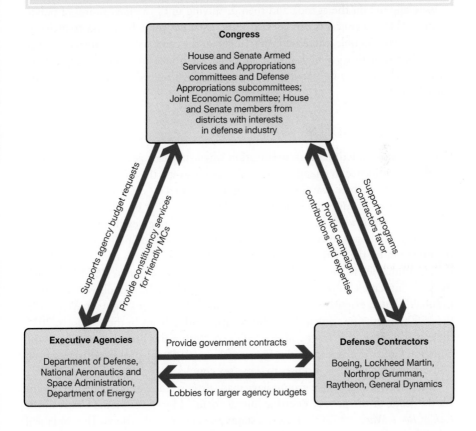

angle in an executive branch program (bureaucratic agency), another angle in a Senate or House committee or subcommittee, and a third angle in some well-organized interest group. In policy areas such as agriculture, energy, or veterans' affairs, interest groups, government agencies, and congressional committees routinely work together for mutual benefit. The interest group provides campaign contributions for members of Congress, lobbies for larger budgets for the agency, and provides policy expertise to lawmakers. The agency, in turn, provides government contracts for the interest group and constituency services for friendly members of Congress. The congressional committee or subcommittee, meanwhile, supports the agency's budgetary requests and the programs the interest group favors. Together the three angles in an iron triangle create a mutually supportive relationship. Figure 8.5 illustrates the iron triangle of the defense industry.

issue network a loose network of elected leaders, public officials, activists, and interest groups drawn together by a specific policy issue

Policy development in a number of important areas, such as the environment, taxes, and immigration, is controlled not by highly structured and unified iron triangles but by broader **issue networks**. These consist of like-minded politicians, consultants, activists, and interest groups who care about the issue in question. Issue networks are more fluid than iron triangles, coming together when an issue appears on the agenda and then dissolving until the next round of policy making. The two concepts can coexist: some issue networks have iron triangles at their core. For example, there are iron triangles at the center of many areas of energy policy, but sometimes a high-profile proposal, such as a new interstate pipeline, activates a broader issue network including landowners, environmentalists, state officials, and so on.

USING THE COURTS

Interest groups sometimes turn to litigation when they lack access or feel they have insufficient influence to change a policy. A group can use the courts to affect public policy in at least three ways: (1) by bringing suit directly on behalf of the group itself, (2) by financing suits brought by individuals, or (3) by filing a companion brief as an *amicus curiae* (literally "friend of the court") to an existing court case.

Among the best-known examples of using the courts for political influence is the litigation by the National Association for the Advancement of Colored People (NAACP) that led to *Brown v. Board of Education of Topeka, Kansas* (1954), in which the U.S. Supreme Court held that legal segregation of public schools was unconstitutional.[47] Later, extensive litigation accompanied the women's rights movement in the 1960s and the movement for rights for gays and lesbians in the 1990s. In 2015 the case of *Obergefell v. Hodges* illustrated the success of this litigation strategy as the Supreme Court declared that the Fourteenth Amendment prohibited states from refusing to issue marriage licenses to same-sex couples.[48]

Since 1973, conservative groups have made extensive use of the courts to diminish the scope of the privacy doctrine initially defined by the Supreme Court in the case of *Roe v. Wade*, which took away a state's power to ban abortions. They obtained rulings, for example, that prohibit the use of federal funds to pay for voluntary abortions and that restore the right of states to place restrictions on abortion, thus undermining the *Roe v. Wade* decision.[49]

HOW INFLUENTIAL ARE INTEREST GROUPS?

Factors in Interest Group Effectiveness Although interest groups are many and varied, most successful groups share certain key organizational components, including strong leadership, an effective strategy, an appropriate structure, and resources such as staff, members, and money.

Strong and charismatic leaders are crucial to interest group success. They can help convince organizations and individuals to join the interest group. They can devise packages of selective benefits that help overcome the free-rider dilemma discussed earlier. They can spearhead recruitment campaigns for members and media campaigns to spread the group's message. And they can engage in lobbying and the other activities of group influence.

Resources are also a factor in group effectiveness. The sheer number of members can be a resource that leaders cite in their interactions with government officials. The fact that AARP has nearly 40 million members—about half the U.S. population age 50 and over—can make lawmakers hesitate to adopt policies that older Americans view as harmful to their interests.[50]

Staff members are another type of group resource—their numbers and their talent for recruiting members, publicizing the group's activities through media, conducting research, monitoring government activity, and lobbying. And money is perhaps the ultimate resource. It funds membership drives and it is necessary for conducting media campaigns aimed both at the public and at policy makers. Having more money means a group can hire more and better-connected lobbyists who can access more government decision makers. Money helps interest groups engage in all of their activities, but studies show that more money doesn't always lead to more interest group success.

MEASURING INTEREST GROUP INFLUENCE

How influential are interest groups? Some people are concerned that interest groups are *too* effective—that their lobbying is too convincing or that their campaign contributions can buy lawmakers' votes on legislation. Indeed, some scholars characterize American politics as less about electoral politics than about "organized combat" among high-resource interest groups fighting over issues far from ordinary Americans' concerns.[51] For analysts, the dilemma is trying to measure the effectiveness of interest groups. We are pretty sure they have an influence on government and policy, but how much? And how do we know?

As noted earlier, the most important way lobbyists win influence is by providing information about policies affecting their clients to busy members of Congress and the bureaucracy. Although interest groups do not necessarily buy roll-call votes, they do "buy time" with lawmakers to promote their preferred policy solutions.[52] Those groups with demonstrated technical expertise have been shown to have more access to lawmakers.[53] Similarly, executive branch officials engaged in rule making are most responsive to the side of an issue that participates the most.[54] The groups with the most expertise and that participate the most tend to be corporate and professional groups.

REGULATING LOBBYING

The role that lobbyists play in policy making raises concerns, and periodically Congress tries to address abuses. Sometimes the actions of lobbyists are outside of the law. In 2005 a prominent Washington lobbyist, Jack Abramoff, was convicted of fraud and violations of federal lobbying laws. Abramoff had collected tens of millions of dollars from several American Indian tribes that operated lucrative gambling casinos. Much of this money found its way into the campaign war chests of Abramoff's friends in Congress, including former House majority leader Tom DeLay (R-Tex.). In exchange for these campaign funds, key Republican members of Congress helped Abramoff's clients shut down rival casino operators. Thus, through a well-connected lobbyist, money had effectively purchased access and influence. Abramoff and several of his associates pleaded guilty to federal bribery and fraud charges, and Abramoff was sentenced to five years in prison.

Because lobbyists are so influential in Washington, D.C., Congress has tried periodically to limit their role by adopting stricter guidelines. For example, businesses may no longer deduct lobbying costs as a business expense. Trade associations must report to members the proportion of their dues that goes toward lobbying, and that proportion may not be reported as a business expense. Congress also passed legislation limiting the size of gifts its members could accept from interest groups, and members cannot accept honoraria for speeches.[55]

Political Parties and Interest Groups: What Do You Think?

We would like to think that government policies are products of legislators representing the public interest. But in truth few programs and policies ever reach the public agenda without the vigorous efforts of the political parties and key interest groups, which help to crystallize a world of possible government actions into a set of distinct choices. The activity of parties and interest groups is of critical importance. As we saw at the start of this chapter, Keli Carender recognized this when she helped found the Tea Party movement.

★ James Madison wrote that "liberty is to faction as air is to fire."[56] By this he meant that the organization and proliferation of political parties and interests are inevitable in a free society. Do you think Keli Carender would agree?

★ Is the two-party system ideal for American politics, or would electoral reforms that encourage more parties to form give more choice to voters?

★ Is party polarization likely to remain high in the near future? Is this a problem? What rules or processes, if any, could reduce party polarization?

★ What do you think of competition among different interests—is it free, open, and vigorous, or are some types of interests more likely to organize? What are the implications for government and politics?

Practice Quiz

1. Political parties are different from interest groups in that political parties *(p. 215)*
   a) seek to control the government by nominating candidates and electing them to office.
   b) are constitutionally exempt from taxation.
   c) are entirely nonprofit.
   d) have much larger memberships.
   e) have much smaller memberships.

2. In a _____ electoral system, political parties are awarded legislative seats based on their share of the total vote cast in the election. *(p. 215)*
   a) plurality
   b) proportional representation
   c) split-ticket
   d) straight-ticket
   e) open primary

3. The congressional election system in the United States is called "first past the post" because *(pp. 215–16)*
   a) candidates must win both a primary election and a general election before taking office.
   b) seats in the House of Representatives and Senate are allocated to political parties based on their share of the total vote cast in the election.
   c) the candidate with the most votes wins even if she did not win a majority of the total.
   d) a candidate can win an election only if he wins a majority of the total vote.
   e) more Americans now vote by mail than at their local polling places.

4. Which of the following is *not* a responsibility of the Democratic National Committee and the Republican National Committee? *(pp. 216–18)*
   a) to work to enhance their party's media image
   b) to set the rules for primaries and caucuses
   c) to give candidates money for their campaigns
   d) to select their party's candidates for elective office
   e) to try to minimize disputes within the party

5. Which of the following best describes the role of factions within the major parties? *(p. 219)*
   a) Factions do not exist; party members largely agree about all issues in a party's platform.
   b) Parties are usually divided into no more than two factions: one liberal and one conservative.
   c) Factions exist within parties because parties are coalitions of people who represent many diverse interests.
   d) Factions are only relevant during elections; they are not relevant among officials who have already been elected.
   e) Factions nearly always result in major parties being split up into smaller parties.

6. Who are "hidden partisans"? *(p. 220)*
   a) independents who lean toward one of the major parties
   b) congressional staffers and other unelected government workers
   c) officials who work for the national party committees
   d) Republicans who identify as liberal and Democrats who identify as conservative
   e) partisans who do not regularly vote

7. Which of the following social groups usually votes for Republicans? *(p. 221)*
   a) women
   b) nonwhite racial and ethnic groups
   c) people with college degrees
   d) organized labor
   e) the very wealthy

8. The so-called New Deal coalition was severely strained *(p. 230)*
   a) during the 1860s by conflicts over slavery and southern secession.
   b) during the 1890s by conflicts over the gold standard.
   c) during the 1930s by conflicts over the Great Depression and America's involvement in World War II.
   d) during the 1960s by conflicts over civil rights and the Vietnam War.
   e) during the 1990s by conflicts over abortion and affirmative action.

9. The National Rifle Association, the Sierra Club, and Mothers Against Drunk Driving are all examples of *(p. 235)*
   a) membership associations.
   b) citizen groups.
   c) professional associations.
   d) ideological groups.
   e) public-sector groups.

10. Gifts, discounts, and health insurance are examples of *(pp. 238–39)*
    a) purposive benefits.
    b) informational benefits.
    c) solidary benefits.
    d) material benefits.
    e) member dues.

11. Friendship and networking are examples of *(p. 239)*
    a) purposive benefits.
    b) informational benefits.
    c) solidary benefits.
    d) material benefits.
    e) member dues.

12. A stable, cooperative relationship between a House or Senate committee or subcommittee, an executive branch program, and one or more well-organized interest groups is called *(pp. 242–43)*
    a) an issue network.
    b) a public interest group.
    c) a political action committee.
    d) pluralism.
    e) an iron triangle.

13. A loose network of like-minded politicians, consultants, activists, and interest groups drawn together by a public policy issue is referred to as *(p. 244)*
    a) an issue network.
    b) a public interest group.
    c) a political action committee.
    d) pluralism.
    e) an iron triangle.

14. Which of the following is a way that interest groups use the courts to influence public policy? *(p. 244)*
    a) supplying judges with solidary benefits
    b) joining an issue network
    c) creating an iron triangle
    d) forming a political action committee
    e) filing amicus briefs

15. Interest groups with _____ have been shown to have more access to lawmakers. *(p. 245)*
    a) a history of supporting successful candidates for office
    b) large constituencies who have an interest in hot-button policy issues
    c) the most money
    d) headquarters in Washington, D.C.
    e) demonstrated technical expertise

Key Terms

political parties *(p. 215)*

partisanship *(p. 215)*

two-party system *(p. 215)*

party organization *(p. 216)*

party identification *(p. 220)*

party activists *(p. 220)*

gender gap *(p. 223)*

third parties *(p. 231)*

interest group *(p. 232)*

collective goods *(p. 235)*

free riders *(p. 235)*

informational benefits *(p. 238)*

material benefits *(p. 238)*

solidary benefits *(p. 239)*

purposive benefits *(p. 239)*

pluralism *(p. 239)*

lobbying *(p. 241)*

iron triangle *(p. 242)*

issue network *(p. 244)*

★ *chapter* ★

09

Participation, Campaigns, and Elections

WHAT GOVERNMENT DOES AND WHY IT MATTERS

Elections are the core of any democracy. In a democratic system like the United States, citizens self-govern by choosing among candidates and electing leaders to represent them in government. The rules of elections affect who runs, how they run, who votes, and who wins.

As you will see in this chapter, one concern with elections in America is that running for office and donating to campaigns is concentrated among the affluent and well connected. Voters in the city of Seattle decided to try an experiment to open up politics to more participants. In 2015 they approved a ballot initiative creating the Seattle Democracy Voucher Program. The city sends residents four $25 vouchers that they can donate to candidates running for city council. The program is funded by an increase in the local property tax.

The Democracy Voucher Program has succeeded in encouraging new types of candidates. Pat Murakami, an IT professional, had lived in Seattle for 40 years and had served on various school- and community-related

In 2019, Seattle city council candidate Shaun Scott was able to use the Seattle Democracy Voucher Program to help publicly fund his campaign. Though he ultimately lost the election, these programs aim to enable candidates of all economic statuses and backgrounds to run successful campaigns for public office.

associations, but decided to run for city council only because of the vouchers. "I never would have attempted to run" without them, she said. In 2017 they made up 90 percent of her funding, and she managed to win the primary election. Although she lost the general election, she was heartened enough to run again in 2019. "I would have been a complete non-contender without the program," she said.[1] Other new candidates from a variety of backgrounds have been inspired by the program as well. Teresa Mosqueda, a first-time candidate in 2017, was a renter paying off student loans.[2] Shaun Scott, a 2019 candidate, described himself on Twitter as a "Black working-class Millennial candidate with a net worth of approximately $10,000. If it weren't for the democracy voucher program, running for office would be a pipe dream."[3]

The program appears to have boosted voter interest and turnout as well. A University of Washington study found that residents who had voted in fewer than half of local elections before 2017 were four times more likely to vote in 2017 if they had used their vouchers. But the program is not without its hiccups. In the first year, some people thought the vouchers were junk mail.

The city ran a commercial with a talking dog to remind people what they were: "That's my human. She's looking for Democracy Vouchers. But she's not going to find them because I ate them." In its early years, the program had high administrative costs as well. But it survived a court challenge, with the Washington State Supreme Court affirming that the program does not violate First Amendment rights, as the plaintiffs, who objected to the property tax increase, alleged.[4] (Many observers expect the case to go to the U.S. Supreme Court.)

Seattle is not alone in attempting to increase electoral participation. Since 2015, city and county governments around the country have enacted at least eight public campaign-finance programs, and many states have enacted same-day voter-registration laws. Of the 10 states with the highest average voting rates, 7 offer same-day registration.[5]

In this chapter, we will learn about how elections work in the United States and how electoral rules and other considerations influence campaign strategy and turnout. We will see how election laws, the candidates' campaigns, and voters' choices determined the outcome of the 2020 presidential and congressional elections, and thus determined who represents the American people in government.

CHAPTER GOALS

★ Describe the patterns of participation among major demographic groups (pp. 253–62)

★ Describe the major rules and types of elections in the United States (pp. 262–69)

★ Explain strategies campaigns use to win elections (pp. 269–77)

★ Identify the major factors that influence voters' decisions (pp. 277–78)

★ Analyze the strategies, issues, and outcomes of the 2020 elections (pp. 278–87)

Who Participates and How?

Describe the patterns of participation among major demographic groups

Political participation refers to a wide range of activities in politics. Participation in politics includes not only voting in elections but also attending campaign events, rallies, and fundraisers; contributing money to campaigns, candidates, and parties; contacting elected officials; working on behalf of candidates and campaigns, such as canvassing voters; displaying campaign signs; and signing political petitions. Protests, demonstrations, and strikes, too, are age-old forms of participatory politics. Participation also includes publicly expressing support for or opposition to candidates or campaigns on social media, as well as organizing campaign events. The expansive world of digital politics includes not only the exchange of information but also new forms of fundraising and voter mobilization.

RIOTS AND PROTESTS

If there is any natural or spontaneous form of popular political participation, it is not the election but the protest or riot. In fact, for much of American history, fewer Americans exercised their right to vote than participated in urban riots and rural uprisings, as voting for a long time was limited to White, male, landowning citizens.

The vast majority of Americans today reject rioting or other violence for political ends, but peaceful **protest** is protected by the First Amendment and generally recognized as a legitimate and important form of political activity. During the height of the civil rights movement in the 1960s, hundreds of thousands of Americans took part in peaceful protests to demand social and political rights for African Americans. Peaceful marches and demonstrations have since been employed by a host of groups across the ideological spectrum. In recent years, even before the protests following George

protest participation that involves assembling crowds to confront a government or other official organization

Floyd's death in May 2020, growing concern over excessive use of police force against African Americans had led to hundreds of protests across the nation. The Black Lives Matter movement prompted national discussion and political action around racial inequity in the criminal justice system and reform, although critics argued that continued instances of excessive force, such as George Floyd's death in police custody, showed continued need for reform.

POLITICAL PARTICIPATION IN ELECTIONS

For most people, voting in elections is the most common form of participation in politics. When asked what makes a good citizen, the top reason mentioned by three in four Americans is voting.[6]

By contacting political officials, attending campaign events and rallies, or volunteering to work on a campaign, citizens can communicate much more detailed information

FIGURE 9.1

Political Participation

Political activities such as volunteering generally take more time and effort than voting. When asked about various forms of political participation, over 40 percent of respondents said they expressed support for a campaign on social media.

PERCENTAGE OF PEOPLE WHO REPORT PARTICIPATING IN EACH ACTIVITY

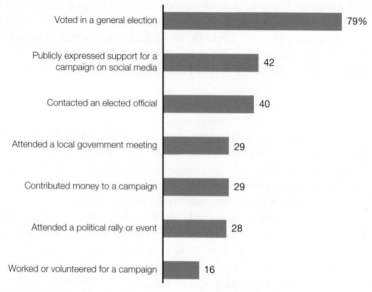

Voted in a general election — 79%
Publicly expressed support for a campaign on social media — 42
Contacted an elected official — 40
Attended a local government meeting — 29
Contributed money to a campaign — 29
Attended a political rally or event — 28
Worked or volunteered for a campaign — 16

SOURCE: Based on a sample made up primarily of registered voters; "Political Engagement, Knowledge, and the Midterms," Pew Research Center, April 26, 2018, www.people-press .org/2018/04/26/10-political-engagement-knowledge-and-the-midterms/ (accessed 10/12/18).

to public officials than they can by voting, thus making these other political activities often more satisfying.[7] But these forms of political action generally require more time, effort, and/or money than voting. As a result, the percentage of the population that participates in ways other than voting is relatively low (see Figure 9.1).

Voting For most Americans, voting is the single most important political act. The right to vote gives ordinary Americans an equal voice in politics, since each vote within the same district or state has the same value. Voting is especially important because it selects the officials who make the laws that the American people must follow.

During early periods of American history, the right to vote, called **suffrage**, was usually restricted to White males over the age of 21. Many states further limited voting to those who owned property or paid more than a specified amount of annual tax. Until the early 1900s, state legislatures elected U.S. senators, and there were

suffrage the right to vote; also called *franchise*

FIGURE 9.2

Voter Turnout* in Presidential and Midterm Elections, 1892–2020

Since the 1890s, participation in elections has declined substantially, with the exception of the 2020 presidential election. One pattern is consistent across time: more Americans tend to vote in presidential election years than in years when only congressional and local elections are held. What are some of the reasons that participation rose and fell during the last century and then rose again in 2020?

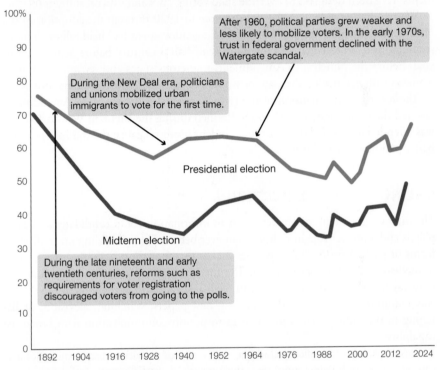

After 1960, political parties grew weaker and less likely to mobilize voters. In the early 1970s, trust in federal government declined with the Watergate scandal.

During the New Deal era, politicians and unions mobilized urban immigrants to vote for the first time.

Presidential election

Midterm election

During the late nineteenth and early twentieth centuries, reforms such as requirements for voter registration discouraged voters from going to the polls.

*Percentage of voting-eligible population

SOURCES: Erik Austin and Jerome Clubb, *Political Facts of the United States since 1789* (New York: Columbia University Press, 1986); United States Election Project, www.electproject .org (accessed 11/14/16); "2018 November General Election Turnout Rates," United States Election Project, November 12, 2020, www.electproject.org/2020g (accessed 11/12/20).

no direct elections for members of the electoral college (who in turn elect the president). As a result, elections for the U.S. House as well as for state legislatures and local offices were how eligible citizens could participate in government. Voter **turnout** as a percentage of the adult U.S. population during this period was relatively low.

During the nineteenth and early twentieth centuries, states often further restricted voting rights, initially through poll taxes (fees charged to vote) and literacy tests (reading tests) designed to limit immigrant voting in northern cities. These strategies

turnout the percentage of eligible individuals who actually vote

were later imported into the southern states to prevent African Americans and poor Whites from voting during the Jim Crow era—the period after the Civil War when African Americans were legally granted the right to vote and before the passage of the 1965 Voting Rights Act (see Chapter 5). Before the 1960s civil rights movement, voting rights often varied greatly from state to state, with many southern states using an array of laws to prevent participation in politics, including all-White primaries and requiring that voters own property in order to be able to vote (see Figure 9.2).[8]

Given the variation in voting rights across states, over the past two centuries of American history many federal statutes, court decisions, and constitutional amendments have been designed to override state voting laws and expand suffrage.[9]

Women nationwide won the right to vote in 1920 through the adoption of the Nineteenth Amendment. The women's suffrage movement had held rallies, demonstrations, and protest marches for more than half a century before achieving this goal. Before the Nineteenth Amendment, numerous states and territories adopted women's suffrage, paving the way for women to earn the right to vote nationally.

The most recent expansion of the right to vote, the Twenty-Sixth Amendment, lowered the voting age from 21 to 18. Ratified during the Vietnam War, in 1971, it was intended to channel the disruptive student protests against the war into peaceful participation at the ballot box.

ONLINE POLITICAL PARTICIPATION

The internet gives citizens greater access to information about candidates and campaigns and a greater role in politics than ever before. While building on traditional forms of participation, digital politics makes many of those activities easier, more immediate, and more personalized. The internet and social media offer an active, two-way form of communication with feedback, rather than the more passive, one-way communication involved in reading newspapers, watching television, or listening to the radio. It combines person-to-person communication with broadcast capability.

Digital political participation includes a wide range of activities: discussing issues and candidates or mobilizing supporters through social media, email, and text messaging; reading online news stories and commenting on them; viewing YouTube videos and campaign ads; contributing money to candidates, parties, and groups; contacting political leaders and following them on Twitter; running campaign ads on social networking sites; organizing petition drives; and organizing face-to-face neighborhood meetings online. With 67 percent of Americans reading the news using social media, digital participation is the most common way average Americans participate in politics outside of voting.[10]

Online mobilization works effectively through emotional appeals, immediacy, personal networks, and social pressure. One's social network plays a

digital political participation activities designed to influence politics using the internet, including visiting a candidate's website, organizing events online, and signing an online petition

Voter Turnout in Comparison

There are many factors that influence whether an individual decides to vote or not. Governments can take several steps to try to increase voter turnout. These include making registration automatic upon reaching voting age, scheduling elections on weekends or a national holiday, conducting elections by mail-in ballot, or even making voting compulsory with the potential for being fined if one does not have a valid excuse.

1. Which of the government policies seem to have the greatest effect on voter turnout?

How does each of these policies make voting easier? Why might even countries with compulsory voting fail to achieve high turnout? How difficult might it be to enforce such a law?

2. What are the downsides to each of these policies? How can a country balance the desire for electoral participation against the desire to protect the right of its citizens to choose to abstain from politics? Which of these policies do you think would be most likely to improve voter turnout in the United States?

COUNTRY	TURNOUT AS PERCENT OF VOTING AGE POPULATION	COMPULSORY VOTING	WEEKEND OR HOLIDAY VOTING	AUTOMATIC OR COMPULSORY REGISTRATION
Australia	81%	Yes	Yes	Yes
Brazil	78	Yes	Yes	Yes
Germany	71		Yes	Yes
India	65		Yes	Yes
South Africa	61		Yes	
Japan	60		Yes	Yes
United Kingdom	60		Yes	
Canada	57			
Mexico	56	Yes	Yes	Yes
Tunisia	54			
United States	45			
Switzerland	39		Yes	Yes

SOURCES: International Institute for Democracy and Electoral Assistance (IDEA) Voter Turnout Database, www.idea.int/data-tools/data/voter-turnout; ACE Electoral Knowledge Network, http://aceproject.org/epic-en/CDTable?view=country&question=VR008 (accessed 8/8/19).

much stronger role in political participation than do individual factors such as income and education. When members of a social network indicate they have voted in an election or contributed to a candidate, for example, that can motivate others in their network to do the same.[11]

Social media can efficiently coordinate the actions of millions of people required for running political campaigns and winning elections. One in three social media users has encouraged others to vote, and roughly the same percentage have shared their own thoughts on politics or government online.[12] Social media make possible tiny acts of political participation—sharing, following a candidate or organization, liking a post, commenting—that can scale up to dramatic changes, leading to real-world political protests, voter-mobilization drives, and the election of candidates and parties to government.[13] Such acts give those who are uninterested in or rarely engaged by politics an easy way of getting involved, which can then encourage them to do more.

Digital politics can create punctuated bursts of collective action. For example, during the 2016 presidential primaries, Bernie Sanders's supporters relied heavily on Reddit to organize rallies and rock concerts on his behalf. After Donald Trump won the 2016 election despite losing the popular vote by nearly 3 million votes, over 700,000 people signed an online petition to eliminate the electoral college and elect the president based on actual votes cast.

Some have dismissed political activity on social media as *clicktivism*—forms of participation that require little effort and may not convert to offline acts of participation in politics. Others argue that so-called clicktivism is the building block for sustained participation in politics. Donald Trump's extensive use of Twitter is evidence that audience-building on social media matters for political leadership and winning votes. A survey analysis of 65,000 registered voters found that frequent social media users were more likely to vote for Trump than for any other candidate in 2016.[14] The clicks of millions of Americans can and do add up.

SOCIOECONOMIC STATUS

Americans with higher levels of education, more income, and higher-level occupations—what social scientists call higher **socioeconomic status**—participate much more in politics than do those with less education and less income.[15] Education is the single most important factor in predicting whether an individual will not only vote but also participate in most other ways, such as by encouraging other people to vote or support an issue and donating to a candidate or cause. Just 52 percent of those with only a high school diploma voted in the 2016 presidential election, compared with 74 percent of college graduates.

Unsurprisingly, income is another important factor when it comes to making contributions, as well as voting. Among people age 45–64, for example, the 2016 census found that 83 percent of individuals earning over $150,000 a year voted compared to 43 percent of those earning less than $20,000 per year.[16] Individuals higher on the socioeconomic scale also tend to have higher levels of interest in politics.[17]

socioeconomic status status in society based on level of education, income, and occupational prestige

Even though much time and effort is spent mobilizing young voters, people who actually vote tend to be older than the average American.

AGE

Older people have much higher rates of participation than do young people, in part because they are more likely to own homes and pay property taxes, which makes them more aware of the importance of government.

The pattern of older people voting more was evident in 2016, with citizens 65 years and older reporting the highest turnout (71 percent), followed by those age 45–66 (67 percent), age 30–44 (58 percent), and age 18–29 (46 percent), according to the census. In midterm elections without a presidential race, youth turnout has historically been extremely low, though youth turnout grew dramatically in the most recent midterm. Among the youngest age cohort, voter turnout went from 20 percent in 2014 to 36 percent in 2018, and increased to 53–56 percent in 2020.

RACE AND ETHNICITY

Increased demographic diversity is rapidly changing U.S. politics. Members of racial and ethnic groups are more likely to vote Democratic, while White non-Latinos are more likely to vote Republican. The 2016 and 2020 electorates were the country's most racially and ethnically diverse ever; combined, African Americans, Latinos, Asian Americans, and other racial or ethnic minorities accounted for 33 percent of all registered voters in 2018, while the share of White non-Hispanic registered voters declined from 76 percent in 2000 to 67 percent by 2018. Latino voters now make up a larger share of the electorate in every state, but their double-digit gains are notable in Nevada, California, and Texas.

African Americans As we mentioned earlier, during much of the twentieth century, the widespread use of the poll tax, literacy tests, and other measures deprived African Americans in the South of the right to vote and meant that they had few avenues for participating in politics. Through a combination of protest, legal action, and political pressure, however, the victories of the civil rights movement made Blacks full citizens and stimulated a tremendous growth in voter turnout. The movement drew a network rooted in Black churches, the National Association for the Advancement of Colored People (NAACP), and historically Black colleges and universities. Because they tended to vote largely as a cohesive bloc, African American voters began to wield considerable political power, and the number of African American elected officials grew significantly. Today, however, state laws requiring government voter identification have created new impediments that tend to have a disproportionate impact on minority voters in some states.

Racial segregation remains a fact of life in the United States, along with Black urban poverty.[18] Participation (for Blacks as well as Whites) is highly correlated with more income, higher education, and higher-level occupations. Nevertheless, African Americans are somewhat more likely to vote than Whites of similar socioeconomic status.[19]

Whites A majority of people who vote in U.S. elections are non-Hispanic Whites (7 in 10 voters in 2016). This group has tended to vote Republican; 59 percent voted for Mitt Romney in 2012 and 57 percent for Trump in 2016. Stated another way, among Whites, just 39 percent voted for the Democratic presidential candidate in 2012 and 37 percent four years later.[20] But there are big differences among Whites based on education levels. A majority of Whites with a college degree support Democratic candidates and turn out at higher rates, while Whites without a college degree support Republicans and are less likely to vote.

In 2016, Donald Trump helped mobilize less-educated and lower-income Whites with a populist campaign promising to "Make America Great Again" and bring back manufacturing jobs. He organized nationwide campaign rallies with high turnout, while his Twitter account provided daily updates and he invested heavily in Facebook political campaign ads. In 2020 Biden won back many blue-collar workers, with Biden and Trump almost evenly split among non-college-educated voters. Biden won 20 percent more White non-college-educated men in 2020 than Hillary Clinton had in 2016.

Latinos and Latinas While 95 percent of Latinos identify racially as White, they are a separate ethnic identity, connected to a shared linguistic heritage. For many years, political analysts called the Latino vote "the sleeping giant" because Latinos and Latinas, while accounting for a large portion of the U.S. population, as a group had relatively low levels of political participation. For instance, 48 percent of Latinos and Latinas voted in the 2016 presidential election, compared with 65 percent of non-Hispanic Whites and just under 60 percent of African Americans.[21] Compared with Whites and African Americans, more Latinos and Latinas are recent immigrants to this country and thus have fewer opportunities, such as access to a quality education.

Therefore, they are more likely to lack resources for participation in politics, such as money, time, and language skills.[22]

Although turnout rates among Latinos are lower than non-Hispanic Whites, there is evidence these are increasing, especially in key swing states. President Trump's anti-immigration policies, which affect many Latinos, increased voter turnout in the 2018 elections by 50 percent compared to the 2014 elections, and increased further in 2020.[23]

Asian Americans Asian Americans are a smaller group than Whites, Latinos, or African Americans, making up roughly 6 percent of the population, or 21 million Americans. In particular states, such as California, home to 33 percent of the nation's Asian American population, the group has become an important political presence. Asian Americans have education and income levels closer to those of Whites than of Latinos and Latinas or African Americans, but they are less likely to participate in politics than Whites or African Americans[24] and have voter turnout rates similar to Latinos.[25] No one national group dominates among the Asian American population, and this diversity has impeded the development of group-based political power.

GENDER

Women register to vote at rates similar to those of men but are more likely to vote. In the high-turnout 2018 midterm election, 55 percent of women voted compared with 52 percent of men, a 3 percentage point gap. The ongoing significance of gender issues in American politics is best exemplified by the **gender gap**—a distinctive pattern of male and female voting decisions—in electoral politics. Women tend to vote in higher numbers for Democratic candidates, whereas Republicans win more male votes. Though the gender gap generally runs around 10 percentage points in presidential elections, the 2016 presidential election saw the first female major-party candidate and a significantly larger gender gap, with 54 percent of women supporting Clinton to 41 percent of men. In 2020, this gap increased even further.[26] Looking at women as a whole, women tend to prefer Democrats, but among White non-Hispanic women with lower education and income, support for Trump in 2016 was high. In presidential elections from 1952 to 2020, White women supported a Democratic candidate for president only twice.

RELIGION

For many Americans, religious groups provide an infrastructure for political participation. African American churches, for example, were instrumental in the civil rights movement, and African American religious leaders continue to play important roles in national and local politics. Jews have also been active as a group in politics, but less through religious bodies than through a variety of social action agencies, including the American

> **gender gap** a distinctive pattern of voting behavior reflecting the differences in views between women and men

Jewish Congress and the Anti-Defamation League. Some of the most divisive conflicts in politics today, such as those over abortion, contraceptives, and LGBTQ rights, hinge on differences over religious beliefs. In the late 1970s, the influence of White evangelical Christians rose to prominence, aligning with the Republican Party and eventually backing Ronald Reagan for president in the 1980 election. Over the next few years, evangelicals strengthened their movement by registering voters and mobilizing them. Their success was evident in the 1984 election, when 8 in 10 evangelical Christian voters cast their ballots for Reagan. This alignment continues today—in 2016 and 2020, most White evangelical Christians supported Trump in the general election.

State Electoral Laws Regulate Most Voting

> **Describe the major rules and types of elections in the United States**

Presidential elections take place every four years and congressional elections every two years, both on the first Tuesday after the first Monday in November. Congressional elections that do not coincide with a presidential election are called **midterm elections**. Localities and states can choose when to hold their elections. Most Americans have the opportunity to vote in several elections each year. Voting in elections is the most common form of participation in American politics, and elections are central to democratic government.

midterm elections
congressional elections that do not coincide with a presidential election; also called *off-year elections*

In the American federal system, the responsibility for running elections is decentralized, resting largely with state and local governments. Elections

Elections are the most important way that Americans participate in politics. Some of the rules of elections have changed over time. (Left) African Americans vote for the first time in Wilcox County, Alabama, after the passage of the Voting Rights Act in 1965. (Right) An 18-year-old woman registers to vote in Illinois after the Twenty-Sixth Amendment in 1971 lowered the nationwide voting age from 21 to 18.

are administered by state, county, and city election boards, which are responsible for establishing and staffing polling places, processing mail-in ballots, and verifying the eligibility of voters. State laws influence who may vote, how they vote, and where they vote. For example, states decide whether to require photo identification to vote and whether to allow residents to vote by mail, to vote in person before Election Day, and to register to vote and then vote on the same day.

Election season begins with **primary elections,** which in most states are held to select each party's candidates for the **general election.** (A few states have "top two primaries," in which candidates from all parties run against one another and then the two who get the most votes face each other in the general election.) Used for offices at the national, state, and often local levels, primary elections are thus usually races where Democrats compete against Democrats and Republicans against Republicans.

The United States is one of the few nations to hold primary elections. In most countries, nominations of candidates are controlled completely by party officials, as they once were in the United States. Primary elections were introduced at the turn of the twentieth century by Progressive Era reformers who hoped to weaken the power of party leaders by enabling voters to pick candidates directly. In states with **closed primaries,** only registered members of a political party may vote in a primary election to select that party's candidates, and independents do not get to participate. States with **open primaries** allow all registered voters, including independents, to choose which party's primary they will participate in.

As stipulated by the Constitution, the states, not the federal government, control voter registration and voting itself. This creates wide variation in the laws governing elections and voting, which affect participation in politics.[27] Voter turnout in presidential elections in the last decade ranges from a high of over 70 percent of eligible voters in Maine to a low of 42 percent in Hawaii. State electoral laws can make voting easier or can impede voting.

primary elections elections held to select a party's candidate for the general election

general election a regularly scheduled election involving most districts in the nation or state, in which voters select officeholders; in the United States, general elections for national office and most state and local offices are held on the first Tuesday after the first Monday in November in even-numbered years (every four years for presidential elections)

closed primary a primary election in which voters can participate in the nomination of candidates but only of the party in which they are enrolled for a period of time prior to primary day

open primary a primary election in which the voter can wait until the day of the primary to choose which party to enroll in to select candidates for the general election

REGISTRATION REQUIREMENTS

One of the most common reasons people in the United States give for not voting is that they are not registered. Young people especially are less likely to register to vote than are older Americans, in part because they tend to change residences more often.[28] Other groups with lower registration rates include people with lower incomes and education, who also tend to change residences more frequently. Once

Register . . . and Vote

MAGGIE BUSH, Programs and Outreach Director for the League of Women Voters of the United States

The League of Women Voters emerged from the fight for women's suffrage in the early twentieth century. Its primary goal today is to help Americans of all descriptions understand and navigate the voting process. Maggie Bush, Programs and Outreach Director for the League of Women Voters of the United States, says, "In most elections, only 50 percent of 18-year-olds are registered to vote, which means that older voters are making decisions that affect all of us. We need to be part of the process. Elections are how we determine how safe our streets are, what kind of health care we have, how community college decisions are made and resources allocated. The first step to participating in these democratic decisions is voting." Here are Maggie's tips for registering to vote and going to the polls:

Registering to Vote

1 How do I know how to register? Consult a website such as Vote411.org, run by the League of Women Voters. Registration procedures and rules vary from state to state. From your state's site at Vote411.org, you can register online (in over 30 states) or print and fill out a paper form. Note that the registration deadline can be up to 30 days prior to the election.

2 What information do I need to provide? On the voter-registration form, you will provide your name and address and will certify that you are eligible—that you are a U.S. citizen and of the appropriate age. The voting age is 18, but some states allow preregistration or primary-election voting at younger ages. You may also need an identification number such as a driver's license, state ID, or the last four digits of your Social Security number, depending on your state.

3 Which address should I use? It is up to the student where they want to vote. You can use your school address or be registered and vote absentee from your home address if it differs.

4 Am I required to register with a political party? In most states, you will be asked to declare an affiliation with a political party or to remain an independent or unaffiliated voter. In many states, if you do not specify a party, you will not be able to vote in primary elections, which parties use to choose their candidates for general elections. Some states have "open primaries," which do not require voters to have a party affiliation.

After you submit your registration electronically or by mail to your local election official, they will follow up, usually by mail, to confirm that you are eligible to vote in the next election. If your address changes—even if you switch apartments in the same building—you need to update your registration. You can update at Vote411.org.

Voting

5 **Where can you vote?** At Vote411. org you can enter your address of residency to find your polling place, its hours of operation, and any early voting options. Many states offer early voting in the evenings and on weekends in the weeks before elections to facilitate voting by busy people such as students.

6 **What's on the ballot?** You can check Vote411.org to see a list of candidates and ballot initiatives for your location. When you go to vote you can take a sample ballot or notes on your phone or on paper with your selections, though some states prohibit taking a selfie with your ballot.

7 **What will happen at the polling place?** You will check in with a poll worker, who will locate your name on the registration list and may check your identification, depending on state rules. You will then be directed to a voting machine or given a paper ballot. Voters have the right to privacy while they vote and the right to accommodations for disabilities. After you vote, you submit your ballot electronically or insert it into a ballot box.

8 **What happens if you have a problem voting?** The first step is to ask a poll worker on-site for help. Another resource is the 866-OUR-VOTE hotline run by volunteers with a legal support staff to make sure people's votes are being counted properly.

That's it. At many polling places you will receive an "I Voted" sticker so you can proudly display your democratic participation.

Voter Registration Application

Before completing this form, review the General, Application, and State specific instructions

This space for office use only.

Are you a citizen of the United States of America?
Will you be 18 years old on or before election day?
If you checked "No" in response to either of these questions, do not complete form.
(Please see state-specific instructions for rules regarding eligibility to register prior to age 18.)

	Last Name	First Name		Middle Name(s)	State
1			Apt. or Lot #	City/Town	State
2	Home Address			City/Town	
3	Address Where You Get Your Mail If Different From Above			ID Number - (See item 6 in the instruction
4	Date of Birth	**5**	Telephone Number (optional)	**6**	
	Month Day Year		Race or Ethnic Group (see item 8 in the instructions for your State)		
	Choice of Party (see item 7 in the instructions foy your State)	**8**			

...er/affirm that:

265

individuals become interested in the election and learn about the candidates, it may be too late for them to register.

In most democratic countries, residents are automatically registered to vote in elections at adult age. In most states except North Dakota, which doesn't require voter registration, individuals who are eligible to vote must take the initiative to register with the state election board before they are actually allowed to vote—sometimes 30 days beforehand.

In 2016 Oregon instituted automatic voter registration (AVR), and as of 2020, 19 states and the District of Columbia have approved AVR. Automatically registering residents to vote is related to another state election reform, **same-day registration**. As of 2020, 17 states plus Washington, D.C., have enacted same-day registration laws, which means that people can both register and vote when they go to the polls on Election Day. Not only is voter turnout in these states higher than the national average, but younger and less educated voters are also more likely to participate.[29] Research shows that same-day registration is the most effective law to boost turnout.[30]

same-day registration the option in some states to register on the day of the election, at the polling place, rather than in advance of the election

VOTER IDENTIFICATION REQUIREMENTS

Another barrier to voting is the requirement that voters provide proof of identity. Recent adoption of voter ID laws in many states has reduced turnout rates, especially among racial minorities, the elderly, the young, and people with low income or disabilities—all of whom disproportionately lack government ID. Thirty-six states have some identification requirements to cast a ballot at the polls, and 8 of them have strict laws that require a government-issued photo.[31] Another 10 states have non-strict laws where photo ID is requested but is not required to vote. On the other end of the spectrum, in 14 states and the District of Columbia no ID is required to vote at the ballot box.

Some reports estimate that these laws reduce turnout by 2 to 3 percentage points, which can amount to millions of people who are prevented from voting nationwide. A recent study found that more stringent forms of these laws lower voter turnout and especially participation by racial and ethnic minorities relative to non-Latino Whites.[32]

Estimates indicate that more than 1 in 10 U.S. citizens does not have government-issued photo identification, including 1 in 5 African Americans. Government identification can be difficult to obtain even if the ID itself is free, because citizens must present a birth certificate to apply for it and applying for a replacement birth certificate costs money. In addition, travel to places where IDs are issued, such as a department of motor vehicles office, can be difficult for elderly and disabled people and residents of rural areas.

THE BALLOT

In the United States, it is the state and county governments, not the federal government, that run elections and create ballots. Some counties still use paper ballots, but most now use computerized electronic voting systems. The controversial 2000 presidential election led to a closer look at different ballot forms and voting systems used across the 3,000 U.S. counties. In 2000 the margin of victory for Republican George W. Bush over Democrat Al Gore in Florida was so small that the state ordered a recount. Careful examination of the results revealed that the punch card voting machines and "butterfly ballot" used in Florida had led to many voting and counting errors.

In the wake of this election, Congress adopted the Help America Vote Act (HAVA) in 2003, requiring the states to use computerized voter-registration databases. Critics of HAVA feared that such systems might be vulnerable to unauthorized use, or hacking. In 2016, 21 states experienced intrusion by Russian hackers into their computerized election systems, although to date there is no evidence that ballots were changed.[33] In the past, computerized voting machines generally worked well and significantly updated America's election system, but all computerized systems have vulnerabilities. Protecting state and county election systems from hackers is a new priority for reform.

Convenience voting, such as early voting and voting by mail, removes the need to stand in a potentially long line to cast a vote and may result in increased voter turnout.

PRESIDENTIAL ELECTIONS

Presidential elections follow unique rules because the president and vice president are the only public officials elected by all American voters (though they are technically elected by the electoral college).

Nominating Presidential Candidates: Primaries and Caucuses Before the presidential election every four years, the major parties start the process of selecting their presidential candidates by holding primary elections and caucuses. Most states hold primaries, but some use caucuses.

Caucuses are party business meetings. At the lowest level, precinct caucuses are meetings of registered voters of the same party within a local geographic area. Each state has thousands of precinct caucuses, whose purpose is to elect delegates supporting particular candidates to county caucuses. The county caucuses in turn elect delegates to represent their preferences at district caucuses, and the district caucuses elect delegates to the state party convention, where delegates to the national convention are chosen. Delegates to the national conventions choose the party's presidential candidate (see below). Compared with primary elections, caucuses involve fewer voters and therefore give party leaders and activists a larger role in selecting candidates.

The primaries and caucuses traditionally begin in January or February of a presidential election year and end in June, with state elections roughly every two weeks.

delegate a representative who votes according to the preferences of his or her constituency

Iowa and New Hampshire's disproportionate role in picking presidential candidates is due to their being the first states to cast votes. In fact, the presidential nomination process today has become "front-loaded," with states vying to increase their political influence by holding their primaries or caucuses earlier in the year. Early voting states are important because they can help candidates gain momentum by securing national media attention, campaign contributions, and higher ratings in public-opinion polls. Candidates who perform well in Iowa, New Hampshire, Nevada, or South Carolina send signals to voters in later voting states that they are viable (can win the nomination) and electable (can win the general election). A candidate who fares poorly in these early voting states may be written off as a loser and drop out of the race.

The result of each state's primary election or caucuses determines how its **delegates** will vote at their party's national convention. When the primaries and caucuses are concluded, it is usually clear which candidates have won their parties' nominations.

Nominating Presidential Candidates: Party Conventions By the time the two party conventions convene in the summer, the candidates usually arrive at the convention knowing who has enough delegate support in hand to assure a victory in the first round of balloting. If one candidate does not win a majority in the first round, a second ballot is issued, and delegates can choose to vote for a different candidate, although no party convention has gone beyond one ballot since 1952.

In addition to delegates chosen in primaries and caucuses and bound to the voting results there, the Democratic Party also designates a number of party leaders as so-called superdelegates, who can vote as they wish. At the 2016 Democratic National Convention, most superdelegates backed Hillary Clinton, giving her a significant advantage over her opponent and independent Bernie Sanders, despite Sanders's strong support among voters. The Republican Party does not use superdelegates, and their use is increasingly controversial among Democrats. In 2020, Democrats reduced the power of superdelegates by instituting a rule that superdelegates will be involved only if no candidate wins a majority of regular delegates in the first round of convention voting.

Even though the party convention usually confirms the choice emerging from the primaries and caucuses, it has other important tasks. The convention makes the rules concerning delegate selection and future presidential primary elections. Another important task for the convention is the drafting of a **party platform**, a statement of principles and pledges around which the delegates can unite.

Most important, the convention allows the party to showcase its candidates in anticipation of the general election. Before a large national audience, the presidential and vice-presidential nominees deliver acceptance speeches that begin their formal general-election campaign and provide them an opportunity to make a positive impression on voters.

party platform a party document, written at a national convention, that contains party philosophy, principles, and policy positions

Picking Presidents: The Electoral College The presidential election differs from other elections in an important way: voters do *not* directly elect the president. The **electoral college** is the group of electors who formally select the president and vice president. No other country in the world uses an electoral college to pick its president.

> **electoral college** the presidential electors from each state who meet after the general election to cast ballots for president and vice president

When Americans vote for president they are technically not voting directly for candidates, even though they mark ballots as such; they are instead choosing among slates of electors selected by each party in the state and pledged, if elected, to support that party's presidential candidate. Electoral votes are allocated to each state based on the size of its congressional delegation (senators plus House members, though members of Congress play no role). North Dakota, for example, has 3 votes in the electoral college (based on its 2 senators plus 1 representative), while California has 55 (2 senators plus 53 representatives). In 2019, each elector in North Dakota (a state with roughly 770,000 people) represents roughly 253,000 people, while each elector in California (39.5 million people) represents 718,000. Because of this, many people argue the electoral college is biased against large-population states and overrepresents small-population states. Under the electoral college, one electoral vote in California is worth about one-third of a vote in North Dakota.

It is the winner of the electoral college who becomes president—the candidate who wins at least 270 of the college's 538 votes—and not necessarily the candidate with the most popular votes, or votes from the people. This is in part because the electoral college and most elections in the United States are governed by plurality, winner-take-all rules. With only two exceptions, each state awards *all* of its electors to the candidate who receives the most votes in the state.[34] Thus, in 2020, Biden received all 16 of Georgia's electoral votes, though he won only 49 percent of the votes in the state.

Since electoral votes are won on a state-by-state basis, it is mathematically possible for a candidate who receives the most popular votes nationwide to fail to carry enough states for their electoral votes to add up to a majority. This has happened four times. Most recently, in 2016 Hillary Clinton won almost 3 million more votes than Donald Trump, but Trump won the majority in the electoral college.

Election Campaigns Are a Political Marathon

> **Explain strategies campaigns use to win elections**

Because of the complexity of the campaign process and the amount of money that candidates must raise, presidential campaigns often begin almost two years before the November election; and congressional campaigns, a year in

campaign an effort by political candidates and their supporters to win the backing of donors, political activists, and voters in their quest for political office

incumbent a candidate running for re-election to a position that he or she already holds

advance. The **campaign** for any office consists of a number of steps (see Figure 9.3). Candidates often form an exploratory committee consisting of supporters who will help them raise funds and bring their names to the attention of the media, potential donors, and voters. Money from corporations and individuals is an important component of U.S. elections, since public funding is limited. **Incumbents** have an advantage in these areas over the candidates challenging them. They usually are already well known and have little difficulty attracting supporters and contributors—unless, of course, they have been subject to damaging publicity while in office.

CAMPAIGN CONSULTANTS

A formal organization and professional campaign managers are critical for campaign success. For a local campaign, candidates generally need hundreds of volunteers and a few paid professionals. State-level campaigns call for thousands of volunteers, and presidential campaigns require tens of thousands of volunteers and hundreds of paid staff nationwide. Virtually all serious contenders for national and statewide office retain the services of professional campaign consultants, including a campaign manager, media consultants, pollsters and a data analytics team, financial advisers, a press spokesperson, and staff directors to coordinate the activities of volunteer and paid workers. Consultants offer candidates the expertise necessary to craft campaign messages, conduct opinion polls, produce television and social media ads, organize direct-mail campaigns, open field offices, and make use of information about their constituents from digital voter files, text messaging, email, political donations, and more.

FUNDRAISING

Candidates generally begin raising funds long before they face an election, and many politicians spend more time on it than on any other campaign activity.[35] Serious fundraising efforts involve appealing to both small and large donors. To have a reasonable chance of winning a seat in the House of Representatives, a candidate may need to raise more than $1 million; in 2014 candidates in the most competitive House races spent $10 million or more. In 2018, candidates in the most competitive House races spent $20 million or more, a huge increase over just four years. In the 2020 congressional races, candidates spent a record $7.2 billion, an increase from $5.9 billion in 2018.[36]

Once elected to office, members of Congress find it much easier to raise funds and are thus able to outspend their challengers.[37] Incumbents out-raise their opponents by significant amounts because most donations from businesses, interest groups, and PACs go to incumbents. These donors seek a voice in government from their investment; thus, they want to invest in the candidate most likely to win, and incumbents win most of the time. Members of the majority party in the House and Senate are particularly attractive to donors who want access to those in power.[38]

Electing the President: Steps in the Process

Formation of an Exploratory Committee
Formed 18 to 24 months before the election, this committee begins fundraising and bringing the candidate's name to the attention of the media and influential groups.

Fundraising
Presidential candidates must develop fundraising strategies, hire expert fundraisers, and quickly build a substantial "war chest" early on to show they are serious contenders.

Campaigning
Months before the primaries, candidates begin meetings with local leaders, public appearances, ad campaigns, and other strategies.

Primaries and Caucuses
Candidates need to do well in early contests such as Iowa and New Hampshire in order to build momentum and win their party's nomination. Party debates give candidates an opportunity to impress large television audiences.

The Convention
The Democratic and Republican parties hold national conventions in September prior to the November general election. The parties' nominees for president and vice president are officially announced.

The General Election Campaign
In the months leading up to the November election, candidates focus on battleground or swing states as they aim to win at least 270 votes in the electoral college. They run television ads and use new media to reach voters. They must continue to raise money throughout this process.

The Debates
In October, the major-party candidates engage in several televised debates along with one vice-presidential debate.

The General Election
On the Tuesday following the first Monday in November, voters in each state cast ballots. In most states, the candidate who wins the most votes in the state wins all of the state's votes in the electoral college.

The Electoral College
The electors meet in their state capitals in December, and their votes are officially counted in January.

The Inauguration
The president is officially inaugurated on January 20.

Candidates with the most campaign dollars often, but don't always, win. In 2008 and 2012, Barack Obama raised more than his Republican opponents. In 2016, though Hillary Clinton spent more than her opponent, Donald Trump, she did not win in the electoral college. Nonetheless, the 2016 election shattered previous records. The total cost of the 2020 elections (congressional and presidential) was an unprecedented $14 billion, making it the most expensive election in history and twice as expensive as the 2016 presidential election. In 2020, roughly half was spent on the congressional races and half on the presidential election.[39]

Candidates and campaigns spend a huge amount of time raising the necessary funds, which are obtained from at least six possible sources.

Individual Donors Politicians ask people for money via direct mail, email, text, phone, and face-to-face meetings. Under federal law, individuals may donate as much as $2,800 per candidate per election, $5,000 per federal PAC per calendar year, $35,500 per national party committee per calendar year, and $10,000 to state and local committees per calendar year. (There is no limit to the number of candidates or PACs that an individual can give to, however—the result of a 2014 Supreme Court decision.[40]) Bernie Sanders's 2016 presidential campaign raised an unprecedented $231 million in individual contributions, 58 percent of which was made up of small contributions under $200.[41]

Political Action Committees Political action committees (PACs) are organizations established by corporations, labor unions, or interest or advocacy groups to channel money into political campaigns. Nearly two-thirds of all PACs represent corporations, trade associations, and other business and professional groups. Under the terms of the 1971 Federal Election Campaign Act, PACs are permitted to make larger contributions to any given candidate than individuals are allowed to make. Moreover, related PACs often coordinate their contributions, increasing the amount of money a candidate actually receives from the same interest group. More than 4,600 PACs are registered with the Federal Election Commission, which oversees campaign finance practices in the United States. Many congressional and party leaders have established PACs, known as "leadership PACs," to provide funding for their political allies.

political action committee (PAC) a private group that raises and distributes funds for use in election campaigns

Soft Money Before 2002 most campaign donations took the form of "soft money," unregulated contributions to the national parties that were officially intended for party-building and voter-registration-and-mobilization efforts rather than for particular campaigns. Federal campaign finance legislation enacted in 2002 aimed to ban soft money by prohibiting the national parties from receiving contributions from corporations, unions, or individuals and preventing them from directing such funds to their affiliated state parties. However, it did not reduce money in politics. Under federal rules, a national political party may make unlimited "independent expenditures" advocating support for its own presidential candidate or defeat for an opposing party's candidate as long as these expenditures are not coordinated with the candidate's own campaign.

Outside Spending/Independent Expenditures: Super PACs and Dark Money

527 committees (i.e., Super PACs) and 501(c)(4) committees (i.e., dark money) are forms of independent expenditures that are not covered by the spending restrictions imposed in 2002 by the Bipartisan Campaign Reform Act, but now raise much of the money used for political campaigns. These groups are named for the sections of the tax code under which they are organized. They can raise and spend unlimited amounts of money for political campaigns.

A 527 is a group established specifically for the purpose of political advocacy and is required to report its sources of funding to the IRS. A 501(c)(4) is a nonprofit group that also engages in campaign advocacy but may not spend more than half its revenue for political purposes. Unlike a 527, a 501(c)(4) is not required to disclose where it gets its funds or exactly what it does with them—as a result, its funding has earned the name "dark money." Indeed, it has become a common practice for wealthy and corporate donors, as well as foreigners, to route campaign contributions through 501(c)(4)s to avoid the legal limits on contributions through other channels.

Outside spending by 527s and 501(c)(4)s played an unprecedented role in the 2012, 2016, and 2020 presidential races, as these groups ran extensive television and digital ads. Super PACs on both sides relied on very large contributions. A growing concern is that elections in the United States can be bought with big money from corporations and wealthy donors, who will then hold significant influence when that candidate is elected.

Unlimited Spending by Candidates of Their Own Money On the basis of the *Buckley v. Valeo* decision, the right of individuals to spend their *own* money to campaign for office is a constitutionally protected matter of free speech and is not subject to limitation.[42] Thus, extremely wealthy candidates often contribute millions of dollars to their own campaign; for example, Democrats Tom Steyer and Mike Bloomberg spent millions of dollars of their own money in 2020.

CAMPAIGN STRATEGY

For candidates who win the nomination, the last hurdle is the general election. There are essentially two types of general-election campaigns in the United States today: grassroots campaigns and mass media campaigns. Grassroots campaigns, which include local and many congressional elections, are organizationally driven and labor intensive. Candidates make many public appearances—some involving celebrity supporters— and recruit volunteers to knock on doors, hand out

527 committee (Super PAC) a nonprofit independent political action committee that may raise unlimited sums of money from corporations, unions, and individuals but is not permitted to contribute to or coordinate directly with parties or candidates

501(c)(4) committees (dark money) politically active nonprofits; under federal law, these nonprofits can spend unlimited amounts on political campaigns and not disclose their donors as long as their activities are not coordinated with the candidate campaigns and political activities are not their primary purpose

grassroots campaigns political campaigns that operate at the local level, often using face-to-face communication to generate interest and momentum by citizens

leaflets, and organize rallies and other public events. Such extensive grassroots outreach and mobilization is designed to increase candidate visibility. Statewide campaigns, some congressional races, and the presidential election are mass media campaigns: media driven and money intensive. Barack Obama's campaigns in 2008 and 2012 were notable in combining both types of campaigns.

All campaigns must decide on a strategy: What will their main message be? How will they allocate their resources (to television, social media, face-to-face mobilization)? Which voters will they target? The electoral college is one election rule that influences the campaign strategy of presidential candidates by forcing them to campaign heavily in a small number of battleground, or swing, states—those whose populations are divided roughly evenly between Democrats and Republicans—while often ignoring the rest of the country. In 2016, 94 percent of the presidential campaign events occurred in 12 battleground states, especially the populous ones of Florida, Ohio, Pennsylvania, and Virginia.[43] Residents of battleground states are smothered with attention from the candidates and media as presidential candidates vie for those states' votes, while the millions of residents of states considered safe for Republicans (West Virginia, Utah) or Democrats (New York, Illinois, California) are often ignored.

The Media Contemporary political campaigns rely on a number of communication tools to reach the voters they want to target for support, including television, radio, social media/digital advertising, massive computerized databases, and microtargeting. Digital media are especially important in mobilizing people to vote.

Extensive use of the broadcast media, television in particular, is central to modern political campaigns. Television ads are used to establish candidate name recognition, create a favorable image of the candidate and a negative image of the opponent, link the candidate with desirable groups in the community, and communicate the candidate's stands on selected issues. Often in the later stages of a campaign, candidates and the political advocacy groups that support them (see below) will "go negative," airing ads that criticize their opponents' policy positions, qualifications, or character.

Voters consistently say they reject so-called negative campaigning, but negative ads can benefit voters more than positive ones in some cases.[44] Negative ads are more likely to address important policy differences and provide supporting evidence, while positive ads tend to focus on candidates' personal characteristics. Interestingly, when negative ads are misleading or even patently false, they are effective in that voters remember more from them than from positive ads, possibly because they are designed to elicit emotional responses, such as fear, anxiety, or anger.

In addition to ads sponsored by the candidates, a growing percentage of campaign ads are sponsored by the political parties and by political advocacy groups. The 2010 *Citizens United* Supreme Court decision allowed corporations, unions, and interest groups to form Super PACs that can spend unlimited amounts to advocate for or against candidates, as long as the Super PACs are "independent" of the candidate's campaign.

Candidates also benefit from *free media*, where the cost of advertising is borne by the television and print media themselves when they cover the candidates' statements and activities as news. In 2016, Donald Trump benefited from much free media coverage, largely due to his many controversial statements and tweets.[45]

Digital media have become another major weapon in modern political campaigns as more Americans turn to the internet, and social media in particular, for news. Today, every campaign for presidential, congressional, and major state offices develops a social media strategy for fundraising, mobilizing supporters, and getting out the vote. One reason digital media are so effective at organizing presidential campaigns is cost: digital media enable inexpensive organization of volunteers and offer more opportunities for free advertising, such as on Twitter and YouTube political videos.

Micro-Targeting and Polling The media and televised debates allow candidates to communicate their policy goals and promises to a broad range of voters, but this is also a blunt instrument; different voters care about different issues, after all. The idea behind micro-targeting is to send different campaign ads or messages to different demographic groups of voters and potential voters. Suburban "soccer moms," for instance, would be targeted with ads different from those targeting rural "cowboy dads."

Micro-targeting was first used effectively by Republican president George W. Bush in 2000 and 2004.[46] It became more sophisticated during the 2008 presidential campaign as Democrats built an extensive organization to contact and turn out voters. The Obama campaign made use of an unprecedented volume of survey data, conducting thousands of interviews each week to gauge voters' preferences. Statistical algorithms looked for patterns in the data the campaign had assembled

People are more likely to turn out to vote if someone asks them face-to-face. Direct mail and impersonal phone calls are less likely to have an effect on turnout.

for voters based on massive state voter-registration files, consumer data, and past campaign contacts. The campaign used this mountain of information to generate different, carefully targeted messages for different demographic, regional, and ideological groups to persuade them to turn out and vote for Obama.[47] Because of micro-targeting, millions of Americans heard from the campaign about issues that mattered the most to them. It was the first time "big data" had been used to win a presidential election. Most serious candidates now follow Obama's lead.

"People power" remains critical in modern political campaigns, since research suggests that direct mail and robocalls are less effective than face-to-face and in-person phone contacts.[48] Candidates continue to use the services of tens of thousands of volunteers, especially for get-out-the-vote drives. Still, even the recruitment of volunteers has become a job for electronic technology. Employing a technique called "instant organization," paid staff use phone banks to contact not only potential voters in computer-targeted areas but also potential campaign workers there.

Mobilization People become much more likely to participate when someone—a candidate campaign, a political party, or (especially) someone they know—asks them to get involved. A recent study of the decline in political participation in the United States in the twentieth century found that half of the drop-off could be accounted for by reduced **mobilization** efforts before 2004.[49] This decline has been largely reversed by nationwide political campaigns for president and Congress over the last decade.

Research on political mobilization has shown that face-to-face interaction with a canvasser greatly increased the chances that the person contacted would go to the polls, boosting overall voter turnout by almost 10 percent. The impact of direct mail was much smaller, increasing turnout by just 0.5 percent.[50] "Robocalls" (prerecorded phone calls) had no measurable effect on turnout, while in-person telephone calls were found to have a modest positive effect.

As means of mobilization, social media networks can mimic face-to-face communication. In a study involving 61 million users of Facebook, political scientists found that election appeals from Facebook friends were responsible for increasing turnout by 340,000 people (who otherwise would not have voted). Users' closest connections ("friends" on the network) had the most influence in getting them to vote.[51]

Since 2000, competitive presidential elections have motivated both parties to build strong grassroots organizations to reach voters and turn them out on Election Day. In 2004, Republicans were more successful in this effort, training more than 1.4 million volunteers to make calls, go door-to-door to register voters, write letters in favor of President Bush, create pro-Bush blogs, and phone local radio call-in shows.

In 2008, Barack Obama's campaign made mobilization a centerpiece of its strategy, organizing a base of volunteers to go door-to-door seeking support for their candidate. Many of Obama's crucial primary victories relied on direct voter mobilization. The campaign then created a nationwide organization,

mobilization the process by which large numbers of people are organized for a political activity

opening more than 700 field offices. Obama campaigned in all 50 states, rather than focusing solely on battleground states as his predecessors had done. By mobilizing support in places where Democrats had not seriously contended in the past, the Obama campaign expanded the party's electoral map. For the first time in decades, turnout rates were comparable to those in 1960.

In the 2016 and 2020 elections, political campaigns shifted to social media as a primary way to mobilize voters and directly provide their supporters with election updates. In 2016, three in 10 Americans received digital messages about the elections, with far more people turning to the candidates' social media posts than to their websites or emails.[52]

Voters Decide Based on Party, Issues, and Candidates

> **Identify the major factors that influence voters' decisions**

Even if well-funded groups and powerful individuals influence the electoral process, it is the millions of individual voter decisions that ultimately determine election outcomes. Three factors influence voters' choices: partisan loyalty, issues and policy preferences, and candidate characteristics.

PARTISAN LOYALTY

Most voters feel a certain sense of identification or kinship with the Democratic or Republican Party, predisposing them to favor their party's candidates and oppose those of the other party. Partisanship is the most reliable indicator of which candidates people will vote for, from presidential elections to local elections. While issues and candidate personalities get more national attention in presidential elections compared to down-ballot elections, they often have very little impact on how partisans vote.

Once formed, voters' partisan loyalties seldom change unless some crisis causes them to reexamine their loyalties. During such a crisis, millions of voters can change their party ties. For example, at the beginning of the New Deal era, between 1932 and 1936, millions of former Republicans traumatized by the Great Depression transferred their allegiance to President Franklin Roosevelt and the Democrats.

ISSUES AND POLICY PREFERENCES

Policy preferences are a second factor influencing voters' choices. Voters may cast their ballots for the candidate whose position on health care, climate change, funding college education, or economic issues they believe to be closest to their own, or the one they believe has the best experience in foreign policy. Though candidates for the presidency or Congress are often judged on the basis of their economic policies or promises, other issues vary in importance depending on the election. In 2008, for example, Obama made ending the war in Iraq and providing national health care for all Americans his core issues. In 2020, Biden made curbing the coronavirus pandemic and unifying the nation key issues.

The Economy Election outcomes are affected by a variety of forces that candidates cannot control. Among the most important of these is the condition of the economy at the time of the election. If voters are satisfied with their economic conditions, they tend to support the party in power, while concern about the economy tends to favor the opposition. For example, the 2008 financial crisis gave Barack Obama and the Democrats a significant advantage in that year's election.

CANDIDATE CHARACTERISTICS

Candidates' personal attributes are a third factor influencing voters' decisions, with the more important being race, ethnicity, religion, gender, geography, and socioeconomic background. Voters may be proud to see someone similar to themselves in a position of leadership and may presume that such candidates are likely to have perspectives close to their own.

Just as candidates' personal characteristics may attract some voters, they may repel others. Some voters are prejudiced against candidates from certain ethnic, racial, religious, or gendered groups. The fact that the 2008 Democratic presidential candidate was African American, the 2016 Democratic candidate a woman, and the 2020 Democratic vice-presidential candidate a Black and South Asian woman indicates the increasing diversity of candidates for public office.

Voters also pay attention to candidates' personality characteristics, such as "authenticity," "decisiveness," and "honesty." In recent years, "integrity" has become a key election issue. Nonetheless, Trump supporters saw their candidate as unafraid to speak his mind, while Biden supporters felt he could unite the country and had good judgment.

The 2020 Elections: A Tale of Three Crises

Analyze the strategies, issues, and outcomes of the 2020 elections

In 2020, Democratic former vice president Joseph Biden faced incumbent Republican President Donald Trump in one of the most divisive and bitter presidential elections in American history. The end result was a solid popular and electoral college victory for Biden and his vice-presidential running mate, Senator Kamala Harris. Democrats retained control of the House of Representatives, but with a reduced margin. Control of the Senate remained to be decided by the outcomes of two January runoff elections in Georgia, where state law requires a second round of voting if no candidate has won a majority.

In this section, we analyze how the 2020 election unfolded and look at the major factors that contributed to the results—especially the three crises facing American politics: the coronavirus pandemic and associated economic crisis, the movement

The 2020 elections demonstrated in several ways how polarized the United States has become, culminating with both sides demanding that all legal votes be counted. Trump supporters hoped this would diminish Biden's lead, and Biden supporters hoped it would buoy his winning margins.

for racial justice, and the conflicts over the fairness, transparency, and administration of elections themselves.

THE BACKDROP: POLARIZATION

Over the past several decades, American politics has become increasingly polarized. The Democratic Party has become the political home of those who view themselves as ideologically liberal, while the Republican Party has become the party of conservatives. There are, to be sure, some differences of political perspective within each party. The perspectives in the Democratic camp range from traditional social-welfare liberalism, which traces its roots to the New Deal, to left-liberal progressivism, which envisions a substantially expanded role for the federal government, including a "Green New Deal" of environmental programs, single-payer national health insurance, and reparations to African Americans for slavery and racial injustice. The Republican camp ranges from business conservatives, who favor reducing government regulation and taxes, to social conservatives, who oppose abortion and same-sex marriage, to Trump conservatives, who favor reducing international trade and immigration to the United States.

More than a few party activists have come to view presidential elections as contests between good and evil, democracy and authoritarianism, and they communicate this perspective to the general public as they work to mobilize supporters via social media and the generally partisan mass media outlets. Democratic politicians and activists declare that Republicans are racist, sexist, homophobic, and ignorant.

Republican activists tell their voters that the Democrats are hostile to working American families and indifferent to the nation's values and traditions. More than half of Republicans and Democrats have developed highly negative views of the other party's supporters.[53]

Political acrimony had already come to a head during the third year of the Trump presidency when the majority of congressional Democrats, particularly those in the party's powerful progressive wing, decided that because of what they claimed was abuse of power and obstruction of Congress, Donald Trump must be removed from office. The House of Representatives impeached Trump for allegedly asking the leader of Ukraine to investigate Trump's political opponents in exchange for U.S. military aid to Ukraine, and for obstructing the inquiry by telling White House officials to ignore subpoenas from Congress for documents and testimony. Trump responded by labeling the impeachment a "witch hunt" and castigating the Democrats for making a case "loaded with lies and misrepresentations." The Republican-controlled Senate declined to convict Trump on the charges brought by the Democratic-controlled House. Acquittal, however, did little to soften the president's feelings about his Democratic foes in Congress.

In the final months before the election, the death of liberal Supreme Court Justice Ruth Bader Ginsburg ignited a partisan battle over the vacancy left by her passing. Democrats requested that Republicans honor the precedent Republicans set in 2016 when they would not hold hearings for Obama's nomination to the Court because it was an election year, but Republicans saw an opportunity to establish a long-lasting conservative majority on the Court. In a record 27 days, the Republican-controlled Senate confirmed Justice Amy Coney Barrett, a staunch religious conservative, establishing a six-member conservative majority on the Court. Every Democrat and only one Republican voted against her nomination.

THE CAMPAIGN

2020 Presidential Primaries Against this backdrop of intense partisan rancor, the two parties prepared for the 2020 presidential race. On the Republican side, the incumbent president, Donald Trump, was certain to be renominated and busied himself attacking the Democratic candidates. On the Democratic side more than 20 candidates sought the nomination. These included former vice president Joe Biden, who represented the party's traditional moderate liberal wing; Senators Bernie Sanders and Elizabeth Warren, who spoke for the party's progressive wing; and a variety of others, who spoke for disparate party factions. Biden struggled in three of the early state nominating contests, but with strong support from African American voters, he scored a huge victory in South Carolina. This caused several of his opponents to drop out of the race and endorse the former vice president, securing Biden the nomination. Trump retained Vice President Mike Pence as his running mate, while Biden named California Democratic Senator Kamala Harris as his vice-presidential running mate.

The candidates focused on issues that had long divided the Democratic and Republican parties. The Trump campaign praised the president's record of tax cuts, deregulation, opposition to immigration, suspicion of international organizations and agreements, and increased military spending financed by further cuts in social spending, particularly on health care. The Biden campaign called for new taxes on the wealthy, stronger environmental and financial regulations, liberalization of immigration rules, increases in social spending, a return to an internationalist foreign policy, and a return to "normalcy" and civility in American politics after what it called "the chaos, the tweets, the anger, the hate, the failure" of the Trump administration.[54] Though many of the issues in the campaign indicated a traditional Democratic–Republican divide, the 2020 general election played out amid crises that dominated American political life: the coronavirus pandemic and the movement for racial justice.

The Coronavirus Pandemic Beginning in the spring of 2020, Americans began to fall ill with COVID-19. This deadly disease was caused by a coronavirus that originated in Wuhan, China, and touched off a pandemic that ultimately killed several million people around the world, including more than 250,000 Americans. The Trump administration reacted to the emergency in fits and starts but did partially seal the nation's borders and launched "Operation Warp Speed," an effort to press pharmaceutical companies and medical equipment companies to ramp up research and production for a vaccine to combat the virus. State governors used their own emergency powers to close schools, businesses, factories, and houses of worship and to ban large gatherings. These public-health measures caused social and economic upheaval and threw millions of people out of work. The administration, with the support of Congress, developed an enormous economic stimulus package that was designed to ease the nation's economic pain.

However, Trump frequently attacked scientists and public-health professionals, and sometimes promoted dubious drugs as potential cures for COVID-19. His refusal to wear a mask became a political statement, with many of the president's supporters also refusing to wear masks in public. Joe Biden, by contrast, did not hold large public rallies and observed COVID-19 precautions. Wearing a face mask became an outward symbol of the party polarization of the nation, with Democratic leaders and partisans regularly wearing them but Republicans sometimes not.

Racial Strife and Mass Protests The second crisis affecting the campaign began in the summer of 2020 when the killing of an unarmed Black man, George Floyd, by Minneapolis, Minnesota, police sparked nationwide Black Lives Matter protests. While the protests were mostly peaceful, there were significant incidents of violent clashes with the police and counterprotesters and reports of looting, vandalism, and arson.

President Trump supported police actions, accused protesters of causing widespread violence, charged that Democratic governors and mayors were not doing enough to protect public safety, and dispatched federal forces to several cities to help quell disturbances. Democrats said the president's actions only added fuel to the fire and hoped that these events would demonstrate to Americans the importance of going to the polls and voting for Joe Biden.

THE RESULTS

As mentioned previously, Joe Biden defeated Donald Trump in the presidential race, Democrats retained control in the House of Representatives, and Republicans were likely to retain control in the Senate, pending the results of two runoff elections in Georgia in January.

President The 2020 presidential election witnessed historic voter turnout, with nearly 159 million votes cast (66.4 percent of eligible voters, up from 60 percent in 2016).[55]

In order to make voting safer during the coronavirus pandemic, all but six states made it easier to vote by mail and vote early in person. Nationwide, Democrats were much more likely to vote by mail, and Republicans in person, as President Trump vocally claimed mail voting would lead to fraud. This partisan divide created a new dynamic in the vote-counting process. On election night, in many states it seemed as though President Trump had a strong lead. But this was dubbed a "red mirage"—the illusion of Republican strength—because as mail-in votes began to be counted, Biden gained ground—the country saw a "blue shift"—and ultimately overtook Trump in the key states that had led Trump to victory in 2016. This unique and time-consuming process was new to many Americans and led many Republicans, including President Trump, to claim that, at best, there were widespread voting irregularities, and at worst, that Biden and the Democrats had stolen the election.

Biden beat Trump with razor-thin victories in just six of the swing states—a mix of traditional battleground states in the upper Midwest (Wisconsin, Michigan, and Pennsylvania) and untraditional battleground states in the Southwest (Arizona and Nevada) and Southeast (Georgia) (see Figure 9.4). Trump won the presidency in 2016 by a narrow margin of just under 40,000 votes in Pennsylvania, Michigan, and Wisconsin combined. In 2020, those three swing states flipped back to the Democrats by just over 220,000 votes.

Congress While Democrats won the presidency, in Congress, Republicans won back nearly a dozen seats in the House that they had lost in 2018 (though Democrats retained control) and Republicans were likely to hold on to the U.S. Senate.

House Democrats lost seats where voters feared too-aggressive progressivism from the party's left wing. Moderate Democrats voiced concern that the progressive wing of the Democratic Party hurt the party with policy proposals such as single-payer health insurance, the Green New Deal, and defunding the police, which are unpopular.[56] Republicans promised to rebuild the economy damaged by the coronavirus pandemic, opposed a national lockdown to prevent the virus's spread, and emphasized restoring law and order to protect families and communities.

Most incumbent Republican U.S. senators were re-elected despite the massive campaign mounted by Democrats to "Flip the Senate" blue. The vote margin for

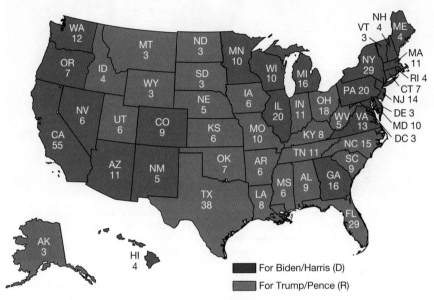

FIGURE 9.4

Distribution of Electoral Votes in the 2020 Election

WA 12
MT 3
ND 3
MN 10
NH
VT 4
ME 4
OR 7
ID 4
WY 3
SD 3
WI 10
MI 16
NY 29
MA 11
RI 4
CT 7
NJ 14
NV 6
UT 6
CO 9
NE 5
IA 6
IL 20
IN 11
OH 18
PA 20
DE 3
MD 10
DC 3
CA 55
AZ 11
NM 5
KS 6
MO 10
KY 8
WV 5
VA 13
NC 15
OK 7
AR 6
TN 11
SC 9
MS 6
AL 9
GA 16
TX 38
LA 8
FL 29
AK 3
HI 4

■ For Biden/Harris (D)
■ For Trump/Pence (R)

Note: Maine and Nebraska allocate electoral college votes by congressional district. Donald Trump won one of Maine's four electoral votes, and Joe Biden won one of Nebraska's five electoral votes.

SOURCE: "Presidential Election Results: Biden Wins," *New York Times*, www.nytimes.com /interactive/2020/11/03/us/elections/results-president.html (accessed 11/19/20).

Senate races closely mirrored the statewide votes for president, with high rates of party-line voting. The three senators who lost re-election were outliers in terms of the partisan composition of their respective states. Republicans Cory Gardner (Colo.) and Martha McSally (Ariz.) lost re-election, but their states also supported Biden for president. Democratic Senator Doug Jones (Ala.), after winning in a special election, lost as Alabama strongly supported Trump. The election was a reality check for Democrats that the electorate is moderate and desires practical policy solutions rather than radical change.

THE AFTERMATH

In addition to the coronavirus pandemic and related economic crisis and the movement for racial justice, the 2020 campaign was affected by a third crisis, the validity of the vote count. Republicans charged that the growing use of mail-in ballots in 2020 had opened the way for systematic electoral fraud. President Trump refused to

In every election, election workers in each state and county meticulously process and count mail-in ballots. Some states are permitted to begin counting before Election Day, but some must wait until after the polls close on Election Day to begin. In 2020, due to the high volume of mail-in ballots, election workers counted mail-in ballots for days after the election.

promise to accept the legitimacy of the outcome if he thought it had been obtained fraudulently.

After nearly all the votes had been tallied and it appeared that Biden won, Trump mounted court challenges to the outcome in several states carried by Biden, including Nevada and Pennsylvania. While these challenges seemed to have little foundation, President Trump and his supporters vowed to continue the fight. Thousands of Trump supporters participated in "Stop the Steal" rallies throughout the nation, and groups quickly formed on social media and attracted hundreds of thousands of followers. This development seemed to indicate that America's bitter political divisions would not dissipate quickly.

ANALYZING THE 2020 ELECTIONS

The winner of this nail-biting election was not known until four days after November 3, the time it took for mail ballots to be counted. However, the nation remained closely and bitterly divided, with the Senate nearly tied, the House nearly tied, and deep partisan polarization ingrained.

Two key shifts in the electorate were at play in 2020, compared to 2016. First, exit polls nationwide and in key battleground states report that ideological moderates supported Biden by nearly two to one, and 54 percent of independents supported Biden, compared to 41 percent for Trump.[57] Second, among first-time voters, Biden won nearly 65 percent of the vote, showing the strength and depth of the Democrats' ground game. Biden won by convincing moderates and independents

Who Participates in Political Campaigns and Elections?

The first step in participating in politics is getting informed about the candidates and the issues. Beyond this basic first step, people can display bumper stickers supporting a candidate, work or volunteer on behalf of a campaign, attend a rally or campaign event, and contribute financially to candidate campaigns. Participation in politics often increases with higher levels of educational attainment and sometimes age.

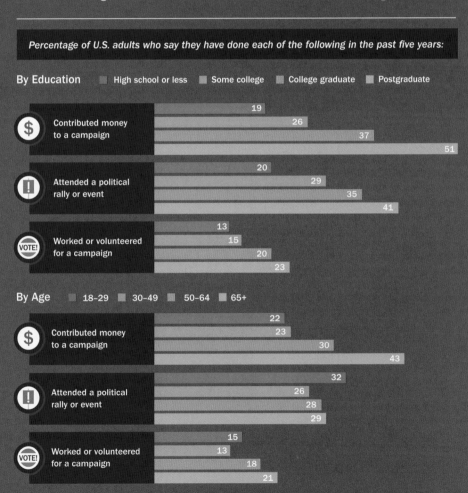

Percentage of U.S. adults who say they have done each of the following in the past five years:

By Education   ■ High school or less   ■ Some college   ■ College graduate   ■ Postgraduate

Contributed money to a campaign
- 19
- 26
- 37
- 51

Attended a political rally or event
- 20
- 29
- 35
- 41

Worked or volunteered for a campaign
- 13
- 15
- 20
- 23

By Age   ■ 18-29   ■ 30-49   ■ 50-64   ■ 65+

Contributed money to a campaign
- 22
- 23
- 30
- 43

Attended a political rally or event
- 32
- 26
- 28
- 29

Worked or volunteered for a campaign
- 15
- 13
- 18
- 21

SOURCE: Michael Dimock, "An Update on Our Research into Trust, Facts and Democracy," Pew Research Center, June 5, 2019; "Political Engagement, Knowledge and the Midterms," Pew Research Center, April 26, 2018.

to support the Democratic ticket and mobilizing a large number of new voters, with overwhelming support from people of color and and young voters.

COVID-19 and the state of the economy also impacted how people voted in the 2020 election. Eight months after the pandemic began, the census's Household Pulse Survey reported that 40 percent of Americans were living in a household where at least one adult had lost employment income, and 24 percent expected someone in their household to experience a loss of employment in the next month. One in 10 were living in a household where there was sometimes or often not enough to eat in the previous week and nearly 3 in 10 households said it had been somewhat or very difficult to pay household expenses and basic necessities. As a result, exit polls indicated the economy was the most important issue influencing how people voted. In separate questions asking what was the most important issue facing the country overall, the coronavirus and the economy were the top two.

CONCLUSION: THE 2020 ELECTION AND AMERICA'S FUTURE

In the 2020 election, each party made a massive push to mobilize voters, and it worked. Nearly 67 percent of those eligible to vote went to the polls, almost 10 percentage points higher than in 2016 and the highest turnout level seen in the United States since 1900. The historic turnout in 2020 showed that when the stakes are high, America can achieve a robust level of political participation, a healthy sign

Joe Biden and Kamala Harris won the 2020 presidential election over Donald Trump and Mike Pence with 306 electoral votes to 232. While their win was decisive and historic, the future of the United States remained uncertain due to the coronavirus pandemic, economic insecurity, and a highly polarized population.

for democracy. Giving cause for concern, however, were multiple warning signs, including deep partisan rancor, an increased belief in political conspiracy theories, and efforts to undermine the election results.

The future will, of course, depend upon the programs and policies of the Biden era and President Biden's ability to heal a fractured and polarized nation. The fact that record numbers of Americans went to the polls in 2020 is a sign of their continuing belief in America and in democracy and their hope for a better future.

Political Participation and Elections: What Do You Think?

The American political community has expanded over the course of history, with new groups winning and asserting political rights. But for much of the twentieth century, the electoral system in the United States failed to mobilize an active citizenry, giving rise to an uneven pattern of political participation that gives some people more voice in politics than others. Since 2000 a series of highly competitive presidential elections has spurred political campaigns to pay more attention to drawing greater numbers of voters into the political process; even so, many Americans still do not participate in politics. Unequal participation has consequences: one important study found that elected officials respond more to the preferences of voters than nonvoters, confirming long-held assumptions that affluent, more educated, and older citizens have more voice in politics and public policy.[58]

★ What would it take to increase political engagement among citizens of all backgrounds?

★ What barriers to participation do you observe among your friends and family? What reforms would help?

★ Will moneyed interests continue to play a large role in the election process? What new laws may be needed to make the rules of the game more fair? What new laws may be needed to make the rules of the game fair? What do you think Pat Murakami, Teresa Mosqueda, and Shaun Scott, the first-time candidates featured at the beginning of the chapter, would say?

★ How might you be involved in campaigns and elections in the future? Do you feel that your voice is heard? What changes would increase electoral participation among young people?

Practice Quiz

1. Which of the following actions is generally considered to be the most common type of participation in politics? *(p. 253)*
   a) directly contacting elected officials
   b) volunteering to work on a campaign
   c) voting in an election
   d) contributing money to candidates, campaigns, and parties
   e) participating in rallies and protests

2. Which group won voting rights most recently? *(p. 256)*
   a) 18- to 20-year-olds
   b) Asian Americans
   c) White property owners
   d) women
   e) African Americans

3. Which of the following best describes the relationship between social media and political participation? *(p. 258)*
   a) Social media is, on the whole, a distraction from forms of political participation that take more time and effort.
   b) When social media users see that others in their network have voted or otherwise engaged in political activity, they are often motivated to participate themselves.
   c) Social media is an ineffective and unwieldy tool for coordinating the political participation of millions of people.
   d) Social media facilitates political participation for ordinary Americans, but it makes it harder for politicians to connect with their constituents.
   e) Actions taken on social media generally do not translate into political participation offline.

4. What is the single most important factor in determining whether an individual will vote or otherwise participate in politics? *(p. 258)*
   a) religion
   b) gender

   c) race and ethnicity
   d) age
   e) level of education

5. In general, when compared with White voters, members of racial and ethnic groups are more likely to vote *(p. 259)*
   a) for Republican candidates.
   b) for Democratic candidates.
   c) for third-party and independent candidates.
   d) with split tickets—voting for Republicans for some offices and Democrats for others.
   e) in state and local elections.

6. The *gender gap* is *(p. 261)*
   a) the gap in the numbers of women and men who hold elective office.
   b) the gap in the numbers of women and men who run for elective office.
   c) a distinctive pattern of male and female voting decisions.
   d) a distinctive pattern of male and female voter turnout.
   e) a distinctive pattern of voting decisions among women of minority racial and ethnic groups.

7. Voter-registration requirements and processes are determined and controlled by *(p. 263)*
   a) local governments.
   b) the federal government.
   c) the U.S. Constitution.
   d) the states.
   e) an independent organization.

8. An open primary is a primary election in which *(p. 263)*
   a) one's vote is made public.
   b) only registered members of the party may vote.
   c) all registered voters are allowed to choose on the day of the primary which party's primary they will participate in.
   d) there are no limits on campaign spending.

e) only superdelegates are allowed to vote.

9. States that allow for same-day registration *(p. 266)*
   a) have lower overall voter turnout rates than the national average.
   b) have the same overall voter turnout rates as the national average.
   c) have higher overall voter turnout rates than the national average.
   d) have overall turnout rates that are very close to 100 percent.
   e) have lower rates of voter turnout among younger and less educated voters than states that do not allow for same-day registration.

10. If a state has 10 members in the U.S. House of Representatives, how many votes in the electoral college does that state have? *(p. 269)*
    a) 2
    b) 10
    c) 12
    d) 20
    e) The number of votes cannot be determined from this information.

11. An incumbent is a candidate who *(p. 270)*
    a) does not currently hold office.
    b) has the support of both major parties.
    c) already holds the office he or she is running for.

d) has won his or her party's primary election.
e) has been nominated at the party convention.

12. The main difference between a 527 committee and a 501(c)(4) is that *(p. 273)*
    a) a 527 is not legally required to disclose where it gets its money, while a 501(c)(4) is legally required to do so.
    b) a 501(c)(4) is not legally required to disclose where it gets its money, while a 527 is legally required to do so.
    c) a 527 can only contribute to one campaign, while a 501(c)(4) can contribute to many.
    d) a 501(c)(4) can only contribute to one campaign, while a 527 can contribute to many.
    e) a 527 can legally coordinate its spending with a candidate's campaign, while a 501(c)(4) cannot.

13. Which of the following techniques is considered most effective in mobilizing voters? *(p. 276)*
    a) direct mailings
    b) "robocalls"
    c) phone calls made by volunteers
    d) face-to-face contact
    e) television advertisements

Key Terms

protest *(p. 253)*
suffrage *(p. 254)*
turnout *(p. 255)*
digital political participation *(p. 256)*
socioeconomic status *(p. 258)*
gender gap *(p. 261)*
midterm elections *(p. 262)*
primary elections *(p. 263)*
general election *(p. 263)*
closed primary *(p. 263)*
open primary *(p. 263)*
same-day registration *(p. 266)*

delegate *(p. 268)*
party platform *(p. 268)*
electoral college *(p. 269)*
campaign *(p. 270)*
incumbent *(p. 270)*
political action committee (PAC) *(p. 272)*
527 committee (Super PAC) *(p. 273)*
501(c)(4) committees (dark money) *(p. 273)*
grassroots campaigns *(p. 273)*
mobilization *(p. 276)*

Congress

WHAT GOVERNMENT DOES AND WHY IT MATTERS

As the nation's chief legislative body, Congress affects Americans every day with its decisions. In early 2020, business owner Glynis Donnelly kept paying her eight part-time employees out of her savings even as the coronavirus pandemic brought sales at her Tampa, Florida, jewelry store to a standstill. "It may not be the most business-smart thing to do," she said, "but I know my employees very well, and I know that they need me as much as I need them." To help small business owners like Donnelly, Congress passed a coronavirus economic stimulus bill in March 2020 that included forgivable loans: if a business with fewer than 500 employees used such a loan to keep its workers on payroll, the amount borrowed would later be forgiven, with the company paying back only the interest. Donnelly planned to apply for the program right away.[1]

Congressional *inaction* affects Americans as well. In Huntington, West Virginia, Police Chief Hank Dial's police force was so overwhelmed by the number of fentanyl-contaminated heroin overdoses in the summer of 2016, with people dying at eight times the national rate, that he called the federal

The members of Congress—100 senators and 435 representatives—represent the voices of the people across America. Yet some observers worry that Congress does not represent all voices equally. From small business owners to police departments, congressional action and inaction can have major consequences.

government for help. Dozens of FBI, Drug Enforcement Agency, and Alcohol, Tobacco and Firearms agents joined his drug unit raiding drug dens and arresting dealers. But for all the arrests, the big problem remained: the seemingly endless supply of opioids—especially deadly fentanyl—continuing to stream into his city from abroad. What was Congress doing to stem the fentanyl tide? For years, nothing. Then-senator Kelly Ayotte, Republican of New Hampshire, introduced legislation in 2015 to increase prison sentences for fentanyl distribution as deaths surged in her state. Senator Rob Portman, Republican of Ohio, raised the alarm, as did Senator Edward Markey, Democrat of Massachusetts, both from states that, like New Hampshire, had been especially hard hit by fentanyl deaths. And yet congressional inaction continued, because of the stigma of the issue, because many lawmakers outside the hardest-hit areas did not think the issue would help them win re-election, because "if Congress had acted sooner and stopped the epidemic before tens of thousands of Americans died, it would have been difficult to publicly claim victory over a theoretical problem," as Mary Bono, a former Republican congresswoman of

California, said. Finally, in October 2018, Congress passed a major opioids bill, but only after 72,000 drug-overdose deaths in 2017 alone—more than the number of people who died in the Vietnam War.[2]

Congress has vast authority over many aspects of American life. Laws related to federal spending, taxing, regulation, and judicial appointments all pass through Congress. While the debates over these laws may seem hard to follow because they are often complex and technical or because heated, partisan struggles distract from the substance of the issue, it is important for the American people to learn about what Congress is doing. As the examples of the coronavirus stimulus and opioid bills indicate, actions taken—or not taken—in Congress affect the everyday experiences we take for granted. With its power to spend and tax, Congress also affects what choices people have and what opportunities they can expect in life.

With so much information about Congress available on the internet, it is not hard to get beyond the heated rhetoric and simplistic headlines and ask your own questions about a proposed law. How will it affect my life and the lives of people I care about? What is the impact on my country? Making laws is a complex and often messy process. Even so, it is vital for citizens to monitor what Congress does, because the laws it passes are so central to their lives.

CHAPTER GOALS

★ Describe who serves in Congress and how they represent their constituents (pp. 293–308)

★ Describe the factors that structure congressional business (pp. 308–13)

★ Describe the regular order and new order processes of how a bill becomes a law (pp. 313–20)

★ Identify the factors that influence which bills Congress passes (pp. 320–24)

★ Describe the powers that Congress uses to influence other branches of government (pp. 324–27)

Congress Represents the American People

Describe who serves in Congress and how they represent their constituents

Congress is the most important representative institution in American government. Each member's primary responsibility in theory is to the people in his or her district or state—his or her **constituency**—not to the congressional leadership, a party, or even Congress itself. Yet the task of representation is not simple. Views about what constitutes fair and effective representation differ, and different constituents may have very different expectations of their representatives. Members of Congress must consider these diverse views and expectations as they represent their constituencies.

HOUSE AND SENATE: DIFFERENCES IN REPRESENTATION

The framers of the Constitution provided for a **bicameral** legislature—that is, a legislative body consisting of two chambers. As we saw in Chapter 2, the framers intended each of these chambers, the House of Representatives and the Senate, to serve a different constituency. Members of the Senate, appointed by state legislatures for six-year terms, were to represent the states, while members of the House were to represent the people of the United States. (Today, members of both the House and the Senate are elected directly by the people.)

The 435 members of the House are elected from districts apportioned according to population; the 100 members of the Senate are elected in statewide votes, with two senators from each state. Senators continue to have much longer terms in office and usually represent much larger and more diverse constituencies than do their counterparts in the House (see Table 10.1).

> **constituency** the residents in the area from which an official is elected
>
> **bicameral** having a legislative assembly composed of two chambers or houses, distinguished from *unicameral*

The House and Senate play different roles in the legislative process. Traditionally, the Senate is the more deliberative of the two bodies—the forum in which any and all ideas that senators raise can receive a thorough public airing. The House is the more centralized and organized of the two bodies. In part, this difference stems from the different rules governing the two bodies. These rules give House leaders more control over the legislative process and allow House members to specialize in certain legislative areas. The rules of the much smaller Senate give its leadership less power and discourage specialization.

Other factors, both formal and informal, also contribute to differences between the two chambers. Differences in the length of terms and the requirements for holding office, specified by the Constitution, generate differences in how members of each body serve their constituencies and exercise their powers of office. For the House, the relatively small size and uniform nature of their constituencies and the need to seek re-election every two years make members more attuned

TABLE 10.1
• •

Differences between the House and the Senate

	HOUSE	SENATE
Minimum age of member	25 years	30 years
U.S. citizenship	At least 7 years	At least 9 years
Length of term	2 years	6 years
Number representing each state	1–53 per state (depends on population)	2 per state
Constituency	Local	Statewide

to the immediate legislative needs of local interest groups. The result is that the constituents they most effectively and frequently serve are well-organized local interests with specific legislative agendas—for instance, used-car dealers seeking relief from regulation, labor unions seeking more favorable workplace laws, or farmers looking for higher subsidies. Senators, on the other hand, serve larger and more diverse constituencies and seek re-election every six years. As a result, they are somewhat more insulated from the pressures of individual, narrow, and immediate interests.

TRUSTEE VERSUS DELEGATE REPRESENTATION

For the Founders, Congress was the national institution that best embodied the ideals of representative democracy. But what is the role of a representative? A member of Congress can interpret her job as representative in two different ways: as a **delegate**, acting on the express preferences of her constituents, or as a **trustee**, more loosely tied to constituents and empowered to make the decisions she thinks best.

The delegate role requires representatives to stay in constant touch with constituents and their wishes. But most constituents do not do this. Many pay little attention and are too busy to become well informed even on issues they care about. Thus, the delegate form of representation runs the risk that the voices of only a few active and informed constituents get heard. Although it seems more democratic at first glance, it may actually open Congress up to even more influence by special interests.

delegate a representative who votes according to the preferences of his or her constituency

trustee a representative who votes based on what he or she thinks is best for his or her constituency

When congressional members act as trustees, on the other hand, they may not pay sufficient attention to the wishes of their constituents, often making decisions based on their own judgment. In this scenario, the only way the public can exercise influence is by voting every two years for representatives and every six years for senators. In fact, most members of Congress

To more effectively promote a legislative agenda addressing issues that disproportionately affect racial and ethnic minority groups, members of Congress from those groups have formed caucuses. Here, Rep. Chuy Garcia (D-Ill.) speaks with fellow members of the Congressional Hispanic Caucus in support of DACA (Deferred Action for Childhood Arrivals).

take this electoral check very seriously. They try to anticipate the wishes of their constituents even when they don't know exactly what those wishes are, because they know that unpopular decisions can be used against them in the coming election.

DESCRIPTIVE VERSUS SUBSTANTIVE REPRESENTATION

We have become so accustomed to the idea of representative government that we tend to forget what a peculiar concept representation really is. A representative claims to act or speak for some other person or group. But how can one person be trusted to speak for another? How do we know that those who call themselves our representatives are actually speaking on our behalf, rather than simply pursuing their own interests?[3]

There are two circumstances under which one person reasonably might be trusted to speak for another. The first occurs if the two individuals are so similar in background, character, interests, and perspectives that anything said by one would very likely reflect the views of the other as well. This principle is at the heart of what is sometimes called **descriptive representation**— the sort that takes place when representatives have the same racial, gender, ethnic, religious, or educational

descriptive representation a type of representation in which representatives have the same racial, gender, ethnic, religious, or educational backgrounds as their constituents; it is based on the principle that if two individuals are similar in background, character, interests, and perspectives, then one can correctly represent the other's views

substantive representation
a type of representation in which a representative is held accountable to a constituency if he or she fails to represent that constituency properly; this is incentive for the representative to provide good representation when his or her personal background, views, and interests differ from those of his or her constituency

backgrounds as their constituents. If demographic, or sociological similarity helps to promote good representation, then the sociological composition of a representative assembly like Congress should mirror the composition of society.

The second circumstance under which one person might be trusted to speak for another occurs if the representative is in some way formally accountable to those he is supposed to represent. If representatives can somehow be punished for failing to speak properly for their constituents, then they have an incentive to provide good representation even if their own personal backgrounds, views, and interests differ from the backgrounds of those they represent. This principle is called substantive representation—the sort of representation that takes place when constituents have the power to hire and fire their representatives, as with an actor's "agent." Both descriptive and substantive representation play a role in the relationship between members of Congress and their constituencies.

The Social Composition of the U.S. Congress The extent to which the U.S. Congress is representative of the American people in a sociological sense can be seen by examining social characteristics of the House and Senate today. African Americans, Latinos, and Asian Americans have increased their congressional representation in the past two decades (see Figure 10.1), but the representation of people of color in Congress is still not comparable to their increasing proportions in the general population. After the 2020 elections, Congress was 11 percent African American, 8 percent Latino, and 3 percent Asian American. By contrast, the American population was 13.4 percent African American, 18.1 percent Latino, and 5.8 percent Asian American.[4]

Similarly, the number of women in Congress continues to trail far behind their proportion of the population. In 2006, Nancy Pelosi (D-Calif.) became the first female Speaker of the House. Following the 2020 elections, the 117th Congress (2021–23) included 117 women in the House and 24 women in the Senate, a total all-time high. Pressure for reform in the representative process is likely to continue until all groups are proportionally represented.

The occupational backgrounds of members of Congress have always been a matter of interest because many issues split along lines relevant to occupations and industries. The legal profession is the most common career of members prior to their election, and public service or politics is also a frequent background. In addition, many members have important ties to business and industry.[5]

Moreover, members of Congress are much more highly educated than most Americans. More than 9 in 10 have college degrees, and more than one-third have law degrees.[6]

On many dimensions, Congress is not a reflection of the U.S. population. Can Congress legislate fairly or take account of a diversity of views and interests if it is not a sociologically representative assembly? Representatives can serve as the agents

FIGURE 10.1

Diversity in Congress, 1971–2020

Congress has become much more socially diverse since the 1970s. After a gradual increase from 1971 to 1990, the number of female and African American members grew quickly during the first half of the 1990s. Do you think these numbers will rise in the future? Why or why not?

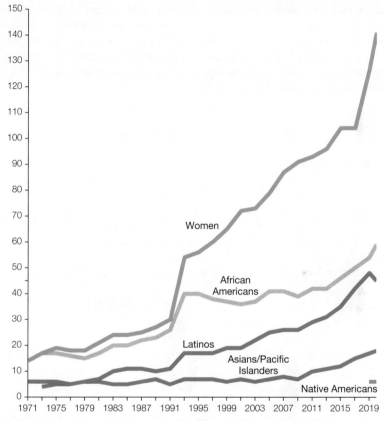

Note: As of mid-November 2020, several races that impact these statistics had still not been called.
SOURCES: Vital Statistics, "Demographics of Members of Congress," Tables 1-16, 1-17, 1-18, 1-19, www.brookings.edu/multi-chapter-report/vital-statistics-on-congress/; Jennifer E. Manning, *Membership of the 116th Congress: A Profile* (Washington, DC: Congressional Research Service, March 31, 2020), https://fas.org/sgp/crs/misc/R45583.pdf (accessed 4/8/20); authors, updates.

of their constituents even if they do not precisely mirror their sociological attributes. Yet descriptive representation is a matter of some importance. At the least, the social composition of a representative assembly is important for symbolic purposes: to demonstrate to groups in the population that the government takes them seriously. If Congress is not representative symbolically, then its own authority, and indeed that of the entire government, is reduced.[7]

Women's Legislative Representation

While the percentage of women in the U.S. House of Representatives has increased over time, reaching an all-time high in 2018, the United States still lags behind much of the rest of the world in this area.

1. Which parts of the world have the highest proportion of women in their legislatures? What do you think may account for certain areas having higher levels of elected women officeholders than others? Are there areas of the world where the percentage of women in the legislature surprises you?

2. How much should a legislature reflect the demographic makeup of its citizens? Should a country create legal requirements, or change its electoral rules, to encourage the election of underrepresented groups?

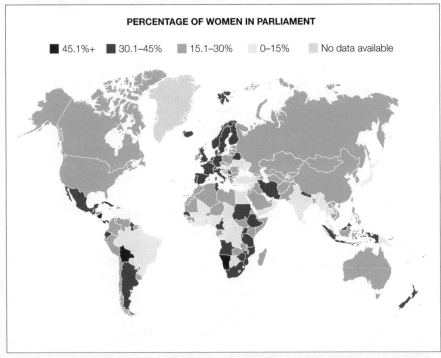

PERCENTAGE OF WOMEN IN PARLIAMENT

■ 45.1%+   ■ 30.1–45%   ■ 15.1–30%   □ 0–15%   □ No data available

SOURCE: Inter-Parliamentary Union (IPU), "Women in National Parliaments," April 1, 2018, http://archive.ipu.org (accessed 5/18/18).

Representatives as Agents A good deal of evidence indicates that whether or not members of Congress share their constituents' sociological characteristics, they *do* work very hard to speak for their constituents' views and to serve their constituents' interests. The idea of representative as agent is similar to the relationship of lawyer and client. True, the relationship between the House member and an average of 710,767 "clients" in the district, or the senator and millions of "clients" in the state, is very different from that of the lawyer and client. But the criteria of performance are comparable. One expects that each representative will seek to discover the interests of the constituency and take those interests into account as she governs. Whether members of Congress always represent the interests of their constituents is another matter, as we will see later in this chapter.[8]

The internet has made communication between constituents and congressional offices constant, and congressional offices have struggled to find effective ways to respond in a timely manner.[9] All congressional offices have websites that describe their achievements, establish a presence on social networking sites, and issue e-newsletters that alert constituents to current issues. Many use blogs and other forms of social media to establish a more informal style of communication with constituents.

The seriousness with which members of Congress attempt to behave as representatives can be seen in the amount of time and resources members spend on constituency service (called "casework"). One measure is the percentage of House and Senate staff assigned to district and state offices as opposed to offices in Washington. In 1972, 22.5 percent of House members' personal staff were located in district offices; by 2016 the number had grown to 47.3 percent. For the Senate, the staff in state offices grew from 12.5 percent in 1972 to 43.2 percent in 2016.[10] The service that these offices provide includes talking to constituents; providing them with minor services; presenting special bills for them; attempting to influence decisions by regulatory commissions on their behalf; helping them apply for federal benefits such as Social Security and Small Business Administration loans; and assisting them with immigration cases.

For example, during his fight for re-election in 2014, Senate Minority Leader Mitch McConnell (R-Ky.) ran a campaign ad featuring Noelle Hunter, a Kentucky resident whose ex-husband had abducted their daughter and taken her to Africa. According to Hunter, McConnell "took up my cause personally" and worked with the State Department to bring her daughter back home.[11]

In many districts and states, there are often two or three issues that are clearly top priorities for constituents and, therefore, for the representatives. For example, representatives from districts that grow wheat, cotton, or tobacco will likely give legislation on these subjects great attention. In oil-rich states such as Oklahoma and Texas, senators and members of the House are likely to be leading advocates of oil interests. On the other hand, on many issues, constituents do not have very strong views, and representatives are free to act as they think best. Foreign policy issues often fall into this category.

CONGRESSIONAL ELECTIONS

Elections have an enormous impact on Congress. Three factors are especially important in understanding who serves as a member of Congress. The first concerns who decides to run for office. The second is that of incumbency advantage. Finally, the way in which congressional district lines are drawn can greatly affect electoral outcomes.

Who Runs for Congress In the past, decisions about who would run for a particular elected office were made by local party officials. A person who had a record of service to the party, who was owed a favor, or whose "turn" had come up might be nominated by party leaders.

Today, few party organizations have the power to slate candidates in this way. Instead, parties try to ensure that their congressional candidates are well qualified. Even so, the decision to run for Congress is a personal one, and one of the most important factors determining who runs for office is an individual candidate's ambition.[12] A potential candidate may also assess whether he can raise enough money to mount a credible campaign. Fundraising ability depends on connections with other politicians, interest groups, and national party organizations.

Incumbency Incumbency plays a very important role in the American electoral system and in the kind of representation citizens get in Washington. Once in office, members of Congress gain access to an array of tools they can use to stack the deck in favor of their re-election. Their success in doing so is evident in the high rates of re-election for congressional

> **incumbency** holding the political office for which one is running

incumbents (see Figure 10.2). It is also evident in what is called "sophomore surge"—the tendency for first-term incumbents to win a higher percentage of the vote when seeking subsequent terms in office. As of mid-November 2020, roughly 90 percent of House and Senate incumbents seeking re-election had been successful, with most winning by comfortable margins.[13] The electoral success of incumbents does not mean that Congress is immutable, though—over the course of a decade, it is likely that nearly half the members of Congress will be replaced by new individuals.[14]

Incumbents have a number of political advantages. To begin with, members of Congress and their staffs are in a position to provide many individual services to constituents—the casework described on the previous page. Also, under a law enacted in 1789, members of Congress may send mail free of charge to their constituents informing them of governmental business and public affairs. Currently, members receive an average of $100,000 in free postage for mailings to voters in their own states or districts, including regular newsletters to all constituent households highlighting

FOR CRITICAL ANALYSIS ▶

1. What kinds of voters tend to vote in midterm elections? Should the electorate closely match the U.S. population?

2. Though the 2018 midterm elections saw historic turnout, turnout rates tend to be low in midterm elections. Why do you think that is?

Who Elects Congress?

During non-presidential election years, congressional elections are the highest-profile races on the ballot. While members of the House of Representatives are re-elected every two years, Senators are re-elected every six years.

2018 Voters as Compared with U.S. Population

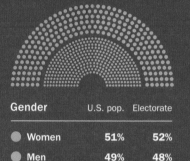

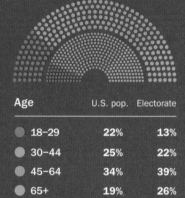

Electorate
U.S. population

Gender	U.S. pop.	Electorate
Women	51%	52%
Men	49%	48%

Age	U.S. pop.	Electorate
18–29	22%	13%
30–44	25%	22%
45–64	34%	39%
65+	19%	26%

Race	U.S. pop.	Electorate
White	62%	72%
Black	13%	11%
Latino	17%	11%
Asian	5%	3%
Other	3%	3%

Income	U.S. pop.	Electorate*
Under $30k	52%	17%
$30–$50k	20%	21%
$50–$100k	20%	29%
$100–$200k	6%	25%
Over $200k	2%	9%

*Numbers may not add up to 100 percent due to rounding.

SOURCES: CNN House Exit Polls, www.cnn.com/election/2018/exit-polls(accessed 11/12/18); U.S. Census Bureau, 2014 American Community Survey, www.census.gov/programs-surveys/acs/data.html (accessed 10/22/15).

FIGURE 10.2

The Power of Incumbency

Members of Congress who run for re-election have a very good chance of winning. Has the incumbency advantage generally been greater in the House or in the Senate? What are the consequences of the incumbency advantage for who serves in Congress?

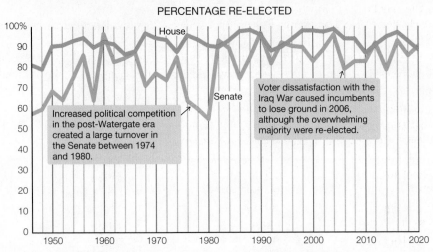

PERCENTAGE RE-ELECTED

Increased political competition in the post-Watergate era created a large turnover in the Senate between 1974 and 1980.

Voter dissatisfaction with the Iraq War caused incumbents to lose ground in 2006, although the overwhelming majority were re-elected.

SOURCES: Norman J. Ornstein et al., eds., *Vital Statistics on Congress, 1999–2000* (Washington, DC: AEI Press, 2000), 57–58; "Reelection Rates over the Years," www.opensecrets.org; and authors' update.

the many efforts and initiatives the incumbent has undertaken on behalf of the community.

Members of Congress lose no opportunity to garner local publicity and advertise their efforts on the constituency's behalf. Events that are ignored by the national media may nevertheless be of considerable significance to local voters. Senators and representatives seek to associate themselves with these events and send out press releases highlighting their involvement.

For example, a press release issued by the office of Congressman Eric Swalwell of California's 15th District honored the managers and employees of a new sanitation facility in his district. In fact, at the ribbon-cutting ceremony for the new plant, a staffer from Swalwell's office presented the facility's general manager with a "Certificate of Special Congressional Recognition" for the facility's "commitment and dedication to renewable energy."[15] Thousands of these certificates, suitable for framing, are awarded by members of Congress every year. Generally, the recipients are grateful and the event is covered by the local media and vigorously tweeted about by all concerned.[16]

Unlike challengers, who can offer only promises, incumbents have a chance to promote legislation favored by important groups and interests in their districts. If the constituency includes a major industry, representatives will almost always promote legislation that will please the workers and managers of that industry. The late senator Henry M. Jackson of Washington took pleasure in being known as the Senator from Boeing (a large aerospace manufacturer then based in Seattle).

Incumbents make it their business to support the interests of local companies and labor unions and of the district or state more generally when it comes to federal projects and contracts. Such efforts, known as **pork barreling**, provide tangible benefits and achievements for which they can claim credit and which can be crucial to their re-election.[17] The late senator Robert Byrd of West Virginia, longtime chair of the Senate Appropriations Committee, was sometimes called the King of Pork for his skill at steering federal projects to his state. During Byrd's tenure in office several billion dollars in federal funds for highways, dams, and government facilities flowed into West Virginia.

> **pork barrel (or pork)** appropriations made by legislative bodies for local projects that are often not needed but that are created so that local representatives can win re-election in their home districts

Often, representatives find it useful to strongly support essentially symbolic legislation that will please constituency groups. For example, representatives from New York and Florida, states with large numbers of Jewish voters, vote for symbolic resolutions such as calling for recognition of Jerusalem as Israel's capital. Similarly, members with large numbers of African American constituents were eager to support recognition of Dr. Martin Luther King, Jr.'s birthday as a national holiday. These symbolic gestures are one form of what is sometimes called "position taking."[18] Generally, position taking is a more effective tactic when it comes to pleasing ordinary voters. Organized interests are more likely to look for tangible benefits.

Another important electoral advantage for incumbents is superior access to campaign funds. Incumbents are usually far more able than challengers to raise money. For most senators and representatives, fundraising is a year-round activity. Incumbents hope not only to outspend challengers but to deter prospective challengers from even undertaking the race knowing they probably face an insurmountable fundraising disadvantage. Incumbents also fear the possibility that outside interests will target their own race. In recent years, national liberal and conservative "Super PACs" have raised tens of millions of dollars to attempt to sway the congressional balance of power, as well as presidential contests.

The electoral success of congressional incumbents is often cast in a negative light as though it was undeserved or a result of improper activities. It is worth noting, however, that incumbents are re-elected, at least in part, because of the vigorous efforts they make on behalf of their constituents. Incumbents undertake constituency casework, try to make certain that the flow of funds from the federal pork barrel favors their own districts, and work to identify legislative responses to the constituents' concerns.

Apportionment and Redistricting The drawing of congressional district lines also has a major impact on election outcomes. Districting, of course, affects only the House of Representatives. (Senators are chosen from states and these boundaries do not change.) At least every 10 years, and sometimes more frequently, state legislatures redistrict, or redraw the borders of their state's districts. Decennial redistricting is required by the Constitution to reflect population changes in accordance with the federal census.

apportionment the process, occurring after every decennial census, that allocates congressional seats among the 50 states

Because the number of House seats has been fixed by law at 435 since 1929, the census results mean that every 10 years some states gain or lose seats. **Apportionment**, the redistribution of seats among the states, is a zero-sum process: for one state to gain a seat, another must lose one. So some states with population growth over the previous decade gain additional seats; some with population decline or lower growth lose seats.

Over the past several decades, the shift of the American population to the South and the West has greatly increased the size of the congressional delegations from those regions. This trend will likely continue after the 2020 census (see Figure 10.3). Texas is likely to gain three seats (after gaining four after 2010), and Florida will likely gain two. States in the Northeast and "Rust Belt" will likely lose seats. Proportionally, Latino voters are nearly three times as numerous in states that gained seats

FIGURE 10.3

Projected Congressional Reapportionment, 2020

States in the South and the West will likely be the big winners in the reapportionment of House seats following the 2020 census. The old manufacturing states in the Midwest and Mid-Atlantic regions will be the biggest losers. Is this shift likely to favor Democrats or Republicans?

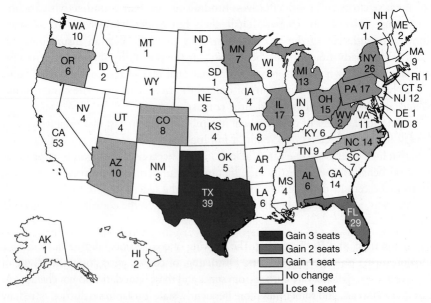

SOURCE: Rebecca Tippett, "2020 Congressional Reapportionment: An Update," December 21, 2017, Carolina Population Center, University of North Carolina, www.demography.cpc.unc.edu (accessed 6/8/18).

Redrawing legislative districts is a difficult task because it has implications for who will be elected. Here, the attorney for Arizona's Independent Redistricting Commission discusses a possible layout with a city council member from Casa Grande. Arizona gained one congressional seat following the 2010 census.

compared with states that lost seats, suggesting that the growth of the Latino population is a major factor in the American political landscape.[19]

In most states, **redistricting** is controlled by the state legislature and is a highly political process to create an advantage for the party with a majority in the legislature. For example, redistricting can put two incumbents of the opposing party into the same district, ensuring that one of them will lose, while creating an open seat that favors the redistricting party. Redistricting can also give an advantage to one party by clustering voters with similar ideological or sociological characteristics in a single district or by separating those voters into two or more districts. The manipulation of electoral districts to serve the interests of a particular group is known as **gerrymandering**.

redistricting the process of redrawing election districts and redistributing legislative representatives; this happens every 10 years to reflect shifts in population or in response to legal challenges to existing districts

gerrymandering the apportionment of voters in districts in such a way as to give unfair advantage to one racial or ethnic group or political party

Some analysts claim that the Republican Party has benefited from partisan gerrymandering since the 2010 redistricting cycle, because it controlled the majority of state legislatures at the time. To support this argument, they point to recent congressional elections in which the Republican Party generally has won a higher percentage of House seats than its percentage of the popular vote. But other analysts argue that districting that favors Republicans may reflect the natural clustering of Democrats in urban areas, not deliberate bias.[20]

Contact Your Member of Congress

NATHAN BARKER, Legislative Correspondent for a Republican member of the House of Representatives

Let's say you feel strongly about an issue, and you want to contact those in power who can make a difference. One important way is to reach out to your member of Congress. Nathan Barker says, "I love my job. I love being able to connect people, connect the constituent and the member each and every day because this republic of ours wouldn't work without it." Here are his tips for contacting legislators in the most effective way:

1 **It's important to do some research first.** You can convey your opinion about a general issue area, but it's even better to refer to a specific piece of legislation by title or the House H.R. number or the Senate S. number. At Congress.gov you can search by key word or member name and follow bills through the process. Also make sure you're contacting about a federal issue, not a state legislative bill.

2 **Identify which office to contact about your issue.** If you want to voice your opinion about an issue or a piece of legislation, contact your representative or senator's Washington, D.C., office, as that's where the experts on policy issues are. If you need casework assistance—help with a federal agency, for example—contact the member's local office.

3 **Should you write, email, or call?** If you want a response, a letter or email is best (keep in mind that a response may take a couple of weeks due to volume). If you simply want to register your opinion, a phone call is good. Leave a voice mail with your full name, your city or town, your subject, and a short message, and staff will log your call.

4 **Always contact your own representative or senator.** They very much want to hear from their constituents. Contacting officials from other districts or states, who have no obligation to respond, or every single Republican or Democrat, or those in leadership, is not an effective use of your time. Better to contact your own member and urge them to speak with leadership or other members of the congressional delegation about your issue.

5 **Always state your name, your location, your background, and your opinion or call for action.** There is no single script to follow. Saying "I'm a veteran" or "I'm a teacher" provides a helpful frame of reference. It's important to be specific and succinct ("I'm a student worried about student loans, and I support bill H.R. ____ for ____ reason"). If you're calling about a specific piece of legislation, better to call and voice support or opposition *before* it comes up for a vote. And feel free to contact them again. The status quo is always shifting, and new bills are constantly coming up.

To follow up, sign up for legislators' newsletters to keep informed about their activities, legislation under consideration, and upcoming events such as town hall meetings or coffee meetups. Most have Facebook and Twitter accounts as well. You may even be able to set up a one-on-one meeting, especially with a House member. It helps to be persistent but also kind and respectful in interacting with the office—hard-working staff members really appreciate that—as well as being informed about your issue.

There is nothing that should stop a student in college from contacting a member about an issue they find important. If you're passionate about an issue, just do it.

Even so, concern about partisan gerrymandering has led some states to take redistricting power away from state legislatures and give it to independent bipartisan commissions that try to develop congressional district maps that do not give an unfair advantage to either party. Currently, seven states—California, Arizona, Hawaii, Idaho, New Jersey, Washington, and Montana—require district lines to be drawn by commissions.[21] The Supreme Court has upheld the legality of relying on commissions to draw congressional district lines.[22]

The federal courts have often sought to intervene in cases involving partisan gerrymandering. In 2019, however, the Supreme Court ruled that gerrymandering was a "political question" beyond the reach of the federal judiciary.[23] The Court's decision left open the possibility that state courts might continue to intervene in gerrymandering cases. And the decision applied only to partisan gerrymandering, not to claims of racial gerrymandering.

Since the passage of the 1982 amendments to the Voting Rights Act of 1965, race has become a major, and controversial, consideration in drawing voting districts. These amendments, which encouraged the creation of districts in which people of color have decisive majorities, have greatly increased the number of representatives of color in Congress. After the 1990 redistricting cycle, the number of predominantly minority districts doubled, rising from 26 to 52. Among the most fervent supporters of creating these districts were White Republicans, who used the opportunity to create more districts dominated by White Republican voters. Some analysts argue that this pattern grants people of color greater descriptive representation but makes it more difficult for them to win substantive policy goals.[24]

Congressional Organization Determines Power

Describe the factors that structure congressional business

The building blocks of congressional organization include the political parties, the committee system, congressional staff, the caucuses, and the parliamentary rules of the House and Senate. Each of these factors plays a key role in the organization of Congress and in the process through which Congress formulates and enacts laws.

PARTY LEADERSHIP IN THE HOUSE

Political parties are not mentioned in the Constitution, but soon after the nation's founding, a party system developed in the Congress. Much of the actual work of Congress is controlled by the parties, which write most of the rules of congressional procedure and select the leaders who direct the flow of congressional business. Without party leadership and party organization, Congress could not function as a lawmaking body.

Every two years, at the beginning of a new Congress, the members of each party gather to elect their House leaders. House Republicans call their gathering the conference. House Democrats call theirs the **caucus**. The elected leader of the majority party is later proposed to the whole House and is automatically elected to the position of **Speaker of the House**, with voting along straight party lines. The House majority conference or caucus then also elects a **majority leader**. The minority party goes through the same process and selects a **minority leader**. Each party also elects a **whip** to line up party members on important votes and to relay voting information to the leaders.

Next in order of importance for each party after the Speaker and majority or minority leader is what Democrats call the Steering and Policy Committee (Republicans have a separate steering committee and a separate policy committee). These committees' tasks are to assign new legislators to committees and to deal with the requests of incumbent members for transfers from one committee to another. At one time, party leaders strictly controlled committee assignments, using them to enforce party discipline. Today, in principle, representatives receive the assignments they want. But often too many individuals seek assignments to the most important committees, which gives the leadership an opportunity to curry favor with their members when it resolves conflicting requests.

Generally, representatives seek assignments that will allow them to influence decisions of special importance to their districts. Representatives from farm districts, for example, often request seats on the Agriculture Committee.[25] Especially popular seats are those on powerful committees such as Ways and Means, which is responsible for tax legislation, and Appropriations.

conference a gathering of House Republicans every two years to elect their House leaders; Democrats call their gathering the "caucus"

caucus (political) a normally closed political party business meeting of citizens or lawmakers to select candidates, elect officers, plan strategy, or make decisions regarding legislative matters

Speaker of the House the chief presiding officer of the House of Representatives; the Speaker is the most important party and House leader and can influence the legislative agenda, the fate of individual pieces of legislation, and members' positions within the House

majority leader the elected leader of the majority party in the House of Representatives or in the Senate; in the House, the majority leader is subordinate in the party hierarchy to the Speaker of the House

minority leader the elected leader of the minority party in the House or Senate

whip a party member in the House or Senate responsible for coordinating the party's legislative strategy, building support for key issues, and counting votes

PARTY LEADERSHIP IN THE SENATE

Within the Senate, the majority party designates a member with the greatest seniority to serve as president pro tempore, a position of primarily ceremonial leadership. Real power is in the hands of the majority leader and minority leader, who together control the Senate's calendar, or agenda for legislation.

THE COMMITTEE SYSTEM

The committee system is a prominent feature of Congress. At each stage of the legislative process, Congress makes use of committees and subcommittees to sort through alternatives, secure information, and write legislation. There are several different kinds of congressional committees: standing committees, select committees, joint committees, and conference committees.

Standing Committees The most important arenas of congressional policy making are **standing committees**. These committees remain in existence from one session of Congress to the next; they have the power to propose and write legislation. The jurisdiction of each one covers a particular subject matter, which in most cases parallels a major department or agency in the executive branch.

standing committee a permanent committee with the power to propose and write legislation that covers a particular subject, such as finance or agriculture

Among the most important standing committees are those in charge of finances. The House Ways and Means Committee and the Senate Finance Committee are powerful because of their jurisdiction over taxes, trade, and expensive entitlement programs such as Social Security and Medicare. The Senate and House Appropriations committees also play important roles because they decide how much funding various programs will actually receive and exactly how the money will be spent.

Except for the House Rules Committee, all standing committees receive numerous legislative proposals. The House Rules Committee decides the order in which bills come up for a vote on the House floor and determines the specific rules that govern the length of debate and opportunity for amendments. The Senate Rules and Administration Committee, however, does not write the rules governing debate and has little power compared to its House counterpart.

Most standing committees are broken into subcommittees that specialize in particular aspects of the committee's work. For example, the Senate Committee on Foreign Relations has seven subcommittees, each specializing in a different geographic region. When a bill is referred to committee, the committee leadership will determine which subcommittee is most appropriate for the matter in question. Subcommittee jurisdictions are loosely defined and committee chairs have considerable discretion in assigning bills. Much of the hard work of deliberating, holding hearings, and "marking up," as the process of amending and rewriting a bill is called, takes place in the subcommittees, though further markup may occur in the full committee after the amended bill leaves the subcommittee.

One important power of the standing committees is the power to conduct hearings and launch investigations. There are two types of legislative hearings. In the most common variety of oversight hearing, Congress listens to testimony, quizzes executive branch officials, and hears complaints from members of the public in order to better fulfill its legislative responsibilities. A second type of hearing, called an investigative hearing or ethics probe, has no immediate legislative intent, though it may eventually result in legislation. The chief purpose of such a hearing is to look into allegations of misconduct on the part of one or more public officials, possibly culminating in a recommendation that the officials in question be dismissed or even subjected to criminal prosecution. These are discussed in the following pages.

Select Committees Select committees are usually not permanent and usually do not have the power to present legislation to the full Congress. (The House and Senate Select Intelligence committees are exceptions.) These committees hold hearings and serve as focal points for the issues they are charged with considering. Congressional leaders form select committees when they want to take up issues that fall outside the jurisdictions of existing committees, to highlight an issue, or to investigate a particular problem.

For example, the Senate set up the Senate Watergate Committee in 1973 to investigate the Watergate break-in and cover-up. More recently, the House Select Committee on Benghazi was established to investigate the 2012 attack on the U.S. embassy in Benghazi, Libya. In 2015 the committee held hearings to investigate Hillary Clinton's use of a private email server during her tenure as secretary of state.

Joint Committees Joint committees involve members from both the Senate and the House. There are four such committees—economic, taxation, library, and printing; they are permanent, but do not have the power to present legislation. The Joint Economic Committee and the Joint Taxation Committee have often played important roles in collecting information and holding hearings on economic and financial issues.

select committees (usually) temporary legislative committees set up to highlight or investigate a particular issue or address an issue not within the jurisdiction of existing committees

joint committees legislative committees formed of members of both the House and Senate

conference committees joint committees created to work out a compromise on House and Senate versions of a piece of legislation

seniority the ranking given to an individual on the basis of length of continuous service on a committee in Congress

Conference Committees Finally, **conference committees** are temporary committees whose members are appointed by the Speaker of the House and the presiding officer of the Senate. These committees are charged with reaching a compromise on legislation once it has been passed by the House and the Senate. Conference committees can play an important role in determining the laws that are actually passed because they must reconcile any differences in the legislation passed by the House and Senate.

Politics and the Organization of Committees Within each committee, leadership has usually been based on **seniority**, determined by years of continuous service on that particular committee. In general, each committee is chaired by the most senior member of the majority party. But the principle of seniority is not absolute. When the Republicans took over the House in 1995, they disregarded it in the selection of key committee chairs. House Speaker Newt Gingrich defended the new practice, saying, "You've got to carry the moral responsibility of fielding the team that can win or you cheat the whole conference."[26]

Since then, Republicans have continued to depart from the seniority principle, often choosing committee chairs on the basis of loyalty to the party leadership's legislative priorities or the member's fundraising abilities rather than seniority. In 2007, Democrats returned to the seniority principle for choosing committee chairs but altered traditional practices in other ways by offering freshman Democrats choice committee assignments to increase their chances of re-election.[27]

Over the years, Congress has reformed its organizational structure and operating procedures. Most changes have been made to improve efficiency, but some reforms have also been a response to political considerations. For example, the Republican leadership of the 104th Congress (1995–97), seeking to concentrate its authority, reduced the number of subcommittees and limited the time committee chairs could serve to three terms. They made good on this limit in 2001, when they replaced 13 committee chairs.

As a consequence of these changes, committees no longer have as central a role as they once held in policy making. Furthermore, sharp partisan divisions have made it difficult for committees to deliberate and bring bipartisan expertise to bear on policy making as in the past. Today they typically do not deliberate for very long or call witnesses, and it has become more common in recent years for party-driven legislation to go directly to the floor, bypassing committees altogether.[28] Nonetheless, committees continue to play a role in the legislative process, especially on issues that are not sharply partisan.[29]

THE STAFF SYSTEM

The congressional institution third in importance to the leadership structure and the committee system is the staff system. Every member of Congress employs many staff members (the total is set by law), whose tasks include handling constituent requests and, to a large extent, dealing with legislative details and the activities of administrative agencies. Staffers often bear the primary responsibility for formulating and drafting proposals, organizing hearings, dealing with administrative agencies, and negotiating with lobbyists. Indeed, legislators typically deal with one another through staff, rather than through direct personal contact. Representatives and senators together employ roughly 11,500 staffers—about half in each chamber—in their Washington and home offices.

In addition, Congress employs more than 2,000 committee staffers.[30] These make up the permanent staff that stays attached to every House and Senate committee regardless of turnover in Congress and that is responsible for organizing and administering the committee's work, including doing research, scheduling, organizing hearings, and drafting legislation. Committee staffers can play key roles in the legislative process.

Not only does Congress employ personal and committee staff, but it has also established **staff agencies** designed to provide the legislative branch with resources and expertise independent of the executive branch. These agencies include the Congressional Research Service, which performs research for legislators who wish to know the facts and competing arguments relevant to policy proposals or other legislative business; the Government Accountability Office, through which Congress can investigate the financial and administrative affairs of any government agency or program; and the

staff agencies legislative support agencies responsible for policy analysis

Congressional Budget Office, which assesses the economic implications and likely costs of proposed federal programs.

Rules of Lawmaking Explain How a Bill Becomes a Law

> **Describe the regular order and new order processes of how a bill becomes a law**

The institutional structure of Congress is a key factor in shaping the legislative process. A second and equally important set of factors is the rules of congressional procedure, which govern everything from the introduction of a **bill** through its submission to the president for signing (see Figure 10.4). Not only do these regulations influence the fate of every bill, but they also help determine the distribution of power in Congress.

We will begin the story of how a bill becomes a law with what is called "regular order." This is the set of procedures Congress claims to follow and often does. As we will see in the following pages, however, many important bills do not follow regular order but, instead, follow a less formal and more leadership-driven process that we will call the "new order."

COMMITTEE DELIBERATION

The first step in getting a law passed is drafting legislation. Members of Congress, the White House, and federal agencies all take roles in developing and drafting initial legislation. Bills can originate in the House or the Senate, but only the House can introduce "money bills," those that spend or raise revenues. The framers inserted this provision in the Constitution because they believed that the chamber closest to the people should exercise greater authority over taxing and spending.

After the bill is drafted, it is officially submitted by a senator or representative to the clerk of the Senate or House and referred to the appropriate committee for deliberation. During the course of its deliberations, the committee typically refers the bill to one of its subcommittees, which may hold hearings, listen to expert testimony, and amend the proposed legislation before referring it to the full committee for consideration. The full committee may then accept the recommendation of the subcommittee or hold its own hearings and prepare its own amendments.

The next steps in the process are the **committee markup** sessions, in which committees rewrite bills to reflect changes discussed during the hearings. Frequently, the committee and subcommittee do little or nothing with a bill that has been submitted to them. Many bills are simply allowed to die in committee without serious consideration. Often, members of Congress introduce legislation that they neither

bill a proposed law that has been sponsored by a member of Congress and submitted to the clerk of the House or Senate

committee markup the session in which a congressional committee rewrites legislation to incorporate changes discussed during hearings on a bill

How a Bill Becomes a Law

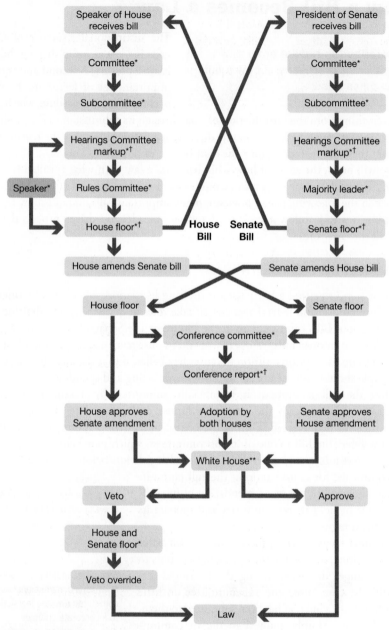

*Points at which a bill can be amended.
**If the president neither signs nor vetoes a bill within 10 days, it automatically becomes law.
†Points at which a bill can die by vote.

expect nor even want to see enacted into law but present mainly to please a constituency group by taking a stand. Other pieces of legislation have ardent supporters and die in committee only after a long battle. But in either case, most bills are never reported out of the committees to which they are assigned. In a typical congressional session, 80 to 90 percent of the more than 10,000 bills introduced die in committee.[31]

closed rule a provision by the House Rules Committee limiting or prohibiting the introduction of amendments during debate

open rule a provision by the House Rules Committee that permits floor debate and the addition of new amendments to a bill

In the House, the relative handful of bills that are reported out of committee must pass one last hurdle within the committee system—the Rules Committee, which determines the rules that will govern action on the bill on the House floor. In particular, the Rules Committee allots the time for debate and decides to what extent amendments to the bill can be proposed from the floor. A bill's supporters generally prefer a **closed rule**, which puts severe limits on floor debate and amendments. Opponents of a bill usually prefer an **open rule**, which makes it easier to add amendments that may cripple the bill or weaken its chances for passage. Thus, the outcome of the Rules Committee's deliberations can be extremely important, and the committee's hearings can be occasions for sharp conflict. In recent years, however, the Rules Committee has become less powerful because the House leadership exercises so much influence over its decisions.

DEBATE

The next step in getting a law passed is debate on the floor of the House and Senate. Party control of the agenda is reinforced by the rule giving the presiding officer of each chamber, the Speaker of the House and the president of the Senate, the power to "recognize" individual members who wish to speak on the floor during debate on a bill—that is, to grant or deny them permission to do so. Usually the presiding officer knows the purpose for which a member intends to speak well in advance of the occasion, and spontaneous efforts to gain recognition often fail. For example, the Speaker may ask, "For what purpose does the member rise?" before deciding whether to grant recognition.

In the House, virtually all the time allotted by the Rules Committee for debate on a given bill is controlled by the bill's sponsor and by its leading opponent. In almost every case, these two people are the chair and the ranking minority member of the committee that processed the bill—or those they designate. These two participants are, by rule and tradition, granted the power to allocate most of the debate time in small amounts to members seeking to speak for or against the measure.

Filibuster In the Senate, the leadership has much less control over floor debate. Indeed, the Senate is unique among the world's legislative bodies for its commitment to unlimited debate. Once given the floor, a senator may speak as long as she wishes. On a number of memorable occasions, senators have used this opportunity to prevent action on legislation that they opposed. Through this tactic, called

filibuster a tactic used by members of the Senate to prevent action on legislation they oppose by continuously holding the floor and speaking until the majority backs down; once given the floor, senators have unlimited time to speak, and it requires a vote of three-fifths of the Senate to end a filibuster

cloture a rule or process in a legislative body aimed at ending debate on a given bill; in the U.S. Senate, 60 senators (three-fifths) must agree in order to impose a time limit and end debate

the **filibuster**, small minorities or even one individual in the Senate can force the majority to give in. The threat of a filibuster ensures that, in crafting legislation, the majority takes into account the viewpoint of the political minority.

Filibusters can be ended by a Senate vote to cut off debate, called **cloture**. From 1917 to 1975, it took two-thirds of the Senate, or 67 votes, to end a filibuster. In 1975 the Senate reduced the requirement to three-fifths of the Senate, or 60 votes.

In 2013 the Democratic Senate leader Harry Reid (Nev.) mobilized his party to alter the filibuster rules for the first time in many decades. Frustrated by the repeated failure of the Senate to vote on many of President Obama's nominees to executive and judicial positions, Reid imposed what senators had come to call "the nuclear option": nominees for positions in the executive branch and the federal courts—except the Supreme Court—could no longer be filibustered and could be approved by a simple majority vote. Republicans denounced the change, but after winning control of both houses of Congress and the White House in 2016 they expanded it to include Supreme Court justices as well. Thus they were able to secure the appointment of Justices Neil Gorsuch, Brett Kavanaugh, and Amy Coney Barrett, who would undoubtedly have been blocked by Senate Democrats under the old rules. Legislation is still subject to filibuster.

Amendments and Holds The filibuster is not the only technique used to block Senate debate. Under Senate rules, members have virtually unlimited ability to propose amendments to a pending bill. Each amendment must be voted on before the bill can come to a final vote, and the introduction of new amendments can be stopped only by unanimous consent of the Senate. These rules permit a determined minority to filibuster by amendment, indefinitely delaying the passage of a bill.

Senators can also place "holds" on bills to delay debate when they fear that more openly opposing the bills will be unpopular. Before 2007, holds were kept secret, so the senators placing them did not have to take public responsibility for their actions. Since 2007, senators who impose a hold have been required to identify themselves in the *Congressional Record* after six days and to state the reasons for the hold.[32] Nevertheless, senators continue to impose holds on legislation and especially on presidential appointees. In 2013, for example, Senator Lindsey Graham (R-S.C.) threatened to use holds on all of President Obama's nominees unless the administration made survivors of the 2012 terrorist attack on the U.S. mission in Benghazi, Libya, available to Congress for questioning.[33]

Voting Once a bill is debated on the floor of the House and the Senate, the leaders schedule it for a vote on the floor of each chamber. Leaders do not bring legislation to the floor unless they are fairly certain it is going to pass. On rare occasions, however, the last moments of the floor vote can be very dramatic as each party's leadership puts its whip organization into action to make sure that wavering members vote with the party.

CONFERENCE COMMITTEE: RECONCILING HOUSE AND SENATE VERSIONS OF LEGISLATION

Getting a bill out of committee and through both houses of Congress is no guarantee that the bill will be enacted into law. If the versions passed by both houses are not identical, then the bill must be sent to a conference committee to work out the differences. The bill produced by the committee must then be approved on the floor of each chamber before it can be sent to the president for signing. Usually such approval is given quickly. Occasionally, however, a bill's opponents use this as one last opportunity to defeat a piece of legislation.

PRESIDENTIAL ACTION

The final step in passing a law is presidential approval. Once adopted by the House and Senate, a bill goes to the president, who may choose to sign the bill into law or to veto it. If the president does neither within 10 days and Congress is in session, the bill automatically becomes law. The **veto** is the president's constitutional power to reject a piece of legislation. To veto a bill, the president returns it unsigned within 10 days to the house of Congress in which it originated. If Congress adjourns during the 10-day period and the president has taken no action, the bill is also considered to be vetoed. This latter method is known as the **pocket veto.**

The possibility of a presidential veto affects how willing members of Congress are to push for a piece of legislation at a particular time; if they think it is likely to be vetoed, they might shelve it until later. There is also the possibility that a veto may be overridden by a two-thirds vote in both the House and the Senate. A veto override is rare and delivers a stinging blow to the executive branch. Presidents will often back down from a veto threat if they believe that Congress will override the veto.

> **veto** the president's constitutional power to turn down acts of Congress; a presidential veto may be overridden by a two-thirds vote of each house of Congress

> **pocket veto** a presidential veto that is automatically triggered if the president does not act on a given piece of legislation passed during the final 10 days of a legislative session

IS REGULAR ORDER STILL REGULAR? THE RISE OF THE NEW ORDER IN CONGRESS

The foregoing discussion summarizes regular order in Congress. Regular order guarantees that a bill's journey to becoming a law will be long and arduous. Indeed, the process can be maddeningly slow for a bill's proponents. Regular order, however, ensures a deliberative process in which many voices are heard and both the majority and minority parties play a role. In short, regular order exemplifies deliberative democracy at its best. In modern times, however, regular order is often abandoned in favor of procedures designed to move bills along more quickly, or with fewer layers of review, trading deliberation for speed.

Today, instead of regular order, bills tend to follow a set of paths that collectively might be called the "new order." Regular order enhanced the power of committees and subcommittees. The new order generally reflects the strengthening of partisanship and the power of party leaders, in particular the Speaker of the House and the Senate majority leader, but also leaves room for individual action by the members of Congress. One thing the new order does not emphasize is deliberation. The new order allows party leaders to push the president's agenda if the president is of their own party or to do battle with the president if the president is of the opposite party. This is primarily why Congress is prone to deadlock today—an era of high levels of partisan division and frequently divided control of government. Some in Congress call for a return to regular order, but it is not clear how realistic that is.[34] The forces that led to the new order were set in motion by institutional reforms of the 1970s and other factors that are not likely to be reversed.[35]

"FOLLOW-THE-LEADER" LAWMAKING

The most important element of the new order is what we can call "follow-the-leader" lawmaking. This is when party leaders rather than committees control the legislative process. These leaders use various tactics to achieve their legislative goals and move legislation more quickly than regular order would allow.

Closed Rules The first element of follow-the-leader lawmaking is the frequent use of closed rules to prevent rank-and-file members—and the minority party—from amending legislation approved by the leadership. Closed rules, which some critics call "gag rules," prohibit most floor amendments and often limit debate to a short period of time. Debate on a complex measure may be limited to one hour—hardly enough time to begin to read, much less debate, a bill that may be more than 1,000 pages long.

For many years, tax bills have been considered under closed rules because most members have agreed that tax provisions are too complex and the provisions too intertwined to be amended from the floor.[36] What once was limited mainly to tax bills has now become what Walter Oleszek calls the "new normal."[37] Whether Congress is controlled by the Democrats or the Republicans, party leaders use closed rules and strict time limits on debate to enhance their own power, compel the rank and file to follow the leader, and restrict the influence of the other party on legislation.

multiple referral the practice of referring a bill to more than one committee for consideration

Multiple Referral A second element of follow-the-leader lawmaking is **multiple referral**. In the House multiple referral was introduced by a rule change in 1975 and has since become commonplace. Used more often in the House than the Senate, multiple referral means that bills are sent to several committees rather than just one for consideration and markup. Multiple referral often works to expand the power of party leaders and reduce the power of committees by preventing any one committee from blocking a piece of legislation.

Ping-ponging A third element of follow-the-leader lawmaking is the declining use of the conference committee. Conference committees can expand the number of voices heard in discussions of a piece of legislation. However, the effort to create a conference committee, particularly in the case of a controversial bill, gives the Senate minority, in particular, many opportunities to block enactment of the bill. Under Senate rules, the minority party has opportunities to filibuster several steps in the process, to propose amendments, and to move to instruct its conferees to insist upon provisions known to be unacceptable to the House. The House minority also has procedural weapons with which it might derail a conference. To deal with these problems, House and Senate leaders have developed procedures for "ping-ponging" amendments back and forth between the relevant House and Senate committees to reconcile differences between bills or major measures without convening a conference committee at all. The ping-pong approach to legislating strengthens the House and Senate leadership and further marginalizes the role of the minority parties.[38]

Catching the Omnibus: The New Order Budget Process A key element of follow-the-leader lawmaking is the use of the omnibus budget bill. The U.S. Congress is one of the few legislatures in the world to have the primary role in its government's budgetary process. This "power of the purse" derives directly from Article I, Section 8, of the Constitution, which asserts that Congress "shall have the Power to lay and collect Taxes, Duties, Imposts, and Excises [and] To borrow Money on the credit of the United States." According to Article I, Section 9, moreover, "no Money shall be drawn from the Treasury, but in Consequence of Appropriations made by Law." The Constitution also specifies that revenue measures must originate in the House.

While giving Congress the power of the purse, the Constitution does not prescribe the procedures to be used for actually drafting the government's budget. Over the years Congress has enacted legislation specifying budgetary procedures and has developed a "regular order" for appropriations bills. Every federal program requires both an authorization and an appropriation. Authorization bills, which might cover multiple years, must be passed by Congress to grant the actual legal authority for government agencies to spend budget money. Appropriations bills are the funding mechanisms that specify how much money will be given to different government agencies and programs. If a program is authorized but no money is appropriated, the program cannot be implemented. In principle, authorizing bills set policies and appropriations bills pay for them. In practice, the line is sometimes not so clear. Appropriations committees sometimes attach limitation riders to the appropriations bill, prohibiting funds from being spent for particular purposes. Republicans, for example, have sought to use limitation riders to prevent federal dollars from being spent on abortions.

As is true for much of the rest of contemporary congressional policy making, the "regular order" of the budget process, as set out by the 1974 Congressional Budget and Impoundment Act, is not typically followed in Congress today. Partisan division and struggles between Congress and the White House have made it difficult to secure the enactment of the 12 separate appropriations bills reported by the 12 House and Senate Appropriations committees. In 2016, for example, congressional Republicans and Democrats agreed in January to cooperate in passing the 12 regular spending bills. By mid-year, though, failed appropriations bills had "piled up in the Senate like a multicar crash on the highway."[39] Similar problems in 2019 led to a brief government shutdown. Republicans were especially outraged that Senate Democrats filibustered the defense appropriations bill. Republicans said Democrats were willing to compromise national security for partisan reasons. Democrats said it was the GOP that demonstrated indifference to the nation's real security needs. Indeed, since 1999, the "regular" budget process has failed to produce a budget as often as it has succeeded.

omnibus appropriations bill a bill that deals with a number of unrelated topics

Departing from regular order, Congress has come to rely on the **omnibus appropriations bill** crafted by party leaders. The omnibus bill combines all or many of the smaller appropriations bills into a single package that can be passed with one vote in each house of Congress. For the most part, the legislative minority is excluded from the process, though in some instances the support of minority party members can be garnered by giving them influence over the omnibus process.

In sum, the omnibus bill is the budgetary component of the new order that gives congressional leaders more power. Omnibus bills discourage deliberation because of their sheer size. Members may have only a couple of days to digest a bill that can be 2,000 pages long and include many complex funding provisions. Rather than read, members seek to make sure that their own favored programs are included in the omnibus spending bill. Like harried commuters throughout the nation's capital, members must run to "catch the omnibus." The idea of deliberation is lost in the rush.

Taken together, closed rules, multiple referrals, ping-ponging, and omnibus bills strengthen party leader power in Congress, reduce the power of the committees and subcommittees, and compel members to follow the leader. Though there have been pleas from current and former members of Congress to return to regular order, it appears unlikely that party leaders will be willing to give up control over the legislative process.

Who Influences Congressional Decision-Making?

Identify the factors that influence which bills Congress passes

The process of creating a legislative agenda, drawing up a list of possible measures, and deciding among them is a very complex one, in which a variety of influences from inside and outside government play important roles. External influences include a legislator's constituency and various interest groups. Influences from inside government include party leadership, congressional colleagues, and the president.

Representatives spend a lot of time meeting with constituents in their districts to explain how they have helped their district and learn what issues their constituents care about. Such meetings are often informal events at local restaurants or fairs, or town halls where constituents can ask questions. Here, Rep. Elissa Slotkin (D-Mich.) speaks with a constituent at an event for local veterans.

CONSTITUENCY

Because members of Congress, for the most part, want to be re-elected, we would expect the views of their constituents to be a primary influence on the decisions that they make. In fact, most constituents pay little attention to politics and often do not even know what policies their representatives support. Nonetheless, members of Congress spend a lot of time worrying about what their constituents think because they realize that the choices they make may be used as ammunition by an opposing candidate in a future election.[40]

For example, in 2017, despite lobbying by President Trump, the House Republican leadership could not muster enough votes to pass a measure that would have repealed Obamacare. Some Republicans from swing districts—those where voters are closely divided between the parties—feared upsetting constituents who favored Obamacare, while more conservative Republicans thought the bill did not go far enough in dismantling government-sponsored health insurance.

INTEREST GROUPS

Interest groups are another important influence on congressional policies. Members of Congress pay close attention to interest groups for a number of reasons: they can mobilize constituents, serve as watchdogs on congressional action, and supply candidates with information and money.

Many interest groups also use legislative "scorecards" that rate how members of Congress vote on issues of importance to that group, often posting them on their websites for members and the public to see. A high or low rating by an important interest group may provide a potent weapon in the next election. Interest groups can increase their influence over a particular piece of legislation by signaling their intention to include it in their scoring. Among the most influential groups that use scorecards are the National Federation of Independent Business, the American Federation of Labor and Congress of Industrial Organizations (AFL-CIO), National Right to Life, the League of Conservation Voters, and the National Rifle Association.

Interest groups also have substantial influence in setting the legislative agenda and, working with members and staffers of congressional committees, in helping to craft specific language in legislation. Today, lobbyists representing such groups provide information about policies, as well as campaign contributions, to busy members of Congress. The $1.1 trillion end-of-year spending bill passed at the end of 2014 included an amendment exempting many financial transactions from federal regulation under the Dodd-Frank Act. The amendment language was taken from a bill originally written by Citigroup lobbyists, with 70 of 85 lines of the bill directly copying Citigroup's language.[41] After further lobbying by the banking industry, legislation enacted in 2018 loosened a number of other Dodd-Frank rules.

Close financial ties between members of Congress and interest group lobbyists often raise concerns that interest groups get favored treatment in exchange for political donations. Interest groups are influential in Congress, but the character of their influence is often misunderstood. Interest groups seldom "buy" votes, in the sense of pressuring members of Congress to radically change their positions on issues. Their main effect is to encourage members already inclined to agree with them to work harder on behalf of the group's goals.

PARTY

In both the House and Senate, party leaders have a good deal of influence over the behavior of their party members. This influence, sometimes called "party discipline," is today at an all-time high.

party unity vote a roll-call vote in the House or Senate in which at least 50 percent of the members of one party take a particular position and are opposed by at least 50 percent of the members of the other party

roll-call vote a vote in which each legislator's yes or no vote is recorded as the clerk calls the names of the members alphabetically

A vote in which half or more of the members of one party take one position while at least half of the members of the other party take the opposing position is called a **party unity vote**. At the beginning of the twentieth century, nearly half of all **roll-call votes** in the House of Representatives were party unity votes. For much of the twentieth century, the number of party unity votes declined as bipartisan legislation became more common. The 1990s, however, witnessed a return to strong party discipline as partisan polarization increased between Democrats and Republicans, and congressional party leaders aggressively used their powers to keep their members in line. That high level of party discipline continues today.

Party unity has been on the rise in recent years because the divisions between the parties have deepened on many high-profile issues such as abortion, health care, and financial reform (see Figure 10.5). Party unity also rises when congressional leaders try to put a partisan stamp on legislation. For example, in 1995 then-Speaker Newt Gingrich sought to enact a Republican "Contract with America" that few Democrats supported. The result was more party unity in the House than in any year since 1954. Since then, increasing polarization has resulted in very high party unity scores. Initial results for the 116th Congress indicate that party unity scores will increase, particularly in the House. Typically, party unity is greater in the House than in the Senate. House rules grant greater procedural control of business to the majority party leaders, which gives them more influence over House members.

To some extent, party unity is based on ideology and background. In the House, Republican members of the House are more likely to have been elected by rural or suburban districts and Democrats by urban ones; in both houses, Democrats are more liberal on economic and social questions than their Republican colleagues.

FIGURE 10.5

Party Unity Votes in Congress

Party unity votes are roll-call votes in which a majority of one party lines up against a majority of the other party. Party unity votes increase when the parties are polarized and when the party leadership can enforce discipline. Why did the percentage of party unity votes decline in the 1970s? Why has it risen in recent years?

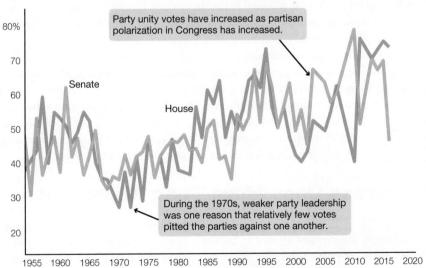

PERCENTAGE OF ALL VOTES

Party unity votes have increased as partisan polarization in Congress has increased.

Senate

House

During the 1970s, weaker party leadership was one reason that relatively few votes pitted the parties against one another.

SOURCES: CQ Roll Call's Vote Studies, http://media.cq.com/votestudies (accessed 6/9/14); Eliza Newlin Carney, "Standing Together against Any Action," *CQ Weekly*, March 16, 2015; and "2015 Vote Studies: Party Unity Remained Strong," *CQ Weekly*, February 8, 2016; Brookings, *Vital Statistics on Congress*, "Table 8-3: Party Unity Votes in Congress, 1953–2016," May 21, 2018, www.brookings.edu/multi-chapter-report/vital-statistics-on-congress/ (accessed 11/9/18).

WHEN CONGRESS HAS TROUBLE DECIDING

The 116th Congress (2019–20) was the least productive in modern history, enacting only 163 pieces of legislation. The previous record was held by the 112th Congress (2011–13), which had enacted 284 laws.[42] Perhaps the most important legislative success of the 116th Congress was the enactment of a multibillion dollar stimulus package to help cushion the economic effects of the coronavirus pandemic. But Congress's attention was often focused on major nonlegislative matters such as the 2019 Mueller probe into Russian efforts to influence the 2016 election, and the monthslong struggle over President Trump's impeachment.

In 2018, the 115th Congress enacted a major government spending bill, but the spending authority given to the government under that bill was due to lapse on September 30, 2020. After months of partisan battles, the 116th Congress was able only to enact a stopgap bill that would extend funding for federal agencies through December 11, 2020.[43]

Many critics of Congress charge that America's legislative body is too slow and cumbersome to deal with crises. Yet, when faced with emergencies, Congress can act quickly. Witness Congress's ability to enact major funding programs in March 2020 in response to the coronavirus pandemic and resulting financial collapse. Some pundits became impatient as Congress debated, but argument, debate, and partisanship are part of democracy. Self-government is never smooth, but it can be effective.

Congressional Polarization Congress's sometime inability to decide reflects the deep ideological distance between the two parties. Efforts to measure this distance show that Republicans and Democrats have been diverging sharply since the mid-1970s and are now more polarized than at any time in the last century. Democrats have become more liberal and Republicans have become more conservative.[44] The Republican Party has experienced the greater shift, becoming sharply more conservative.

Moreover, because congressional districts are increasingly unified in their ideology—due in part to gerrymandering but mainly to natural clustering of the population—most members of Congress are in safe seats. Their constituents will not punish them for failing to compromise. In addition, organizations on the right, such as the National Rifle Association (NRA), often punish Republican members of Congress who do support compromises, by recruiting and financing alternative candidates to challenge members who vote against the organization's positions.[45]

Congress Does More Than Make Laws

> **Describe the powers that Congress uses to influence other branches of government**

In addition to the power to make the law, Congress has a number of other ways to influence the process of government. The Constitution gives the Senate the power to approve treaties and appointments. And Congress has a number of other powers through which it can help administer laws.

OVERSIGHT

Oversight, as applied to Congress, usually refers to the effort to oversee or to supervise how the executive branch carries out legislation. Sometimes committees can look into the actions of private firms, as exemplified by recent hearings into Facebook's privacy policies and business practices. Oversight is carried out by committees or subcommittees of the Senate or the House, which conduct hearings and investigations to analyze and evaluate bureaucratic agencies and the effectiveness of their programs. Their purpose may be to locate inefficiencies or abuses of power, to explore the relationship between what an agency does and what a law intends, or to change or abolish a program. Most programs and agencies are subject to some oversight every year during the course of hearings on **appropriations**, the funding of agencies and government programs.

Committees or subcommittees have the power to subpoena witnesses, administer oaths, cross-examine, compel testimony, and bring criminal charges for contempt (refusing to cooperate) and perjury (lying under oath). Hearings and investigations are similar in many ways, but a hearing is usually held on a specific bill, and the questions asked are usually intended to build a record with regard to that bill.

In recent years, congressional oversight power has increasingly been used as a tool of partisan politics. After 2010 the Republican House used the oversight power to highlight the political weak points in President Obama's record, holding extensive hearings on the Affordable Care Act and on the militant attack of the American consulate in Benghazi, Libya, that resulted in four American deaths.[46] First convened in 2014, the Select Committee on Benghazi became enmeshed in partisan contention after Hillary Clinton, secretary of state during the attacks, announced that she would run for president. In 2015, as revelations emerged that Clinton had used a private email server during her tenure as secretary of state, the committee began to investigate whether appropriate procedures had been followed and whether national security had been compromised.[47] When the FBI undertook an investigation into the matter in 2016, FBI director James Comey recommended no criminal charges against Clinton but also questioned her judgment and called her actions "extremely careless."

Almost as soon as Donald Trump took office in 2017, Democrats called for investigations into allegations that his campaign had colluded with Russian operatives to help Trump win the 2016 election. House and Senate committees, chaired by Republicans, failed to find evidence of presidential wrongdoing. Democrats, however, demanded the appointment of a special counsel after President Trump's firing of FBI director James Comey. Over the course of the investigation, the special counsel, Robert Mueller, indicted several close Trump aides for improper contacts with Russian officials. In 2018, four former Trump aides—George Papadopoulos, Paul Manafort, Rick Gates, and Michael Flynn—pleaded guilty to a variety of crimes related to the investigation. However, in 2019, Mueller's final report indicated no conclusive evidence of collusion between the Trump campaign and the Russians, but congressional Democrats were not convinced.

ADVICE AND CONSENT: SPECIAL SENATE POWERS

The Constitution says the president has the power to make treaties and to appoint top executive officers, ambassadors, and federal judges—but only "with the Advice and Consent of the Senate" (Article II, Section 2). For treaties, two-thirds of senators present must consent; for appointments, a simple majority is required.

The power to approve or reject presidential requests includes the power to set conditions. In fact, the Senate only occasionally exercises its power to reject treaties and appointments, and despite recent debate surrounding judicial nominees, during the past century only a small number of them have been rejected by the Senate or withdrawn by the president to avoid rejection, whereas hundreds have been approved.

IMPEACHMENT

The Constitution also grants Congress the power of **impeachment**, which means formally charging a federal official with "Treason, Bribery, or other high Crimes and Misdemeanors"; officials found guilty are removed from office. Impeachment is thus like a criminal indictment in which the House of Representatives acts like a grand jury, voting (by simple majority) on whether the accused ought to be impeached. If the House votes to impeach, the Senate then acts like a trial jury, voting on whether to convict and remove the official (which requires a two-thirds majority of the Senate).

The impeachment power is the power of Congress to remove the president and is a safeguard against the executive tyranny so greatly feared by the framers of the Constitution. The House has initiated impeachment proceedings more than 60 times in U.S. history. Fewer than 20 officials were ultimately impeached, however, and only 8—all federal judges—were convicted by the Senate and removed from office.[48]

Controversy over Congress's impeachment power has arisen over the grounds for impeachment, especially the meaning of "high Crimes and Misdemeanors." An impeachable offense could be a crime but is not necessarily one, as the phrase also covers a noncriminal offense that is an abuse of the powers of office. Yet the vagueness of the term also means that impeachment is political, too, sometimes defined as "whatever the majority of the House of Representatives considers it to be at a given moment in history."[49]

In 2019, House Democrats voted to impeach President Trump on charges that he had sought to pressure the Ukrainian government to investigate Joe Biden and Biden's son, Hunter, for their business activities in Ukraine. Democrats asserted that Trump had threatened the Ukrainians with a cutoff of military aid if they did not help him undermine a major political foe. Despite a leaked phone call that seemed to support the allegation, Trump denied the charge and averred that the Democrats and liberal media were conspiring against him. After a short Senate trial,

impeachment the formal charge by the House of Representatives that a government official has committed "Treason, Bribery, or other high Crimes and Misdemeanors"

The House possesses the power to impeach federal officials. In American history, 17 federal officials have been impeached, including three presidents. In 2019–20, the House impeached Donald Trump for abuse of power and obstruction of Congress after aid to Ukraine was allegedly withheld, though he was acquitted in February 2020.

Trump was acquitted, with all but one GOP senator (Mitt Romney) choosing to support the president. Most Republican voters agreed that the charges against the president did not merit his removal from office.

Congress: What Do You Think?

Much of this chapter has described the major institu-tional components of Congress and has shown how they work as Congress makes policy. But what do these institutional features mean for how Congress represents the American public?

★ Does the organization of Congress promote the equal representation of all Americans? Or are there institutional features of Congress that allow some interests more access and influence than others? What can we learn from a stimulus bill that passes Congress and an opioids bill that almost fails? What might Huntington, West Virginia, police chief Hank Dial or business owner Glynis Donnelly say?

★ What areas of public policy might suffer if Congress continues its inability to decide?

★ What types of institutional changes would make Congress work better? Some suggest the appointment of citizen commissions to draw district lines in order to elect more moderate candidates and make compromise in Congress easier. Others argue for eliminating the filibuster in the Senate to reduce gridlock. What do you think the effects would be?

★ Will continued partisan gridlock hurt Congress as an institution?

STUDY GUIDE

Practice Quiz

1. Which of the following is one way in which the House and the Senate are different? *(pp. 293–94)*
   a) Senators are more interested in attending to their constituents' immediate legislative needs, while members of the House are more insulated from the pressures of immediate interests.
   b) Members of the House are more interested in attending to their constituents' immediate legislative needs, while senators are more insulated from the pressures of immediate interests.
   c) Senators serve smaller and more homogeneous constituencies than members of the House.
   d) Senators are often more attuned to the legislative needs of local interest groups than members of the House.
   e) There are no important differences between the House and the Senate.

2. Which type of representation is described when constituents have the power to hire and fire their representative? *(p. 296)*
   a) substantive representation
   b) descriptive representation
   c) philosophical representation
   d) ideological representation
   e) economic representation

3. Which of the following statements best describes the social composition of the U.S. Congress? *(p. 296)*
   a) The majority of representatives do not have university degrees.
   b) Men and women are equally represented in Congress.
   c) Most members of Congress do not affiliate with any specific religion.
   d) The legal profession is the most common career of members of Congress prior to their election.

   e) The number of African American, Latino, and Asian American representatives has decreased over the last 20 years.

4. The Supreme Court has ruled that *(p. 308)*
   a) only the House of Representatives has the constitutional authority to redraw congressional district lines.
   b) states may use independent bipartisan commissions to redraw congressional districts.
   c) states may not use independent bipartisan commissions to redraw congressional districts.
   d) states can forgo the redistricting process if they lose more than 10 percent of their population between censuses.
   e) only the Senate has the constitutional authority to redraw congressional district lines.

5. Which of the following types of committees includes members of both the House and the Senate on the same committee? *(p. 311)*
   a) standing committee
   b) conference committee
   c) select committee
   d) All committees include both House members and senators.
   e) No committees include both House members and senators.

6. Which of the following statements about the filibuster is most accurate? *(p. 316)*
   a) The filibuster was first used in 1975.
   b) The votes of 67 senators are currently required to end a filibuster.
   c) The filibuster was used far more frequently in the 1930s and '40s than it has been in the last two decades.

d) Nominees for federal executive and judicial positions cannot currently be filibustered.

e) Filibusters were declared unconstitutional by the Supreme Court in 2013.

7. Which of the following distinguishes the "new order" from the "regular order" when it comes to passing legislation? *(p. 318)*

a) The new order reflects the enhanced power of committees and subcommittees in both houses of Congress.

b) The new order reflects the diminished power of party leaders in both houses of Congress.

c) The new order relies heavily on conference committees to draft legislation.

d) The new order is meant to move bills along more slowly, with more deliberation.

e) The new order is meant to move bills along more quickly, with less deliberation.

8. Members of Congress take their constituents' views into account because *(p. 321)*

a) the Supreme Court can invalidate laws passed without majority support in the public.

b) interest groups are forbidden from lobbying during legislative votes.

c) most constituents pay close attention to what's going on in Congress at all times.

d) they worry that their voting record will be used as ammunition by their opponents at election time.

e) they can be impeached if they go against their constituents' policy preferences.

9. Congressional polarization *(p. 324)*

a) has decreased since the mid-1970s.

b) has increased since the mid-1970s.

c) has remained the same since the mid-1970s.

d) has been driven entirely by Democrats becoming more liberal since the mid-1970s.

e) has not been measured since the mid-1970s.

10. When Congress conducts an investigation to explore the relationship between what a law intended and how an executive agency has implemented it, it is engaged in *(p. 325)*

a) oversight.

b) advice and consent.

c) appropriations.

d) executive agreement.

e) direct patronage.

11. Which of the following statements about impeachment is not true? *(p. 326)*

a) The president is not the only official who can be impeached by Congress.

b) Impeachment means to charge a government official with "Treason, Bribery, or other high Crimes and Misdemeanors."

c) The House of Representatives decides by simple majority vote whether the accused ought to be impeached.

d) The Senate decides whether to convict and remove the person from office.

e) Only criminal offenses are impeachable.

Key Terms

constituency *(p. 293)*

bicameral *(p. 293)*

delegate *(p. 294)*

trustee *(p. 294)*

descriptive representation *(p. 295)*

substantive representation *(p. 296)*

incumbency *(p. 300)*

pork barrel (or pork) *(p. 303)*

apportionment *(p. 304)*

redistricting *(p. 305)*

gerrymandering *(p. 305)*

conference *(p. 309)*

caucus (political) *(p. 309)*

Speaker of the House *(p. 309)*

majority leader *(p. 309)*

minority leader *(p. 309)*

whip *(p. 309)*

standing committee *(p. 310)*

select committees *(p. 311)*

joint committees *(p. 311)*

conference committees *(p. 311)*

seniority *(p. 311)*

staff agencies *(p. 312)*

bill *(p. 313)*

committee markup *(p. 313)*

closed rule *(p. 315)*

open rule *(p. 315)*

filibuster *(p. 316)*

cloture *(p. 316)*

veto *(p. 317)*

pocket veto *(p. 317)*

multiple referral *(p. 318)*

omnibus appropriations bill *(p. 320)*

party unity vote *(p. 322)*

roll-call vote *(p. 322)*

oversight *(p. 325)*

appropriations *(p. 325)*

impeachment *(p. 326)*

The Presidency

WHAT GOVERNMENT DOES AND WHY IT MATTERS

Presidents inevitably face challenges during their time in office. Donald Trump was no exception, as the coronavirus pandemic of 2020 strained the nation's health care system, killing thousands, and forced millions out of work. Indeed, Trump declared himself a "wartime president," an apt title given the magnitude of the pandemic's devastating effects on the nation.

Enacted in 1950 during the Korean War, the Defense Production Act (DPA) allows a presidential administration to secure or ramp up production of needed equipment from private businesses. In March 2020, President Trump invoked the DPA for a nonmilitary purpose: to compel auto manufacturer GM to produce much-needed ventilators for hospitals.

Some observers urged the president not to stop there but to use the DPA to force production of additional medical equipment, such as masks, eye protection, and other types of personal protective equipment (PPE). Dr. Craig Spencer, director of global health in emergency medicine at New York-Presbyterian/Columbia University Medical Center, made such a plea, saying

During the coronavirus pandemic, President Trump took several actions to mobilize the government to respond to the virus. One was invoking the Defense Production Act, overseen by Peter Navarro, pictured here on the left, which allowed the government to block exports of masks and other personal protective equipment. Health care workers across the country, experiencing a shortage of PPE, urged the president to use the power of the Defense Production Act to force private companies to manufacture PPE.

that supplies were running out at his hospital and others in New York, a virus hot spot. "If we don't take decisive and aggressive action now, many more of my colleagues will be infected."[1] A number of governors and members of Congress, as well as the American Medical Association, called for the further use of the DPA as well.

Through March 2020, President Trump declined to invoke the DPA further. "We're a country not based on nationalizing our businesses," Trump said. Some parts of the business community had urged him not to invoke the DPA, worrying that it would introduce government bureaucracy at the precise time when streamlined processes were acutely important. Congressional Democrats contemplated passing a law that would force President Trump to use his DPA powers more broadly.[2]

Then, in April 2020, President Trump changed course, invoking the DPA, but not in a way his earlier critics anticipated. Under DPA Policy Coordinator Peter Navarro, the Trump administration sought to commandeer face masks made by 3M. First it threatened to block 3M's export of American-made masks to

Canada and Latin America, which 3M resisted, saying this would have "significant humanitarian implications." Then the administration seized a shipment of masks made by 3M in Thailand that was headed to Berlin. A German spokesperson said, "We view this as an act of modern piracy. That's not how you treat trans-Atlantic partners." In the global scramble for supplies to combat the coronavirus pandemic, fears arose that the Trump administration's attempts to protect the American populace would lead instead to retaliation by other countries.[3]

In this chapter, we examine the foundations of the American presidency and assess the origins and character of presidential power. Presidents are empowered by democratic political processes and, increasingly, by their ability to control and expand the institutional resources of the office. They sit atop the executive branch, a large bureaucracy of departments and agencies. They influence policy with their appointments to the Cabinet, to the White House staff, and to the Executive Office of the President, choosing officials who are sympathetic to their policy goals and using regulatory review and executive orders and proclamations to make policy. They set the tone for government as the sole elected official representing the entire country. As we will see, the framers thought a powerful and energetic president would make America's government more effective but knew that presidential power needed to be subject to constraints to prevent it from becoming a threat to citizens' liberties. The checks and balances in the constitutional design not only constrain each branch's powers but also ensure that those powers are shared.

CHAPTER GOALS

★ Identify the expressed, implied, delegated, and inherent powers of the presidency (pp. 335–46)

★ Describe the institutional resources presidents have to help them exercise their powers (pp. 346–50)

★ Explain how modern presidents have become even more powerful (pp. 352–60)

Presidential Power Is Rooted in the Constitution

The presidency was established by Article II of the Constitution, which begins: "The executive power shall be vested in a President of the United States of America." This language is known as the Constitution's "vesting clause." The president's executive power is underscored in Section 3 of Article II, which confers upon the president the duty to "take care that the laws be faithfully executed." The president's oath of office in Section 1, moreover, obligates—and thus empowers—the chief executive to "preserve, protect and defend the Constitution of the United States."

This language seems to require the president to take action, without specifying any limits to that action, if constitutional government is threatened. In 1861, during the Civil War, President Abraham Lincoln cited his oath of office as justification for suspending the writ of habeas corpus, which protects against arbitrary government detention of individuals. He declared that his oath would be broken if the government were overthrown and that suspension of habeas corpus was necessary to prevent that calamity from taking place.

Abraham Lincoln, like many other presidents, cited the presidential oath of office as providing the president the authority to take all the necessary actions to protect the nation.

By vesting the executive power in the president, Article II also implies that the president serves as America's head of state and is therefore entitled to special deference and respect.

On the basis of Article II, presidents have three types of powers: expressed powers, implied powers, and delegated powers. A fourth type of power claimed by presidents does not appear in Article II. This is called the inherent power of the office.

EXPRESSED POWERS

The **expressed powers** of the presidency are those specifically established by the language of the Constitution. These fall into several categories:

1. *Military.* Article II, Section 2, provides for the power as "Commander in Chief of the Army and Navy of the United States, and of the Militia of the several States, when called in to the actual Service of the United States."

2. *Judicial.* Article II, Section 2, also provides the power to "grant Reprieves and Pardons for Offences against the United States, except in Cases of Impeachment."

3. *Diplomatic.* Article II, Section 2, further provides the power "by and with the Advice and Consent of the Senate to make Treaties." Article II, Section 3, provides the power to "receive Ambassadors and other public Ministers."

4. *Executive.* Article II, Section 3, authorizes the president to see to it that all the laws are faithfully executed; Section 2 gives the power to appoint, remove, and supervise all executive officers and to appoint all federal judges.

5. *Legislative.* Article I, Section 7, and Article II, Section 3, give the president the power to participate authoritatively in the legislative process.

Military Power The president's military powers are among the most important ones of the office. The position of **commander in chief** makes the president the highest military authority in the United States, with control of the entire defense establishment. The president is also head of the nation's intelligence network, which includes not only the Central Intelligence Agency (CIA) but also the National Security Council (NSC), the National Security Agency (NSA), the Federal Bureau of Investigation (FBI), and a host of less well-known but very powerful international and domestic security agencies.

expressed powers specific powers granted by the Constitution to Congress (Article I, Section 8) and to the president (Article II)

commander in chief the role of the president as commander of the national military and the state National Guard units (when called into service)

The president's military powers extend into the domestic sphere. Article IV, Section 4, provides that the "United States shall [protect] every State . . . against . . . Invasion . . . and . . . domestic Violence." Congress has made this an explicit presidential power through statutes directing the president as commander in chief to discharge these obligations.[4] The Constitution restrains the president's use of domestic force, however, by providing that a state legislature (or governor) must request federal troops before the president can send them into the state to provide public order.

One of the president's responsibilities is the maintenance of public order in times of crisis. In 1951, President Eisenhower used this to justify sending the troops to Little Rock to enforce racial integration of public schools (left). During the coronavirus crisis of 2020, President Trump sent the USNS *Mercy*, a navy hospital ship, to Los Angeles to treat patients suffering from COVID-19 as hospitals became overwhelmed (right).

Yet presidents are not obligated to deploy national troops merely because the state legislature or governor makes such a request. More important, the president may deploy troops without a specific request from the state legislature or governor if the president considers them necessary to keep order, maintain an essential national service during an emergency, enforce a federal judicial order, or protect federally guaranteed civil rights.[5]

A historic example of the unilateral use of presidential emergency power when a state did not request or even want it is the decision by President Dwight D. Eisenhower in 1957 to send troops into Little Rock, Arkansas, against the wishes of the Arkansas government, to enforce court orders to integrate Little Rock's Central High School. The state's governor, Orval Faubus, had posted the Arkansas National Guard at the school entrance to prevent the court-ordered admission of nine Black students. After an effort to negotiate with Governor Faubus failed, President Eisenhower reluctantly sent 1,000 paratroopers from the U.S. Army's 101st Airborne Division to Little Rock; they stood watch while the Black students took their places in the previously all-White classrooms.

In 2020, Trump considered issuing orders to mobilize as many as 10,000 federal troops to help quell protests that broke out in the wake of the killing of George Floyd, an African American man, by a Minneapolis police officer. Military officials balked at Trump's proposed use of troops and Trump did not issue the order. The president did, however, dispatch federal law enforcement agents to Portland, Oregon, and several other cities to guard federal property and help local police. These agents were withdrawn after local officials declared that they were not needed.

Judicial Power The president has power to grant reprieves, pardons, and amnesty. Presidents may use this power on behalf of a particular individual, as did Gerald Ford when he pardoned Richard Nixon in 1974 "for all offenses against the United States which he . . . has committed or may have committed." Or they may use it on a large scale, as did President Andrew Johnson in 1868, when he gave full amnesty to all southerners who had participated in the Civil War.

As the head of state, the president is America's chief representative in dealings with other countries. Here, President Trump meets with North Korea's Supreme Leader Kim Jong-un in 2018 to discuss nuclear disarmament on the Korean Peninsula.

Presidents' use of the pardon power can be very controversial. President Trump was criticized for pardoning former Arizona sheriff Joe Arpaio after Arpaio was found guilty of criminal contempt for ignoring a court order that directed his office to halt illegal racial-profiling practices. The pardon was criticized because Trump did not first consult with the Justice Department's office of pardons, because Arpaio was a political supporter of Trump, and because the pardon was issued before Arpaio had been sentenced.

Diplomatic Power The president is America's chief representative in dealings with other nations, having the power to make treaties for the United States (with the advice and consent of the Senate) as well as the power to "recognize" the governments of other countries. Diplomatic recognition means that the United States acknowledges a government's legitimacy—that is, its claim to be the legal and rightful government of the country.

In recent years, presidents have expanded the practice of using executive agreements instead of treaties to establish contracts with other countries.[6] An **executive agreement** is exactly like a treaty except that it does not require approval by two-thirds of the Senate. The courts have held that executive agreements have the force of law, as though they were formal treaties.

> **executive agreement** an agreement, made between the president and another country, that has the force of a treaty but does not require the Senate's "advice and consent"

Executive Power The Constitution focuses executive power and legal responsibility on the president. The most important constitutional basis of the president's power as chief executive is found in Article II, Section 3, which stipulates that the president must see that all the laws are faithfully executed, and Section 2, which provides that the president will appoint and supervise all executive officers and appoint all federal judges (with Senate approval). The power to appoint the principal executive officers and to require each of them to report to the president on subjects relating to the duties of their departments makes the president the true chief executive officer (CEO) of the nation.

Another component of the president's power as chief executive is **executive privilege**, the claim that confidential communications between a president and close advisers should not be revealed without presidential consent. Presidents have made this claim ever since George Washington refused a request from the House of Representatives to deliver documents concerning negotiations of an important treaty. Washington refused (successfully) on the grounds that, first, the House was not constitutionally part of the treaty-making process and, second, diplomatic negotiations required secrecy.

> **executive privilege** the claim that confidential communications between a president and close advisers should not be revealed without the consent of the president

Although many presidents have claimed executive privilege, the concept was not tested in the courts until the "Watergate" affair of the early 1970s, when President Richard Nixon refused congressional demands that he turn over secret White House tapes that congressional investigators suspected would establish his involvement in illegal activities. In *United States v. Nixon* (1974), the Supreme Court ordered Nixon to turn over the tapes.[7] The president complied with the order and was eventually forced to resign from office as a result.

In *United States v. Nixon* the Court ruling recognized for the first time the legal validity of executive privilege, though noting that it was not absolute and could be set aside in the face of a criminal inquiry. An executive privilege claim would be much stronger if it involved national security. Subsequent presidents have cited the case in support of executive privilege claims. The Obama administration invoked executive privilege once, in response to congressional demands for records from Attorney General Eric Holder relating to Operation Fast and Furious, an arms-trafficking sting operation that went awry, with federal agents losing track of hundreds of guns they had sold to suspected gun smugglers. In 2019, President Trump asserted executive privilege to block the release of portions of the Mueller Report on Russian meddling in the 2016 election and again to prevent the release of certain documents relating to the Census Bureau's deliberations over the proposed addition of a citizenship question to the 2020 census. Trump's use of executive privilege to withhold information from Congress became the basis for one of the articles of impeachment drafted by the House to impeach the president in 2019.

Legislative Power—Agenda Setting Two constitutional provisions are the primary sources of the president's power in the legislative process. The first of these, in Article II, Section 3, provides that the president "shall from time to time give to the Congress Information of the State of the Union, and recommend to their Consideration such Measures as he shall judge necessary and expedient." Delivering a "State of the Union" address may at first appear to be little more than the president's obligation to make recommendations for Congress's consideration. But in the twentieth century, as political and social conditions began to favor an increasingly prominent presidential role, each president, especially since Franklin Roosevelt, increasingly relied on this provision to become the primary initiator of proposals for legislative action in Congress and the most important single participant in legislative decision-making. The address has also become the principal source for public awareness of national issues.[8]

With some important exceptions, Congress depends on the president to set the agenda of public policy. For example, under the terms of the 1921 Budget and Accounting Act, the president is required to submit a budget to Congress. This gives presidents the power to set the terms of debate about budgetary matters. Presidents also often set the country's policy agenda, beyond the budget. During the weeks immediately following the September 11, 2001, terrorist attacks, President George W. Bush took many presidential initiatives to Congress, and each was given almost unanimous support. President Obama made health care his chief domestic priority and negotiated with divided congressional Democrats to bring about the enactment of the Affordable Care Act, known as "Obamacare." Congress enacted President Trump's proposals for a sweeping tax reform bill and a budget that substantially increased spending on military programs.

Legislative Power—the Veto The second of the president's constitutionally authorized legislative powers is the **veto** power to reject acts of Congress (see Figure 11.1), which is provided in Article I, Section 7.[9] This power effectively makes the president the most important single legislative leader,[10] since no vetoed bill can become law unless both the House and Senate override the veto by a two-thirds vote. In the case of a **pocket veto**, as explained in Chapter 10, Congress does not even have the chance to override the veto but must pass the bill again in its next session.

Use of the veto varies according to the political situation each president confronts. During his last two years in office, when Democrats had control of both houses of Congress, Republican president George W. Bush vetoed 10 bills, including legislation designed to prohibit the use of harsh interrogation tactics, saying it "would take away one of the most valuable tools in the war on terror."[11] Similarly, 10 of President Obama's 12 vetoes occurred during his last two years in office, when Republicans held the majority in both houses. Among the most significant was his 2015 veto of a bill authorizing construction of the Keystone XL pipeline, which would have carried oil from Canada to U.S. refineries but was opposed by environmentalists.

veto the president's constitutional power to turn down acts of Congress; a presidential veto may be overridden by a two-thirds vote of each house of Congress

pocket veto a presidential veto that is automatically triggered if the president does not act on a given piece of legislation passed during the final 10 days of a legislative session

Since the time of George Washington, presidents have used their veto power almost 2,600 times, and on only 111 occasions has Congress overridden them. As of October 2020, President Trump had issued eight vetoes, including a veto of a House resolution seeking to terminate the state of national emergency that the president had declared along America's southern border.

The Veto Process

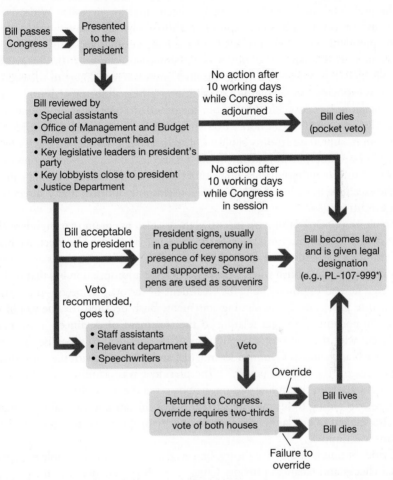

*PL—public law; 107—number of Congress (107th was 2001–02); 999—number of the law.

IMPLIED POWERS

Each expressed power has become the foundation of a second set of presidential powers, the **implied powers** of the office. An implied power is one that can be said to be necessary to allow presidents to exercise their expressed power. For example, the Constitution expressly gives the president the power to appoint "all other officers of the United States . . . which shall be established

implied powers powers derived from the necessary and proper clause of Article I, Section 8, of the Constitution; such powers are not specifically expressed but are implied through the expansive interpretation of delegated powers

by law." Article II does not, however, expressly grant the president the power to remove such officials from office. From the earliest years of the Republic, though, presidents have claimed that the removal power was implied by the appointment power.

The vesting and "take care" clauses of the Constitution, discussed earlier, as well as the president's oath of office, have also been cited by successive White Houses as justifications for actions not expressly authorized by the Constitution. In recent years, presidents and their advisers have used the vesting clause to support what has come to be known as the "theory of the unitary executive."[12] This theory holds that all executive power within the national government belongs to the president except as explicitly limited by the Constitution.[13] Thus, all the officials of the executive branch must take their orders from the president. Moreover, according to this view, Congress has little authority over the executive branch and the president is a sovereign or supreme authority subject only to specific restraints, such as Congress's control of revenues, its impeachment power, and its power to override presidential vetoes. Thus, the unitary theory holds that the president controls all policy making by the executive branch and that Congress wields only limited, if any, direct power over executive agencies.

Some proponents of unitary executive theory also maintain that presidents have their own power to interpret the Constitution as it applies to the executive branch and do not necessarily have to defer to the judiciary. This claim was advanced by President George W. Bush when he signed a defense appropriation bill that included language he had opposed about the treatment of terrorist suspects—the so-called antitorture provision. In his signing statement, Bush declared that he would construe the portion of the act relating to the treatment of detainees "in a manner consistent with the constitutional authority of the President to supervise the unitary executive branch and as Commander in Chief and consistent with the constitutional limitations on the judicial power."[14] The president was claiming, in other words, that particularly in the military realm, he possessed the authority to execute acts of Congress according to his own understanding of the law and the nation's interests. He also seemed to be claiming that the authority of the courts to interfere with his actions was limited.

Critics of unitary executive theory, however, argue that the principle of constitutional checks and balances provides Congress with powers over executive agencies through "congressional oversight" of the executive branch. Article I of the Constitution gives Congress a number of powers, including the power to appropriate funds, to raise and support armies and navies, to regulate interstate commerce, and to impeach officials of the executive branch. Article I also gives Congress the authority "to make all laws which shall be necessary and proper for carrying into execution the foregoing powers."

Congressional oversight, which includes hearings, investigations, studies, and reports, is arguably implied by this language. If Congress is to carry out its constitutional responsibilities, it must be able to obtain information about the activities of executive branch agencies and officials. Thus, the stage is set for conflict between the implied powers of Congress and those of the president.

Comparing Executive Authority

The American president is the face of the federal government. While the role has become much more powerful since the founding, the president is actually quite weak compared to his or her peer executives in other countries. While most countries have constitutions that outline the powers of the executive, such as the power to dissolve the legislature, or the power to initiate legislation, in practice, executives often claim powers beyond what is explicitly granted to them. The figure below shows the countries with the most and least powerful executives.

1. What are the benefits of having a strong executive in a country? Do you think the office of the president in the American system has too much power? Not enough? Does seeing the data in this graphic change your opinion?
2. What might be an argument for giving an executive the ability to dissolve the legislature or declare a state of emergency? How do you put checks on such a strong executive while still granting him or her some powers?

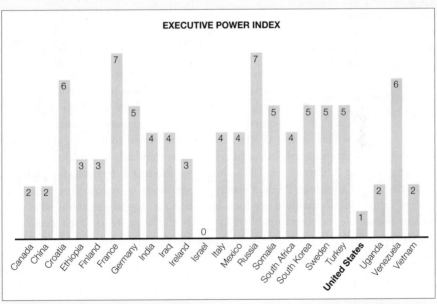

EXECUTIVE POWER INDEX

Country	Value
Canada	2
China	2
Croatia	6
Ethiopia	3
Finland	3
France	7
Germany	5
India	4
Iraq	4
Ireland	3
Israel	0
Italy	4
Mexico	4
Russia	7
Somalia	5
South Africa	4
South Korea	5
Sweden	5
Turkey	5
United States	1
Uganda	2
Venezuela	6
Vietnam	2

SOURCE: Comparative Constitutions Project, http://comparativeconstitutionsproject.org/ccp-rankings/ (accessed 8/12/19).

DELEGATED POWERS

Many of the powers exercised by the president and the executive branch are not found in the Constitution but are **delegated powers**, the products of congressional statutes and resolutions. Over the past century, Congress has voluntarily delegated a great deal of its own legislative authority to the executive branch. To some extent, this delegation of power has been an almost inescapable consequence of the expansion of government activity in the United States since the New Deal.

In the nineteenth century, the federal government was small and had relatively few domestic responsibilities, so Congress could pay close attention to details. Given the vast range of the federal government's responsibilities today, however, Congress cannot possibly execute all federal laws and administer all of the thousands of federal programs. Inevitably, it must turn more and more to the hundreds of departments and agencies in the executive branch or, when necessary, create new agencies to implement its goals. Thus, for example, in 2002, to strengthen protection against terrorist attacks, it established the Department of Homeland Security, with broad powers in the realms of law enforcement, public health, and immigration.

delegated powers constitutional powers that are assigned to one governmental agency but are exercised by another agency with the express permission of the first

inherent powers powers claimed by a president that are not expressed in the Constitution but are inferred from it

As they implement congressional legislation, federal agencies collectively develop thousands of rules and regulations and issue thousands of orders and findings every year. Agencies interpret Congress's intent, publish rules aimed at implementing that intent, and issue orders to individuals, firms, and organizations to compel them to conform to the law. Such administrative rules have the effect of law; the courts treat them like congressional statutes.

Since the New Deal of the 1930s, Congress has tended to draft legislation that defines a broad goal for agencies but offers few clear standards or guidelines for how that goal is to be achieved. The 1972 Consumer Product Safety Act, for example, authorizes the Consumer Product Safety Commission to reduce "unreasonable" risks of injury from household products but offers no suggestions about what constitutes reasonable and unreasonable risks or how the latter are to be reduced.[15] As a result, the executive branch, under the president's direction, has wide discretion to make rules that impact American citizens and businesses.

INHERENT POWERS

Presidents have also claimed a set of powers not specified in the Constitution but said to stem from the rights, duties, and obligations of the presidency. These are referred to as **inherent powers** and are most often asserted by presidents in time of war or national emergency. Presidents Roosevelt (World War II), Truman (Korean War), and both Presidents Bush (Persian Gulf and Middle East wars) claimed inherent powers to defend the nation.

Since the Korean War, presidents have used their claim of inherent powers along with their constitutional power as commander in chief to bypass the constitutional provision giving Congress the power to declare war. Congress declared war after the Japanese attack on Pearl Harbor on December 7, 1941. Since that time, American forces have been sent to fight foreign wars on more than 100 occasions, but not once was Congress asked for a declaration of war. In 1973, Congress passed the War Powers Resolution, designed to restore its role in military policy. Presidents, however, have regarded the resolution as an improper limitation on their inherent powers and have sometimes ignored its provisions.

The difference between inherent and implied powers is often subtle, and the two are frequently jointly claimed in support of presidential action. Implied powers can be traced to the powers expressed in the actual language of the Constitution.[16] Inherent powers, on the other hand, derive from national sovereignty. Under international law and custom, sovereign states possess a number of inherent rights and powers, the most important being the rights to engage in relations with other nations, to defend themselves against attacks from other states, and to curb internal violence and unrest.

No president has acted so frequently on the basis of inherent powers as President George W. Bush. He claimed that they authorized him to create military commissions; designate U.S. citizens as enemy combatants; engage in "extraordinary renditions" of captured suspects, who would be moved to unknown facilities in unnamed countries for interrogation; and order the National Security Agency (NSA) to monitor phone conversations between the United States and other nations.[17] When challenged, some but not all of these actions were overturned by the courts.

Bush's successor, President Obama, continued to rely on the concept of inherent power in ordering drone strikes against suspected terrorists and ordering American air strikes in Libya. Testifying before Congress in 2014, Attorney General Eric Holder defended the president's unilateral actions, saying, "Given what the president's responsibility is in running the executive branch, I think there is an inherent power there for him to act in the way that he has."[18]

In 2017, President Trump's order banning travelers from several Muslim countries was based mainly on a claim that the president had the inherent power to bar any class of immigrants he thought to be a threat to the United States. In 2018, the Supreme Court[19] overruled lower-court decisions that had sought to block Trump's travel ban, saying that the president was entitled to deference in judging whether a particular group of immigrants represented a threat to the United States. In 2020, President Trump asserted that he had the inherent power to determine whether businesses could reopen or must remain closed in the face of the coronavirus threat.

Congress has tried to place some limits on powers that presidents claim to be inherent. For example, although presidents believe they have the inherent power to deal with emergencies, Congress has passed legislation to restrict and guide the use of this power. Under the 1976 National Emergencies Act, the president is authorized to declare a national emergency in the event of major threats to America's national security or economy.[20] An emergency declaration relating to foreign threats allows the president to embargo trade, seize foreign assets, and prohibit transactions with whatever foreign nations are involved.

The 1976 act provided, however, that an emergency declaration does not remain in force indefinitely but expires in one year unless renewed by the president. Congress may also terminate a state of emergency by a joint resolution of the two houses. Nevertheless, several declarations have been renewed for quite some time.[21]

Presidents Claim Many Institutional Powers

> **Describe the institutional resources presidents have to help them exercise their powers**

Since the ratification of the Constitution, the president has been joined by thousands of officials and staffers who work for, assist, or advise the chief executive (see Figure 11.2). Collectively, these individuals could be said to make up the institutional presidency and to give the president a capacity for action that no single individual could duplicate. The first component of the institutional presidency is the president's Cabinet.

THE CABINET

In the American system of government, the **Cabinet** is the traditional but informal designation for the heads of all the major federal government departments. The Cabinet has no constitutional status. Unlike in Great Britain and many other parliamentary countries, where the cabinet *is* the government, the American Cabinet is not a formal organized body. It meets but makes no decisions as a group. Each appointment to it must be approved by the Senate, but Cabinet members are not responsible to the Senate or to Congress at large. However, Cabinet secretaries and their deputies frequently testify before congressional committees to justify budgets and policy objectives, or to explain policies or recent major events or issues.

Each of the 15 government departments is led by a secretary, who is a member of the president's Cabinet. Reporting to the secretary is a deputy secretary, while individual offices and activities are led by undersecretaries and assistant secretaries. Government departments range in size from the Department of Education, which employs only about 4,200 people, to the Department of Defense (DoD), which oversees some 700,000 civilian employees and 1.3 million military personnel and is also responsible for maintaining the military readiness of 1.1 million reserve and National Guard troops.

Cabinet the secretaries, or chief administrators, of the major departments of the federal government; Cabinet secretaries are appointed by the president with the consent of the Senate

In addition to the Cabinet agencies, the executive branch also includes a number of "independent" agencies reporting to the president. Like Cabinet secretaries, the chief executives of the independent agencies are appointed by the president and usually require senatorial confirmation. Congress engages in oversight of these agencies as it does the Cabinet departments.

FIGURE 11.2
. . . .

The Institutional Presidency

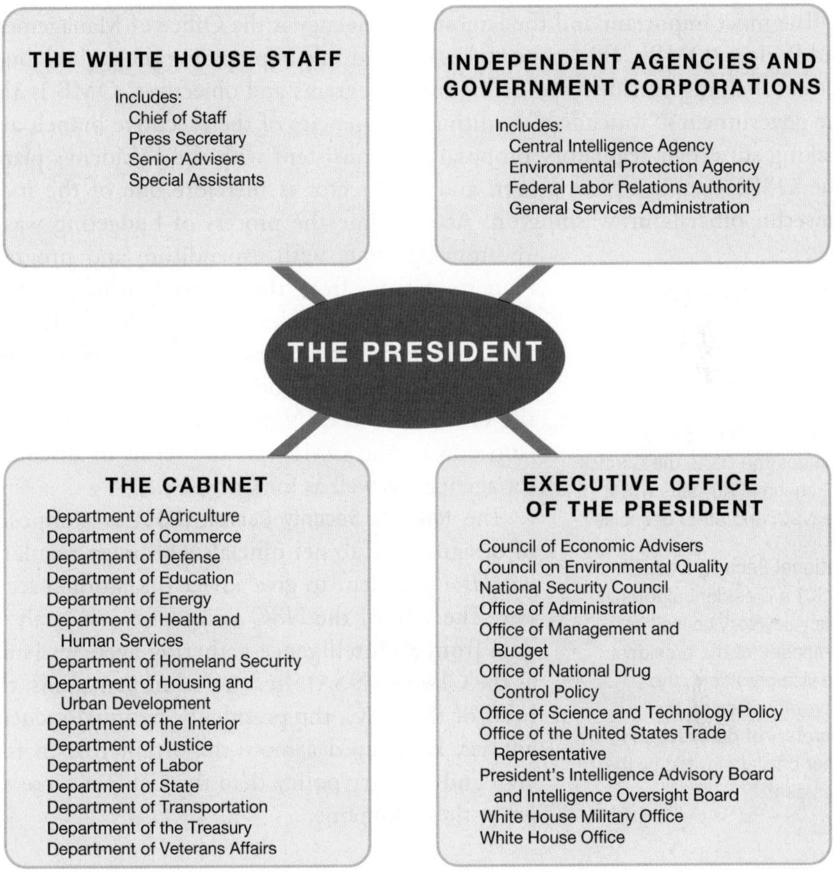

THE WHITE HOUSE STAFF

Includes:
    Chief of Staff
    Press Secretary
    Senior Advisers
    Special Assistants

INDEPENDENT AGENCIES AND GOVERNMENT CORPORATIONS

Includes:
    Central Intelligence Agency
    Environmental Protection Agency
    Federal Labor Relations Authority
    General Services Administration

THE PRESIDENT

THE CABINET

Department of Agriculture
Department of Commerce
Department of Defense
Department of Education
Department of Energy
Department of Health and
   Human Services
Department of Homeland Security
Department of Housing and
   Urban Development
Department of the Interior
Department of Justice
Department of Labor
Department of State
Department of Transportation
Department of the Treasury
Department of Veterans Affairs

EXECUTIVE OFFICE OF THE PRESIDENT

Council of Economic Advisers
Council on Environmental Quality
National Security Council
Office of Administration
Office of Management and
   Budget
Office of National Drug
   Control Policy
Office of Science and Technology Policy
Office of the United States Trade
   Representative
President's Intelligence Advisory Board
   and Intelligence Oversight Board
White House Military Office
White House Office

THE WHITE HOUSE STAFF

The White House staff is composed mainly of analysts and advisers.[22] Although many of the top **White House staff** members hold such titles as "adviser to the president," "assistant to the president," "deputy assistant," and "special assistant" for a particular task or sector, the judgments and advice they are supposed to provide are a good deal broader and more generally political than those coming from the Executive Office of the President or from the Cabinet departments. The members of the White House staff are more closely associated with the president than are other presidentially appointed officials.

> **White House staff** analysts and advisers to the president, each of whom is often given the title "special assistant"

THE EXECUTIVE OFFICE OF THE PRESIDENT

Created in 1939, the **Executive Office of the President (EOP)** is a major part of the institutional presidency. Somewhere between 1,500 and 2,000 highly specialized people work for EOP agencies.[23] The importance of each agency in the EOP varies according to the personal orientation of each president.

The most important and the largest EOP agency is the Office of Management and Budget (OMB). This agency takes the lead role in preparing the nation's budget and helping presidents to define their programs and objectives. OMB is also the government's "watchdog," auditing the agencies of the executive branch and making sure their regulatory proposals are consistent with the president's plans. The OMB exercises great power, and its director is therefore one of the most powerful officials in Washington. At one time the process of budgeting was a "bottom-up" one, with expenditure and program requests passing from the lowest bureaus through the departments to "clearance" in the OMB and then to Congress, where each agency could be called in to explain what its "original request" was before the OMB revised it. Now the budgeting process is "top-down": the OMB sets the terms of discourse for agencies as well as for Congress.

The **National Security Council (NSC)** is composed of designated Cabinet officials who meet regularly with the president to give advice on national security. The staff of the NSC assimilates and analyzes data from all intelligence-gathering agencies (such as the CIA and NSA). In some administrations, the head of the NSC, the president's national security adviser, has played a more important role in foreign and military policy than the Cabinet secretaries in these domains.

Executive Office of the President (EOP) the permanent agencies that perform defined management tasks for the president; created in 1939, the EOP includes the OMB, the Council of Economic Advisers (CEA), the NSC, and other agencies

National Security Council (NSC) a presidential foreign policy advisory council composed of the president, the vice president, the secretary of state, the secretary of defense, and other officials invited by the president

THE VICE PRESIDENCY

The vice presidency is a constitutional peculiarity, even though the office was created along with the presidency by the Constitution. The vice president exists for two purposes only: to succeed the president in case of death, resignation, or incapacity, and to preside over the Senate, casting a tie-breaking vote when necessary.[24]

The main value of the vice president as a political resource for the president is electoral. Sometimes, presidential candidates choose running mates who they feel can win the support of at least one state that may not otherwise support the ticket. Presidents often choose a vice-presidential nominee who provides some regional, gender, ideological, or ethnic balance as well.

During the course of American history, eight vice presidents have had to replace presidents who died in office, and one, Gerald Ford, became president

Kamala Harris served as a U.S. senator from California and was the first woman and person of color ever elected to the vice presidency. She helped improve Biden's appeal with younger voters and nonwhite voters.

when his predecessor resigned. Until the ratification of the Twenty-Fifth Amendment in 1965, the succession of the vice president to the presidency was merely a tradition, launched by John Tyler when he assumed the presidency after William Henry Harrison's death in 1841. The Twenty-Fifth Amendment codified this tradition by providing that the vice president would assume the presidency in the event of the chief executive's death or incapacity and setting forth the procedures that would be followed. The amendment also provides that if the vice presidency becomes vacant, the president is to nominate an individual who must be confirmed by a majority vote of both houses of Congress. Thus, in 1973 when Vice President Spiro Agnew was forced to resign, President Nixon nominated Gerald Ford, who was confirmed. In 1974, when Nixon was forced to resign as a result of the Watergate scandal, Ford became president.

In the event that both the president and vice president are killed, the Presidential Succession Act of 1947 establishes an order of succession, beginning with the Speaker of the House and continuing with the president pro tempore of the Senate and the Cabinet secretaries.

THE PRESIDENT'S PARTY

Presidents have another tool: their own political party. Most presidents have sought to use their own party to implement their legislative agenda. For example, in 2009–10, President Obama relied on congressional Democrats to pass the Affordable Care Act ("Obamacare") in the face of virtually unanimous Republican opposition. All but one Republican senator voted to acquit President Trump in his impeachment trial before the Senate in 2020, thus blocking the president's removal from office. President Trump was unable to rally enough Republican legislators to repeal Obamacare, although he was able to bring about the enactment of tax reform. Although the party is valuable, it has not been a fully reliable presidential tool.

Moreover, in America's system of separated powers, the president's party may be in the minority in Congress and unable to do much to advance the president's agenda. When the 2018 elections gave Democrats control of the House of Representatives, very few of Trump's policy initiatives could be enacted even with full GOP support.

THE FIRST SPOUSE

The president serves as both chief executive and head of state—the equivalent of Great Britain's prime minister and monarch rolled into one, simultaneously leading the government and representing the nation at official ceremonies and functions. Presidential spouses, because they are traditionally associated with the head-of-state aspect of the presidency, are usually not subject to the same sort of media scrutiny or partisan attack as that aimed at the president. Historically, most first ladies have limited their activities to the ceremonial portion of the presidency: greeting foreign dignitaries, visiting other countries, and attending important national ceremonies. Some take up causes and advocate for them—in 2018, Melania Trump launched the "Be Best" public awareness campaign, focusing on well-being for youth and especially advocating against cyberbullying and drug use by young people.

Some first spouses, however, have had considerable influence over policy. Franklin Roosevelt's wife, Eleanor, was widely popular but also widely criticized for her active role in many elements of her husband's presidency. During the 1992 campaign, Bill Clinton often implied that his wife would be active in the administration; he joked that voters would get "two for the price of one." After the election, Hillary Clinton took a leading role in many policy areas, most notably health care reform. She also became the first presidential spouse to seek public office on her own, winning a seat in the U.S. Senate from New York in 2000 and then running for president in 2008 and 2016, having served in between as President Obama's secretary of state.

Jill Biden, wife of President Joe Biden, is a community college professor and has long been her husband's closest political adviser. It is assumed that she will continue to advise the president and to advocate for causes she had long supported like expansion of educational opportunities.

> **FOR CRITICAL ANALYSIS ▶**
>
> 1. Should the president aim to gain votes from both parties, or just his or her own? Why?
>
> 2. What are some of the differences between those who supported Barack Obama and those who supported Donald Trump? What are the similarities?

Who Supports the President's Agenda?

Many factors contribute to why a person supports a certain president—from their support of policies he or she has enacted, to their gender, to which region of the country they live in. Recently, however, party identification has been the most influential feature of a candidate that voters consider. As polarization in the country has increased, fewer Democrats have approved of Republican presidents, and vice versa.

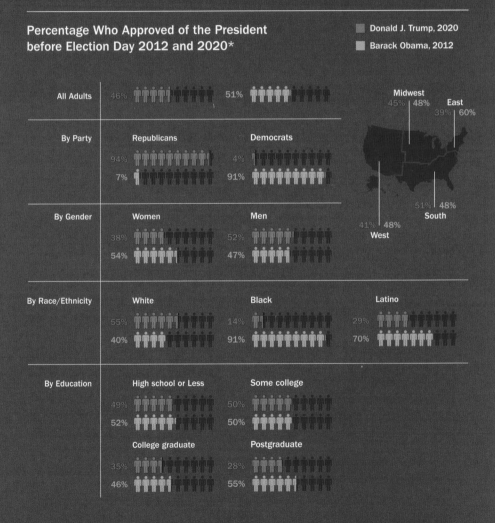

Percentage Who Approved of the President before Election Day 2012 and 2020*

- Donald J. Trump, 2020
- Barack Obama, 2012

All Adults 46% / 51%

By Party
Republicans 94% / 7%
Democrats 4% / 91%

By Gender
Women 38% / 54%
Men 52% / 47%

By Race/Ethnicity
White 55% / 40%
Black 14% / 91%
Latino 29% / 70%

By Education
High school or Less 49% / 52%
Some college 50% / 50%
College graduate 35% / 46%
Postgraduate 28% / 55%

Midwest 45% / 48%
East 39% / 60%
South 51% / 48%
West 41% / 48%

* Based on data collected the week of the presidential elections in 2012 and 2020.

SOURCE: Gallup, "Presidential Job Approval Center," gallup.com (accessed 10/27/20).

Presidential Power Grew in the Twentieth Century

> **Explain how modern presidents have become even more powerful**

During the nineteenth century, Congress was America's dominant institution of government, and its members sometimes treated the president with disdain. Today, however, presidents seek to dominate the policy-making process and claim the power to lead the nation in time of war. The expansion of presidential power over the course of the past century has come about as the result of an ongoing effort by successive presidents to enlarge the powers of the office. Generally, presidents can expand their power in two primary ways: by "going public,"[25] and by taking steps to reduce their dependence on Congress and to give themselves a more independent governing and policy-making capability.

GOING PUBLIC

In the nineteenth century, it was considered inappropriate for presidents to engage in personal campaigning on their own behalf or in support of programs and policies. In the twentieth century, though, popular mobilization became a favored weapon in the political arsenals of most presidents. The first to make systematic use of appeals to the public were Theodore Roosevelt and Woodrow Wilson, but the president who used them most effectively was Franklin Delano Roosevelt. In particular, he made effective use of a relatively new medium, the radio, to reach millions of Americans. In his famous "fireside chats," Roosevelt's voice could be heard in almost every living room in the country, discussing programs and policies, assuring Americans that he was aware of their difficulties and working diligently toward solutions.

Roosevelt was also an innovator in press relations. When he entered the White House, he faced a press mainly controlled by conservative members of the business establishment.[26] To bypass these generally hostile editors and publishers, the president worked to cultivate the reporters who covered the White House. FDR made himself available for biweekly press conferences, where he offered candid answers to reporters' questions and made important policy announcements that would provide the reporters with significant stories for their papers.[27]

Every president since FDR has sought to craft a public-relations strategy that would emphasize his strengths and maximize his popular appeal. For John F. Kennedy, who was handsome and quick witted, the televised press conference was an excellent public-relations vehicle. Both Bill Clinton and Barack Obama held televised town hall meetings—carefully staged events that let these presidents appear to consult with rank-and-file citizens about their goals and policies without having to face pointed questions from reporters.

An innovation introduced by Clinton and continued by his successors was to make the White House Communications Office an important institution within the EOP. The Communications Office became responsible not only for responding to reporters' queries but also for developing and implementing a

> **Donald J. Trump** ✔
> @realDonaldTrump
>
> ## The Ballots being returned to States cannot be accurately counted. Many things are already going very wrong!
>
> ⚠ Learn how voting by mail is safe and secure

To combat misinformation from politicians and foreign influence, social media platforms began flagging posts that contained misleading information. During the 2020 election and the coronavirus pandemic, President Trump's tweets were often labeled by Twitter as containing misinformation, with links to reliable sources of information.

coordinated communications strategy—promoting the president's policy goals, developing responses to adverse news stories, and making certain that a favorable image of the president would, insofar as possible, dominate the news.

Going Public Online President Obama was the first chief executive to make full use of another new communication medium—the internet. Drawing on the interactive tools of the web, Obama's 2008 and 2012 campaigns changed the way politicians organize supporters, advertise to voters, defend against attacks, and communicate with their constituents.[28]

In the 2016 presidential campaign, candidates Hillary Clinton and especially Donald Trump made particular use of Twitter to communicate with millions of voters, bypassing traditional media. Trump usually tweeted many times a day, often making outrageous claims that guaranteed that he would dominate media coverage as reporters rushed to analyze and criticize his assertions. While Trump may have pioneered the social media campaign, by 2020 the Democrats followed suit and both campaigns made extensive use of social media including YouTube, Twitter, Facebook, and Instagram. In August 2020, the major social media platforms announced a partnership to guard against misinformation and foreign efforts to use American social media to influence the outcome of the election.

The internet has changed not only the way modern presidents campaign but also how they govern. Circumventing television and other older media, it allows them to broadcast their policy ideas directly to citizens. Whitehouse.gov keeps constituents abreast of the president's policy agenda with a weekly streaming video address by the president, press briefings, speeches and remarks, a daily blog, photos of the president, the White House schedule, and other information.

In the Trump administration, every presidential **legislative initiative** and policy proposal was preceded by a flurry of tweets repeated by the broadcast and print media. And Trump's language seemed tailored to the Twitter age. For example, calling North Korean leader Kim Jong-un "Little Rocket Man" in his tweets allowed Trump to boil down his contempt and harsh posture toward North Korea into a tweet-sized threat to use force.

> **legislative initiative** the president's inherent power to bring a legislative agenda before Congress

The Limits of Going Public Some presidents have been able to make effective use of popular appeals to overcome congressional opposition. Popular support, though, has not been a firm foundation for presidential power. President George W. Bush maintained an approval rating of over 70 percent for more than a year following the September 11, 2001, terrorist attacks. By the end of 2005, however, Bush's approval rating had dropped to 39 percent as a result of the growing unpopularity of the Iraq War, the administration's handling of hurricane relief, and a number of White House scandals.

President Obama's public approval ranged from a high of 76 percent in 2009 to a low of 36 percent in 2014.[29] By the end of his term in 2016, Obama's popularity had recovered to about 56 percent. Declines in popular approval during a president's term in office are nearly inevitable and follow a predictable pattern.[30] Both before and after they are elected, presidents generate popular support by promising to undertake important programs that will contribute directly to the well-being of large numbers of Americans. Almost without exception, presidential performance falls short of promises and popular expectations, leading to a decline in public support and the ensuing weakening of presidential influence.[31] It is a rare American president, such as Bill Clinton, who exits the White House more popular than when he went in. Donald Trump's approval rating has been the lowest of any president, with a low of 35 percent in 2017; as of October 2020, Trump's approval rating stood at 46 percent, with 52 percent disapproving of the president's performance.[32]

THE ADMINISTRATIVE STRATEGY

Contemporary presidents have increased the administrative capabilities of their office in three ways. First, they have enhanced the reach and power of the EOP. Second, they have increased White House control over the federal bureaucracy. Third, they have expanded the role of executive orders and other instruments of direct presidential governance. Taken together, these three components of what might be called the White House "administrative strategy" have given presidents a capacity to achieve their programmatic and policy goals even when they are unable to secure congressional approval. Indeed, some recent presidents have been able to accomplish a great deal with remarkably little congressional, partisan, or even public support.

The Growth of the EOP The EOP has grown from six administrative assistants in 1939 to several hundred employees today, along with some 2,500 individuals staffing the several EOP divisions. The White House staff has given the president enormous capacity to gather information, plan programs and strategies, communicate with constituencies, and exercise supervision over the executive branch. The staff multiplies the president's eyes, ears, and arms, becoming a critical instrument of presidential power.[33]

In particular, the Office of Management and Budget serves as a key instrument of presidential control over federal spending and hence as a mechanism through which the White House has greatly expanded its power. The OMB has the capacity to analyze and approve all legislative proposals, not only budgetary requests, emanating from all federal agencies before being submitted to Congress. This procedure, now a matter of routine, greatly enhances the president's control over the entire executive branch. All legislation originating in the White House and all executive orders also go through the OMB.[34] Thus, through one White House agency, the president has the means to exert major influence over the flow of money and the shape and content of national legislation.

Regulatory Review A second instrument that presidents have used to increase their power and reach is an agency within OMB called the Office of Information and Regulatory Affairs (OIRA), which supervises the process of regulatory review. Whenever Congress enacts a law, implementing it requires the promulgation of hundreds of rules by the agency charged with administering the law and giving effect to what Congress intended. For example, if Congress wishes to improve air quality, it must delegate to an agency—say, the Environmental Protection Agency (EPA)—the power to establish numerous regulations governing actions by businesses, individuals, and government agencies (including the EPA itself) that may affect the atmosphere.

The agency rule-making process is governed by a number of statutory requirements concerning public notice (the most important being publication in the *Federal Register*), hearings, and appeals. Once completed and published in the massive *Code of Federal Regulations*, administrative rules have the effect of law and will be enforced by the federal courts. Beginning with little fanfare during the Nixon administration, recent presidents gradually have tried to take control of the rule-making process and to use it in effect to make laws without the interference of the legislature.

For example, during the course of his presidency, Clinton issued 107 directives ordering agency administrators to propose specific rules, such as one ordering the Food and Drug Administration (FDA) to develop rules designed to restrict the marketing of tobacco products to children.[35] Presidents George W. Bush and Obama continued this practice.[36] In his final two years in office, Obama sought new regulations governing power plant emissions, overtime pay for workers, the educational practices of career (for-profit) colleges, and a host of other matters.

President Trump moved aggressively to reverse these and other Obama directives by issuing new rules or repealing existing ones. Trump's actions reduced or eliminated regulations related to the environment, banking, and workplace safety and removed protections for transgender workers, among others. In the four years of his presidency, Trump eliminated or began the process of rescinding 95 environmental regulations.[37]

In June 2020, the Trump administration eliminated Obama-era regulations prohibiting health care facilities from discriminating against transgender patients. Within a few days, however, the Supreme Court ruled that existing civil rights laws protected gay and transgender individuals in the workplace. This decision cast doubt on the legality of discrimination against transgender patients. The administration also proposed new rules that would rewrite the nation's asylum rules, blocking asylum in most new cases and likely foreclosing asylum to the more than 300,000 individuals whose cases have already been filed.

Governing by Decree: Executive Orders and Memoranda A third mechanism through which contemporary presidents have sought to enhance their power to govern unilaterally is the use of executive orders and other forms of presidential decrees.

An **executive order** is a presidential directive to the bureaucracy to undertake some action. Executive orders have a long history in the United States and have been the means for imposing a number of important policies, including the purchase of the Louisiana Territory, the annexation of Texas, the emancipation of enslaved people, the wartime internment of Japanese Americans, the desegregation of the military, the initiation of affirmative action, and the creation of federal agencies, including the Environmental Protection Agency, the Food and Drug Administration, and the Peace Corps (although the creation of these agencies was later approved by Congress).[38] Historically, executive orders were most often used during times of war or national emergency. In recent years, though, executive orders have become routine instruments of presidential governance (Figure 11.3).

executive order a rule or regulation issued by the president that has the effect and formal status of legislation

President George W. Bush issued more than 300 executive orders, many relating to the war on terrorism but others pertaining to domestic policy matters, such as his ban on the use of federal funds to support international family-planning groups and his prohibition of the use of embryonic stem cells in federally funded research projects. President Obama issued executive orders halting the deportation of undocumented immigrants who had come to the United States as children, prohibiting federal agencies and contractors from discriminating against transgender employees, and declaring more than 700,000 square miles of the central Pacific Ocean off-limits to fishing. In addition to his orders on immigration, by the first three months of 2020, President Trump had issued more than 150 executive orders on such matters as the COVID-19 pandemic, other health care issues, regulatory reform, cybersecurity, freedom of speech at colleges and universities, and the imposition of new sanctions on Iran. Trump's orders included several that rescinded some of former president Obama's orders; for example, he invalidated several environmental protections and limits on gun purchases. During the same month, in the wake of two weeks of protests over police violence, President Trump issued an executive order placing limits on police use of force. Critics charged that the order was too little, too late.

When presidents issue executive orders, in principle they do so using the powers granted to them by the Constitution or delegated to them by Congress, and they generally must state the constitutional or statutory basis for their actions. For example, when President Lyndon Johnson ordered U.S. government contractors to initiate programs of affirmative action in hiring, he said the order was designed to implement the 1964 Civil Rights Act, which prohibited employment discrimination. Where the courts have found no constitutional or statutory basis for a presidential order, they have invalidated it. Such cases, however, are rare. Generally, the judiciary has accepted executive orders as the law of the land.

FIGURE 11.3

Presidential Executive Orders*

Executive orders are a tool presidents have for influencing policy. Their use has varied considerably over time. Each bar in the graph shows the average number of executive orders each president issued per year in office. Which presidents issued the most executive orders? What events in U.S. history were occurring when those presidents were in office?

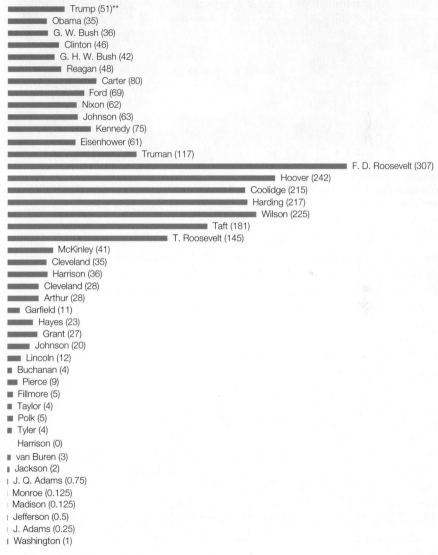

Trump (51)**
Obama (35)
G. W. Bush (36)
Clinton (46)
G. H. W. Bush (42)
Reagan (48)
Carter (80)
Ford (69)
Nixon (62)
Johnson (63)
Kennedy (75)
Eisenhower (61)
Truman (117)
F. D. Roosevelt (307)
Hoover (242)
Coolidge (215)
Harding (217)
Wilson (225)
Taft (181)
T. Roosevelt (145)
McKinley (41)
Cleveland (35)
Harrison (36)
Cleveland (28)
Arthur (28)
Garfield (11)
Hayes (23)
Grant (27)
Johnson (20)
Lincoln (12)
Buchanan (4)
Pierce (9)
Fillmore (5)
Taylor (4)
Polk (5)
Tyler (4)
Harrison (0)
van Buren (3)
Jackson (2)
J. Q. Adams (0.75)
Monroe (0.125)
Madison (0.125)
Jefferson (0.5)
J. Adams (0.25)
Washington (1)

*Does not include memoranda or other forms of executive action.
**As of October 2020.
SOURCE: The American Presidency Project, "Executive Orders," August 26, 2020, www.presidency.ucsb.edu (accessed 10/6/20).

In 2020, President Trump signed an executive order to prevent hoarding and price gouging after the coronavirus pandemic sparked a climate of panic in its early days, causing many to hoard groceries and cleaning supplies, and prices surged on sought-after items like hand sanitizer.

Additional forms of presidential decree include administrative orders, national security findings and directives, presidential memoranda, and presidential proclamations.[39] Like executive orders, they establish policy and have the force of law, and presidents often use them interchangeably. Generally speaking, though, administrative orders apply to matters of administrative procedure and organization; directives seem most often associated with national or homeland security; memoranda are used to clarify or modify presidential positions and orders; and proclamations are usually used to emphasize an especially important decree, such as Lincoln's proclamation emancipating all enslaved people.

Congress can overturn orders based on the president's legislative authority by passing legislation declaring that the order "shall not have legal effect" or by actually repealing the statute upon which the order was based.

Efforts to overturn the orders of sitting presidents are, however, hindered by the fact that any such legislation can be vetoed. Thus, two-thirds of the members of both houses of Congress would have to agree to the move. One study indicates that only about 4 percent of all presidential orders have ever been rescinded by legislation.[40] Failure by Congress to act strengthens the legal validity of a presidential order. The Supreme Court has held that congressional inaction tends to validate an order by indicating congressional "acquiescence" to the president's decision.[41]

Signing Statements Recent presidents have also increasingly found ways other than vetoes to negate congressional actions to which they objected. In particular, they have made frequent and calculated use of presidential **signing statements**.[42] The signing statement is an announcement made by the president, at the time of signing a bill into law, that offers the president's interpretation of the law and usually innocuous remarks predicting the many benefits the new law will bring to the nation.

> **signing statements**
> announcements made by the president when signing bills into law, often presenting the president's interpretation of the law

Occasionally, however, presidents have used signing statements to point to sections of the law they consider improper or even unconstitutional, and to instruct executive branch agencies in how to execute the law.[43] In 2018, for example, when President Trump signed the 2019 National Defense Authorization Act, he issued a signing statement declaring "constitutional concerns" with more than 50 of the act's provisions. The president said he would interpret these provisions in a manner consistent with his authority as president rather than simply accepting the law as written.

Presidential Nonenforcement of Laws A final instrument of direct presidential governance is nonenforcement of statutes. Congress may make the law, but if the president decides that a particular law is not to his or her liking and refuses to enforce it, Congress may find that its intent is stymied. President Obama, for example, suspended enforcement of portions of the Affordable Care Act when the rollout of "Obamacare" produced public confusion and inefficient implementation. President Trump, in an effort to undercut the ACA, effectively ordered the IRS to not enforce a provision of it that required taxpayers to indicate on their tax returns that they had health insurance—a major blow to the law's mandate.

The Advantages of the Administrative Strategy Because presidents can act on their own, the unilateral administrative powers of the office are tempting as means of achieving their policy goals. In recent decades, the expansion of the Executive Office of the President, the development of regulatory review, and the use of executive orders and signing statements have allowed presidents to achieve significant policy results despite congressional opposition to their legislative agendas.

In principle, Congress could respond more vigorously to unilateral policy making by the president than it has. But the president has significant advantages in such struggles. In battles over presidential directives and orders, Congress is on the defensive. When the president issues a decree, Congress must respond through the cumbersome and time-consuming lawmaking process, overcome internal divisions, and enact legislation that the president may ultimately veto.

THE LIMITS OF PRESIDENTIAL POWER: CHECKS AND BALANCES

While the framers of the Constitution wanted an energetic executive, they were also concerned that executive power could be abused and might stifle citizens' liberties. To guard against this possibility, the framers contrived a number of checks on executive power. The president's term is limited to four years, though with the possibility of re-election. Congress is empowered to impeach and remove the president, to reject presidential appointments and refuse to ratify treaties, to refuse to enact laws requested by the president, to deny funding for the president's programs, and to override presidential vetoes of legislation. And only Congress can enact legislation, levy taxes, and appropriate funds. Despite fears that the executive would be too weak and the potential energy of executive power lost, presidential power has grown significantly beyond the framers' vision.

Although the requirement that the Senate consent to presidential appointments was seen by the framers as another important check on executive power, in recent years severe partisan disagreements have often led presidents to resort to—and the Senate to resist—"recess appointments." These are authorized by Article II, Section 2, which states, "The President shall have power to fill up all Vacancies that may happen during the Recess of the Senate, by granting Commissions which shall expire at the End of their next Session."

Until recent years, recess appointments were made only when the Senate was between sessions or when a regular session of the Senate was adjourned for holidays or other lengthy periods. However, presidents have sometimes sought to make recess appointments even when the Senate was only briefly recessed. The Senate has responded with a strategy also sometimes used to prevent pocket vetoes. During periods when the Senate is recessed, one senator is assigned the task of calling the chamber to order for a few moments every day for a pro forma session so that the president cannot claim the Senate was actually in recess. Presidents have viewed this procedure as nothing more than a subterfuge, since the Senate is incapable of actually conducting business during these periods. The Supreme Court, however, has supported the Senate's strategy.[44]

Presidential Power: What Do You Think?

The framers of the Constitution created a system of government in which the Congress and the executive branch were to share power. At least since the New Deal, however, the powers of Congress have waned, whereas those of the presidency have expanded dramatically. There is no doubt that Congress continues to be able to confront presidents and even, on occasion, hand the White House a sharp rebuff. In the larger view, however, presidents' occasional defeats, however dramatic, have to be seen as temporary setbacks in a gradual but decisive shift toward increased presidential power.

A powerful presidency, a weak Congress, and a partially apathetic electorate make for a dangerous mix. Who we vote into the office of the president matters. Presidential power, to be sure, can be a force for good. To cite one example from the not-so-distant past, it was President Lyndon Johnson, more than Congress or the judiciary, who faced up to the task of smashing America's racial segregation system. Yet, as the framers knew, unchecked power—whether executive or legislative—is always dangerous. The framers of the Constitution believed that liberty required checks and balances. Conversely, sometimes presidential *inaction* can be a concern, as President Trump's reluctance to use the Defense Production Act during the coronavirus pandemic demonstrates.

★ Presidential strength works both ways. The growth of executive power means that policies an individual favors can more easily become the law of the land, because Congress works slowly while the president can work quickly. But what if the president fails to act? What would Craig Spencer, featured at the start of this chapter, have to say about presidential power?

★ How have the checks and balances between branches in the Constitution changed in practice over the decades?

★ Are there some issue areas—or certain conditions—in which presidential rather than congressional policy making is necessary?

★ Have you been affected by a presidential decision? Do you think the policy outcome would have been different if Congress had been more involved?

Practice Quiz

1. Which article of the Constitution describes the basic powers of the presidency and the means of selecting presidents? *(p. 335)*
   a) Article I
   b) Article II
   c) Article III
   d) Article IV
   e) Article V

2. Executive agreements are exactly like treaties except that *(p. 338)*
   a) executive agreements involve only domestic, not international, affairs.
   b) the Constitution explicitly mentions the president's ability to make executive agreements.
   c) executive agreements do not require approval by two-thirds of the Senate.
   d) executive agreements are ordinarily used to carry out commitments not already made in treaties or laws.
   e) executive agreements require a two-thirds approval vote in the Senate.

3. What is executive privilege? *(p. 339)*
   a) the president's ability to exercise unlimited and unconditional veto power over acts of Congress
   b) the president's role in creating the national budget
   c) the idea that the president has access to the highest levels of classified governmental information
   d) the idea that constituents tend to support the president's policy initiatives more than they support policies initiated by Congress
   e) the claim that confidential communications between a president and close advisers should not be revealed without presidential consent

4. What are the requirements for overriding a presidential veto? *(p. 340)*
   a) 50 percent plus one vote in both houses of Congress
   b) two-thirds vote in both houses of Congress
   c) two-thirds vote in the Senate only
   d) three-fourths vote in both houses of Congress
   e) A presidential veto cannot be overridden by Congress.

5. The War Powers Resolution of 1973 was an act passed by Congress that *(p. 345)*
   a) required the CIA to collect intelligence on all Americans born in a foreign country.
   b) outlawed presidential use of executive agreements.
   c) created the National Security Council.
   d) granted the president the authority to declare war.
   e) was designed to restore Congress's role in military policy.

6. Which of the following statements about presidential declarations of national emergency is not accurate? *(pp. 345–46)*
   a) Presidents can only declare a state of national emergency in response to foreign threats after receiving the approval of Congress.
   b) The president's power to declare national emergencies is one of the office's expressed powers.
   c) A declaration of national emergency in response to foreign threats allows the president to embargo trade, seize foreign assets, and prohibit transactions with whatever foreign nations are involved.
   d) Declarations of national emergency remain in force for only one year unless they are renewed by the president.
   e) Congress may, by a joint resolution of the two houses, terminate a declaration of national emergency.

7. Approximately how many people work for agencies within the Executive Office of the President? *(p. 348)*
   a) 25 to 50
   b) 500 to 750
   c) 1,500 to 2,000
   d) 4,500 to 5,000
   e) over 10,000

8. Which of the following statements about vice presidents is not true? *(pp. 348–49)*
   a) The vice president succeeds the president in case of death, resignation, or incapacitation.
   b) The vice president casts the tie-breaking vote in the Senate when necessary.
   c) The vice president serves as an honorary member of the Supreme Court.
   d) Eight vice presidents have had to replace American presidents who died in office.
   e) Presidential candidates typically select a vice-presidential candidate who they feel can win the support of a state that may not otherwise support the ticket.

9. What are two primary ways that presidents can expand their power? *(p. 352)*
   a) avoiding "going public" and creating a closer relationship with Congress
   b) "going public" and reducing their dependence on Congress
   c) "going public" and creating a closer relationship with Congress
   d) avoiding "going public" and reducing their dependence on Congress
   e) weakening national partisan institutions and creating a closer relationship with Congress

10. The Environmental Protection Agency and the Food and Drug Administration were created through the use of *(p. 356)*
    a) a pocket veto.
    b) a signing statement.
    c) an executive agreement.
    d) an executive order.
    e) executive privilege.

11. When the president makes an announcement about his or her interpretation of a bill that he or she is signing into law, it is called *(p. 359)*
    a) a signing statement.
    b) a line-item veto.
    c) an executive order.
    d) legislative initiative.
    e) executive privilege.

Key Terms

expressed powers *(p. 336)*
commander in chief *(p. 336)*
executive agreement *(p. 338)*
executive privilege *(p. 339)*
veto *(p. 340)*
pocket veto *(p. 340)*
implied powers *(p. 341)*
delegated powers *(p. 344)*
inherent powers *(p. 344)*

Cabinet *(p. 346)*
White House staff *(p. 347)*
Executive Office of the President (EOP) *(p. 348)*
National Security Council (NSC) *(p. 348)*
legislative initiative *(p. 353)*
executive order *(p. 356)*
signing statements *(p. 359)*

The Bureaucracy

WHAT GOVERNMENT DOES AND WHY IT MATTERS

In late January 2020, Dr. Helen Y. Chu, an infectious-disease expert in Seattle, heard that the first confirmed case in the United States of a new corona-virus had been detected in her area. She realized that she had a way to verify whether the virus was spreading in the community—she could repurpose nasal samples she had already collected for a flu study of the region. But to do so, she needed approval from state and federal officials. They denied her requests, both because her lab did not have permission from the research subjects and because her lab was not certified for clinical work. She argued that these strictures should be lifted in an emergency. Officials were unmoved. Her lab performed tests for the virus anyway and discovered that it had infected not just those who had traveled to impacted countries like China but also people with no travel history. Community transmission of the disease—what every public-health expert fears—had already started. "It must have been here this entire time," she thought. "It's just everywhere already." Nonethe-less, in early March state regulators ordered her lab to stop testing.

In early 2020, Dr. Helen Chu attempted to test a sample of nasal swabs for coronavirus after collecting them for a separate study on influenza. The FDA refused to certify her lab to do so, but in testing the samples, she found community spread of the virus as the CDC sent out faulty test kits to labs across the country.

In the meantime, the Centers for Disease Control and Prevention (CDC) had sent virus test kits to public-health labs around the country, but the tests didn't work. Labs started doing their own tests, but the FDA was slow to approve them and insisted that the labs first get an Emergency Use Authorization from the agency. When working test kits were finally available, there were not enough of them for widespread testing. Only patients who had traveled outside the country or who were already sick were tested. Throughout February and early March it seemed as if there were relatively few cases in the United States, but that was because so few people were being tested. In fact, the corona-virus was spreading rapidly throughout this time period. "We just twiddled our thumbs as the coronavirus waltzed in," said Harvard epidemiologist William Hanage. Without data from testing, mayors and governors were reluctant to issue lockdown orders, which were the best public-health intervention in the absence of a vaccine but which also had severe economic effects. And without data, hospitals could not prepare properly. Meanwhile, the nation's Strategic National Stockpile—reserves of medical equipment and other disaster-relief goods—had not been replenished after the 2009 swine flu epidemic because of budget cuts. States and localities would end up bidding against one another in a mad scramble to secure supplies on the open market.[1]

The coronavirus testing and supply missteps are a dramatic, tragic example of bureaucratic failure. Americans depend on public bureaucracies for providing services they use both in emergencies and every day. On a typical day, a college student might check the weather forecast, drive on an interstate highway, mail the rent check, drink from a public water fountain, attend a class, go online, and meet a relative at the airport. Each of these activities is possible because of the work of a government bureaucracy: the National Weather Service, the U.S. Department of Transportation, the U.S. Postal Service, the Environmental Protection Agency, the student loan programs of the U.S. Department of Education, the Advanced Research Projects Agency (which developed the internet in the 1960s), and the Federal Aviation Administration. Without the ongoing work of these agencies, many of these common activities would be impossible, unreliable, or more expensive. When bureaucracies work well, we barely notice.

But when they fail, the results can be truly alarming, like the botched virus testing, or the September 11, 2001, terror attacks, widely viewed as a failure of the national security bureaucracy.[2] Such failures play into Americans' ambivalence about the role of government. Some disasters prompt politicians to promise that they will slash the bureaucracy, especially at the federal level. Yet others result in an increase in the bureaucracy, like the creation of the federal Department of Homeland Security after September 11. Each instance raises a number of questions: Should the bureaucracy be smaller or larger? How can it become more efficient and effective? How can the bureaucracy be made more responsive to the needs of the American people?

CHAPTER GOALS

★ Describe the characteristics and roles of bureaucrats and bureaucracies (pp. 367–80)

★ Explain civil service hiring, political appointments, and the use of federal contracting (pp. 380–83)

★ Explain how the president, Congress, and the judiciary try to manage the bureaucracy (pp. 383–91)

What Is the Federal Bureaucracy?

Describe the characteristics and roles of bureaucrats and bureaucracies

Bureaucracy is the complex structure of offices, tasks, rules, and principles that organize all large-scale institutions to coordinate the work of their personnel. The bureaucracy of the federal executive branch plays a crucial role in administering national policy on the ground. Bureaucrats carry out the policies that Congress and the president have passed and that the court system may have weighed in on. The teachers you had in elementary school, the Social Security officer who approved your grandmother's retirement pension, the air traffic controller who guided the plane on your last vacation, the engineers who designed the roads that carried you to class, and the inspector who approved the meat in this morning's breakfast sausage are all bureaucrats.

> **bureaucracy** the complex structure of offices, tasks, rules, and principles of organization that is employed by all large-scale institutions to coordinate the work of their personnel

At its best, bureaucracy ensures fair, accountable administration performed by expert professionals. To provide services, government bureaucracies employ specialists such as meteorologists, doctors, and scientists. To do their jobs effectively, these specialists require resources and tools (ranging from paper to complex computer software). They must coordinate their work with others (for example, traffic engineers must communicate with construction engineers). And they must effectively reach out to the public (for example, people must be made aware of health warnings). Bureaucracy is a means of coordinating the many different parts that must work together for the government to provide useful services.

When bureaucracy runs well, it can be virtually invisible. When it fails, the results can be spectacularly public (and even tragic), as when Hurricane Katrina breached levies built by the Army Corps of Engineers in 2005 and the Federal Emergency Management Agency reacted ineffectually, or when the Department of Veterans Affairs was criticized in 2014 for long waiting lists for veterans seeking medical care and was even blamed for veteran deaths in Phoenix.[3] Or when FDC and CDC missteps delayed coronavirus testing as the pandemic swept across the nation. How bureaucrats carry out their responsibilities shapes individuals' experiences of government in profound ways.

WHAT BUREAUCRATS DO

Bureaucrats execute and implement laws. They determine who is eligible for Medicare, for example, or study whether a new medicine is safe and effective. They deliver mail, tell national park campers that they can build a fire *here* but not *there*, calculate how long it would take a spacecraft to reach the edge of the solar system. They gather data and conduct research. Some, like customs officials, are "street-level bureaucrats" who regularly interact with the public. Yet others, like researchers at the National Institutes of Health, work in specialized facilities with other experts.

As bureaucrats carry out their responsibilities, implementing and enforcing laws, making rules, and innovating, they exercise discretion and help define how public policy gets expressed.

Bureaucrats Implement Laws Congress is responsible for making the laws, but the federal bureaucracy is responsible for putting laws into effect. In most cases legislation sets only the broad parameters for government action. Bureaucracies are responsible for filling in the details by determining how the laws should be implemented. This requires bureaucracies to draw up detailed rules that guide the process of **implementation** and to play a key role in enforcing the laws. For example, during the coronavirus pandemic, while Congress appropriated funds for direct payments to individuals and for economic relief for small businesses, these programs were implemented by the Internal Revenue Service (part of the Treasury Department) and the Small Business Administration, an independent agency of the federal government. Congress also increased unemployment insurance benefits and broadened eligibility, but had to rely on the state-level bureaucracies that run the program, which were overwhelmed by the enormous rise in jobless claims. Administrative capacity is an important factor in bureaucracies' ability to implement laws effectively.

implementation the efforts of departments and agencies to translate laws into specific bureaucratic rules and actions

Bureaucrats Make Rules One of the most important activities that government agencies do is issue rules that provide more detailed and specific indications of what a given congressional policy will actually mean. For example, the Clean Air Act empowers the Environmental Protection Agency (EPA) to assess whether current or projected levels of air pollutants pose a threat to public health, determine whether motor vehicle emissions are contributing to such pollution, and create rules designed to regulate these emissions. During the coronavirus pandemic, the Department of Labor's Occupational Safety and Health Administration (OSHA) and the CDC jointly released guidance for meatpacking plants to increase employees' protection from the coronavirus, after infections soared at several facilities.[4]

Once Congress passes a new law, the relevant agency studies the legislation and proposes a set of rules to guide implementation. These proposed rules are submitted to the White House Office of Management and Budget (OMB) for review. If OMB approves, the proposed rule is published in the *Federal Register*, a daily publication of the federal government, which anyone can read and where they can leave comments, which are also published. After reviewing public comments and making changes, the agency proposes a final rule, which goes back to OMB for clearance, upon which it is published in the *Federal Register*. The agency's rules have the force of law.

Although bureaucratic rule making has the force of law, it is easier to change than laws passed by Congress.[5] If Congress passes a new law, changing it usually requires another congressional action, while rules made by the bureaucracy in one administration can be easily reversed by the next. For example, during the Obama administration, the EPA imposed new emission standards for automobiles that raised the average fuel economy for new vehicles to 35.5 miles per gallon starting in 2016, a standard later boosted to 54.4 miles per gallon by 2025.[6] But under President

An example of bureaucratic rules that affect Americans both positively and negatively are the regulations set forth by the Environmental Protection Agency (EPA). When President Obama extended the EPA's authority to regulate greenhouse gas emissions in 2014, many people applauded the benefits to the environment, but at the same time, thousands lost jobs because of the new rules.

Trump the EPA both rolled back the Obama-era rules and ended California's special status under the 1970 Clean Air Act that allows it to set its own vehicle pollution standards, although both moves prompted court battles.[7]

Bureaucrats Enforce Laws In addition to rule making, bureaucracies play an essential role in enforcing the laws, thus exercising considerable power over private actors. In 2015 the EPA charged Volkswagen with cheating on emissions tests of its diesel vehicles. For over seven years, the company had installed software that showed emissions at legal levels during testing conditions, but once the cars were on the road emissions were actually 10 to 40 percent higher. After the EPA threatened to bar the company from selling some of its 2016 cars in the United States, Volkswagen admitted that it had cheated and agreed to a $15.8 billion settlement that required it to buy back the faulty vehicles and compensate owners and to fund several clean-air programs.[8]

Bureaucrats Innovate A good case study of the important role agencies can play is the story of how ordinary federal bureaucrats created the internet. It's true: what became the internet was developed largely by the U.S. Department of Defense, and defense considerations still shape the basic structure of the internet. In 1957, immediately following the profound American embarrassment over the Soviet Union's launching of *Sputnik*, the first satellite to orbit the Earth, Congress authorized the establishment of the Advanced Research Projects Agency (ARPA) to develop, among other things, a means of maintaining communications in the event of a strategic attack on the existing telecommunications network (the telephone system). Since the telephone network was highly centralized and therefore could have been completely disabled by a single attack, ARPA developed a decentralized, highly redundant network with an improved probability of functioning after an attack. The full design, called ARPANET, took almost a decade to create. By 1971 around 20 universities were connected to the ARPANET. The forerunner to the internet was born.[9]

Key Characteristics of Bureaucracies In the United States, bureaucracies are typically defined by mission statements, which lay out each agency's role and responsibilities. For example, the mission of the Department of Health and Human Services (HHS) is to "enhance the health and well-being of all Americans, by providing for effective health and human services and by fostering sound, sustained advances in the sciences underlying medicine, public health, and social services."

Another key characteristic is expertise. Bureaucracies are populated by policy-specific experts who are deeply knowledgeable about the issue areas they oversee. Expertise is one of the main resources and distinguishing characteristics of the federal bureaucracy. Bureaucrats often have specialized training, such as advanced degrees, and may spend their careers working on a given set of issues, developing deep knowledge.

Bureaucracies are also characterized by hierarchical structures with clear lines of authority and standardized procedures governed by rules. These structures are intended to foster equal treatment of citizens. In the United States, the bureaucracy is supposed to be insulated from politics as well. The long length of employment of many career civil servants—whose service may persist through many presidencies and congressional terms—is one form of protection. There are also merit systems in place for hiring and promotion, meant to maximize the political neutrality of the bureaucracy regardless of which party controls the presidency or Congress. In addition, the nonpartisan nature of the bureaucracy is underscored by the 1939 Hatch Act and its amendments, which prevent federal employees from engaging in certain types of political activities, such as wearing political buttons while on duty or using their official authority to interfere with an election.

The Decision to Delegate Thus federal bureaucrats shape the nation's public policy. We might wonder why Congress writes laws but then delegates such significant policy-making responsibility to the bureaucracy. One reason is that bureaucracies employ people who have much more specialized expertise in specific policy areas than do members of Congress. Decisions about how to achieve many policy goals—from managing the national parks to regulating air quality to ensuring a sound economy—rest on the judgment of specialized experts. A second reason that Congress needs bureaucracy is that updating legislation can take many years, and bureaucratic flexibility can ensure that laws are administered in ways that take new conditions into account more quickly. Finally, members of Congress often prefer to delegate politically difficult decision-making to bureaucrats, thus avoiding having to deal with controversial issues that might anger constituents or interest groups and threaten their chances for re-election. For example, when Congress wrote the Affordable Care Act, it required health insurance plans to cover "essential health benefits" but did not define what those benefits are. Instead, lawmakers provided some general guidelines and instructed the bureaucracy—the Department of Health and Human Services—to specify which benefits must be covered.[10]

Delegation comes with risks. In delegating, Congress gives agencies discretion to use their expertise as they implement laws and create rules. But such discretion can lead to the **principal-agent problem**, which occurs when one entity (the principal) gives decision-making authority to another (the agent), but the agent makes decisions that are different from what the principal may have wanted. For example, Congress might delegate aspects of air quality standards to the Environmental Protection Agency, but the EPA may write rules that are stricter than Congress would have written. Congress delegated implementation of the Paycheck Protection Program, the small business pandemic-relief program, to the Small Business Administration, which in turn used banks as the intermediaries to which businesses applied for funds. Problems arose in spring 2020 when numerous small businesses were unable to secure loans before the funds ran out, because many banks accepted applications only from their existing business customers, met the needs of larger businesses first, or quickly hit their program lending limits. Amid great outcry, Congress responded by passing a second round of small business relief with tighter rules and by pressuring larger, publicly traded companies, like Shake Shack and AutoNation, to return the program funds they had received.[11] Later we will consider the tools that Congress uses to overcome the principal-agent problem and try to control the bureaucracy.

principal-agent problem
a conflict in priorities between an actor and the representative authorized to act on the actor's behalf

executive departments the 15 departments in the executive branch headed by Cabinet secretaries and constituting the majority of the federal bureaucracy

HOW THE BUREAUCRACY IS ORGANIZED

Currently there are 15 **executive departments** in the federal government. The first 4 were established in 1789 under President George Washington: State, Treasury, Defense, and Justice. Others were added over time: Interior, Agriculture, Commerce, Labor, Health and Human Services, Housing and Urban Development, Transportation, Energy, Education, Veterans Affairs, and most recently, in 2002, Homeland Security. These 15 executive departments employ over 80 percent of the federal civilian workforce, with Defense, Veterans Affairs, and Homeland Security having the most employees.[12] The rest work in agencies in the Executive Office of the President (for example, the Council of Economic Advisers or the Office of the United States Trade Representative) or in agencies outside of the executive departments (for example, the Central Intelligence Agency or the National Aeronautics and Space Administration). At the top of each department is an official who is called the secretary of the department (though the head of the Justice Department is the attorney general). The executive department secretaries, along with the vice president and attorney general, make up the president's "Cabinet." Presidents can also confer Cabinet-level status on additional agencies.

Beyond the executive departments, the federal bureaucracy also consists of independent agencies that are not part of executive departments but that have independent

Bureaucracy in Comparison

As the third-largest country by area, with over 330 million residents, the United States has a sizable bureaucracy to run government programs and services. As a percentage of the labor force, however, the number of government employees in the United States is not especially high compared to other nations. We can also see differences in whether most government employees work at the national level or the subnational (state and local) level in each country.

1. What factors might lead a country like Norway or Japan to have a significantly larger or smaller government workforce as a percentage of its population? Would you expect these percentages to be going up or down over time? How might you expect them to change during times of economic growth versus during recessions?

2. What might explain the differences in how some countries have most of their government employment at the national level whereas others focus their employment at the subnational level? How does America's federal structure influence its bureaucratic hiring?

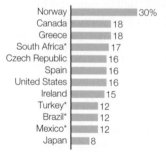

TOTAL GOVERNMENT EMPLOYMENT AS A PERCENTAGE OF THE LABOR FORCE MARKET

Country	Percentage
Norway	30%
Canada	18
Greece	18
South Africa*	17
Czech Republic	16
Spain	16
United States	16
Ireland	15
Turkey*	12
Brazil*	12
Mexico*	12
Japan	8

Note: Includes national and subnational government employees.
*Brazil, Mexico, South Africa, and Turkey data are from 2014.

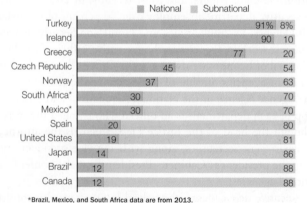

GOVERNMENT EMPLOYMENT BY LEVEL OF GOVERNMENT

■ National ■ Subnational

Country	National	Subnational
Turkey	91%	8%
Ireland	90	10
Greece	77	20
Czech Republic	45	54
Norway	37	63
South Africa*	30	70
Mexico*	30	70
Spain	20	80
United States	19	81
Japan	14	86
Brazil*	12	88
Canada	12	88

*Brazil, Mexico, and South Africa data are from 2013.

SOURCE: OECD, "Public Employment and Pay," Government at a Glance, 2017, www.stats.oecd.org (accessed 4/16/18).

authority to implement policy and design regulations in their particular area. Some are called administrations, including NASA, the Small Business Administration, and the Social Security Administration. There are also **independent regulatory commissions**, such as the Federal Trade Commission (FTC), Federal Communications Commission (FCC), and Securities and Exchange Commission (SEC). These commissions are typically run by a small number of commissioners appointed by the president for fixed terms. And there are **government corporations**, which receive federal funding and are subject to federal control but function like private businesses in charging for a service, such as transporting railroad passengers (Amtrak) or delivering the mail (United States Postal Service).

independent regulatory commission a government agency outside the executive department usually headed by commissioners

government corporation a government agency that performs a market-oriented public service and raises revenues to fund its activities

For simplicity we will call all of these bureaucratic entities "agencies." As Figure 12.1 shows, the federal bureaucracy handles a vast number of important functions, as a few examples illustrate. Some agencies work to promote national security, such as the State Department, whose primary mission is diplomacy, sending foreign-service officers and ambassadors to other countries where they work to promote American perspectives and interests in the world; and the Defense Department, one of the largest bureaucracies in the world. Headquartered at the Pentagon, across the Potomac River from Washington, D.C., the Department of Defense includes the Office of the Secretary

The National Aeronautics and Space Administration (NASA), an independent agency of the federal government, was established by President Eisenhower in 1958. Its mission is "To reach for new heights and reveal the unknown so that what we do and learn will benefit all humankind." Here, NASA public affairs officer Dwayne Brown announces the presence of water on Mars.

of Defense, which provides civilian oversight of the military; the Joint Chiefs of Staff, which includes the five military service chiefs; the six regional Unified Combatant Commands, which execute military operations in different parts of the world; and a number of additional agencies that supply and service the military.

While the State and Defense Departments confront threats from outside the nation, the Department of Homeland Security has responsibility for maintaining domestic security, and was created after the September 11, 2001, terrorist attacks to reorganize existing agencies and expand their mission from fighting crime to preventing terrorism as well. The antiterrorism mandate requires the DHS to integrate information from intelligence agencies and law enforcement to protect the nation. The DHS is also responsible for securing the nation's borders; administering and enforcing its immigration laws; addressing cybersecurity and energy security issues; running the Secret Service, which protects federal officials; administering disaster relief through FEMA; and any number of other responsibilities, from running the national flood insurance program to coordinating national health security response to infectious-disease outbreaks and natural disasters with the Department of Health and Human Services.[13] Little wonder that the Government Accountability Office—an agency that works for Congress as a "watchdog" over executive branch functions, as we will see below—has issued hundreds of recommendations for managerial improvements over the DHS's two-decade history.[14]

Yet other federal agencies work to maintain a strong economy. The Treasury Department collects taxes through the Internal Revenue Service (IRS), manages the national debt, prints currency, and performs economic policy analysis. The Federal Reserve System (called the Fed) is the nation's key monetary agency and is headed by the Federal Reserve Board. The Fed has authority over the interest rates and lending activities of the nation's most important banks. It was established by Congress in 1913 as a clearinghouse for adjusting the supply of money and credit to the needs of commerce and industry in different parts of the country. Many other agencies work to strengthen other parts of the economy, for example the Agriculture Department, which disseminates information on effective farming practices; the Transportation Department, which promotes economic growth by overseeing the nation's highway and air traffic systems; and the Commerce Department, whose Small Business Administration provides loans and technical assistance to small businesses across the country.

Another set of agencies promotes citizen well-being. The Department of Health and Human Services (HHS) includes the National Institutes of Health, which conducts cutting-edge biomedical research; the Food and Drug Administration (FDA), which monitors the safety and efficacy of human and veterinary drugs, cosmetics, and the nation's food supply; the Centers for Disease Control and Prevention (CDC), which protects public health and safety; and the Medicaid and Medicare programs, which provide health insurance to low-income and elderly Americans. The Department of Agriculture's Food and Nutrition Service administers the federal school-lunch program and Supplemental Nutrition Assistance Program (SNAP, formerly known as food stamps). The Interior Department's National Park Service maintains natural areas for the public to enjoy. Yet other agencies, such as the Food and Drug Administration (FDA, within HHS); the Occupational Safety and Health

FIGURE 12.1

The Executive Branch of the Federal Government

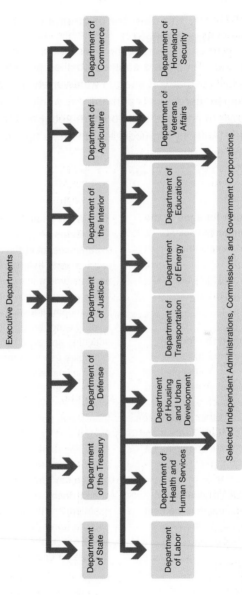

Executive Departments

Department of State | Department of the Treasury | Department of Defense | Department of Justice | Department of the Interior | Department of Agriculture | Department of Commerce

Department of Labor | Department of Health and Human Services | Department of Housing and Urban Development | Department of Transportation | Department of Energy | Department of Education | Department of Veterans Affairs | Department of Homeland Security

Selected Independent Administrations, Commissions, and Government Corporations

Amtrak
Central Intelligence Agency
Consumer Financial Protection Bureau
Consumer Product Safety Commission
Environmental Protection Agency
Equal Employment Opportunity Commission
Federal Communications Commission
Federal Deposit Insurance Corporation
Federal Election Commission

Federal Maritime Commission
Federal Reserve System
Federal Trade Commission
General Services Administration
National Aeronautics and Space Administration
National Endowment for the Arts
National Labor Relations Board
Office of Personnel Management

Office of the Director of National Intelligence
Peace Corps
Postal Regulatory Commission
Securities and Exchange Commission
Small Business Administration
Social Security Administration
Tennessee Valley Authority
U.S. Agency for International Development
U.S. Postal Service

SOURCE: Based on GPO Access: Guide to the U.S. Government, http://bensguide.gpo.gov /files/gov_chart.pdf (accessed 9/22/12).

Apply for a Federal Job

ANTHONY MARUCCI, the director of communications at the Office of Personnel Management

The federal government employs a couple of million people, mostly outside of Washington, D.C. Now that you see the wide variety of responsibilities the federal government carries out, perhaps you would like to apply your skills and knowledge to an issue that you care about and that the federal government tackles. Anthony Marucci gave us these tips to getting a job in the federal government:

1 Where can I look for a job in the federal government? Look at USAJobs (www.usajobs.gov), the official federal government portal. You can also look at the "employment" or "careers" section of any government agency website.

2 Can I find a job in the federal government outside of Washington, D.C.? Yes. You should set up a profile on USAJobs, where you can add work preferences such as desired work location. This and other preferences you include on your profile will refine and improve your results when searching for jobs on USAJobs.

3 How can I tell if I'm qualified? Read the entire job announcement and focus on the critical information in three key sections: Duties and Qualifications, How to Apply, and How You Will Be Evaluated. You will be able to see the level and amount of experience, education, and training needed.

4 What should I include on my résumé? Show how your skills and experiences meet the qualifications and requirements listed in the job announcement in order to be considered. List your experiences, beginning with the most recent, and include dates, hours, level of experience, and examples of your activities and accomplishments. The best examples use numbers to highlight your accomplishments, such as "Managed a student organization budget of more than $7,000" or "Wrote 25 news releases in a three-week period under daily deadlines." Also, provide greater detail for experiences that are relevant to the job for which you are applying. And be sure to use the key terms in the job listing: if the qualifications section says you need experience with MS Project you need to use the words "MS Project" in your résumé. You should customize your résumé for each job to which you apply.

5 **Will I have to take a civil service exam?** Federal government hiring in the civil service positions in the executive branch, with some exceptions, must be done through a competitive process. This typically means an evaluation of the individual's education and experience, and/or an evaluation of other attributes necessary for successful performance in the position to be filled. In some cases the process may also consist of a written test.

6 **Can I apply for more than one position?** Yes, you can apply for multiple jobs at USAJobs, but note that you must apply for each under the specific job announcement. One key thing to remember (and this is likely true for any job to which you apply): hiring agencies often receive dozens or even hundreds of résumés for certain positions, so you want to look at your résumé and ask, "Can a hiring manager see my main credentials within 10 to 15 seconds? Does critical information jump off the page? Do I effectively sell myself on the top quarter of the first page?" Working for the federal government can be rewarding. As with pursuing any job, it can take time. So if you do apply, be patient and persistent. Best of luck!

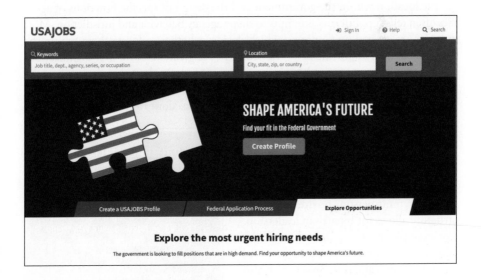

The president regularly meets with the Cabinet to discuss the affairs of each department or agency. Here, President Trump delivers remarks before beginning a Cabinet meeting.

Administration, within the Labor Department; and the Consumer Product Safety Commission, an independent regulatory commission, make rules to protect the public's health and welfare.

The location within the government and the design of specific functions of agencies often reflect politicians' attempts to shape agency behavior and jurisdiction. Most agencies are created by Congress, which decides whether to locate them within the executive branch or outside of it. The president has greater control over organizations contained within executive departments, whereas independent agencies, such as the Securities and Exchange Commission (SEC), which oversees the security industry, including the nation's stock exchanges, have more freedom from both the president and Congress.

In creating agencies, Congress also decides whether they will be headed by one person (who reports to the president, if the agency is in the executive branch) or by a multiperson board. A board structure allows for bipartisan leadership. For example, no more than three of the SEC's five commissioners can be from the same political party. Boards may also have members with staggered terms of office, which reduces the power of any one president to name the entire agency leadership. Other structural features can

FOR CRITICAL ANALYSIS ▶

1. What factors might explain why some federal agencies receive higher evaluations than others? In particular, why might the EPA and the VA be rated so low? Why would the Postal Service, the CDC, and the Secret Service be rated so high?

2. What might explain the differences (or similarities) between Democrats' and Republicans' ratings of federal agencies?

What Do People Think of Federal Agencies?

Despite the stereotype of being staffed by apathetic employees mired in red tape, federal government agencies provide important services, and most get positive ratings from the people using them. When is the last time you interacted with a federal government agency? What was your experience?

By Party ● Democrat ● Republican   Performance Rating ● Excellent/good ● Only fair ● Poor

Agency	Approval by Party		Overall Performance Rating*		
	Democrat	Republican	Excellent/good	Only fair	Poor
U.S. Postal Service	76%	69%	74%	18%	8%
U.S. Secret Service	66%	74%	69%	19%	8%
Centers for Disease Control and Prevention (CDC)	61%	71%	64%	22%	12%
Central Intelligence Agency (CIA)	61%	59%	60%	25%	12%
NASA	60%	61%	60%	26%	5%
FBI	66%	46%	57%	23%	19%
Department of Homeland Security	42%	65%	55%	26%	17%
Federal Emergency Management Agency (FEMA)	38%	64%	52%	29%	16%
Internal Revenue Service (IRS)	52%	53%	50%	30%	19%
Federal Reserve Board	45%	51%	48%	34%	13%
Food and Drug Administration (FDA)	37%	52%	44%	33%	22%
Environmental Protection Agency (EPA)	38%	54%	43%	30%	26%
Veterans Affairs (VA)	35%	45%	39%	31%	28%

*"No opinion" category has been omitted and numbers may not add up to 100 percent.

SOURCE: Gallup, "Postal Service Still Americans' Favorite Federal Agency" https://news.gallup.com (accessed 6/11/20).

increase independence as well, for example the fact that the president appoints SEC commissioners but cannot fire them. Independent agencies and regulatory commissions are meant to be relatively insulated from politics, hence their location outside of the executive departments, but escaping politics entirely is impossible. Since presidents appoint agency heads or commissioners, they may do so on the basis of party loyalty. Also, the budgets of most such agencies are proposed by the president and approved by Congress, and agencies must therefore be responsive to congressional oversight.

Who Are Bureaucrats?

Explain civil service hiring, political appointments, and the use of federal contracting

The vast majority of bureaucrats are members of the "civil service" and work under the **merit system** created by the Pendleton Civil Service Reform Act of 1883. With this act, the federal government required bureaucratic personnel to be qualified for the jobs to which they were hired. The goal was to end the "spoils system" that dominated federal hiring during the 1800s and awarded government jobs based on political connections and support for the political party in office. The Pendleton Act replaced such patronage with a system of competitive examinations through which the very best candidates were to be hired for every job.

As a further safeguard against political interference, merit-system employees were given legal protection against being fired without a show of cause. The objective of this job protection was to shield bureaucracy from political interference while upgrading performance. The 1883 civil service reform was updated by the Civil Service Reform Act of 1978, which set up new processes to ensure that the recruitment and promotion of civil servants remained merit based rather than political. The 1978 act created the Merit Systems Protection Board to defend competitive and merit-based recruitment and promotion of civil servants from efforts to make these personnel policies more political. The Federal Labor Relations Authority was set up to administer collective bargaining and to address individual personnel grievances. A third new agency, the Office of Personnel Management, was created to manage the recruiting, testing, and training of federal employees, as well as their retirement system.[15]

merit system a product of civil service reform, in which appointees to positions in public bureaucracies must objectively be deemed qualified for those positions

political appointees the presidentially appointed layer of the bureaucracy on top of the civil service

At the higher levels of government agencies are several thousand **political appointees**, who fill posts as Cabinet secretaries and assistant secretaries and who are not part of the civil service. Of the 4,000-plus political appointees, just over 1,000 require Senate confirmation. Many political appointees have ties to the president or the president's party—they may have worked on the president's campaign, for example—and serve to advance the president's agenda through agency action. Presidents also often use Cabinet secretary nominations—the handful of appointed positions at the very top of the bureaucracy, which are the most visible to the public—to make political statements or to send messages about their style of management or expectations for government. For example, President Obama, the nation's first Black president, nominated seven women and ten people of color to his first Cabinet. Both President George W. Bush (the first president with an MBA) and President Trump came from business backgrounds, and nominated many business leaders to their Cabinets.

In addition to political appointees, in many agencies there are top executives who are members of the **Senior Executive Service (SES)**, a top management rank for career civil servants—and sometimes individuals from outside of government. The SES was created by

> **Senior Executive Service (SES)**
> the top, presidentially appointed management rank for career civil servants

the 1978 civil service reform and intended to foster "public management" as a profession. For career bureaucrats, moving to the SES means losing their civil service protections, but it also provides an opportunity to pursue a top position. The SES also provides the president with an additional layer of high-level managers to select beyond the political appointees.

Compared to those in past administrations, appointments to senior leadership positions in the Trump administration have stood out for several reasons. Many of the political appointment slots in the bureaucracy remained unfilled well into President Trump's term. He also had a large number of agency leaders in "acting" positions. The Federal Vacancies Reform Act of 1998 allows a president to name officials to top posts on a temporary basis while awaiting Senate confirmation of permanent personnel. President Trump used the FVRA provisions in a more permanent manner and, as of summer 2019, two years into his presidency, had acting leaders as secretary of Defense, secretary of the Department of Homeland Security, UN ambassador, Immigration and Customs Enforcement (ICE) director, Federal Emergency Management Administration (FEMA) director, and Federal Aviation Administration (FAA) administrator, among others. "I sort of like 'acting,'" he said in 2019. "It gives me more flexibility." Critics say that the seemingly permanent use of "acting" heads undermines congressional oversight of the executive branch by skirting the Senate confirmation process.[16]

The size of the federal service has been a subject of political contention for decades. Particularly in the post–Watergate era of low trust in government, politicians from both parties, from Reagan to Clinton, have asserted that the federal government is too big. Bill Clinton's vice president, Al Gore, headed a National Performance Review during the 1990s, which sought to reduce paperwork, improve communications across agencies, streamline government purchasing procedures, and cut the federal workforce; by 2000 the number of federal jobs had fallen by more than 400,000.[17] While President Barack Obama struck a different note in his first inaugural address, saying, "The question we ask today is not whether our government is too big or too small, but whether it works."[18] President Trump's first budget proposed major decreases in federal departments outside of Defense and Homeland Security. Under President Trump, some agencies were reorganized or had positions relocated, such as the relocation of two USDA research groups from Washington, D.C., to Kansas City, which reduced the workforce when over half of the researchers declined to move.[19]

Despite fears of bureaucratic growth getting out of hand—or perhaps because of such fears—the federal service has shrunk in size both absolutely and relative to the total population. The number of civil federal employees has fallen from its postwar peak of 3.0 million in 1968 to 2.8 million in 2019, while the number of military personnel has fallen from 3.6 million to 1.29 million over the same period.[20] As a percentage of the total workforce, federal employment has declined since 1950, as Figure 12.2 indicates.

While the federal bureaucracy has decreased in size, both state and local government employment and government contracting have grown. State and local civil service employment has increased from about 6.5 percent of the country's workforce in 1950 to nearly 13 percent in 2020.[21] Federal employment, in contrast, exceeded

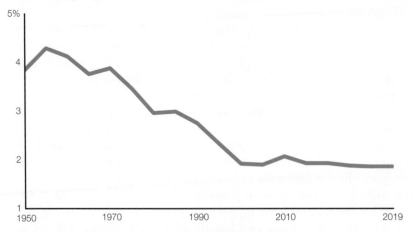

FIGURE 12.2

Employees in the Federal Service as a Percentage of the National Workforce, 1950–2019

Since the 1950s, the ratio of federal employment to the total workforce has gradually declined. Today, federal employees make up less than 2 percent of the total workforce in the United States. Even at the federal bureaucracy's height, federal employees made up less than 5 percent. What do these numbers suggest about the size of the federal government today?

SOURCES: Office of Personnel Management, "Executive Branch Civilian Employment since 1940," www.opm.gov (accessed 4/24/20); United States Postal Service, "Number of Postal Employees since 1926," https://about.usps.com/who-we-are/postal-history/employees-since-1926.pdf (accessed 4/24/20).

6 percent of the workforce only during World War II, and almost all of that temporary growth was military.

The number of federal contractors has also grown, and exceeds the number of federal employees. Private contractors of all types provide an enormous range of goods and services, from nonprofit firms that run Head Start day-care centers, to military contractors that build fighter jets, to universities that conduct government-funded basic science research. **Privatization** downsizes the government in that the workers providing the service are no longer counted as part of the government bureaucracy—and pointing to a small federal government has appealed to both Republican and Democratic elected officials over the past several decades. Contracting may or may not lead to reduced costs, depending on the performance of the contractors and the competitiveness of the bidding process. And while contracting reduces the size of the federal workforce, it also requires a new role for government, to manage and oversee the private companies carrying out government work.[22] Critics of contracting worry that oversight and accountability are insufficient and that the emphasis on contracting has detracted from efforts to recruit and retain talented employees in the career civil service itself.[23]

> **privatization** the process by which a formerly public service becomes a service provided by a private company but paid for by the government

The Bureaucracy Needs to Be Managed

Explain how the president, Congress, and the judiciary try to manage the bureaucracy

By their very nature, bureaucracies pose challenges to democratic governance. Although they provide the expertise needed to implement the public will, they can also become entrenched organizations that serve their own interests. The challenge is to take advantage of the bureaucracy's strengths while making it accountable to the demands of democratic politics and representative government, including the president and Congress.

The word *bureaucracy* does not appear in the Constitution, but the bureaucracy has constitutional roots nonetheless. Article II, Section 2, gives the president the power to nominate with the "Advice and Consent of the Senate" the officers of the United States. It also tells the president to "require the Opinion, in writing, of the principal Officer in each of the executive Departments, upon any subject relating to the duties of their respective Offices." These sections establish the existence of executive departments whose heads are nominated by the president and confirmed by the Senate and which are tasked with giving the president advice. Article II, Section 3, then gives the president broad executive powers to "take Care that the Laws be faithfully executed," making the president the administrator in chief. The Constitution thus lays the groundwork for a federal bureaucracy that carries out the duties of government under the president with congressional oversight.

This structure raises two ongoing questions for American governance. One concerns whether the amount of control the democratically elected president and Congress have over the unelected bureaucracy is sufficient. The other concerns relations between the president and Congress: both have levers of control over the bureaucracy—one of the many ways in which the Constitution creates what Richard Neustadt termed "separated institutions sharing powers"[24]—and this framework ensures that the president and Congress will disagree at times about bureaucratic action. Much of the controversy that we observe in federal government is a result of the push-and-pull between the president and Congress that the constitutional framework makes inevitable.

THE PRESIDENT AS CHIEF EXECUTIVE

The Constitution charges the president with seeing that the laws are faithfully executed. The president heads the federal government, which is the largest employer in the country and the largest purchaser of goods and services in the world.[25] As the CEO of this enormous organization, the president may have goals associated with both management (striving for efficiency) and control (shaping policy outcomes). Presidents have several tools at their disposal.

One major tool of bureaucratic control that presidents possess is appointment power over the political appointees atop the career civil service. Presidents have an incentive to appoint officials who are loyal to them and who they believe are likely to pursue their policy agendas. And such appointments require Senate approval, as the Constitution gives both the president and the Congress mechanisms for controlling the bureaucracy. The Senate rarely rejects nominees; more commonly, if it is clear that Senate support is weak, a president will withdraw a nominee before the confirmation vote. For example, Andrew Puzder, the CEO of the parent company of Hardee's and Carl's Jr., withdrew his nomination to be President Trump's secretary of labor after liberals criticized his treatment of fast-food workers and conservatives criticized his employment of an undocumented immigrant as his housekeeper.[26]

Another instrument of presidential control over the bureaucracy is the Executive Office of the President (EOP). The EOP was established during the presidency of Franklin Roosevelt, when the rapid growth of the national government led a Committee on Administrative Management to note in 1937, "The president needs help." The EOP includes key staffs reporting directly to the president on budgetary, military, and economic policies, such as the National Security Council and the Council of Economic Advisers. The EOP is usually considered the component of the bureaucracy most responsive to the presidency because it has the highest share of political appointees and because Congress gives the president greater control over its structure.[27]

Office of Management and Budget (OMB) the agency in the Executive Office of the President with control over the federal budget and regulations

One of the most important EOP agencies is the **Office of Management and Budget (OMB)**. All federal rules go through OMB. OMB also collects the budgets for all government agencies, allowing presidents to emphasize their own priorities and policy goals in the federal budget submitted annually to Congress. The centralization of these regulatory and budgetary functions is another indicator of increased presidential power relative to Congress.

In addition to making political appointments at the top of the bureaucracy, presidents may also appoint "policy czars" with responsibilities for addressing a specific policy need, often working across agencies. President Roosevelt was the first to appoint policy czars; Presidents Bush and Obama each had dozens in their administrations. President Trump has not tended to use czars, having a smaller presidential staff, although he did appoint a coronavirus pandemic task force in late January 2020, headed first by Health and Human Services Secretary Alex Azar and later by Vice President Mike Pence.[28] Presidents often appoint czars to signal responsiveness to some acute policy problem. There have been multiple illicit-drug czars, several AIDS czars, a car czar (who managed the auto industry bailout during the Great Recession), an Ebola czar (who managed the response to an outbreak in 2014), an Asian carp czar, cybersecurity czars, and so on. These advisers are directly under presidential control, as they report to the president and do not require Senate confirmation.[29]

Although the president is ostensibly in charge of the federal bureaucracy and has the tools of control just discussed, influence over the bureaucracy remains a challenge. Even though presidents nominate their own department secretaries, and try to select like-minded individuals, sometimes those officials pursue their own agendas, or become advocates for the agency itself rather than the president's agenda. Sometimes presidential appointees turn out to be poor managers, and their agency is unable to execute its duties optimally.[30] Interest groups also have ongoing relationships with agencies and may try to shape agency agendas, interfering with presidential preferences (some critics say, for example, that the pharmaceutical industry has too much influence over its regulatory agency, the Food and Drug Administration).[31] One reason that bureaucratic action may seem inefficient is that the bureaucracy answers to many players, such as Congress, not just to the president.

CONGRESSIONAL CONTROL

The Constitution gives Congress several tools of control over the bureaucracy as it interprets and implements the laws Congress has passed. Most important, Congress approves agencies' annual funding. At hearings on appropriations, members of Congress can evaluate agency performance and may reduce funding if they are not satisfied. Agencies wish to avoid this fate and so take congressional opinion—and by extension public opinion—into account as they implement programs. In addition, the Senate approves presidential nominations to the top levels of the executive agencies.

Like the president, Congress can change the location or structure of agencies, creating new ones or reorganizing policy responsibilities across existing agencies in an effort to shape agency behavior or to reduce presidential control. For example, Congress may choose to place a regulatory body or commission outside of the 15 executive departments. Or it can designate a multimember board rather than a single person to head an agency, which limits presidential control by allowing for a partisan-balance requirement (members have to come from both parties, not just the president's), or staggered terms of office (so that a president cannot replace all board members at once). Fixed terms of office, especially long ones, also diminish presidential control (members of the Board of Governors of the Fed serve 14-year terms, for example, far longer than a president). And one of the most important ways Congress can check presidential control of the bureaucracy is by limiting the president's ability to *remove* agency officials. In many instances the congressional statutes creating or reorganizing agencies do not allow presidents to remove officials except "for cause," such as neglect of duty or wrongdoing, not merely for policy disagreements.

Congress can also make political or policy statements with its organizational choices. For example, Congress first created the Department of Health, Education, and Welfare in 1953. Then, 25 years later, during the Carter administration, Congress divided the agency into the Department of Health and Human Services and the Department of Education to underscore the federal role in education. When Congress placed the Transportation Security Administration, in charge of airport security, in the Department of Homeland Security rather than the Department of Transportation, it signaled that domestic security concerns were to be a more central aspect of the administration's mission than facilitating transportation, as those who have stood in long TSA lines at airports can attest.[32]

Congress can also hold the bureaucracy accountable through **oversight**. Congressional committees and subcommittees have jurisdictions roughly parallel to the departments and agencies in the executive branch, and members of Congress who sit on these committees can develop expertise in these policy areas. For example, both the House and Senate have Agriculture Committees and subcommittees that oversee the Department of Agriculture.

The most visible indication of Congress's oversight efforts is the use of public hearings, before which bureaucrats and other witnesses are summoned to discuss and defend agency budgets and decisions. Congress can also pass laws requiring agencies to submit regular reports on their activities and can create advisory committees to make recommendations to agencies and to help Congress oversee them. For example, the Food and Drug Administration (FDA) has several dozen advisory committees consisting of physicians, scientists, statisticians, pharmaceutical industry representatives, and members of the public, including an FDA Patient Representative, which provide independent advice on scientific and policy questions concerning the safety and effectiveness of new medical and drug therapies.[33]

In recent years, there appears to be less **"police patrol" oversight**—regular or even anticipatory hearings on agency operations—and more **"fire alarm" oversight** prompted by media attention or advocacy group complaints. For example, consumer outrage

oversight the effort by Congress, through hearings, investigations, and other techniques, to exercise control over the activities of executive agencies

"police patrol" oversight regular or even preemptive congressional hearings on bureaucratic agency operations

"fire alarm" oversight episodic, as-needed congressional hearings on bureaucratic agency operations, usually prompted by media attention or advocacy group complaints

prompted the 2016 inquiry by the House Oversight and Government Reform Committee into a 500 percent price hike on EpiPens, used to treat severe allergic reactions.[34]

As a result, Congress has created additional sources of oversight. The Inspector General Act of 1978 established **inspectors general (IGs)**, which are nonpartisan, independent organizations now located in most agencies, which investigate agency

> **inspectors general (IGs)**
> independent audit organizations located in most federal agencies

activities on Congress's behalf. IGs audit agency operations to uncover cases of waste, fraud, or misconduct. They alert agency heads of any severe problems, and the agency head must then send the IG's report, along with comments and corrective plans, to Congress. Inspectors general of the Cabinet-level agencies are appointed by the president and approved by the Senate, another example of shared control over the bureaucracy; in other federal agencies, the agency head appoints the IG. In both cases, agency heads cannot interfere with IG audits or investigations. On several occasions, President Trump exerted control over inspectors general. For example, during the coronavirus pandemic, he replaced a deputy inspector general in HHS whose report revealed extensive supply shortages at hospitals, and he blocked a Defense Department inspector general from heading a new Pandemic Response Accountability Committee to oversee the government's coronavirus relief spending. Critics alleged that while the president did have the authority to remove these officials, he did so in an effort to avoid transparency and congressional oversight.[35]

Another source of oversight involves the three large agencies Congress created for itself to research the executive branch: the Government Accountability Office (GAO), the Congressional Research Service, and the Congressional Budget Office. These organizations provide information independent from what Congress gets from the executive branch. The GAO is the nation's "supreme audit institution," providing Congress with information about how tax dollars are spent and how the government could be made more efficient.[36] The Congressional Research Service (CRS), part of the Library of Congress, provides expert analysis to congressional committees and members of Congress on policy issues. The CRS responds to inquiries from individual congresspeople; creates tailored memos, briefings, and consultations; runs seminars and workshops; and provides congressional testimony.[37] And the Congressional Budget Office provides independent analyses of budgetary and economic issues to assist Congress in its budget process, for example estimating the cost of proposed legislation.[38]

PRESIDENTIAL–CONGRESSIONAL STRUGGLE FOR BUREAUCRATIC CONTROL: A CASE STUDY

A look at the birth of a new agency, the Consumer Financial Protection Board (CFPB), helps illustrate the struggle between the president and Congress over the bureaucracy. The financial crisis that began in 2007 had its roots in the collapse of the housing market. Many borrowers had taken on home mortgages that were difficult to understand and unaffordable, and when they could no longer pay, they lost their

The Consumer Financial Protection Bureau is an agency created by President Obama under the Department of the Treasury. Here, President Obama, with Timothy Geithner, Treasury secretary at the time, nominates Elizabeth Warren as its head (although congressional Republicans later blocked the nomination).

homes to foreclosure, which in turn caused their neighbors' home values to fall. Critics of this system believed there were insufficient consumer protections in place and proposed creating the CFPB. This new agency would address consumer complaints and regulate banks, credit unions, payday lenders, debt collectors, and other firms that provide consumer financial products and services such as mortgages, credit cards, and student loans. In 2010, Congress passed the Dodd-Frank Wall Street Reform and Consumer Protection Act, which imposed new banking regulations and also created the CFPB.[39]

President Obama and congressional Republicans disagreed about the structure, funding, and location of the CFPB. The 2010 legislation made the CFPB an independent agency located inside the Federal Reserve System, with automatic funding based on a fixed percentage of the Fed's operating expenses and with a single director appointed by the president with the consent of the Senate. Congressional Republicans argued that the CFPB's funding should be annually appropriated by Congress instead, obviously increasing Congress's influence over the agency, and that it should be headed by a multimember board rather than a single person, diminishing any president's influence over the agency's leadership. Proponents argued that the automatic funding and the location inside the Fed, which is already an independent institution, were necessary to give the CFPB independence from political forces and the muscle it needed to help consumers confronting powerful financial institutions. They felt Senate consent for the director was a sufficient check on the president's influence.

Disagreements over the CFPB's design have continued ever since. The idea for the agency came from Massachusetts senator and 2020 Democratic presidential candidate Elizabeth Warren, back when she was a law professor studying bankruptcy. President Obama had planned to appoint her the first head of the agency but, in the face of Republican opposition, selected former Ohio attorney general and Ohio treasurer Richard Cordray. But that nomination was held up by Senate Republicans, who continued to urge a multimember board structure. (Cordray became head in a recess appointment.) Later, President Trump appointed Mick Mulvaney as the acting head of the agency. As a congressman, Mulvaney had proposed legislation eliminating the CFPB. After some members of the CFPB's consumer advisory board criticized him in 2018, Mulvaney had the entire 25-member board removed. Controversy over the CFPB's structure and role continues.

JUDICIAL OVERSIGHT

The third branch of government serves an important role as well. The bureaucracy's decisions are subject to judicial review; the *Marbury v. Madison* decision in 1803 posited that the Supreme Court has final authority to judge the constitutionality of executive actions, whether taken by the president or the bureaucracy. The courts also settle disputes between Congress and executive agencies about the interpretations of laws. In addition, they monitor the implementation of laws by creating an arena in which individuals or groups who are negatively affected by a regulation or program can bring lawsuits.

WHISTLEBLOWING

Sometimes a form of control comes from within bureaucratic agencies themselves. **Whistleblowers** are federal employees who report wrongdoing within agencies. Congress passed the Whistleblower Protection Act in 1989 to protect those reporting mismanagement or corruption from punishment by their colleagues or superiors. In 2019 a whistleblower from the U.S. intelligence community filed a complaint about a phone call between President Trump and the president of Ukraine in which the whistleblower feared that the president was "using the power of his office to solicit interference from a foreign country in the 2020 U.S. election," including "pressuring a foreign country to investigate one of the president's main domestic political rivals," Joe Biden and his son Hunter Biden.[40] The whistleblower complaint prompted an impeachment investigation by the House Democrats that began in fall 2019.

whistleblowers federal employees who report wrongdoing in federal agencies

CITIZEN OVERSIGHT

The Freedom of Information Act of 1966 (FOIA) provides ordinary citizens and journalists the right to request records from any federal agency. Congress's intent in passing the law was to increase bureaucratic transparency and executive branch oversight.[41] Agencies must comply with the requests unless they fall under one of nine exemptions, which concern issues such as personal privacy, national security, or law enforcement, or unless disclosure of the information is prohibited by another federal law. Agencies are required by law to produce records within 20 days, but frequently there are backlogs. Agencies can also disclose portions rather than entire records.

FOIA requests sometimes prompt congressional oversight and investigation when agency misbehavior is revealed. In 2017, a *USA Today* story revealed that the Centers for Disease Control and Prevention, an agency within the Department of Health and Human Services that conducts research and provides information to protect people from health threats, had tried to keep secret a series of accidents from 2013 to 2015 involving dangerous pathogens such as anthrax and Ebola. The article was based on heavily redacted lab incident reports that a reporter had obtained through a FOIA request. After the article was published, the House Committee on Energy and Commerce sent a letter to the director of the CDC stating that "the details in the article seem to indicate that most, if not all, of these incidents were not disclosed to the Committee," and demanding that the CDC turn over the unredacted reports.[42]

THE DIFFICULTIES OF BUREAUCRATIC CONTROL

Controlling the bureaucracy is difficult. On the one hand, having a federal branch populated by experts who implement laws and issue regulations in an impartial, uniform manner, with minimal political interference, is necessary to make the government operate as efficiently and responsibly as possible. On the other hand, bureaucrats may pursue their own goals rather than those of the president, who oversees the bureaucracy, or Congress, which writes the laws the bureaucracy implements. The tools of control are imperfect.

In addition, there are sometimes outright bureaucratic failures. In 2014 a waiting-list scandal rocked the Veterans Health Administration, the organization within the Veterans Administration that provides health care to military veterans. Some VHA hospitals that had not met the target of providing appointments for veterans within 14 days had created unofficial lists to make their waiting times look better. A VA audit and FBI investigation found that over 120,000 veterans were left waiting or never got appointments. In response, VA Secretary Eric Shinseki resigned, and Congress passed and President Obama signed legislation that added funding, allowed some veterans to get private health care at government expense, and gave the VA secretary increased authority to fire poorly performing managers.[43]

Bureaucracies can also be subject to **regulatory capture**. This occurs when an agency, rather than acting in the public interest, becomes too favorable toward the organized interests or corporations it is supposed to be regulating. Critics point to two 737 Max airliner crashes in 2018 and 2019, which killed nearly 400 people, as a classic example of regulatory capture, in which the Federal Aviation Administration allowed the Boeing Corporation to handle key aspects of safety assessments needed to get the new airliner model approved for commercial service. The FAA approved Boeing's safety analysis, which was later revealed to have critical lapses.[44]

regulatory capture a form of government failure in which regulatory agencies become too sympathetic to interests or businesses they are supposed to regulate

Many presidents have proposed or enacted broad-based reorganization schemes to enhance their control or increase bureaucratic efficiency, or in response to bureaucratic failures. The September 11, 2001, terrorist attacks not only prompted the creation of the Department of Homeland Security in 2002, as we have seen, but also the creation of the Office of the Director of National Intelligence (DNI) in 2004. With that reform, the DNI became the head of the intelligence community, a role previously played by the director of the CIA. Similarly, both the savings-and-loan crisis of the 1980s and the financial crisis of 2007–09 prompted reorganized or new entities regulating the financial industry.[45]

Bureaucracy: What Do You Think?

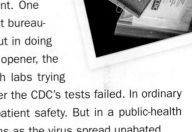

Americans' views about the federal government bureaucracy present something of a paradox. On the one hand, the public expresses dislike for "big government," exemplified by bureaucracy. From this perspective, the federal government is too large, inherently wasteful, and at odds with individual freedom. On the other hand, Americans support many government programs and have high expectations for government. One consequence of these divergent views can be that bureaucracies try to maximize one benefit for citizens but in doing so undermine others. As we saw in the chapter opener, the FDA put up bureaucratic hurdles for public-health labs trying to develop their own tests for the coronavirus after the CDC's tests failed. In ordinary times, such processes are intended to ensure patient safety. But in a public-health emergency, they endangered the lives of Americans as the virus spread unabated.

★ Some argue that Americans' liberties are threatened when the bureaucracy grows too large, while others contend that a bureaucracy with too few resources is the real threat. What do you think Helen Chu would say?

★ Are there ways in which you have benefited from bureaucratic action, or been harmed by it? What types of bureaucratic activity are most noticeable to you, and what types are most hidden?

★ What kinds of reforms would make the bureaucracy more accountable to the public?

STUDY GUIDE

Practice Quiz

1. Which of the following statements about Congress and the bureaucracy is not true? *(pp. 368–70)*
   a) Bureaucracies employ people who have much more specialized expertise in specific policy areas than do members of Congress.
   b) Members of Congress often prefer to delegate politically difficult decision-making to bureaucrats.
   c) While Congress is responsible for making laws, the bureaucracy is responsible for filling in the details by determining how the laws should be implemented.
   d) Congress banned rule making by the federal bureaucracy in 1995.
   e) Congress relies heavily on bureaucratic flexibility in implementing laws because updating legislation can take many years, and bureaucrats can ensure that laws are administered in ways that take new conditions into account.

2. Which of the following is an example of a government corporation? *(p. 373)*
   a) National Aeronautics and Space Administration
   b) Amtrak
   c) Federal Bureau of Investigation
   d) Environmental Protection Agency
   e) Department of Justice

3. The State Department's primary mission is *(p. 373)*
   a) gathering intelligence.
   b) unifying the nation's military departments.
   c) engaging in diplomacy.
   d) investigating terrorism.
   e) overseeing domestic security efforts.

4. Which of the following organizations is responsible for adjusting the supply of money and credit in the economy? *(p. 374)*
   a) the Office of Management and Budget
   b) the Treasury Department
   c) the Federal Reserve System
   d) the Internal Revenue Service
   e) the Commerce Department

5. If Congress wants to create an agency with independent, bipartisan leadership, it will likely *(p. 378)*
   a) locate the agency within the executive branch.
   b) refrain from exercising its oversight powers on the agency.
   c) allow the president to decide how the agency should be organized.
   d) provide for the election, rather than the appointment, of the agency's leadership.
   e) install a multiperson board at the head of the agency.

6. The Pendleton Civil Service Reform Act of 1883 required that bureaucratic personnel *(p. 380)*
   a) pledge an oath of loyalty to the United States.
   b) register as independents rather than as members of an organized political party.
   c) be qualified for the job to which they were appointed.
   d) serve for no more than ten years.
   e) serve for no fewer than ten years.

7. Which president's administration instituted the National Performance Review? *(p. 381)*
   a) Richard Nixon
   b) Lyndon Johnson
   c) Jimmy Carter
   d) Bill Clinton
   e) George W. Bush

8. Which of the following best describes the size of the federal service? *(p. 382)*
   a) The size of the federal service has grown exponentially since 1980.
   b) The size of the federal service has changed very little since 1980.
   c) As a percentage of the total workforce, federal employment has declined since 1950.

d) The federal service has employed at least 15 percent of the American workforce every year since 1950.
e) The federal service was eliminated during the 1990s in order to hire more state government employees.

9. The number of federal contractors _____ the number of federal employees. *(p. 383)*
a) exceeds
b) is slightly less than
c) is significantly less than
d) is roughly the same as
e) is projected to soon overtake

10. When congressional hearings on bureaucratic agency operations are prompted by media attention or advocacy group complaints, it is an example of *(p. 386)*
a) "police patrol" oversight.
b) "fire alarm" oversight.
c) "watchdog" oversight.
d) devolution.
e) preemption.

11. Which of the following statements about the Freedom of Information Act (FOIA) is most accurate? *(pp. 389–90)*
a) It was passed following the September 11, 2001, terrorist attacks.

b) FOIA is primarily meant to help bureaucratic agencies request information from other bureaucratic agencies.
c) All agencies are required to comply with FOIA requests, with no exceptions.
d) FOIA requests sometimes prompt congressional oversight and investigation when agency misbehavior is revealed.
e) President Trump instructed federal agencies to reject all FOIA requests made during his term in office.

12. What is regulatory capture? (p. 390)
a) when Congress uses its oversight powers to block agencies from creating regulations
b) when an executive department assumes control over an agency that is outside of its traditional jurisdiction
c) when regulations get stuck in the notice-and-comment stage for over a year
d) when Congress refuses to confirm the president's nominees to high-level bureaucratic offices
e) when an agency becomes too favorable toward the organized interests or corporations it is supposed to be regulating

Key Terms

bureaucracy *(p. 367)*

implementation *(p. 368)*

principal-agent problem *(p. 371)*

executive departments *(p. 371)*

independent regulatory commission *(p. 373)*

government corporation *(p. 373)*

merit system *(p. 380)*

political appointees *(p. 380)*

Senior Executive Service (SES) *(p. 381)*

privatization *(p. 383)*

Office of Management and Budget (OMB) *(p. 384)*

oversight *(p. 386)*

"police patrol" oversight *(p. 386)*

"fire alarm" oversight *(p. 386)*

inspectors general (IGs) *(p. 387)*

whistleblowers *(p. 389)*

regulatory capture *(p. 390)*

The Federal Courts

WHAT GOVERNMENT DOES AND WHY IT MATTERS

Mark Janus worked for the Illinois Department of Healthcare and Family Services as a child-support specialist. He is not a member of the union representing many public-sector workers in the state, the American Federation of State, County, and Municipal Employees (AFSCM). Nonetheless, he is required to pay a "fair-share" fee to the union on the grounds that nonmembers benefit from the union's bargaining activities over issues such as pay and benefits. Nonmembers do not have to contribute to the union's political activities, such as endorsements of political candidates.[1]

Janus argues, however, that *all* activity that public-sector unions engage in is inherently political, and he disagrees with the union's bargaining for increased benefits when Illinois was facing a budget crisis due in part to mismanagement of the state pension program. "The union's fight is not my fight," he says. He believes that being forced to pay a fee that supports the union's activities violates his First Amendment rights.

Although the Supreme Court is often viewed as the least political of the three branches, its rulings touch on major political issues that affect Americans in many ways. Here, Mark Janus (left) celebrates with supporters after winning his Supreme Court case, which could have a profound effect on how unions operate.

His case went to the Supreme Court. Janus's lawsuit challenged a 1977 case in which the Court allowed state and local governments to require public employees to pay union fees, a practice in 22 states.[2] The Court almost overturned a case in 2015 in which a California teacher sued the local teachers' union over such fees. But after Justice Antonin Scalia died in 2016, the Court split 4–4 in the California case.

President Barack Obama nominated Merrick Garland to replace Scalia, but the Republican-controlled Senate took no action on the nomination in the hope, which was fulfilled, of a Republican victory in the 2016 presidential election. After taking office in 2017, President Donald Trump nominated conservative appeals court judge Neil Gorsuch to the vacant seat. With the Gorsuch appointment, conservatives once again enjoyed a 5–4 Supreme Court majority. The Gorsuch appointment resulted in a conservative decision in *Janus v. AFSCME*, and Janus's First Amendment rights would be upheld. But union supporters say the decision will have devastating effects on public-sector unions' ability to protect workers.

The Supreme Court's 5–4 decision underscored the significance of Supreme Court appointments. Had Garland rather than Gorsuch been seated on the Court, the mandatory-dues requirement would likely have been upheld. With the *Janus* decision in mind, Democrats and Republicans intensified their efforts to win subsequent battles over judicial appointments. After Justice Anthony Kennedy announced his retirement from the Court in July 2018, Trump nominated Brett Kavanaugh, another conservative judge, to take his place. After a divisive political battle, Kavanaugh was confirmed by the Senate and joined the Court in October. In September 2020, Justice Ruth Bader Ginsburg passed away, and Trump nominated conservative judge Amy Coney Barrett to the Court days before the presidential election.

Every year, approximately 25 million cases are tried in American courts. Cases can arise from disputes between citizens, from efforts by government agencies to punish wrongdoing, from citizens' efforts to prove that government action—or inaction—has infringed on their rights, and from efforts by interest groups to promote their agendas. Many critics of the U.S. legal system assert that Americans have become too litigious, too ready to use the courts for all purposes. But given the existence of social conflict, it is far better that Americans seek to settle their differences through the courts than resort to violence or otherwise take matters into their own hands.

The framers of the Constitution called the Supreme Court the "least dangerous branch" of American government. Today, though, it is not unusual to hear the Court described as an all-powerful "imperial judiciary."

CHAPTER GOALS

★ **Identify the general types of cases and types of courts in America's legal system (pp. 397–402)**

★ **Describe the different levels of federal courts and the process of appointing federal judges (pp. 402–6)**

★ **Explain the Supreme Court's judicial review of national law (pp. 407–11)**

★ **Describe the process by which cases are considered and decided by the Supreme Court (pp. 411–19)**

★ **Describe the factors that influence Court decisions (pp. 420–23)**

The Legal System Settles Disputes

Originally, a "court" was the place where a monarch ruled. Settling disputes between one's subjects was part of governing. In modern democracies, courts made up of judges and juries have taken over the power to settle conflicts, which they do by hearing the facts on both sides of a case and applying the relevant law or constitutional principle to the facts to decide which side has the stronger argument. Courts have been given the authority to settle disputes not only between citizens but also between citizens and the government itself, where judges and juries must maintain the same impartiality as they do in disputes involving two citizens. This is the essence of the "rule of law": that "the state" and its officials must be judged by the same laws as the citizenry.

CASES AND THE LAW

Court cases in the United States proceed under two broad categories of law: criminal law and civil law.

Cases of **criminal law** are those in which the government charges an individual with violating a statute enacted to protect public health, safety, morals, or welfare. In criminal cases, the government is always the **plaintiff** (the party that brings charges)

criminal law the branch of law that regulates the conduct of individuals, defines crimes, and specifies punishment for proscribed conduct

plaintiff the individual or organization that brings a complaint in court

In criminal cases, the government charges an individual with violating a statute protecting health, safety, morals, or welfare. Most such cases arise in state and municipal courts. Here, an Illinois county court hears testimony in a murder case.

defendant the one against whom a complaint is brought in a criminal or civil case

civil law the branch of law that deals with disputes that do not involve criminal penalties

precedent a prior case whose principles are used by judges as the basis for their decision in a present case

and alleges that a criminal violation has been committed by a named **defendant**. Most criminal cases arise in state and municipal courts and involve matters ranging from traffic offenses to robbery and murder. However, a large and growing body of federal criminal law deals with matters ranging from tax evasion and mail fraud to acts of terrorism and the sale of narcotics. Defendants found guilty of criminal violations may be fined or sent to jail or prison.

Cases of **civil law** involve disputes among individuals, groups, corporations, and other private entities or between such litigants and the government, in which no criminal violation is charged. Unlike in criminal cases, the losers in civil cases cannot be incarcerated, although they may be required to pay monetary damages to the winners.

The two most common types of civil cases involve contracts and torts. In a typical contract case, an individual or corporation charges that it has suffered because of another's violation of an agreement between the two. For example, the Smith Manufacturing Corporation may charge that Jones Distributors failed to honor an agreement to deliver raw materials at a specified time, causing Smith to lose business. Smith asks the court to order Jones to compensate it for the damage it allegedly suffered. In a typical tort case, one individual charges that he has been injured by another's negligence or bad conduct. Medical malpractice suits are one example of tort cases.

Another important area of civil law is administrative law, which involves disputes over the jurisdiction, procedures, or authority of administrative agencies. A plaintiff may assert, for example, that an agency did not follow proper procedures when issuing new rules and regulations. A court will then examine the agency's conduct in light of the Administrative Procedure Act, the legislation that governs agency rule making.

In deciding cases, courts apply statutes (laws) and legal **precedents** (prior decisions). Jones Distributors might argue that it was not obliged to fulfill its contract with the Smith Manufacturing Corporation because actions by Smith, such as the failure to make promised payments, constituted fraud under state law. Precedents established in previous cases also guide courts' decisions in new cases. Attorneys for a physician being sued for malpractice might search for prior instances in which courts ruled that actions similar to those of their client did not constitute negligence. Such precedents are applied using the legal principle of stare decisis, a Latin phrase meaning "let the decision stand."

If a case involves the actions of the federal government or a state government, a court may also be asked to examine whether the government's conduct was consistent with the Constitution. In a criminal case, for example, defendants might assert that their constitutional rights were violated when the police searched their property. Similarly, in a civil case involving federal or state restrictions on land development, plaintiffs might assert that government actions violated the Fifth

Amendment's prohibition against taking private property without just compensation. Thus, both civil and criminal cases may raise questions of constitutional law.

TYPES OF COURTS

In the United States, systems of courts have been established both by the federal government and by the governments of the individual states. Both systems have several levels, as shown in Figure 13.1. More than 97 percent of all court cases

FIGURE 13.1

The U.S. Court System

The state and federal court systems both include several types of courts. The Supreme Court hears appeals from both systems.

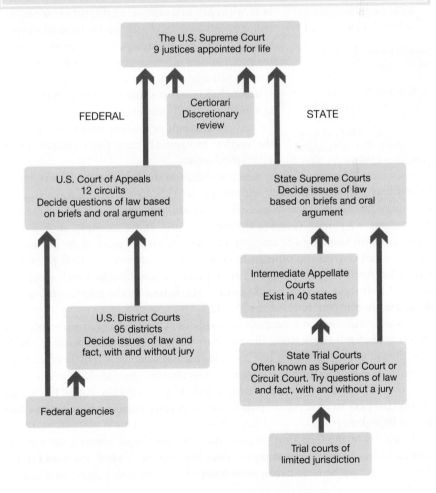

trial court the first court to hear a criminal or civil case

court of appeals a court that hears appeals of trial court decisions

supreme court the highest court in a particular state or in the United States; this court primarily serves an appellate function

plea bargain a negotiated agreement in a criminal case in which a defendant agrees to plead guilty in return for the state's agreement to reduce the severity of the criminal charge or prison sentence the defendant is facing

jurisdiction the sphere of a court's power and authority

original jurisdiction the authority to initially consider a case; distinguished from appellate jurisdiction, which is the authority to hear appeals from a lower court's decision

in the United States are heard in state courts. The overwhelming majority of criminal cases, for example, involve violations of state laws prohibiting such actions as murder, robbery, fraud, theft, and assault. If such a case is brought to trial, it will be heard at a state **trial court**, in front of a judge and sometimes a jury, who will determine whether the defendant violated state law. If the defendant is convicted, she may appeal the conviction to a higher court, such as a state **court of appeals**, and from there to a court of last resort, usually called the state's **supreme court**. The government is not entitled to appeal if the defendant is found not guilty.

The party filing an appeal, known as an *appellant*, usually must show that the trial court made a legal error in deciding the case. Appeals courts do not hear witnesses or examine additional evidence and will consider new facts only under unusual circumstances. Thus, for example, a physician who loses a malpractice case might appeal on the basis that the trial court misapplied the relevant law or incorrectly instructed the jury. It should be noted that in both criminal and civil matters most cases are settled before trial through negotiated agreements between the parties. In criminal cases these agreements are called **plea bargains.**

Cases are heard in the federal courts if they involve federal laws, treaties with other nations, or the U.S. Constitution; these areas are the official **jurisdiction** of the federal courts. In addition, any case in which the U.S. government is a party is heard in the federal courts. If, for example, an individual is charged with violating a federal criminal statute, such as evading the payment of income taxes, charges are brought before a federal judge by a federal prosecutor. Civil cases involving the citizens of more than one state and in which more than $75,000 is at stake may be heard in either the federal or the state courts, usually depending on the preference of the plaintiff.

Congress has assigned federal court jurisdictions on the basis of geography. The nation is currently, by statute, divided into 94 judicial districts. Each of the 94 U.S. district courts, including one court for each of three U.S. territories, exercises jurisdiction over federal cases arising within its district. The judicial districts are, in turn, organized into 11 regional circuits and the D.C. circuit (see Figure 13.2). Each circuit court exercises appellate jurisdiction over cases heard by the district courts within its region.

Article III of the Constitution gives the Supreme Court **original jurisdiction** in a limited variety of cases, including (1) cases between the United States and one of the states, (2) cases between two or more states, (3) cases involving foreign ambassadors

FIGURE 13.2
....

Federal Appellate Court Circuits

The 94 federal district courts are organized into 12 regional circuits: the 11 shown here, plus the District of Columbia, which has its own circuit. Each circuit court hears appeals from lower federal courts within the circuit. A thirteenth federal circuit court, the U.S. Court of Appeals for the Federal Circuit, hears appeals from a number of specialized courts, such as the U.S. Court of Federal Claims.

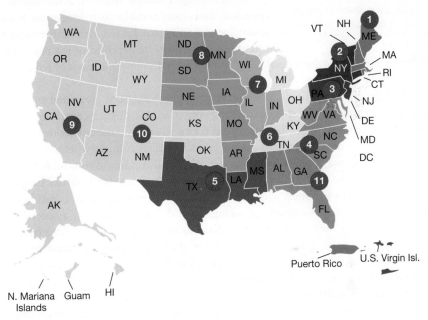

SOURCE: "Federal Court Finder," www.uscourts.gov/court_locator.aspx (accessed 7/27/10).

or other ministers, and (4) cases brought by one state against citizens of another state or against a foreign country. Courts of original jurisdiction discover the facts in a controversy and create the record on which a judgment is based. In all other federal cases, Article III assigns original jurisdiction to the lower courts that Congress was authorized to establish. The Constitution gives the Supreme Court appellate jurisdiction in all federal cases, and almost all cases heard by the Supreme Court today are appealed from lower courts. In courts that have appellate jurisdiction, judges receive cases after the factual record is established by the trial court. Ordinarily, new facts cannot be presented before appellate courts.

Congress has also established several specialized courts that have nationwide original jurisdiction in certain types of cases, such as the U.S. Court of International Trade, created to deal with trade and customs issues; and the U.S. Court of Federal Claims, which handles damage suits against the United States. Congress

due process of law the right of every individual against arbitrary action by national or state governments

writ of habeas corpus a court order that the individual in custody be brought into court and shown the cause for detention; habeas corpus is guaranteed by the Constitution and can be suspended only in cases of rebellion or invasion

has also established a court with nationwide appellate jurisdiction, the U.S. Court of Appeals for the Federal Circuit, which hears appeals involving patent law and those arising from the decisions of the trade and claims courts.

The appellate jurisdiction of the federal courts extends to cases originating in the state courts. In both civil and criminal cases, a decision of the highest state court can be appealed to the U.S. Supreme Court by raising a federal issue. A defendant who appeals a state court decision in federal court might assert, for example, that he was denied the right to counsel or was otherwise deprived of the **due process of law** guaranteed by the federal Constitution or that important issues of federal law were at stake in the case.

In addition, in criminal cases, defendants who have been convicted in a state court may request a **writ of habeas corpus** from a federal district court. Sometimes known as the "Great Writ," habeas corpus is a court order to the authorities to show cause for a prisoner's incarceration. The court will then evaluate whether the cause is sufficient and may order the release of a prisoner if it is found not to be. In 1867 Congress's distrust of southern courts led it to authorize federal district judges to issue such writs to prisoners who they believed had been deprived of constitutional rights in state court. Generally speaking, state defendants seeking a federal writ of habeas corpus must show that they have exhausted all available state remedies and must raise issues not previously raised in their state appeals. Federal courts of appeals and, ultimately, the U.S. Supreme Court have appellate jurisdiction for federal district court habeas decisions.

Although the federal courts hear only a small fraction of all the civil and criminal cases decided each year in the United States, their decisions are extremely important. It is in the federal courts that the Constitution and federal laws that govern all Americans are interpreted. Moreover, it is in the federal courts that the powers and limitations of the increasingly powerful national government are tested. Finally, through their power to review state court decisions, it is ultimately the federal courts that dominate the American judicial system.

Federal Courts Hear a Small Percentage of All Cases

Describe the different levels of federal courts and the process of appointing federal judges

During the year ending in September 2019, federal district courts (the lowest federal level) received 390,555 cases. Though large, this number is less than 3 percent of the number of cases heard by state courts. The federal courts of appeal listened to 48,486 cases during the same period. Generally, about 15 percent of the verdicts rendered by these courts are appealed to the U.S. Supreme Court.

Most of the 6,500 or so cases filed with the Supreme Court each year are dismissed without a ruling on their merits. The Court has broad latitude to decide what cases it will hear and generally listens to only those it believes raise the most important issues. In recent years, fewer than 100 cases per year have received full-dress Supreme Court reviews.[3]

FEDERAL TRIAL COURTS

Most federal cases begin in the lowest courts—the 94 federal district courts. Congress has authorized the appointment of 678 federal district judges to staff these courts, although at any given time, some of these positions may be vacant. District judges are assigned to district courts according to the workload; the busiest courts may have as many as 28 judges. Only 1 judge is assigned to each case, except where statutes provide for 3-judge courts to deal with special issues.

FEDERAL APPELLATE COURTS

Roughly 20 percent of all lower-court cases, along with appeals from some federal agency decisions, are subsequently reviewed by federal appeals courts. As noted earlier, the country is divided geographically into 11 regional circuits and the D.C. circuit, each of which has a U.S. Court of Appeals. A thirteenth appellate court, the U.S. Court of Appeals for the Federal Circuit, has a subject-matter jurisdiction, rather than a geographical one. Congress has authorized the appointment of 179 court-of-appeals judges, though, as in the case of the district courts, some spots may be vacant at any given point in time.

Except for the few cases selected for review by the Supreme Court, appeals court decisions are final. Because of this finality, certain safeguards have been built into the system. The most important is the provision of more than one judge for every appeals case. Each court of appeals has from 6 to 28 permanent judgeships, depending on the workload of the circuit. Normally three of these judges hear each case, and in some instances a larger number sit together "en banc."

Another safeguard is provided by the assignment of a Supreme Court justice as the circuit justice for each of the 12 circuits. The circuit justice deals with requests for special action by the Supreme Court. The most frequent and best-known action of circuit justices is that of reviewing requests for stays of execution when the full Court is unable to do so—primarily during the summer, when the Court is in recess.

THE SUPREME COURT

Article III of the Constitution vests "the judicial power of the United States" in the Supreme Court, and this court is supreme in fact as well as name. The Supreme Court is the only federal court established by the Constitution. The lower federal courts were created by Congress and can be restructured or, presumably, even abolished.

The Supreme Court is made up of the chief justice of the United States and eight associate justices. The **chief justice** presides over the Court's public sessions and conferences and is always the first to speak and vote when the justices deliberate. In deliberations and decisions, however, the chief justice has no more authority than her colleagues. Each justice casts one vote. If the chief justice has voted with the majority, he decides which of the justices will write the formal opinion for the Court. The character of the opinion can be an important means of influencing the evolution of the law beyond the mere affirmation or denial of the appeal on hand.

chief justice justice on the Supreme Court who presides over the Court's public sessions and whose official title is "chief justice of the United States"

To some extent, the influence of the chief justice is a function of her own leadership ability. Some chief justices, such as the late Earl Warren, have been able to lead the Court in a new direction.

The Constitution does not specify the number of justices on the Supreme Court, so Congress has the authority to change its size. In the early nineteenth century, there were six justices; later there were seven. Congress set the number at nine in 1869, and the Court has remained that size ever since.

HOW JUDGES ARE APPOINTED

Federal judges are nominated by the president and must be confirmed by the Senate. They are generally selected from among the more prominent or politically active members of the legal profession, and many previously served as state court judges or state or local prosecutors. However, there are no formal qualifications for service as a federal judge. In general, presidents try to appoint judges whose partisan and ideological views are similar to their own.

Once the president has formally nominated someone, the nominee must be considered by the Senate Judiciary Committee and confirmed by a majority vote in the full Senate. In recent years, a good deal of partisan conflict has surrounded judicial appointments. Senate Democrats have sought to prevent Republican presidents from appointing conservative judges, while Senate Republicans have worked to prevent Democratic presidents from appointing liberal judges.

During the early months of the Obama administration, Republicans were able to slow the judicial appointment process through filibusters and other procedural maneuvers so that only 3 of the president's 23 nominees were confirmed by the Senate.[4] Some of Obama's allies urged the president to take a more aggressive stance because he risked allowing Republicans to block what had been considered a key Democratic priority. In 2013 the Senate voted to end the use of the filibuster against all executive branch and judicial nominees except those to the Supreme Court, allowing President Obama to quickly secure the appointment of more than 300 new district court judges and 55 new appeals court judges. In 2017, Republicans turned the tables and extended these rule changes to include Supreme Court nominees, thus blocking Democratic efforts to prevent President Trump from appointing Neil Gorsuch to the Court.

Senate Republicans' strategy to not take up Obama's nomination of Merrick Garland, and to eliminate filibusters on Supreme Court nominations, paid off when President Trump nominated Neil Gorsuch in 2017 and Brett M. Kavanaugh in 2018. When Justice Ruth Bader Ginsburg passed away in 2020, the Trump administration nominated another justice to the bench, Judge Amy Coney Barrett, pictured here.

Supreme Court Appointments Political factors are decisive when it comes to Supreme Court appointments. Because the high court has so much influence over American law and politics, virtually all presidents have made an effort to select justices who share their political philosophies.

Six of the nine current justices, as of October 2020, were appointed by Republican presidents (see Table 13.1). With the exception of the months between the death of Antonin Scalia in February 2016 and the confirmation of Gorsuch in April 2017, the Court has had a conservative majority for 46 years, most recently consisting of Chief Justice John Roberts and justices Samuel Alito, Clarence Thomas, Neil Gorsuch, Brett Kavanaugh, and Amy Coney Barrett. This majority propelled the Court in a more conservative direction in a variety of areas, including civil rights and election law.

In recent decades, Supreme Court nominations have come to involve intense partisan struggle. Typically, after the president has named a nominee, interest groups opposed to the nomination mobilize opposition in the media, among the public, and in the Senate. Republicans severely criticized Obama's nomination of Sonia Sotomayor in 2009 and Elena Kagan in 2010, though both were ultimately confirmed by the Senate. In 2016, however, as we saw in the chapter opening, Republicans refused to act on Obama's nomination of Merrick Garland. In 2017 newly elected President Trump secured the appointment of a conservative, Neil Gorsuch, and Republicans used their Senate majority to change the rules and prevent a Democratic filibuster.

TABLE 13.1
. . . .

Supreme Court Justices, 2020*
(in Order of Seniority)

NAME	YEAR OF BIRTH	LAW SCHOOL ATTENDED	PRIOR EXPERIENCE	APPOINTED BY	YEAR OF APPOINTMENT
Clarence Thomas	1948	Yale	Federal judge	G. H. W. Bush	1991
Stephen Breyer	1938	Harvard	Federal judge	Clinton	1994
John Roberts, Jr. (Chief Justice)	1955	Harvard	Federal judge	G. W. Bush	2005
Samuel Alito	1950	Yale	Federal judge	G. W. Bush	2006
Sonia Sotomayor	1954	Yale	Federal judge	Obama	2009
Elena Kagan	1960	Harvard	Solicitor general	Obama	2010
Neil Gorsuch	1967	Harvard	Federal judg	Trump	2017
Brett Kavanaugh	1965	Yale	Federal judge	Trump	2018
Amy Coney Barrett	1972	Notre Dame	Federal judge	Trump	2020

*As of October 2020.

In 2018, President Trump nominated the judge Brett Kavanaugh to replace retiring justice Anthony Kennedy. The Kavanaugh nomination touched off one of the most intense political struggles in recent American history when three women accused Kavanaugh of sexual impropriety from high school and college. Kavanaugh vehemently denied the allegations. Democrats argued that Kavanaugh was unfit to serve on the Court, while Republicans asserted that the charges against him had been invented for political reasons. An FBI investigation failed to shed light on the allegations, and Kavanaugh was confirmed, receiving the votes of all but one Republican and only one Democrat.[5] In September 2020, the death of Ruth Bader Ginsburg gave President Trump an opportunity to appoint a third Supreme Court justice. With only weeks remaining before the presidential election, Trump nominated former Notre Dame law professor and federal appeals court judge Amy Coney Barrett to replace Ginsburg. Republicans used their Senate majority to expedite the confirmation process and Justice Barrett was duly sworn in on October 26, 2020, just days before the presidential election. Her appointment solidified the Court's conservative majority.

The Power of the Supreme Court Is Judicial Review

Explain the Supreme Court's judicial review of national law

The term *judicial review* refers to the power of the judiciary to examine actions undertaken by the legislative and executive branches and, if necessary, invalidate them if it finds them unconstitutional.

JUDICIAL REVIEW OF ACTS OF CONGRESS

The Constitution does not explicitly give the Supreme Court the power of **judicial review** over congressional enactments, although the idea was discussed at the Constitutional Convention. Some delegates expected the courts to exercise this power, while others were "departmentalists," believing that each branch of the new government would interpret the Constitution as it applied to that branch's own actions, with the judiciary mainly ensuring that individuals did not suffer injustices.

> **judicial review** the power of the courts to review actions of the legislative and executive branches and, if necessary, declare them invalid or unconstitutional; the Supreme Court asserted this power in *Marbury v. Madison* (1803)

Ambiguity over the framers' intentions was settled in 1803 in the case of *Marbury v. Madison.*[6] This case arose after Thomas Jefferson succeeded John Adams as president. Jefferson's secretary of state, James Madison, refused to deliver an official commission to William Marbury, who had been appointed to a minor office by Adams and approved by the Senate just before Adams left the presidency. Marbury petitioned the Supreme Court to order Madison to deliver the commission.

Jefferson and his allies did not believe that the Court had the power to issue such an order and might have resisted it. Chief Justice John Marshall was determined to assert the power of the judiciary but wanted to avoid a direct confrontation with the president. Accordingly, he turned down Marbury's petition but gave as his reason the unconstitutionality of the legislation upon which Marbury had based his claim. Thus, Marshall asserted the power of judicial review but did so in a way that would not provoke a battle with Jefferson. The Supreme Court's decision in this case established the power of judicial review.

The Court's legal power to review acts of Congress has not been seriously questioned since 1803. One reason for that is that the Supreme Court makes a self-conscious effort to give acts of Congress an interpretation that will make them constitutional. For example, in its 2012 decision upholding the constitutionality of the Affordable Care Act, the Court agreed with the many legal scholars who had argued that the Congress had no power under the Constitution's commerce clause to order Americans to purchase health insurance. But, rather than invalidate the act, the Court declared that the law's requirement that all Americans purchase insurance was actually a tax and, thus, represented a constitutionally acceptable use of Congress's power to levy taxes.[7]

In more than two centuries, the Court has concluded that fewer than 160 acts of Congress directly violated the Constitution.[8] These cases are often highly controversial.

JUDICIAL REVIEW OF STATE ACTIONS

The power of the Supreme Court to review state legislation or other state action to determine its constitutionality is also not explicitly granted by the Constitution. But the logic of the **supremacy clause** of Article VI, which declares the Constitution itself and laws made under its authority to be the supreme law of the land, is very strong. Furthermore, in the Judiciary Act of 1789, Congress conferred on the Supreme Court the power to reverse state constitutions and laws whenever they are clearly in conflict with the U.S. Constitution, federal laws, or treaties.[9] This power gives the Supreme Court appellate jurisdiction over all the millions of cases that American courts handle each year.

supremacy clause Article VI of the Constitution, which states that laws passed by the national government and all treaties are the supreme law of the land and superior to all laws adopted by any state or any subdivision

The supremacy clause not only established the federal Constitution, statutes, and treaties as the "supreme Law of the Land" but also provided that "the Judges in every State shall be bound thereby, any Thing in the Constitution or Laws of the State to the Contrary notwithstanding." Under this authority, the Supreme Court has

The courts may be called on to review the actions of the president. After President Trump's "travel ban" was implemented in early 2017, many court cases challenged this policy, and eventually one case was tried before the Supreme Court. In a 5–4 decision, the Court upheld the travel ban, sparking outrage from Democratic lawmakers like Representative Joe Kennedy III (Mass.).

Courts in Comparison

Constitutional courts (courts with the power of judicial review) aim to preserve judicial independence, as they play an important role in checking executive and legislative overreach. Different countries have sought to balance the need for judicial independence with having a more responsive court. Here we see that countries have very diverse approaches to the selection and composition of their courts, including in how many justices serve, how long they serve, and who is responsible for appointing them.

1. How does the United States compare with other countries when it comes to term limits, or lack thereof, for judges? What are the benefits and drawbacks to having term limits for judges?
2. Why might some countries choose to have larger courts than others?
3. We see a variety of systems for appointing judges, including some where only one branch appoints them, others where multiple branches each appoint some judges, and still others, such as the United States, where one branch nominates judges and a second branch confirms them. Which system do you prefer, and why?

NAME	TERM LIMITS	MANDATORY RETIREMENT AGE	SIZE	HOW SELECTED?
Chilean Constitutional Court	9	—	9	Each branch appoints some
French Constitutional Council	9	—	9	Each branch appoints some
German Constitutional Court	12	68	18	Legislature
High Court of Australia	Life	70	7	Executive
Indian Supreme Court	Life	65	28	Executive
South African Constitutional Court	12	70	11	Executive
South Korean Constitutional Court	6	65	9	Each branch appoints some
Supreme Court of Canada	Life	75	9	Executive
Supreme Federal Court of Brazil	Life	75	11	Executive with Legislative confirmation
United States Supreme Court	Life	—	9	Executive with Legislative confirmation

SOURCE: CIA World Factbook, www.cia.gov/index.html (accessed 8/12/19).

frequently overturned state constitutional provisions or statutes, state court decisions, and local ordinances it finds in violation of rights or privileges guaranteed under the federal Constitution or federal statutes.

One realm in which the Court constantly monitors state conduct is that of law enforcement. Over the years, the Supreme Court has developed a number of principles to ensure that police conduct does not violate constitutional liberties. These principles, however, must often be updated to keep pace with changes in technology. In a 2012 decision, the Supreme Court found that police use of a GPS tracker— a device invented more than 200 years after the adoption of the Bill of Rights— constituted a "search" as defined by the Fourth Amendment.[10] And in the 2014 case of *Riley v. California*, the Court held that the police could not undertake a warrantless search of the digital contents of a cell phone—another device hardly imagined by the framers.[11]

JUDICIAL REVIEW OF FEDERAL AGENCY ACTIONS

Although Congress makes the law, to administer the thousands of programs it has enacted it must delegate power to the president and to a huge bureaucracy. For example, if Congress wishes to improve air quality, it cannot anticipate all the conditions that may arise with respect to that general goal. Inevitably, it must delegate to the executive substantial discretionary power to make judgments about the best ways to bring about improved air quality in the face of changing circumstances. Thus, almost any congressional program will result in thousands upon thousands of pages of administrative regulations developed by executive agencies.

Over the past two centuries, a number of court decisions have dealt with the scope of the delegation of power. Courts have also had to decide whether regulations adopted by federal agencies are consistent with Congress's express or implied intent.

JUDICIAL REVIEW AND PRESIDENTIAL POWER

The federal courts are also called on to review the actions of the president. On many occasions, members of Congress as well as individuals and groups have challenged presidential orders and actions in the federal courts. In recent years, the judiciary has usually upheld assertions of presidential power in such realms as foreign policy, war and emergency powers, legislative power, and administrative authority.[12] In 2004, however, in two of three cases involving President George W. Bush's antiterrorism initiatives, the Supreme Court appeared to place some limits on presidential authority.

One important case was *Hamdi v. Rumsfeld*.[13] Yaser Esam Hamdi, apparently a Taliban soldier, was captured by American forces in Afghanistan and brought to the United States. Hamdi was classified as an "enemy combatant" and denied civil rights, including the right to counsel, despite the fact that he was an American-born citizen. In 2004 the Supreme Court ruled that Hamdi was entitled to a lawyer and "a fair opportunity to rebut the government's factual assertions."

The Court asserted that it could review and place some constraints on the president's power, but it also affirmed that the president had unilateral power to declare individuals, including U.S. citizens, enemy combatants, who could be detained by federal authorities under adverse legal circumstances.

Judicial review of presidential actions is not limited to presidential war powers and the realm of terrorism. In 2014 the Supreme Court upheld a lower-court ruling that President Obama had violated the Constitution when he made so-called recess appointments to the National Labor Relations Board in order to avoid the need to secure Senate confirmation. Recess appointments are customarily used only when the Senate adjourns at the end of the year, but the president had made the appointments in question when the Senate had recessed for only 3 days. A recess of less than 10 days was "presumptively too short" to justify a recess appointment.[14]

In a 2018 decision, however, the Court upheld the use of presidential power.[15] Through an executive order, President Trump had prohibited travel into the United States by people from several Muslim-majority countries. The Court held that the president had broad authority, given by statute, to determine that certain travelers might pose a risk to the security of the United States. In July 2020, the Court decided two cases that affected presidential power.[16] The decisions ultimately did not require President Trump to make his tax records public, which his critics have demanded since his election in 2016. However, they did allow for the possibility that lower courts could require President Trump make his tax records public.

Most Cases Reach the Supreme Court by Appeal

| Describe the process by which cases are considered and decided by the Supreme Court |

Given the millions of legal disputes that arise every year, the Supreme Court could not possibly do its job if it were not able to control the flow of cases and its own caseload. Over the years, the courts have developed specific rules that govern which cases within their jurisdiction they will and will not hear. These rules of access can be broken down into three major categories: case or controversy, standing, and mootness.

ACCESSING THE COURT

Article III of the Constitution and Supreme Court decisions define judicial power as extending only to "cases and controversies." This means that the case before a court must be an actual controversy, not a hypothetical one, with two truly adversarial parties. The courts have interpreted this language to mean that they do not have the power to render advisory opinions to legislatures or agencies about the constitutionality of proposed laws or regulations. Furthermore, even after a law is enacted, the courts will generally refuse to consider its constitutionality until it is actually applied.

Parties to a case must also have **standing**—that is, they must show that they have a substantial stake in the outcome of the case. The traditional requirement for standing has been to show injury to oneself; that injury can be personal, economic, or even aesthetic, such as a neighbor's building a high fence that blocks one's view of the ocean. In order for a group or class of people to have standing, each member must show specific injury. This means that a general interest in the environment, for instance, does not provide a group with sufficient basis for standing.

The Supreme Court also uses a third criterion in determining whether it will hear a case: that of **mootness**. In theory, this requirement disqualifies cases that are brought too late—after the relevant facts have changed or the problem has been resolved by other means. The criterion of mootness, however, is subject to the discretion of the courts, which have begun to relax it, particularly in cases where a situation that has been resolved is likely to come up again. In the abortion case *Roe v. Wade*, for example, the Supreme Court rejected the lower court's argument that because the pregnancy in question had already come to term, the case was moot. The Court agreed to hear the case because no pregnancy was likely to outlast the lengthy appeals process.[17]

The Supreme Court is often likely to accept cases that involve conflicting decisions by the federal circuit courts, important questions of civil rights or civil liberties, or appeals by the federal government. Ultimately, however, the question of which cases to accept can come down to the preferences and priorities of the justices. If a group of justices believes that the Court should intervene in a particular area of policy or politics, the justices are likely to look for a case or cases that will serve as vehicles for doing so.

Writs Most cases reach the Supreme Court through a **writ of certiorari**, an order to a lower court to deliver the records of a particular case to be reviewed for legal errors. The term *certiorari* is sometimes shortened to *cert*, and cases deserving certiorari are referred to as "certworthy." An individual who loses in a lower federal court or state court and wants the Supreme Court to review the decision has 90 days to file a petition for a writ of certiorari with the clerk of the U.S. Supreme Court. Petitions for thousands of cases are filed with the Court every year (see Figure 13.3).

Since 1972 most of the justices have participated in a "certiorari pool," in which they make recommendations for cases to be placed on a "discuss list," which is circulated by the chief justice. If a case is not placed on the discuss list, it is automatically denied certiorari.

Cases placed on the discuss list are considered and voted on during the justices' closed-door conference. For certiorari to be granted, four justices must

FIGURE 13.3

Cases Filed in the U.S. Supreme Court, 1938–2018 Terms*

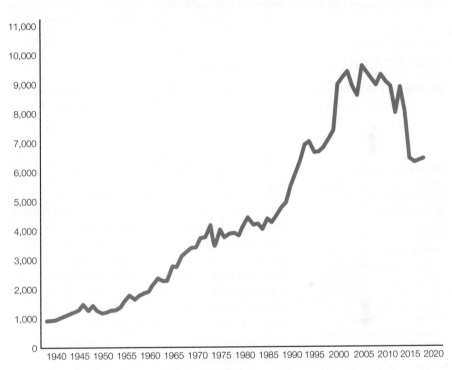

NUMBER OF CASES FILED PER YEAR

*Number of cases filed in term starting in year indicated.
SOURCES: Years 1938–69, 1970–83, 1984–99: reprinted with permission from *The United States Law Week* (Washington, DC: Bureau of National Affairs) (copyright © Bureau of National Affairs Inc.); 2000–05: U.S. Bureau of the Census, *Statistical Abstract of the United States*; 2006–07: Office of the Clerk, Supreme Court of the United States; and Supreme Court of the United States, Cases on Docket, www.uscourts.gov; Supreme Court, 2018 Year-End Report on the Federal Judiciary, www.supremecourt .govcou (accessed 10/7/20).

be convinced that the case satisfies rule 10 of the Rules of the Supreme Court of the United States, which states that certiorari is to be granted only when there are special and compelling reasons. These include conflicting decisions by two or more circuit courts, by circuit courts and state courts of last resort, or by two or more state courts of last resort; decisions by circuit courts on matters of federal law that should be settled by the Supreme Court; and a circuit court decision on an important question that conflicts with previous Supreme Court decisions.

Few cases are able to gain the support of four justices needed for certiorari. In recent sessions, the Court has granted it to barely more than 80 petitioners each year—about 1 percent of those seeking a Supreme Court review.

A handful of cases reach the Supreme Court through avenues other than certiorari. One of these is the writ of certification, which can be used when a U.S. Court of Appeals asks the Supreme Court for instructions on a point of law that has never been decided. A second alternative avenue is the writ of appeal, which is used to appeal the decision of a three-judge district court.

BEYOND THE JUDGES: KEY PLAYERS IN THE FEDERAL COURT PROCESS

In addition to the judges, other actors play important roles in how (and which) cases proceed through the federal courts: the solicitor general and federal law clerks.

solicitor general the top government lawyer in all cases before the Supreme Court where the government is a party

amicus curiae literally, "friend of the court"; individuals or groups who are not parties to a lawsuit but who seek to assist the Supreme Court in reaching a decision by presenting additional briefs

The Solicitor General If any single person has greater influence than individual judges over the federal courts, it is the solicitor general of the United States. The solicitor general is the third-ranking official in the Justice Department (below the attorney general and the deputy attorney general) but is the top government lawyer in virtually all cases before the Supreme Court in which the government is a party. More than half the Supreme Court's total workload consists of cases under the direct charge of the solicitor general, whose actions are not reviewed by any higher authority in the executive branch.

The solicitor general exercises especially strong influence by screening cases that any federal agency wishes to appeal to the Supreme Court.[18] Agency heads may lobby the president or otherwise try to circumvent the solicitor general, and a few of the independent agencies have a statutory right to make direct appeals, but requests that lack the solicitor general's support are seldom accepted for review by the Court.

The solicitor general can enter a case even when the federal government is not a direct party to it by writing an **amicus curiae** ("friend of the court") brief. A friend of the court is not a direct party to a case but has a vital interest in its outcome. Thus, when the government has such an interest, the solicitor general can file an amicus brief or a federal court can

FOR CRITICAL ANALYSIS ▶

1. What are the advantages of nonpartisan elections to select judges? Which method of selection do you think is the best, and why?

2. Are there regional patterns in how judges are selected? If so, why do you think that is?

Comparing How States Select Judges

States vary in their methods for selecting judges. Some elect judges through partisan election, where voters generally decide whom to vote for based on party affiliation. Most states employ a merit selection method through nominating commissions that make recommendations to the governor. Other states have judges elected by the governor without nominating commissions. Thirteen states elect their judges in nonpartisan elections, meaning that the role of political parties in judicial elections is minimized. The state legislature chooses judges in the remaining two states.

Judicial Selection Methods by State, 2017

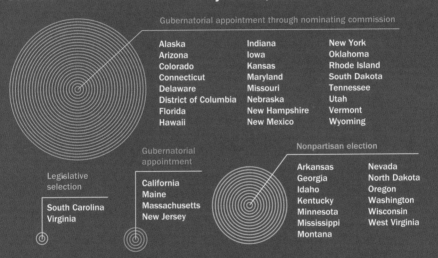

Gubernatorial appointment through nominating commission

Alaska	Indiana	New York
Arizona	Iowa	Oklahoma
Colorado	Kansas	Rhode Island
Connecticut	Maryland	South Dakota
Delaware	Missouri	Tennessee
District of Columbia	Nebraska	Utah
Florida	New Hampshire	Vermont
Hawaii	New Mexico	Wyoming

Gubernatorial appointment

California
Maine
Massachusetts
New Jersey

Legislative selection

South Carolina
Virginia

Nonpartisan election

Arkansas	Nevada
Georgia	North Dakota
Idaho	Oregon
Kentucky	Washington
Minnesota	Wisconsin
Mississippi	West Virginia
Montana	

Judicial Selection Methods: A Regional View

- Gubernatorial appointment through nominating commission
- Gubernatorial appointment
- Nonpartisan election
- Partisan election
- Legislative selection

Partisan election

Alabama
Illinois
Louisiana
Michigan
North Carolina
Ohio
Pennsylvania
Texas

SOURCES: American Judicature Society, Judicial Selection in the States, www.judicialselection.us/; and IAALS, the Institute for the Advancement of the American Legal System at the University of Denver, "Selection and Retention of State Judges," *Texas Bar Journal* (February 2016): 92–97.

invite such a brief because it wants an opinion in writing. Other interested parties may file briefs as well.

In addition to exercising substantial control over the flow of cases, the solicitor general can shape the arguments used before the federal courts. Indeed, the Supreme Court tends to give special attention to the way the solicitor general characterizes the issues.

Law Clerks Every federal judge employs law clerks to research legal issues and assist with the preparation of opinions. Each Supreme Court justice is assigned four clerks, almost always honors graduates of the nation's top law schools. A clerkship with a Supreme Court justice is a great honor and generally indicates that the fortunate individual is likely to reach the very top of the legal profession. The work of the Supreme Court clerks is a closely guarded secret, but it is likely that some justices rely heavily on their clerks for advice in writing opinions and in deciding whether the Court should hear specific cases. A former law clerk to the late justice Harry Blackmun charged that Supreme Court justices yielded "excessive power to immature, ideologically driven clerks, who in turn use that power to manipulate their bosses."[19]

LOBBYING FOR ACCESS: INTERESTS AND THE COURT

While the Court exercises discretion over which cases it will review, groups and forces in society try various ways to persuade the justices to listen to their grievances. Lawyers representing interest groups try to choose the proper client and the proper case so that the issues in question are most dramatically and appropriately portrayed. When possible, they also pick a court with a sympathetic judge in which to bring the case. Sometimes they even wait for an appropriate political climate. They must also attempt to develop a proper record at the trial court level, one that includes some constitutional arguments and even, when possible, legal errors on the part of the trial court.

One of the most effective strategies in getting cases accepted for review by the Supreme Court is to bring the same type of suit in more than one circuit (that is, to develop a "pattern of cases") in the hope that inconsistent rulings will improve the chance of a review. The two most notable users of the pattern-of-cases strategy in recent years have been the National Association for the Advancement of Colored People (NAACP) and the American Civil Liberties Union (ACLU).

THE SUPREME COURT'S PROCEDURES

The Supreme Court's decision to accept a case is the beginning of what can be a lengthy and complex process (see Figure 13.4). After a petition is filed and certiorari is granted, the Court considers the reasoning on both sides as presented in briefs and oral argument, the justices discuss the case in conference, and opinions are carefully drafted.

FIGURE 13.4

Time Line of a Supreme Court Case

This calendar of events in the case of *Janus v. American Federation of State, County, and Municipal Employees* illustrates the steps of the process a case goes through as it moves through the Supreme Court. The total time from petition to the Supreme Court to the decision is just over one year, although the initial case was filed years ago in a lower court.

June 6, 2017

Petition for a writ of certiorari filed.

July 7, 2017

Filing of briefs and amicus curiae briefs in support of the petitioner.

August 11, 2017

Brief of respondent American Federation of State, County, and Municipal Employees, Council 31 in opposition filed.

August 30, 2017

The case is distributed for conference.

September 28, 2017

The petition (certiorari) is granted.

December 20, 2017

Date for oral argument is set for February 26, 2018.

December 2017

Briefs and amicus curiae briefs are filed on behalf of petitioner.

January 2018

Briefs and amicus curiae briefs are filed on behalf of respondent.

February 26, 2018

Oral argument of one hour

June 27, 2018

Decision

briefs written documents in which attorneys explain, using case precedents, why the court should find in favor of their client

oral argument the stage in the Supreme Court procedure in which attorneys for both sides appear before the Court to present their positions and answer questions posed by the justices

opinion the written explanation of the Supreme Court's decision in a particular case

Briefs First, the attorneys on both sides must prepare **briefs**, written documents in which the attorneys explain why the Court should rule in favor of their client. Briefs are filled with references to precedents chosen to show that other courts have frequently ruled in the same way the attorneys are requesting that the Supreme Court rule. The attorneys for both sides muster the most compelling precedents they can in support of their arguments.

As the attorneys prepare their briefs, they often ask sympathetic interest groups to file amicus curiae briefs that support their claims. Often, dozens of briefs will be filed on each side of a major case. Amicus filings are one of the primary methods used by interest groups to lobby the Court.

Oral Argument The next stage of a case is **oral argument**, in which an attorney for each side appears before the Court to present his position and answer the justices' questions. Each attorney has only a half hour to present a case, and this time includes interruptions for questions. Certain justices, such as the late Antonin Scalia, are known to interrupt attorneys dozens of times. Others, such as Clarence Thomas, seldom ask questions.

For an attorney, the opportunity to argue a case before the Supreme Court is an honor and a mark of professional distinction. It can also be harrowing, as when justices interrupt a carefully prepared presentation. Oral argument can be very important to the outcome of a case because it allows justices to understand better the heart of the case and to raise questions that might not have been addressed in the opposing sides' briefs. It is not uncommon for justices to go beyond the strictly legal issues and ask opposing counsel to discuss the implications of the case for the Court and the nation at large.

The Conference Following oral argument, the Court discusses the case in its Wednesday or Friday conference, a strictly private meeting that no outsiders are permitted to attend. The chief justice presides over the conference and speaks first; the other justices follow in order of seniority. The justices discuss the case and eventually reach a decision on the basis of a majority vote. If the Court is divided, a number of votes may be taken before a final decision is reached. As the case is discussed, justices may try to influence or change one another's opinions, a process that may result in compromise decisions.

Opinion Writing After a decision has been reached, one of the members of the majority is assigned to write the **opinion**. This assignment, which is made by the chief justice or by the most senior justice in the majority if the chief justice is on the losing side, can make a significant difference to the interpretation of a decision. Every opinion of the Supreme Court sets a major precedent for future cases throughout the judicial system. Lawyers and judges in the lower courts will examine it carefully to determine the Supreme Court's intent, since differences in wording and emphasis can have important implications.

One of the more dramatic instances of the importance of opinion assignment occurred in 1944, when Chief Justice Harlan F. Stone chose Justice Felix Frankfurter to write the opinion in the "White primary" case *Smith v. Allwright*.[20] The chief justice believed that this sensitive case, which overturned the southern practice of prohibiting Black participation in nominating primaries, required the efforts of the most brilliant and scholarly member of the Court. But the day after Stone made the assignment, Justice Robert H. Jackson wrote a letter to him urging a change of assignment on the grounds that Frankfurter, a foreign-born Jew from New England, would not win over the South with his opinion, regardless of its brilliance. Stone accepted the advice and substituted Justice Stanley Reed, an American-born Protestant from Kentucky.

Once the majority opinion is drafted, it is circulated to the other justices. Some members of the majority may wish to emphasize a particular point in the majority opinion. For that purpose, they draft a **concurring opinion**, called a *regular concurrence*. In other instances, one or more justices may agree with the majority decision but disagree with the rationale for it that is presented in the majority opinion. These justices may draft *special concurrences*, explaining their own rationale and how it differs from the majority's.

Dissent Justices who disagree with the majority decision may choose to publicize the character of their disagreement in the form of a **dissenting opinion**, which is generally assigned by the senior justice among the dissenters. Dissents can be used to express opposition to an outcome or to signal to the losing side that its position is supported by at least some members of the Court. Because there is no need to please a majority, dissenting opinions can be more eloquent and less guarded than majority opinions.

concurring opinion a written opinion by a judge agreeing with the majority opinion but giving different reasons for his or her decision

The current Supreme Court often produces 5–4 decisions, with dissenters writing long and detailed opinions that, they hope, will help them persuade a swing justice to join their side in future similar cases. Dissenting justices will sometimes read their dissents aloud from the bench to dramatize their concerns.

dissenting opinion a decision written by a justice in the minority in a particular case, in which the justice wishes to express his or her reasoning in the case

Dissent plays a special role in the work and impact of the Court because it amounts to an appeal to lawyers all over the country to keep bringing similar cases. Ironically, a dependable way an individual justice can exercise influence on the Court is to write an effective dissent, which influences the future flow of cases through the Court and the arguments that lawyers will use in later cases. Even more important, dissent points out that the Court's ruling is the opinion only of the majority—and one day the majority might go the other way.

Supreme Court Decisions Are Influenced by Activism and Ideology

> **Describe the factors that influence Court decisions**

Like other actors in government, justices are influenced by institutional concerns, prior experience, and personal philosophy.

INFLUENCES ON SUPREME COURT DECISION-MAKING

The Supreme Court explains its decisions in terms of law and precedent. But it is the Court itself that decides what the laws actually mean and what importance the precedent will actually have. Throughout its history, the Court has shaped and reshaped the law.

In the late nineteenth and early twentieth centuries, for example, the Supreme Court held that the Constitution, law, and precedent permitted racial segregation in the United States. Beginning in the 1950s, however, the Court found that the Constitution prohibited segregation and that the use of racial categories in legislation was always suspect. By the 1970s and '80s the Court once again held that the Constitution permitted the use of racial categories—when they were needed to help members of minority groups achieve full participation in American society. Since the 1990s the Court has retreated from this position, too, indicating that governmental efforts to provide extra help to racial minorities could represent an unconstitutional infringement on the rights of the majority.

Institutional Interests The Supreme Court's justices are acutely aware of the Court's place in history, and their desire to protect its power and reputation for integrity can sometimes influence judicial thinking. During the 1935–36 term, for example, the Court struck down several of President Franklin Roosevelt's New Deal programs in a series of 5–4 votes. Furious, the president responded by proposing a reform plan that would have enlarged the Court to as many as 15 justices. Roosevelt hoped to pack the Court with his own appointees and, thus, win future cases over New Deal programs. Justice Owen Roberts, one of the five justices who had been voting against the president's initiatives, then made a sudden reversal, voting in favor of an important New Deal policy he had been expected to oppose. The media dubbed Roberts's shift "the switch in time that saved nine."

More recently, Chief Justice John Roberts seemed to have institutional concerns in mind when he surprised fellow conservatives by casting the deciding vote in favor of the constitutionality of the Affordable Care Act in 2012 and again in 2015. The Court's conservative majority had come under increasing political fire for its positions on such matters as campaign finance and affirmative action. Roberts, according to one commentator, saw himself as "uniquely entrusted with the custodianship of the Court's legitimacy, reputation, and stature" and was determined to show that the Court stood above mere political ideology.[21]

Since the retirement of Justice Anthony Kennedy, Chief Justice John Roberts has sometimes served as a swing vote on the Court to protect the precedents set by past decisions. In 2020, he ruled with the liberal justices to reject the Trump administration's suit against DACA, a program that protects young undocumented immigrants from deportation.

In 2020, Chief Justice Roberts once again demonstrated his concern for the reputation of the institution of the Court. He angered conservatives and President Trump, in particular, when he sided with the Court's liberals in supporting transgender rights, in blocking a restrictive state abortion law, and in blocking the administration's efforts to proceed quickly with the deportation of young undocumented immigrants—the so-called DREAMers. In the immigration and abortion cases, Roberts cast the deciding fifth vote. Trump responded angrily, declaring that the Supreme Court needed new justices.

Activism and Restraint Judicial philosophy also plays a role in the decisions of all judges, including those on the Supreme Court. One element of judicial philosophy is the issue of activism versus restraint. Over the years, some justices have believed that courts should interpret the Constitution according to the stated intentions of its framers and defer to the views of Congress when interpreting federal statutes. Justice Felix Frankfurter, for example, advocated judicial deference to legislative bodies and avoidance of the "political thicket" in which the Court would entangle itself by deciding questions that were essentially political rather than legal in character. Some, but not all, advocates of **judicial restraint** are also called "strict constructionists" because they look strictly to the words of the Constitution in interpreting its meaning.

> **judicial restraint** judicial philosophy whose adherents refuse to go beyond the clear words of the Constitution in interpreting the document's meaning

judicial activism judicial philosophy that posits that the Court should go beyond the words of the Constitution or a statute to consider the broader societal implications of its decisions

The alternative to restraint is **judicial activism**. Activist judges such as Chief Justice Earl Warren believed that the Court should go beyond the words of the Constitution or a statute to consider the broader societal implications of its decisions. Such judges sometimes strike out in new directions, putting forth new interpretations or inventing new legal and constitutional concepts when they believe these to be socially desirable. For example, Justice Harry Blackmun's opinion in *Roe v. Wade* was based on a constitutional right to privacy that is not found in the words of the Constitution but was, rather, from the Court's prior decision in *Griswold v. Connecticut*.[22] Blackmun and the other members of the majority in the *Roe* case argued that the right to privacy was implied by other constitutional provisions.

Activism and restraint can overlap with but are not always the same as liberalism and conservatism. For example, conservative politicians often castigate "liberal activist" judges and call for the appointment of conservative judges who will refrain from reinterpreting the law. But the Supreme Court from 1986 to 2005, dominated by conservatives under Chief Justice William Rehnquist, was among the most activist in American history, particularly in such areas as federalism and election law.

The Roberts Court is continuing along the same route. For example, in the 2014 case of *McCutcheon v. Federal Election Commission*, the Court struck down one of the major remaining elements of Congress's efforts to regulate campaign finance. The Court's five more conservative justices said that limits on how much individuals could contribute in any given election were a restraint on free speech.[23] This decision could be described as "activist" because it broadens the interpretation of "speech" and overturns congressional legislation that has significant public support. As these examples illustrate, a judge may be philosophically conservative and believe in strict construction of the Constitution but also believe that the courts must play an active and energetic role in policy making, if necessary striking down acts of Congress to ensure that the intent of the framers is fulfilled.

Political Ideology and Partisanship The philosophy of activism versus restraint is indeed sometimes a smoke screen for political ideology, and justices' liberal or conservative attitudes and Democratic or Republican leanings play an important role in their decisions.[24] In the past, liberal judges have often been activists, willing to use the law to achieve social and political change, whereas conservatives have been associated with judicial restraint. Democrats who opposed the appointment of Justice Amy Coney Barrett to the Court in 2020 were suspicious of her commitment to the principle of judicial restraint. They feared that Barrett might be a conservative activist who would work to undo Obamacare as well as the Court's long-standing positions on abortion.

From the 1950s to the 1980s the Supreme Court took a liberal role in such areas as civil rights, civil liberties, abortion, voting rights, and police procedures. For example, it was more responsible than any other governmental institution for breaking down America's system of racial segregation. In the following decades, however, the conservative justices appointed by Presidents Ronald Reagan, George H. W.

Bush, George W. Bush, and Donald Trump became the dominant bloc on the Court and moved the Court to the right on a number of issues, including affirmative action and abortion.

The political struggles of recent years amply illustrate the importance of judicial ideology. Is abortion a fundamental right or a criminal activity? How much separation must there be between church and state? Does application of the Voting Rights Act to increase minority representation constitute a violation of the rights of Whites? The answers to these questions cannot be found in the words of the Constitution. They must be located, instead, in the hearts and minds of the judges who interpret that text.

Judicial philosophy, ideology, and institutional interest all influence the thinking of justices. In the end, however, the Supreme Court is a court of law and must pay heed to statutes and legal precedent. A decision that cannot be justified by law and precedent cannot be issued. To ignore the law would be to undermine the rule of law and to destroy the constitutional structure in which the Supreme Court occupies such a prominent place.

JUDICIAL POWER AND POLITICS

One of the most important institutional changes to occur in the United States over the last 75 years has been the striking transformation of the role and power of the federal courts, and of the Supreme Court in particular. Understanding how this transformation came about is the key to understanding the contemporary role of the courts in America.

Traditional Limitations on the Federal Courts For much of American history, the power of the federal courts was subject to a number of limitations.[25] First, unlike other governmental institutions, the courts are "passive" institutions in that they cannot exercise power on their own initiative. Judges must wait until a case is brought to them before they can make authoritative decisions.

Second, courts were traditionally limited in the kind of remedies they could provide to those who won cases. In general, courts acted to offer relief or assistance only to individuals and not to broad social classes.

Third, courts lacked enforcement powers and had to rely on executive or state agencies to ensure compliance with their rulings. If the executive or state agencies were unwilling to do so, judicial decisions could go unheeded, as when President Andrew Jackson declined to enforce Chief Justice John Marshall's 1832 order that the state of Georgia release two missionaries it had arrested on Cherokee lands. Marshall asserted that the state had no right to enter the lands without the Cherokees' assent.[26] Jackson is reputed to have said, "John Marshall has made his decision, now let him enforce it."

A fourth limitation on the federal courts is that because their judges are appointed by the president and require Senate confirmation, the president and Congress can shape their composition and ultimately, perhaps, the character of judicial decisions.

Finally, Congress has the power to change both the size and the jurisdiction of the Supreme Court and other federal courts. In many areas, federal courts obtain their jurisdiction not from the Constitution but from congressional statutes.

The Federal Judiciary: What Do You Think?

In their original conception, the framers intended the judiciary to be the institution that would protect individual liberty from the government. As we saw in Chapter 2, they believed that "tyranny of the majority" was a great threat to democracy, fearing that a popular majority, "united or actuated by some common impulse or passion," would "trample on the rules of justice."[27] For most of American history, the federal courts' most important decisions were those that protected the freedoms—to speak, worship, publish, vote, and attend school—of groups and individuals whose political views, religious beliefs, or racial or ethnic backgrounds made them unpopular. But today, Americans of all political persuasions seem to view the courts as useful instruments through which to pursue their policy goals. Conservatives want to ban abortion and help business maintain its profitability, whereas liberals want to enhance the power of workers in the workplace and reduce the role of private money in political campaigns.

★ These may all be noble goals, but they present a basic dilemma for students of American government. If the courts are simply one more set of policy-making institutions, who is left to protect the liberty of individuals? What would Mark Janus say about the role of the courts in American government?

★ Can you think of ways that Supreme Court decisions affect your life? For example, how might the Court's campaign-finance decisions affect who will govern the nation you inherit? How could its decisions on health care influence the type of care you receive and its cost? How will its decisions in the realm of immigration affect who will and will not be able to call themselves Americans? How might the Court's decision in Mark Janus's case against public-sector unions influence your future job and taxes?

★ Given what you know now, do you view the Court as the "least dangerous branch" or an "imperial judiciary"? What evidence do you see for each characterization?

STUDY GUIDE

Practice Quiz

1. What is the name for the body of law that deals with disputes in which no criminal violation is charged? *(p. 398)*
   a) civil law
   b) privacy law
   c) plea bargains
   d) household law
   e) common law

2. The legal principle that previous court decisions should apply as precedents in similar cases is known as *(p. 398)*
   a) habeas corpus.
   b) a writ of certiorari.
   c) stare decisis.
   d) the rule of four.
   e) senatorial courtesy.

3. Which courts hear the majority of all cases in the United States? *(pp. 399–400)*
   a) state courts
   b) appellate courts
   c) federal courts
   d) federal circuit courts
   e) the Supreme Court

4. Which of the following is not included in the original jurisdiction of the Supreme Court? *(pp. 400–401)*
   a) cases between the United States and one of the states
   b) cases brought by one state against citizens of another state or against a foreign country
   c) cases involving challenges to the constitutionality of state laws
   d) cases between two or more states
   e) cases involving foreign ambassadors or other ministers

5. The term *writ of habeas corpus* refers to *(p. 402)*
   a) a short, unsigned decision by an appellate court that rejects a petition to review the decision of a lower court.

   b) a criterion used by courts to screen cases that no longer require resolution.
   c) a decision of at least four of the nine Supreme Court justices to review a decision of a lower court.
   d) a court order to authorities to show cause for a prisoner's incarceration.
   e) a brief filed by the solicitor general when the federal government is not a direct litigant in a Supreme Court case.

6. The size of the Supreme Court is determined by *(p. 404)*
   a) the president.
   b) the chief justice.
   c) the Department of Justice.
   d) Congress.
   e) the Constitution.

7. The Supreme Court's decision in *Marbury v. Madison* was important because *(p. 407)*
   a) it invalidated state laws prohibiting interracial marriage.
   b) it ruled that the recitation of prayers in public schools is unconstitutional under the establishment clause of the First Amendment.
   c) it established that arrested people have the right to remain silent, the right to be informed that anything they say can be held against them, and the right to counsel before and during police interrogation.
   d) it provided an expansive definition of *commerce* under the interstate commerce clause.
   e) it established the power of judicial review.

8. Which of the following is *not* included as a "special and compelling" reason to hear a case under rule 10 of the Rules of the Supreme Court of the United States? *(p. 413)*
   a) The president of the United States authors an amicus curiae brief on the issue in question.
   b) A circuit court decision on the issue in question conflicts with previous Supreme Court decisions.
   c) There are conflicting decisions by two or more state courts of last resort on the issue in question.
   d) There are conflicting decisions between circuit courts and state courts of last resort on the issue in question.
   e) There are conflicting decisions by two or more circuit courts on the issue in question.

9. Which of the following play an important role in shaping the flow of cases heard by the Supreme Court? *(p. 414)*
   a) the attorney general and the secretary of state
   b) the solicitor general and federal law clerks
   c) the president and Congress
   d) state legislatures
   e) the federal district and circuit courts

10. Which of the following is a brief submitted to the Supreme Court by someone who is not a direct party to the case? *(p. 414)*
    a) amicus curiae brief
    b) writ of habeas corpus
    c) writ of certiorari
    d) ex post brief
    e) de jure brief

11. A dissenting opinion is written by *(p. 419)*
    a) the chief justice of the Supreme Court.
    b) a Supreme Court justice who agrees with the majority's ultimate decision but wishes to offer a different rationale or emphasis.
    c) a Supreme Court justice who disagrees with the majority decision.
    d) the solicitor general.
    e) a Supreme Court justice assigned by the chief justice.

12. If a justice looks strictly to the words of the Constitution in interpreting its meaning, he or she would be considered an advocate of which judicial philosophy? *(p. 421)*
    a) judicial restraint
    b) judicial activism
    c) *stare decisis*
    d) judicial liberalism
    e) judicial conservatism

Key Terms

criminal law *(p. 397)*

plaintiff *(p. 397)*

defendant *(p. 398)*

civil law *(p. 398)*

precedent *(p. 398)*

trial court *(p. 400)*

court of appeals *(p. 400)*

supreme court *(p. 400)*

plea bargain *(p. 400)*

jurisdiction *(p. 400)*

original jurisdiction *(p. 400)*

due process of law *(p. 402)*

writ of habeas corpus *(p. 402)*

chief justice *(p. 404)*

judicial review *(p. 407)*

supremacy clause *(p. 408)*

standing *(p. 412)*

mootness *(p. 412)*

writ of certiorari *(p. 412)*

solicitor general *(p. 414)*

amicus curiae *(p. 414)*

briefs *(p. 418)*

oral argument *(p. 418)*

opinion *(p. 418)*

concurring opinion *(p. 419)*

dissenting opinion *(p. 419)*

judicial restraint *(p. 421)*

judicial activism *(p. 422)*

chapter 14

Domestic Policy

WHAT GOVERNMENT DOES AND WHY IT MATTERS

To gain flexibility to care for her oldest son, who has a disability, C. Shonda Woods, of Yeadon, Pennsylvania, has worked as a contract worker for home health companies and as a driver for ride-hailing apps rather than in a traditional nine-to-five job. When her latest home health contract was cancelled and ride-hailing jobs dried up in March 2020 in the face of the coronavirus pandemic, she applied for unemployment insurance benefits. She was fortunate to be eligible—part-time, contract, and gig-economy workers are normally ineligible for unemployment compensation. But Congress passed several stimulus bills in 2020 to try to offset the pandemic's devastating economic effects. For individuals, the rescue legislation expanded unemployment insurance, provided direct one-time payments ($1,200 per adult, $500 per child), and allowed student-loan borrowers to defer payments through September 2020. Aid to businesses, meant to minimize layoffs and to prevent bankruptcies, included hundreds of billions in grants and loans. The stimulus bills also included direct aid for state and local governments, which faced

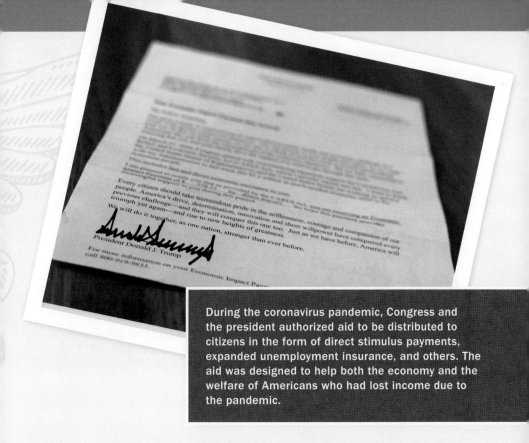

During the coronavirus pandemic, Congress and the president authorized aid to be distributed to citizens in the form of direct stimulus payments, expanded unemployment insurance, and others. The aid was designed to help both the economy and the welfare of Americans who had lost income due to the pandemic.

sharply increased health care spending but deep declines in tax revenue, and increased funding for hospitals and community health centers. Woods put her stimulus check toward her house and bills. But she had to wait to receive unemployment insurance, as the state's computer system had to be changed to enroll the newly eligible. "Everything was up in the air." She was told, "'You should see this.' 'This should happen at this point.' 'Should, should, should.'" The anxiety of waiting gave her stress-induced insomnia, which she tried to ward off with video games.[1]

American social policy has three main goals. It addresses the risks that people might face in their everyday lives: illness, disability, loss of income due to aging or, as in Wood's case, unemployment. It provides opportunity, such as student loans to expand access to higher education. And it seeks to alleviate poverty, the most controversial goal. Social policy contributes to the government's larger goals in economic policy: ensuring economic stability and growth, promoting business development, and protecting employees and consumers.

In this chapter, we will examine these two types of domestic public policy. Both social policy and economic policy have profound effects on societal resources and benefits: who gets what, and why.

CHAPTER GOALS

★ Describe how the government uses fiscal, monetary, and regulatory policies to influence the economy (pp. 431–38)

★ Explain the key debates in economic policy making (pp. 438–41)

★ Trace the history of government programs designed to promote economic security (pp. 441–45)

★ Describe how education, health, and housing policies try to advance equality of opportunity (pp. 445–51)

★ Explain how contributory, noncontributory, and tax expenditure programs benefit different groups of Americans (pp. 451–57)

The Government Shapes Economic Policy with Three Tools

> **Describe how the government uses fiscal, monetary, and regulatory policies to influence the economy**

The U.S. economy is the result of specific policies that have expanded American markets and sustained massive economic growth. The Constitution provides that Congress shall have the power "to lay and collect Taxes . . . to pay the Debts and provide for the common Defence and general Welfare . . . To borrow Money . . . To coin Money [and] regulate the Value thereof." These clauses of Article I, Section 8, are the constitutional sources of the fiscal and monetary policies of the national government.

The Constitution says nothing, however, about *how* these powers can be used. As it works to meet the multiple goals of economic policy, the federal government relies on a broad set of tools that has evolved over time. Decisions about which tools to use are not simply technical; they are highly political and reflect conflicts over whether the government should act at all and, if so, how.

FISCAL POLICIES

Fiscal policy includes the government's taxing and spending powers. Fiscal policy shapes the economy and can be used to counteract the business cycle, which is the pattern of highs and lows that nations' economies experience over time. For example, during economic slowdowns the government may decide to stimulate the economy by increasing spending, as it did during the coronavirus pandemic, or by reducing taxes. Conversely, if the economy is growing too fast, which might bring **inflation** (a consistent increase in prices), the government might cut back on spending or raise taxes. Through fiscal policy the government also influences the distribution of resources in the economy when it decides what programs to spend more or less on and which groups to tax at higher or lower rates.

Taxation During the nineteenth century, the scope of the federal government was quite modest, and most of its revenue came from **tariffs** on imported goods, and from excise taxes, which are taxes levied on specific products, such as tobacco and alcohol. As federal activities expanded in the twentieth century, the federal government added new sources of tax revenue, including the corporate income tax in 1909 and the individual income tax in 1913. At first only top earners paid the individual income tax; it became a tax that most households paid during World War II, when the government's revenue needs increased dramatically. With the creation of the Social Security system in 1935, social insurance taxes became an additional source of federal revenue.

The largest share of federal revenue today comes from the individual income tax. It accounts for

fiscal policy the government's use of taxing, monetary, and spending powers to manipulate the economy

inflation a consistent increase in the general level of prices

tariff a tax on imported goods

FIGURE 14.1

Federal Revenues by Type of Tax

The federal government collects revenue from a variety of different taxes. Most important is the individual income tax, which has grown over the last 50 years, now accounting for approximately 50 percent of federal revenue. Revenues from corporate income tax have fallen considerably over this time period, from 23 percent in 1966 to 7 percent in 2020. In the same period, taxes for social insurance and retirement have grown substantially. Does the federal government draw more of its revenue from progressive taxes or regressive taxes?

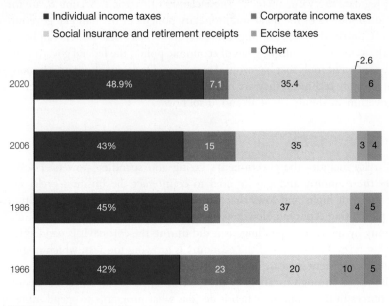

■ Individual income taxes   ■ Corporate income taxes
■ Social insurance and retirement receipts   ■ Excise taxes
■ Other

Year	Individual income taxes	Corporate income taxes	Social insurance and retirement receipts	Excise taxes	Other
2020	48.9%	7.1	35.4	2.6	6
2006	43%	15	35	3	4
1986	45%	8	37	4	5
1966	42%	23	20	10	5

NOTE: Data for 2020 are estimated.
SOURCE: Office of Management and Budget, "Table 2.2—Percentage Composition of Receipts by Source: 1934–2025," www.whitehouse.gov/omb/budget/Historicals (accessed 5/13/20).

nearly half of federal revenues. At the same time, social insurance taxes have risen as a share of federal revenues while corporate income taxes have declined significantly (see Figure 14.1).

redistribution a policy whose objective is to tax or spend in such a way as to reduce the disparities of wealth between the lowest and the highest income brackets

progressive taxation taxation that hits upper-income brackets more heavily

The federal tax system has several goals, including raising revenue for government operations, achieving some income **redistribution** (reducing gaps between the lowest and highest income groups), and providing incentives for activities policy makers deem desirable, such as investment. One of the most important features of the individual income tax is that it is a "progressive," or "graduated," tax, with the heaviest burden carried by those most able to pay. A tax is called **progressive** if people with higher incomes pay a greater

Global Tax Rates

Tax rates can be difficult to compare across countries. For example, some countries set different income tax rates for married people and those with children, whereas other countries levy similar tax rates regardless of marital or family status. Income taxes are just one form of tax that governments collect; they also collect sales tax, property tax, and Social Security contributions.

1. Why might a country want to have a different tax rate for a single person without children than for a married couple with a single wage earner, raising two children? What kinds of policy goals might a country be trying to achieve with different tax rates? What might be an argument for having the same tax rate regardless of marital or family status?

2. Do you believe a government should favor lowering taxes or collecting revenue to provide services? How much does your answer change depending on the quality of the services the government is providing its residents for those dollars?

Average Income Tax Rate on Average Wage, 2018

	SINGLE PERSON, NO CHILD	ONE-EARNER MARRIED COUPLE, TWO CHILDREN	INCOME TAX REVENUE AS A PERCENTAGE OF GDP, 2017
Australia	25%	25%	28%*
France	29	21	46
Germany	40	22	38
Japan	22	21	31*
Mexico	10	10	16
Republic of Korea	15	13	27
Sweden	25	25	44
Turkey	28	26	25
United Kingdom	23	23	33
United States	24	12	27

* Data are from 2016.

SOURCES: Organization for Economic Cooperation and Development, "All-In Average Personal Income Tax Rates at Average Wage by Family Type," Table I.6, 2018, and "Revenue Statistics," 2018, https://stats.oecd.org (accessed 7/17/19).

share of their income in tax. A tax is **regressive** if people with higher incomes pay a small share of their income in tax. The individual income tax is progressive because taxable income is divided into brackets, with higher tax rates imposed on higher brackets. For example, in 2020, a single person pays no tax on the first $12,000 of income. Then the next $9,875 is taxed at 10 percent, the next $30,250 at 12 percent, and so on through the top bracket, which taxes income above $518,400 at 37 percent.[2] In contrast, the Social Security tax is regressive. In 2020, Social Security law applied a tax of 6.2 percent on the first $137,700 of income for the retirement program.[3] This means that a person earning $137,700 pays $8,540 and a person making twice as much, $275,400, pays the same $8,540, a rate of 3.1 percent. And a CEO earning $5 million in income also pays the same $8,540, for a rate of 0.17 percent.

Over time the individual income tax and the corporate income tax have become less progressive. Tax cuts passed under President Reagan in the 1980s, President George W. Bush in the 2000s, and President Trump in 2017 reduced income taxes for most individuals and families, with the largest reductions going to the highest earners. The 2017 tax cut also lowered corporate and small business taxes substantially. Advocates of tax cuts directed toward high earners and businesses argue that such cuts will provide incentives for those individuals and companies to increase their investments in the economy and that the cuts will not harm federal revenues. Critics say such cuts will undermine the government's revenue-raising capacity and reduce redistribution.

Spending and Budgeting The federal government's power to spend is one of the most important tools of economic policy. Decisions about how much to spend affect the overall health of the economy. They also affect every aspect of American life, from the distribution of income to the availability of different modes of transportation to the level of education in society.

Government spending is sometimes used to counteract the effect of economic recessions, when the economy slows down and consumers and businesses spend less. Unlike state governments, most of which have to balance their budgets from year to year, the federal government can run a **budget deficit**, which means that government spending exceeds revenues, with the federal government borrowing the difference by selling government bonds on which the government pays interest. The sum of all federal government borrowing is called the **national debt**. The government used deficit spending to stimulate the economy during both the Great Recession that began in 2007 and the coronavirus pandemic of 2020.

Government spending can also incentivize certain behaviors, through subsidies and contracts. **Subsidies** are government grants of cash or other valuable

regressive taxation taxation that hits lower-income brackets more heavily

budget deficit the amount by which government spending exceeds government revenue in a fiscal year

national debt the total amount of money the government has borrowed

subsidies government grants of cash or other valuable commodities, such as land, to an individual or an organization; used to promote activities desired by the government, reward political support, or buy off political opposition

commodities, such as land. During the nineteenth century the federal government tried to persuade pioneers to settle the vast western lands by giving away plots of land contingent on improvements. Today, economic sectors receiving substantial subsidies include agriculture, energy, transportation, health, and national defense. **Contracting** is also an important technique of policy. Like any corporation, a government agency must purchase goods and services by contract. Contracting can be used to encourage corporations to improve themselves, to build up whole sectors of the economy, and to promote certain desirable goals or behavior, such as equal employment opportunity. For example, the infant airline industry of the 1930s was nurtured by the national government's lucrative contracts to carry airmail. More recently, President Obama required federal contractors to pay a minimum wage of $10.10 per hour even though the prevailing federal minimum wage set by Congress was (and still is) $7.25 per hour.

contracting the power of government to set conditions on companies seeking to sell goods or services to government agencies

monetary policies efforts to regulate the economy through the manipulation of the supply of money and credit; America's most powerful institution in this area of monetary policy is the Federal Reserve Board

Decisions about spending are so important that both the president and Congress have each created institutions to assert control over the budget process. The Office of Management and Budget (OMB) in the Executive Office of the President is responsible for preparing the president's budget, which contains the president's spending priorities and the estimated costs of the president's policy proposals. The president's budget may have little influence on the budget that Congress ultimately adopts, but the president's budget is viewed as the starting point for the annual budget debate.

Congress created the Congressional Budget Office (CBO) in 1974 so that it could have reliable information about the costs and economic impact of the policies it considers. At the same time, it set up a budget process designed to establish spending priorities and to consider individual expenditures in light of the entire budget. A key element of the process is the annual budget resolution, which designates broad targets for spending. By estimating the costs of policy proposals, Congress hoped to control spending and reduce deficits.

MONETARY POLICIES

Monetary policies manipulate the growth of the entire economy by controlling the availability of money to banks. With very few exceptions, banks in the United States are privately owned and locally operated. Many are chartered by states, which give banks permission to make loans, hold deposits, and make investments within that state. However, the most important banks are members of the federal banking system.

Federal Reserve System Banks did not become the core of American capitalism without intense political controversy. In 1791 Congress, led by Treasury Secretary Alexander Hamilton, established a Bank of the United States, but it was vigorously opposed by agricultural interests, led by Thomas Jefferson, who feared that it would be dominated by the interests of urban, industrial capitalism. The Bank of the United States was terminated during the administration of Andrew Jackson in the 1830s, and the fear of a central, public bank lingered when, in 1913, Congress established an institution, the **Federal Reserve System**, to integrate private banks into a single national system.

The Federal Reserve System is composed of 12 Federal Reserve banks, each located in a major commercial city. The Federal Reserve banks are not ordinary banks; they are bankers' banks that make loans to other banks, clear checks, and supply the economy with currency. They also play a regulatory role over the member banks. Every national bank must be a member of the Federal Reserve System and must follow national banking rules. State banks and savings-and-loan associations may also join if they accept national rules.

At the top of the system is the Federal Reserve Board—"the Fed"—comprising seven members appointed by the president (with Senate confirmation) for 14-year terms. The chair of the Fed is selected by the president from among the seven members for a 4-year term. In all other concerns, however, the Fed is an independent agency inasmuch as its members cannot be removed during their terms except "for cause," and the president's executive power does not extend to them or their policies.

The major advantage that a bank gains from being in the Federal Reserve System is that it can borrow from the system. Borrowing enables banks to expand their loan operations continually, as long as there is demand for loans in the economy.

Financial markets closely watch the statements of the Federal Reserve. Here, Fed chair Jerome Powell speaks about widening income inequality in the United States.

On the other hand, it is this very access of member banks to the Federal Reserve System that gives the Fed its power: the ability to expand or contract the amount of credit available in the United States. During the coronavirus pandemic, the Fed under Chairman Jerome Powell used monetary policy to stimulate the economy, cutting interest rates and buying Treasury securities (the nation's debt) to keep credit markets functioning.

REGULATION AND ANTITRUST POLICY

In addition to fiscal and monetary policy, another tool of economic policy making is regulation and antitrust policy. Federal economic regulation aims to protect the public against potential abuses by concentrated economic power in two ways. First, the federal government can establish rules for the operation of big businesses to ensure fair competition, for example, requiring businesses to make information about their activities and account books publicly available. Second, it can force a large business to break up into smaller companies if it finds that the business has established a **monopoly**. This is called **antitrust policy**. In addition to economic regulation, the federal government engages in social regulation, which establishes conditions on businesses to protect workers, the environment, and consumers.

monopoly a single firm in a market that controls all the goods and services of that market; absence of competition

antitrust policy government regulation of large businesses that have established monopolies

Federal regulatory policy has evolved, in part, as a reaction to public demands. In the nineteenth century, some companies grew so large that they were recognized as possessing "market power," dominant enough to eliminate competitors, collude on prices, and impose conditions on consumers rather than cater to consumer demand.

Small businesses, laborers, farmers, and consumers all began to clamor for protective regulation. The Interstate Commerce Act of 1887 created the first national independent regulatory commission, the Interstate Commerce Commission (ICC), designed to control the monopolistic practices of the railroads. Regulatory power to cover all monopolistic practices was later extended by the Sherman Antitrust Act of 1890 and the Clayton Antitrust Act of 1914. The ICC was abolished in 1995, but the enforcement of antitrust law continues under the Federal Trade Commission, also created in 1914. Social regulation protecting consumers got a start when Upton Sinclair's best-seller about the meatpacking industry, *The Jungle*, led to the Federal Meat Inspection Act of 1906. In the late 1930s, the Food and Drug Administration was given broad powers to test and regulate products viewed as essential to public health.

Indeed, the modern era of national regulation began in the 1930s. Many agencies were established to regulate companies in a variety of economic sectors, including the securities, radio (and eventually television), banking, coal-mining, and agriculture industries. For example, the Securities and Exchange Commission (SEC), created after the stock market crash of 1929, requires companies to disclose information about the stocks and bonds they are selling, inform buyers of the investment

deregulation a policy of reducing or eliminating regulatory restraints on the conduct of individuals or private institutions

laissez-faire capitalism an economic system in which the means of production and distribution are privately owned and operated for profit with minimal or no government interference

risks, and protect investors against fraud. In this way the SEC helps maintain investor confidence and a strong supply of capital for American business.

Also during the 1930s and '40s, Congress set the basic framework of American labor regulation, including the rules for collective bargaining and the minimum wage. Regulation increased in the 1970s, with increased scope for agencies such as the Occupational Safety and Health Administration, the Consumer Product Safety Commission, and the Environmental Protection Agency (EPA).

Despite occasional high-profile regulatory cases, the trend since the late 1970s has been against regulation. Over the years, businesses complained about the burden of the new regulations they confronted, and many economists began to argue that excessive regulation was hurting the economy. In the 1980s, Congress and the president responded with a wave of **deregulation**. For example, shortly after taking office, President Reagan gave the OMB authority to review all executive branch proposals for new regulations, decreasing the total number of regulations issued by federal agencies and dropping the number of pages in the *Federal Register* from 74,000 in 1980 to 49,600 in 1987.[4] Similarly, President Trump signed an executive order within days of assuming office in 2017 requiring that two significant regulations be eliminated for every one added. How much government regulation is necessary remains a subject of considerable partisan disagreement.

Economic Policy Making Is Inherently Political

Explain the key debates in economic policy making

Addressing economic challenges and maintaining a strong economy are extremely important to political leaders. As was discovered by presidents from Herbert Hoover (who presided over the beginning of the Great Depression of the 1930s) to Jimmy Carter (who faced double-digit inflation in the 1970s) to Donald Trump (who faced the economic fallout of the coronavirus pandemic), voters will punish politicians for poor economic conditions. Because the state of the economy is so important to voters, politicians of both parties strive to ensure a strong economy, but they differ over which goals and tools are appropriate. Indeed, disagreements about the role of the government in the economy are some of the defining differences between the political parties.

HOW MUCH SHOULD THE GOVERNMENT INTERVENE IN THE ECONOMY?

Until 1929 most Americans believed that government should not actively manage the economy. The world was guided by the theory—called **laissez-faire capitalism**—that the economy, if left to its own devices, would produce full employment and maximum production. This traditional view crumbled beginning in 1929 before the stark reality of the Great Depression, when around 20 percent of the workforce lost their jobs. Many had no savings or family farm to fall back on, and when banks failed, those with savings were wiped out as well. Thousands of businesses closed, throwing middle-class Americans onto the bread lines alongside unemployed laborers and farmers who had lost their land. The Great Depression proved to Americans that the economic system was not, in fact, perfectly self-regulating. Demands grew for the federal government to act.

When President Franklin Delano Roosevelt took office in 1933, he energetically threw the federal government into the business of fighting the Depression. He proposed a variety of temporary relief and work programs, most of them financed by the federal government but administered by the states. Roosevelt also created several important federal programs designed to provide future economic security for Americans. Since that time, the public has held the government, and the president in particular, responsible for ensuring a healthy economy.

After World War II, Republicans and Democrats broadly agreed that Keynesian ideas, such as running deficits during periods of recession to stimulate demand, could best guide economic policy. By the 1960s, **Keynesians** believed that economic policy did not need to provoke political controversy because they could ensure ongoing prosperity by "fine-tuning" the economy. Democrats and Republicans often disagreed about how much the government should do to alleviate unemployment or inflation, but they shared a pragmatic view that government intervention could solve economic problems.

> **Keynesians** followers of the economic theories of John Maynard Keynes, who argued that the government can stimulate the economy by increasing public spending or by cutting taxes

Partisan Divisions over the Role of Government in the Economy By the 1980s, a growing number of Republicans began to reject the idea that government could help ensure prosperity. Instead, they argued that freeing markets from government intervention would produce the best economic results. As Ronald Reagan put it in his first inaugural address, "Government is not the solution to our problem, government is the problem."[5] The ideas of laissez-faire capitalism began to make a comeback in American politics.

Although only a few politicians would entirely remove government from the economy, Republicans today draw on the ideas of laissez-faire economics as they argue for significant reductions in nonmilitary spending. Many Democrats, on the other hand, stress the important role of government in promoting a strong economy. This fundamental disagreement between the parties underlies the fierce contemporary political debates over taxes, government spending, and economic regulation. These debates reemerged in spring 2020 when Democrats urged more coronavirus pandemic rescue spending after Congress passed the $2 trillion CARES Act, while Republicans hesitated to engage in more deficit spending.

Taxes As Republicans embraced the idea that reducing the role of government in the economy would promote investment and spur growth, they made tax cuts

In response to the economic catastrophe caused by the coronavirus pandemic, Congress passed and the president signed the Families First and CARES acts to provide cash payments to individuals, assistance to businesses, and expanded unemployment benefits.

their highest priority. Rejecting Keynesian ideas, they adopted **supply-side economics**, the idea that lower tax rates create incentives for more productive and efficient use of resources. When individuals know they can keep more of their earnings, they are more likely to be productive workers and creative investors. This greater productivity, Republicans argue, ultimately produces more revenue, and therefore more taxes. In this perspective, low taxes are not just a temporary measure to stimulate the economy; taxes should remain low at all times to ensure a growing economy.

Spending The two parties have long battled over government spending. Contending that the federal government has become too big, Republicans argue that government spending is excessive and creates deficits that harm the economy. It is not hard to convince Americans that government spending is wasteful, that government is too big, or that deficits are bad. When asked, a majority of Americans regularly say they would prefer a smaller government with fewer services (although in 2017 slightly more said they would prefer a bigger government with more services—48 percent, compared to 45 percent preferring smaller government).[6]

Yet polls reveal little support for cutting specific government programs.[7] In fact, the public shows the strongest support for the most expensive programs: Social Security and Medicare, which provide pensions and health insurance to the elderly. Only the most ardent spending foes among Republicans have argued for cutting these programs. Indeed, in 2003 Republicans agreed to a major expansion in Medicare spending by adding a prescription drug benefit to the program.

Because neither party wishes to cut big, expensive, popular programs and because tax increases have been so difficult to enact, budget deficits have grown periodically over the past three decades. Democratic critics and most economists point to rising deficits as proof that supply-side economics does not work; they argue that the economy would be better off without tax cuts. Some go further, arguing that Republicans deliberately reduced taxes in order to force spending cuts, a strategy called "starving the beast."[8]

supply-side economics an economic theory that posits that reducing the marginal rate of taxation will create a productive economy by promoting levels of work and investment that would otherwise be discouraged by higher taxes

Because raising taxes or reducing big-spending programs is politically difficult, most cuts have fallen on smaller programs, where spending has decreased substantially since 2010. Nondefense discretionary spending includes everything the government does outside of defense and mandatory programs such as Social Security and Medicare. For 2020 such spending was the smallest share of the economy ever recorded, with data going back to 1962.[9]

Economic Regulation The federal government regulates business to promote economic stability, maintain workplace safety, set minimum wages and define overtime work, ensure consumer satisfaction, and protect the environment. However, regulation often attracts intense political conflict as businesses seek to limit the government role and other interests press for stronger government action. While Democrats usually favor regulation more than Republicans do, each party can point to public-opinion polls to support its position. Americans agree that government regulation of business does more harm than good on the whole, but as with spending, they often express strong support for maintaining or even strengthening current regulations.[10] One area of regulation that sharply divides the parties is the minimum wage, which has become a regular target of political conflict as Democrats aim to raise it to keep pace with inflation. When President Obama signed an executive order increasing the minimum wage for federal contractors to $10.10 an hour in 2014, he urged Congress to raise the federal minimum wage from $7.25 to $10.10 an hour as well. However, opposition from Republican lawmakers has prevented an increase, perhaps because, while a 2019 poll found that two-thirds of Americans—and 86 percent of Democrats—favored a $15-an-hour minimum wage, only 43 percent of Republicans agreed.[11] As of November 2020, 30 states and nearly four dozen cities and counties had enacted minimum wages higher than the federal wage.[12]

The Welfare State Was Created to Address Inequality

> **Trace the history of government programs designed to promote economic security**

For much of American history, local governments and private charities were in charge of caring for the poor. During the 1930s, when this system collapsed in the face of widespread economic destitution, the federal government created the beginnings of an American **welfare state**, the term given to the collection of social policies a nation uses to address well-being. The idea of the welfare state was new; it meant that the national government would oversee programs designed to promote economic security for all Americans—not just the poor. Today, the American system of social welfare includes many different policies enacted over the years since the Great Depression. Because each program is governed by distinct rules, the type and level of assistance available vary widely.

> **welfare state** the collection of policies a nation has to promote and protect the economic and social well-being of its citizens

FOUNDATIONS OF THE WELFARE STATE

The modern welfare state in the United States consists of three separate categories of welfare: contributory and noncontributory programs, many created by the Social Security Act of 1935, and the tax expenditure system, first established by the new federal income tax in 1913 and expanded over time.

During the Great Depression, the government took a more active role in helping poor and struggling Americans. Here, people line up to receive free bread.

Contributory Programs Welfare programs financed in advance by taxation are essentially a form of "mandatory savings." These programs, also known as social insurance, require working Americans to contribute a portion of their earnings to provide income and benefits for present-day retirees, with the understanding that younger workers will one day provide for them in the same way. **Social Security**, the best-known **contributory program**, is funded by an employer and an employee paying equal amounts. Their contributions in 2020 were 6.2 percent each on the first $137,700 of income.[13]

Social Security does not work like ordinary private insurance; workers' contributions do not accumulate in a personal account. The contributions are pooled across all workers, and while one's benefits are based on one's earnings—the higher one's income, the higher one's retirement pension—the benefits formula is redistributive, providing lower-income workers with a higher proportion of their contributions than higher-income workers receive. This is because the goal of Social Security, a form of *social* insurance, is to ensure a basic income to all workers once they retire.

Senior citizens' purchasing power is protected by **indexing**, whereby benefits are raised annually by **cost-of-living adjustments (COLAs)** tied to the rate of inflation. The average payment for retired workers in

Social Security a contributory welfare program into which working Americans contribute a percentage of their wages and from which they receive cash benefits after retirement or if they become disabled

contributory programs social programs financed in whole or in part by taxation or other mandatory contributions by their present or future recipients

indexing a periodic process of adjusting social benefits or wages to account for increases in the cost of living

cost-of-living adjustments (COLAs) changes made to the level of benefits of a government program based on the rate of inflation

2020 was $1,503 each month.[14] The program also plays a vital role for young people by providing survivor benefits to those whose parents die, retire, or become disabled. Surviving spouses also receive survivor benefits. In addition, in 1956 Social Security Disability Insurance (SSDI) was created to provide a monthly cash benefit to the permanently disabled.[15]

The biggest single expansion in contributory programs since 1935 was the establishment in 1965 of **Medicare**, which provides substantial medical services to elderly people and the permanently disabled. Employees and their employers pay a tax of 1.45 percent on all earnings for Medicare; households earning over $250,000 a year pay an extra 0.9 percent due to a provision in the Patient Protection and Affordable Care Act (ACA).

Unemployment insurance, another contributory program, is funded by a combination of federal and state taxes. In most states, benefits last for a maximum of 26 weeks. In periods of high unemployment, Congress can authorize an additional 13 weeks, as it did in 2020 in response to the coronavirus pandemic; such extended benefits are generally funded by federal taxes. For most workers, unemployment benefits replace only half of their lost wages. Moreover, because states impose criteria about how long a person must work or how much she must earn to become eligible for unemployment insurance, only about half of workers who lose their jobs receive benefits.[16] Independent contractors, gig employees, and part-time workers are normally ineligible for unemployment benefits, but pandemic rescue legislation in 2020 temporarily extended coverage to them.

Noncontributory Programs Programs to which beneficiaries do not have to contribute—**noncontributory programs**—are also known as "social assistance programs" or, more commonly, as "welfare." Eligibility is determined by **means testing**, which requires applicants to show a financial need for assistance. The 1935 Social Security Act created programs for cash assistance to families with children (later known as AFDC) and to poor elderly, blind, and disabled people (Old Age Assistance, later changed to Supplemental Security Income or SSI). In the ensuing decades the government also created programs to provide housing assistance, food stamps, and school lunches. The largest single category of expansion was the establishment in 1965 of **Medicaid**, which provides medical services to low-income Americans.

Like contributory programs, the noncontributory ones also made their most significant advances during the 1960s and '70s. The creation of SSI in 1974 made benefits for the elderly, blind, and disabled uniform across the nation. The number of people receiving AFDC benefits expanded in the 1970s, in part because of the establishment in the 1960s of Medicaid and food stamps, later renamed the

Medicare a form of national health insurance for the elderly and the disabled

noncontributory programs social programs that provide assistance to people on the basis of demonstrated need rather than any contribution they have made

means testing a procedure by which potential beneficiaries of a social assistance program establish their eligibility by demonstrating a genuine need for the assistance

Medicaid a federally and state-financed, state-operated program providing medical services to low-income people

Supplemental Nutrition Assistance Program (SNAP) the largest antipoverty program, which provides recipients with a debit card for food at most grocery stores; formerly known as food stamps

in-kind benefits noncash goods and services provided to needy individuals and families by the federal government

equality of opportunity a widely shared American ideal that all people should have the freedom to use whatever talents and wealth they have to reach their fullest potential

Supplemental Nutrition Assistance Program (SNAP). These programs provide what are called **in-kind benefits**— noncash goods and services that would otherwise have to be paid for in cash by the beneficiary. At the time, AFDC recipients were automatically eligible for Medicaid and food stamps. After the mid-1970s, AFDC benefits fell because they were not indexed to inflation (unlike Social Security), and the number of recipients decreased after the 1996 welfare reform broke the linkages among Medicaid, food stamps, and cash welfare and replaced AFDC with Temporary Assistance for Needy Families (TANF).

State Variation in Welfare Benefits Some means-tested, noncontributory programs are run by the federal government, with uniform eligibility criteria and benefits nationwide, such as SNAP, the school lunch program, and SSI. However, many such programs are run jointly by the federal government and the states. Because states provide some of the funding and have considerable flexibility to set program criteria, benefits can vary greatly by state.

For example, in 2019 states' monthly TANF benefits for a family of three varied from $170 in Mississippi to $1,066 in New Hampshire, which passed legislation in 2017 to increase TANF benefits to 60 percent of the federal poverty level.[17] Most TANF payments are well below the federal poverty line, which was $21,330 per year or $1,778 per month in 2019 (see Figure 14.2).[18]

Tax Expenditures In addition to contributory and noncontributory programs, the United States provides social welfare benefits through tax breaks—credits, deductions, and preferential tax rates that some analysts call tax expenditures or the shadow welfare state. These include subsidies for benefits that employers may offer to their workers, such as medical insurance and retirement plans—both traditional pensions and 401(k)s. The federal government subsidizes such benefits by not taxing the payments that employers and employees make for them.

The shadow welfare state also includes tax breaks that individuals can file for when they prepare their federal tax returns. For example, taxpayers can deduct from their income the amount they paid in home mortgage interest and in state and local taxes (up to a limit). There are also tax deductions for out-of-pocket medical expenses, child care, charitable contributions, and so on. These tax breaks lower the effective cost of homeownership, health insurance, child-rearing, and other subsidized activities. But such benefits are concentrated among middle- and upper-income people who are most likely to have employer-provided benefits at work and to engage in subsidized activities such as buying a house.

People often do not think of these tax expenditures as part of social policy because they are not as visible as the programs that provide direct payments or services to beneficiaries.[19] But they cost the national treasury over $1 trillion in forgone revenue each year.[20]

Maximum Monthly TANF Benefits

Spending on TANF benefits varies widely across the country. In 14 states, monthly benefits for a single-parent family of three are below $300; in 21 states and Washington, D.C., they are above $500. In which regions does spending on TANF benefits tend to be highest? In which regions is it generally lower?

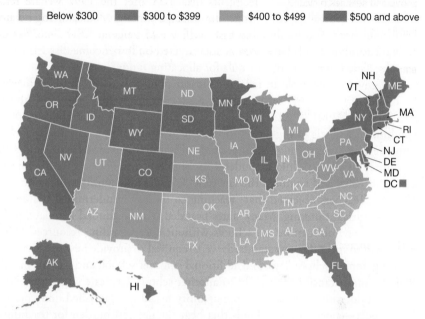

Below $300 $300 to $399 $400 to $499 $500 and above

SOURCE: Ashley Burnside and Ife Floyd, "More States Raising TANF Cash Benefits to Boost Families' Economic Security," December 9, 2019, Center on Budget and Policy Priorities, www.cbpp.org/sites/default/files/atoms /files/10-30-14tanf.pdf (accessed 5/9/20).

Social Policies Open Opportunity

> **Describe how education, health, and housing policies try to advance equality of opportunity**

The welfare state aims at providing not only a measure of economic security but also **equality of opportunity**. Programs that provide opportunity keep people from falling into poverty and offer a hand up to those who are poor. Three types of policies are most significant in opening opportunity: education policies, health policies, and housing policies.

EDUCATION POLICIES

Although education policies are the most important single force in the distribution and redistribution of opportunity in America, they are largely set by state and local governments.

Elementary and Secondary Education (K–12) Embarrassment that the Soviet Union had beaten the United States into space with the launch of *Sputnik,* the world's first satellite, prompted national government involvement in K–12 education. In 1958 the National Defense Education Act set forth a federal policy of improving education in science and mathematics. Soon after, the federal government officially recognized the role of education in promoting equality of opportunity. In 1965 the Elementary and Secondary Education Act offered federal funds to school districts with substantial numbers of children whose parents were unemployed or low income.

Today the federal government accounts for 10 percent of all spending on K–12 education; states and localities each account for 45 percent. Over time, however, federal education funds have become less targeted on low-income districts as Congress has failed to update the formula for allocating funds.[21]

The government's role in federal education policy was substantially increased by President George W. Bush's signature education initiative, the No Child Left Behind Act of 2001 (NCLB). Supported by Democrats and Republicans, the law combined the goals of higher standards and equality of opportunity. It aimed to improve standards through stronger federal requirements for testing and school accountability. Every child in grades 3 through 8 had to be tested yearly for proficiency in math and reading. The law quickly generated considerable controversy, however. Teachers objected that "teaching to the test" undermined the development of critical thinking. Many states branded it an unfunded mandate, placing expensive new obligations on schools without corresponding resources. Schools that failed to meet the new standards were required to provide new services such as tutoring, longer school days, and additional summer school, and parents in failing schools could transfer their child to another school. Critics charged that NCLB actually undermined equality of opportunity because it punished underperforming schools—mostly those schools that bear the greatest burden for teaching the neediest students.[22]

Over the course of the Obama administration, K–12 education policy was once again decentralized toward the states. At first, the administration overhauled NCLB, allowing states to get exemptions from its requirements in return for adopting a strong set of education standards and linking teacher evaluations to test results. Most states endorsed the Common Core State Standards, drawn up by representatives of the National Governors Association and the Council of Chief State School Officers in 2010, although critics alleged that the Common Core testing regime too closely resembled the failed policies of NCLB.[23] Later, in 2015, a bipartisan coalition in Congress enacted a major new education law entitled Every Student Succeeds, which eliminated federal requirements for teachers' evaluations and mandated standards, and which returned control to the states by making them responsible for devising their own methods of ensuring accountability. Like NCLB, Every Student Succeeds continues to require testing and sorting of testing results by racial and ethnic minorities, English learners, and disability, and it requires states to intervene to correct problems in the lowest-scoring 5 percent of schools. But it leaves the specific remedies up to the states.[24]

The Obama administration also supported charter schools—publicly funded schools that are free from the bureaucratic rules of the school district in which they are located and free to design specialized curricula and to use resources in ways they think most effective. It created a new $4.3 billion program of grants to state education programs, Race to the Top. To be eligible for the grants, states had to agree to lift the caps on creation of charter schools. In the end, 18 states and Washington, D.C., received grants,[25] although several years after the program began, it was clear that system-wide improvements in school performance were elusive.[26]

The Secretary of Education under Donald Trump, Betsy DeVos, strongly supported charter schools and vouchers, which allow students to use public funds to attend private schools. In 2020 the Supreme Court sided with voucher supporters in ruling that voucher-like private school state scholarship programs cannot exclude religious schools.[27]

Higher Education The federal government also plays an important role in helping to fund higher education, another important pathway toward opportunity. College graduates earn 50 percent more than high school graduates, and this "wage premium" has stabilized at around $30,000 since 2000.[28]

As with K–12 education, most higher education has historically been funded by the states, not the federal government. However, federal programs have made a big difference in promoting equal access to higher education. The GI Bill of 1944 put higher education in reach of a whole generation of World War II veterans who had never thought they would attend college. In the 1950s and '60s, the federal government built on this role with the National Defense Education Act, which offered low-interest loans to college students, and the Higher Education Act, which supplied assistance directly to colleges and offered additional need-based grants allocated to students by universities. In 1972, Congress created the Pell Grant program, which offered grants directly to lower-income students.

Since the mid-1970s, however, as states have sharply reduced funding for higher education and college tuition has risen dramatically, these financial assistance programs have not kept pace. Whereas Pell Grants had initially provided enough to pay for tuition plus room and board at a four-year public college, by 2019–20, they covered only 59 percent of tuition and fees.[29] The growing costs of higher education have put college out of reach for many lower-income students and have left those who do attend with a heavy load of debt. In the two decades between 1996 and 2016, average student debt among seniors graduating from four-year colleges more than doubled after accounting for inflation, from $12,750 to $29,650, with lower-income students carrying greater debt loads.[30]

HEALTH POLICIES

Until recent decades, no government in the United States (national, state, or local) concerned itself directly with individual health. But public responsibility was always accepted for *public* health. After New York City's newly created Board of Health was credited with holding down a cholera epidemic in 1867, most states created statewide public-health agencies, recognizing that government can play an important role in preventing the spread of disease and reducing the likelihood of injury.

At the federal level, agencies committed to public health gained new visibility with the outbreak of the coronavirus pandemic in 2020. The U.S. Public Health Service, headed by the U.S. surgeon general, was established in 1798 and includes, among other agencies, the National Institutes of Health (NIH), dedicated to biomedical research, and the Centers for Disease Control and Prevention, which monitors outbreaks of disease and implements prevention measures and awareness campaigns about HIV/AIDS, Ebola, Zika, COVID-19, and other public-health threats. Additional federal commitments to the improvement of public health include the numerous laws aimed at cleaning up and defending the environment (including the creation in 1970 of the Environmental Protection Agency) and laws to improve the safety of consumer products (regulated by the Consumer Product Safety Commission, created in 1972).

Health policies aimed directly at the poor include nutritional programs, such as SNAP and the school lunch program, and Medicaid. Medicaid is the single largest medical insurance program in the United States, covering 70.7 million people, a number that rose by 23 percent after the ACA's expansion provisions were put into place.[31] Medicaid covers the poor and people who are disabled; it also assists the elderly poor who cannot pay Medicare premiums. Because there is no government provision for long-term care, Medicaid has become the de facto program financing nursing home residents when they have exhausted their savings. In fact, the disabled and elderly account for two-thirds of all Medicaid spending.[32]

Health Care Reform The United States is the only advanced industrial nation without universal access to health care. Opposition from the American Medical Association, the main lobbying organization of doctors, prevented President Roosevelt from proposing national health insurance during the 1930s, when other elements of the welfare state became law. As a result, the United States developed a patchwork system: in 2016, 56 percent of the nonelderly population received health insurance through their employers, older Americans were covered through Medicare, and the poor and disabled were assisted with Medicaid.[33] However, the growing cost of employer-provided insurance means that increasing numbers of workers cannot afford it and that many small employers cannot even afford to offer it. And both Medicaid and Medicare face severe fiscal strain due to rising costs.

The Affordable Care Act ("Obamacare") After the 2008 election, the Obama administration and the Democratic Congress implemented comprehensive health care reform. The administration aimed to cover most Americans who lacked health insurance with a reform strategy that built on the existing system.

The plan that ultimately passed had three key features. The first was the creation of exchanges where individuals could buy health insurance, along with regulations prohibiting insurers from denying benefits for a variety of reasons, such as preexisting conditions. With a few exceptions, the legislation also made insurers cover preventive care, such as vaccinations, mammograms, and other screenings, in full. The second key provision of the ACA, known as "the individual mandate," required uninsured individuals to purchase health insurance; those who did not would be subject to a fine.

Some Americans opposed the 2010 Affordable Care Act because they were concerned that decisions previously left to patients and their doctors would be made by the government.

The third major provision of the ACA was a set of subsidies to help the uninsured and small businesses purchase insurance, as well as an expansion of Medicaid and the Children's Health Insurance Program (CHIP) for low-income children. The Medicaid expansion made more people eligible for the program by opening it up to people with incomes up to 138 percent of the poverty level ($29,974 a year for a family of three in 2020).[34] The reform also allowed working-age adults without dependent children to qualify for the program for the first time.

The new health reform law faced challenges from state governments: 21 states filed lawsuits against it, arguing that the individual mandate was unconstitutional as were provisions stipulating that states would lose all federal Medicaid funds if they did not expand their Medicaid programs, even though the federal government initially paid for 100 percent of the expansion and starting in 2016 would cover 90 percent of new costs.

The Supreme Court ruled in 2012 that most of the act was constitutional, including the individual mandate.[35] Regarding Medicaid, the Court ruled that Congress did not have the power to take existing Medicaid funds away from states if they did not comply with the expansion requirements. Several governors announced their intention to opt out of the expansion. Although some states later decided to expand, as of August 2020, 12 had not, leaving 2.3 million people who would have qualified for Medicaid without access to health care (see Figure 14.3).[36]

Health care reform remains a focus of partisan contention. By 2016 Republican members of the House of Representatives had voted 62 times to repeal the ACA.[37] After Republicans won control of the presidency and both houses of Congress in the 2016 election, they drafted a replacement bill that would have ended the Medicaid entitlement by turning the program into a block grant to the states, and would have effectively ended some regulatory protections for people with preexisting conditions.

FIGURE 14.3

Health Insurance Coverage, 1972–2018

The percentage of Americans under 65 without health insurance reached 17.7 percent in 2010, when the ACA was enacted. With implementation beginning in 2014, the uninsured rate fell to 10 percent in 2016. It began to rise in 2018 with reductions in the ACA enrollment period and advertising and is predicted to rise further with the repeal of the individual mandate, effective 2019, and with job losses from the coronavirus pandemic.

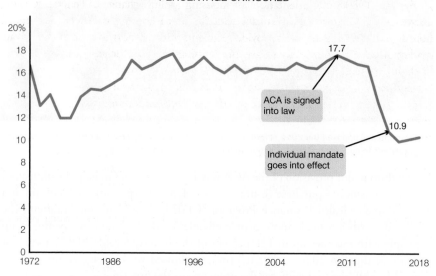

PERCENTAGE UNINSURED

ACA is signed into law

17.7

10.9

Individual mandate goes into effect

SOURCES: 1972–2007: Centers for Disease Control and Prevention, "Trends in Health Care Coverage and Insurance for 1968–2011," November 6, 2015, www.cdc.gov/nchs/health_policy/trends_hc_1968_2011 .htm (accessed 8/9/18); 2008–2018: U.S. Census Bureau, "Trends in Health Care Coverage Status and Type of Coverage by State—Persons under 65: 2008–2018," Table HIC-6, www.census.gov/data/tables/time-series /demo/health-insurance/historical-series/hic.html (accessed 5/12/20).

Though the bill failed in the Senate, the individual mandate was ultimately repealed with the 2017 Tax Cuts and Jobs Act.

HOUSING POLICIES

Economic opportunity is also closely connected to housing. Access to quality, affordable housing provides individuals and families with stability and protection from pollution, disease, injury, and anxiety and depression. The effects of quality housing are especially strong for children.[38]

Federal housing programs were first created during the Great Depression of the 1930s, when many Americans found themselves unable to afford housing. Through public housing for low-income families, which originated in 1937 with the Wagner-Steagall National Housing Act, the percentage of American families living in overcrowded conditions (defined by the U.S. Census Bureau as more than one person per room) fell from 20 percent in 1940 to 9 percent in 1970. Over the same period, the proportion of American households living in "substandard" housing, defined by the Census Bureau as lacking complete kitchen or bathroom facilities, fell from almost 50 percent to 8 percent.[39]

Despite these improvements in housing standards, public-housing policy through the 1970s was largely seen as a failure. Restricted to the poorest of the poor and marked by racial segregation and inadequate maintenance, public housing contributed to the problems of the poor by isolating them from shopping, jobs, and urban amenities. Dilapidated high-rise housing projects stood as a symbol of the failed American policy of "warehousing the poor."

By the 1980s the orientation of housing policy changed. Federal housing assistance for low-income Americans shifted toward housing vouchers (now called housing choice vouchers) that provide recipients with support to rent in the private market. Most cities and suburbs have long waiting lists for vouchers; only one-quarter of eligible individuals and families receive them.[40] Another concern is that vouchers provide too little money to cover rental costs in very active housing markets.

Other types of federal housing policy have had a discriminatory effect, worsening patterns of residential segregation by race. For decades the federal government permitted banks to engage in "redlining," refusing to issue mortgage loans or extend credit in predominantly minority neighborhoods. Federal programs that encouraged homeownership by providing insurance for loans made by private lenders (called underwriting) also discriminated against minority home buyers and contributed to segregation by allowing "restrictive covenants," which prevented owners from selling their houses to racial or religious minorities.[41] Such policies exacerbated vast Black–White differences in personal wealth that exist to this day.[42]

Beginning in 2007, a home loan foreclosure crisis presented the government with a different kind of housing problem (although one that also disproportionately affected minority groups). During the housing boom of the early 2000s, many Americans bought homes using loans from "predatory lenders" they later could not afford to repay. As growing numbers defaulted on their loans, banks foreclosed on their houses and the value of housing began to drop, a downward spiral that set off the major recession that began in 2008. Although new federal programs tried to slow the rising interest rates burdening some homeowners or otherwise help those facing foreclosure, their success was limited. The effects of the housing bubble were felt for years beyond the official end of the Great Recession in June 2009.

Who Gets What from Social Policy?

Explain how contributory, noncontributory, and tax expenditure programs benefit different groups of Americans

The elderly and the middle class receive the most benefits from the government's social policies, and children and the poor receive the fewest. In addition, America's social policies do little to change the fact that minorities and women are more likely than White men to be poor.

THE ELDERLY

The elderly are the beneficiaries of the two strongest and most generous social policies: retirement pensions (Social Security) and health insurance for older Americans (Medicare). As these programs have grown, they have provided most elderly Americans with economic security and have dramatically reduced the poverty rate among the elderly. Social Security has been called the most effective antipoverty program in the United States: the elderly poverty rate fell from 35 percent in 1959, before many older people received social insurance benefits, to 8.9 percent in 2019.[43] This does not mean that the elderly are rich, however; in 2019 the median income of elderly households was $47,357, well below the median of $77,873 for those under age 65.[44] Also, older African Americans and Latinos are much more likely to be poor than are White seniors, with comparative rates of 18.0 percent, 17.1 percent, and 6.8 percent respectively in 2019.[45] The difference is due in part to the lower wages of these groups during their working years, since Social Security benefits are pegged to wages.

Social Security and Medicare are politically strong because they serve a constituency that has become quite powerful electorally. The elderly are not only a very large group—in 2019, there were 52.8 million Americans over the age of 65, just over 16 percent of the population—they also vote at higher rates than the rest of the population.[46] In addition, the elderly have developed strong and sophisticated lobbying organizations that can influence policy making and mobilize older Americans to defend these programs against proposals to cut them. The largest and most influential such organization, AARP, had 38 million members in 2018, amounting to one-quarter of all voters. It also has a lobbying organization in Washington that employs 57 lobbyists and nearly 50 policy analysts.[47]

THE MIDDLE AND UPPER CLASSES

Americans don't usually think of the middle and upper classes as benefiting from social welfare policies, but government action promotes their welfare in a variety of ways. First, health insurance and pensions for the elderly, as well as Medicaid coverage of nursing home bills, help relieve the middle class of the burden of caring for elderly relatives. Before these programs existed, old people were more likely to live with and depend financially on their adult children.

Second, the middle and upper classes are the chief beneficiaries of the shadow welfare state of tax expenditures.[48] Beyond the Earned Income Tax Credit (EITC), which benefits the working poor, the great majority of tax expenditure benefits go to middle- and upper-income households. For example, while households with incomes under $30,000 receive 68 percent of the EITC, households with incomes

> **FOR CRITICAL ANALYSIS ▶**
>
> 1. What are some of the major differences among the demographics of those receiving each program?
>
> 2. What underlying social patterns about poverty and government help do these data suggest?

Who Receives Benefits from Social Programs?

Almost all Americans benefit from social policy programs at some point in their lives. Two important programs in America's safety net are Medicaid, which provides health insurance to the poor, and Social Security Disability Insurance, which helps Americans who are permanently disabled. Children make up a disproportionate number of the Medicaid recipients, while people over 50 make up a disproportionate share of SSDI recipients. The Earned Income Tax Credit benefits low- to moderate-income working individuals, especially those with children. Middle- and upper-class people also benefit from governmental programs, like the home mortgage deduction.

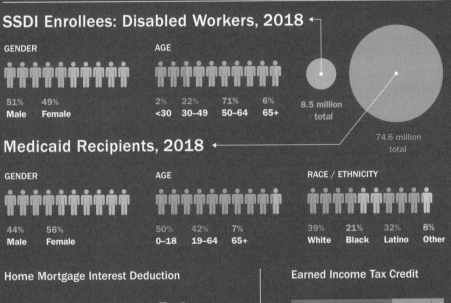

SSDI Enrollees: Disabled Workers, 2018

GENDER

51% Male   49% Female

AGE

2% <30   22% 30–49   71% 50–64   6% 65+

8.5 million total

74.6 million total

Medicaid Recipients, 2018

GENDER

44% Male   56% Female

AGE

50% 0–18   42% 19–64   7% 65+

RACE / ETHNICITY

39% White   21% Black   32% Latino   8% Other

Home Mortgage Interest Deduction

0.1% <$30,000   0.6% $30,000–$50,000   9% $50,000–$100,000

27% $100,000–$200,000   64% >$200,000

Earned Income Tax Credit

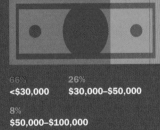

66% <$30,000   26% $30,000–$50,000

8% $50,000–$100,000

* Percentages are of total value to each income group.

SOURCES: MACStats: Medicaid and CHIP Data Book 2019, www.macpac.gov; Estimates of Federal Tax Expenditures for Fiscal Years 2019–2023, www.jct.gov; 2018 SSDI Annual Statistical Report, www.ssa.gov (accessed 6/15/20).

over $200,000 claim 49 percent of the state and local tax deduction (the figure was 71 percent before the deduction was limited by the 2017 Tax Cuts and Jobs Act), 58 percent of the home-mortgage deduction, and 83 percent of the deduction for charitable contributions.[49]

THE WORKING POOR

Even though people who are working but poor or just above the poverty line may be seen as deserving, they receive only limited assistance from government social programs. They typically hold jobs that do not provide pensions or health insurance; often, they are renters because they cannot afford to buy homes. This means they cannot benefit from the shadow welfare state that subsidizes the social benefits enjoyed by most middle-class Americans. Because the wages of less educated workers have declined significantly since the 1980s and minimum wages have not kept pace with inflation, the problems of the working poor remain acute.

Government programs that assist the working poor include the Earned Income Tax Credit (EITC), SNAP, and the ACA. Implemented in 1976, the EITC refunds some or all of the Social Security and income taxes the working poor pay, particularly those with children, providing a modest wage supplement and allowing them to catch up on utility bills or pay for children's clothing. SNAP is available to

The Supplemental Nutrition Assistance Program (SNAP), formerly known as "food stamps," helps people in need buy food. Today recipients use a government-provided debit card that is accepted at most grocery stores. In 2020, 38 million Americans were enrolled in SNAP.

households earning below 130 percent of the poverty line (about $27,700 a year for a three-person family in 2019). The average monthly benefit for a family of three is $376 a month.[50] Both the EITC and SNAP serve tens of millions of families because, unlike many social assistance programs like TANF and housing subsidies, they do not have waiting lists.

The ACA was intended in part to address lack of health insurance among the working poor. The law expanded Medicaid to cover workers who earn up to 138 percent of the poverty line ($29,974 for a family of three in 2020). However, as we saw earlier, the decision of 12 states to opt out of Medicaid expansion has left a gap in coverage in which 2.3 million people have incomes above the Medicaid eligibility limits in their states but below 100 percent of the federal poverty line, the income level at which subsidies for purchasing private insurance on the marketplaces begin. About half of Americans falling into this coverage gap and lacking insurance live in Texas or Florida. Latinos and African Americans disproportionately fall into the coverage gap.[51]

Even though the working poor may be seen as deserving, they are not politically powerful because they are not organized. There is no equivalent to AARP for this group. Nonetheless, because work is highly valued in American society, these programs enjoy more support among politicians than those for the nonworking poor.

THE NONWORKING POOR

Americans generally don't like to subsidize adults who are not working, but they do not want to harm children. Thus the only nonworking, able-bodied poor people who receive federal cash assistance are parents caring for children. The primary source of cash assistance for these families is the state-run TANF program; they also rely on SNAP and Medicaid. Able-bodied adults not caring for children are not eligible for federal assistance other than food stamps. Such individuals may receive small amounts of cash through "general assistance" in some states and Medicaid in the states that chose to expand the program under the ACA.

Restrictions have been added to many programs for the poor. The federal funds states receive for TANF are fixed at 1996 levels, unadjusted for inflation, whether the welfare rolls rise or fall. Also, the term *nonworking poor* is a bit of a misnomer, because work requirements have been imposed on TANF since 1996 and on SNAP and Medicaid (in some states) more recently.

Welfare recipients have little political power to resist cuts to their benefits. Because they are widely viewed as undeserving and are not politically organized, they have played little part in debates about welfare.

MINORITIES, WOMEN, AND CHILDREN

Members of some ethnic and racial minorities, as well as women and children in general, are disproportionately poor. In 2019 the poverty rates for African Americans and Latinos were 18.8 percent and 15.7 percent, more than double that for non-Hispanic Whites, 7.3 percent. Median household incomes were $45,438 for African Americans, $56,113 for Latinos, and $76,057 for non-Hispanic Whites.[52]

Much of this economic inequality occurs because minority workers tend to have lower-wage jobs than White Americans—often without employer-provided benefits—and to become unemployed more often and for longer periods. African Americans, for example, typically have experienced twice as much unemployment as other Americans. Scholars have argued that deep-seated patterns of structural racism affect the access of American racial and ethnic minorities not just to jobs but also to quality education, housing, and health care. As a result these groups

FIGURE 14.4

Poverty Levels in the United States, 1966–2018

Poverty rates in the U.S. population vary considerably. The rate of poverty among female-headed households declined significantly in the 1990s, increased again after 2000, and declined again after 2010. Which group has seen the greatest reduction in its poverty level since 1966? How might poverty levels change with the effects of the coronavirus pandemic?

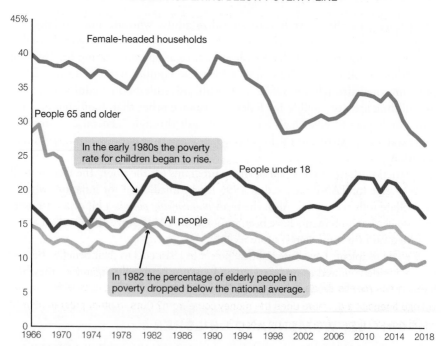

PERCENTAGE LIVING BELOW POVERTY LINE

Female-headed households

People 65 and older

In the early 1980s the poverty rate for children began to rise.

People under 18

All people

In 1982 the percentage of elderly people in poverty dropped below the national average.

SOURCES: U.S. Census Bureau, Historical Poverty Tables, "Table 2. Poverty Status of People by Family Relationship, Race, and Hispanic Origin: 1959 to 2018," and "Table 3. Poverty Status of People, by Age, Race, and Hispanic Origin: 1969 to 2018," www.census.gov/data/tables/time-series/demo/income-poverty /historical-poverty-people.html (accessed 5/12/20).

are disproportionately vulnerable to financial insecurity, risk, poverty, and lack of opportunity.[53]

More than 30 years ago, policy analysts began to talk about the "feminization of poverty," or the fact that women are more likely than men to be poor. For example, single mothers are more than twice as likely to be poor as the average American (see Figure 14.4). When the Social Security Act was passed in 1935, lawmakers did not envision that so many single women would be heading families or that so many women with children would also be working. This combination of changes helped make AFDC more controversial. Many people asked why welfare recipients shouldn't work, if the majority of women not on welfare worked. Such questions led to the welfare reform of 1996, which created TANF.

One of the most troubling issues related to American social policy is the number of children who live in poverty. The rate of child poverty in 2019 was 14.4 percent— 5 percentage points higher than that of the population as a whole—and the rates for African American children (30.2 percent) and Latino children (20.9 percent) were much higher than for White children (8.3 percent).[54] These high rates of poverty stem in part from the design of American social policies. Because these policies offer little help to poor adults, either working or nonworking, the children of these adults are likely to be poor as well.

As child poverty has grown, several lobbying groups have emerged to represent children's interests; the best known of these is the Children's Defense Fund. But even with a sophisticated lobbying operation on their behalf, and although their numbers are large, poor children do not vote and therefore cannot wield much political power.[55]

Domestic Policy: What Do You Think?

Economic and social policies raise issues that cut to the core of Americans' lives and livelihoods. You may have frustrations with government economic policies that affect your life in areas such as college funding, wages, taxes, and transportation, or with social policies that help particular groups.

Government policy affects your future job opportunities, what kinds of further education or training you can access, and where you may live. Yet changing policy in any of these areas means tough decisions: If more government funding is provided for, say, college financial aid, where does the money come from? Cuts to other programs? If so, which ones? Higher taxes, but on whom?

★ Most conservatives have pressed for freer markets and less government, while most liberals have defended the need for market regulation and more government intervention in the economy. Where do you stand on this debate?

★ Do you tend to agree with liberals, who often argue that more generous social policies are needed if the United States is truly to ensure equality of opportunity? Or do you tend to agree with conservatives, who often argue that social policies that offer income support take the ideal of equality too far and do for individuals what those individuals should be doing for themselves?

★ What do you think is the government's most effective tool in economic policy making: fiscal policy, monetary policy, or regulation?

★ Look back at C. Shonda Woods's story at the beginning of the chapter. What views do you imagine she has about the role of government? Do you think the coronavirus pandemic will change people's views about social and economic policy? Why or why not?

★ Which do you think the government should increase spending on (if any): social insurance, social assistance, or tax expenditures? Who would benefit most from your plan?

Practice Quiz

1. Government attempts to manipulate the economy by using its taxing and spending powers are called *(p. 431)*
   a) antitrust policies.
   b) expropriation policies.
   c) monetary policies.
   d) fiscal policies.
   e) redistributive policies.

2. A policy whose objective is to reduce the gaps between the highest and lowest income groups is called *(p. 432)*
   a) antitrust policy.
   b) deregulation.
   c) discretionary spending.
   d) equalization.
   e) redistribution.

3. Monetary policy manipulates the growth of the economy by *(p. 435)*
   a) taxing and spending.
   b) privatizing and nationalizing selected industries.
   c) controlling the availability of money to banks.
   d) regulating the foreign exchange of currency.
   e) distributing welfare benefits.

4. The most powerful institution in determining America's monetary policy is *(pp. 435–36)*
   a) the Department of Commerce.
   b) the Department of the Treasury.
   c) the federal judiciary.
   d) the Federal Reserve System.
   e) the president.

5. The United States' welfare state was constructed initially in response to *(p. 441)*
   a) the Civil War.
   b) World War II.
   c) political reforms of the Progressive Era.
   d) the Great Depression.
   e) the growth of the military–industrial complex.

6. Which of the following is an example of a contributory program? *(pp. 442–43)*
   a) Medicaid
   b) Medicare
   c) Temporary Assistance for Needy Families
   d) Supplemental Nutrition Assistance Program
   e) Aid to Families with Dependent Children

7. Means testing requires that applicants for welfare benefits show *(p. 443)*
   a) that they are capable of getting to and from their workplace.
   b) that they have the ability to store and prepare food.
   c) a financial need for assistance.
   d) that they have the time and resources to take full advantage of federal educational opportunities.
   e) that they are natural-born citizens who have never been convicted of a felony.

8. Which of the following are examples of in-kind benefits? *(pp. 443–44)*
   a) Medicaid and the Supplemental Nutrition Assistance Program
   b) Social Security and the Troubled Assets Relief Program
   c) Medicare and unemployment compensation
   d) the GI Bill of Rights and the Equal Rights Amendment
   e) the Earned Income Tax Credit and No Child Left Behind

9. What event prompted the federal government to enter the field of public education? *(p. 446)*
   a) the Civil War
   b) the Great Depression
   c) World War II
   d) the Soviet Union's launching of *Sputnik*
   e) the civil rights movement

10. Which of the following was *not* part of the No Child Left Behind Act? *(p. 446)*
    a) a provision allowing parents whose child is attending a failing school to transfer the child to a better school
    b) a requirement that states failing to meet national standards improve student performance by providing tutoring, longer school days, and additional summer school
    c) federal requirements for testing and school accountability
    d) a requirement that a national test be used to evaluate every student around the country
    e) a requirement that every child in grades 3 through 8 be tested yearly for proficiency in math and reading

11. Who are the chief beneficiaries of the "shadow welfare state"? *(p. 452)*
    a) children
    b) the elderly
    c) the nonworking poor
    d) the working poor
    e) the middle and upper classes

12. Which three government programs provide assistance to the working poor? *(p. 454)*
    a) Temporary Assistance for Needy Families, Medicare, and the Supplemental Nutrition Assistance Program
    b) the Earned Income Tax Credit, the Supplemental Nutrition Assistance Program, and the Affordable Care Act
    c) Temporary Assistance for Needy Families, Social Security, and the Earned Income Tax Credit
    d) Temporary Assistance for Needy Families, Medicare, and the Affordable Care Act
    e) Social Security, Medicaid, and Medicare

Key Terms

fiscal policy *(p. 431)*

inflation *(p. 431)*

tariff *(p. 431)*

redistribution *(p. 432)*

progressive taxation *(p. 432)*

regressive taxation *(p. 434)*

budget deficit *(p. 434)*

national debt *(p. 434)*

subsidies *(p. 434)*

contracting *(p. 435)*

monetary policies *(p. 435)*

Federal Reserve System *(p. 436)*

monopoly *(p. 437)*

antitrust policy *(p. 437)*

deregulation *(p. 438)*

laissez-faire capitalism *(p. 438)*

Keynesians *(p. 439)*

supply-side economics *(p. 440)*

welfare state *(p. 441)*

Social Security *(p. 442)*

contributory programs *(p. 442)*

indexing *(p. 442)*

cost-of-living adjustments (COLAs) *(p. 442)*

Medicare *(p. 443)*

noncontributory programs *(p. 443)*

means testing *(p. 443)*

Medicaid *(p. 443)*

Supplemental Nutrition Assistance Program (SNAP) *(p. 444)*

in-kind benefits *(p. 444)*

equality of opportunity *(p. 444)*

Foreign Policy

WHAT GOVERNMENT DOES AND WHY IT MATTERS

Foreign policy carries tremendous consequences for ordinary people. In January 2017, President Trump signed an executive order banning travel to the United States for people from Iran, Iraq, Libya, Somalia, Sudan, Syria, and Yemen. The president's purpose was to protect U.S. borders and prohibit entry from countries with lax security standards.

As with any public policy, Americans' views on the travel ban varied. Amanda Patrick of Georgia, a 38-year-old tax associate with a young son, supported the ban, saying, "The biggest thing for me, especially with having a child now, is the safety factor. Just people coming in that we aren't properly vetting."[1]

Yet for others, the travel ban has meant personal turmoil. Mohamed Iye, an American citizen born in Somalia, was about to be reunited with his Somali wife and two American daughters after a two-year separation when the travel ban was issued, stranding his family in Nairobi, Kenya. He, and many others, joined lawsuits against the ban. "It was never my intention to go against the

America's foreign policy can have profound effects on the lives of individuals here and abroad. President Trump's decision to ban immigration from certain countries put many lives in limbo, like that of Mohamed Iye (pictured here). Iye was reunited with his family after being stranded in Kenya when the ban was declared. Supporters of the ban maintain it is necessary to protect America from foreign threats.

president of the United States," Iye said. "I was just following the law and doing everything the way it's in the books. And it came to this."[2]

The Trump administration's travel ban, which was challenged in the federal courts, was finally upheld by the U.S. Supreme Court in the 2018 case of *Trump v. Hawaii*. But the travel ban took on additional significance as the coronavirus pandemic affected countries around the globe. In January 2020, President Trump expanded the travel ban to include six additional countries: Nigeria (Africa's largest economy and most populous nation), Myanmar, Eritrea, Sudan, Tanzania, and Kyrgyzstan. When Berea College in Kentucky announced the next month that it was canceling the rest of the spring 2020 semester due to the pandemic, Stephen Nwalorizi, a senior from Nigeria, thought it was "going to end my education." Most students from the travel-ban countries rely on single-entry student visas, which means that if they return home they need to get a new visa to return to school. This was already difficult with the travel ban, but became a near impossibility with the pandemic raging. Fortunately Nwalorizi's college granted him an exemption to stay on campus, allowing him to remain in the United States.[3]

These examples illustrate just one of the complexities of foreign policy. A government's first duty is to protect its citizens, but should protection mean the exclusion of citizens of other countries from America's shores? Foreign trade raises equally complicated issues. America's interests and those of foreign countries are so closely intertwined that the Trump administration's tariffs against foreign auto companies, and subsequent retaliation from America's trading partners, hurt workers in South Carolina, where BMWs (a German car) are assembled and then shipped all over the world.

Or in the realm of security interests, when dealing with America's rivals such as Russia, China, and North Korea, what is the proper mix of such foreign policy tools as diplomacy, economic pressure, and the threat of force? To make matters even more complicated, some threats require international rather than national responses, but achieving international cooperation is sometimes problematic. President Trump has demanded that America's NATO allies pay a larger share of the collective cost of defense, though his demands threaten to undermine the NATO alliance. The United States, like other nations, struggles to strike the right balance between competition and cooperation in the international arena.

CHAPTER GOALS

★ Explain how foreign policy is designed to promote security, prosperity, and humanitarian goals (pp. 465–71)

★ Describe the structure and roles of the major organizations and players in U.S. foreign-policy making (pp. 471–79)

★ Describe the means the United States uses to carry out foreign policy today (pp. 479–84)

★ Explain the foreign policy problems facing American policy makers today (pp. 486–89)

The Goals of Foreign Policy

Explain how foreign policy is designed to promote security, prosperity, and humanitarian goals

The term *foreign policy* refers to the programs and policies that determine America's relations with other nations and foreign entities. Foreign policy includes diplomacy, military and security policy, international human rights policy, and various forms of economic policy, such as trade policy and international energy policy. In fact, foreign policy and domestic policy are not completely separate categories but are closely intertwined. As we will see, domestic politics affects foreign policy, and foreign policy certainly affects domestic politics.

Although U.S. foreign policy has a number of purposes, two main goals stand out: security and prosperity. Some Americans also favor a third goal—improving the quality of life for all the world's people. Others say the United States should remain focused on its own challenges and not get involved in solving the world's problems. These foreign policy goals overlap with one another, and none can be pursued fully in isolation.

SECURITY

To many Americans, the chief goal of the nation's foreign policy is protection of U.S. security in an often hostile world. Traditionally, the United States has been concerned about possible threats from other countries, such as Nazi Germany during the 1940s and then the Soviet Union until the late 1980s. Today, American security policy is concerned with the actions not only of other nations but also of terrorists and other hostile groups and individuals, often called **non-state actors**.[4] To protect the nation's security from foreign threats, the United States has built an enormous military apparatus and a complex array of intelligence-gathering institutions, such as the Central Intelligence Agency (CIA), charged with evaluating and anticipating challenges from abroad.[5]

Security is, of course, a broad term. Policy makers must be concerned with Americans' physical security. The September 11, 2001, terrorist attacks killed and injured thousands, and new attacks could be even more catastrophic. Policy makers must also be concerned with such matters as the security of food supplies, transportation infrastructure, and energy supplies. Many American efforts in the Middle East, for example, are aimed at ensuring continuing American access to vital oil fields.

In recent years, cyberspace has become a new security concern. The nation's dependence on computers means that the government must be alert to efforts by hostile governments, groups, or even individual "hackers" to damage computer networks or access sensitive or proprietary information. The U.S. government has often charged Chinese and Russian government and military agencies with

non-state actors groups other than nation-states that attempt to play a role in the international system; terrorist groups are one type of non-state actor

stealing American secrets through cyber espionage. In 2017 it appeared that a popular antivirus software marketed by a Russian company was being used by the Russian government to spy on American corporations and government agencies.

During the eighteenth and nineteenth centuries, American security was based mainly on the geographic isolation of the United States. Separated by oceans from European and Asian powers, many Americans thought that the country's security would be best preserved by remaining aloof from international power struggles. This policy was known as **isolationism**. In his 1796 Farewell Address, President George Washington warned Americans to avoid permanent alliances with foreign powers; and in 1823, President James Monroe warned foreign powers not to meddle in the Western Hemisphere. Washington's warning and what came to be called the Monroe Doctrine were the cornerstones of U.S. foreign policy until the end of the nineteenth century. The United States saw itself as the dominant power in the Western Hemisphere and, indeed, believed that its "manifest destiny" was to expand from sea to sea. The rest of the world, however, should remain at arm's length.

In the twentieth century, technology made oceans less of a barrier to foreign threats, and the world's growing economic interdependence meant that the nation could no longer ignore events abroad. The United States entered World War I in 1917 on the side of Great Britain and France when President Woodrow Wilson concluded that a German victory would adversely affect U.S. economic and security interests. In 1941 the United States was drawn into World War II when Japan, hoping to become the dominant power in the Pacific, attacked the U.S. Pacific naval fleet anchored at Pearl Harbor, Hawaii. Even before the attack, President Franklin Roosevelt had concluded that the United States must act to prevent a victory by the German–Japanese–Italian Axis alliance. Until Pearl Harbor, however, he had been unable to overcome isolationist arguments that American security was best served by leaving foreigners to their own devices. The attack proved that the Pacific Ocean could not protect the United States from foreign foes and effectively discredited isolationism as a security policy.

isolationism avoidance of involvement in the affairs of other nations

containment a policy designed to curtail the political and military expansion of a hostile power

preventive war a policy of striking first when a nation fears that a foreign foe is contemplating hostile action

appeasement the effort to forestall war by giving in to the demands of a hostile power

Following World War II, the United States developed a new security policy known as **containment** to check or "contain" the growing power of the Soviet Union, which by the end of the 1940s had built a huge empire and enormous military forces, including nuclear weapons and bombers capable of attacking the United States. The United States committed itself to maintaining its own military might as a means of deterrence, to discourage the Soviets from attacking the United States or its allies.

Some Americans wanted a more aggressive policy and argued that we should attack the Soviets before it was too late, a policy known as **preventive war**. Others said that we should show our peaceful intentions and attempt to placate the Soviets, a policy called **appeasement**. The disastrous results of the British effort to prevent World War II by appeasing Nazi Germany, however, had left most Americans with little confidence in appeasement as a policy.

The policies that the United States actually adopted, **deterrence** and containment, could be seen as midway between preventive war and appeasement. Deterrence signals, on the one hand, peaceful intentions but also, on the other hand, a willingness and ability to fight if attacked. Thus, during the era of confrontation with the Soviet Union, known as the **Cold War**, the United States frequently asserted that it had no intention of attacking the Soviet Union but also built a huge military force, including an arsenal of over 1,500 nuclear warheads, and frequently asserted that it had the ability and will to respond to a Soviet attack with overwhelming force. The Soviet Union, which had also built powerful nuclear and conventional military forces, announced that its nuclear weapons were also intended for deterrent purposes.

Eventually, the two sides possessed such enormous arsenals of nuclear missiles that each had the ability to destroy the other many times over. This heavily armed standoff came to be called a posture of "mutually assured destruction," which discouraged either side from attacking the other. Eventually, this situation led to a period of "détente," in which a number of arms control agreements were signed and the threat of war was reduced. The Soviet Union collapsed in 1991, and the new Russia, though still a formidable power, at the time seemed to pose less of a threat to the United States.

A policy of deterrence requires that a nation not only possess large military forces but also convince potential adversaries with *certainty* that it is willing to fight if attacked. Thus, during the Cold War the United States engaged in wars in Korea and Vietnam, where it had no particular interests, because American policy makers believed that if it did not, the Soviets would be emboldened to pursue an expansionist policy elsewhere, thinking that the Americans would not respond.

This arrangement may not be valid or relevant in the context of some contemporary security threats. The September 11, 2001, terrorist attacks,

During the Cold War, the United States and the Soviet Union engaged in an arms race, each acquiring nuclear weapons to deter the other from attacking.

for example, demonstrated the threat that non-state actors and so-called rogue states might acquire significant military capabilities, including nuclear weapons, and would not be affected by America's deterrent capabilities. Unlike **nation-states**, which are countries with governments and fixed borders, terrorist groups have no fixed geographic location that can be attacked. Terrorists may believe they can attack and melt away, leaving the United States with no one against whom to retaliate. Hence, the threat of massive retaliation does not deter them. Rogue states are nations with often unstable and erratic leaders who seem to pursue policies driven by ideological or religious fervor rather than careful consideration of economic or human costs. The United States considers North Korea and Iran to be rogue states, though most academic analysts see both nations' leaders as behaving belligerently but not necessarily irrationally.

To counter these new security threats, the George W. Bush administration shifted from a policy of deterrence to one of preventive war—the willingness to strike first in order to prevent an attack, particularly by enemies that might be armed with weapons of mass destruction. The United States declared that, if necessary, it would take action to disable terrorist groups and rogue states before they could develop the capacity to harm the United States.[6] The Bush administration's "global war on terror" was an expression of prevention, as was the U.S. invasion of Iraq in 2003. The United States also refused to rule out the possibility that it would attack North Korea or Iran if it deemed those nations' nuclear programs to be imminent threats to American security. Accompanying this shift in military doctrines was an enormous increase in overall U.S. military spending (see Figure 15.1).

President Obama took a less aggressive line, saying that the United States would rely on diplomacy and economic sanctions. President Trump, however, said that the United States was prepared to use overwhelming force against its adversaries. Trump called North Korean leader Kim Jong-un "Little Rocket Man" and declared that only force would thwart Kim's ambitions. Nevertheless, in 2018 and 2019, Trump met with Kim three times to discuss ways of reducing tensions on the Korean Peninsula. Yet no agreements were reached. Also in 2018, Trump met with Russian president Vladimir Putin. Trump called the meeting a great success, but critics charged that Trump had not demanded an accounting for Russian attempts to influence the 2016 American election. In April 2020, Kim temporarily dropped from sight, leading to speculation that he might have serious health problems. The United States began to ponder the impact of a leadership change in North Korea.

Generally speaking, President Trump has taken a belligerent tone toward America's adversaries while seeking to avoid military involvements. President Theodore Roosevelt once declared that in foreign affairs it was important to speak softly and carry a big stick. Critics have accused Trump of speaking loudly while carrying a small stick. Thus, in 2019, while denouncing the Assad regime in Syria, Trump withdrew most American troops from the region, leaving America's longtime Kurdish allies without protection. President Trump said America could not afford to be drawn into every regional conflict.

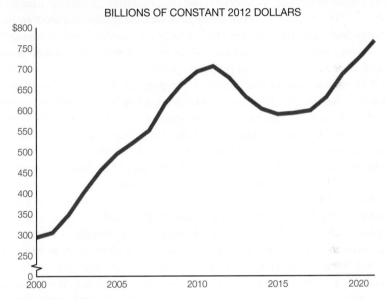

BILLIONS OF CONSTANT 2012 DOLLARS

*Data for 2020 and 2021 are estimated.
SOURCE: Office of Management and Budget, "Table 3.1—Outlays by Superfunction and Function: 1940–2025," www.whitehouse.gov/omb/historical-tables/ (accessed 7/15/20).

ECONOMIC PROSPERITY

A second major goal of U.S. foreign policy is promoting American prosperity. America's international economic policies are intended to expand employment opportunities in the United States, to maintain access to foreign energy supplies, to promote foreign investment in the United States, and to lower the prices Americans pay for goods and services.

Among the key elements of U.S. international economic policy is trade policy, which seeks to promote American goods and services abroad. The United States is the world's largest importer and exporter of goods and services. In 2017 it exported more than $2.3 trillion in goods and services while importing $2.9 trillion. Roughly 40 million jobs in the United States are directly or indirectly tied to international

World Trade Organization (WTO) an international organization promoting free trade that grew out of the General Agreement on Tariffs and Trade

United States-Mexico-Canada Agreement (USMCA) a trade treaty between the United States, Canada, and Mexico to lower and eliminate tariffs among the three countries

trade. Accordingly, America has a vital interest in maintaining international trade and monetary practices that promote American prosperity.

This effort involves a complex arrangement of treaties, tariffs, and other mechanisms of policy formation. Trade policy is always complicated because Americans have a complicated relationship to trade. Most Americans benefit from a policy of free trade, which tends to reduce the cost of goods and services. Consumer electronics such as televisions and smartphones, for example, would be far more expensive if they were not imported from all over the world. However, many American industries and their employees are hurt by free trade if it results in factories and jobs moving abroad. Hence, trade policy always produces huge political battles between those who stand to benefit and those who stand to lose from particular policies.

In 2016 one of Donald Trump's main campaign pledges was to end free-trade policies that he deemed harmful to American workers. In 2018 the president imposed tariffs on foreign imports that sparked retaliation from U.S. trading partners. Some American manufacturers benefited from the tariffs, while others were hurt by foreign retaliation against U.S. goods. Ironically, America's farm states generally supported Donald Trump in 2016 and 2020 but American agricultural exports were hurt by the trade war the president sparked.

The United States is a member of the most important international organization for promoting trade, the **World Trade Organization (WTO)**, as well as a number of regional arrangements designed to reduce trade barriers. These include the **United States-Mexico-Canada Agreement (USMCA)**, formerly known as NAFTA, a trade treaty among the United States, Canada, and Mexico that the Trump administration renegotiated in 2018. Under the terms of the new agreement, the United States was able to obtain better access to the Canadian dairy market and obtained concessions from Mexico on auto imports. Dairy farmers and auto workers are important Trump constituencies, and the president was anxious to please both groups.

HUMAN RIGHTS

Many Americans believe that the United States has an obligation to protect human rights and to provide assistance throughout the world. Other Americans say we should spend our resources at home and let other nations look after their own people. Still a third group of Americans view human rights and humanitarian policies as a form of "soft power," serving American interests and winning friends by demonstrating our concern for the oppressed and less fortunate throughout the world. This third group has generally been dominant within the American foreign policy community.

The United States has a long-standing commitment to human rights and is a party to most major international human rights agreements. This commitment has a lower priority in American foreign policy than security concerns and economic interests, however; thus, the United States is likely to overlook human rights violations by its major trading partners, such as China, and such allies as Saudi Arabia. Nevertheless, human rights concerns do play a role in American foreign policy. For example, beginning in 2007 the United States has annually made available several million dollars in small grants to pay medical and legal expenses of individuals who have been the victims of retaliation in their own countries for working against their governments' repressive practices. In this small way, the United States is backing its often-asserted principles.

As the world's wealthiest nation, the United States also recognizes an obligation to assist nations facing emergencies. For example, between 2010 and 2017 the United States provided more than $5 billion in assistance to Haiti after a huge earthquake devastated the island nation.[7] In 2020, the United States provided assistance to the Republic of Uzbekistan after a dam collapse displaced 70,000 people; to Pacific Island nations that suffered millions of dollars in damage from Tropical Cyclone Harold; and millions of dollars in emergency assistance to the people of war-torn Yemen.

In many ways, the coronavirus pandemic revealed the limits on international cooperation in the face of global emergencies. Every nation, including the United States, worked to secure medical supplies and future supplies of potential vaccines for its own people with little concern for the interests of others. While quarreling with one another, the wealthy nations paid little heed to the needs of poor countries not in a position to secure favorable treatment from pharmaceutical companies.

American Foreign Policy Is Shaped by Government and Nongovernment Actors

> **Describe the structure and roles of the major organizations and players in U.S. foreign-policy making**

As we have seen, domestic policies are made by governmental institutions and influenced by a variety of interest groups, political movements, and even the mass media. The same is true in the realm of foreign policy. The president and the chief advisers are the principal architects of U.S. foreign policy. However, Congress, the bureaucracy, the courts, political parties, interest groups, and trade associations also play important roles in this realm.

THE PRESIDENT AND THE EXECUTIVE BRANCH

The president is the leading figure in the conduct of American foreign policy. The president's foreign policy powers today, particularly in the military realm, are far greater than the Constitution's framers had thought wise. The framers gave the power to declare war to Congress and made the president the nation's top military commander if and when Congress chose to go to war. Today, presidents both command the troops and decide when to go to war.

Among America's 15 presidents during the past century only 5—Hoover, Eisenhower, Nixon, George H. W. Bush, and Joe Biden—had any extensive foreign policy experience before taking office. The others were forced to learn on the job.[8]

All recent presidents, like most of their predecessors, were nevertheless faced with momentous challenges to American security and to America's international interests. George W. Bush, in particular, was compelled to develop a response to the September 11, 2001, terror attacks. In a 2002 speech at West Point, the president announced a policy of unilateral action and preemptive war—what came to be called the **Bush Doctrine**. Bush said, "Our security will require all Americans . . . to be ready for preemptive action when necessary to defend our liberty and to defend our lives."

In his own West Point speech in 2014, President Obama articulated a different policy when he said the United States must reduce its reliance on military force and make more use of diplomacy. But even though he expressed reservations about unilateral preemption, during his administration the United States continued to launch many attacks against suspected terrorists before they were able to strike.

President Trump rattled America's allies by declaring an "America first" foreign policy and adopting a confrontational posture toward North Korea and Iran. In terms of actions, however, through 2020, Trump seemed to have given diplomacy a greater emphasis, as evidenced by his meetings with North Korea's leader and Russian president Putin, and the establishment of diplomatic relations between Israel and two of its neighbors, Bahrain and the United Arab Emirates.

As the dominant figure in American foreign and military policy, the president is in a position to decide with whom, when, and how the United States will interact in the international arena. Since World War II, American military forces have fought in many parts of the world. The decision to commit troops to battle was generally made by the president, often without much consultation with the Congress. When President Obama ordered special operations soldiers to attack Osama bin Laden's compound in Pakistan, members of Congress learned of the operation and bin Laden's death from news broadcasts—just like other Americans. And it is the president and his representatives who conduct negotiations with other nations to deal with international problems and crises.

Presidents can also make use of **executive agreements** to partially bypass congressional power in foreign relations. Executive agreements are agreements made by the president with other countries that have the force of a treaty but do not require Senate ratification. Thus, the importance of the Senate's constitutional power to block treaties has sharply diminished. Since 1947 the United States has entered into more than 17,000 different agreements with other nations and international entities. Of these, only 6 percent were submitted to the Senate for approval.[9]

Foreign Aid in Comparison

Many Americans overestimate both the amount that the government spends on foreign aid and the percent of GNI (a representation of the size of the overall economy) spent. In these figures we see that the United States is the clear leader globally if one looks at the dollars spent on foreign aid. However, if we take account of the size and wealth of a country's economy, the United States falls much further down the rankings.

1. Why would a country choose to spend money on foreign aid? What factors would limit the amount a country was willing or able to spend on such aid?
2. Do the data in these figures imply that America is less generous with aid than other nations are? What other explanations are there for the differences across countries?

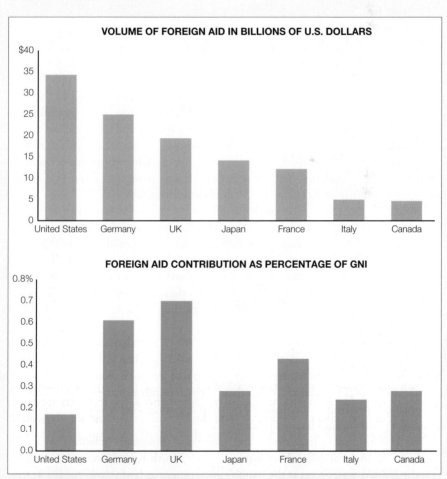

SOURCE: Organization for Economic Cooperation and Development, "Development Cooperation Profiles, 2019," www.oecd.org (accessed 5/22/20).

Beyond the president, several government agencies within the executive branch play important roles in shaping and executing American foreign policy.

The National Security Council The National Security Council (NSC) was created in 1947 as an entity within the Executive Office of the President (EOP) to oversee America's foreign policy institutions, synthesize information coming from the bureaucracy, and help the president develop foreign policy.[10] The NSC is a "sub-cabinet" made up of the president, the vice president, and the secretaries of defense, state, and homeland security, plus other presidential appointees, including the director of the CIA and the director of national intelligence. The heart of the NSC is its staff, consisting of about 200 foreign policy experts capable of evaluating political, economic, and military issues throughout the world. The head of the NSC staff is the president's national security adviser (NSA).[11] Some NSAs have been close presidential confidants and have exercised considerable power because they had the president's ear and trust.

The State Department Routine matters of international diplomacy come under the authority of the Department of State, the first federal agency created by the first Congress in 1789. The State Department is headed by the secretary of state, a member of the president's Cabinet and, nominally, the most important foreign policy official after the president. The secretary's actual importance varies with his or her relationship to the president. Franklin Delano Roosevelt, for example, was barely aware that Cordell Hull existed, relegating the secretary to observer of the diplomatic scene. On the other end of the spectrum, George W. Bush worked very closely with Condoleezza Rice, who served as his chief foreign policy adviser. In some instances, presidents use their secretaries less as advisers and more as roving ambassadors, like John Kerry in the Obama administration.

Donald Trump relied occasionally on his first secretary of state, Rex Tillerson, but severely criticized him for his belief that diplomacy could reduce the nuclear threat from North Korea; Trump asserted that only force could end the threat. In 2018, Trump fired Tillerson and replaced him with CIA director Mike Pompeo. The relationship between the two became strained during the Trump impeachment process when several State Department officials testified against the president. Trump faulted Pompeo for hiring officials the president deemed disloyal to his administration.

The State Department oversees more than 300 U.S. embassies, consulates, and diplomatic missions around the world. Embassies are headed by ambassadors. While most embassy staff members are officers of the U.S. Foreign Service, the State Department's professional diplomatic corps, a number of ambassadors have no diplomatic expertise and are, instead, political appointees being rewarded for their campaign contributions to the president.

The United States "recognizes" and maintains diplomatic relations with 195 countries. It does not officially recognize Iran or North Korea. Recognition means that the United States accepts the nation's government as lawful, will engage in routine trade and diplomatic exchanges with it, and will accept its citizens' passports

The president meets with many foreign leaders, often after key agreements have been hammered out by the president's staff. In a highly controversial move, President Trump met alone with Russian president Vladimir Putin in July 2018, leaving many staffers and observers wondering what the two said.

for travel into America. At the various embassies and missions, State Department officials monitor American treaty and trade relations with the host country, provide assistance for American business interests and tourists, and deal with foreign nationals attempting to emigrate to or visit the United States.

President Trump generally did not follow this well-established set of procedures. He preferred to begin with a face-to-face meeting with a foreign leader and leave it to staff to fill in details later. In the case of Trump's 2018 meeting with Putin, the two leaders met alone, without staff. State Department and other staff were left trying to determine exactly what had been said during the meeting.

Trump's undisciplined style caused a number of problems. In 2019, during a phone call with Ukraine's newly elected president, Volodymyr Zelensky, Trump departed from his script to discuss allegations that the former vice president and potential 2020 Democratic presidential candidate, Joe Biden, along with Biden's son, Hunter, might have been tied to corrupt activities in Ukraine. Trump seemed to link U.S. military aid to Ukraine to Zelensky's willingness to cooperate in investigating the Bidens. When the contents of Trump's phone call leaked, Democrats charged that Trump had committed the impeachable offense of inviting a foreign government's interference in an American election, and the phone call became the centerpiece of House impeachment hearings and subsequent impeachment in 2019.

Department of Defense Since its creation in 1947, the Defense Department (DoD) has played a major role in the making of American foreign policy. DoD employs more than 2 million military and civilian personnel and is a huge and complex bureaucratic entity.[12] Each of the military services—the army, navy, air force, marines, and National Guard—is led by a chief of staff and collectively these leaders constitute the Joint Chiefs of Staff (JCS), led by the chairman of the Joint Chiefs, a presidential appointee who serves as the nation's top military commander. The chairman reports directly to the secretary of defense, who, in turn, answers to the president. Each of the three main services—army, navy, and air force—possesses its own civilian and military bureaucracies to administer and support its combat forces.

In recent years, American ambassadors have complained that they have been relegated to secondary status as the White House has looked to military commanders for information, advice, and policy implementation. For every region of the world, the U.S. military has assigned a "combatant commander," a senior general or admiral, to take charge of operations in that area. In many instances, these combatant commanders, who control troops, equipment, and intelligence capabilities, have become the real eyes, ears, and voices for American foreign policy in their designated regions. The combatant commanders report to the Joint Chiefs of Staff.

Intelligence Agencies The CIA is the United States' chief civilian intelligence agency, collecting information throughout the world, preparing analyses, and launching covert operations if the president wishes to use force but is unwilling to publicly acknowledge America's involvement. CIA operators also pilot many of the drones used to attack and kill suspected terrorists. Although the CIA and DoD were created by the same piece of legislation, the CIA director and secretary of defense have generally viewed one another as rivals in the intelligence field.

In 2005, Congress created the position of director of national intelligence (DNI) to coordinate intelligence activities and prepare the president's daily intelligence summary—a responsibility previously held by the CIA's director. This change came about because Congress concluded that the intelligence community's failure to anticipate the September 11, 2001, attacks was the result of a lack of coordination among the various agencies. Both the CIA and DoD resented the creation of the DNI, however, and put aside their mutual suspicions to join forces against the new position. Both agencies generally refuse to share information with the DNI, who, having no operational capabilities, has been left in the dark on many intelligence matters. National intelligence agencies seem generally to regard one another as rivals.[13]

The National Security Agency The National Security Agency (NSA) is a highly influential, and controversial, intelligence agency. Though housed within DoD, the NSA effectively reports directly to the president, providing the results of its worldwide electronic surveillance efforts. Surveillance of electronic communication has a long history in the United States, going back to a World War I government effort to read suspicious telegrams.[14] During the 1970s, however, Congress became concerned about secret White House surveillance efforts and, in 1978, enacted the Foreign Intelligence Surveillance Act (FISA), designed to regulate electronic surveillance by government agencies. In 2019, the FISA Court, the judicial body that must approve surveillance warrants requested by intelligence agencies, charged that the

FBI had made a practice of providing false information to the court and demanded immediate changes in FBI procedures.

CONGRESS

Through its general legislative powers, Congress can exercise broad influence over foreign policy. Congress may, for example, refuse to appropriate funds for presidential actions it finds unwise or inappropriate. This power of the purse also extends to military action. Not only does Congress have the constitutional power to declare war, but under its general legislative powers it must appropriate the funds needed to support military activities. In *Federalist* 69, Hamilton argues that Congress's power of the purse provides it with an ultimate check on the president's power as commander in chief.[15]

Presidents, as we saw, control several enormous bureaucracies through which to develop and implement foreign and security policies. Congress has far less bureaucratic capacity of its own, but it has committees that can influence the nation's international and military programs. Chief among these are the House and Senate committees charged with overseeing foreign policy, military affairs, and the collection and analysis of intelligence.

Key Congressional Committees in the Foreign Policy Realm On the Senate side, the most influential committee dealing with foreign policy is the U.S. Senate Committee on Foreign Relations. Established in 1816 as one of the original 10 standing committees of the Senate, it oversees the State Department, other foreign policy agencies, and executive branch compliance with several statutes, including the War Powers Resolution. Each of its seven subcommittees has jurisdiction over a specific region or subject matter.

Throughout its history, the Foreign Relations Committee has viewed its role as the guardian of congressional power in the foreign policy realm. Its power stems from its responsibility to confirm State Department officials and the requirement that it review treaties proposed by the executive branch before they can be referred to the full Senate for a vote on ratification. In recent years, the committee's efforts to influence presidential foreign policy initiatives have become less successful because presidents, as we noted above, have made use of executive agreements (not requiring senatorial approval) rather than treaties. Nevertheless, the committee occasionally flexes its muscles.

Paralleling the jurisdiction of the Senate Foreign Relations Committee is the House Committee on Foreign Affairs. The House committee is considerably less influential than its Senate counterpart, however, because it is involved neither in appointments nor in the ratification of treaties. For the most part, its hearings focus on symbolic questions.

In both houses of Congress, standing subcommittees of the Appropriations Committees are responsible for funding the State Department, foreign aid programs, and other matters in the foreign policy realm. Through these subcommittees as well as through the Foreign Relations and Foreign Affairs Committees, the Senate and House can indicate their displeasure with presidential programs by cutting or withholding funds. In 2017, for example, the Senate Appropriations Committee restored $11 billion in funding for the State Department and foreign operations that had been slashed by the Trump administration.

Armed Services and Intelligence The House and Senate Armed Services Committees oversee the Department of Defense and the Department of Energy (which houses America's nuclear weapons programs). In both houses of Congress, other standing committees are responsible for such matters as veterans' affairs. Defense appropriations are the domains of the House and Senate Defense Appropriations Subcommittees.

Generally, the House and Senate Armed Services Committees are friendly to the military and the defense contractors who provide support and equipment for America's military services. Sometimes, however, they make use of their staff resources and contacts in the military community to advocate for military programs not currently in the Pentagon's plans. In 2015, for example, both committees released reports calling for the armed services to focus on the growing threat of cyberattacks against U.S. weapons and communications software, and authorized spending $200 million for this purpose.[16]

The House and Senate Intelligence Committees were established during the 1970s to oversee America's growing intelligence bureaucracies and to review their activities at home and abroad. These committees have focused on such matters as American intelligence failures (notably the failure to predict and prevent the September 11, 2001, terrorist attacks), the use of private military contractors in missions organized by the CIA, clandestine CIA missions in other nations, and the use of drones to carry out military and intelligence missions in other nations. In 2019, the House Intelligence Committee reviewed allegations that President Trump had behaved improperly in dealing with Ukraine. Information reviewed by the Intelligence Committee helped to persuade congressional Democrats to support the president's impeachment.

INTEREST GROUPS

Although the president, the executive branch bureaucracy, and Congress are the true makers of foreign policy, the "foreign policy establishment" is a much larger arena. Many unofficial players exert varying degrees of influence on foreign policy, depending on their prestige and socioeconomic standing and, most important, the party and ideology that are dominant at a given moment.

The most important unofficial players are the interest groups. Economic groups are reputed to wield the most influence, but in fact it varies enormously from issue to issue and year to year. Some business groups represent industries dependent on exports, and others represent ones threatened by imports. Hence, "business" has more than one view on trade policy.

Another type of interest group with significant foreign policy influence comprises people who strongly identify with a particular country. For example, many Jewish Americans and evangelical Protestants possess strong emotional ties to Israel. In 2015 many, though not all, Jewish and evangelical groups lobbied heavily but ultimately unsuccessfully against the Obama administration's agreement with Iran, which they

Cuban Americans have strong voices in Congress in Senator Marco Rubio (R-Fla.), among others.

argued posed a threat to both the United States and Israel. Similarly, Cuban Americans, most recently represented by two powerful senators, Marco Rubio and Ted Cruz, have long been a strong voice in support of maintaining sanctions against the Castro regime in Cuba. Their influence helps explain why U.S. relations with Cuba were not normalized until 2015 and remain tenuous today.

A third type of interest group, more prominent in recent decades, is devoted to human rights or other global causes such as protection of the environment. An example is Amnesty International, whose exposés of human rights abuses have led to reforms in some countries. Environmental groups often depend more on demonstrations than on lobbying and electoral politics. Demonstrations in strategically located areas can have significant influence on American foreign policy. In recent years environmental activists have staged major protests, including at the 2015 Paris environmental summit that led to the signing of a series of international accords aimed at limiting the production of greenhouse gases. Environmental groups were furious when the Trump administration announced in 2017 that the United States would withdraw from the Paris Agreement.

Tools of American Foreign Policy: Diplomacy, Money, and Force

Describe the means the United States uses to carry out foreign policy today

Governments possess a variety of instruments, or tools, to implement foreign policy. We examine those instruments of American foreign policy most important today: diplomacy, the United Nations, the international monetary structure, economic aid and sanctions, collective security, military force, soft power, and arbitration.

DIPLOMACY

Diplomacy is a national government's representation of itself to foreign governments. Its purpose is to promote national values or interests by peaceful means. As mentioned earlier, the United States maintains diplomatic missions throughout the world. American ambassadors are tasked with maintaining good relations with foreign governments, promoting a positive view of the United States abroad, and securing information about foreign governments that might be helpful to the United States in its international dealings. When it comes to major diplomatic initiatives, however, such as new international agreements, presidents or their personal representatives usually take charge.

THE UNITED NATIONS

The **United Nations (UN)** is a very large and unwieldy institution with few powers, no standing armed forces of its own to implement its rules and resolutions, and little organization to make it an effective decision-making body. However, the usefulness of the UN to the United States as an instrument of foreign policy can be too easily underestimated. Its defenders maintain that although it lacks armed forces, it relies on the power of world opinion—and this is not to be taken lightly. The UN can serve as a useful forum for international discussions and as an instrument for multilateral action. Most peacekeeping efforts to which the United States contributes, for example, are undertaken under UN auspices.

diplomacy the representation of a government to other governments

United Nations (UN) an organization of nations founded in 1945 to be a channel for negotiation and a means of settling international disputes peaceably

The United Nations' supreme body is the UN General Assembly, comprising one representative of each of the 193 member states; each member representative has one vote, regardless of the size of the country. Important issues require a two-thirds majority vote, and the annual session of the General Assembly runs only from September to December (although it can call extra sessions). The powers of the UN belong mainly to its "executive committee," the UN Security Council, which alone has the real power to make decisions that member states are obligated by the UN Charter to implement. The Security Council may be called into session at any time, and the representative of each member (or a designated alternate) must be present at UN headquarters in New York at all times.

The Security Council is composed of 15 members: 5 are permanent (the major countries on the winning side in World War II), and 10 are elected by the General Assembly for two-year terms. The 5 permanent members are China, France, Russia, the United Kingdom, and the United States. Each of the 15 members has only one vote, and a 9-vote majority is required on all substantive matters. But each of the 5 permanent members also has a negative vote, a "veto"; and one veto is sufficient to reject any substantive proposal.

THE INTERNATIONAL MONETARY STRUCTURE

Fear of a repeat of the economic devastation that had followed World War I brought the United States together with its World War II allies (except the Soviet Union) to Bretton Woods, New Hampshire, in 1944 to create a new international economic structure for the postwar world. One major goal was to prevent economic instability that might lead to political instability and war, like the economic collapse in Germany that had opened the way for Nazism. At the same time, the new structure would give the United States and its allies greater leverage in the economic and political affairs of developing countries.

The Bretton Woods conference resulted in two institutions: the International Bank for Reconstruction and Development, commonly called the World Bank, and the **International Monetary Fund (IMF)**. The World Bank's chief mission is development aid to poor countries through long-term capital investments. The IMF was set up to provide for the short-term flow of money. After the war, the U.S. dollar replaced gold as the chief means by which the currency of one country would be "changed into" the currency of another country for purposes of making international transactions. To permit debtor countries with no international credit to make purchases and investments, the IMF was prepared to lend them dollars or other appropriate currencies to help them overcome temporary trade deficits.

> **International Monetary Fund (IMF)** an institution established in 1944 that provides loans and facilitates international monetary exchange

During the 1990s the importance of the IMF increased through its efforts to reform some of the largest debtor nations and formerly communist countries to bring them more fully into the global capitalist economy. Today, IMF loans total nearly $200 billion to 35 countries, including 16 in sub-Saharan Africa where drought and war have undermined local economies.

ECONOMIC AID AND SANCTIONS

Every year, the United States, acting on its own, provides nearly $50 billion in economic and military assistance to other nations. Some aid has a humanitarian purpose, such as health care, shelter for refugees, or famine relief. A good deal of it, however, is designed to promote American security interests or economic concerns. For example, the United States provides military assistance to a number of its allies in the form of advanced weapons or loans to help them purchase such weapons. These loans generally stipulate that the weapons must be purchased from American firms. In this way, the United States hopes to bolster its security and economic interests with one grant. The two largest recipients of American military assistance are Israel and Egypt, American allies that fought two wars against each other. The United States believes that its military assistance allows both countries to feel sufficiently secure to remain at peace with each other.

Aid is an economic carrot. Sanctions are an economic stick. Economic sanctions that the United States employs against other nations include trade embargoes, bans on investment, and efforts to prevent the World Bank or other international institutions from extending credit. Sanctions are most often imposed when the United States wants to weaken what it considers a hostile regime or to compel some particular action. In 2017, for example, existing economic sanctions against North Korea were tightened in response to that nation's missile tests. The United States also uses economic sanctions to advance its international humanitarian and human rights policy goals. U.S. sanctions are currently in place against a number of governments with records of serious violations of civil and political rights.[17]

COLLECTIVE SECURITY

Collective security refers to the development of alliances and agreements among a group of nations that pledge to aid one another in fending off or confronting security threats. In the aftermath of World War II, the United States' first collective security agreement was the Rio Treaty (1947), which created the Organization of American States. This was the model for all later collective security treaties, providing that an armed attack against any of its members "shall be considered as an attack against all the American [Western Hemisphere] States," including the United States. It was followed by the North Atlantic Treaty (signed in 1949), which created the North Atlantic Treaty Organization (NATO), joining the United States, Canada, and Western European nations. The Australian, New Zealand, United States Security (ANZUS) Treaty was signed in 1951. Three years later, the Southeast Asia Treaty created the Southeast Asia Treaty Organization (SEATO).

Since 1998, NATO has expanded to include formerly Communist Eastern European states such as the Czech Republic, Hungary, and Poland. After the collapse of the Soviet Union, the importance of NATO as a military alliance seemed to diminish. However, since 2014 the resurgence of Russia as a military power has forced NATO members once again to look to one another for support. In 2014, Russia seized the Crimean Peninsula from Ukraine and appeared to pose a threat to the Baltic states and other portions of the old Soviet empire. Russia has also sent military forces to support the Assad regime in Syria. In 2019, Russia sought to take advantage of President Trump's decision to withdraw most American forces from Syria by expanding its own power in the region. Facing an aggressive new Russia, NATO's period of relative quiet seemed to be coming to a close.

MILITARY FORCE

The most visible instrument of foreign policy is, of course, military force. The United States has built the world's most imposing military, with units stationed in virtually every corner of the globe, and accounts for one-third of the world's total military expenditures. The Prussian military strategist Carl von Clausewitz famously called war "politics by other means." By this he meant that force or the threat of it is a tool nations must sometimes use to achieve their foreign policy goals. Military force may be needed not only to protect a nation's security and economic interests but also, ironically, even to achieve humanitarian goals. For example, in 2014 and 2015, international military force was required to protect tens of thousands of Yazidi refugees threatened by ISIS forces in Iraq. Without the use of military force, humanitarian assistance to the Yazidis would have been irrelevant.[18]

Military force is generally considered a last resort and is avoided if possible, for several reasons. First, its use is extremely costly in both human and financial terms. Over the past 50 years, tens of thousands of Americans have been killed and hundreds of billions of dollars spent in America's military operations. Before they use military force to achieve national goals, policy makers must be certain that achieving those goals is essential and that other means are unlikely to succeed.

Second, the use of military force is inherently extremely risky. However carefully policy makers and generals plan, variables ranging from the weather to opponents' unexpected weapons and tactics may turn calculated operations into chaotic disasters, or operations expected to be quick and decisive into long, drawn-out, expensive struggles. In 2003, American policy makers expected to defeat the Iraqi army quickly and easily—and they did. They did not anticipate, however, that American forces would still be struggling years later to defeat the insurgency that arose in the war's aftermath.

Finally, in a democracy, any government that addresses policy problems through military means is almost certain to encounter political difficulties. Generally speaking, the American public will support relatively short and decisive military engagements.

Often, military efforts abroad do not turn out as the government or the public expected. Though most Americans were in favor of U.S. involvement in Afghanistan following September 11, 2001, public opinion on the issue has shifted.

If, however, a conflict drags on, producing casualties and expenses with no clear outcome, the public loses patience, and opposition politicians point to the government's lies and ineptitude. The wars in Korea, Vietnam, and Iraq are all examples of protracted conflicts whose domestic political repercussions became serious liabilities for the governments that launched them.

SOFT POWER

The term *soft power* refers to efforts by one nation to influence the people and governments of other nations by persuasion rather than coercion. The instruments of soft power include development aid, cultural diplomacy, student-exchange programs, and other mechanisms designed to shape perceptions. Cultural programs that send American actors, athletes, and musicians around the world are thought to offer a positive view of the United States that will encourage foreign governments and their citizens to see America as the "good guy" in international disputes. Exchange programs that bring foreign students to the United States serve a similar purpose. Although the effects of soft power are difficult to measure, the United States makes an effort to promote its "brand" of freedom and democracy throughout the world.

ARBITRATION

The final foreign policy tool to be considered is dispute arbitration. *Arbitration* means referring an international disagreement to a neutral third party for resolution. Arbitration is itself sometimes seen as a form of soft power, as distinguished from military force, economic sanctions, and other coercive foreign policy instruments. The United States will occasionally turn to international tribunals to resolve disputes with other countries—in 2008 it asked the International Court of Justice to resolve a long-standing dispute with Italy over American property confiscated by the Italian government more than 40 years earlier. The Trump administration has generally rejected the authority of international bodies that it sees as limitations on American sovereignty.

The United States continues to rely heavily on the work of arbitral panels to maintain the flow of international trade on which the U.S. economy depends. U.S. firms would be reluctant to do business abroad if they could not be certain that their property and contractual rights would be honored by other nations. Arbitration helps produce that certainty. Almost every international contract contains an arbitration clause requiring that disputes between the parties be resolved not by their governments but by impartial arbitral panels accepted by both sides.

FOR CRITICAL ANALYSIS ▶

1. The move to an all-volunteer military in the United States in 1973 resulted in a more educated and professionalized force. However, the United States has used the draft in the past, and some countries require military service of all citizens. Can you think of some arguments for and against each approach? What groups have increased in their U.S. military service over the past few years?

2. Does it matter if some groups are more heavily represented in the armed forces than others?

Who Serves in the U.S. Military?

The Department of Defense and the military are often responsible for implementing foreign policy that relates to security. Who are the men and women in the armed forces? The military has a far greater proportion of men to women than the general population, but in terms of race and ethnicity, the military is fairly similar to the United States as a whole. Residents of southern states are significantly more likely to enlist than those from other regions.

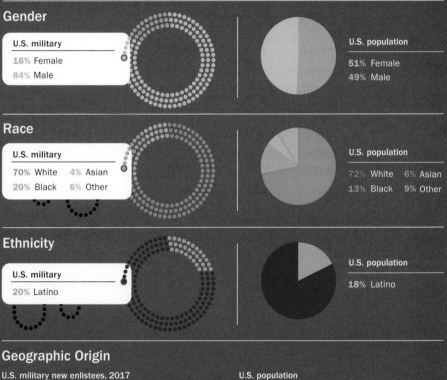

Gender

U.S. military
16% Female
84% Male

U.S. population
51% Female
49% Male

Race

U.S. military
70% White   4% Asian
20% Black   6% Other

U.S. population
72% White   6% Asian
13% Black   9% Other

Ethnicity

U.S. military
20% Latino

U.S. population
18% Latino

Geographic Origin

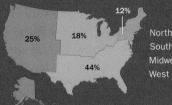

U.S. military new enlistees, 2017

12%
25%   18%
44%

Northeast 12%
South   44%
Midwest   18%
West   25%

U.S. population

17%
24%   21%
38%

Northeast 17%
South   38%
Midwest   21%
West   24%

SOURCES: CNA Analysis & Solutions, "Population Representation in the Military Services 2017," https://www.cna.org/pop-rep/2017/summary/summary.pdf; U.S. Census Bureau, "Data Profile of the United States of America," census.gov.

Daunting Foreign Policy Issues Face the United States

Explain the foreign policy problems facing American policy makers today

The United States currently faces many foreign policy problems, but this section will examine only a few major issues that stand out: relations with China and Russia, relations with Iran and North Korea, international trade policy, and the global environment. Each reveals how the key players in foreign policy use the tools at their disposal to achieve their policy goals.

A POWERFUL CHINA AND A RESURGENT RUSSIA

After the United States, China and Russia are the world's greatest military powers. China is an economic power as well, with an economy that in some respects already outpaces America's and continues to grow. China seems determined to expand its military capabilities and to replace the United States as the dominant power in Asia. The United States has no desire to engage in a military conflict with China but, at the same time, would prefer to blunt Chinese ambitions.

The relationship between the United States and China represents a growing concern for American policy makers, who have worked to strengthen U.S. alliances with other Asian nations, including India, Japan, and Vietnam, in order to increase American power in the region and prevent the rise of China. President Trump has also sought to use trade policy, especially tariff barriers and stricter efforts to prevent China from acquiring American intellectual property, to forestall the rise of Chinese power.

While relations with China are a long-term problem, those with Russia present a more immediate set of issues. Once the center of a global superpower that was America's chief rival, Russia remains heavily armed but economically weak. Under its current leader, Vladimir Putin, Russia has challenged the United States in Europe and in the Middle East, and has even meddled in American politics.[19]

The first in this series of direct Russian challenges to the United States came in 2014, when Russian forces seized control of the Crimean Peninsula, an area that had been part of Ukraine and that was important to Russia because of its strategic location on the Black Sea, giving Russia a significant naval base. Russian troops next massed along other portions of the Ukrainian border. The Obama administration urged the Russians to withdraw, announced a program of economic sanctions, and encouraged NATO allies to impose sanctions as well.

The result illustrated the difficulties inherent in collective action and the use of sanctions. Many of the United States' European allies depend on Russian energy supplies and engage in a good deal of trade with the Russians. As a result, while all agreed in principle that Russia should withdraw from Crimea, none were prepared to follow the American lead of imposing sanctions. Later in 2014 Russia formally annexed Crimea, though the action was not officially recognized by the United

States. Subsequently, Russian forces supported separatist groups in several other parts of Ukraine.

In 2016, Russia also intruded into American presidential politics, as Russian agents purchased ads on Facebook and other social media designed to cause ethnic and economic tensions within the United States. For the most part, these efforts seemed to favor Donald Trump and oppose Hillary Clinton. Whether these had any effect or not is open to question.[20]

Both the Chinese and the Russians have made use of extensive electronic "hacking" to break into the computer systems of American government agencies and American firms. Both countries deny these allegations—as does the United States when accused of hacking into Russian and Chinese systems.[21]

NUCLEAR PROLIFERATION IN IRAN AND NORTH KOREA

Unlike China and Russia, Iran and North Korea are not great powers, but both present challenges to the United States, especially in the realm of nuclear proliferation. Though it is a nuclear power, the United States has generally seen nuclear proliferation as leading to a more dangerous world and has done what it can to prevent more countries from developing nuclear weapons.

Iran and the United States have been adversaries since 1979, when Iranians overthrew an unpopular U.S.-backed leader, Shah Reza Pahlavi. For years the United States has worried that Iran is working toward obtaining nuclear weapons with which it could threaten Saudi Arabia and Israel—both close U.S. allies—and bring Middle Eastern oil fields under its control. To prevent Iran from obtaining nuclear weapons, U.S. presidents have used a mix of carrots (in the form of diplomacy) and sticks (in the form of sanctions). Sanctions made it more difficult for Iran to sell its oil, its major export, hurting its economy. In this case, U.S. allies mostly cooperated with the sanctions.

In 2015 the United States and Iran signed an agreement in which the Iranians pledged not to build nuclear weapons in exchange for a lifting of the economic sanctions. Critics of the agreement charged it would not deter the Iranians from continuing with their nuclear program, and during his presidential campaign Donald Trump promised to abandon the agreement. In 2018, Trump withdrew from the agreement. In 2019, Iran resumed parts of its nuclear program.

As for North Korea, U.S. efforts to undermine its regime have been difficult because China, North Korea's major backer and trading partner, will not cooperate. China regards North Korea as a useful pawn on the geopolitical chessboard, preventing the United States and two of its allies, Japan and South Korea, from dominating the Sea of Japan. As a result, the North Koreans have continued to build nuclear warheads and to test missiles capable of carrying them.

TRADE POLICY

Trade is one of the most contentious issues in contemporary international relations. The United States persistently imports more than it exports, producing a substantial trade deficit with the rest of the world. The United States has accused China and other nations of unfair trade practices that limit the sale of imported goods in their markets while they export billions of dollars in goods to the United States. Trade also affects job growth in the United States. Populist politicians like Donald Trump charge that this is the result of trade policies that allowed American jobs to be exported to Asia and Mexico, where labor is cheaper. Trade, as we saw above, supports many millions of jobs in the United States. However, U.S. workers whose jobs were lost when industries moved abroad call for tariffs and other remedies they hope might bring their jobs back to the United States.

Many workers voted for Trump, who during his 2016 campaign promised to bring these jobs back. One of Trump's first acts in office was to withdraw from the Trans-Pacific Partnership (TPP), a free-trade agreement between the United States and 11 Pacific Rim nations. Trump said the TPP would allow foreign countries to profit at America's expense.

Trade disputes have especially complicated America's relationship with China. President Trump declared that the Chinese act unfairly and promised to change the rules in America's favor—a move that increased Chinese hostility toward the United States. In 2018, he announced the imposition of $50 billion in tariffs on Chinese steel, aluminum, and electronic goods sold to the United States, and China quickly announced that it would retaliate with tariffs on U.S. farm products, seafoods, and autos sold in China. These moves raised the prospect of an all-out trade war between the world's two largest economies. In January 2020, however, the United States and China signed a new trade agreement that reduced some U.S. tariffs in exchange for a Chinese agreement to purchase more American agricultural goods.

GLOBAL ENVIRONMENTAL POLICY

A final trouble spot for American policy makers is international environmental policy. The environment is a global matter, since pollutants produced in one country affect all others, and America, along with other industrial nations like China, is a major producer of pollution. Generally speaking, the United States supports various international efforts to protect the environment. These include the United Nations Framework Convention on Climate Change, an international agreement to study and ameliorate harmful changes in the global environment, and the Montreal Protocol, an agreement by over 150 countries to limit the production of substances potentially harmful to the world's ozone layer.

Other nations have criticized the United States for withdrawing from the 1997 Kyoto Protocol, an agreement setting limits on industrial countries' emissions of greenhouse gases. The United States asserted that the limits would harm American economic interests. The Kyoto Protocol expired in 2012, but 37 of the original signatories signed the Doha Amendment to renew their commitment to reduce greenhouse gas emissions. The United States refrained from signing this new agreement as well.

In 2015, however, the United States did agree to the Paris Agreement to reduce greenhouse gas emissions. Each country agreed to reduce emissions but would determine its own contribution to the effort. Many Republicans, including Donald Trump, opposed the agreement, and as president, Trump ended U.S. participation in it, stating that strict environmental controls would undermine American manufacturing interests and cause more jobs to leave the United States to the benefit of developing nations without such standards. America's Western European allies, on the other hand, remain committed to the Paris Agreement and view the American decision as uninformed and reckless.[22]

Foreign Policy: What Do You Think?

The foreign policy areas discussed above are only a few of the problems facing America in the world. Policy makers must constantly monitor, assess, and determine a response to these and other challenges facing the nation.

★ America's history and ideals hold that U.S. foreign policies should have a higher purpose than the pursuit of self-interest and that the United States should use force only as a last resort. In what ways do American responses to various security, trade, and humanitarian challenges reflect these historic ideals, and in what ways do they sometimes clash? What do you think Amanda Patrick, Mohamed Iye, and Stephen Nwalorizi (all featured at the start of this chapter) would say?

★ Greater trade reduces the price of many products for American and international consumers. Yet globalization also creates economic winners and losers. What can U.S. leaders do in the future to make sure that globalization is a positive force that promotes U.S. security and prosperity?

★ Under what conditions do you think it is appropriate for the United States to use military force? Under what conditions do you think diplomacy is the appropriate channel?

STUDY GUIDE

Practice Quiz

1. Which of the following terms best describes the American posture toward the world prior to the twentieth century? *(p. 466)*
   a) interventionist
   b) isolationist
   c) appeasement
   d) humanitarian
   e) internationalist

2. Which of the following terms describes an effort to forestall war by placating a hostile power? *(p. 466)*
   a) appeasement
   b) deterrence
   c) détente
   d) containment
   e) "Minuteman" theory of defense

3. The World Trade Organization is *(p. 470)*
   a) an agency in the federal executive branch that analyzes trade deficits.
   b) an American interest group that lobbies Congress for the passage of agricultural and manufacturing tariffs.
   c) an American interest group that lobbies Congress for the passage of so-called Fair Trade laws.
   d) a regional organization regulating trade in North America.
   e) an important international organization for promoting trade.

4. The Bush Doctrine refers to the idea that the United States should *(p. 472)*
   a) not allow foreign powers to meddle in the Western Hemisphere.
   b) avoid future wars by giving in to the demands of hostile foreign powers.
   c) take preemptive, unilateral action against threats to its national security.
   d) never take preemptive, unilateral action against threats to its national security.

   e) always secure international approval before taking any military action.

5. An agreement made between the president and another country that has the force of a treaty but does not require Senate ratification is called *(p. 472)*
   a) an executive order.
   b) an executive privilege.
   c) an executive agreement.
   d) a diplomatic decree.
   e) arbitration.

6. The Constitution assigns the power to declare war to *(p. 477)*
   a) the National Security Council.
   b) the president.
   c) the chief justice of the United States.
   d) the secretary of defense.
   e) Congress.

7. Which of the following statements about the U.S. Senate Committee on Foreign Relations is *not* accurate? *(p. 477)*
   a) The Committee can overturn executive agreements.
   b) The Committee was established in 1816 as one of the original 10 standing committees of the Senate.
   c) The Committee oversees the State Department.
   d) The Committee must review all treaties before they are put to the Senate for a vote.
   e) The Committee includes seven subcommittees, each with a regional or subject-matter jurisdiction.

8. Which of the following statements about the United Nations is not true? *(p. 480)*
   a) It has a powerful army to implement its decisions.
   b) It gives every country one vote in the General Assembly.
   c) The five permanent members of the UN Security Council are China, France, Russia, the United Kingdom, and the United States.
   d) It is a forum for international discussions and as an instrument for multilateral action.
   e) Important issues require a two-thirds majority vote.

9. Which of the following were founded during the 1940s in order to create a new international monetary structure for the postwar world? *(p. 481)*
   a) the Federal Reserve System and the Council of Economic Advisers
   b) the North Atlantic Treaty Organization and the Southeast Asia Treaty Organization
   c) the International Monetary Fund and the World Bank
   d) the International Court of Justice and the Warsaw Pact
   e) the Office of Management and Budget and the General Agreement on Tariffs and Trade

10. The North Atlantic Treaty Organization was formed by the United States, Canada, and *(p. 482)*
    a) Eastern Europe.
    b) the Soviet Union.
    c) Mexico.
    d) Western Europe.
    e) Australia and New Zealand.

11. Cultural programs that send American actors, athletes, and musicians around the world in order to promote a positive view of the United States are examples of the use of *(p. 484)*
    a) soft power.
    b) star power.
    c) arbitration.
    d) détente.
    e) hard power.

12. In 2015 the United States entered into an international agreement to reduce greenhouse gas emissions called the *(p. 488)*
    a) Kyoto Protocol.
    b) Doha Amendment.
    c) Trans-Pacific Partnership.
    d) Montreal Protocol.
    e) Paris Agreement.

Key Terms

non-state actors *(p. 465)*

isolationism *(p. 466)*

containment *(p. 466)*

preventive war *(p. 466)*

appeasement *(p. 466)*

deterrence *(p. 467)*

Cold War *(p. 467)*

nation-states *(p. 468)*

World Trade Organization (WTO) *(p. 470)*

United States–Mexico–Canada Agreement (USMCA) *(p. 470)*

Bush Doctrine *(p. 472)*

executive agreement *(p. 472)*

diplomacy *(p. 480)*

United Nations (UN) *(p. 480)*

International Monetary Fund (IMF) *(p. 481)*

Appendix

The Declaration of Independence
In Congress, July 4, 1776

The unanimous Declaration of the thirteen united States of America,

When in the Course of human events, it becomes necessary for one people to dissolve the political bands which have connected them with another, and to assume among the powers of the earth, the separate and equal station to which the Laws of Nature and of Nature's God entitle them, a decent respect to the opinions of mankind requires that they should declare the causes which impel them to the separation.

We hold these truths to be self-evident, that all men are created equal, that they are endowed by their Creator with certain unalienable Rights, that among these are Life, Liberty and the pursuit of Happiness.—That to secure these rights, Governments are instituted among Men, deriving their just powers from the consent of the governed.—That whenever any Form of Government becomes destructive of these ends, it is the Right of the People to alter or to abolish it, and to institute new Government, laying its foundation on such principles and organizing its powers in such form, as to them shall seem most likely to effect their Safety and Happiness. Prudence, indeed, will dictate that Governments long established should not be changed for light and transient causes; and accordingly all experience hath shewn, that mankind are more disposed to suffer, while evils are sufferable, than to right themselves by abolishing the forms to which they are accustomed. But when a long train of abuses and usurpations, pursuing invariably the same Object evinces a design to reduce them under absolute Despotism, it is their right, it is their duty, to throw off such Government, and to provide new Guards for their future security.—Such has been the patient sufferance of these Colonies; and such is now the necessity which constrains them to alter their former Systems of Government. The history of the present King of Great Britain is a history of repeated injuries and usurpations, all having in direct object the establishment of an absolute Tyranny over these States. To prove this, let Facts be submitted to a candid world.

He has refused his Assent to Laws, the most wholesome and necessary for the public good.

He has forbidden his Governors to pass Laws of immediate and pressing importance, unless suspended in their operation till his Assent should be obtained; and when so suspended, he has utterly neglected to attend to them.

He has refused to pass other Laws for the accommodation of large districts of people, unless those people would relinquish the right of Representation in the Legislature, a right inestimable to them and formidable to tyrants only.

He has called together legislative bodies at places unusual, uncomfortable, and distant from the depository of their public Records, for the sole purpose of fatiguing them into compliance with his measures.

He has dissolved Representative Houses repeatedly, for opposing with manly firmness his invasions on the rights of the people.

He has refused for a long time, after such dissolutions, to cause others to be elected; whereby the Legislative powers, incapable of Annihilation, have returned to the People at large for their exercise; the State remaining in the mean time exposed to all the dangers of invasion from without, and convulsions within.

He has endeavoured to prevent the population of these States; for that purpose obstructing the Laws for Naturalization of Foreigners; refusing to pass others to encourage their migrations hither, and raising the conditions of new Appropriations of Lands.

He has obstructed the Administration of Justice, by refusing his Assent to Laws for establishing Judiciary powers.

He has made Judges dependent on his Will alone, for the tenure of their offices, and the amount and payment of their salaries.

He has erected a multitude of New Offices, and sent hither swarms of Officers to harrass our people, and eat out their substance.

He has kept among us, in times of peace, Standing Armies without the Consent of our legislatures.

He has affected to render the Military independent of and superior to the Civil power.

He has combined with others to subject us to a jurisdiction foreign to our constitution, and unacknowledged by our laws; giving his Assent to their Acts of pretended Legislation:

For Quartering large bodies of armed troops among us:

For protecting them, by a mock Trial, from punishment for any Murders which they should commit on the Inhabitants of these States:

For cutting off our Trade with all parts of the world:

For imposing Taxes on us without our Consent:

For depriving us in many cases, of the benefits of Trial by Jury:

For transporting us beyond Seas to be tried for pretended offences:

For abolishing the free System of English Laws in a neighboring Province, establishing therein an Arbitrary government, and enlarging its Boundaries so as to render it at once an example and fit instrument for introducing the same absolute rule into these Colonies:

For taking away our Charters, abolishing our most valuable Laws, and altering fundamentally the Forms of our Governments:

For suspending our own Legislatures, and declaring themselves invested with power to legislate for us in all cases whatsoever.

He has abdicated Government here, by declaring us out of his Protection and waging War against us.

He has plundered our seas, ravaged our Coasts, burnt our towns, and destroyed the lives of our people.

He is at this time transporting large Armies of foreign Mercenaries to compleat the works of death, desolation and tyranny, already begun with circumstances of Cruelty & perfidy scarcely paralleled in the most barbarous ages, and totally unworthy the Head of a civilized nation.

He has constrained our fellow Citizens taken Captive on the high Seas to bear Arms against their Country, to become the executioners of their friends and Brethren, or to fall themselves by their Hands.

He has excited domestic insurrections amongst us, and has endeavoured to bring on the inhabitants of our frontiers, the merciless Indian Savages, whose known rule of warfare, is an undistinguished destruction of all ages, sexes and conditions.

In every stage of these Oppressions We have Petitioned for Redress in the most humble terms: Our repeated Petitions have been answered only by repeated injury. A Prince whose character is thus marked by every act which may define a Tyrant, is unfit to be the ruler of a free people.

Nor have We been wanting in attentions to our Brittish brethren. We have warned them from time to time of attempts by their legislature to extend an unwarrantable jurisdiction over us. We have reminded them of the circumstances of our emigration and settlement here. We have appealed to their native justice and magnanimity, and we have conjured them by the ties of our common kindred to disavow these usurpations, which, would inevitably interrupt our connections and correspondence. They too have been deaf to the voice of justice and of consanguinity. We must, therefore, acquiesce in the necessity, which denounces our Separation, and hold them, as we hold the rest of mankind, Enemies in War, in Peace Friends.

We, Therefore, the Representatives of the United States of America, in General Congress, Assembled, appealing to the Supreme Judge of the world for the rectitude of our intentions, do, in the Name, and by Authority of the good People of these Colonies, solemnly publish and declare, That these United Colonies are, and of Right ought to be Free and Independent States; that they are Absolved from all Allegiance to the British Crown, and that all political connection between them and the State of Great Britain, is and ought to be totally dissolved; and that as Free and Independent States, they have full Power to levy War, conclude Peace, contract Alliances, establish Commerce, and to do all other Acts and Things which Independent States may of right do. And for the support of this Declaration, with a firm reliance on the protection of divine Providence, we mutually pledge to each other our Lives, our Fortunes and our sacred Honor.

The foregoing Declaration was, by order of Congress, engrossed, and signed by the following members:

John Hancock

NEW HAMPSHIRE
Josiah Bartlett
William Whipple
Matthew Thornton

MASSACHUSETTS BAY
Samuel Adams
John Adams
Robert Treat Paine
Elbridge Gerry

RHODE ISLAND
Stephen Hopkins
William Ellery

CONNECTICUT
Roger Sherman
Samuel Huntington
William Williams
Oliver Wolcott

NEW YORK
William Floyd
Philip Livingston
Francis Lewis
Lewis Morris

NEW JERSEY
Richard Stockton
John Witherspoon
Francis Hopkinson
John Hart
Abraham Clark

PENNSYLVANIA
Robert Morris
Benjamin Rush
Benjamin Franklin
John Morton
George Clymer
James Smith
George Taylor
James Wilson
George Ross

DELAWARE
Caesar Rodney
George Read
Thomas M'Kean

MARYLAND
Samuel Chase
William Paca
Thomas Stone
Charles Carroll,
*   of Carrollton*

VIRGINIA
George Wythe
Richard Henry Lee
Thomas Jefferson
Benjamin Harrison
Thomas Nelson, Jr.
Francis Lightfoot Lee
Carter Braxton

NORTH CAROLINA
William Hooper
Joseph Hewes
John Penn

SOUTH CAROLINA
Edward Rutledge
Thomas Heyward, Jr.
Thomas Lynch, Jr.
Arthur Middleton

GEORGIA
Button Gwinnett
Lyman Hall
George Walton

Resolved, That copies of the Declaration be sent to the several assemblies, conventions, and committees, or councils of safety, and to the several commanding officers of the continental troops; that it be proclaimed in each of the United States, at the head of the army.

The Articles of Confederation

Agreed to by Congress November 15, 1777;
ratified and in force March 1, 1781

To all whom these Presents shall come, we the undersigned Delegates of the States affixed to our Names, send greeting. Whereas the Delegates of the United States of America, in Congress assembled, did, on the fifteenth day of November, in the Year of Our Lord One thousand Seven Hundred and Seventy seven, and in the Second Year of the Independence of America, agree to certain articles of Confederation and perpetual Union between the States of Newhampshire, Massachusetts-bay, Rhodeisland and Providence Plantations, Connecticut, New-York, New-Jersey, Pennsylvania, Delaware, Maryland, Virginia, North-Carolina, South-Carolina and Georgia in the words following, viz. "Articles of Confederation and perpetual Union between the states of Newhampshire, Massachusettsbay, Rhodeisland and Providence Plantations, Connecticut, New-York, New-Jersey, Pennsylvania, Delaware, Maryland, Virginia, North-Carolina, South-Carolina and Georgia.

Art. I. The Stile of this confederacy shall be "The United States of America."

Art. II. Each state retains its sovereignty, freedom and independence, and every Power, Jurisdiction and right, which is not by this confederation expressly delegated to the United States, in Congress assembled.

Art. III. The said states hereby severally enter into a firm league of friendship with each other, for their common defence, the security of their Liberties, and their mutual and general welfare, binding themselves to assist each other, against all force offered to, or attacks made upon them, or any of them, on account of religion, sovereignty, trade, or any other pretence whatever.

Art. IV. The better to secure and perpetuate mutual friendship and intercourse among the people of the different states in this union, the free inhabitants of each of these states, paupers, vagabonds and fugitives from Justice excepted, shall be entitled to all privileges and immunities of free citizens in the several states; and the people of each state shall have free ingress and regress to and from any other state, and shall enjoy therein all the privileges of trade and commerce, subject to the same duties, impositions and restrictions as the inhabitants thereof respectively, provided that such restriction shall not extend so far as to prevent the removal of property imported into any state, to any other state, of which the Owner is an inhabitant; provided also that no imposition, duties or restriction shall be laid by any state, on the property of the united states, or either of them.

If any Person guilty of, or charged with treason, felony, or other high misdemeanor in any state, shall flee from Justice, and be found in any of the united states, he shall, upon demand of the Governor or executive power, of the state from which he fled, be delivered up and removed to the state having jurisdiction of his offence.

Full faith and credit shall be given in each of these states to the records, acts and judicial proceedings of the courts and magistrates of every other state.

Art. V. For the more convenient management of the general interests of the united states, delegates shall be annually appointed in such manner as the legislature of each state shall direct, to meet in Congress on the first Monday in November, in every year, with a power reserved to each state, to recall its delegates, or any of them, at any time within the year, and to send others in their stead, for the remainder of the Year.

No state shall be represented in Congress by less than two, nor by more than seven Members; and no person shall be capable of being a delegate for more than three years in any term of six years; nor shall any person, being a delegate, be capable of holding any office under the united states, for which he, or another for his benefit receives any salary, fees or emolument of any kind.

Each state shall maintain its own delegates in a meeting of the states, and while they act as members of the committee of the states.

In determining questions in the united states, in Congress assembled, each state shall have one vote.

Freedom of speech and debate in Congress shall not be impeached or questioned in any Court, or place out of Congress, and the members of congress shall be protected in their persons from arrests and imprisonments, during the time of their going to and from, and attendance on congress, except for treason, felony, or breach of the peace.

Art. VI. No state without the Consent of the united states in congress assembled, shall send any embassy to, or receive any embassy from, or enter into any conference, agreement, or alliance or treaty with any King, prince or state; nor shall any person holding any office or profit or trust under the united states, or any of them, accept of any present, emolument, office or title of any kind whatever from any king, prince or foreign state; nor shall the united states in congress assembled, or any of them, grant any title of nobility.

No two or more states shall enter into any treaty, confederation or alliance whatever between them, without the consent of the united states in congress assembled, specifying accurately the purposes for which the same is to be entered into, and how long it shall continue.

No state shall lay any imposts or duties, which may interfere with any stipulations in treaties, entered into by the united states in congress assembled, with any king, prince or state, in pursuance of any treaties already proposed by congress, to the courts of France and Spain.

No vessels of war shall be kept up in time of peace by any state, except such number only, as shall be deemed necessary by the united states in congress assembled, for the defence of such state, or its trade; nor shall any body of forces be kept up by any state, in time of peace, except such number only, as in the judgment of the united states, in congress assembled, shall be deemed requisite to garrison the forts necessary for the defence of such state; but every state shall always keep up a well regulated and disciplined militia, sufficiently armed and accoutred, and shall provide and constantly have ready for use, in public stores, a due number of field pieces and tents, and a proper quantity of arms, ammunition and camp equipage.

No state shall engage in any war without the consent of the united states in congress assembled, unless such state be actually invaded by enemies, or shall have received certain advice of a resolution being formed by some nation of Indians to invade such state, and the danger is so imminent as not to admit of a delay, till the united states in congress asssembled can be consulted; nor shall any state grant commissions to any ships or vessels of war, nor letters of marque or reprisal, except it be after a declaration of war by the united states in congress assembled, and then only against the kingdom or state and the subjects thereof, against which war has been so declared, and under such regulations as shall be established by the united states in congress assembled, unless such state be infested by pirates; in which case vessels of war may be fitted out for that occasion, and kept so long as the danger shall continue, or until the united states in congress assembled shall determine otherwise.

Art. VII. When land-forces are raised by any state for the common defence, all officers of or under the rank of colonel, shall be appointed by the legislature of each state respectively, by whom such forces shall be raised, or in such manner as such state shall direct, and all vacancies shall be filled up by the state which first made the appointment.

Art. VIII. All charges of war, and all other expences that shall be incurred for the common defence or general welfare, and allowed by the united states in congress assembled, shall be defrayed out of a common treasury, which shall be supplied by the several states in proportion to the value of all land within each state, granted to or surveyed for any Person, as such land and the buildings and improvements thereon shall be estimated according to such mode as the united states in congress assembled, shall from time to time direct and appoint.

The taxes for paying that proportion shall be laid and levied by the authority and direction of the legislatures of the several states within the time agreed upon by the united states in congress assembled.

Art. IX. The united states in congress assembled, shall have the sole and exclusive right and power of determining on peace and war, except in the cases mentioned in the sixth article—of sending and receiving ambassadors—entering into treaties and alliances, provided that no treaty of commerce shall be made whereby the legislative power of the respective states shall be restrained from imposing such imposts and duties on foreigners, as their own people are subjected to, or from prohibiting the exportation of any species of goods or commodities whatsoever—of establishing rules for deciding in all cases, what captures on land or water shall be legal, and in what manner prizes taken by land or naval forces in the service of the united states shall be divided or appropriated—of granting letters of marque and reprisal in times of peace—appointing courts for the trial of piracies and felonies committed on the high seas and establishing courts for receiving and determining finally appeals in all cases of captures, provided that no member of congress shall be appointed a judge of any of the said courts.

The united states in congress assembled shall also be the last resort on appeal in all disputes and differences now subsisting or that hereafter may arise between two or more states concerning boundary, jurisdiction or any other cause whatever; which authority shall always be exercised in the manner following. Whenever the legislative or executive authority or lawful agent of any state in controversy with another shall present a petition to congress stating the matter in question and praying for a hearing, notice thereof shall be given by order of congress to the legislative or executive authority of the other state in controversy, and a day assigned for the appearance of the parties by their lawful agents, who shall then be directed to appoint by joint consent, commissioners or judges to constitute a court for hearing and determining the matter in question: but if they cannot agree, congress shall name three persons out of each of the united states, and from the list of such persons each party shall alternately strike out one, the petitioners beginning, until the number shall be reduced to thirteen; and from that number not less than seven, nor more than nine names as congress shall direct, shall in the presence of congress be drawn out by lot, and the persons whose names shall be so drawn or any five of them, shall be commissioners or judges, to hear and finally determine the controversy, so always as a major part of the judges who shall hear the cause shall agree in the determination: and if either party shall neglect to attend at the day appointed, without shewing reasons, which congress shall judge sufficient, or being present shall refuse to strike, the congress shall proceed to nominate three persons out of each state, and the secretary of congress shall strike in behalf of such party absent or refusing; and the judgment and sentence of the court to be appointed, in the manner before prescribed, shall be final and conclusive; and if any of the parties shall refuse to submit to the authority of such court, or to appear to defend their claim or cause, the court shall nevertheless proceed to pronounce sentence, or judgment, which shall in like manner be final and decisive, the judgment or sentence and other proceedings being in either case transmitted to congress, and lodged among the acts of congress for the security of the parties concerned: provided that every commissioner, before he sits in judgment, shall take an oath to be administered by one of the judges of the supreme or superior court of the state, where the cause shall be tried, "well and truly to hear and determine the matter in question, according to the best of his judgment, without favour, affection or hope of reward:" provided also, that no state shall be deprived of territory for the benefit of the united states.

All controversies concerning the private right of soil claimed under different grants of two or more states, whose jurisdictions as they may respect such lands, and the states which passed such grants are adjusted, the said grants or either of them being at the same time claimed to have originated antecedent to such settlement of jurisdiction, shall on the petition of either party to the congress of the united states, be finally determined as near as may be in the same manner as is before prescribed for deciding disputes respecting territorial jurisdiction between different states.

The united states in congress assembled shall also have the sole and exclusive right and power of regulating the alloy and value of coin struck by their own authority, or by that of the respective states—fixing the standard of weights and measures throughout the united states—regulating the trade and managing all affairs with the Indians, not members of any of the states, provided that the legislative right of any state within its own limits be not infringed or violated—establishing and regulating post-offices from one state to another, throughout all the united states, and exacting such postage on the papers passing thro' the same as may be requisite to defray the expences of the said office—appointing all officers of the land forces, in the service of the united states, excepting regimental officers—appointing all the officers of the naval forces, and commissioning all officers whatever in the service of the united states—making rules for the government and regulation of the said land and naval forces, and directing their operations.

The united states in congress assembled shall have authority to appoint a committee, to sit in the recess of congress, to be denominated "A Committee of the States," and to consist of one delegate from each state; and to appoint such other committees and civil officers as may be necessary for managing the general affairs of the united states under their direction—to appoint one of their number to preside, provided that no person be allowed to serve in the office of president more than one year in any term of three years; to ascertain the necessary sums of Money to be raised for the service of the united states, and to appropriate and apply the same for defraying the public expenses—to borrow money, or emit bills on the credit of the united states, transmitting every half year to the respective states an account of the sums of money so borrowed or emitted,—to build and equip a navy—to agree upon the number of land forces, and to make requisitions from each state for its quota, in proportion to the number of white inhabitants in such state; which requisition shall be binding, and thereupon the legislature of each state shall appoint the regimental officers, raise the men and cloath, arm and equip them in a soldier like manner, at the expense of the united states; and the officers and men so cloathed, armed and equipped shall march to the place appointed, and within the time agreed on by the united states in congress assembled: But if the united states in congress assembled shall, on consideration of circumstances judge proper that any state should not raise men, or should raise a smaller number than its quota, and that any other state should raise a greater number of men than the quota thereof, such extra number shall be raised, officered, cloathed, armed and equipped in the same manner as the quota of such state, unless the legislature of such state shall judge that such extra number cannot be safely spared out of the same, in which case they shall raise officer, cloath, arm and equip as many of such extra number as they judge can be safely spared. And the officers and men so cloathed, armed and equipped, shall march to the place appointed, and within the time agreed on by the united states in congress assembled.

The united states in congress assembled shall never engage in a war, nor grant letters of marque and reprisal in time of peace, nor enter into any treaties or alliances, nor coin money, nor regulate the value thereof, nor ascertain the sums and expenses necessary for the defence and welfare of the united states, or any of them, nor emit bills, nor borrow money on the credit of the united states, nor appropriate money, nor agree upon the number of vessels of war, to be built or purchased, or the number of land or sea forces to be raised, nor appoint a commander in chief of the army or navy, unless nine states assent to the same: nor shall a question on any other point, except for adjourning from day to day be determined, unless by the votes of a majority of the united states in congress assembled.

The congress of the united states shall have power to adjourn to any time within the year, and to any place within the united states, so that no period of adjournment be for a longer duration than the space of six Months, and shall publish the Journal of their proceedings monthly, except such parts thereof relating to treaties, alliances or military operations, as in their judgment require secrecy; and the yeas and nays of the delegates of each state on any question shall be entered on the Journal, when it is desired by any delegate; and the delegates of a state, or any of them, at his or their request shall be furnished with a transcript of the said Journal, except such parts as are above excepted, to lay before the legislatures of the several states.

Art. X. The committee of the states, or any nine of them, shall be authorised to execute, in the recess of congress, such of the powers of congress as the united states in congress assembled, by the consent of nine states, shall from time to time think expedient to vest them with; provided that no power be delegated to the said committee, for the exercise of which, by the articles of confederation, the voice of nine states in the congress of the united states assembled is requisite.

Art. XI. Canada acceding to this confederation, and joining in the measures of the united states, shall be admitted into, and entitled to all the advantages of this union: but no other colony shall be admitted into the same, unless such admission be agreed to by nine states.

Art. XII. All bills of credit emitted, monies borrowed and debts contracted by, or under the authority of congress, before the assembling of the united states, in pursuance of the present confederation, shall be deemed and considered as a charge against the united states, for payment and satisfaction whereof the said united states and the public faith are hereby solemnly pledged.

Art. XIII. Every state shall abide by the determinations of the united states in congress assembled, on all questions which by this confederation are submitted to them. And the Articles of this confederation shall be inviolably observed by every state, and the union shall be perpetual; nor shall any alteration at any time hereafter be made in any of them; unless such alteration be agreed to in a congress of the united states, and be afterwards confirmed by the legislatures of every state.

And Whereas it hath pleased the Great Governor of the World to incline the hearts of the legislatures we respectively represent in congress, to approve of, and to authorize us to ratify the said articles of confederation and perpetual union. Know Ye that we the undersigned delegates, by virtue of the power and authority to us given for that purpose, do by these presents, in the name and in behalf of our respective constituents, fully and entirely ratify and confirm each and every of the said articles of confederation and perpetual union, and all and singular the matters and things therein contained: And we do further solemnly plight and engage the faith of our respective constituents, that they shall abide by the determinations of the united states in congress assembled, on all questions, which by the said confederation are submitted to them. And that the articles thereof shall be inviolably observed by the states we respectively represent, and that the union shall be perpetual. In Witness whereof we have hereunto set our hands in Congress. Done at Philadelphia in the state of Pennsylvania the ninth day of July, in the Year of our Lord one Thousand seven Hundred and Seventy-eight, and in the third year of the independence of America.

The Constitution of the United States of America

We the People of the United States, in Order to form a more perfect Union, establish Justice, insure domestic Tranquility, provide for the common defence, promote the general Welfare, and secure the Blessings of Liberty to ourselves and our Posterity, do ordain and establish this Constitution for the United States of America.

ARTICLE I

SECTION 1
[LEGISLATIVE POWERS]

All legislative Powers herein granted shall be vested in a Congress of the United States, which shall consist of a Senate and House of Representatives.

SECTION 2
[HOUSE OF REPRESENTATIVES, HOW CONSTITUTED, POWER OF IMPEACHMENT]

The House of Representatives shall be composed of Members chosen every second Year by the People of the several States, and the Electors in each State shall have the Qualifications requisite for Electors of the most numerous Branch of the State Legislature.

No Person shall be a Representative who shall not have attained to the Age of twenty five Years, and been seven Years a Citizen of the United States, and who shall not, when elected, be an Inhabitant of that State in which he shall be chosen.

Representatives and *direct Taxes*[1] shall be apportioned among the several States which may be included within this Union, according to their respective Numbers, *which shall be determined by adding to the whole Number of free Persons, including those bound to Service for a Term of Years, and excluding Indians not taxed, three fifths of all other Persons.*[2] The actual Enumeration shall be made within three Years after the first Meeting of the Congress of the United States, and within every subsequent Term of ten Years, in such Manner as they shall by Law direct. The Number of Representatives shall not exceed one for every thirty Thousand, but each State shall have at Least one Representative; *and until such enumeration shall be made, the State of New Hampshire shall be entitled to chuse three, Massachusetts eight, Rhode-Island and Providence Plantations one, Connecticut five, New-York six, New Jersey four, Pennsylvania eight, Delaware one, Maryland six, Virginia ten, North Carolina five, South Carolina five, and Georgia three.*[3]

When vacancies happen in the Representation from any State, the Executive Authority thereof shall issue Writs of Election to fill such Vacancies.

The House of Representatives shall chuse their Speaker and other Officers; and shall have the sole Power of Impeachment.

---

[1]Modified by Sixteenth Amendment.
[2]Modified by Fourteenth Amendment.
[3]Temporary provision.

SECTION 3
[THE SENATE, HOW CONSTITUTED, IMPEACHMENT TRIALS]

The Senate of the United States shall be composed of two Senators from each State, *chosen by the Legislature thereof,*[4] for six Years; and each Senator shall have one Vote.

Immediately after they shall be assembled in Consequence of the first Election, they shall be divided as equally as may be into three Classes. The Seats of the Senators of the first Class shall be vacated at the Expiration of the second Year, of the second Class at the Expiration of the fourth Year, and of the third Class at the Expiration of the sixth Year, so that one third may be chosen every second Year; *and if Vacancies happen by Resignation, or otherwise, during the Recess of the Legislature of any State, the Executive thereof may make temporary Appointments until the next Meeting of the Legislature, which shall then fill such Vacancies.*[5]

No Person shall be a Senator who shall not have attained to the Age of thirty Years, and been nine Years a Citizen of the United States, and who shall not, when elected, be an Inhabitant of that State for which he shall be chosen.

The Vice President of the United States shall be President of the Senate, but shall have no Vote, unless they be equally divided.

The Senate shall chuse their other Officers, and also a President pro tempore, in the Absence of the Vice President, or when he shall exercise the Office of President of the United States.

The Senate shall have the sole Power to try all Impeachments. When sitting for that Purpose, they shall be on Oath or Affirmation. When the President of the United States is tried, the Chief Justice shall preside: And no Person shall be convicted without the Concurrence of two thirds of the Members present.

Judgment in Cases of Impeachment shall not extend further than to removal from Office, and disqualification to hold and enjoy any Office of honor, Trust or Profit under the United States: but the Party convicted shall nevertheless be liable and subject to Indictment, Trial, Judgment and Punishment, according to Law.

SECTION 4
[ELECTION OF SENATORS AND REPRESENTATIVES]

The Times, Places and Manner of holding Elections for Senators and Representatives, shall be prescribed in each State by the Legislature thereof; but the Congress may at any time by Law make or alter such Regulations, except as to the Places of chusing Senators.

The Congress shall assemble at least once in every Year, and such Meeting shall be on the first Monday in December, unless they shall by Law appoint a different Day.[6]

SECTION 5
[QUORUM, JOURNALS, MEETINGS, ADJOURNMENTS]

Each House shall be the Judge of the Elections, Returns and Qualifications of its own Members, and a Majority of each shall constitute a Quorum to do Business; but a smaller Number may adjourn from day to day, and may be authorized to compel the Attendance of absent Members, in such Manner, and under such Penalties as each House may provide.

---

[4]Modified by Seventeenth Amendment.
[5]Modified by Seventeenth Amendment.
[6]Modified by Twentieth Amendment.

Each House may determine the Rules of its Proceedings, punish its Members for disorderly Behaviour, and, with the Concurrence of two thirds, expel a Member.

Each House shall keep a Journal of its Proceedings, and from time to time publish the same, excepting such Parts as may in their Judgment require Secrecy; and the Yeas and Nays of the Members of either House on any questions shall, at the Desire of one fifth of those Present, be entered on the Journal.

Neither House, during the Session of Congress, shall, without the Consent of the other, adjourn for more than three days, nor to any other Place than that in which the two Houses shall be sitting.

SECTION 6
[COMPENSATION, PRIVILEGES, DISABILITIES]

The Senators and Representatives shall receive a Compensation for their Services, to be ascertained by Law, and paid out of the Treasury of the United States. They shall in all Cases, except Treason, Felony and Breach of the Peace, be privileged from Arrest during their Attendance at the Session of their respective Houses, and in going to and returning from the same; and for any Speech or Debate in either House, they shall not be questioned in any other Place.

No Senator or Representative shall, during the Time for which he was elected, be appointed to any civil Office under the Authority of the United States, which shall have been created, or the Emoluments whereof shall have been encreased during such time; and no Person holding any Office under the United States, shall be a Member of either House during his Continuance in Office.

SECTION 7
[PROCEDURE IN PASSING BILLS AND RESOLUTIONS]

All Bills for raising Revenue shall originate in the House of Representatives; but the Senate may propose or concur with Amendments as on other Bills.

Every Bill which shall have passed the House of Representatives and the Senate, shall, before it become a Law, be presented to the President of the United States: If he approve he shall sign it, but if not he shall return it, with his Objections to that House in which it shall have originated, who shall enter the Objections at large on their Journal, and proceed to reconsider it. If after such Reconsideration two thirds of that House shall agree to pass the Bill, it shall be sent, together with the Objections, to the other House, by which it shall likewise be reconsidered, and if approved by two thirds of that House, it shall become a Law. But in all such Cases the Votes of both Houses shall be determined by yeas and Nays, and the Names of the Persons voting for and against the Bill shall be entered on the Journal of each House respectively. If any Bill shall not be returned by the President within ten Days (Sundays excepted) after it shall have been presented to him, the Same shall be a Law, in like Manner as if he had signed it, unless the Congress by their Adjournment prevent its Return, in which Case it shall not be a Law.

Every Order, Resolution, or Vote to which the Concurrence of the Senate and House of Representatives may be necessary (except on a question of Adjournment) shall be presented to the President of the United States; and before the Same shall take Effect, shall be approved by him, or being disapproved by him, shall be repassed by two thirds of the Senate and House of Representatives, according to the Rules and Limitations prescribed in the Case of a Bill.

SECTION 8

The Congress shall have Power

To lay and collect Taxes, Duties, Imposts and Excises, to pay the Debts and provide for the common Defence and general Welfare of the United States; but all Duties, Imposts and Excises shall be uniform throughout the United States;

To borrow Money on the credit of the United States;

To regulate Commerce with foreign Nations, and among the several States, and with the Indian Tribes;

To establish an uniform Rule of Naturalization, and uniform Laws on the subject of Bankruptcies throughout the United States;

To coin Money, regulate the Value thereof, and of foreign Coin, and fix the Standard of Weights and Measures;

To provide for the Punishment of counterfeiting the Securities and current Coin of the United States;

To establish Post Offices and post Roads;

To promote the Progress of Science and useful Arts, by securing for limited Times to Authors and Inventors the exclusive Right to their respective Writings and Discoveries;

To constitute Tribunals inferior to the supreme Court;

To define and punish Piracies and Felonies committed on the high Seas, and Offences against the Law of Nations;

To declare War, grant Letters of Marque and Reprisal, and make Rules concerning Captures on Land and Water;

To raise and support Armies, but no Appropriation of Money to that Use shall be for a longer Term than two Years;

To provide and maintain a Navy;

To make Rules for the Government and Regulation of the land and naval Forces;

To provide for calling forth the Militia to execute the Laws of the Union, suppress Insurrections and repel Invasions;

To provide for organizing, arming, and disciplining, the Militia, and for governing such Part of them as may be employed in the Service of the United States, reserving to the States respectively, the Appointment of the Officers, and the Authority of training the Militia according to the discipline prescribed by Congress;

To exercise exclusive Legislation in all Cases whatsoever, over such District (not exceeding ten Miles square) as may, by Cession of particular States, and the Acceptance of Congress, become the Seat of the Government of the United States, and to exercise like Authority over all Places purchased by the Consent of the Legislature of the State in which the Same shall be, for the Erection of Forts, Magazines, Arsenals, dock-Yards, and other needful Buildings;—And

To make all Laws which shall be necessary and proper for carrying into Execution the foregoing Powers, and all other Powers vested by this Constitution in the Government of the United States, or in any Department or Officer thereof.

SECTION 9

The Migration or Importation of such Persons as any of the States now existing shall think proper to admit, shall not be prohibited by the Congress prior to the Year one thousand eight hundred

and eight, but a Tax or duty may be imposed on such Importation, not exceeding ten dollars for each Person.[7]

The Privilege of the Writ of Habeas Corpus shall not be suspended, unless when in Cases of Rebellion or Invasion the public Safety may require it.

No Bill of Attainder or ex post facto Law shall be passed.

No Capitation, or other direct, Tax shall be laid, unless in Proportion to the Census or Enumeration herein before directed to be taken.[8]

No Tax or Duty shall be laid on Articles exported from any State.

No Preference shall be given by any Regulation of Commerce or Revenue to the Ports of one State over those of another; nor shall Vessels bound to, or from, one State, be obliged to enter, clear, or pay Duties in another.

No Money shall be drawn from the Treasury, but in Consequence of Appropriations made by Law; and a regular Statement and Account of the Receipts and Expenditures of all public Money shall be published from time to time.

No Title of Nobility shall be granted by the United States: And no Person holding any Office of Profit or Trust under them, shall, without the Consent of the Congress, accept of any present, Emolument, Office, or Title, of any kind whatever, from any King, Prince, or foreign State.

SECTION 10
[RESTRICTIONS UPON POWERS OF STATES]

No State shall enter into any Treaty, Alliance, or Confederation; grant Letters of Marque and Reprisal; coin Money; emit Bills of Credit; make any Thing but gold and silver Coin a Tender in Payment of Debts; pass any Bill of Attainder, ex post facto Law, or Law impairing the Obligation of Contracts, or grant any Title of Nobility.

No State shall, without the Consent of the Congress, lay any Imposts or Duties on Imports or Exports, except what may be absolutely necessary for executing its inspection Laws: and the net Produce of all Duties and Imposts, laid by any State on Imports or Exports, shall be for the Use of the Treasury of the United States; and all such Laws shall be subject to the Revision and Control of the Congress.

No State shall, without the Consent of Congress, lay any Duty of Tonnage, keep Troops, or Ships of War in time of Peace, enter into any Agreement or Compact with another State, or with a foreign Power, or engage in War, unless actually invaded, or in such imminent Danger as will not admit of delay.

ARTICLE II

SECTION 1
[EXECUTIVE POWER, ELECTION, QUALIFICATIONS OF THE PRESIDENT]

The executive Power shall be vested in a President of the United States of America. *He shall hold his Office during the Term of four Years, and, together with the Vice President, chosen for the same Term, be elected, as follows*[9]

---

[7]Temporary provision.

[8]Modified by Sixteenth Amendment.

[9]Number of terms limited to two by Twenty-Second Amendment.

Each State shall appoint, in such Manner as the Legislature thereof may direct, a Number of Electors, equal to the whole Number of Senators and Representatives to which the State may be entitled in the Congress: but no Senator or Representative, or Person holding an Office of Trust or Profit under the United States, shall be appointed an Elector.

The electors shall meet in their respective States, and vote by ballot for two Persons, of whom one at least shall not be an Inhabitant of the same State with themselves. And they shall make a List of all the Persons voted for, and of the Number of Votes for each; which List they shall sign and certify, and transmit sealed to the Seat of the Government of the United States, directed to the President of the Senate. The President of the Senate shall, in the Presence of the Senate and House of Representatives, open all the Certificates, and the Votes shall then be counted. The Person having the greatest Number of Votes shall be the President, if such Number be a Majority of the whole Number of Electors appointed; and if there be more than one who have such Majority, and have an equal Number of Votes, then the House of Representatives shall immediately chuse by Ballot one of them for President; and if no Person have a Majority, then from the five highest on the List the said House shall in like Manner chuse the President. But in chusing the President, the Votes shall be taken by States, the Representation from each State having one Vote; A quorum for this Purpose shall consist of a Member or Members from two thirds of the States, and a Majority of all the States shall be necessary to a Choice. In every Case, after the Choice of the President, the person having the greatest Number of Votes of the Electors shall be the Vice President. But if there should remain two or more who have equal Votes, the Senate shall chuse from them by Ballot the Vice President.[10]

The Congress may determine the Time of chusing the Electors, and the Day on which they shall give their Votes; which Day shall be the same throughout the United States.

No Person except a natural born Citizen, or a Citizen of the United States, at the time of the Adoption of this Constitution, shall be eligible to the Office of President; neither shall any Person be eligible to that Office who shall not have attained to the Age of thirty five Years, and been fourteen Years a Resident within the United States.

In Case of the Removal of the President from Office, or his Death, Resignation, or Inability to discharge the Powers and Duties of the said Office, the Same shall devolve on the Vice President, and the Congress may by Law provide for the Case of Removal, Death, Resignation or Inability, both of the President and Vice President, declaring what Officer shall then act as President, and such Officer shall act accordingly, until the Disability be removed, or a President shall be elected.

The President shall, at stated Times, receive for his Services, a Compensation, which shall neither be increased nor diminished during the Period for which he shall have been elected, and he shall not receive within that Period any other Emolument from the United States, or any of them.

Before he enter on the Execution of his Office, he shall take the following Oath or Affirmation:—"I do solemnly swear (or affirm) that I will faithfully execute the Office of President of the United States, and will to the best of my Ability, preserve, protect and defend the Constitution of the United States."

SECTION 2
[POWERS OF THE PRESIDENT]

The President shall be Commander in Chief of the Army and Navy of the United States, and of the Militia of the several States, when called into the actual Service of the United States;

---

[10]Modified by Twelfth and Twentieth Amendments.

he may require the Opinion, in writing, of the principal Officer in each of the executive Departments, upon any Subject relating to the Duties of their respective Offices, and he shall have Power to grant Reprieves and Pardons for Offences against the United States, except in Cases of Impeachment.

He shall have Power, by and with the Advice and Consent of the Senate, to make Treaties, provided two thirds of the Senators present concur; and he shall nominate, and by and with the Advice and Consent of the Senate, shall appoint Ambassadors, other public Ministers and Consuls, Judges of the supreme Court, and all other Officers of the United States, whose Appointments are not herein otherwise provided for, and which shall be established by Law: but the Congress may by Law vest the Appointment of such inferior Officers, as they think proper, in the President alone, in the Courts of Law, or in the Heads of Departments.

The President shall have Power to fill up all Vacancies that may happen during the Recess of the Senate, by granting Commissions which shall expire at the End of their next Session.

SECTION 3
[POWERS AND DUTIES OF THE PRESIDENT]

He shall from time to time give to the Congress Information of the State of the Union, and recommend to their Consideration such Measures as he shall judge necessary and expedient; he may, on extraordinary Occasions, convene both Houses, or either of them, and in Case of Disagreement between them, with Respect to the Time of Adjournment, he may adjourn them to such Time as he shall think proper; he shall receive Ambassadors and other public Ministers; he shall take Care that the Laws be faithfully executed, and shall Commission all the Officers of the United States.

SECTION 4
[IMPEACHMENT]

The President, Vice President and all civil Officers of the United States, shall be removed from Office on Impeachment for, and Conviction of, Treason, Bribery, or other high Crimes and Misdemeanors.

ARTICLE III

SECTION 1
[JUDICIAL POWER, TENURE OF OFFICE]

The judicial Power of the United States, shall be vested in one supreme Court, and in such inferior Courts as the Congress may from time to time ordain and establish. The Judges, both of the supreme and inferior Courts, shall hold their Offices during good Behaviour, and shall, at stated Times, receive for their Services, a Compensation, which shall not be diminished during their Continuance in Office.

SECTION 2
[JURISDICTION]

The judicial Power shall extend to all Cases, in Law and Equity, arising under this Constitution, the Laws of the United States, and Treaties made, or which shall be made, under their Authority;—to all Cases affecting Ambassadors, other public Ministers and Consuls;—to all Cases of admiralty and maritime Jurisdiction;—to Controversies to which the United States shall be a Party;—to Controversies between two or more States;—*between a State and Citizens of another State;*—between Citizens of different States,—between Citizens of the same State claiming Lands under Grants of different States, *and between a State,* or the Citizens thereof, *and foreign States, Citizens or Subjects.*[11]

In all Cases affecting Ambassadors, other public Ministers and Consuls, and those in which a State shall be Party, the supreme Court shall have original Jurisdiction. In all the other Cases before mentioned, the supreme Court shall have appellate Jurisdiction, both as to Law and Fact, with such Exceptions, and under such Regulations as the Congress shall make.

The Trial of all Crimes, except in Cases of Impeachment, shall be by Jury; and such Trial shall be held in the State where the said Crimes shall have been committed; but when not committed within any State, the Trial shall be at such Place or Places as the Congress may by Law have directed.

SECTION 3
[TREASON, PROOF, AND PUNISHMENT]

Treason against the United States, shall consist only in levying War against them, or in adhering to their Enemies, giving them Aid and Comfort. No Person shall be convicted of Treason unless on the Testimony of two Witnesses to the same overt Act, or on Confession in open Court.

The Congress shall have Power to declare the Punishment of Treason, but no Attainder of Treason shall work Corruption of Blood, or Forfeiture except during the Life of the Person attainted.

ARTICLE IV

SECTION 1
[FAITH AND CREDIT AMONG STATES]

Full Faith and Credit shall be given in each State to the public Acts, Records, and judicial Proceedings of every other State. And the Congress may by general Laws prescribe the Manner in which such Acts, Records and Proceedings shall be proved, and the Effect thereof.

SECTION 2
[PRIVILEGES AND IMMUNITIES, FUGITIVES]

The Citizens of each State shall be entitled to all Privileges and Immunities of Citizens in the several States.

A Person charged in any State with Treason, Felony or other Crime, who shall flee from Justice, and be found in another State, shall on Demand of the executive Authority of the State from which he fled, be delivered up, to be removed to the State having Jurisdiction of the Crime.

No person held to Service or Labour in one State, under the Laws thereof, escaping into another, shall, in Consequence of any Law or Regulation therein, be discharged from such Service or Labour, but shall be delivered up on Claim of the Party to whom such Service or Labour may be due.[12]

---

[11]Modified by Eleventh Amendment.

[12]Repealed by the Thirteenth Amendment.

SECTION 3

New States may be admitted by the Congress into this Union; but no new State shall be formed or erected within the Jurisdiction of any other State; nor any State be formed by the Junction of two or more States, or Parts of States, without the Consent of the Legislatures of the States concerned as well as of the Congress.

The Congress shall have Power to dispose of and make all needful Rules and Regulations respecting the Territory or other Property belonging to the United States; and nothing in this Constitution shall be so construed as to Prejudice any Claims of the United States, or of any particular State.

SECTION 4

[GUARANTEE OF REPUBLICAN GOVERNMENT]

The United States shall guarantee to every State in this Union a Republican Form of Government, and shall protect each of them against Invasion; and on Application of the Legislature, or of the Executive (when the Legislature cannot be convened), against domestic Violence.

ARTICLE V

[AMENDMENT OF THE CONSTITUTION]

The Congress, whenever two thirds of both Houses shall deem it necessary, shall propose Amendments to this Constitution, or, on the Application of the Legislatures of two thirds of the several States, shall call a Convention for proposing Amendments, which, in either Case, shall be valid to all Intents and Purposes, as Part of this Constitution, when ratified by the Legislatures of three fourths of the several States, or by Conventions in three fourths thereof, as the one or the other Mode of Ratification may be proposed by the Congress; *Provided that no Amendment which may be made prior to the Year One thousand eight hundred and eight shall in any Manner affect the first and fourth Clauses in the Ninth Section of the first Article;*[13] and that no State, without its Consent, shall be deprived of its equal Suffrage in the Senate.

ARTICLE VI

[DEBTS, SUPREMACY, OATH]

All Debts contracted and Engagements entered into, before the Adoption of this Constitution, shall be as valid against the United States under this Constitution, as under the Confederation.

This Constitution, and the Laws of the United States which shall be made in Pursuance thereof; and all Treaties made, or which shall be made, under the Authority of the United States, shall be the supreme Law of the Land; and the Judges in every State shall be bound thereby, any Thing in the Constitution or Laws of any State to the Contrary notwithstanding.

The Senators and Representatives before mentioned, and the Members of the several State Legislatures, and all executive and judicial Officers, both of the United States and of the

---

[13]Temporary provision.

several States, shall be bound by Oath or Affirmation, to support this Constitution; but no religious Test shall be required as a Qualification to any Office or public Trust under the United States.

ARTICLE VII

[RATIFICATION AND ESTABLISHMENT]

The Ratification of the Conventions of nine States, shall be sufficient for the Establishment of this Constitution between the States so ratifying the Same.[14]

Done in Convention by the Unanimous Consent of the States present the Seventeenth Day of September in the Year of our Lord one thousand seven hundred and Eighty seven and of the Independence of the United States of America the Twelfth. *In Witness* whereof We have hereunto subscribed our Names,

G:⁰ WASHINGTON—
Presidt. and deputy from Virginia

NEW HAMPSHIRE
John Langdon
Nicholas Gilman

MASSACHUSETTS
Nathaniel Gorham
Rufus King

CONNECTICUT
Wm. Saml. Johnson
Roger Sherman

NEW YORK
Alexander Hamilton

NEW JERSEY
Wil: Livingston
David Brearley
Wm. Paterson
Jona: Dayton

PENNSYLVANIA
B Franklin
Thomas Mifflin
Robt. Morris
Geo. Clymer
Thos. FitzSimons
Jared Ingersoll
James Wilson
Gouv Morris

DELAWARE
Geo: Read
Gunning Bedford jun
John Dickinson
Richard Bassett
Jaco: Broom

MARYLAND
James McHenry
Dan of St Thos. Jenifer
Danl. Carroll

VIRGINIA
John Blair—
James Madison Jr.

NORTH CAROLINA
Wm. Blount
Richd. Dobbs Spaight
Hu Williamson

SOUTH CAROLINA
J. Rutledge
Charles Cotesworth
 Pinckney
Charles Pinckney
Pierce Butler

GEORGIA
William Few
Abr Baldwin

[14]The Constitution was submitted on September 17, 1787, by the Constitutional Convention, was ratified by the conventions of several states at various dates up to May 29, 1790, and became effective on March 4, 1789.

Amendments to the Constitution

Proposed by Congress and Ratified by the Legislatures of the Several States, Pursuant to Article V of the Original Constitution.

Amendments I–X, known as the Bill of Rights, were proposed by Congress on September 25, 1789, and ratified on December 15, 1791.

AMENDMENT I

[FREEDOM OF RELIGION, OF SPEECH, AND OF THE PRESS]

Congress shall make no law respecting an establishment of religion, or prohibiting the free exercise thereof; or abridging the freedom of speech, or of the press; or the right of the people peaceably to assemble, and to petition the Government for a redress of grievances.

AMENDMENT II

[RIGHT TO KEEP AND BEAR ARMS]

A well regulated Militia, being necessary to the security of a free State, the right of the people to keep and bear Arms, shall not be infringed.

AMENDMENT III

[QUARTERING OF SOLDIERS]

No Soldier shall, in time of peace be quartered in any house, without the consent of the Owner, nor in time of war, but in a manner to be prescribed by law.

AMENDMENT IV

[SECURITY FROM UNWARRANTABLE SEARCH AND SEIZURE]

The right of the people to be secure in their persons, houses, papers, and effects, against unreasonable searches and seizures, shall not be violated, and no Warrants shall issue, but upon probable cause, supported by Oath or affirmation, and particularly describing the place to be searched, and the persons or things to be seized.

AMENDMENT V

[RIGHTS OF ACCUSED PERSONS IN CRIMINAL PROCEEDINGS]

No person shall be held to answer for a capital, or otherwise infamous crime, unless on a presentment or indictment of a Grand Jury, except in cases arising in the land or naval forces, or in the Militia, when in actual service in time of War or in public danger; nor shall any person be subject for the same offence to be twice put in jeopardy of life or limb; nor shall be compelled in any criminal case to be a witness against himself, nor be deprived of life, liberty, or property, without due process of law; nor shall private property be taken for public use, without just compensation.

AMENDMENT VI

[RIGHT TO SPEEDY TRIAL, WITNESSES, ETC.]

In all criminal prosecutions, the accused shall enjoy the right to a speedy and public trial, by an impartial jury of the State and district wherein the crime shall have been committed, which district shall have been previously ascertained by law, and to be informed of the nature and cause of the accusation; to be confronted with the witnesses against him; to have compulsory process for obtaining witnesses in his favor, and to have the Assistance of Counsel for his defence.

AMENDMENT VII

[TRIAL BY JURY IN CIVIL CASES]

In suits at common law, where the value in controversy shall exceed twenty dollars, the right of trial by jury shall be preserved, and no fact tried by a jury, shall be otherwise reexamined in any Court of the United States, than according to the rules of the common law.

AMENDMENT VIII

[BAILS, FINES, PUNISHMENTS]

Excessive bail shall not be required, nor excessive fines imposed, nor cruel and unusual punishments inflicted.

AMENDMENT IX

[RESERVATION OF RIGHTS OF PEOPLE]

The enumeration in the Constitution, of certain rights, shall not be construed to deny or disparage others retained by the people.

AMENDMENT X

[POWERS RESERVED TO STATES OR PEOPLE]

The powers not delegated to the United States by the Constitution, nor prohibited by it to the States, are reserved to the States respectively, or to the people.

AMENDMENT XI

[PROPOSED BY CONGRESS ON MARCH 4, 1794; DECLARED RATIFIED ON JANUARY 8, 1798.]

[RESTRICTION OF JUDICIAL POWER]

The Judicial power of the United States shall not be construed to extend to any suit in law or equity, commenced or prosecuted against one of the United States by Citizens of another State, or by Citizens or Subjects of any Foreign State.

AMENDMENT XII

[PROPOSED BY CONGRESS ON DECEMBER 9, 1803; DECLARED RATIFIED ON SEPTEMBER 25, 1804.]

[ELECTION OF PRESIDENT AND VICE PRESIDENT]

The Electors shall meet in their respective states and vote by ballot for President and Vice-President, one of whom, at least, shall not be an inhabitant of the same state with themselves; they shall name in their ballots the person voted for as President, and in distinct ballots the person voted for as Vice-President, and they shall make distinct lists of all persons voted for as President, and of all persons voted for as Vice-President, and of the number of votes for each, which lists they shall sign and certify, and transmit sealed to the seat of the government of the United States, directed to the President of the Senate;—the President of the Senate shall, in presence of the Senate and House of Representatives, open all the certificates and the votes shall then be counted;—The person having the greatest number of votes for President, shall be the President, if such number be a majority of the whole number of Electors appointed; and if no person have such majority, then from the persons having the highest numbers not exceeding three on the list of those voted for as President, the House of Representatives shall choose immediately, by ballot, the President. But in choosing the President, the votes shall be taken by states, the representation from each state having one vote; a quorum for this purpose shall consist of a member or members from two-thirds of the states, and a majority of all the states shall be necessary to a choice. And if the House of Representatives shall not choose a President whenever the right of choice shall devolve upon them, before the fourth day of March next following, then the Vice-President shall act as President, as in the case of the death or other constitutional disability of the President.—The person having the greatest number of votes as Vice-President, shall be the Vice-President, if such number be a majority of the whole number of Electors appointed, and if no person have a majority, then from the two highest numbers on the list, the Senate shall choose the Vice-President; a quorum for the purpose shall consist of two-thirds of the whole number of Senators, and a majority of the whole number shall be necessary to a choice. But no person constitutionally ineligible to the office of President shall be eligible to that of Vice-President of the United States.

AMENDMENT XIII

[PROPOSED BY CONGRESS ON JANUARY 31, 1865; DECLARED RATIFIED ON DECEMBER 18, 1865.]

SECTION 1
[ABOLITION OF SLAVERY]

Neither slavery nor involuntary servitude, except as a punishment for crime whereof the party shall have been duly convicted, shall exist within the United States, or any place subject to their jurisdiction.

SECTION 2
[POWER TO ENFORCE THIS ARTICLE]

Congress shall have power to enforce this article by appropriate legislation.

AMENDMENT XIV

[PROPOSED BY CONGRESS ON JUNE 13, 1866; DECLARED RATIFIED ON JULY 28, 1868.]

SECTION 1
[CITIZENSHIP RIGHTS NOT TO BE ABRIDGED BY STATES]

All persons born or naturalized in the United States, and subject to the jurisdiction thereof, are citizens of the United States and of the State wherein they reside. No State shall make or enforce any law which shall abridge the privileges or immunities of citizens of the United States; nor shall any State deprive any person of life, liberty, or property, without due process of law; nor deny to any person within its jurisdiction the equal protection of the laws.

SECTION 2
[APPORTIONMENT OF REPRESENTATIVES IN CONGRESS]

Representatives shall be apportioned among the several States according to their respective numbers, counting the whole number of persons in each State, excluding Indians not taxed. But when the right to vote at any election for the choice of electors for President and Vice-President of the United States, Representatives in Congress, the Executive and Judicial officers of a State, or the members of the Legislature thereof, is denied to any of the male inhabitants of such State, being twenty-one years of age, and citizens of the United States, or in any way abridged, except for participation in rebellion, or other crime, the basis of representation therein shall be reduced in the proportion which the number of such male citizens shall bear to the whole number of male citizens twenty-one years of age in such State.

SECTION 3
[PERSONS DISQUALIFIED FROM HOLDING OFFICE]

No person shall be a Senator or Representative in Congress, or elector of President and Vice-President, or hold any office, civil or military, under the United States, or under any State, who, having previously taken an oath, as a member of Congress, or as an officer of the United States, or as a member of any State legislature, or as an executive or judicial officer of any State, to support the Constitution of the United States, shall have engaged in insurrection or rebellion against the same, or given aid or comfort to the enemies thereof. But Congress may by a vote of two-thirds of each House, remove such disability.

SECTION 4
[WHAT PUBLIC DEBTS ARE VALID]

The validity of the public debt of the United States, authorized by law, including debts incurred for payment of pensions and bounties for services in suppressing insurrection or rebellion, shall not be questioned. But neither the United States nor any State shall assume or pay any debt or obligation incurred in aid of insurrection or rebellion against the United States, or any claim for the loss or emancipation of any slave; but all such debts, obligations and claims shall be held illegal and void.

SECTION 5
[POWER TO ENFORCE THIS ARTICLE]

The Congress shall have power to enforce, by appropriate legislation, the provisions of this article.

AMENDMENT XV

[PROPOSED BY CONGRESS ON FEBRUARY 26, 1869; DECLARED RATIFIED ON MARCH 30, 1870.]

SECTION 1
[NEGRO SUFFRAGE]

The right of citizens of the United States to vote shall not be denied or abridged by the United States or by any State on account of race, color, or previous condition of servitude.

SECTION 2
[POWER TO ENFORCE THIS ARTICLE]

The Congress shall have power to enforce this article by appropriate legislation.

AMENDMENT XVI

[PROPOSED BY CONGRESS ON JULY 2, 1909; DECLARED RATIFIED
ON FEBRUARY 25, 1913.]

[AUTHORIZING INCOME TAXES]

The Congress shall have power to lay and collect taxes on incomes, from whatever source derived, without apportionment among the several States, and without regard to any census or enumeration.

AMENDMENT XVII

[PROPOSED BY CONGRESS ON MAY 13, 1912; DECLARED RATIFIED ON MAY 31, 1913.]

[POPULAR ELECTION OF SENATORS]

The Senate of the United States shall be composed of two Senators from each State, elected by the people thereof, for six years; and each Senator shall have one vote. The electors in each State shall have the qualifications requisite for electors of the most numerous branch of the State legislatures.

When vacancies happen in the representation of any State in the Senate, the executive authority of such State shall issue writs of election to fill such vacancies: *Provided,* That the legislature of any State may empower the executive thereof to make temporary appointments until the people fill the vacancies by election as the legislature may direct.

This amendment shall not be so construed as to affect the election or term of any Senator chosen before it becomes valid as part of the Constitution.

AMENDMENT XVIII

[PROPOSED BY CONGRESS DECEMBER 18, 1917; DECLARED RATIFIED
ON JANUARY 29, 1919.]

SECTION 1
[NATIONAL LIQUOR PROHIBITION]

After one year from the ratification of this article the manufacture, sale, or transportation of intoxicating liquors within, the importation thereof into, or the exportation thereof from the United States and all territory subject to the jurisdiction thereof for beverage purposes is hereby prohibited.

SECTION 2
[POWER TO ENFORCE THIS ARTICLE]

The Congress and the several States shall have concurrent power to enforce this article by appropriate legislation.

SECTION 3
[RATIFICATION WITHIN SEVEN YEARS]

This article shall be inoperative unless it shall have been ratified as an amendment to the Constitution by the legislatures of the several States, as provided in the Constitution, within seven years from the date of the submission hereof to the States by the Congress.[1]

---

[1]Repealed by the Twenty-First Amendment.

AMENDMENT XIX

[PROPOSED BY CONGRESS ON JUNE 4, 1919; DECLARED RATIFIED ON AUGUST 26, 1920.]
[WOMAN SUFFRAGE]

The right of citizens of the United States to vote shall not be denied or abridged by the United States or by any State on account of sex.

Congress shall have power to enforce this article by appropriate legislation.

AMENDMENT XX

[PROPOSED BY CONGRESS ON MARCH 2, 1932; DECLARED RATIFIED ON FEBRUARY 6, 1933.]

SECTION 1
[TERMS OF OFFICE]

The terms of the President and Vice President shall end at noon on the 20th day of January, and the terms of Senators and Representatives at noon on the 3rd day of January, of the years in which such terms would have ended if this article had not been ratified; and the terms of their successors shall then begin.

SECTION 2
[TIME OF CONVENING CONGRESS]

The Congress shall assemble at least once in every year, and such meeting shall begin at noon on the 3rd day of January, unless they shall by law appoint a different day.

SECTION 3
[DEATH OF PRESIDENT-ELECT]

If, at the time fixed for the beginning of the term of the President, the President elect shall have died, the Vice President elect shall become President. If a President shall not have been chosen before the time fixed for the beginning of his term, or if the President elect shall have failed to qualify, then the Vice President elect shall act as President until a President shall have qualified; and the Congress may by law provide for the case wherein neither a President elect nor a Vice President elect shall have qualified, declaring who shall then act as President, or the manner in which one who is to act shall be selected, and such person shall act accordingly until a President or Vice President shall have qualified.

SECTION 4
[ELECTION OF THE PRESIDENT]

The Congress may by law provide for the case of the death of any of the persons from whom the House of Representatives may choose a President whenever the right of choice shall have devolved upon them, and for the case of the death of any of the persons from whom the Senate may choose a Vice President whenever the right of choice shall have devolved upon them.

SECTION 5
[AMENDMENT TAKES EFFECT]

Sections 1 and 2 shall take effect on the 15th day of October following the ratification of this article.

SECTION 6
[RATIFICATION WITHIN SEVEN YEARS]

This article shall be inoperative unless it shall have been ratified as an amendment to the Constitution by the legislatures of three-fourths of the several States within seven years from the date of its submission.

AMENDMENT XXI
[PROPOSED BY CONGRESS ON FEBRUARY 20, 1933; DECLARED RATIFIED ON DECEMBER 5, 1933.]

SECTION 1
[NATIONAL LIQUOR PROHIBITION REPEALED]

The eighteenth article of amendment to the Constitution of the United States is hereby repealed.

SECTION 2
[TRANSPORTATION OF LIQUOR INTO "DRY" STATES]

The transportation or importation into any State, Territory, or Possession of the United States for delivery or use therein of intoxicating liquors, in violation of the laws thereof, is hereby prohibited.

SECTION 3
[RATIFICATION WITHIN SEVEN YEARS]

This article shall be inoperative unless it shall have been ratified as an amendment to the Constitution by conventions in the several States, as provided in the Constitution, within seven years from the date of the submission hereof to the States by the Congress.

AMENDMENT XXII
[PROPOSED BY CONGRESS ON MARCH 21, 1947; DECLARED RATIFIED ON FEBRUARY 27, 1951.]

SECTION 1
[TENURE OF PRESIDENT LIMITED]

No person shall be elected to the office of President more than twice, and no person who has held the office of President or acted as President, for more than two years of a term to which some other person was elected President shall be elected to the office of the President more than once. But this Article shall not apply to any person holding the office of President when this Article was proposed by the Congress, and shall not prevent any person who may be holding the office of President, or acting as President, during the term within which this Article becomes operative from holding the office of President or acting as President during the remainder of such term.

SECTION 2
[RATIFICATION WITHIN SEVEN YEARS]

This article shall be inoperative unless it shall have been ratified as an amendment to the Constitution by the legislatures of three-fourths of the several States within seven years from the date of its submission to the States by the Congress.

AMENDMENT XXIII

[PROPOSED BY CONGRESS ON JUNE 16, 1960; DECLARED RATIFIED ON MARCH 29, 1961.]

SECTION 1
[ELECTORAL COLLEGE VOTES FOR THE DISTRICT OF COLUMBIA]

The District constituting the seat of Government of the United States shall appoint in such manner as the Congress may direct:

A number of electors of President and Vice President equal to the whole number of Senators and Representatives in Congress to which the District would be entitled if it were a State, but in no event more than the least populous State; they shall be in addition to those appointed by the States, but they shall be considered, for the purposes of the election of President and Vice President, to be electors appointed by a State; and they shall meet in the District and perform such duties as provided by the twelfth article of amendment.

SECTION 2
[POWER TO ENFORCE THIS ARTICLE]

The Congress shall have power to enforce this article by appropriate legislation.

AMENDMENT XXIV

[PROPOSED BY CONGRESS ON AUGUST 27, 1962; DECLARED RATIFIED ON JANUARY 23, 1964.]

SECTION 1
[ANTI-POLL TAX]

The right of citizens of the United States to vote in any primary or other election for President or Vice President, for electors for President or Vice President, or for Senator or Representative of Congress, shall not be denied or abridged by the United States or any State by reason of failure to pay any poll tax or other tax.

SECTION 2
[POWER TO ENFORCE THIS ARTICLE]

The Congress shall have power to enforce this article by appropriate legislation.

AMENDMENT XXV

[PROPOSED BY CONGRESS ON JULY 6, 1965; DECLARED RATIFIED ON FEBRUARY 10, 1967.]

SECTION 1
[VICE PRESIDENT TO BECOME PRESIDENT]

In case of the removal of the President from office or his death or resignation, the Vice President shall become President.

SECTION 2
[CHOICE OF A NEW VICE PRESIDENT]

Whenever there is a vacancy in the office of the Vice President, the President shall nominate a Vice President who shall take the office upon confirmation by a majority vote of both houses of Congress.

SECTION 3
[PRESIDENT MAY DECLARE OWN DISABILITY]

Whenever the President transmits to the President pro tempore of the Senate and the Speaker of the House of Representatives his written declaration that he is unable to discharge the powers and duties of his office, and until he transmits to them a written declaration to the contrary, such powers and duties shall be discharged by the Vice President as Acting President.

SECTION 4
[ALTERNATE PROCEDURES TO DECLARE AND TO END PRESIDENTIAL DISABILITY]

Whenever the Vice President and a majority of either the principal officers of the executive departments, or of such other body as Congress may by law provide, transmit to the President pro tempore of the Senate and the Speaker of the House of Representatives their written declaration that the President is unable to discharge the powers and duties of his office, the Vice President shall immediately assume the powers and duties of the office as Acting President.

Thereafter, when the President transmits to the President pro tempore of the Senate and the Speaker of the House of Representatives his written declaration that no inability exists, he shall resume the powers and duties of his office unless the Vice President and a majority of either the principal officers of the executive department, or of such other body as Congress may by law provide, transmit within four days to the President pro tempore of the Senate and the Speaker of the House of Representatives their written declaration that the President is unable to discharge the powers and duties of his office. Thereupon Congress shall decide the issue, assembling within forty eight hours for that purpose if not in session. If the Congress, within twenty one days after receipt of the latter written declaration, or, if Congress is not in session, within twenty one days after Congress is required to assemble, determines by two-thirds vote of both Houses that the President is unable to discharge the powers and duties of his office, the Vice President shall continue to discharge the same as Acting President; otherwise, the President shall resume the powers and duties of his office.

AMENDMENT XXVI

[PROPOSED BY CONGRESS ON MARCH 23, 1971; DECLARED RATIFIED ON JULY 1, 1971.]

SECTION 1
[EIGHTEEN-YEAR-OLD VOTE]

The right of citizens of the United States, who are eighteen years of age or older, to vote shall not be denied or abridged by the United States or by any State on account of age.

SECTION 2
[POWER TO ENFORCE THIS ARTICLE]

The Congress shall have power to enforce this article by appropriate legislation.

AMENDMENT XXVII

[PROPOSED BY CONGRESS ON SEPTEMBER 25, 1789; DECLARED RATIFIED ON MAY 8, 1992.]

[CONGRESS CANNOT RAISE ITS OWN PAY]

No law varying the compensation for the services of the Senators and Representatives, shall take effect, until an election of representatives shall have intervened.

The Federalist Papers

NO. 10: MADISON

Among the numerous advantages promised by a well constructed Union, none deserves to be more accurately developed than its tendency to break and control the violence of faction. The friend of popular governments never finds himself so much alarmed for their character and fate, as when he contemplates their propensity to this dangerous vice. He will not fail therefore to set a due value on any plan which, without violating the principles to which he is attached, provides a proper cure for it. The instability, injustice, and confusion introduced into the public councils have, in truth, been the mortal diseases under which popular governments have everywhere perished, as they continue to be the favorite and fruitful topics from which the adversaries to liberty derive their most specious declamations. The valuable improvements made by the American constitutions on the popular models, both ancient and modern, cannot certainly be too much admired; but it would be an unwarrantable partiality to contend that they have as effectually obviated the danger on this side, as was wished and expected. Complaints are everywhere heard from our most considerate and virtuous citizens, equally the friends of public and private faith and of public and personal liberty, that our governments are too unstable, that the public good is disregarded in the conflicts of rival parties, and that measures are too often decided, not according to the rules of justice and the rights of the minor party, but by the superior force of an interested and overbearing majority. However anxiously we may wish that these complaints had no foundation, the evidence of known facts will not permit us to deny that they are in some degree true. It will be found, indeed, on a candid review of our situation, that some of the distresses under which we labor have been erroneously charged on the operation of our governments; but it will be found, at the same time, that other causes will not alone account for many of our heaviest misfortunes; and, particularly, for that prevailing and increasing distrust of public engagements and alarm for private rights which are echoed from one end of the continent to the other. These must be chiefly, if not wholly, effects of the unsteadiness and injustice with which a factious spirit has tainted our public administration.

By a faction I understand a number of citizens, whether amounting to a majority or minority of the whole, who are united and actuated by some common impulse of passion, or of interest, adverse to the rights of other citizens, or to the permanent and aggregate interests of the community.

There are two methods of curing the mischiefs of faction: the one, by removing its causes; the other, by controlling its effects.

There are again two methods of removing the causes of faction: the one, by destroying the liberty which is essential to its existence; the other, by giving to every citizen the same opinions, the same passions, and the same interests.

It could never be more truly said than of the first remedy, that it is worse than the disease. Liberty is to faction what air is to fire, an aliment without which it instantly expires. But it could not be a less folly to abolish liberty, which is essential to political life, because it nourishes faction, than it would be to wish the annihilation of air, which is essential to animal life, because it imparts to fire its destructive agency.

The second expedient is as impracticable, as the first would be unwise. As long as the reason of man continues fallible, and he is at liberty to exercise it, different opinions will be formed. As long as the connection subsists between his reason and his self-love, his opinions and his passions will have a reciprocal influence on each other; and the former will be objects to which the latter will attach themselves. The diversity in the faculties of men, from which the rights of property originate, is not less an insuperable obstacle to a uniformity of interests. The protection of these faculties is the first object of Government. From the protection of different and unequal faculties of acquiring property, the possession of different degrees and kinds of property immediately results; and from the influence of these on the sentiments and views of the respective proprietors, ensues a division of the society into different interests and parties.

The latent causes of faction are thus sown in the nature of man; and we see them everywhere brought into different degrees of activity, according to the different circumstances of civil society. A zeal for different opinions concerning religion, concerning Government, and many other points, as well of speculation as of practice; an attachment to different leaders ambitiously contending for pre-eminence and power; or to persons of other descriptions whose fortunes have been interesting to the human passions, have in turn divided mankind into parties, inflamed them with mutual animosity, and rendered them much more disposed to vex and oppress each other, than to co-operate for their common good. So strong is this propensity of mankind to fall into mutual animosities, that where no substantial occasion presents itself, the most frivolous and fanciful distinctions have been sufficient to kindle their unfriendly passions, and excite their most violent conflicts. But the most common and durable source of factions has been the various and unequal distribution of property. Those who hold and those who are without property have ever formed distinct interests in society. Those who are creditors, and those who are debtors, fall under a like discrimination. A landed interest, a manufacturing interest, a mercantile interest, a moneyed interest, with many lesser interests, grow up of necessity in civilized nations, and divide them into different classes, actuated by different sentiments and views. The regulation of these various and interfering interests forms the principal task of modern Legislation, and involves the spirit of party and faction in the necessary and ordinary operations of Government.

No man is allowed to be judge in his own cause, because his interest would certainly bias his judgment and, not improbably, corrupt his integrity. With equal, nay with greater reason, a body of men are unfit to be both judges and parties at the same time; yet what are many of the most important acts of legislation but so many judicial determinations, not indeed concerning the rights of single persons, but concerning the rights of large bodies of citizens; and what are the different classes of legislators but advocates and parties to the causes which they determine? Is a law proposed concerning private debts? It is a question to which the creditors are parties on one side and the debtors on the other. Justice ought to hold the balance between them. Yet the parties are, and must be, themselves the judges; and the most numerous party, or in other words, the most powerful faction must be expected to prevail. Shall domestic manufacturers be encouraged, and in what degree, by restrictions on foreign manufacturers? are questions which would be differently decided by the landed and the manufacturing classes, and probably by neither with a sole regard to justice and the public good. The apportionment of taxes on the various descriptions of property is an act which seems to require the most exact impartiality; yet there is, perhaps, no legislative act in which greater opportunity and temptation are given to a predominant party to trample on the rules of justice. Every shilling with which they overburden the inferior number is a shilling saved to their own pockets.

It is in vain to say that enlightened statesmen will be able to adjust these clashing interests and render them all subservient to the public good. Enlightened statesmen will not always be at the helm. Nor, in many cases, can such an adjustment be made at all without taking into view indirect and remote considerations, which will rarely prevail over the immediate interest which one party may find in disregarding the rights of another or the good of the whole.

The inference to which we are brought is that the *causes* of faction cannot be removed and that relief is only to be sought in the means of controlling its *effects.*

If a faction consists of less than a majority, relief is supplied by the republican principle, which enables the majority to defeat its sinister views by regular vote. It may clog the administration, it may convulse the society; but it will be unable to execute and mask its violence under the forms of the Constitution. When a majority is included in a faction, the form of popular government, on the other hand, enables it to sacrifice to its ruling passion or interest both the public good and the rights of other citizens. To secure the public good and private rights against the danger of such a faction, and at the same time to preserve the spirit and the form of popular government, is then the great object to which our enquiries are directed. Let me add that it is the great desideratum by which alone this form of government can be rescued from the opprobrium under which it has so long labored and be recommended to the esteem and adoption of mankind.

By what means is this object attainable? Evidently by one of two only. Either the existence of the same passion or interest in a majority at the same time must be prevented, or the majority, having such co-existent passion or interest, must be rendered, by their number and local situation, unable to concert and carry into effect schemes of oppression. If the impulse and the opportunity be suffered to coincide, we well know that neither moral nor religious motives can be relied on as an adequate control. They are not found to be such on the injustice and violence of individuals, and lose their efficacy in proportion to the number combined together, that is, in proportion as their efficacy becomes needful.

From this view of the subject it may be concluded that a pure Democracy, by which I mean a Society consisting of a small number of citizens, who assemble and administer the Government in person, can admit of no cure for the mischiefs of faction. A common passion or interest will, in almost every case, be felt by a majority of the whole; a communication and concert results from the form of Government itself; and there is nothing to check the inducements to sacrifice the weaker party or an obnoxious individual. Hence it is that such Democracies have ever been spectacles of turbulence and contention; have ever been found incompatible with personal security or the rights of property; and have in general been as short in their lives as they have been violent in their deaths. Theoretic politicians, who have patronized this species of Government, have erroneously supposed that by reducing mankind to a perfect equality in their political rights, they would at the same time be perfectly equalized and assimilated in their possessions, their opinions, and their passions.

A Republic, by which I mean a Government in which the scheme of representation takes place, opens a different prospect and promises the cure for which we are seeking. Let us examine the points in which it varies from pure Democracy, and we shall comprehend both the nature of the cure and the efficacy which it must derive from the Union.

The two great points of difference between a Democracy and a Republic are: first, the delegation of the Government, in the latter, to a small number of citizens elected by the rest; secondly, the greater number of citizens and greater sphere of country over which the latter may be extended.

The effect of the first difference is, on the one hand, to refine and enlarge the public views by passing them through the medium of a chosen body of citizens, whose wisdom may best discern the true interest of their country and whose patriotism and love of justice will be least likely to sacrifice it to temporary or partial considerations. Under such a regulation it may well happen that the public voice, pronounced by the representatives of the people, will be more consonant to the public good than if pronounced by the people themselves, convened for the purpose. On the other hand, the effect may be inverted. Men of factious tempers, of local prejudices, or of sinister designs, may, by intrigue, by corruption, or by other means, first obtain the suffrages, and then betray the interests of the people. The question resulting is, whether small or extensive Republics are most favorable to the election of proper guardians of the public weal; and it is clearly decided in favor of the latter by two obvious considerations.

In the first place it is to be remarked that however small the Republic may be, the Representatives must be raised to a certain number in order to guard against the cabals of a few; and that however large it may be they must be limited to a certain number in order to guard against the confusion of a multitude. Hence, the number of Representatives in the two cases not being in proportion to that of the Constituents, and being proportionally greatest in the small Republic, it follows that if the proportion of fit characters be not less in the large than in the small Republic, the former will present a greater option, and consequently a greater probability of a fit choice.

In the next place, as each Representative will be chosen by a greater number of citizens in the large than in the small Republic, it will be more difficult for unworthy candidates to practise with success the vicious arts by which elections are too often carried; and the suffrages of the people being more free, will be more likely to centre on men who possess the most attractive merit and the most diffusive and established characters.

It must be confessed that in this, as in most other cases, there is a mean, on both sides of which inconveniencies will be found to lie. By enlarging too much the number of electors, you render the representative too little acquainted with all their local circumstances and lesser interests; as by reducing it too much, you render him unduly attached to these, and too little fit to comprehend and pursue great and national objects. The Federal Constitution forms a happy combination in this respect; the great and aggregate interests being referred to the national, the local and particular to the State legislatures.

The other point of difference is the greater number of citizens and extent of territory which may be brought within the compass of Republican than of Democratic Government; and it is this circumstance principally which renders factious combinations less to be dreaded in the former than in the latter. The smaller the society, the fewer probably will be the distinct parties and interests composing it; the fewer the distinct parties and interests, the more frequently will a majority be found of the same party; and the smaller the number of individuals composing a majority, and the smaller the compass within which they are placed, the more easily will they concert and execute their plans of oppression. Extend the sphere and you take in a greater variety of parties and interests; you make it less probable that a majority of the whole will have a common motive to invade the rights of other citizens; or if such a common motive exists, it will be more difficult for all who feel it to discover their own strength and to act in unison with each other. Besides other impediments, it may be remarked, that where there is a consciousness of unjust or dishonorable purposes, communication is always checked by distrust in proportion to the number whose concurrence is necessary.

Hence, it clearly appears that the same advantage which a Republic has over a Democracy in controlling the effects of faction is enjoyed by a large over a small republic—is enjoyed by the Union over the States composing it. Does this advantage consist in the substitution of representatives whose enlightened views and virtuous sentiments render them superior to local prejudices and to schemes of injustice? It will not be denied that the representation of the Union will be most likely to possess these requisite endowments.

Does it consist in the greater security afforded by a greater variety of parties, against the event of any one party being able to outnumber and oppress the rest? In an equal degree does the increased variety of parties comprised within the Union increase this security? Does it, in fine, consist in the greater obstacles opposed to the concert and accomplishment of the secret wishes of an unjust and interested majority? Here again the extent of the Union gives it the most palpable advantage.

The influence of factious leaders may kindle a flame within their particular States but will be unable to spread a general conflagration through the other States: a religious sect may degenerate into a political faction in a part of the Confederacy; but the variety of sects dispersed over the entire face of it must secure the national Councils against any danger from that source: a rage for paper money, for an abolition of debts, for an equal division of property, or for any other improper or wicked project, will be less apt to pervade the whole body of the Union than a particular member of it; in the same proportion as such a malady is more likely to taint a particular county or district than an entire State.

In the extent and proper structure of the Union, therefore, we behold a republican remedy for the diseases most incident to Republican Government. And according to the degree of pleasure and pride we feel in being republicans ought to be our zeal in cherishing the spirit and supporting the character of federalist.

PUBLIUS
November 22, 1787

NO. 51: MADISON

To what expedient, then, shall we finally resort, for maintaining in practice the necessary partition of power among the several departments as laid down in the constitution? The only answer that can be given is that as all these exterior provisions are found to be inadequate the defect must be supplied, by so contriving the interior structure of the government as that its several constituent parts may, by their mutual relations, be the means of keeping each other in their proper places. Without presuming to undertake a full development of this important idea I will hazard a few general observations which may perhaps place it in a clearer light, and enable us to form a more correct judgment of the principles and structure of the government planned by the convention.

In order to lay a due foundation for that separate and distinct exercise of the different powers of government, which to a certain extent is admitted on all hands to be essential to the preservation of liberty, it is evident that each department should have a will of its own; and consequently should be so constituted that the members of each should have as little agency as possible in the appointment of the members of the others. Were this principle rigorously adhered to, it would require that all the appointments for the supreme executive, legislative, and judiciary magistracies should be drawn from the same fountain of authority, the people, through channels having no communication whatever with one another. Perhaps such a plan of constructing the several departments would be less difficult in practice than it may in contemplation appear. Some difficulties, however, and some additional expense would attend the execution of it. Some deviations, therefore, from the principle must be admitted. In the constitution of the judiciary department in particular, it might be inexpedient to insist rigorously on the principle: first, because peculiar qualifications being essential in the members, the primary consideration ought to be to select that mode of choice which best secures these qualifications; second, because the permanent tenure by which the appointments are held in that department must soon destroy all sense of dependence on the authority conferring them.

It is equally evident that the members of each department should be as little dependent as possible on those of the others for the emoluments annexed to their offices. Were the executive magistrate, or the judges, not independent of the legislature in this particular, their independence in every other would be merely nominal.

But the great security against a gradual concentration of the several powers in the same department consists in giving to those who administer each department the necessary constitutional means and personal motives to resist encroachments of the others. The provision for defence must in this, as in all other cases, be made commensurate to the danger of attack. Ambition must be made to counteract ambition. The interest of the man must be connected with the constitutional rights of the place. It may be a reflection on human nature that such devices should be necessary to control the abuses of government. But what is government itself but the greatest of all reflections on human nature? If men were angels, no government would be necessary. If angels were to govern men, neither external nor internal controls on government would be necessary. In framing a government which is to be administered by men over men, the great difficulty lies in this: You must first enable the government to control the governed; and in the next place oblige it to control itself. A dependence on the people is, no doubt, the primary control on the government; but experience has taught mankind the necessity of auxiliary precautions.

This policy of supplying, by opposite and rival interests, the defect of better motives, might be traced through the whole system of human affairs, private as well as public. We see it particularly displayed in all the subordinate distributions of power, where the constant aim is to divide and arrange the several offices in such a manner as that each may be a check on the other; that the private interest of every individual may be a sentinel over the public rights. These inventions of prudence cannot be less requisite in the distribution of the supreme powers of the State.

But it is not possible to give to each department an equal power of self-defense. In republican government, the legislative authority necessarily predominates. The remedy for this inconveniency is to divide the legislature into different branches; and to render them, by different modes of election and different principles of action, as little connected with each other as the nature of their common functions and their common dependence on the society will admit. It may even be necessary to guard against dangerous encroachments by still further precautions. As the weight of the legislative authority requires that it should be thus divided, the weakness of the executive may require, on the other hand, that it should be fortified. An absolute negative on the legislature appears, at first view, to be the natural defense with which the executive magistrate should be armed. But perhaps it would be neither altogether safe nor alone sufficient. On ordinary occasions it might not be exerted with the requisite firmness, and on extraordinary occasions it might be perfidiously abused. May not this defect of an absolute negative be supplied by some qualified connection between this weaker branch of the stronger department, by which the latter may be led to support the constitutional rights of the former, without being too much detached from the rights of its own department?

If the principles on which these observations are founded be just, as I persuade myself they are, and they be applied as a criterion to the several State constitutions, and to the federal Constitution, it will be found that if the latter does not perfectly correspond with them, the former are infinitely less able to bear such a test.

There are, moreover, two considerations particularly applicable to the federal system of America, which place that system in a very interesting point of view.

First. In a single republic, all the power surrendered by the people is submitted to the administration of a single government; and usurpations are guarded against by a division of the government into distinct and separate departments. In the compound republic of America, the power surrendered by the people is first divided between two distinct governments, and then the portion allotted to each subdivided among distinct and separate departments. Hence a double security arises to the rights of the people. The different governments will control each other, at the same time that each will be controlled by itself.

Second. It is of great importance in a republic not only to guard the society against the oppression of its rulers, but to guard one part of the society against the injustice of the other part. Different interests necessarily exist in different classes of citizens. If a majority be united by a common interest, the rights of the minority will be insecure. There are but two methods of providing against this evil: The one by creating a will in the community independent of the majority—that is, of the society itself; the other, by comprehending in the society so many separate descriptions of citizens as will render an unjust combination of a majority of the whole very improbable, if not impracticable. The first method prevails in all governments possessing an hereditary or self-appointed authority. This, at best, is but a precarious security; because a power independent of the society may as well espouse the unjust views of the major as the rightful interests of the minor party, and may possibly be turned against both parties. The second method will be exemplified in the federal republic of the United States. Whilst all authority in it will be derived from and dependent on the society, the society itself will be broken into so many parts, interests and classes of citizens, that the rights of individuals, or of the minority, will be in little danger from interested combinations of the majority. In a free government the security for civil rights must be the same as that for religious rights. It consists in the one case in the multiplicity of interests, and in the other in the multiplicity of sects. The degree of security in both cases will depend on the number of interests and sects; and this may be presumed to depend on the extent of country and number of people comprehended under the same government. This view of the subject must particularly recommend a proper federal system to all the sincere and considerate friends of republican government: Since it shows that in exact proportion as the territory of the Union may be formed into more circumscribed Confederacies, or States, oppressive combinations of a majority will be facilitated; the best security, under the republican form, for the rights of every class of citizens, will be diminished; and consequently the stability and independence of some member of the government, the only other security, must be proportionally increased. Justice is the end of government. It is the end of civil society. It ever has been and ever will be pursued until it be obtained, or until liberty be lost in the pursuit. In a society under the forms of which the stronger faction can readily unite and oppress the weaker, anarchy may as truly be said to reign as in a state of nature, where the weaker individual is not secured against the violence of the stronger: And as, in the latter state, even the stronger individuals are prompted, by the uncertainty of their condition, to submit to a government which may protect the weak as well as themselves: So, in the former state, will the more powerful factions or parties be gradually induced, by a like motive, to wish for a government which will protect all parties, the weaker as well as the more powerful. It can be little doubted that if the State of Rhode Island was separated from the Confederacy and left to itself, the insecurity of rights under the popular form of government within such narrow limits would be displayed by such reiterated oppressions of factious majorities that some power altogether independent of the people would soon be called for by the voice of the very factions whose misrule had proved the necessity of it. In the extended republic of the United States, and among the great variety of interests, parties, and sects which it embraces, a coalition of a majority of the whole society could seldom take place on any other principles than those of justice and the general good; and there being thus less danger to a minor from the will of the major party, there must be less pretext, also, to provide for the security of the former, by introducing into the government a will not dependent on the latter, or, in other words, a will independent of the society itself. It is no less certain than it is important, notwithstanding the contrary opinions which have been entertained, that the larger the society, provided it lie within a practicable sphere, the more duly capable it will be of self-government. And happily for the *republican cause,* practicable sphere may be carried to a very great extent by a judicious modification and mixture of the *federal principle.*

PUBLIUS
February 6, 1788

The Anti-Federalist Papers

Essay by Brutus in the *New York Journal*

When the public is called to investigate and decide upon a question in which not only the present members of the community are deeply interested, but upon which the happiness and misery of generations yet unborn is in great measure suspended, the benevolent mind cannot help feeling itself peculiarly interested in the result.

In this situation, I trust the feeble efforts of an individual, to lead the minds of the people to a wise and prudent determination, cannot fail of being acceptable to the candid and dispassionate part of the community. Encouraged by this consideration, I have been induced to offer my thoughts upon the present important crisis of our public affairs.

Perhaps this country never saw so critical a period in their political concerns. We have felt the feebleness of the ties by which these United-States are held together, and the want of sufficient energy in our present confederation, to manage, in some instances, our general concerns. Various expedients have been proposed to remedy these evils, but none have succeeded. At length a Convention of the states has been assembled, they have formed a constitution which will now, probably, be submitted to the people to ratify or reject, who are the fountain of all power, to whom alone it of right belongs to make or unmake constitutions, or forms of government, at their pleasure. The most important question that was ever proposed to your decision, or to the decision of any people under heaven, is before you, and you are to decide upon it by men of your own election, chosen specially for this purpose. If the constitution, offered to your acceptance, be a wise one, calculated to preserve the invaluable blessings of liberty, to secure the inestimable rights of mankind, and promote human happiness, then, if you accept it, you will lay a lasting foundation of happiness for millions yet unborn; generations to come will rise up and call you blessed. You may rejoice in the prospects of this vast extended continent becoming filled with freemen, who will assert the dignity of human nature. You may solace yourselves with the idea, that society, in this favoured land, will fast advance to the highest point of perfection; the human mind will expand in knowledge and virtue, and the golden age be, in some measure, realised. But if, on the other hand, this form of government contains principles that will lead to the subversion of liberty—if it tends to establish a despotism, or, what is worse, a tyrannic aristocracy; then, if you adopt it, this only remaining assylum for liberty will be shut up, and posterity will execrate your memory.

Momentous then is the question you have to determine, and you are called upon by every motive which should influence a noble and virtuous mind, to examine it well, and to make up a wise judgment. It is insisted, indeed, that this constitution must be received, be it ever so imperfect. If it has its defects, it is said, they can be best amended when they are experienced. But remember, when the people once part with power, they can seldom or never resume it again but by force. Many instances can be produced in which the people have voluntarily increased the powers of their rulers; but few, if any, in which rulers have willingly abridged their authority. This is a sufficient reason to induce you to be careful, in the first instance, how you deposit the powers of government.

With these few introductory remarks, I shall proceed to a consideration of this constitution:

The first question that presents itself on the subject is, whether a confederated government be the best for the United States or not? Or in other words, whether the thirteen United States should be reduced to one great republic, governed by one legislature, and under the direction of one executive and judicial; or whether they should continue thirteen confederated republics, under the direction and controul of a supreme federal head for certain defined national purposes only?

This enquiry is important, because, although the government reported by the convention does not go to a perfect and entire consolidation, yet it approaches so near to it, that it must, if executed, certainly and infallibly terminate in it.

This government is to possess absolute and uncontroulable power, legislative, executive and judicial, with respect to every object to which it extends, for by the last clause of section 8th, article 1st, it is declared "that the Congress shall have power to make all laws which shall be necessary and proper for carrying into execution the foregoing powers, and all other powers vested by this constitution, in the government of the United States; or in any department or office thereof." And by the 6th article, it is declared "that this constitution, and the laws of the United States, which shall be made in pursuance thereof, and the treaties made, or which shall be made, under the authority of the United States, shall be the supreme law of the land; and the judges in every state shall be bound thereby, any thing in the constitution, or law of any state to the contrary notwithstanding." It appears from these articles that there is no need of any intervention of the state governments, between the Congress and the people, to execute any one power vested in the general government, and that the constitution and laws of every state are nullified and declared void, so far as they are or shall be inconsistent with this constitution, or the laws made in pursuance of it, or with treaties made under the authority of the United States.—The government then, so far as it extends, is a complete one, and not a confederation. It is as much one complete government as that of New-York or Massachusetts, has as absolute and perfect powers to make and execute all laws, to appoint officers, institute courts, declare offences, and annex penalties, with respect to every object to which it extends, as any other in the world. So far therefore as its powers reach, all ideas of confederation are given up and lost. It is true this government is limited to certain objects, or to speak more properly, some small degree of power is still left to the states, but a little attention to the powers vested in the general government, will convince every candid man, that if it is capable of being executed, all that is reserved for the individual states must very soon be annihilated, except so far as they are barely necessary to the organization of the general government. The powers of the general legislature extend to every case that is of the least importance—there is nothing valuable to human nature, nothing dear to freemen, but what is within its power. It has authority to make laws which will affect the lives, the liberty, and property of every man in the United States; nor can the constitution or laws of any state, in any way prevent or impede the full and complete execution of every power given. The legislative power is competent to lay taxes, duties, imposts, and excises;—there is no limitation to this power, unless it be said that the clause which directs the use to which those taxes, and duties shall be applied, may be said to be a limitation: but this is no restriction of the power at all, for by this clause they are to be applied to pay the debts and provide for the common defence and general welfare of the United States; but the legislature have authority to contract debts at their discretion; they are the sole judges of what is necessary to provide for the common defence, and they only are to determine what is for the general welfare; this power therefore is neither more nor less, than a power to lay and collect taxes, imposts, and excises, at their pleasure; not only [is] the power to lay taxes unlimited, as to the amount they may require, but it is perfect and absolute to raise them in any mode they please. No state legislature, or any power in the state governments, have any more to do in carrying this into effect, than the authority of one state has to do with that of another. In the business therefore of laying and collecting taxes, the idea of confederation is totally lost, and that of one entire republic is embraced. It is proper here to remark, that the authority to lay and collect taxes is the most important of any power that can be granted; it connects with it almost all other powers, or at least will in process of time draw all other after it; it is the great mean of protection, security, and defence, in a good government, and the great engine of oppression and tyranny in a bad one. This cannot fail of being the case, if we consider the contracted limits which are set by this constitution, to the late [state?] governments, on this article of raising money. No state can emit paper money—lay any duties, or imposts, on imports, or exports, but by consent of the Congress; and then the net produce shall be for the benefit of the United States: the only mean therefore left, for any state to support its government and discharge its debts, is by direct taxation; and the United States have also power to lay and collect taxes, in any way they please. Every one who has thought on the subject, must be convinced that but small sums of money can be collected in any country, by direct taxe[s], when the foederal government begins to exercise the right of taxation in all its parts, the legislatures of the several states will find it impossible to raise monies to support their governments. Without money they cannot be supported, and they must dwindle away, and, as before observed, their powers absorbed in that of the general government.

It might be here shewn, that the power in the federal legislative, to raise and support armies at pleasure, as well in peace as in war, and their controul over the militia, tend, not only to a consolidation of the government, but the destruction of liberty.—I shall not, however, dwell upon these, as a few observations upon the judicial power of this government, in addition to the preceding, will fully evince the truth of the position.

The judicial power of the United States is to be vested in a supreme court, and in such inferior courts as Congress may from time to time ordain and establish. The powers of these courts are very extensive; their jurisdiction comprehends all civil causes, except such as arise between citizens of the same state; and it extends to all cases in law and equity arising under the constitution. One inferior court must be established, I presume, in each state, at least, with the necessary executive officers appendant thereto. It is easy to see, that in the common course of things, these courts will eclipse the dignity, and take away from the respectability, of the state courts. These courts will be, in themselves, totally independent of the states, deriving their authority from the United States, and receiving from them fixed salaries; and in the course of human events it is to be expected, that they will swallow up all the powers of the courts in the respective states.

How far the clause in the 8th section of the 1st article may operate to do away all idea of confederated states, and to effect an entire consolidation of the whole into one general government, it is impossible to say. The powers given by this article are very general and comprehensive, and it may receive a construction to justify the passing almost any law. A power to make all laws, which shall be *necessary and proper*, for carrying into execution, all powers vested by the constitution in the government of the United States, or any department or officer thereof, is a power very comprehensive and definite [indefinite?], and may, for ought I know, be exercised in a such manner as entirely to abolish the state legislatures. Suppose the legislature of a state should pass a law to raise money to support their government and pay the state debt, may the Congress repeal this law, because it may prevent the collection of a tax which they may think proper and necessary to lay, to provide for the general welfare of the United States? For all laws made, in pursuance of this constitution, are the supreme lay of the land, and the judges in every state shall be bound thereby, any thing in the constitution or laws of the different states to the contrary notwithstanding.—By such a law, the government of a particular state might be overturned at one stroke, and thereby be deprived of every means of its support.

It is not meant, by stating this case, to insinuate that the constitution would warrant a law of this kind; or unnecessarily to alarm the fears of the people, by suggesting, that the federal legislature would be more likely to pass the limits assigned them by the constitution, than that of an individual state, further than they are less responsible to the people. But what is meant is, that the legislature of the United States are vested with the great and uncontroulable powers, of laying and collecting taxes, duties, imposts, and excises; of regulating trade, raising and supporting armies, organizing, arming, and disciplining the militia, instituting courts, and other general powers. And are by this clause invested with the power of making all laws, *proper and necessary*, for carrying all these into execution; and they may so exercise this power as entirely to annihilate all the state governments, and reduce this country to one single government. And if they may do it, it is pretty certain they will; for it will be found that the power retained by individual states, small as it is, will be a clog upon the wheels of the government of the United States; the latter therefore will be naturally inclined to remove it out of the way. Besides, it is a truth confirmed by the unerring experience of ages, that every man, and every body of men, invested with power, are ever disposed to increase it, and to acquire a superiority over every thing that stands in their way. This disposition, which is implanted in human nature, will operate in the federal legislature to lessen and ultimately to subvert the state authority, and having such advantages, will most certainly succeed, if the federal government succeeds at all. It must be very evident then, that what this constitution wants of being a complete consolidation of the several parts of the union into one complete government, possessed of perfect legislative, judicial, and executive powers, to all intents and purposes, it will necessarily acquire in its exercise and operation.

Let us now proceed to enquire, as I at first proposed, whether it be best the thirteen United States should be reduced to one great republic, or not? It is here taken for granted, that all agree in this, that whatever government we adopt, it ought to be a free one; that it should be so framed as to secure the liberty of the citizens of America, and such an one as to admit of a full, fair, and equal representation of the people. The question then will be, whether a government thus constituted, and founded on such principles, is practicable, and can be exercised over the whole United States, reduced into one state?

If respect is to be paid to the opinion of the greatest and wisest men who have ever thought or wrote on the science of government, we shall be constrained to conclude, that a free republic cannot succeed over a country of such immense extent, containing such a number of inhabitants, and these encreasing in such rapid progression as that of the whole United States. Among the many illustrious authorities which might be produced to this point, I shall content myself with quoting only two. The one is the baron de Montesquieu, spirit of laws, chap. xvi. vol. I [book VIII]. "It is natural to a republic to have only a small territory, otherwise it cannot long subsist. In a large republic there are men of large fortunes, and consequently of less moderation; there are trusts too great to be placed in any single subject; he has interest of his own; he soon begins to think that he may be happy, great and glorious, by oppressing his fellow citizens; and that he may raise himself to grandeur on the ruins of his country. In a large republic, the public good is sacrificed to a thousand views; it is subordinate to exceptions, and depends on accidents. In a small one, the interest of the public is easier perceived, better understood, and more within the reach of every citizen; abuses are of less extent, and of course are less protected." Of the same opinion is the marquis Beccarari.

History furnishes no example of a free republic, any thing like the extent of the United States. The Grecian republics were of small extent; so also was that of the Romans. Both of these, it is true, in process of time, extended their conquests over large territories of country; and the consequence was, that their governments were changed from that of free governments to those of the most tyrannical that ever existed in the world.

Not only the opinion of the greatest men, and the experience of mankind, are against the idea of an extensive republic, but a variety of reasons may be drawn from the reason and nature of things, against it. In every government, the will of the sovereign is the law. In despotic governments, the supreme authority being lodged in one, his will is law, and can be as easily expressed to a large extensive territory as to a small one. In a pure democracy the people are the sovereign, and their will is declared by themselves; for this purpose they must all come together to deliberate, and decide. This kind of government cannot be exercised, therefore, over a country of any considerable extent; it must be confined to a single city, or at least limited to such bounds as that the people can conveniently assemble, be able to debate, understand the subject submitted to them, and declare their opinion concerning it.

In a free republic, although all laws are derived from the consent of the people, yet the people do not declare their consent by themselves in person, but by representatives, chosen by them, who are supposed to know the minds of their constituents, and to be possessed of integrity to declare this mind.

In every free government, the people must give their assent to the laws by which they are governed. This is the true criterion between a free government and an arbitrary one. The former are ruled by the will of the whole, expressed in any manner they may agree upon; the latter by the will of one, or a few. If the people are to give their assent to the laws, by persons chosen and appointed by them, the manner of the choice and the number chosen, must be such, as to possess, be disposed, and consequently qualified to declare the sentiments of the people; for if they do not know, or are not disposed to speak the sentiments of the people, the people do not govern, but the sovereignty is in a few. Now, in a large extended country, it is impossible to have a representation, possessing the sentiments, and of integrity, to declare the minds of the people, without having it so numerous and unwieldly, as to be subject in great measure to the inconveniency of a democratic government.

The territory of the United States is of vast extent; it now contains near three millions of souls, and is capable of containing much more than ten times that number. Is it practicable for a country, so large and so numerous as they will soon become, to elect a representation, that will speak their sentiments, without their becoming so numerous as to be incapable of transacting public business? It certainly is not.

In a republic, the manners, sentiments, and interests of the people should be similar. If this be not the case, there will be a constant clashing of opinions; and the representatives of one part will be continually striving against those of the other. This will retard the operations of government, and prevent such conclusions as will promote the public good. If we apply this remark to the condition of the United States, we shall be convinced that it forbids that we should be one government. The United States includes a variety of climates. The productions of the different parts of the union are very variant, and their interests, of consequence, diverse. Their manners and habits differ as much as their climates and productions; and their sentiments are by no means coincident. The laws and customs of the several states are, in many respects, very diverse, and in some opposite; each would be in favor of its own interests and customs, and, of consequence, a legislature, formed of representatives from the respective parts, would not only be too numerous to act with any care or decision, but would be composed of such heterogenous and discordant principles, as would constantly be contending with each other.

The laws cannot be executed in a republic, of an extent equal to that of the United States, with promptitude.

The magistrates in every government must be supported in the execution of the laws, either by an armed force, maintained at the public expence for that purpose; or by the people turning out to aid the magistrate upon his command, in case of resistance.

In despotic governments, as well as in all the monarchies of Europe, standing armies are kept up to execute the commands of the prince or the magistrate, and are employed for this purpose when occasion requires: But they have always proved the destruction of liberty, and [are] abhorrent to the spirit of a free republic. In England, where they depend upon the parliament for their annual support, they have always been complained of as oppressive and unconstitutional, and are seldom employed in executing of the laws; never except on extraordinary occasions, and then under the direction of a civil magistrate.

A free republic will never keep a standing army to execute its laws. It must depend upon the support of its citizens. But when a government is to receive its support from the aid of the citizens, it must be so constructed as to have the confidence, respect, and affection of the people. Men who, upon the call of the magistrate, offer themselves to execute the laws, are influenced to do it either by affection to the government, or from fear; where a standing army is at hand to punish offenders, every man is actuated by the latter principle, and therefore, when the magistrate calls, will obey: but, where this is not the case, the government must rest for its support upon the confidence and respect which the people have for their government and laws. The body of the people being attached, the government will always be sufficient to support and execute its laws, and to operate upon the fears of any faction which may be opposed to it, not only to prevent an opposition to the execution of the laws themselves, but also to compel the most of them to aid the magistrate; but the people will not be likely to have such confidence in their rulers, in a republic so extensive as the United States, as necessary for these purposes. The confidence which the people have in their rulers, in a free republic, arises from their knowing them, from their being responsible to them for their conduct, and from the power they have of displacing them when they misbehave: but in a republic of the extent of this continent, the people in general would be acquainted with very few of their rulers: the people at large would know little of their proceedings, and it would be extremely difficult to change them. The people in Georgia and New-Hampshire would not know one another's mind, and therefore could not act in concert to enable them to effect a general change of representatives. The different parts of so extensive a country could not possibly be made acquainted with the conduct of their representatives, nor be informed of the reasons upon which measures were founded. The consequence will be, they will have no confidence in their legislature, suspect them of ambitious views, be jealous of every measure they adopt, and will not support the laws they pass. Hence the government will be nerveless and inefficient, and no way will be left to render it otherwise, but by establishing an armed force to execute the laws at the point of the bayonet—a government of all others the most to be dreaded.

In a republic of such vast extent as the United-States, the legislature cannot attend to the various concerns and wants of its different parts. It cannot be sufficiently numerous to be acquainted with the local condition and wants of the different districts, and if it could, it is impossible it should have sufficient time to attend to and provide for all the variety of cases of this nature, that would be continually arising.

In so extensive a republic, the great officers of government would soon become above the controul of the people, and abuse their power to the purpose of aggrandizing themselves, and oppressing them. The trust committed to the executive offices, in a country of the extent of the United-States, must be various and of magnitude. The command of all the troops and navy of the republic, the appointment of officers, the power of pardoning offences, the collecting of all the public revenues, and the power of expending them, with a number of other powers, must be lodged and exercised in every state, in the hands of a few. When these are attended with great honor and emolument, as they always will be in large states, so as greatly to interest men to pursue them, and to be proper objects for ambitious and designing men, such men will be ever restless in their pursuit after them. They will use the power, when they have acquired it, to the purposes of gratifying their own interest and ambition, and it is scarcely possible, in a very large republic, to call them to account for their misconduct, or to prevent their abuse of power.

These are some of the reasons by which it appears, that a free republic cannot long subsist over a country of the great extent of these states. If then this new constitution is calculated to consolidate the thirteen states into one, as it evidently is, it ought not to be adopted.

Though I am of opinion, that it is a sufficient objection to this government, to reject it, that it creates the whole union into one government, under the form of a republic, yet if this objection was obviated, there are exceptions to it, which are so material and fundamental, that they ought to determine every man, who is a friend to the liberty and happiness of mankind, not to adopt it. I beg the candid and dispassionate attention of my countrymen while I state these objections—they are such as have obtruded themselves upon my mind upon a careful attention to the matter, and such as I sincerely believe are well founded. There are many objections, of small moment, of which I shall take no notice—perfection is not to be expected in any thing that is the production of man—and if I did not in my conscience believe that this scheme was defective in the fundamental principles—in the foundation upon which a free and equal government must rest—I would hold my peace.

BRUTUS

October 18, 1787

Presidents and Vice Presidents

PRESIDENT	VICE PRESIDENT
1 George Washington *(Federalist 1789)*	John Adams *(Federalist 1789)*
2 John Adams *(Federalist 1797)*	Thomas Jefferson *(Dem.-Rep. 1797)*
3 Thomas Jefferson *(Dem.-Rep. 1801)*	Aaron Burr *(Dem.-Rep. 1801)*
	George Clinton *(Dem.-Rep. 1805)*
4 James Madison *(Dem.-Rep. 1809)*	George Clinton *(Dem.-Rep. 1809)*
	Elbridge Gerry *(Dem.-Rep. 1813)*
5 James Monroe *(Dem.-Rep. 1817)*	Daniel D. Tompkins *(Dem.-Rep. 1817)*
6 John Quincy Adams *(Dem.-Rep. 1825)*	John C. Calhoun *(Dem.-Rep. 1825)*
7 Andrew Jackson *(Democratic 1829)*	John C. Calhoun *(Democratic 1829)*
	Martin Van Buren *(Democratic 1833)*
8 Martin Van Buren *(Democratic 1837)*	Richard M. Johnson *(Democratic 1837)*
9 William H. Harrison *(Whig 1841)*	John Tyler *(Whig 1841)*
10 John Tyler *(Whig and Democratic 1841)*	
11 James K. Polk *(Democratic 1845)*	George M. Dallas *(Democratic 1845)*
12 Zachary Taylor *(Whig 1849)*	Millard Fillmore *(Whig 1849)*
13 Millard Fillmore *(Whig 1850)*	
14 Franklin Pierce *(Democratic 1853)*	William R. D. King *(Democratic 1853)*

PRESIDENT	VICE PRESIDENT
15 James Buchanan *(Democratic 1857)*	John C. Breckinridge *(Democratic 1857)*
16 Abraham Lincoln *(Republican 1861)*	Hannibal Hamlin *(Republican 1861)*
	Andrew Johnson *(Unionist 1865)*
17 Andrew Johnson (Unionist 1865)	
18 Ulysses S. Grant *(Republican 1869)*	Schuyler Colfax *(Republican 1869)*
	Henry Wilson *(Republican 1873)*
19 Rutherford B. Hayes *(Republican 1877)*	William A. Wheeler *(Republican 1877)*
20 James A. Garfield *(Republican 1881)*	Chester A. Arthur *(Republican 1881)*
21 Chester A. Arthur *(Republican 1881)*	
22 Grover Cleveland *(Democratic 1885)*	Thomas A. Hendricks *(Democratic 1885)*
23 Benjamin Harrison *(Republican 1889)*	Levi P. Morton *(Republican 1889)*
24 Grover Cleveland *(Democratic 1893)*	Adlai E. Stevenson *(Democratic 1893)*
25 William McKinley *(Republican 1897)*	Garret A. Hobart *(Republican 1897)*
	Theodore Roosevelt *(Republican 1901)*
26 Theodore Roosevelt *(Republican 1901)*	Charles W. Fairbanks *(Republican 1905)*
27 William H. Taft *(Republican 1909)*	James S. Sherman *(Republican 1909)*
28 Woodrow Wilson *(Democratic 1913)*	Thomas R. Marshall *(Democratic 1913)*
29 Warren G. Harding *(Republican 1921)*	Calvin Coolidge *(Republican 1921)*
30 Calvin Coolidge *(Republican 1923)*	Charles G. Dawes *(Republican 1925)*

PRESIDENT	VICE PRESIDENT
31 Herbert Hoover *(Republican 1929)*	Charles Curtis *(Republican 1929)*
32 Franklin D. Roosevelt *(Democratic 1933)*	John Nance Garner *(Democratic 1933)* Henry A. Wallace *(Democratic 1941)* Harry S. Truman *(Democratic 1945)*
33 Harry S. Truman *(Democratic 1945)*	Alben W. Barkley *(Democratic 1949)*
34 Dwight D. Eisenhower *(Republican 1953)*	Richard M. Nixon *(Republican 1953)*
35 John F. Kennedy *(Democratic 1961)*	Lyndon B. Johnson *(Democratic 1961)*
36 Lyndon B. Johnson *(Democratic 1963)*	Hubert H. Humphrey *(Democratic 1965)*
37 Richard M. Nixon *(Republican 1969)*	Spiro T. Agnew *(Republican 1969)* Gerald R. Ford *(Republican 1973)*
38 Gerald R. Ford *(Republican 1974)*	Nelson Rockefeller *(Republican 1974)*
39 James E. Carter *(Democratic 1977)*	Walter Mondale *(Democratic 1977)*
40 Ronald Reagan *(Republican 1981)*	George H. W. Bush *(Republican 1981)*
41 George H. W. Bush *(Republican 1989)*	J. Danforth Quayle *(Republican 1989)*
42 William J. Clinton *(Democratic 1993)*	Albert Gore, Jr. *(Democratic 1993)*
43 George W. Bush *(Republican 2001)*	Richard Cheney *(Republican 2001)*
44 Barack H. Obama *(Democratic 2009)*	Joseph R. Biden, Jr. *(Democratic 2009)*
45 Donald J. Trump *(Republican 2017)*	Michael R. Pence *(Republican 2017)*
46 Joseph R. Biden, Jr. *(Democratic 2021)*	Kamala Harris *(Democratic 2021)*

Endnotes

CHAPTER 1

1. Lydia DePillis et al., "Here's Why Florida Got All the Emergency Medical Supplies It Requested While Other States Did Not," ProPublica, March 20, 2020, www .propublica.org/article/heres-why-florida-got-all-the-emergency-medical-supplies-it -requested-while-other-states-did-not (accessed 3/23/20).
2. V-Dem Institute, "Democracy for All? V-Dem Annual Democracy Report 2018," May 2018, www.v-dem.net/media/filer_public/3f/19/3f19efc9-e25f-4356-b159 -b5c0ec894115/v-dem_democracy_report_2018.pdf (accessed 1/19/20).
3. Harold Lasswell, *Politics: Who Gets What, When, How* (New York: Meridian Books, 1958).
4. "2020 Ballot Measures," Ballotpedia, https://ballotpedia.org/2020_ballot _measures#Notable_topics_and_trends_in_2020 (accessed 10/12/20).
5. U.S. Citizenship and Immigration Services, "Citizenship Rights and Responsibilities," www.uscis.gov/citizenship/learners/citizenship-rights-and-responsibilities (accessed 6/1/19).
6. This definition is taken from Norman H. Nie, Jane Junn, and Kenneth Stehlik-Barry, *Education and Democratic Citizenship in America* (Chicago: University of Chicago Press, 1996).
7. Kyle Dropp and Brendan Nyhan, "One-Third Don't Know Obamacare and Affordable Care Act Are the Same," *New York Times*, The Upshot, February 7, 2017, www.nytimes.com/2017/02/07/upshot/one-third-dont-know-obamacare-and -affordable-care-act-are-the-same.html?_r=0 (accessed 12/28/17).
8. Annenberg Constitution Day Civics Survey, August 16–27, 2019, https://cdn .annenbergpublicpolicycenter.org/wp-content/uploads/2019/09/Annenberg _civics_2019_Appendix.pdf (accessed 1/19/20).
9. Pew Research Center, Global Attitudes & Trends, "Attitudes toward Elected Officials, Voting, and the State," February 26, 2020, pewresearch.org/global/2020/02/27 /attitudes-toward-elected-officials-voting-and-the-state/pg_2020-02-27_global -democracy_02-1/ (accessed 3/21/20).
10. Pew Research Center, "Attitudes toward Elected Officials, Voting, and the State."
11. U.S. Census Bureau, Population Clock, April 15, 2018, www.census.gov/popclock/ (accessed 4/15/18).
12. Susan B. Carter et al., eds., *Historical Statistics of the United States: Millennial Edition Online* (New York: Cambridge University Press, 2006), Table Aa145-184, Population, by Sex and Race: 1790–1990, 23. Data from 2016 available at U.S. Census Bureau, "2016 American Community Survey 1-Year Estimates: Selected Characteristics of the Native and Foreign-Born Populations," https://factfinder.census.gov/faces /tableserVices/jsf/pages/productview.xhtml?pid=ACS_16_1YR_S0501&prodType =table (accessed 12/26/17).

13. Carter et al., *Historical Statistics of the United States*, Table Aa145-184, Population, by Sex and Race: 1790–1990, 23.
14. Carter et al., *Historical Statistics of the United States*, Table Aa145-184, Population, by Sex and Race: 1790–1990, 23; Table Aa2189-2215, Hispanic Population Estimates.
15. Campbell J. Gibson and Emily Lennon, "Historical Census Statistics on the Foreign-Born Population of the United States: 1850–1990," February 1999, www.census.gov/population/www/documentation/twps0029/twps0029.html (accessed 4/10/16).
16. Carter et al., *Historical Statistics of the United States*, Table Aa22-35, Selected Population Characteristics.
17. Michael B. Katz and Mark J. Stern, *One Nation Divisible: What America Was and What It Is Becoming* (New York: Russell Sage Foundation, 2006), 16.
18. Carter et al., *Historical Statistics of the United States*, Table Aa145-184, Population, by Sex and Race: 1790–1990, 23. Karen R. Humes, Nicholas A. Jones, and Roberto R. Ramirez, "Overview of Race and Hispanic Origin: 2010. *2010 Census Briefs*," no. C2010BR-02 (Washington, DC: U.S. Census Bureau, March 2011), 4, www.census.gov/prod/cen2010/briefs/c2010br-02.pdf (accessed 10/14/2011).
19. U.S. Census Bureau, "American Community Survey 2018, 1-year Estimates Data Profiles, Table DP05," https://data.census.gov/cedsci/table?t=Hispanic%20or%20Latino&tid=ACSDP1Y2018.DP05&hidePreview=false (accessed 3/23/2020).
20. U.S. Census Bureau, "2016 American Community Survey 1-Year Estimates: Selected Characteristics of the Native and Foreign-Born Populations."
21. U.S. Census Bureau, "2016 American Community Survey 1-Year Estimates: Selected Characteristics of the Foreign-Born Population by Region of Birth: Latin America," https://factfinder.census.gov/faces/tableservices/jsf/pages/productview.xhtml?pid=ACS_16_1YR_S0506&prodType=table (accessed 12/26/17).
22. U.S. Census Bureau, "2016 American Community Survey 1-Year Estimates: Selected Characteristics of the Foreign-Born Population by Region of Birth: Asia," https://factfinder.census.gov/faces/tableservices/jsf/pages/productview.xhtml?pid=ACS_16_1YR_S0505&prodType=table (accessed 12/2/17).
23. U.S. Census Bureau, "2016 American Community Survey 1-Year Estimates: Selected Characteristics of the Foreign-Born Population by Region of Birth: Europe," https://factfinder.census.gov/faces/tableservices/jsf/pages/productview.xhtml?pid=ACS_16_1YR_S0503&prodType=table (accessed 12/26/17).
24. Bryan Baker, "Estimates of the Illegal Alien Population Residing in the United States: January 2015," Department of Homeland Security, December 2018, www.dhs.gov/sites/default/files/publications/18_1214_PLCY_pops-est-report.pdf (accessed 1/17/20).
25. *Plyler v. Doe*, 457 U.S. 202 (1982).
26. National Conference of State Legislatures, "Federal Benefit Eligibility for Unauthorized Immigrants," February 24, 2014, www.ncsl.org/research/immigration/federal-benefits-to-unauthorized-immigrants.aspx (accessed 5/22/19); National Conference of State Legislatures, "Undocumented Student Tuition: Overview," March 14, 2019, www.ncsl.org/research/education/undocumented-student-tuition-overview.aspx (accessed 5/22/19).
27. Gallup, "Religion," https://news.gallup.com/poll/1690/religion.aspx (accessed 10/12/20).
28. Gallup, "Religion."
29. U.S. Census Bureau, "Demographic Trends in the 20th Century, Table 5: Population by Age and Sex for the United States: 1900 to 2000," www.census.gov/prod/2002pubs/censr-4.pdf (accessed 4/11/16); U.S. Census Bureau, "Population Estimates, Age and Sex," www.census.gov/quickfacts/fact/table/US/PST045217 (accessed 12/26/17).

30. World Bank, "Population Ages 65 and Above (% of Total)," March 1, 2018, http://data.worldbank.org/indicator/SP.POP.65UP.TO.ZS (accessed 4/15/18).

31. U.S. Census Bureau, "2010 Census Urban Area Facts," www.census.gov/geo/reference/ua/uafacts.html (accessed 4/11/16); Central Intelligence Agency, "World Factbook: Urbanization," 2017, www.cia.gov/library/publications/the-world-factbook/fields/2212.html (accessed 4/15/18).

32. See, for example, David B. Grusky and Tamar Kricheli-Katz, eds., *The New Gilded Age: The Critical Inequality Debates of Our Time* (Stanford: Stanford University Press, 2012).

33. Thomas Piketty and Emmanuel Saez, "Income Inequality in the United States, 1913–1998," *Quarterly Journal of Economics* 118, no. 1 (2003) (tables and figures updated to 2018), https://eml.berkeley.edu/~saez/ (accessed 1/17/20).

34. U.S. Census Bureau, "Income: Historical Income Data. Tables F-2, F-3, and F-6," www.census.gov/hhes/www/income/data/historical/index.html (accessed 4/12/16).

35. U.S. Census Bureau, "Historical Poverty Tables, Table 2: Poverty Status of People by Family Relationship, Race, and Hispanic Origin: 1959 to 2014," www.census.gov/hhes/www/poverty/data/historical/hstpov2.xls (accessed 4/11/16).

36. Jesse Sussell and James A. Thomson, "Are Changing Constituencies Driving Rising Polarization in the U.S. House of Representatives?" RAND Corporation Research Report RR-396-RC, 2015, www.rand.org/pubs/research_reports/RR896.html (accessed 1/15/18).

37. See Judith N. Shklar, *American Citizenship: The Quest for Inclusion* (Cambridge, MA: Harvard University Press, 1991).

38. Herbert McClosky and John Zaller, *The American Ethos: Public Attitudes toward Capitalism and Democracy* (Cambridge, MA: Harvard University Press, 1984), 19.

39. J. R. Pole, *The Pursuit of Equality in American History* (Berkeley: University of California Press, 1978), 3.

40. Veronique de Rugy and Donald J. Boudreaux, "COVID-19 Is Not a Good Reason to Enact a Permanent Federal Leave Entitlement," National Review, March 13, 2020, www.nationalreview.com/2020/03/covid-19-is-not-a-good-reason-to-enact-a-permanent-federal-paid-leave-entitlement/?itm_source=parsely-api" (accessed 3/23/20).

41. "Americans' Views of Government: Low Trust, but Some Positive Performance Ratings," September 14, 2020, www.pewresearch.org/politics/2020/09/14/americans-views-of-government-low-trust-but-some-positive-performance-ratings/ (accessed 10/12/20).

42. Frank Newport, "10 Key Findings: Public Opinion on Coronavirus," Gallup Polling Matters, March 20, 2020, https://news.gallup.com/opinion/polling-matters/296681/ten-key-findings-public-opinion-coronavirus.aspx (accessed 3/23/20).

43. Joseph S. Nye, Jr., "Introduction: The Decline of Confidence in Government," in *Why People Don't Trust Government*, eds. Joseph S. Nye, Jr., Philip D. Zelikow, and David C. King (Cambridge, MA: Harvard University Press, 1997), 4.

CHAPTER 2

1. "Jim Obergefell," Biography.com, www.biography.com/people/jim-obergefell (accessed 3/4/18).

2. Jim Obergefell, "Gay Activist Jim Obergefell: Love, Loss and Steadfast Commitment Lead a Nation Forward," *Variety*, June 29, 2015, http://variety.com/2015/biz/news/gay-activist-jim-obergefell-love-loss-commitment-lead-nation-forward-1201529672/ (accessed 3/4/18).

3. *Obergefell v. Hodges*, 576 U.S. — (2015).

4. Richard E. Neustadt, *Presidential Power and the Modern Presidents: The Politics of Leadership from Roosevelt to Reagan* (New York: Simon and Schuster, 1991), 29.

5. George B. Tindall and David E. Shi, *America: A Narrative History*, 8th ed. (New York: W. W. Norton, 2010), 202.
6. For a discussion of events leading up to the Revolution, see Charles M. Andrews, *The Colonial Background of the American Revolution* (New Haven, CT: Yale University Press, 1924).
7. See Carl Becker, *The Declaration of Independence* (New York: Knopf, 1942).
8. An excellent and readable account of the development from the Articles of Confederation to the Constitution will be found in Alfred H. Kelly, Winfred A. Harbison, and Herman Belz, *The American Constitution: Its Origins and Development*, 7th ed., vol. 1 (New York: W. W. Norton, 1991), chap. 5.
9. Reported in Samuel E. Morrison, Henry Steele Commager, and William Leuchtenburg, *The Growth of the American Republic*, vol. 1 (New York: Oxford University Press, 1969), 244.
10. Quoted in Morrison, Commager, and Leuchtenburg, *Growth of the American Republic*, 242.
11. Charles A. Beard, *An Economic Interpretation of the Constitution of the United States* (New York: Macmillan, 1913).
12. Max Farrand, ed., *The Records of the Federal Convention of 1787*, vol. 1 (New Haven, CT: Yale University Press, 1966).
13. Madison's notes, along with the somewhat less complete records kept by several other participants in the convention, are available in a four-volume set. See Max Farrand, ed., *The Records of the Federal Convention of 1787*, 4 vols., rev. ed. (New Haven, CT: Yale University Press, 1966).
14. Alexander Hamilton, James Madison, and John Jay, *The Federalist Papers*, ed. Clinton L. Rossiter (New York: New American Library, 1961), no. 71.
15. *Federalist Papers*, no. 70.
16. Melancton Smith, quoted in Herbert J. Storing, *What the Anti-Federalists Were For* (Chicago: University of Chicago Press, 1981), 17.
17. *Federalist Papers*, no. 57.
18. *Federalist Papers*, no. 10.
19. "Essays of Brutus," no. 7, in Storing, *Complete Anti-Federalist*.
20. "Essays of Brutus," no. 6, in Storing, *Complete Anti-Federalist*.
21. Storing, *What the Anti-Federalists Were For*, 28.
22. *Federalist Papers*, no. 51.

CHAPTER 3

1. White House, "Remarks by President Trump after Tour of the Centers for Disease Control and Prevention," March 6, 2020, www.whitehouse.gov/briefings-statements/remarks-president-trump-tour-centers-disease-control-prevention-atlanta-ga/ (accessed 3/27/20).
2. Robert P. Baird, "Why Widespread Coronavirus Testing Isn't Coming Anytime Soon," *New Yorker*, March 24, 2020, www.newyorker.com/news/news-desk/why-widespread-coronavirus-testing-isnt-coming-anytime-soon (accessed 3/26/20).
3. Pietro S. Nivola, "Why Federalism Matters," Brookings Institution Policy Brief #146, October 2005, www.brookings.edu/wp-content/uploads/2016/06/pb146.pdf (accessed 7/15/19).
4. The public policy exception stems from developments in case law tracing back to the 1930s. In Section 283 of the Restatement (Second) of Conflict of Laws (1971) a group of judges and academics codified existing case law related to marriage: "A marriage which satisfies the requirements of the state where the marriage was contracted will

everywhere be recognized as valid unless it violates the strong public policy of another state which had the most significant relationship to the spouses and the marriage at the time of the marriage." However, in *Baker v. General Motors Corp*, 522 U.S. 222 (1998), the Supreme Court explicitly stated that its decision "creates no general exception to the full faith and credit command."

5. Adam Liptak, "Bans on Interracial Unions Offer Perspective on Gay Ones," *New York Times*, March 17, 2004, A22.

6. *Loving v. Virginia*, 388 U.S. 1 (1967). The Lovings were charged with violating Virginia's miscegenation laws and were sentenced to one year in jail, which would be suspended if they left the state for 25 years. Five years later, with the assistance of the American Civil Liberties Union, the Lovings filed a motion to vacate their conviction. The Supreme Court heard the case and overturned the Lovings' conviction, finding Virginia's miscegenation law unconstitutional under the due process clause and equal protection clause of the Fourteenth Amendment.

7. *Obergefell v. Hodges*, 576 U.S. — (2015).

8. *Hicklin v. Orbeck*, 437 U.S. 518 (1978).

9. A good discussion of the constitutional position of local governments is in Richard Briffault, "Our Localism: Part I, the Structure of Local Government Law," *Columbia Law Review* 90, no. 1 (January 1990): 1–115. For more on the structure and theory of federalism, see Larry N. Gerston, *American Federalism: A Concise Introduction* (Armonk, NY: M. E. Sharpe, 2007), and Martha Derthick, "Up-to-Date in Kansas City: Reflections on American Federalism" (1992 John Gaus Lecture), *PS: Political Science and Politics* 25 (December 1992): 671–75.

10. *McCulloch v. Maryland*, 4 Wheaton 316 (1819).

11. *Gibbons v. Ogden*, 9 Wheaton 1 (1824).

12. The Sherman Antitrust Act, adopted in 1890, for example, was enacted not to restrict commerce but rather to protect it from monopolies, or trusts, in order to prevent unfair trade practices and to enable the market again to become self-regulating. Moreover, the Supreme Court sought to uphold liberty of contract to protect businesses. For example, in *Lochner v. New York*, 198 U.S. 45 (1905), the Court invalidated a New York law regulating the sanitary conditions and hours of labor of bakers on the grounds that the law interfered with liberty of contract.

13. The key case in this process of expanding the power of the national government is generally considered to be *NLRB v. Jones & Laughlin Steel Corporation*, 301 U.S. 1 (1937), in which the Supreme Court approved federal regulation of the workplace and thereby virtually eliminated interstate commerce as a limit on the national government's power.

14. Morton Grodzins, *The American System*, ed. Daniel J. Elazar (Chicago: Rand McNally, 1966).

15. See Donald F. Kettl, *The Regulation of American Federalism* (Baton Rouge: Louisiana State University Press, 1983).

16. Evan Halper, "Trump and California Are Set to Collide Head-On over Fuel Standards," *Los Angeles Times*, April 27, 2018, www.latimes.com/politics/la-na-pol -mileage-20180427-story.html (accessed 5/1/18).

17. Brady Dennis and Juliet Eilperin, "California and Nearly Two Dozen Other States Sue Trump Administration for the Right to Set Fuel-Efficiency Standards," *Washington Post*, November 15, 2019, www.washingtonpost.com/climate-environment /2019/11/15/california-nearly-two-dozen-other-states-sue-trump-administration -right-require-more-fuel-efficient-cars/ (accessed 1/21/20).

18. The phrase "laboratories of democracy" was coined by Supreme Court Justice Louis Brandeis in his dissenting opinion in *New State Ice Co. v. Liebmann*, 285 U.S. 262 (1932).

19. W. John Moore, "Pleading the 10th," *National Journal*, July 29, 1996.
20. Timothy Conlan, *New Federalism: Intergovernmental Reform from Nixon to Reagan* (Washington, DC: Brookings Institution Press, 1988); U.S. Advisory Commission on Intergovernmental Relations, *Federal Regulation of State and Local Governments*.
21. For an assessment of the achievements of the 104th and 105th Congresses, see Timothy Conlan, *From New Federalism to Devolution: Twenty-Five Years of Intergovernmental Reform* (Washington, DC: Brookings Institution Press, 1998).
22. Education Commission of the States, "50-State Comparison: Charter School Policies," January 2018, www.ecs.org/charter-school-policies/ (accessed 6/5/18).
23. Robert Jay Dilger and Richard S. Beth, "Unfunded Mandates Reform Act: History, Impact, and Issues" (Washington, DC: Congressional Research Service, April 19, 2011), 40, http://digital.library.unt.edu/ark:/67531/metadc40084/m1/1/high_res_d /R40957_2011Apr19.pdf (accessed 11/16/13).
24. Elissa Cohen et al., "Welfare Rules Databook: State TANF Policies as of July 2015," OPRE Report 2016-67 (Washington, DC: Office of Planning, Research and Evaluation, Administration for Children and Families, U.S. Department of Health and Human Services, 2016), http://wrd.urban.org/wrd/data/databooks/2015%20Welfare %20Rules%20Databook%20(Final%2009%2026%2016).pdf (accessed 7/30/17); and Mary Jo Pitzi, "Arizona Limits Poverty Aid to 1 Year; Strictest in U.S.," AZcentral.com, July 1, 2016, www.azcentral.com/story/news/politics/arizona/2016 /07/01/arizona-limits-poverty-aid-1-year-strictest-us/86499262/ (accessed 7/30/17).
25. Ashley Burnside and Ife Floyd, "TANF Benefits Remain Low despite Recent Increases in Some States," Center on Budget and Policy Priorities, October 12, 2018, www .cbpp.org/sites/default/files/atoms/files/10-30-14tanf.pdf (accessed 10/12/18).
26. Kate Linthicum, "Obama Ends Secure Communities Program as Part of Immigration Action," *Los Angeles Times*, November 21, 2014, www.latimes.com/local/california /la-me-1121-immigration-justice-20141121-story.html (accessed 8/16/15).
27. "Enhancing Public Safety in the Interior of the United States," Executive Order 13768, January 25, 2017, www.federalregister.gov/documents/2017/01/30/2017 -02102/enhancing-public-safety-in-the-interior-of-the-united-states (accessed 7/27/17).
28. Camila Domonoske, "Judge Blocks Trump Administration from Punishing 'Sanctuary Cities,'" NPR, November 21, 2017, www.npr.org/sections/thetwo-way/2017/11/21 /565678707/enter-title (accessed 2/18/18).
29. Tal Axelrod, "9th Circuit Rules in Favor of Trump Admin in 'Sanctuary City' Case," The Hill, July 12, 2019, https://thehill.com/regulation/court-battles/452862-9th -circuit-rules-in-favor-of-trump-admin-in-sanctuary-city-case (accessed 7/15/19).
30. *Gonzales v. Raich*, 545 U.S. 1 (2005). For more, see William Yardley, "New Federal Crackdown Confounds States That Allow Medical Marijuana," *New York Times*, May 8, 2011, A13.
31. Local Solutions Support Center, The Growing Shadow of State Interference: Preemption in the 2019 State Legislative Sessions," August 2019, https://static1 .squarespace.com/static/5ce4377caeb1ce00013a02fd/t/5d66a3c36044f700019a7efd /1567007722604/LSSCSiXReportAugust2019.pdf (accessed 3/21/20).
32. Lisa L. Miller, "The Representational Biases of Federalism: Scope and Bias in the Political Process, Revisited," *Perspectives on Politics* 50, no. 2, June 2007, 305–21.
33. U.S. Department of Labor, "Consolidated Minimum Wage Table," January 1, 2020, www.dol.gov/agencies/whd/mw-consolidated (accessed 3/27/20).

CHAPTER 4

1. This account taken from April Baer, "The Slants: Trading in Stereotypes," NPR, June 11, 2008, www.npr.org/templates/story/story.php?storyId=90278746; Katy Steinmetz, "The Slants' Suit: Asian-American Band Goes to Court over Name," *Time*, October 23, 2013, http://entertainment.time.com/2013/10/23/the-slants-suit -asian-american-band-goes-to-court-over-name/; Kat Chow, "The Slants: Fighting for the Right to Rock a Racial Slur," NPR, January 19, 2017, www.npr.org/sections /codeswitch/2017/01/19/510467679/the-slants-fighting-for-the-right-to-rock-a-racial -slur; *Matal v. Tam*, 582 U.S. — (2017); Ian Shapira and Ann E. Marimow, "Wash-ington Redskins Win Trademark Fight over the Team's Name," *Washington Post*, June 29, 2017, www.washingtonpost.com/local/public-safety/2017/06/29/a26f52f0 -5cf6-11e7-9fc6 c7ef4bc58d13_story.html?utm_term=.22ed3bf39917 (accessed 2/4/18).
2. Alexander Hamilton, James Madison, and John Jay, *The Federalist Papers*, ed. Clinton Rossiter (New York: New American Library, 1961), no. 84, 513.
3. *Federalist Papers*, no. 84, 513.
4. Clinton Rossiter, *1787: The Grand Convention* (New York: W. W. Norton, 1987), 302.
5. Rossiter, *1787*, 303. Rossiter also reports that "in 1941 the States of Connecticut, Massachusetts, and Georgia celebrated the sesquicentennial of the Bill of Rights by giving their hitherto withheld and unneeded assent."
6. *Barron v. Baltimore*, 7 Peters 243, 246 (1833).
7. The Fourteenth Amendment also seems designed to introduce civil rights. The final clause of the all-important Section 1 provides that no state can "deny to any person within its jurisdiction the equal protection of the laws." It is not unreasonable to conclude that the purpose of this provision was to obligate state governments as well as the national government to take positive actions to protect citizens from arbitrary and discriminatory actions, at least those based on race. Civil rights will be explored in Chapter 5.
8. For example, *The Slaughterhouse Cases*, 16 Wallace 36 (1883).
9. *Chicago, Burlington and Quincy Railroad Company v. Chicago*, 166 U.S. 226 (1897).
10. *Gitlow v. New York*, 268 U.S. 652 (1925).
11. *Near v. Minnesota*, 283 U.S. 697 (1931); *Hague v. C.I.O.*, 307 U.S. 496 (1939).
12. *Abington School District v. Schempp*, 374 U.S. 203 (1963).
13. *Engel v. Vitale*, 370 U.S. 421 (1962).
14. *Wallace v. Jaffree*, 472 U.S. 38 (1985).
15. *Van Orden v. Perry*, 545 U.S. 677 (2005).
16. *McCreary County v. American Civil Liberties Union of Kentucky*, 545 U.S. 844 (2005).
17. *West Virginia State Board of Education v. Barnette*, 319 U.S. 624 (1943). The case reversed an earlier decision, *Minersville School District v. Gobitus*, 310 U.S. 586 (1940), in which the Court upheld such a requirement and permitted schools to expel students for refusing to salute the flag. But the entry of the United States into a war to defend democracy in 1941, coupled with the ugly treatment to which the Jehovah's Witnesses' children had been subjected, persuaded the Court to reverse itself and to endorse the free exercise of religion even when it may be offensive to the beliefs of the majority.
18. *Burwell v. Hobby Lobby Stores*, 573 U.S. 682 (2014).
19. *Abrams v. United States*, 250 U.S. 616 (1919).
20. *United States v. Carolene Products Company*, 304 U.S. 144 (1938), n4. This footnote is one of the Court's most important doctrines. See Alfred H. Kelly, Winfred A. Harbison, and Herman Belz, *The American Constitution: Its Origins and Development*, 7th ed. (New York: W. W. Norton, 1991), 2:519–23.

21. *Schenck v. United States*, 249 U.S. 47 (1919).
22. *Citizens United v. Federal Election Commission*, 558 U.S. 310 (2010).
23. *McCutcheon v. Federal Election Commission*, 572 U.S. 185 (2014).
24. Arthur Delaney, "Supreme Court Rolls Back Campaign Finance Restrictions," Huffington Post, March 23, 2010, updated May 25, 2011, www.huffingtonpost.com /2010/01/21/supreme-court-rolls-back_n_431227.html (accessed 7/9/12).
25. *Chaplinsky v. State of New Hampshire*, 315 U.S. 568 (1942).
26. *Dennis v. United States*, 341 U.S. 494 (1951), which upheld the infamous Smith Act of 1940 that provided criminal penalties for those who "willfully and knowingly conspire to teach and advocate the forceful and violent overthrow and destruction of the government."
27. *United States v. Schwimmer*, 279 U.S. 644 (1929).
28. *Bethel School District No. 403 v. Fraser*, 478 U.S. 675 (1986).
29. *Hazelwood School District v. Kuhlmeier*, 484 U.S. 260 (1988).
30. *Morse v. Frederick*, 551 U.S. 393 (2007).
31. *City Council v. Taxpayers for Vincent*, 466 U.S. 789 (1984).
32. *Bigelow v. Virginia*, 421 U.S. 809 (1975).
33. *Hague v. Committee for Industrial Organization*, 307 U.S. 496 (1939).
34. *Near v. Minnesota*, 283 U.S. 697 (1931).
35. *New York Times Co. v. United States*, 403 U.S. 713 (1971).
36. *Branzburg v. Hayes*, 408 U.S. 665 (1972).
37. *New York Times Co. v. Sullivan*, 376 U.S. 254 (1964).
38. See *Zeran v. America Online*, 129 F3d 327 (4th Cir. 1997).
39. *Roth v. United States*, 354 U.S. 476 (1957).
40. Concurring opinion in *Jacobellis v. Ohio*, 378 U.S. 184 (1964).
41. *Reno v. American Civil Liberties Union*, 521 U.S. 844 (1997).
42. *United States v. Williams*, 553 U.S. 285 (2008).
43. *United States v. Playboy Entertainment Group*, 529 U.S. 803 (2000).
44. *Brown v. Entertainment Merchants Association*, 564 U.S. 786 (2011).
45. *United States v. Miller*, 307 U.S. 174 (1939).
46. *District of Columbia v. Heller*, 554 U.S. 570 (2008).
47. *McDonald v. Chicago*, 561 U.S. 742 (2010).
48. *Horton v. California*, 496 U.S. 128 (1990).
49. *Mapp v. Ohio*, 367 U.S. 643 (1961). Although Mapp went free in this case, she was later convicted in New York on narcotics trafficking charges and served 9 years of a 20-year sentence.
50. For a good discussion of the issue, see Louis Fisher, *American Constitutional Law* (New York: McGraw-Hill, 1990), 884–89.
51. *National Treasury Employees Union v. Von Raab*, 489 U.S. 656 (1989).
52. *Skinner v. Railway Labor Executives' Association*, 489 U.S. 602 (1989).
53. *Florida v. Jardines*, 569 U.S. 1 (2013).
54. *United States v. Jones*, 132 S. 565 U.S. 400 (2012).
55. *Maryland v. King*, 569 U.S. 435 (2013).
56. Edwin S. Corwin and J. W. Peltason, *Understanding the Constitution* (New York: Holt, 1967), 286.
57. *Benton v. Maryland*, 395 U.S. 784 (1969).
58. *Miranda v. Arizona*, 348 U.S. 436 (1966).
59. *Gideon v. Wainwright*, 372 U.S. 335 (1963).
60. *Furman v. Georgia*, 408 U.S. 238 (1972).
61. *Gregg v. Georgia*, 428 U.S. 153 (1976).

62. J. Baxter Oliphant, "Public Support for the Death Penalty Ticks Up," Pew Research Center, June 11, 2018, www.pewresearch.org/fact-tank/2018/06/11/us-support-for -death-penalty-ticks-up-2018/ (accessed 2/3/20).

63. Death Penalty Information Center, "Facts about the Death Penalty," October 11, 2018, https://deathpenaltyinfo.org/documents/FactSheet.pdf (accessed 10/12/18).

64. *Kennedy v. Louisiana*, 554 U.S. 407 (2008).

65. *Snyder v. Louisiana*, 552 U.S. 472 (2008).

66. *Glossip v. Gross*, 576 U.S. — (2015).

67. *Timbs v. Indiana*, 586 U.S. — (2019).

68. *Olmstead v. United States*, 277 U.S. 438 (1928). See also David M. O'Brien, *Constitutional Law and Politics*, 6th ed. (New York: W. W. Norton, 2005), 1:76–84.

69. *Griswold v. Connecticut*, 381 U.S. 479 (1965).

70. *Roe v. Wade*, 410 U.S. 113 (1973).

71. *Planned Parenthood of Southeastern Pennsylvania v. Casey*, 505 U.S. 833 (1992).

72. *June Medical Services L.L.C. v. Russo*, 591 U.S. _ (2020).

73. *Bowers v. Hardwick*, 478 U.S. 186 (1986).

74. *Lawrence v. Texas*, 539 U.S. 558 (2003).

75. *Lawrence* (2003). It is worth recalling here the provision of the Ninth Amendment: "The enumeration in the Constitution, of certain rights, shall not be construed to deny or disparage others retained by the people."

76. *Obergefell v. Hodges*, 576 U.S. — (2015).

77. *Bostock v. Clayton County*, 590 U.S. _ (2020).

CHAPTER 5

1. Shannon Green, "Desmond Meade Helps Restore Voting Rights to Millions of Ex-felons across Florida," *Orlando Sentinel*, February 5, 2019, www.orlandosentinel.com/opinion /os-ae-desmond-meade-ex-felon-voting-rights-20190130-story.html (accessed 7/27/19).

2. Stacey Abrams, "Desmond Meade," *Time*, April 17, 2019, https://time.com/collection /100-most-influential-people-2019/5567673/desmond-meade/ (accessed 7/27/19).

3. Lawrence Mower, "Ron DeSantis Signs Amendment 4 Bill, Limiting Felon Voting," *Tampa Bay Times*, June 28, 2019, www.tampabay.com/florida-politics /buzz/2019/06/28/ron-desantis-signs-amendment-4-bill-limiting-felon-voting/ (accessed 7/27/19); "A Punishing Poll Tax in Florida," *New York Times*, August 11, 2019, www.nytimes.com/2019/08/10/opinion/sunday/florida-vote.html (accessed 8/12/19).

4. P. R. Lockhart, "Florida Faces an Intense Legal Battle over Restoring Former Felons' Voting Rights," Vox, July 2, 2019, www.vox.com/policy-and-politics/2019/7/2 /20677955/amendment-4-florida-felon-voting-rights-lawsuits-fines-fees (accessed 7/27/19).

5. Patricia Mazzei, "Ex-Felons in Florida Must Pay Fines Before Voting, Appeals Court Rules," *The New York Times*, September 11, 2020, https://www.nytimes .com/2020/09/11/us/florida-felon-voting-rights.html (accessed 11/15/20).

6. Paula Baker, "The Domestication of Politics: Women and American Political Society, 1780–1920," *American Historical Review* 89 (June 1984): 620–47.

7. *Dred Scott v. Sandford*, 60 U.S. 393 (1857).

8. August Meier and Elliott Rudwick, *From Plantation to Ghetto* (New York: Hill and Wang, 1976), 184–88; Nikole Hannah-Jones, "Our Founding Ideals of Liberty and Equality Were False," *New York Times Magazine*, August 18, 2019, 20–21.

9. Jill Dupont, "Susan B. Anthony," New York Notes (Albany: New York State Commission on the Bicentennial of the U.S. Constitution, 1988), 3.

10. *Missouri ex rel. Gaines v. Canada*, 305 U.S. 337 (1938).

11. *Sweatt v. Painter*, 339 U.S. 629 (1950).

12. *Brown v. Board of Education of Topeka, Kansas*, 347 U.S. 483 (1954).

13. The Supreme Court first declared that race was a suspect classification requiring strict scrutiny in the decision *Korematsu v. United States*, 323 U.S. 214 (1944). In this case, the Court upheld President Roosevelt's executive order of 1941 allowing the military to exclude persons of Japanese ancestry from the West Coast and to place them in internment camps. It is one of the few cases in which classification based on race survived strict scrutiny.

14. For good treatments of this long stretch of the struggle of the federal courts to integrate the schools, see Paul Brest and Sanford Levinson, *Processes of Constitutional Decision-Making: Cases and Materials*, 2nd ed. (Boston: Little, Brown, 1983), 471–80; and Alfred H. Kelly, Winfred A. Harbison, and Herman Belz, *The American Constitution: Its Origins and Development*, 6th ed. (New York: W. W. Norton, 1983), 610–16.

15. Aimee Green, "Elmer's Restaurant Says It Made Black Man Prepay Because He Sat in a Bar, Ordered Alcohol," *Oregon Live*, October 29, 2015, www.oregonlive.com/clark -county/index.ssf/2015/10/elmers_told_state_investigator.html (accessed 8/2/18).

16. See Hamil Harris, "For Blacks, Cabs Can Be Hard to Get," *Washington Post*, July 21, 1994, J1.

17. For a thorough analysis of the Office for Civil Rights, see Jeremy Rabkin, "Office for Civil Rights," in *The Politics of Regulation*, ed. James Q. Wilson (New York: Basic Books, 1980).

18. This was an accepted way of using quotas or ratios to determine statistically that blacks or other minorities were being excluded from schools or jobs and then, on the basis of that statistical evidence, to authorize the Justice Department to bring suits in individual cases and class-action suits. In most segregated situations outside the South, it is virtually impossible to identify and document an intent to discriminate.

19. *Swann v. Charlotte-Mecklenberg Board of Education*, 402 U.S. 1 (1971).

20. *Milliken v. Bradley*, 418 U.S. 717 (1974).

21. *Board of Education v. Dowell*, 498 U.S. 237 (1991).

22. *Parents Involved in Community Schools v. Seattle School District No. 1*, 551 U.S. 701 (2007).

23. In 1970 this act was amended to outlaw for five years literacy tests as a condition for voting in all states.

24. *Shelby County v. Holder*, 570 U.S. 529 (2013).

25. *Crawford v. Marion County Election Board*, 553 U.S. 181 (2008). See also David Stout, "Supreme Court Upholds Voter Identification Law in Indiana," *New York Times*, April 29, 2008, www.nytimes.com/2008/04/29/washington/28cnd-scotus .html (accessed 1/13/14).

26. See Douglas S. Massey and Nancy A. Denton, *American Apartheid: Segregation and the Making of the Underclass* (Cambridge, MA: Harvard University Press, 1993), chap. 7.

27. *Loving v. Virginia*, 388 U.S. 1 (1967).

28. See *Frontiero v. Richardson*, 411 U.S. 677 (1973).

29. See *Craig v. Boren*, 429 U.S. 190 (1976).

30. *Franklin v. Gwinnett County Public Schools*, 503 U.S. 60 (1992).

31. Jennifer Halperin, "Women Step Up to Bat," *Illinois Issues* 21 (September 1995): 11–14.

32. Joan Biskupic and David Nakamura, "Court Won't Review Sports Equity Ruling," *Washington Post*, April 22, 1997, A1.

33. Debra DeMeis and Rosanna Hertz, "Sex, Sports, and Title IX on Campus: The Triumphs and Travails," Daily Beast, June 22, 2012, www.dailybeast.com/articles/2012/06/22/sex -sports-and-title-ix-on-campus-the-triumphs-and-travails.html (accessed 6/22/12).

34. *Meritor Savings Bank v. Vinson*, 477 U.S. 57 (1986). See also Gwendolyn Mink, *Hostile Environment: The Political Betrayal of Sexually Harassed Women* (Ithaca, NY: Cornell University Press, 2000), 28–32.

35. *Burlington Industries v. Ellerth*, 524 U.S. 742 (1998); *Faragher v. City of Boca Raton*, 524 U.S. 775 (1998).

36. Laura Kipness, *Unwanted Advances: Sexual Paranoia Comes to Campus* (New York: Harper, 2017).

37. New Mexico had a different history because not many Anglos settled there initially. (*Anglo* is the term for a non-Hispanic white, generally of European background.) Mexican Americans had considerable power in territorial legislatures between 1865 and 1912. See Lawrence H. Fuchs, *The American Kaleidoscope* (Hanover, NH: University Press of New England, 1990), 239–40.

38. 347 U.S. 475 (1954).

39. Ted Hesson, "Trump to Deny Green Cards to Immigrants Receiving Public Benefits," Politico, August 12, 2019, www.politico.com/story/2019/08/12/trumop -immigration-public-benefits-1413690 (accessed 8/12/19).

40. *United States v. Wong Kim Ark*, 169 U.S. 649 (1898).

41. *Korematsu v. United States*, 323 U.S. 214 (1944). In 2018 the Supreme Court repudiated, though did not actually overturn, the Court's World War II–era Japanese internment rulings in *Trump v. Hawaii*, 585 U.S. — (2018).

42. Children of the Camps, "Historical Documents: Civil Liberties Act of 1988," http://pbs.org/childofcamp/history/civilact.html (accessed 2/17/08).

43. 21 U.S. 543 (1823).

44. On the resurgence of Native American political activity, see Stephen Cornell, *The Return of the Native: American Indian Political Resurgence* (New York: Oxford University Press, 1990); and Dee Brown, *Bury My Heart at Wounded Knee* (New York: Holt, Rinehart, 1971).

45. See the discussion in Robert A. Katzmann, *Institutional Disability: The Saga of Transportation Policy for the Disabled* (Washington, DC: Brookings Institution Press, 1986).

46. For example, after pressure from the Justice Department, one of the nation's largest rental-car companies agreed to make special hand controls available to any customer requesting them. See "Avis Agrees to Equip Cars for Disabled," *Los Angeles Times*, September 2, 1994, D1.

47. For more, see Dale Carpenter, *Flagrant Conduct: The Story of* Lawrence v. Texas (New York: W. W. Norton, 2013).

48. *Romer v. Evans*, 517 U.S. 620 (1996).

49. *Obergefell v. Hodges*, 576 U.S. — (2015).

50. The Department of Health, Education, and Welfare (HEW) was the cabinet department charged with administering most federal social programs. In 1980, when education programs were transferred to the newly created Department of Education, HEW was renamed the Department of Health and Human Services.

51. *Regents of the University of California v. Bakke*, 438 U.S. 265 (1978).

52. *Gratz v. Bollinger*, 539 U.S. 244 (2003).

53. *Grutter v. Bollinger*, 539 U.S. 306 (2003).

54. The Court reaffirmed the *Grutter* decision in 2013 in *Fisher v. University of Texas* when it rejected a white student's suit challenging the use of race as one factor among many in admissions decisions.

CHAPTER 6

1. Suzanna Hupp, "In Their Own Words: The Gun Rights Advocate," *Texas Monthly*, March 23, 2016, www.texasmonthly.com/list/in-their-own-words/the-gun-rights -advocate/ (accessed 3/3/18).

2. Brianna Sacks, "After Florida School Shooting, Several Survivors and Victims' Parents Pan Trump's Idea to Arm Teachers," BuzzFeed News, February 24, 2018, www.buzzfeed.com/briannasacks/students-and-parents-react-to-armed-teacher -proposal?utm_term=.rtNPqM580#.xrVbnry1A (accessed 3/3/18).

3. Jeffrey M. Jones, "U.S. Preference for Stricter Gun Laws Highest since 1993," Gallup Social & Policy Issues, March 14, 2018, http://news.gallup.com/poll/229562 /preference-stricter-gun-laws-highest-1993.aspx (accessed 5/30/18).

4. Alvin Chang, "Gun Sales Usually Skyrocket after Mass Shootings. But Not This Time," Vox, March 7, 2018, www.vox.com/2018/3/7/17066352/gun-sales-mass -shooting-data (accessed 5/30/18).

5. Richard Wike and Katie Simmons, "Global Support for Principle of Free Expression, but Opposition to Some Forms of Speech: Americans Especially Likely to Embrace Individual Liberties," Pew Research Center, November 18, 2015, www.pewglobal .org/2015/11/18/global-support-for-principle-of-free-expression-but-opposition-to -some-forms-of-speech/ (accessed 11/18/15).

6. Paul R. Abramson, *Political Attitudes in America* (San Francisco: Freeman, 1983).

7. Pew Research Center, "In Views of U.S. Democracy, Widening Partisan Divides Over Freedom to Peacefully Protest," September 2, 2020, www.pewresearch.org /politics/2020/09/02/in-views-of-u-s-democracy-widening-partisan-divides-over -freedom-to-peacefully-protest/ (accessed 10/12/20).

8. Matt Grossmann and David A. Hopkins, *Asymmetric Politics: Ideological Republicans and Group Interest Democrats* (New York: Oxford University Press, 2016).

9. Lydia Saad, "U.S. Still Leans Conservative, but Liberals Keep Recent Gains," Gallup News, January 8, 2019, https://news.gallup.com/poll/245813/leans-conservative -liberals-keep-recent-gains.aspx (accessed 1/15/20).

10. See Angus Campbell et al., *The American Voter* (New York: Wiley, 1960), 147.

11. Betsy Sinclair, *The Social Citizen: Peer Networks and Political Behavior* (Chicago: University of Chicago Press, 2012).

12. Pew Research Center, "Gun Policy Remains Divisive, but Several Proposals Still Draw Bipartisan Support," October 18, 2018, www.people-press.org/2018/10/18 /gun-policy-remains-divisive-but-several-proposals-still-draw-bipartisan-support /#impact-of-changes-in-access-to-guns-on-crime-mass-shootings (accessed 1/15/20).

13. Raymond E. Wolfinger and Steven J. Rosenstone, *Who Votes?* (New Haven, CT: Yale University Press, 1980). See also Steven J. Rosenstone and John Mark Hansen, *Mobilization, Participation, and Democracy in America* (New York: Macmillan, 1993).

14. Katherine Tate, *Black Faces in the Mirror* (Princeton, NJ: Princeton University Press, 1993).

15. Pew Research Center. "On Views of Race and Inequality, Blacks and Whites Are Worlds Apart: About Four-in-Ten Blacks Are Doubtful That the U.S. Will Ever Achieve Racial Equality," June 27, 2016, www.pewsocialtrends.org/2016/06/27/on -views-of-race-and-inequality-blacks-and-whites-are-worlds-apart/ (accessed 4/3/18).

16. Tate, *Black Faces in the Mirror*.

17. Kim Parker, Juliana Menasce Horowitz, and Monica Anderson, "Amid Protests, Majorities Across Racial and Ethnic Groups Express Support for the Black Lives Matter Movement," Pew Research Center, June 12, 2020, www.pewsocialtrends .org/2020/06/12/amid-protests-majorities-across-racial-and-ethnic-groups-express -support-for-the-black-lives-matter-movement/ (accessed 10/15/20).

18. National Conference of State Legislatures, "Legislative Responses for Policing—State Bill Tracking Database," October 28, 2020, www.ncsl.org/research/civil-and-criminal-justice/legislative-responses-for-policing.aspx (accessed 10/28/20).

19. Jens Manuel Krogstad, "Key Facts about the Latino Vote in 2016," October 14, 2016, Pew Research Center, www.pewresearch.org/fact-tank/2016/10/14/key-facts-about-the-latino-vote-in-2016/ (accessed 3/17/18); Antonio Flores, "Facts on U.S. Latinos, 2015. Statistical Portrait of Hispanics in the United States," September 18, 2017, Pew Research Center, www.pewhispanic.org/2016/04/19/statistical-portrait-of-hispanics-in-the-united-states-key-charts/ (accessed 3/17/18).

20. Anna Brown and Renee Stepler, "Statistical Portrait of the Foreign-Born Population in the United States, 1960–2013," Pew Research Center, September 28, 2015, www.pewhispanic.org/2015/09/28/statistical-portrait-of-the-foreign-born-population-in-the-united-states-1960-2013-key-charts/#2013-fb-origin (accessed 12/22/15).

21. Pew Research Center, "Shifting Public Views on Legal Immigration into the U.S.," June 28, 2018, www.people-press.org/2018/06/28/shifting-public-views-on-legal-immigration-into-the-u-s/ (accessed 1/15/20).

22. Amanda Barroso, "Key Takeaway on Americans' Views On Gender Equality a Century After U.S. Women Gained the Right to Vote," Pew Research Center, August 13, 2020, www.pewresearch.org/fact-tank/2020/08/13/key-takeaways-on-americans-views-on-gender-equality-a-century-after-u-s-women-gained-the-right-to-vote/ (accessed 10/20/20).

23. Michael Lipka, "Religious 'Nones' Are Not Only Growing, They're Becoming More Secular," Pew Research Center, Fact Tank, November 11, 2015, www.pewresearch.org/fact-tank/2015/11/11/religious-nones-are-not-only-growing-theyre-becoming-more-secular/ (accessed 11/11/15).

24. 2014 Cooperative Comparative Election Study.

25. See Richard Lau and David Redlawsk, *How Voters Decide: Information Processing during an Election Campaign* (New York: Cambridge University Press, 2006).

26. Peter Marks, "Adept in Politics and Advertising, 4 Women Shape a Campaign," *New York Times*, November 11, 2001, B6.

27. John R. Zaller, *The Nature and Origins of Mass Opinion* (New York: Cambridge University Press, 1992).

28. Carroll Glynn et al., *Public Opinion*, 2nd ed. (Boulder, CO: Westview, 2004), 293. See also Michael X. Delli Carpini and Scott Keeter, *What Americans Know about Politics and Why It Matters* (New Haven, CT: Yale University Press, 1996).

29. Delli Carpini and Keeter, *What Americans Know.*

30. Adam J. Berinsky, "Assuming the Costs of War: Events, Elites and American Support for Military Conflict," *Journal of Politics* 69, no. 4 (2007): 975–97; Zaller, *Nature and Origins.*

31. Lee Rainie et al., "Social Media and Political Engagement," Pew Research Center, October 19, 2012, www.pewinternet.org/2012/10/19/social-media-and-political-engagement (accessed 8/14/14).

32. Tony Dokoupil, "Is the Internet Making Us Crazy? What the New Research Says," *Newsweek*, July 9, 2012, http://mag.newsweek.com/2012/07/08/is-the-internet-making-us-crazy-what-the-new-research-says.html (accessed 3/19/14); Nicholas Carr, *The Shallows: What the Internet Is Doing to Our Brains* (New York: W. W. Norton, 2011).

33. Kim Parker, Juliana Menasce Horowitz, and Anna Brown, "About Half of Lower-Income Americans Report Household Job or Wage Loss Due to COVID-19," Pew Research Center, April 21, 2020 (accessed 5/4/2020).

34. Benjamin I. Page and Robert Y. Shapiro, *The Rational Public: Fifty Years of Trends in Americans' Policy Preferences* (Chicago: University of Chicago Press, 1992).

35. Christopher Wlezien, "The Public as Thermostat: Dynamics of Preferences for Spending," *American Journal of Political Science* 39, no. 4 (1995): 981–1000.

36. See Julianna Pacheco, "Attitudinal Policy Feedback and Public Opinion: The Impact of Smoking Bans on Attitudes toward Smokers, Secondhand Smoke, and Anti-Smoking Policies," *Political Research Quarterly* 77, no. 3 (2013): 714–34; Barbara Norrander, "The Multi-Layered Impact of Public Opinion on Capital Punishment Implementation in the American States," *Political Research Quarterly* 53, no. 4 (2000): 771–93; Suzanne Mettler and Joe Soss, "The Consequences of Public Policy for Democratic Citizenship: Bridging Policy Studies and Mass Politics," *Perspectives on Politics* 2, no. 1 (2004): 55–73; Andrea Hetling and Monika L. McDermott, "Judging a Book by Its Cover: Did Perceptions of the 1996 U.S. Welfare Reforms Affect Public Support for Spending on the Poor?" *Journal of Social Policy* 37, no. 3 (2008): 471–87; Joe Soss, "Lessons of Welfare: Policy Design, Political Learning, and Political Action," *American Political Science Review* 93, no. 2 (1999): 363–80; Joe Soss and Sanford F. Schram, "A Public Transformed? Welfare Reform as Policy Feedback," *American Political Science Review* 101, no. 1 (2007): 111.

37. Malcolm E. Jewell, *Representation in State Legislatures* (Lexington: University Press of Kentucky, 1982).

38. Lawrence R. Jacobs and Robert Y. Shapiro, *Politicians Don't Pander: Political Manipulation and the Loss of Democratic Responsiveness* (Chicago: University of Chicago Press, 2000).

39. John Griffin and Brian Newman, "Are Voters Better Represented?," *Journal of Politics* 67 (2005): 1206–27.

40. Larry M. Bartels, *Unequal Democracy: The Political Economy of the New Gilded Age* (Princeton, NJ: Princeton University Press, 2008).

41. Other authors have endorsed Bartels's view that government policy exacerbates income inequality. See, for example, Jacob S. Hacker and Paul Pierson, *Winner-Take-All Politics: How Washington Made the Rich Richer—and Turned Its Back on the Middle Class* (New York: Simon and Schuster, 2010).

42. Herbert Asher, *Polling and the Public* (Washington, DC: CQ Press, 2001), 64.

43. Courtney Kennedy and Hannah Hartig, "Response Rates in Telephone Surveys Have Resumed Their Decline," Pew Research Center, February 27 2019, www.pewresearch.org/fact-tank/2019/02/27/response-rates-in-telephone-surveys-have-resumed-their-decline/ (accessed 1/15/20).

44. Michael Kagay and Janet Elder, "Numbers Are No Problem for Pollsters, Words Are," *New York Times*, August 9, 1992, E6.

45. Berinsky, "Two Faces of Public Opinion." See also Adam Berinsky, "Political Context and the Survey Response: The Dynamics of Racial Policy Opinion," *Journal of Politics* 64, no. 2 (2002): 567–84.

46. Nate Silver, "Which Polls Fared Best (and Worst) in the 2012 Presidential Race," *FiveThirtyEight* (blog), November 10, 2012, http://fivethirtyeight.blogs.nytimes.com/2012/11/10/which-polls-fared-best-and-worst-in-the-2012-presidential-race/ (accessed 2/24/16).

47. Ruth Igielnik et al., "Commercial Voter Files and the Study of U.S. Politics," Pew Research Center, February 15, 2018, www.pewresearch.org/methods/2018/02/15/commercial-voter-files-and-the-study-of-u-s-politics/ (accessed 1/15/20).

48. David Redlawsk, Caroline J. Tolbert, and Todd Donovan, *Why Iowa? How Caucuses and Sequential Elections Improve the Presidential Nominating Process* (Chicago: University of Chicago Press, 2010).

CHAPTER 7

1. This account taken from Anisa Subedar, "The Godfather of Fake News," BBC News, November 27, 2018, www.bbc.co.uk/news/resources/idt-sh/the_godfather_of_fake _news (accessed 12/10/19); and Eli Saslow, "Nothing on This Page Is Real: How Lies Become Truth in Online America," *Washington Post*, November 17, 2018, www .washingtonpost.com/national/nothing-on-this-page-is-real-how-lies-become-truth -in-online-america/2018/11/17/edd44cc8-e85a-11e8-bbdb-72fdbf9d4fed_story.html (accessed 12/10/19).
2. Subedar, "The Godfather of Fake News."
3. A. W. Geiger, "Key Findings about the Online News Landscape in America," Pew Research Center Fact Tank, September 11, 2019, www.pewresearch.org/fact-tank/2019 /09/11/key-findings-about-the-online-news-landscape-in-america/ (accessed 12/10/19).
4. Pew Research Center, "Public Broadcasting Fact Sheet," July 23, 2019, www.journalism .org/fact-sheet/public-broadcasting/ (accessed 12/4/19).
5. Shanto Iyengar, *Media Politics* (New York: W. W. Norton, 2019).
6. Iyengar, *Media Politics.*
7. Quoted in Rodney Tiffen, "Journalism in the Trump Era," Inside Story, February 24, 2017, http://insidestory.org.au/journalism-in-the-trump-era (accessed 4/4/18).
8. David Folkenflik, "AT&T Deal for Time Warner Casts Renewed Attention on CNN," NPR, October 25, 2016, www.npr.org/2016/10/25/499299869/at-t-deal-for -time-warner-casts-renewed-attention-on-cnn (accessed 5/21/18).
9. Columbia Journalism Review, "Resources," https://archives.cjr.org/resources/index .php (accessed 8/2/18).
10. For a criticism of the increasing consolidation of the media, see the essays in Patricia Aufderheide et al., *Conglomerates and the Media* (New York: New Press, 1997).
11. Amy Mitchell, "Americans Still Prefer Watching to Reading the News—and Mostly Still through Television," Pew Research Center, December 13, 2018, https://www .journalism.org/2018/12/03/americans-still-prefer-watching-to-reading-the-news-and -mostly-still-through-television/ (accessed 4/22/2020).
12. Elisa Shearer and Elizabeth Grieco, "Americans Are Wary of the Role Social Media Sites Play in Delivering the News," Pew Research Center, October 2, 2019, www .journalism.org/2019/10/02/americans-are-wary-of-the-role-social-media-sites-play-in delivering-the-news/; (accessed 12/4/19).
13. Pew Research Center, "Amid Criticism, Support for Media's 'Watchdog' Role Stands Out," August 8, 2013, www.people-press.org/2013/08/08/amid-criticism-support-for -medias-watchdog-role-stands-out (accessed 4/27/14).
14. Pew Research Center, "Digital News Fact Sheet," www.journalism.org/fact-sheet /digital-news/ (accessed 11/23/20).
15. Clay Shirky, *Here Comes Everybody: The Power of Organizing without Organizations* (New York: Penguin Books, 2008).
16. Pew Research Center, "State of the News Media," www.pewresearch.org/topics/state -of-the-news-media/ (accessed 12/4/19).
17. Shirky, *Here Comes Everybody*; Amy Mitchell, Jesse Holcomb, and Rachel Weisel, "State of the News Media 2016," Pew Research Center, June 15, 2016, www.journalism .org/2016/06/15/state-of-the-news-media-2016 (accessed 3/19/18).
18. Elisa Shearer and Elizabeth Grieco, "Americans Are Wary of the Role Social Media Sites Play in Delivering the News," Pew Research Center, October 2, 2019, www .journalism.org/2019/10/02/americans-are-wary-of-the-role-social-media-sites-play-in -delivering-the-news/ (accessed 12/4/19).

19. "The Washington Post Records 86.6 Million Unique Visitors in March 2019," April 17, 2019, *WashPost PR* (blog), www.washingtonpost.com/pr/2019/04/17/washington -post-records-million-unique-visitors-march/ (accessed 12/4/19).

20. Robert McChesney and John Nichols, *The Death and Life of American Journalism: The Media Revolution That Will Begin the World Again* (New York: Nation Books, 2010).

21. Elizabeth Grieco, "U.S. Newspapers have shed half of their newsroom employees since 2008," Pew Research Center, April 20, 2020, https://www.pewresearch.org/fact -tank/2020/04/20/u-s-newsroom-employment-has-dropped-by-a-quarter-since-2008/ (accessed 5/26/2020).

22. Darrell West, *The Next Wave: Using Digital Technology to Further Social and Political Innovation* (Washington, DC: Brookings Institution Press, 2011).

23. Laura Wamsley, "Big Newspapers Are Booming: 'Washington Post' to Add 60 Newsroom Jobs," NPR, December 27, 2016, www.npr.org/sections/thetwo -way/2016/12/27/507140760/big-newspapers-are-booming-washington-post-to-add -sixty-newsroom-jobs (accessed 1/22/18).

24. Michael Barthel, Elizabeth Grieco, and Elisa Shearer, "Older Americans, Black Adults, and Americans with Less Education More Interested in Local News," Pew Research Center, August, 14, 2019, www.journalism.org/2019/08/14/older-americans -black-adults-and-americans-with-less-education-more-interested-in-local-news/ (accessed 12/4/19).

25. Pew Research Center, "Local TV News Fact Sheet," June 25, 2019, www.journalism .org/fact-sheet/local-tv-news/ (accessed 12/4/19).

26. Elisa Shearer, "Social Media Outpaces Print Newspapers in the U.S. as News Source," Pew Research Center, December 10, 2019, www.pewresearch.org/fact-tank /2018/12/10/social-media-outpaces-print-newspapers-in-the-u-s-as-a-news-source/ (accessed 12/4/19).

27. Pew Research Center, "Audio and Podcasting Fact Sheet," July 9, 2019, www .journalism.org/fact-sheet/audio-and-podcasting/ (accessed 12/4/19).

28. Pew Research Center, "Audio and Podcasting Fact Sheet."

29. Pew Research Center, "Audio and Podcasting Fact Sheet."

30. West, *The Next Wave*; Edward Glaeser, *Triumph of the City: How Our Greatest Invention Makes Us Richer, Smarter, Greener, Healthier, and Happier* (New York: Penguin Press, 2011).

31. Aaron Smith and Maeve Duggan, "Online Political Videos and Campaign 2012," Pew Research Center, November 2, 2012, www.pewinternet.org/2012/11/02/online -political-videos-and-campaign-2012 (accessed 4/29/14).

32. Karen Mossberger, Caroline Tolbert, and Ramona McNeal, "Digital Citizenship," MIT Press, Internet Broadband Fact Sheet, 2008; Elisa Shearer and Katerina Eva Matsa, "News Use across Social Media Platforms 2018," Pew Research Center, September 10, 2018, www.pewresearch.org/internet/fact-sheet/internet-broadband/ (accessed 12/4/19).

33. U.S. Census Bureau, "Nearly 8 in 10 Americans Have Access to High-Speed Internet," American Community Survey, November 13, 2014, www.census.gov/newsroom /press-releases/2014/cb14-202.html (accessed 3/2/16).

34. Karen Mossberger, Caroline J. Tolbert, and Mary Stansbury, *Virtual Inequality: Beyond the Digital Divide* (Washington, DC: Georgetown University Press, 2003).

35. Pew Research Center, "Mobile Fact Sheet," June 12, 2019, www.pewresearch.org /internet/fact-sheet/mobile/ (accessed 12/4/19).

36. Amy Mitchell, Jeffrey Gottfried, and Katerina Eva Matsa, "Political Interest and Awareness Lower among Millennials," Pew Research Center, June 1, 2015, www .journalism.org/2015/06/01/political-interest-and-awareness-lower-among-millennials/ (accessed 12/7/15).

37. Jordan Misra, "Voter Turnout Rates among All Voting Age and Major Racial and Ethnic Groups Were Higher Than in 2014," U.S. Census Bureau, April 23, 2019, www.census.gov/library/stories/2019/04/behind-2018-united-states-midterm-election -turnout.html (accessed 12/4/19).

38. Pew Research Center, "Social Media Fact Sheet," June 12, 2019, www.pewresearch .org/internet/fact-sheet/social-media/ (accessed 12/4/19).

39. Politifact, "Donald Trump's File," www.politifact.com/personalities/donald-trump/ (accessed 6/1/20).

40. Richard Davis, "Interplay: Political Blogging and Journalism," in *iPolitics: Citizens, Elections, and Governing in the New Media Era*, eds. Richard L. Fox and Jennifer M. Ramos (Cambridge: Cambridge University Press, 2012), 76–99.

41. Karen Mossberger and Caroline J. Tolbert, "Digital Democracy: How Politics Online Is Changing Electoral Participation," in *Oxford Handbook of American Elections and Political Behavior*, ed. Jan E. Leighley (New York: Oxford University Press, 2010), 200–218.

42. Caroline Tolbert and Ramona McNeal, "Unraveling the Effects of the Internet on Political Participation," *Political Research Quarterly* 56, no. 2 (2003): 175–85.

43. W. R. Neuman, M. R. Just, and A. N. Crigler, *Common Knowledge: News and the Construction of Political Meaning* (Chicago: University of Chicago Press, 1992).

44. A. Healy and D. McNamara, "Verbal Learning and Memory: Does the Modal Model Still Work?" in *Annual Review of Psychology*, 47, eds. J. Spense, J. Darley, and D. Foss (Palo Alto, CA: Annual Reviews, 1996), 143–72.

45. Hannah Roberts, "This Is What Fake News Actually Looks Like—We Ranked 11 Election Stories That Went Viral on Facebook," Business Insider, November 17, 2016, www.businessinsider.com/fake-presidential-election-news-viral-facebook-trump -clinton-2016-11 (accessed 5/21/18).

46. Krysten Crawford, "Stanford Study Examines Fake News and the 2016 Presidential Election," *Stanford News*, January 18, 2017, www.news.stanford.edu/2017/01/18 /stanford-study-examines-fake-news-2016-presidential-election/ (accessed 5/21/18).

47. Amy Mitchell, Jeffrey Gottfried, Galen Stocking, Mason Walker, and Sophia Fedeli, "Many Americans Say Made-Up News is a Critical Problem That Needs to Be Fixed," Pew Research Center, June 5, 2019, https://www.journalism.org/2019/06/05/many -americans-say-made-up-news-is-a-critical-problem-that-needs-to-be-fixed/ (accessed 5/30/2020).

48. Amy Mitchell, Jeffrey Gottfried, Galen Stocking, Mason Walker, and Sophia Fedeli, "Many Americans Say Made-Up News Is a Critical Problem That Needs to Be Fixed," Pew Research Center, June 5, 2019, www.journalism.org/2019/06/05/many-americans -say-made-up-news-is-a-critical-problem-that-needs-to-be-fixed/ (accessed 12/4/19).

49. Mitchell et al., "Many Americans Say Made-Up News."

50. Pew Research Center, "Public Highly Critical of State of Political Discourse in the U.S.," June 19, 2019, www.people-press.org/2019/06/19/public-highly-critical-of -state-of-political-discourse-in-the-u-s/ (accessed 12/4/19).

51. Matthew A. Baum, "Preaching to the Choir or Converting the Flock: Presidential Communication Strategies in the Age of Three Medias," in *iPolitics: Citizens, Elections, and Governing in the New Media Era*, ed. Richard L. Fox and Jennifer M. Ramos (Cambridge: Cambridge University Press, 2012), 183–205.

52. Eli Pariser, *The Filter Bubble: What the Internet Is Hiding from You* (New York: Penguin Press, 2011).

53. Michael X. Delli Carpini and Scott Keeter, *What Americans Know about Politics* (New Haven, CT: Yale University Press, 1996); Cass Sunstein, *Republic.com* (Princeton, NJ: Princeton University Press, 2001).

54. Mossberger, Tolbert, and Stansbury, *Virtual Inequality.*

55. Jeffrey Gottfried, Galen Stocking, and Elizabeth Grieco, "Partisans Remain Sharply Divided in Their Attitudes about the News Media," Pew Research Center, September 25, 2018, www.journalism.org/2018/09/25/partisans-remain-sharply-divided-in-their -attitudes-about-the-news-media/ (accessed 12/4/19).

56. Jeffrey Gottfried, Mason Walker, and Amy Mitchell, "Americans' Views of the News Media During the COVID-19 Outbreak," Pew Research Center, www.journalism .org/2020/05/08/americans-views-of-the-news-media-during-the-covid-19-outbreak/ (accessed 5/12/20).

57. David J. Garrow, *Protest at Selma: Martin Luther King, Jr., and the Voting Rights Act of 1965* (New Haven, CT: Yale University Press, 2001).

58. See Todd Gitlin, *The Whole World Is Watching* (Berkeley: University of California Press, 1980).

59. Tim Groseclose, *Left Turn: How Liberal Media Bias Distorts the American Mind* (New York: St. Martin's Press, 2011).

60. Pew Research Center, "How Journalists See Journalists in 2004: Views on Profits, Performance and Politics," May 2004, http://people-press.org/files/legacy-pdf/214.pdf (accessed 9/7/12).

61. "Media Bias Ratings," AllSides, www.allsides.com/media-bias/media-bias-ratings (accessed 3/25/20).

62. Doris Graber, ed., *Media Power in American Politics*, 5th ed. (Washington, DC: CQ Press, 2006).

63. Amber E. Boydstun, Stefaan Walgrave, and Anne Hardy, "Two Faces of Media Attention: Media Storms vs. General Coverage," *Political Communication* 31, no. 4 (2014): 509–31.

64. Larry M. Bartels, *Presidential Primaries and the Dynamics of Public Choice* (Princeton, NJ: Princeton University Press, 1988).

65. David P. Redlawsk, Caroline J. Tolbert, and Todd Donovan, *Why Iowa? How Caucuses and Sequential Elections Improve the Presidential Nominating Process* (Chicago: University of Chicago Press, 2011).

66. Larry M. Bartels, *Unequal Democracy: The Political Economy of the New Gilded Age* (Princeton, NJ: Princeton University Press, 2008).

67. Robert Entman, "Framing: Toward Clarification of a Fractured Paradigm," *Journal of Communication* 43, no. 4 (1993): 51–58.

68. Shanto Iyengar and Donald R. Kinder, *News That Matters: Television and American Opinion* (Chicago: University of Chicago Press, 1987), 63; John Zaller, *The Nature and Origins of Mass Opinion* (New York: Cambridge University Press, 1992).

69. *New York Times v. United States*, 403 U.S. 713 (1971).

CHAPTER 8

1. Taxdayteaparty.com, "Meet Keli Carender, Tea Party Organizer in Seattle, Washington," March 15, 2009, http://taxdayteaparty.com/2009/03/meet-keli-carender-tea-party -organizer-in-seattle-washington/ (accessed 1/26/18).

2. James Madison, *The Federalist Papers*, no. 10.

3 For an excellent analysis of the parties' role in recruitment, see Paul Herrnson, *Congressional Elections: Campaigning at Home and in Washington* (Washington, DC: CQ Press, 1995).

4. Katherine Schaeffer, "Far More Americans See 'Very Strong' Partisan Conflicts Now Than in the Last Two Presidential Election Years," Pew Research Center, March 4,

2020, www.pewresearch.org/fact-tank/2020/03/04/far-more-americans-see-very-strong
-partisan-conflicts-now-than-in-the-last-two-presidential-election-years/ (accessed 4/30/20).

5. Donald Green, Bradley Palmquist, and Eric Schickler, *Partisan Hearts and Minds* (New Haven, CT: Yale University Press, 2004).

6. Samara Klar and Yanna Krupnikov, *Independent Politics: How American Disdain for Parties Leads to Political Inaction* (Cambridge: Cambridge University Press, 2016).

7. Pew Research Center, "Political Independents: Who They Are, What They Think," March 14, 2019, www.people-press.org/2019/03/14/political-independents-who-they -are-what-they-think/ (accessed 1/16/20).

8. Alan Abramowitz, *The Great Alignment: Race, Party Transformation, and the Rise of Donald Trump* (New Haven, CT: Yale University Press, 2018).

9. Lilliana Mason, *Uncivil Agreement: How Politics Became Our Identity* (Chicago: University of Chicago Press, 2018); Christopher Achen and Larry M. Bartels, *Democracy for Realists: Why Elections Do Not Produce Responsive Government* (Princeton, NJ: Princeton University Press, 2017).

10. Pew Research Center, "Amid Campaign Turmoil, Biden Holds Wide Leads on Coronavirus, Unifying the Country," October 9, 2020, www.pewresearch.org /politics/2020/10/09/the-trump-biden-presidential-contest/ (accessed 11/3/20); *The New York Times*, "National Exit Polls: How Different Groups Voted," November 18, 2020, https://www.nytimes.com/interactive/2020/11/03/us/elections/exit-polls -president.html?action=click&pgtype=Article&state=default&module=styln-elections -2020&region=TOP_BANNER&context=election_recirc (accessed 11/20/20).

11. Chris Alcantara, Scott Clement, and Emily Guskin, "Battleground District Poll: What Voters in Key Districts Said on Election Day," *Washington Post*, November 7, 2018, www.washingtonpost.com/graphics/2018/politics/midterm-battleground -districts/ (accessed 1/16/20).

12. Pew Research Center, "Amid Campaign Turmoil, Biden Holds Wide Leads on Coronavirus, Unifying the Country"; *The New York Times*, "National Exit Polls: How Different Groups Voted."

13. Alex Leary, "Hispanics Voting in Record Numbers in Florida, Other States, Boosting Hillary Clinton," *Miami Herald*, November 6, 2016, www.miamiherald.com/news /politics-government/election/article112958953.html (accessed 11/11/16).

14. Pew Research Center, "Religious Landscape Study: Party Affiliation," 2014, www .pewforum.org/religious-landscape-study/party-affiliation/ (accessed 1/16/20).

15. Alcantara, Clement, and Guskin, "Battleground District Poll."

16. Larry M. Bartels, *Unequal Democracy: The Political Economy of the New Gilded Age* (Princeton, NJ: Princeton University Press, 2008).

17. Shaun Bowler, Gary Segura, and Stephen Nicholson, "Earthquakes and Aftershocks: Race, Direct Democracy, and Partisan Change," *American Journal of Political Science* 50 (January 2006): 146–59.

18. *The New York Times*, "National Exit Polls: How Different Groups Voted."

19. Pew Research Center, "Partisan Antipathy: More Intense, More Personal," October 10, 2019, www.people-press.org/2019/10/10/partisan-antipathy-more-intense-more -personal/ (accessed 1/16/20).

20. Pew Research Center, "Partisan Antipathy."

21. Nathan P. Kalmoe and Lilliana Mason, "Lethal Mass Partisanship: Prevalence, Correlates, and Electoral Contingencies," presented at APSA 2018, www.dropbox .com/s/bs618kn939gq0de/Kalmoe%20%26%20Mason%20APSA%202018%20-%20 Lethal%20Mass%20Partisanship.pdf.

22. Stephen Skowronek, *Building a New American State: The Expansion of National Administrative Capacities, 1877–1920* (Cambridge: Cambridge University Press, 1982).

23. Stephen Gruber-Miller, "Chuck Grassley Says He Tried to Remind President That Tariffs 'Brought about Adolf Hitler,'" *Des Moines Register*, May 15, 2019, www .desmoinesregister.com/story/news/politics/2019/05/15/chuck-grassley-tariffs-donald -trump-brought-great-depression-hitler-world-war-2-smoot-hawley-trade/ 3683407002/ (accessed 1/16/20).

24. Thomas Mann and Norman J. Ornstein, *It's Even Worse Than It Looks: How the American Constitutional System Collided with the New Politics of Extremism* (New York: Basic Books, 2016).

25. For a discussion of third parties in the United States, see Daniel Mazmanian, *Third Parties in Presidential Elections* (Washington, DC: Brookings Institution Press, 1974).

26. Lee Drutman, *The Business of America Is Lobbying: How Corporations Became Politicized and Politics Became More Corporate* (New York: Oxford University Press, 2015).

27. Kay Lehman Schlozman, Henry E. Brady, and Sidney Verba, *Unequal and Unrepresented: Political Inequality and the People's Voice in the New Gilded Age* (Princeton, NJ: Princeton University Press, 2018), Table 8.3.

28. Center for Responsive Politics, "Lobbying Database: Ranked Sectors," www.opensecrets .org/lobby/top.php?showYear=2018&indexType=c (accessed 9/10/19).

29. Drutman, *The Business of America Is Lobbying*, 13.

30. Schlozman, Brady, and Verba, *Unequal and Unrepresented*, Table 8.3.

31. G. William Domhoff, "The Rise and Fall of Labor Unions in the U.S.," Who Rules America?, February 2013, https://whorulesamerica.ucsc.edu/power/history_of_labor _unions.html (accessed 9/10/19); and Bureau of Labor Statistics, "Union Members Summary," January 18, 2019, www.bls.gov/news.release/union2.nr0.htm (accessed 9/10/19).

32. Sean McElwee, "How Unions Boost Democratic Participation," *American Prospect*, September 16, 2015, https://prospect.org/article/how-unions-boost-democratic -participation (accessed 9/10/19).

33. Schlozman, Brady, and Verba, *Unequal and Unrepresented*, Table 8.3.

34. Anthony J. Nownes, *Interest Groups in American Politics*, 2nd ed. (New York: Routledge, 2013).

35. Schlozman, Brady, and Verba, *Unequal and Unrepresented*, Table 8.3.

36. See, for example, the Singles Section of the New Jersey Sierra Club: www.sierraclub .org/new-jersey/sierra-singles (accessed 9/4/19).

37. Martin Gilens and Benjamin I. Page, "Testing Theories of American Politics: Elites, Interest Groups, and Average Citizens," *Perspectives on Politics* 12, no. 3 (September 2014): 564–81; Martin Gilens, *Affluence and Influence: Economic Inequality and Political Power in America* (Princeton, NJ: Princeton University Press, 2012); Benjamin I. Page and Martin Gilens, *Democracy in America? What Has Gone Wrong and What We Can Do about It* (Chicago: University of Chicago Press, 2017).

38. E. E. Schattschneider, *The Semisovereign People: A Realist's View of Democracy in America* (New York: Holt, Rinehart and Winston, 1960).

39. Kay Lehman Schlozman and John T. Tierney, *Organized Interests and American Democracy* (New York: Harper and Row, 1986), 60.

40. Center for Responsive Politics, "Lobbying Database," www.opensecrets.org/lobby/ (accessed 5/15/18).

41. See Sean McMinn and Kate Ackley, "Lobbying Hits $3.9 Billion in Trump's First Year," Roll Call, January 23, 2018, www.rollcall.com/news/politics/lobbying-trump -first-year; and Derek Kravitz and Alex Mierjeski, "Trump's Appointees Pledged Not to Lobby After They Leave. Now They're Lobbying," ProPublica, May 3, 2018, www .propublica.org/article/trump-appointees-pledged-not-to-lobby-after-they-leave-now -lobbying (accessed 9/5/19).

42. U.S. PIRG, "Lobbyist Registrations Hit 18-Year Low," January 30, 2017, https://uspirg
    .org/news/usp/lobbyist-registrations-hit-18-year-low (accessed 9/5/19).

43. For discussions of lobbying, see Allan J. Cigler and Burdett A. Loomis, eds., *Interest
    Group Politics* (Washington, DC: CQ Press, 1983). See also Jeffrey M. Berry,
    Lobbying for the People (Princeton, NJ: Princeton University Press, 1977).

44. Brookings Institution, *Vital Statistics on Congress*, Table 5.1, March 4, 2019, www
    .brookings.edu/multi-chapter-report/vital-statistics-on-congress/ (accessed 9/5/19).

45. Drutman, *The Business of America Is Lobbying*, 33–34.

46. Christine Stapleton, "Trump's Mar-a-Lago Transitions from Society Galas to
    Political Hub," *Palm Beach Daily News*, May 10, 2019, www.palmbeachdailynews
    .com/news/20190510/trumps-mar-a-lago-transitions-from-society-galas-to-political
    -hub (accessed 3/28/20); Luke Darby, "Political Group Spending at Trump Hotels
    Rocketed up to $19 Million," *GQ*, November 11, 2019, www.gq.com/story/trump
    -hotels-millions-from-politics (accessed 3/28/20).

47. *Brown v. Board of Education of Topeka, Kansas*, 347 U.S. 483 (1954).

48. *Obergefell v. Hodges*, 575 U.S. 947 (2015).

49. *Webster v. Reproductive Health Services*, 492 U.S. 490 (1989). The *Webster* case brought more
    than 300 interest groups on both sides of the abortion issue to the Supreme Court's door.

50. Christine Day, *AARP: America's Largest Interest Group and Its Impact* (Westport, CT:
    Praeger, 2017).

51. Jacob S. Hacker and Paul Pierson, *Winner-Take-All Politics: How Washington Made the Rich
    Richer, and Turned Its Back on the Middle Class* (New York: Simon and Schuster, 2010).

52. Richard L. Hall and Frank W. Wayman, "Buying Time: Moneyed Interests and the
    Mobilization of Bias in Congressional Committees," *American Political Science Review*
    84 (1990): 797–820.

53. Kevin M. Esterling, *The Political Economy of Expertise: Information and Efficiency in
    American National Politics* (Ann Arbor: University of Michigan Press, 2004).

54. Amy McKay and Susan Webb Yackee, "Interest Group Competition on Federal
    Agency Rules," *American Politics Research* 35, no. 3 (May 2007): 336–57.

55. Ida A. Brudnick, "Congressional Salaries and Allowances: In Brief," Congressional
    Research Service, April 11, 2018, www.senate.gov/CRSpubs/9c14ec69-c4e4-4bd8
    -8953-f73daa1640e4.pdf (accessed 9/24/19).

56. Mancur Olson, *The Logic of Collective Action* (Cambridge, MA: Harvard University
    Press, 1965).

CHAPTER 9

1. Associated Press, "Seattle Is Giving Voters $100 Worth of 'Democracy Vouchers' to
   Donate to Politicians," June 19, 2019, www.marketwatch.com/story/seattle-is-giving-voters
   -100-worth-of-democracy-vouchers-to-donate-to-politicians-2019-06-19 (accessed 8/3/19).

2. Sarah Kliff and Kenny Malone, "Seattle's Voucher Test Tried to Flood Local Politics
   with Small Money," NPR, December 21, 2018, www.npr.org/2018/12/21/679036745
   /seattle-s-voucher-test-tried-to-flood-politics-with-small-money (accessed 8/3/19).

3. Associated Press, "Seattle Is Giving Voters $100."

4. Daniel Beekman, "Washington State Supreme Court Unanimously Upholds Seattle's
   Pioneering Democracy Vouchers Program," *Seattle Times*, July 11, 2019, www
   .seattletimes.com/seattle-news/politics/washington-state-supreme-court-unanimously
   -upholds-seattles-pioneering-democracy-vouchers-program/ (accessed 8/3/19).

5. Associated Press, "Seattle Is Giving Voters $100"; National Conference of State
   Legislatures, "Same Day Voter Registration," June 28, 2019, www.ncsl.org/research
   /elections-and-campaigns/same-day-registration.aspx (accessed 8/3/19).

6. John Gramlich, "What Makes a Good Citizen? Voting, Paying Taxes, Following the Law Top List," Pew Research Center, July 2, 2019, www.pewresearch.org/fact -tank/2019/07/02/what-makes-a-good-citizen-voting-paying-taxes-following-the-law -top-list/ (accessed 12/6/19).

7. Sidney Verba, Kay Lehman Schlozman, and Henry E. Brady, *Voice and Equality: Civic Voluntarism in American Politics* (Cambridge, MA: Harvard University Press, 2005), chap. 3, for kinds of participation; 66–67 for prevalence of local activity.

8. Michael P. McDonald, "American Voter Turnout in Historical Perspective," in *The Oxford Handbook of American Elections and Political Behavior*, ed. Jan Leighley (New York: Oxford University Press, 2010), 125–43.

9. Todd Donovan and Shaun Bowler, *Reforming the Republic: Democratic Institutions for the New America* (Upper Saddle River, NJ: Pearson Education, 2004).

10. Elisa Shearer and Jeffrey Gottfried, "News Use across Social Media Platforms 2017," Pew Research Center, www.journalism.org/2017/09/07/news-use-across-social-media -platforms-2017/ (accessed 3/29/18).

11. Meredith Rolfe, *Voter Turnout: A Social Theory of Political Participation* (New York: Cambridge University Press, 2012).

12. Lee Rainie et al., "Social Media and Political Engagement," Internet, Science & Tech, Pew Research Center, www.pewinternet.org/2012/10/19/social-media-and-political -engagement/ (accessed 6/24/14).

13. Helen Margetts, Peter John, Scott Hale, and Taha Yasseri, *Political Turbulence: How Social Media Shape Collective Action* (New York: Oxford University Press, 2017).

14. Philip Bump, "'60 Minutes' Profiles the Genius Who Won Trump's Campaign: Face-book," *Washington Post*, October 9, 2017, www.washingtonpost.com/news /politics/wp/2017/10/09/60-minutes-profiles-the-genius-who-won-trumps-campaign -facebook/?utm_term=.ad2bd8d8194a (accessed 3/29/18).

15. Angus Campbell et al., *The American Voter* (New York: Wiley, 1960); Steven Rosenstone and John Mark Hansen, *Mobilization, Participation, and Democracy in America* (New York: Macmillan, 1993); Kay Lehman Scholzman, Sidney Verba, and Henry E. Brady, *The Unheavenly Chorus: Unequal Political Voice and the Broken Promise of American Democracy* (Princeton, NJ: Princeton University Press, 2012).

16. U.S. Census Bureau, "Table 7. Reported Voting and Registration of Family Members, by Age and Family Income: November 2016," Voting and Registration, www.census .gov/data/tables/time-series/demo/voting-and-registration/p20-580.html (accessed 3/29/18).

17. Sidney Verba and Norman H. Nie, *Participation in America: Political Democracy and Social Equality* (New York: Harper and Row, 1972); and U.S. Census Bureau, "Voting and Registration in the Election of November 2018," Table 7, www.census.gov/data /tables/time-series/demo/voting-and-registration/p20-583.html (accessed 3/8/20).

18. Jessica Trounstine, *Segregation by Design: Local Politics and Inequality in American Cities* (New York: Cambridge University Press, 2018).

19. Jan E. Leighley and Jonathan Nagler, "Individual and Systemic Influences on Turnout: Who Votes? 1984," *Journal of Politics* 54, no. 3 (1992): 718–40.

20. "2016 Election Exit Polls," *Washington Post*, November 29, 2019, www.washingtonpost .com/graphics/politics/2016-election/exit-polls/ (accessed 12/6/19).

21. Thom File, "The Diversifying Electorate—Voting Rates by Race and Hispanic Origin in 2012 (and Other Recent Elections)," Current Population Survey, U.S. Census Bureau, May 2013, www.census.gov/prod/2013pubs/p20-568.pdf (accessed 4/11/16).

22. Matt Barreto and Gary Segura, *Latino America: How America's Most Dynamic Population Is Poised to Transform the Politics of the Nation* (New York: Public Affairs, 2014).

23. Mark Hugo Lopez, Ana Gonzalez-Barrera, and Jens Manuel Krogstad, "Hispanic Voters and the 2018 Midterm Elections," Pew Research Center, October 25, 2018, www.pewresearch.org/hispanic/2018/10/25/hispanic-voters-and-the-2018-midterm-elections/ (accessed 12/6/19).

24. File, "The Diversifying Electorate."

25. File, "Voting in America."

26. *The New York Times*, "National Exit Polls: How Different Groups Voted," November 18, 2020, https://www.nytimes.com/interactive/2020/11/03/us/elections/exit-polls-president.html?action=click&pgtype=Article&state=default&module=styln-elections-2020&region=TOP_BANNER&context=election_recirc (accessed 11/20/20).

27. Bruce E. Cain, Todd Donovan, and Caroline J. Tolbert, *Democracy in the States: Experiments in Election Reform* (Washington, DC: Brookings Institution Press, 2008).

28. U.S. Census Bureau, "Table 10. Reasons for Not Voting, by Selected Characteristics: November 2012," Voting and Registration, www.census.gov/hhes/www/socdemo/voting/publications/p20/2012/tables.html.

29. Robert A. Jackson, Robert D. Brown, and Gerald C. Wright, "Registration, Turnout and the Electoral Representativeness of U.S. State Electorates," *American Politics Quarterly* 26, no. 3 (July 1998): 259–87. See also Benjamin Highton, "Easy Registration and Voter Turnout," *Journal of Politics* 59, no. 2 (April 1997): 565–87.

30. Michael Hanmer, *Discount Voting: Voting Registration Reforms and Their Effects* (New York: Cambridge University Press, 2009); Melanie Springer, *How the States Shaped the Nation: American Electoral Institutions and Voter Turnout, 1920–2000* (Chicago: University of Chicago Press, 2014); Mary Fitzgerald, "Greater Convenience but Not Greater Turnout: The Impact of Alternative Voting Methods on Electoral Participation in the United States," *American Politics Research* 33, no. 6 (2005): 842–67; Craig Leonard Brians and Bernard Grofman, "When Registration Barriers Fall, Who Votes? An Empirical Test of a Rational Choice Model," *Public Choice* 99 (1999): 161–76.

31. National Conference of State Legislatures, "Voter Identification Requirements," www.ncsl.org/research/elections-and-campaigns/voter-id.aspx (accessed 10/12/18).

32. Zoltan Hajnal, Nazita Lajevardi, and Lindsey Nielson, "Voter Identification Laws and the Suppression of Minority Votes," *Journal of Politics* 79, no. 2 (2017): 363–79.

33. Sarah Zimmerman, "Illinois Protecting against Russian Election Tampering," *U.S. News and World Reports*, February 28, 2018, www.usnews.com/news/best-states/illinois/articles/2018-02-28/illinois-protecting-against-russian-election-tampering (accessed 5/14/18).

34. State legislatures determine the system by which electors are selected. Almost all states use this "winner-take-all" system. Maine and Nebraska, however, provide that one electoral vote goes to the winner in each congressional district and two electoral votes go to the winner statewide.

35. Jeffrey Karp and Caroline J. Tolbert, "Polls and Elections: Support for Nationalizing Presidential Elections," *Presidential Studies Quarterly* 40, no. 4 (2010): 771–93.

36. OpenSecrets.org, "2020 Election to Cost $14 Billion, Blowing Away Spending Records," October 28, 2020, www.opensecrets.org/news/2020/10/cost-of-2020-election-14billion-update (accessed 11/15/20).

37. "Most Expensive Races," Center for Responsive Politics, February 19, 2020, www.opensecrets.org/overview/topraces.php?cycle=2018&display=currcands (accessed 2/19/20).

38. Stephen Ansolabehere and James Snyder, "Campaign War Chests and Congressional Elections," *Business and Politics* 2 (2000): 9–34.
39. OpenSecrets.org, "2020 Election to Cost $14 Billion, Blowing Away Spending Records."
40. *McCutcheon et al. v. Federal Election Commission*, 572 U.S. 185 (2014).
41. OpenSecrets.org, Sen. Bernie Sanders, www.opensecrets.org/politicians/summary .php?cid=N00000528 (accessed 6/23/16).
42. *Buckley v. Valeo* (1975).
43. "Two-Thirds of Presidential Campaign Is in Just 6 States," Nationalpopularvote.com, www.nationalpopularvote.com/campaign-events-2016 (accessed 5/14/18); Daron Shaw, *The Race to 270: The Electoral College and the Campaign Strategies of 2000 and 2004* (Chicago: University of Chicago Press, 2006).
44. John Geer, *In Defense of Negativity: Attack Ads in Presidential Campaigns* (Chicago: University of Chicago Press, 2006).
45. Nicholas Confessore and Karen Yourish, "$2 Billion of Free Media for Donald Trump," *New York Times*, March 16, 2016, www.nytimes.com/2016/03/16/upshot /measuring-donald-trumps-mammoth-advantage-in-free-media.html (accessed 7/25/18).
46. D. Sunshine Hillygus and Todd G. Shields, *The Persuadable Voter: Wedge Issues in Political Campaigns* (Princeton, NJ: Princeton University Press, 2009). Bush's campaign focused on wedge issues—issues where a voter's preferences diverge from those of that individual's political party. By targeting Democratic voters with messages focusing on Bush's opposition to same-sex marriage, the campaign hoped to convince socially conservative Democrats to cast a ballot for Bush rather than for his opponent.
47. Sasha Issenberg, *The Victory Lab: The Secret Science of Winning Campaigns* (New York: Crown, 2012).
48. Alan S. Gerber and Donald P. Green, "The Effects of Canvassing, Telephone Calls, and Direct Mail on Voter Turnout: A Field Experiment," *American Political Science Review* 94, no. 3 (2000): 660.
49. Rosenstone and Hansen, *Mobilization, Participation, and Democracy*, 59.
50. Gerber and Green, "The Effects of Canvassing."
51. Robert M. Bond et al., "A 61-Million-Person Experiment in Social Influence and Political Mobilization," *Nature* 489 (2012): 295–98.
52. Katerina Eva Matsa and Kristine Lu, "10 Facts about the Changing Digital News Landscape," Pew Research Center, September 14, 2016, www.pewresearch.org /fact-tank/2016/09/14/facts-about-the-changing-digital-news-landscape/ (accessed 10/16/16).
53. Kim Hart, "Most Democrats See Republicans as Racist, Sexist," *Axios*, November 12, 2018, www.axios.com/poll-democrats-and-republicans-hate -each-other-racist-ignorant-evil-99ae7afc-5a51-42be-8ee2-3959e43ce320.html (accessed 11/13/20).
54. Noah Bierman, "Tensions Flare in Fight for Key States, and Trump Cheers a Truck Caravan Swarming a Biden Bus," *Los Angeles Times*, October 31, 2020, www .latimes.com/politics/story/2020-10-31/trump-biden-campaigns-turnout (accessed 11/15/20).
55. United States Election Project, "2020 November General Election: Turnout Rates," November 10, 2020, www.electproject.org/2020g (accessed 11/11/20).
56. Astead W. Herndon, "Conor Lamb, House Moderate, on Biden's Win, 'the Squad' and the Future of the Democratic Party," *New York Times*, November 8, 2020, www .nytimes.com/2020/11/08/us/politics/conor-lamb-democrats-biden.html (accessed 11/15/20).

57. "National Exit Polls: How Different Groups Voted," *New York Times*, www.nytimes
    .com/interactive/2020/11/03/us/elections/exit-polls-president.html (accessed 11/15/20).
58. John Griffin and Michael Keane, "Are Voters Better Represented?," *Journal of Politics*
    65, no. 4 (2005): 1206–27.

CHAPTER 10

1. Emily Flitter, "Small Businesses Will Get Help Paying Workers, If They Can Wait,"
   New York Times, March 26, 2020, www.nytimes.com/2020/03/26/business
   /coronavirus-stimulus-small-business.html (accessed 3/26/20).
2. This account from Kate Zezima and Colby Itkowitz, "Flailing on Fentanyl,"
   Washington Post, September 20, 2019, www.washingtonpost.com/graphics/2019
   /investigations/fentanyl-epidemic-congress/?wpisrc=nl_most&wpmm=1 (accessed
   11/18/19); Sharyn Alfonsi, "Cops Bring Addiction Counselor on Drug Raids to Fight
   Opioid Crisis," CBS News, June 16, 2019, www.cbsnews.com/news/cops-bring
   -addiction-counselor-on-drug-raids-to-fight-opioid-crisis/ (accessed 11/18/19);
   Colby Itkowitz, "Senate Easily Passes Sweeping Opioids Legislation, Sending to
   President Trump," *Washington Post*, October 3, 2018, www.washingtonpost.com
   /politics/2018/10/03/senate-is-poised-send-sweeping-opioids-legislation-president
   -trump/ (accessed 11/18/19).
3. David Mayhew, *Congress: The Electoral Connection* (New Haven, CT: Yale University
   Press, 1974).
4. Claire Hansen, "116th Congress by Party, Race, Gender and Religion," U.S. News,
   December 19, 2019, www.usnews.com/news/politics/slideshows/116th-congress-by
   -party-race-gender-and-religion?slide=3 (accessed 3/16/20).
5. Jennifer E. Manning, *Membership of the 116th Congress: A Profile* (Washington,
   DC: Congressional Research Service, March 31, 2020), https://fas.org/sgp/crs/misc
   /R45583.pdf (accessed 4/8/20).
6. Manning, *Membership of the 116th Congress.*
7. Manning, *Membership of the 116th Congress.*
8. For a discussion, see Benjamin Ginsberg, *The Consequences of Consent* (New York:
   Random House, 1982), chap. 1.
9. See Kristen D. Burnett, *Congressional Apportionment*, U.S. Census Bureau,
   November 2011, www.census.gov/prod/cen2010/briefs/c2010br-08.pdf (accessed
   1/23/12). For some interesting empirical evidence, see Angus Campbell et al.,
   Elections and the Political Order (New York: Wiley, 1966), chap. 11; for more recent
   considerations about the relationship between members of Congress and their
   constituents, see Lawrence Jacobs and Robert Y. Shapiro, *Politicians Don't Pander:
   Political Manipulation and the Loss of Democratic Responsiveness* (Chicago: University
   of Chicago Press, 2000); and Larry M. Bartels, *Unequal Democracy: The Political
   Economy of the New Gilded Age* (Princeton, NJ: Princeton University Press, 2008).
10. Norman J. Ornstein et al., *Vital Statistics on Congress* (Washington, DC: Brookings
    Institution Press, 2017), Tables 5–3 and 5–4, www.brookings.edu/,/media/Research
    /Files/Reports/2013/07/vital-statistics-congress-mann-ornstein/Vital-Statistics-Full
    -Data-Set.pdf?la5en (accessed 3/22/18); Norman J. Ornstein, Thomas E. Mann, and
    Michael J. Malbin, *Vital Statistics on Congress 2008* (Washington, DC: Brookings
    Institution Press, 2009), 111–12.
11. Ashley Parker, "Spotlighting Constituents to Buoy Congressional Candidates," *New
    York Times*, October 8, 2014, www.nytimes.com/2014/10/09/us/politics/out-of-the
    -mouths-of-constituents-candidates-find-a-message.html (accessed 9/14/15); Juana
    Summers, "Constituent Services Give Voters Something to Remember," NPR, www

.npr.org/2014/10/28/359615965/constituent-services-give-voters-something-to
-remember (accessed 9/14/15).

12. Linda Fowler and Robert McClure, *Political Ambition: Who Decides to Run for Congress* (New Haven, CT: Yale University Press, 1989); and Alan Ehrenhalt, *The United States of Ambition: Politicians, Power, and the Pursuit of Office* (New York: Three Rivers Press, 1992).

13. Center for Responsive Politics, "Incumbent Advantage," www.opensecrets.org /elections-overview/reelection-rates (accessed 11/15/20).

14. Center for Responsive Politics, "Reelection Rates over the Years."

15. Autumn Johnson, "Union Sanitary District Dedicates New Green Energy Facility," Patch, April 6, 2015, https://patch.com/california/unioncity/union-sanitary-district -dedicates-new-green-energy-facility (accessed 2/18/20).

16. Autumn Johnson, "Union Sanitary District Dedicates New Green Energy Facility."

17. Diana Evans, *Greasing the Wheels: Using Pork Barrel Projects to Build Majority Coalitions in Congress* (New York: Cambridge University Press, 2004).

18. Mayhew, *Congress: The Electoral Connection.*

19. Mark Hugo Lopez and Paul Taylor, "The 2010 Congressional Reapportionment and Latinos," Pew Research Center, www.pewhispanic.org/2011/01/05/the-2010 -congressional-reapportionment-and-latinos/ (accessed 2/24/14).

20. Eric McGhee, "Are the Democrats Still at a Disadvantage in Redistricting?" *Monkey Cage* (blog), July 9, 2013, https://themonkeycage.org/2013/07/09/are-the-democrats -still-at-a-disadvantage-in-redistricting/ (accessed 12/2/13).

21. Royce Crocker, *Congressional Redistricting: An Overview* (Washington, DC: Congressional Research Service, November 21, 2012), www.fas.org/sgp/crs/misc/R42831.pdf (accessed 12/2/13).

22. Adam Liptak, "Supreme Court Rebuffs Lawmakers over Independent Redistricting Plan," *New York Times*, June 29, 2015, www.nytimes.com/2015/06/30/us/supreme -court-upholds-creation-of-arizona-redistricting-commission.html (accessed 9/14/15).

23. *Rucho v. Common Cause*, 588 U.S. __ (2019).

24. R. E. Cohen, "Did Redistricting Sink the Democrats?," *National Journal*, December 17, 1994, 2984.

25. Richard Fenno, Jr., *Home Style: House Members in Their Districts* (Boston: Little, Brown, 1978).

26. Derek Willis, "Republicans Mix It Up When Assigning House Chairmen for the 108th," *Congressional Quarterly Weekly*, January 11, 2003, 89.

27. Rebecca Kimitch, "CQ Guide to the Committees: Democrats Opt to Spread the Power," *Congressional Quarterly Weekly*, April 16, 2007, 1080.

28. Richard E. Cohen, "Crackup of the Committees," *National Journal*, July 31, 1999, 2210–16.

29. See, for example, the announcement of an agreement on the Agricultural Act of 2014, House Committee on Agriculture, "House–Senate Negotiators Announce Bipartisan Agreement on Final Farm Bill," press release, http:// agriculture.house.gov/news/documentsingle.aspx?DocumentID51220 (accessed 9/21/15).

30. Norman J. Ornstein et al., *Vital Statistics on Congress* (Washington, DC: Brookings Institution and American Enterprise Institute, July 2013), chap. 5, www.brookings .edu/research/reports/2013/07/vital-statistics-congress-mann-ornstein (accessed 6/13/16).

31. "Statistics and Historical Comparisons: Bills by Final Status," govtrack.us, www .govtrack.us/congress/bills/statistics (accessed 9/21/15).

32. Jonathan Weisman, "House Votes 411–18 to Pass Ethics Overhaul," *Washington Post*, August 1, 2007, A1.

33. Leigh Munsil, "Graham Won't Lift Nominee-Hold Threat over Benghazi," Politico, November 11, 2013, www.politico.com/blogs/politico-live/2013/11/graham-wont-lift-nomineehold-threat-over-benghazi-177154.html (accessed 11/30/13).

34. Lindsey McPherson, "Paul Ryan Talks Up Return to Regular Order," Roll Call, December 16, 2015, www.rollcall.com; see also "A Better Way: Our Vision for a Confident America," issued by Speaker Ryan's office and the Republican leadership of the House of Representatives, June 16, 2016, www.gop.gov/wp-content/uploads/2016/07/ABetterBooklet_update.pdf.

35. Barbara Sinclair, *Unorthodox Lawmaking: New Legislative Processes in the U.S. Congress* (Washington, DC: Sage/CQ Press, 2012).

36. Walter Oleszek, *Congressional Procedures and the Policy Process* (Washington, DC: CQ Press, 2019), 170.

37. Oleszek, *Congressional Procedures*, 182.

38. Doug Andres, "Congress and Why Process Matters" (master's thesis, Johns Hopkins University, 2015).

39. David M. Herszenhorn, "Failed Spending Bills Pile Up in Senate as Budget Agreement Breaks Down," *New York Times*, July 12, 2016, A11.

40. John W. Kingdon, *Congressmen's Voting Decisions* (New York: Harper and Row, 1973), chap. 3; and R. Douglas Arnold, *The Logic of Congressional Action* (New Haven, CT: Yale University Press, 1990).

41. Eric Lipton and Ben Protess, "Banks' Lobbyists Help in Drafting Financial Bills," *New York Times*, May 23, 2013, https://dealbook.nytimes.com/2013/05/23/banks-lobbyists-help-in-drafting-financial-bills/ (accessed 9/21/15); Michael Corkery, "Citigroup Becomes the Fall Guy in the Spending Bill Battle," *New York Times*, December 12, 2014, https://dealbook.nytimes.com/2014/12/12/citigroup-becomes-the-fall-guy-in-the-spending-bill-battle/ (accessed 9/21/15).

42. Norman J. Ornstein and Thomas E. Mann, *Vital Statistics on Congress* (Washington, DC: Brookings Institution, 2018), Table 6-4.

43. "115th Congress (2017–2018)," www.congress.gov (accessed 11/9/18).

44. Geoffrey C. Layman, Thomas M. Carsey, and Juliana Menasce Horowitz, "Party Polarization in American Politics: Characteristics, Causes, and Consequences," *Annual Review of Political Science* 9 (2006): 83–110.

45. For example, Fredreka Schouten, "Club for Growth Plans New Push in House Races," *USA Today*, August 17, 2015, http://onpolitics.usatoday.com/2015/08/17/club-for-growth-plans-new-push-in-house-races/ (accessed 9/21/15).

46. Eric Lipton and Sheryl Gay Stolberg, "Health Law Rollout Provides Rich Target for Oversight Chief," *New York Times*, November 12, 2013, www.nytimes.com/2013/11/13/us/politics/health-law-rollout-provides-rich-target-for-oversight-chief.html (accessed 12/12/13).

47. Michael S. Schmidt and Maggie Haberman, "Aides for Hillary Clinton and Benghazi Committee Dispute Testimony Plan," *New York Times*, July 25, 2015, www.nytimes.com/2015/07/26/us/clinton-to-testify-publicly-before-house-committee-investigating-benghazi-attacks.html (accessed 9/21/15).

48. *United States v. Pink*, 315 U.S. 203 (1942). For a good discussion of the problem, see James W. Davis, *The American Presidency* (New York: Harper and Row, 1987), chap. 8.

49. U.S. House, "Impeachment," http://history.house.gov/Institution/Origins-Development/Impeachment/ (accessed 4/18/14).

CHAPTER 11

1. Craig Spencer, "Utilizing the Defense Production Act Will Save Health Care Workers' Lives," The Hill, March 28, 2020, https://thehill.com/opinion/healthcare/489976-utilizing-the-defense-production-act-will-save-health-care-workers-lives (accessed 4/1/20).

2. Zolan Kanno-Youngs and Ana Swanson, "Wartime Law Has Been Used Routinely by Trump," *New York Times*, April 1, 2020; Li Zhou, "How Congress Could Force Trump to Use the Defense Production Act," Vox, March 25, 2020, www.vox.com/2020/3/25/21191600/congress-defense-production-act-trump (accessed 4/2/20).

3. Ana Swanson, "Peter Navarro Has Antagonized Multinational Companies. Now He's in Charge," *New York Times*, April 6, 2020, www.nytimes.com/2020/04/06/business/economy/peter-navarro-coronavirus-defense-production-act.html (accessed 4/7/20).

4. These statutes are contained mainly in Title 10 of the U.S. Code, Sections 331, 332, and 333.

5. The best study covering all aspects of the domestic use of the military is that of Adam Yarmolinsky, *The Military Establishment* (New York: Harper and Row, 1971). Probably the most famous instance of a president's unilateral use of the power to protect a state "against domestic violence" was President Grover Cleveland's dealing with the Pullman strike of 1894. The famous Supreme Court case that ensued was *In re Debs*, 158 U.S. 564 (1895).

6. In *United States v. Pink*, 315 U.S. 203 (1942), the Supreme Court confirmed that an executive agreement is the legal equivalent of a treaty, despite the absence of Senate approval. This case approved the executive agreement that was used to establish diplomatic relations with the Soviet Union in 1933. An executive agreement, not a treaty, was used in 1940 to exchange "fifty over-age destroyers" for 99-year leases on some important military bases.

7. *United States v. Nixon*, 418 U.S. 683 (1974); Mark J. Rozell, *Executive Privilege*, 3rd ed. (Lawrence: University Press of Kansas, 2010).

8. For a different perspective, see William F. Grover, *The President as Prisoner: A Structural Critique of the Carter and Reagan Years* (Albany: State University of New York Press, 1988).

9. A third source of presidential power is implied from the provision for "faithful execution of the laws." This is the president's power to impound funds—that is, to refuse to spend money Congress has appropriated for certain purposes. One author referred to this as a "retroactive veto power" (Robert E. Goostree, "The Power of the President to Impound Appropriated Funds," *American University Law Review* 11 [January 1962]: 32–47). This impoundment power has been used freely and to considerable effect by many modern presidents, and Congress has occasionally delegated such power to the president by statute. But in reaction to the Watergate scandal, Congress adopted the Congressional Budget and Impoundment Control Act of 1974, which was designed to circumscribe the president's ability to impound funds by requiring that the president spend all appropriated funds unless both houses of Congress consented to an impoundment within 45 days of a presidential request. Therefore, since 1974, the use of impoundment has declined significantly. Presidents have had either to bite their tongues and accept unwanted appropriations or to revert to the older and more dependable but politically limited method of vetoing the entire bill.

10. For more on the veto, see Robert J. Spitzer, *The Presidential Veto: Touchstone of the American Presidency* (Albany: State University of New York Press, 1989).

11. Dan Eggen, "Bush Announces Veto of Waterboarding Ban," *Washington Post*, March 8, 2008, www.washingtonpost.com/wp-dyn/content/article/2008/03/08 AR2008030800304.html (accessed 6/10/10).

12. John Yoo, *The Powers of War and Peace* (Chicago: University of Chicago Press, 2003). See also Dana D. Nelson, "The 'Unitary Executive' Question," *Los Angeles Times*, October 11, 2008, www.latimes.com/opinion/la-oe-nelson11-2008oct11-story.html (accessed 4/20/18).

13. See Eric Posner and Adrian Vermeule, *The Executive Unbound: After the Madisonian Republic* (Chicago: University of Chicago Press, 2011).

14. "Unchecked Abuse," *Washington Post*, January 11, 2006, www.washingtonpost.com /wp-dyn/content/article/2006/01/10/AR2006011001536.html (accessed 3/25/18).

15. Theodore J. Lowi, *The End of Liberalism*, 2nd ed. (New York: W. W. Norton, 1979), 117.

16. Louis Fisher, "The Unitary Executive and Inherent Executive Power," *Journal of Constitutional Law* 12, no. 1 (February 2010): 586.

17. Louis Fisher, "Invoking Inherent Powers: A Primer," *Presidential Studies Quarterly* 37, no. 1 (March 2007): 1–22.

18. John Gramlich, "Holder Sees Constitutional Basis for Obama's Executive Actions," Roll Call, January 29, 2014, www.rollcall.com/news/holder_sees_constitutional _basis_for_obamas_executive_actions-230528-1.html?pg=1 (accessed 4/20/18).

19. *Trump v. Hawaii*, 585 U.S. __ (2018).

20. Harold C. Relyea, "National Emergency Powers," Congressional Research Service, 2007, http://fas.org/sgp/crs/natsec/98-505.pdf (accessed 3/27/18).

21. Matthew Crenson and Benjamin Ginsberg, *Presidential Power: Unchecked and Unbalanced* (New York: W. W. Norton, 2007), 341–42.

22. A substantial portion of this section is taken from Theodore J. Lowi, *The Personal President* (Ithaca, NY: Cornell University Press, 1985), 141–50.

23. The actual number is difficult to estimate because, as with White House staff, some EOP personnel, especially in national security work, are detailed to the EOP from outside agencies.

24. Article I, Section 3, provides that "the Vice-President . . . shall be President of the Senate, but shall have no Vote, unless they be equally divided." This is the only vote the vice president is allowed.

25. Samuel Kernell, *Going Public: New Strategies of Presidential Leadership*, 3rd ed. (Washington, DC: CQ Press, 1997); also Jeffrey K. Tulis, *The Rhetorical Presidency* (Princeton, NJ: Princeton University Press, 1987).

26. James MacGregor Burns, *Roosevelt: The Lion and the Fox* (New York: Harcourt, Brace, 1956), 317.

27. Kernell, *Going Public*, 79.

28. Claire Cain Miller, "How Obama's Internet Campaign Changed Politics," *New York Times*, November 7, 2008, https://bits.blogs.nytimes.com/2008/11/07/how-obamas-internet -campaign-changed-politics/ (accessed 4/7/14); David Plouffe, *The Audacity to Win: The Inside Story and Lessons of Barack Obama's Historic Victory* (New York: Viking, 2009).

29. "Presidential Job Approval Center," Gallup, www.gallup.com/poll/124922/presidential -approval-center.aspx (accessed 3/14/14).

30. Lowi, *Personal President*.

31. Lowi, *Personal President*, 11.

32. Gallup, "Presidential Job Approval Center," November 3, 2020, https://news.gallup .com/interactives/185273/presidential-job-approval-center.aspx (accessed 11/3/20).

33. Sidney M. Milkis, *The President and the Parties* (New York: Oxford University Press, 1993), 128.

34. Milkis, *President and the Parties*, 160.

35. Elena Kagan, "Presidential Administration," *Harvard Law Review* 114 (June 2001): 2265.

36. John M. Broder, "Powerful Shaper of U.S. Rules Quits, with Critics in Wake," *New York Times*, August 4, 2012, A1.

37. Nadja Popovich, Livia Albeck-Ripka, and Kendra Pierre-Louis, "85 Environmental Rules Being Rolled Back under Trump," *New York Times*, September 12, 2019, www.nytimes.com/interactive/2019/climate/trump-environment-rollbacks.html (accessed 10/4/19).

38. Terry M. Moe and William G. Howell, "The Presidential Power of Unilateral Action," *Journal of Law, Economics and Organization* 15, no. 1 (January 1999): 133–34.

39. Harold C. Relyea, "Presidential Directives: Background and Overview," Congressional Research Service, November 26, 2008, http://fas.org/sgp/crs/misc/98-611.pdf (accessed 3/25/18).

40. Adam L. Warber, *Executive Orders and the Modern Presidency* (Boulder, CO: Lynne Rienner Publishers, 2006), 118–20.

41. *Dames & Moore v. Regan*, 453 U.S. 654 (1981).

42. Philip Cooper, *By Order of the President* (Lawrence: University Press of Kansas, 2002), 201.

43. Edward S. Corwin, *The President: Office and Powers*, 5th ed. (New York: NYU Press, 1984), 283.

44. *National Labor Relations Board v. Noel Canning*, 573 U.S. 513 (2014).

CHAPTER 12

1. This account from Alexis C. Madrigal and Robinson Meyer, "How the Coronavirus Became an American Catastrophe," *The Atlantic*, March 21, 2020, www.theatlantic.com/health/archive/2020/03/how-many-americans-are-sick-lost-february/608521/ (accessed 4/3/20); Sheri Fink and Mike Baker, "'It's Just Everywhere Already': How Delays in Testing Set Back the U.S. Coronavirus Response," *New York Times*, March 10, 2020, www.nytimes.com/2020/03/10/us/coronavirus-testing-delays.html (accessed 4/3/20); and Conor Friedersdorf, "The Government Is Failing by Doing Too Little, and Too Much," *The Atlantic*, March 26, 2020, www.theatlantic.com/ideas/archive/2020/03/two-kinds-pandemic-failures/608767/ (accessed 3/26/20).

2. Amy B. Zegart, *Spying Blind: The CIA, the FBI, and the Origins of 9/11* (Princeton, NJ: Princeton University Press, 2009).

3. Paul C. Light, "A Cascade of Failures: Why Government Fails, and How to Stop It," Brookings Institution, July 14, 2014, www.brookings.edu/research/a-cascade-of-failures-why-government-fails-and-how-to-stop-it/ (accessed 8/5/17).

4. OSHA National News Release, "U.S. Department of Labor's OSHA and CDC Issue Interim Guidance to Protect Workers in Meatpacking and Processing Industries," April 26, 2020, www.osha.gov/news/newsreleases/national/04262020 (accessed 5/4/20).

5. Thanks to Andy Rudalevige for this formulation.

6. Environmental Protection Agency, "Regulations and Standards: Light Duty," www3.epa.gov/otaq/climate/regs-light-duty.htm#new1 (accessed 7/9/16).

7. Nathan Rott and Jennifer Ludden, "Trump Administration Weakens Auto Emissions Standards," NPR, March 31, 2020, www.npr.org/2020/03/31/824431240/trump-administration-weakens-auto-emissions-rolling-back-key-climate-policy (accessed 4/21/20); Ella Nilsen, "Trump Just Started a Huge Legal Battle with California over Lowering Car Emission Standards," Vox, September 18, 2019, www.vox.com

/policy-and-politics/2019/9/18/20872226/trump-california-car-emission-standards (accessed 4/21/20).

8. Margaret Cronin Fisk, Kartikay Mehrotra, Alan Katz, and Jeff Plungis, "Volkswagen Agrees to $15 Billion Diesel-Cheating Settlement," Bloomberg News, June 28, 2016, www.bloomberg.com/news/articles/2016-06-28/volkswagen-to-pay-14-7-billion-to-settle-u-s-emissions-claims (accessed 7/8/16).

9. Gary Bryner, *Bureaucratic Discretion* (New York: Pergamon Press, 1987).

10. Nicholas Bagley, "Legal Limits and the Implementation of the Affordable Care Act," *University of Pennsylvania Law Review* 164, no. 7 (2016): 1715–52.

11. Li Zhou, "Many Small Businesses Are Being Shut Out of a New Loan Program by Major Banks," Vox, April 7, 2020, www.vox.com/2020/4/7/21209584/paycheck-protection-program-banks-access (accessed 5/4/20).

12. Office of Management and Budget, Historical Tables, "Table 16.2, Total Executive Branch Civilian Full-Time Equivalent (FTE) Employees, 1981–2020," www.whitehouse.gov/omb/historical-tables/ (accessed 12/12/19).

13. Congressional Research Service, "Selected Homeland Security Issues in the 116th Congress," November 26, 2019, https://fas.org/sgp/crs/homesec/R45701.pdf (accessed 12/10/19).

14. For example, see Government Accountability Office, "High-Risk Series: Substantial Efforts Needed to Achieve Greater Progress on High-Risk Areas," March 2019, www.gao.gov/assets/700/697245.pdf (accessed 12/10/19).

15. In 2019, the Trump administration announced plans to dismantle the OPM. For more history, see David Rosenbloom, *Public Administration* (New York: Random House, 1986), 186–221; Charles H. Levine and Rosslyn S. Kleeman, *The Quiet Crisis of the Civil Service: The Federal Personnel System at the Crossroads* (Washington, DC: National Academy of Public Administration, 1986).

16. Matt Ford, "An Administration Run by Temp Workers," *New Republic*, June 19, 2019, https://newrepublic.com/article/154243/trump-administration-cabinet-acting-department-secretaries (accessed 12/9/19).

17. Vice President Gore's National Partnership for Reinventing Government, "Appendix F, History of the National Partnership for Reinventing Government: Accomplishments, 1993–2000, A Summary," http://govinfo.library.unt.edu/npr/whoweare/appendixf.html (accessed 3/28/08).

18. President Barack Obama, First Inaugural Address, January 21, 2009, https://obamawhitehouse.archives.gov/blog/2009/01/21/president-barack-obamas-inaugural-address (accessed 8/5/17).

19. Kate Rogers, "USDA's Plan to Relocate Research Agencies to the Midwest Unleashes a Brain Drain," CNBC, July 22, 2019, www.cnbc.com/2019/07/22/usdas-plan-to-move-research-agencies-to-midwest-starts-a-brain-drain.html (accessed 11/14/19).

20. Office of Personnel Management, "Federal Civilian Employment," September 2017, www.opm.gov/policy-data-oversight/data-analysis-documentation/federal-employment-reports/reports-publications/federal-civilian-employment/ (accessed 10/13/18); George M. Reynolds and Amanda Shendruk, "Demographics of the U.S. Military," Council on Foreign Relations, April 24, 2018, www.cfr.org/article/demographics-us-military (accessed 10/13/18).

21. Bureau of Labor Statistics, Current Employment Statistics, "Table B-1a, Employees on Nonfarm Payrolls by Industry Sector and Selected Industry Detail, Seasonally Adjusted," www.bls.gov/web/empsit/ceseeb1a.htm (accessed 4/21/20).

22. John J. Dilulio, Jr., *Bring Back the Bureaucrats: Why More Federal Workers Will Lead to Better (and Smaller!) Government* (West Conshohocken, PA: Templeton Press, 2014); Kimberly J. Morgan and Andrea Louise Campbell, *The Delegated Welfare State* (New York: Oxford University Press, 2011).

23. Jennifer L. Selin and David E. Lewis, *Sourcebook of United States Executive Agencies*, 2nd ed. (Washington, DC: Administrative Conference of the United States, 2018).

24. Richard E. Neustadt, *Presidential Power and the Modern Presidents: The Politics of Leadership from Roosevelt to Reagan* (New York: Free Press, 1990), 29.

25. Daniel P. Gitterman, *Calling the Shots: The President, Executive Orders, and Public Policy* (Washington, DC: Brookings Institution Press, 2017).

26. Alan Rappeport, "Andrew Puzder Withdraws from Consideration as Labor Secretary," *New York Times*, February 15, 2017, www.nytimes.com/2017/02/15/us/politics/andrew-puzder-withdrew-labor-secretary.html (accessed 11/4/19).

27. Selin and Lewis, *Sourcebook of United States Executive Agencies*, 21.

28. Adam Andrzejewski, "Trump's Leaner White House 2019 Payroll Has Already Saved Taxpayers $20 Million," Forbes, June 28, 2019, www.forbes.com/sites/adamandrzejewski/2019/06/28/trumps-leaner-white-house-2019-payroll-has-already-saved-taxpayers-20-million/#5a991169386d (accessed 12/12/19); White House, "Statement from the Press Secretary regarding the President's Coronavirus Task Force," January 29, 2020, www.whitehouse.gov/briefings-statements/statement-press-secretary-regarding-presidents-coronavirus-task-force/ (accessed 5/4/20).

29. Selin and Lewis, *Sourcebook of United States Executive Agencies*, 27.

30. David M. Cohen, "Amateur Government: When Political Appointees Manage the Federal Bureaucracy," (CPM Working Paper 96-1, Brookings Institution, 1996), www.brookings.edu/wp-content/uploads/2016/06/amateur.pdf (accessed 12/12/19).

31. William G. Howell, *An American Presidency: Institutional Foundations of Executive Politics* (Boston: Pearson, 2015).

32. Selin and Lewis, *Sourcebook of United States Executive Agencies*, 34.

33. Food and Drug Administration, "Learn about FDA Advisory Committees," June 21, 2018, www.fda.gov/patients/learn-about-patient-affairs-staff/learn-about-fda-advisory-committees (accessed 12/12/19).

34. Linette Lopez and Lydia Ramsey, "'You Asked for It'—Congress Railed on the Maker of EpiPen," Business Insider, September 21, 2016, www.businessinsider.com/mylan-ceo-heather-bresch-house-oversight-committee-hearing-epipen-2016-9 (accessed 11/9/17); see Mathew D. McCubbins and Thomas Schwartz, "Congressional Oversight Overlooked: Police Patrols versus Fire Alarms," *American Journal of Political Science* 28, no. 1 (1984): 165–79.

35. Charlie Savage and Peter Baker, "Trump Ousts Pandemic Spending Watchdog Known for Independence," *New York Times*, April 7, 2020; Peter Baker, "Trump Moves to Replace a Watchdog Who Irked Him," *New York Times*, May 2, 2020.

36. Government Accountability Office, "About GAO," www.gao.gov/about/ (accessed 12/8/19).

37. Congressional Research Service, "About CRS," www.loc.gov/crsinfo/about/ (accessed 12/8/19).

38. Congressional Budget Office, "Introduction to CBO," www.cbo.gov/about/overview (accessed 12/8/19).

39. Consumer Financial Protection Bureau, "Creating the Consumer Bureau," www.consumerfinance.gov/about-us/the-bureau/creatingthebureau/ (accessed 12/7/19); NPR, "How the Consumer Financial Protection Bureau Came into Creation," November 28, 2017, www.npr.org/2017/11/28/567057893/how-the-consumer-financial-protection-bureau-came-into-creation (accessed 12/7/19).

40. Andrew Prokop, "Read: The Whistleblower Complaint about Trump and Ukraine," Vox, September 26, 2019, www.vox.com/2019/9/26/20884022/whistleblower-complaint-trump-ukraine-read (accessed 11/14/19).

41. See Aram A. Gavoor and Daniel Miktus, "Oversight of Oversight: A Proposal for More Effective FOIA Reform," *Catholic University Law Review* 66, no. 3 (Spring 2017): 528.

42. Alison Young, "Congress Demands Details of Secret CDC Lab Incidents Revealed by *USA Today*," USA Today, January 17, 2017, www.usatoday.com/story/news /2017/01/17/congress-wants-details-of-cdc-lab-accidents/96551636/ (accessed 11/14/19).

43. U.S. Department of Veterans Affairs, "Veterans Access, Choice, and Accountability Act of 2014 Fact Sheet," www.va.gov/opa/choiceact/documents/choice-act-summary .pdf (accessed 8/6/17).

44. Dominic Gates, "Flawed Analysis, Failed Oversight: How Boeing, FAA Certified the Suspect 737 MAX Flight Control System," *Seattle Times*, March 17, 2019, www.seattletimes.com/business/boeing-aerospace/failed-certification-faa -missed-safety-issues-in-the-737-max-system-implicated-in-the-lion-air-crash/ (accessed 11/4/19).

45. Selin and Lewis, *Sourcebook of United States Executive Agencies*, 85–87.

CHAPTER 13

1. This account draws from Austin Berg, "Meet the Man Who Could End Forced Union Fees for Government Workers," Illinois Policy, 2018, www.illinoispolicy.org /story/meet-the-man-who-could-end-forced-union-fees-for-government-workers/ (accessed 3/3/18); and P. R. Lockhart, "What the Latest Union Case before the Supreme Court Could Mean for Workers of Color," Vox, February 26, 2018, www .vox.com/policy-and-politics/2018/2/26/17053328/janus-afscme-supreme-court -unions-minorities (accessed 3/3/18).

2. *Abood v. Detroit Board of Education*, 431 U.S. 209 (1977).

3. U.S. Courts Statistical Tables, www.uscourts.gov/statistics-reports/analysis-reports /statistical-tables-federal-judiciary (accessed 9/19/15).

4. Michael A. Fletcher, "Obama Criticized as Too Cautious, Slow on Judicial Posts," *Washington Post*, October 16, 2009, www.washingtonpost.com/wp-dyn/content /article/2009/10/15/AR2009101504083.html (accessed 3/1/10).

5. John Bowden, "Timeline: Brett Kavanaugh's Nomination to the Supreme Court," The Hill, October 6, 2018, https://thehill.com/homenews/senate/410217-timeline -brett-kavanaughs-nomination-to-the-supreme-court (accessed 10/16/18).

6. *Marbury v. Madison*, 5 U.S. 137 (1803).

7. *National Federation of Independent Business v. Sebelius*, 567 U.S. 519 (2012).

8. "Acts of Congress Held Unconstitutional in Whole or in Part by the Supreme Court of the United States," General Printing Office, www.gpo.gov/fdsys/pkg/GPO -CONAN-2013/pdf/GPO-CONAN-2013-11.pdf (accessed 4/20/14).

9. This review power was affirmed by the Supreme Court in *Martin v. Hunter's Lessee*, 14 U.S. 304 (1816).

10. *United States v. Jones*, 565 U.S. 400 (2012).

11. *Riley v. California*, 573 U.S. 373 (2014).

12. Michael A. Genovese and Robert J. Spitzer, *The Presidency and the Constitution* (New York: Palgrave Macmillan, 2005).

13. *Hamdi v. Rumsfeld*, 542 U.S. 507 (2004).

14. *National Labor Relations Board v. Noel Canning*, 573 U.S. 513 (2014).

15. *Trump v. Hawaii*, 585 U.S. __ (2018).

16. *Trump v. Vance* 591 U.S.__ (2020); *Trump v. Mazars LLP* 591 U.S.__ (2020).

17. *Roe v. Wade*, 410 U.S. 113 (1973).

18. Robert Scigliano, *The Supreme Court and the Presidency* (New York: Free Press, 1971), 162. For an interesting critique of the solicitor general's role during the Reagan administration, see Lincoln Caplan, "Annals of the Law," *New Yorker*, August 17, 1987, 30–62.

19. Edward Lazarus, *Closed Chambers* (New York: Times Books, 1998), 6.

20. *Smith v. Allwright*, 321 U.S. 649 (1944).

21. Charles Krauthammer, "Why Roberts Did It," *Washington Post*, June 29, 2012, www .washingtonpost.com/opinions/charles-krauthammer-why-roberts-did-it/2012/06/28 /gJQA4X0g9V_story.html (accessed 4/22/14).

22. *Griswold v. Connecticut*, 381 U.S. 479 (1965).

23. *McCutcheon v. Federal Election Commission*, 572 U.S. 185 (2014).

24. R. W. Apple, Jr., "A Divided Government Remains, and with It the Prospect of Further Combat," *New York Times*, November 7, 1996, B6.

25. For limits on judicial power, see Alexander Bickel, *The Least Dangerous Branch* (Indianapolis, IN: Bobbs-Merrill, 1962).

26. *Worcester v. Georgia*, 31 U.S. 515 (1832).

27. Alexander Hamilton, James Madison, and John Jay, *The Federalist Papers*, ed. Clinton Rossiter (New York: New American Library, 1961), no. 10, 78.

CHAPTER 14

1. Laura Benshoff, "Unemployed in a 'Black Hole': PA's Jobless Wait for Benefits as Pressure, Bills Mount," WHYY, May 1, 2020, https://whyy.org/articles/unemployed -in-a-black-hole-pa-s-jobless-wait-for-benefits-as-pressure-bills-mount/ (accessed 5/23/20).

2. Tax Foundation, "2020 Tax Brackets," November 14, 2019, https://taxfoundation .org/2020-tax-brackets/ (accessed 1/12/20).

3. There is an additional 1.45 percent tax on all income without limit that funds Medicare benefits, and an additional 0.9 percent Medicare tax for high earners (individuals earning over $200,000 and couples earning over $250,000) that was introduced by the Affordable Care Act.

4. The *Federal Register* is the daily publication of all official acts of Congress, the president, and the administrative agencies. A law or executive order is not legally binding until it is published in the *Federal Register*.

5. Ronald Reagan, Inaugural Address, January 20, 1981, www.presidency.ucsb.edu /ws/?pid543130 (accessed 4/27/14).

6. Pew Research Center, "With Budget Debate Looming, Growing Share of Public Prefers Bigger Government," U.S. Politics & Policy, April 24, 2017, www.people-press .org/2017/04/24/with-budget-debate-looming-growing-share-of-public-prefers-bigger -government/ (accessed 10/6/17).

7. Pew Research Center, "As Sequester Deadline Looms, Little Support for Cutting Most Programs," U.S. Politics & Policy, February 22, 2013, www.people-press .org/2013/02/22/as-sequester-deadline-looms-little-support-for-cutting-most -programs/ (accessed 4/27/14).

8. See, for example, Paul Krugman, "The Bankruptcy Boys," *New York Times*, February 21, 2010, www.nytimes.com/2010/02/22/opinion/22krugman.html?_r50 (accessed 4/27/14).

9. Office of Management and Budget, Historical Table 8.3, "Percentage Distribution of Outlays by Budget Enforcement Act Category: 1962–2025," www.whitehouse.gov /omb/budget/Historicals (accessed 5/13/20).

10. Pew Research Center, "Section 2: Government, Regulation, and the Social Safety Net," U.S. Politics & Policy, October 5, 2017, www.people-press.org/2017/10/05/2 -government-regulation-and-the-social-safety-net/ (accessed 10/6/17).

11. Leslie Davis and Hannah Hartig, "Two-Thirds of Americans Favor Raising Federal Minimum Wage to $15 an Hour," Pew Research Center, July 30, 2019, www.pewresearch.org/fact-tank/2019/07/30/two-thirds-of-americans-favor-raising-federal-minimum-wage-to-15-an-hour/ (accessed 1/13/20).

12. Economic Policy Institute, "Minimum Wage Tracker," January 3, 2020, www.epi.org/minimum-wage-tracker/ (accessed 1/13/20).

13. Social Security Administration, "OASDI and SSI Program Rates and Limits, 2020," www.ssa.gov/policy/docs/quickfacts/prog_highlights/RatesLimits2020.html (accessed 12/16/19).

14. Social Security Administration, "Social Security Fact Sheet: 2020 Social Security Changes," www.ssa.gov/news/press/factsheets/colafacts2020.pdf (accessed 5/9/20).

15. John R. Kearney, "Social Security and the 'D' in OASDI: The History of a Federal Program Insuring Earners against Disability," *Social Security Bulletin* 66, no. 3 (2006), www.ssa.gov/policy/docs/ssb/v66n3/v66n3p1.html (accessed 6/7/17).

16. Workers must have lost their job through no fault of their own. For a full description of the program, see Chad Stone and William Chen, "Introduction to Unemployment Insurance," Center on Budget and Policy Priorities, July 30, 2014, www.cbpp.org/research/introduction-to-unemployment-insurance (accessed 11/18/15).

17. Ashley Burnside and Ife Floyd, "More States Raising TANF Cash Benefits to Boost Families' Economic Security," December 9, 2019, Center on Budget and Policy Priorities, www.cbpp.org/sites/default/files/atoms/files/10-30-14tanf.pdf (accessed 5/9/20).

18. This poverty threshold is for a household of three persons that includes two children. Department of Health and Human Services, Office of the Assistant Secretary for Planning and Evaluation, 2019 Poverty Guidelines, https://aspe.hhs.gov/2019-poverty-guidelines (accessed 5/9/20).

19. Suzanne Mettler, *The Submerged Welfare State* (Chicago: University of Chicago Press, 2011); Christopher Faricy, *Welfare for the Wealthy* (New York: Cambridge University Press, 2015).

20. U.S. Congress, Joint Committee on Taxation, "Estimates of Federal Tax Expenditures for Fiscal Years 2016–2020," January 30, 2017, www.jct.gov/publications.html?func=startdown&id=4971 (accessed 5/29/17). Note that there are tax breaks in the corporate tax code as well, but the tax breaks for individuals and households account for about 80 percent of the total.

21. New America Foundation, "Federal, State and Local K–12 School Finance Overview," June 29, 2015, http://atlas.newamerica.org/school-finance (accessed 7/10/16).

22. David K. Cohen and Susan L. Moffitt, *The Ordeal of Equality: Did Federal Regulation Fix the Schools?* (Cambridge, MA: Harvard University Press, 2009).

23. For a positive view of the standards, see Sonja Brookins Santelises, "Abandoning the Common Core Is Taking the Easy Way Out," *Equity Line* (blog), March 31, 2014, https://edtrust.org/the-equity-line/abandoning-the-common-core-is-taking-the-easy-way-out/ (accessed 4/3/18); for a critique see Valerie Strauss, "The Coming Common Core Meltdown," *Washington Post*, January 23, 2014, www.washingtonpost.com/blogs/answer-sheet/wp/2014/01/23/the-coming-common-core-meltdown (accessed 5/11/14).

24. Valerie Strauss, "The Successor to No Child Left Behind Has, It Turns Out, Big Problems of Its Own," *Washington Post*, December 7, 2015, www.washingtonpost.com/news/answer-sheet/wp/2015/12/07/the-successor-to-no-child-left-behind-has-it-turns-out-big-problems-of-its-own/ (accessed 7/11/16).

25. Department of Education, "Fundamental Change: Innovation in America's Schools under Race to the Top," November 2015, www2.ed.gov/programs/racetothetop/rttfinalrptexecsumm.pdf (accessed 7/11/16).

26. Elaine Weiss, "Mismatches in Race to the Top Limit Educational Improvement: Lack of Time, Resources, and Tools to Address Opportunity Gaps Puts Lofty State Goals out of Reach," Economic Policy Institute, September 12, 2013, www.epi.org/publication/race-to-the-top-goals/ (accessed 5/11/14).

27. Erica L. Green, "Private and Religious School Backers See Broad Victory in Supreme Court Decision," *New York Times,* July 1, 2020, www.nytimes.com/2020/07/01/us/politics/private-religious-schools-supreme-court.html (accessed 7/14/20).

28. Jaison R. Abel and Richard Deitz, "Despite Rising Costs, College Is Still a Good Investment," Federal Reserve Bank of New York, June 5, 2019, https://libertystreeteconomics.newyorkfed.org/2019/06/despite-rising-costs-college-is-still-a-good-investment.html (accessed 5/12/20).

29. College Board, "Trends in Student Aid 2019," 28, https://research.collegeboard.org/pdf/trends-student-aid-2019-full-report.pdf (accessed 12/15/19).

30. The Institute for College Access and Success, "Student Debt and the Class of 2018," September 2019, https://ticas.org/wp-content/uploads/2019/09/classof2018.pdf (accessed 12/16/19).

31. Henry J. Kaiser Family Foundation, "Total Monthly Medicaid and CHIP Enrollment," www.kff.org/health-reform/state-indicator/total-monthly-medicaid-and-chip-enrollment (accessed 5/9/20).

32. Henry J. Kaiser Family Foundation, *Medicaid: A Primer—Key Information on the Nation's Health Coverage Program for Low-Income People,* March 1, 2013, https://kaiserfamilyfoundation.files.wordpress.com/2010/06/7334-05.pdf (accessed 6/2/16) (see p. 26).

33. Henry J. Kaiser Family Foundation, "Health Insurance Coverage of Non-Elderly, 0–64," www.kff.org/other/state-indicator/nonelderly-0-64/?curentTimeframe=0&sortModel=%7B%22colId%22:%22Location%22,%22sort%22:%22asc%22%7D (accessed 4/15/18).

34. Henry J. Kaiser Family Foundation, "Medicaid and CHIP Eligibility, Enrollment and Cost Sharing Policies as of January 2020," March 26, 2020, www.kff.org/medicaid/report/medicaid-and-chip-eligibility-enrollment-and-cost-sharing-policies-as-of-january-2020-findings-from-a-50-state-survey/ (accessed 5/9/20).

35. *National Federation of Independent Businesses v. Sebelius,* 567 U.S. — (2012).

36. Kaiser Family Foundation, "Status of State Action on the Medicaid Expansion Decision," October 1, 2020, www.kff.org/health-reform/state-indicator/state-activity-around-expanding-medicaid-under-the-affordable-care-act (accessed 10/12/20).

37. Jennifer Steinhauer, "House Votes to Send Bill to Repeal Health Law to Obama's Desk," *New York Times,* January 6, 2016, www.nytimes.com/2016/01/07/us/politics/house-votes-to-send-bill-to-repeal-health-law-to-obamas-desk.html (accessed 7/11/16).

38. James Krieger and Donna L. Higgins, "Housing and Health: Time Again for Public Health Action," *American Journal of Public Health* 92, no. 5 (May 2002): 758–68.

39. John E. Schwarz, *America's Hidden Success*, 2nd ed. (New York: W. W. Norton, 1988), 41–42.

40. Congressional Budget Office, "Federal Housing Assistance for Low-Income Households," September 2015, www.cbo.gov/sites/default/files/114th-congress-2015-2016/reports/50782-lowincomehousing-onecolumn.pdf (accessed 5/29/17).

41. Chloe N. Thurston, *At the Boundaries of Homeownership: Credit, Discrimination, and the American State* (New York: Cambridge University Press, 2018).

42. Trymaine Lee, "A Vast Wealth Gap, Driven by Segregation, Redlining, Evictions and Exclusion, Separates Black and White America," *New York Times Magazine*, August 14, 2019, www.nytimes.com/interactive/2019/08/14/magazine/racial-wealth-gap .html (accessed 12/16/19).

43. U.S. Census Bureau, "Income and Poverty in the United States: 2019," September 2020, Figure 8, www.census.gov/content/dam/Census/library/publications/2020 /demo/p60-270.pdf (accessed 10/12/20).

44. U.S. Census Bureau, "Income and Poverty in the United States: 2019," Figure 1.

45. U.S. Census Bureau, "Income and Poverty in the United States: 2019," Table B-6.

46. U.S. Census Bureau, "Age and Sex Composition in the United States: 2019," Table 1, www.census.gov/data/tables/2019/demo/age-and-sex/2019-age-sex-composition.html (accessed 5/12/20).

47. AARP, Annual Report 2018, www.aarp.org/content/dam/aarp/about_aarp /annual_reports/2019/822801-internal-2018-annual-report-web.pdf (accessed 12/16/19); Center for Responsive Politics, "Client Profile: AARP," www.opensecrets .org/federal-lobbying/clients/lobbyists?cycle=2019&id=D000023726 (accessed 12/16/19); AARP, "Public Policy Institute Experts 2019," www.aarp.org/ppi/experts/ (accessed 12/16/19).

48. Christopher Howard, *The Hidden Welfare State: Tax Expenditures and Social Policy in the United States* (Princeton, NJ: Princeton University Press, 1999).

49. U.S. Congress Joint Committee on Taxation, "Estimates of Federal Tax Expenditures for Fiscal Years 2016–2020," www.jct.gov/publications.html?func=startdown&id=4971 (accessed 5/29/17).

50. Center on Budget and Policy Priorities, "A Quick Guide to SNAP Eligibility and Benefits," February 7, 2018, www.cbpp.org/research/food-assistance/a-quick-guide -to-snap-eligibility-and-benefits (accessed 4/15/18).

51. Rachel Garfield, Kendal Orgera, and Anthony Damico, "The Coverage Gap: Uninsured Poor Adults in States That Do Not Expand Medicaid," March 21, 2019, www.kff.org /medicaid/issue-brief/the-coverage-gap-uninsured-poor-adults-in-states-that-do-not -expand-medicaid/ (accessed 12/15/19).

52. U.S. Census Bureau, "Income and Poverty in the United States: 2019," Figure 8 and Figure 1.

53. Thurston, *At the Boundaries of Homeownership*; Jamila Michener, *Fragmented Democracy: Medicaid, Federalism, and Unequal Politics* (New York: Cambridge University Press, 2018); Matthew Desmond, *Evicted: Poverty and Profit in the American City* (New York: Crown, 2016); Monique W. Morris, *Black Stats: African Americans by the Numbers in the Twenty-First Century* (New York: New Press, 2014).

54. U.S. Census Bureau, "Income and Poverty in the United States: 2019," Table B-6.

55. For an argument that children should be given the vote, see Paul E. Peterson, "An Immodest Proposal," *Daedalus* 121, no. 4 (Fall 1992): 151–74.

CHAPTER 15

1. Lyric Lewin, "In Support of a Travel Ban," CNN Politics, March 2017, www .cnn.com/interactive/2017/03/politics/travel-ban-supporters-cnnphotos/ (accessed 2/1/18).

2. Vivian Yee, "Meet the Everyday People Who Have Sued Trump. So Far, They've Won," *New York Times*, March 29, 2017, www.nytimes.com/2017/03/29/us/trump -travel-ban.html (accessed 4/12/18).

3. Saahill Desai, "The Real Lesson of the College Closures," *The Atlantic*, March 16, 2020, www.theatlantic.com/education/archive/2020/03/coronavirus-college-closure -disaster-students/608095 (accessed 3/26/20).

4. Rupert Smith, *The Utility of Force: The Art of War in the Modern World* (New York: Vintage, 2008).

5. D. Robert Worley, *Shaping U.S. Military Forces: Revolution or Relevance in a Post–Cold War World* (Westport, CT: Praeger Security International, 2006).

6. Colin S. Gray, "The Implications of Preemptive and Preventive War Doctrines," Strategic Studies Institute, July 2007, www.strategicstudiesinstitute.army.mil/pdffiles /pub789.pdf (accessed 8/1/14).

7. U.S. Department of State, "U.S. Relations with Haiti," March 2018, www.state.gov/r /pa/ei/bgn/1982.htm (accessed 4/15/18).

8. Kurt M. Campbell and James B. Steinberg, *Difficult Transitions: Foreign Policy Troubles at the Outset of Presidential Power* (Washington, DC: Brookings Institution Press, 2008).

9. U.S. Senate, "Treaties," www.senate.gov/artandhistory/history/common/briefing /Treaties.htm (accessed 4/15/18).

10. P. D. Miller, "Organizing the National Security Council: I Like Ike's," *Presidential Studies Quarterly* 43, no. 3 (2013): 592–606.

11. Ivo H. Daalder and I. M. Destler, *In the Shadow of the Oval Office: Profiles of the National Security Advisers and the Presidents They Served* (New York: Simon and Schuster, 2009).

12. Department of Defense, "About," January 27, 2017, www.defense.gov/About/ (accessed 7/23/18).

13. Mark Riebling, *Wedge: From Pearl Harbor to 9/11* (New York: Touchstone, 2002).

14. Benjamin Ginsberg, *The Worth of War* (New York: Prometheus Books, 2014), chap. 5.

15. Alexander Hamilton, James Madison, and John Jay, *The Federalist Papers*, ed. Clinton L. Rossiter (New York: New American Library, 1961; repr., New York: Signet Classics, 2003), no. 418 (Signet edition).

16. Bill Gertz, "Congress: U.S. Military Highly Vulnerable to Cyber Attacks," *Washington Free Beacon*, June 1, 2015, www.freebeacon.com/national-security/congress-u-s -military-highly-vulnerable-to-cyber-attacks/ (accessed 4/12/18).

17. For information on current U.S. sanctions programs, visit U.S. Department of the Treasury, "Sanctions Programs and Country Information," www.treasury.gov /resource-center/sanctions/Programs/Pages/Programs.aspx (accessed 6/1/14).

18. Loveday Morris, "Yazidis Who Suffered Genocide Are Fleeing Again," *Washington Post*, March 21, 2017, www.washingtonpost.com/world/middle_east/yazidis-who -suffered-genocide-are-fleeing-again-but-this-time-not-from-the-islamic-state/2017 /03/21/6392fe26-0353-11e7-9d14-9724d48f5666_story.html?noredirect=on&utm_ term=.c2dbf2c8c6a1 (accessed 4/15/18).

19. Scott Shane and Mark Mazzetti, "Inside a Three-Year Russian Campaign to Influence U.S. Voters," *New York Times*, Febuary 16, 2018, www.nytimes.com/2018/02/16/us /politics/russia-mueller-election.html (accessed 4/15/18).

20. Shane and Mazzetti, "Inside a Three-Year Russian Campaign to Influence U.S. Voters."

21. Elias Groll, "Feds Quietly Reveal Chinese State-Backed Hacking Operation," *Foreign Policy*, November 30, 2017, www.foreignpolicy.com/2017/11/30/feds-quietly-reveal -chinese-state-backed-hacking-operation/ (accessed 4/15/18).

22. Jonathan Watts and Kate Connolly, "World Leaders React after Trump Rejects Paris Climate Deal," *The Guardian*, June 1, 2017, www.theguardian.com/environment /2017/jun/01/trump-withdraw-paris-climate-deal-world-leaders-react (accessed 4/15/18).

Answer Key

Chapter 1
1. c
2. d
3. b
4. d
5. d
6. a
7. d
8. b
9. e
10. d
11. c
12. c
13. c
14. d
15. d

Chapter 2
1. b
2. a
3. b
4. c
5. c
6. e
7. d
8. b
9. d
10. e
11. d
12. b
13. a

Chapter 3
1. b
2. c
3. c
4. e
5. a
6. a
7. d
8. b
9. b

10. c
11. b
12. d
13. d
14. c
15. a

Chapter 4
1. c
2. a
3. a
4. e
5. d
6. a
7. a
8. a
9. c
10. d
11. b
12. b
13. c

Chapter 5
1. b
2. b
3. e
4. a
5. c
6. d
7. a
8. b
9. a
10. b
11. d
12. c
13. d
14. c
15. d

Chapter 6
1. b
2. c

3. a
4. d
5. e
6. e
7. d
8. a
9. c
10. c
11. c
12. b
13. c
14. a
15. b

Chapter 7
1. b
2. a
3. e
4. b
5. d
6. d
7. c
8. e
9. c
10. c
11. b

Chapter 8
1. c
2. a
3. b
4. e
5. b
6. c
7. d
8. d
9. c
10. c
11. c
12. c
13. b

14. b
15. c

Chapter 9
1. c
2. a
3. b
4. e
5. b
6. c
7. d
8. c
9. c
10. c
11. c
12. b
13. d

Chapter 10
1. b
2. a
3. d
4. b
5. b
6. b
7. d
8. e
9. b
10. a
11. e

Chapter 11
1. b
2. c
3. e
4. b
5. e
6. a
7. c
8. c
9. b
10. d
11. a

Chapter 12	Chapter 13	Chapter 14	Chapter 15
1. d	1. a	1. d	1. b
2. b	2. c	2. e	2. a
3. c	3. a	3. c	3. e
4. c	4. c	4. d	4. c
5. e	5. d	5. d	5. c
6. c	6. d	6. b	6. e
7. d	7. e	7. c	7. a
8. c	8. a	8. a	8. a
9. a	9. b	9. d	9. b
10. b	10. a	10. d	10. d
11. d	11. c	11. e	11. a
12. e	12. a	12. b	12. e

Credits

PHOTOGRAPHS

Front Matter: Page vii: Paul Hennessy/NurPhoto via Getty Images; p. viii: Alex Wong/Getty Images; p. ix (top): Bing Guan/Bloomberg via Getty Images; p. ix (bottom): Anthony Pidgeon/ Redferns/Getty Images; p. x: Scott Mcintyre/The New York Times/Redux; p. xi (top) Jay Mallin/ ZUMAPRESS.com/Alamy Live News; p. xi (bottom): Jabin Botsford/The Washington Post via Getty Images; p. xii: Rod Lamkey/Getty Images; p. xiii: AP Photo/Elaine Thompson; p. xiv: Ryan Fisher/The Herald-Dispatch via AP; p. xv (top): Leonard Ortiz/MediaNews Group/ Orange County Register via Getty Images; p. xv (bottom): John Vicory; p. xvi (top): AP Photo/Andrew Harnik; p. xvi (bottom): Chip Somodevilla/Getty Images; p. xvii: Jerry Hotl/ TNS via ZUMA Wire.

Chapter 1: Page 2: Shutterstock; p. 3 (left): Paul Hennessy/NurPhoto via Getty Images; p. 3 (right): Air National Guard photo by Master Sgt. Christopher Schepers; p. 7: Bettmann/ Corbis via Getty Images; p. 10: Erik McGregor/ Pacific Press/LightRocket via Getty Images; p. 11: Rue des Archives/Granger NYC — All rights reserved; p. 15: Reproduced by permission of The Economist Intelligence Unit; p. 20: Frederic J. Brown/AFP via Getty Images; p. 22 (top): Courtesy of April Lawson; p. 23: Courtesy of April Lawson; p. 24 (top): AP Photo/Patrick Semansky; p. 24 (middle): Paul Hennessy/ NurPhoto via Getty Images; p. 24 (bottom): Air National Guard photo by Master Sgt. Christopher Schepers.

Chapter 2: Page 28: Shutterstock; p. 29: Alex Wong/Getty Images; p. 32: IanDagnall Computing/ Alamy Stock Photo; p. 36: Sarin Images/Granger NYC — All rights reserved; p. 38: Samuel Jennings (active 1789-1834). *Liberty Displaying the Arts and Sciences, or The Genius of America Encouraging the Emancipation of the Blacks*, 1792. Oil on canvas. 60 1/4" x 74" Library Company of Philadelphia. Gift of the artist, 1792; p. 50: Paul J. Richards/AFP/Getty Images; p. 56: Alex Wong/Getty Images.

Chapter 3: Page 60: rehab-icons/Shutterstock; p. 61 (left): Bing Guan/Bloomberg via Getty Images; p. 61 (right): White House Photo/Alamy Stock Photo; p. 66: Christian Petersen/Getty Images; p. 68: Courtesy of Domingo Morel; p. 69: Derek Davis/Portland Portland Press Herald via Getty Images; p. 73: Library of Congress; p. 79: Ilene MacDonald/Alamy Stock Photo; p. 83: AP Photo/Skip Foreman; p. 84 (top): Bing Guan/Bloomberg via Getty Images; p. 84 (bottom): White House Photo/Alamy Stock Photo.

Chapter 4: Page 88: Shutterstock p. 89: Anthony Pidgeon/Redferns/Getty Images; p. 96: Jerry Holt/Star Tribune via Getty Images; p. 99: Chine Nouvelle/SIPA/Newscom; p. 101: Clay Good/ ZUMA Press; p. 105: Sandy Huffaker/Getty Images; p. 110: Bettmann/Getty Images; p. 115: Anthony Pidgeon/Redferns/Getty Images.

Chapter 5: Page 118: Shutterstock; p. 119: Scott Mcintyre/The New York Times/Redux; p. 122 (left): Lanmas/Alamy Stock Photo; p. 122 (right): Historic Collection/Alamy Stock Photo; p. 124: Library of Congress; p. 126: Bettmann/ Getty Images; p. 131: Francis Miller/The LIFE Picture Collection via Getty Images; p. 137: Kent Sievers/The World-Herald via AP; p. 138: Eliot Elisofon/The LIFE Picture Collection via Getty Images; p. 140: Alex Wong/Getty Images; p. 143: Scott Mcintyre/The New York Times/ Redux.

Chapter 6: Page 148: Shutterstock; p. 149 (left): Jay Mallin/ZUMAPRESS.com/Alamy

TEXT

Figure 3.3 (p. 82): State Marijuana Laws in 2018 Map, originally published by Governing .com, March 30, 2018. Reprinted by permission of Governing.

Chapter 4, America Side by Side Map (p. 103): Global Press Freedom in Peril from Freedom and the Media 2019, Media Freedom: A Downward Spiral, by Sarah Repucci. © 2019 Freedom House. Reprinted by permission of Freedom House.

Figure 7.2 (p. 194): Figure: Profile of Social Media News Consumers in the U.S." from "Americans Are Wary of the Role Social Media Sites Play in Delivering the News," Pew Research Center, Washington, DC (October 2019) https://www.journalism.org/2019/10/02/americans-are-wary-of-the-role-social-media-sites-play-in-delivering-the-news/.

Figure 9.1 (p. 254): Figure: "More Engage with Politics Digitally than by Volunteering or Attending Rallies," from "Political Engagement, Knowledge and the Midterms," Pew Research Center, Washington, DC (April 2018) https://www.pewresearch.org/politics/2018/04/26/10-political-engagement-knowledge-and-the-mid terms/.

Glossary/Index

Page numbers in *italic* refer to figures or photos.

African Americans (*continued*)
    unemployment and, 456
    in U.S. population, 11, 12
    voter turnout, 259, 260
African American voting rights
    civil rights movement and, 256, 260
    current suppression of, 119–20, 266
    Fifteenth Amendment and, *53*, 123
    Jim Crow era restrictions on, 256, 260, 419
    political parties and, 228, 231
    protest and, *128*
    Reconstruction and, 8
    Twenty-Fourth Amendment and, 129
    Voting Rights Act (1965) and, *128*,
        129–30, *130*, 231, 256, *262*, 308
age
    See also demographics; older Americans; voter
        demographics; young Americans
    media and, 191
    political participation and, *285*
    political parties and, 224
    public opinion and, 162–63
    social media use and, *194*
    U.S. population and, 14
    voter turnout and, 259, *259*
    voting rights and, 256, *262*

agenda setting (media), 202–4, 202   the
    power of the media to bring public
    attention to particular issues and problems

agenda setting (presidential legislative initiative),
    339–40, 353

agents of socialization, 156–58, 156, *157,*
    160–63, 220   social institutions, including
    families and schools, that help to shape
    individuals' basic political beliefs and values

Agnew, Spiro, 349
agriculture, 73, 470
Agriculture, Department of, 374
Alabama, 126
Alien and Sedition Acts (1791), 98
Alito, Samuel, 405, *406*
Alphabet, 188
Amazon, 188

amendments, 51, 316   changes added to bills,
    laws, or constitutions
    See also specific amendments to the U.S.
        Constitution, e.g. First Amendment

American Civil Liberties Union (ACLU), 416
American Federation of State, County, and
    Municipal Employees (AFSCME), 394

American Jewish Congress, 262
American Medical Association, 333, 448
American people. *See* demographics
American Revolution, 31–33
    See also Founding
Americans with Disabilities Act (ADA)
    (1990), 140

amicus curiae, 244, 414, 416, 418   literally,
    "friend of the court"; individuals or groups
    who are not parties to a lawsuit but who
    seek to assist the Supreme Court in reaching
    a decision by presenting additional briefs

amnesty, 337
Amnesty International, 479
Annapolis Convention (1786), 35, 36
Anthony, Susan B., 123
Anti-Defamation League, 261–62

Antifederalists, 47–48, 47, *48,* **50–51, 64,**
    92, 226   those who favored strong
    state governments and a weak national
    government and who were opponents of
    the Constitution proposed at the American
    Constitutional Convention of 1787

antislavery movement, 121, *122*, 228
anti-terrorism
    bin Laden raid, 472
    bureaucracy and, 374
    drone strikes, 345, 472
    inherent powers and, 345
    judicial review and, 410–11
    preventive war and, 468
    unitary executive theory and, 342
    veto and, 340

antitrust policy, 437   government regulation
    of large businesses that have established
    monopolies

ANZUS (Australian, New Zealand, United
    States Security) Treaty, 482

appeasement, 466–67, 466   the effort to
    forestall war by giving in to the demands of
    a hostile power

appellate courts, , 400, 401, *401*, 403, 414
Apple, *50*, 188
appointments. *See* presidential appointments

apportionment, 14, 304–5, *304,* **304**   the
    process, occurring after every decennial
    census, that allocates congressional seats
    among the 50 states

bills, 313 proposed laws that have been sponsored by a member of Congress and submitted to the clerk of the House or Senate *See also* lawmaking

bin Laden, Osama, 472
Bipartisan Campaign Reform Act (BCRA) (2002), 273
birth control, 97, 112
Black Americans. *See* African Americans
Black Lives Matter, 126, 160
    See also racial injustice protests (2020)
Blackmun, Harry, 416, 422
Black Power movement, *128*
Blair, Christopher, 180–82, *181*

block grants, 78, 79 federal grants-in-aid that allow states considerable discretion in how the funds are spent

blogging. *See* social media
Bloomberg, Mike, 273
Boeing Corporation, 303, 390
Bono, Mary, 291–92
Boston Massacre (1770), 31–32
Boston Tea Party (1773), 33
Bowers v. Hardwick, 114–15, 140
Brandeis, Louis, 77, 112
Bretton Woods conference (1944), 481
Breyer, Stephen, 96, *406*

briefs, 418 written documents in which attorneys explain, using case precedents, why the court should find in favor of their client

British Broadcasting Company (BBC), 207

broadcast media, 191 television, radio or other media that transmit audio and/or video content to the public *See also* media

    campaign strategy and, 274
    free media and, 274–75
    government regulation of, 104, 207–8
    ownership of, 185, 187, 191, 202, 207–8
    presidency and, 163, *163*
    public, 185, 192
    radio, 163, *163*, 185, 192, 206, 207, 352
    sound bites and, 191, 195
    television, 104, 191–92, 202, 207, 216, 218, 274
Brown, Dwayne, *373*

Brown v. Board of Education, 124–25, **125,** 126, *128,* 141, 244 the 1954 Supreme Court decision that struck down the "separate but equal" doctrine as fundamentally unequal; this case eliminated state power to use race as a criterion of discrimination in law and provided the national government with the power to intervene by exercising strict regulatory policies against discriminatory actions

Bryan, William Jennings, 229
Buckley v. Valeo, 273
Budget and Accounting Act (1921), 340

budget deficits, 434, 440 amount by which government spending exceeds government revenue in a fiscal year

budget process
    See also government spending
    bureaucratic control and, 384–85, 387
    congressional "power of the purse" and, 313, 319, 477
    foreign policy and, 477, 478
    new order and, 319–20
    presidency and, 340, 348, 354–55, 435

bureaucracy, 364–93, 367 the complex structure of offices, tasks, rules, and principles of organization that is employed by all large-scale institutions to coordinate the work of their personnel
    See also bureaucratic control; Executive Office of the President; government regulation; *specific agencies, e.g. Food and Drug Administration*

    administrative law and, 398
    agency locations, 378, 382, 385
    characteristics of, 370
    civil rights and, 127
    Congress and, 355, 367, 368, 370–71, 378, 410
    congressional staff agencies, 312–13
    coronavirus pandemic and, 364–66, *367,* 368, 371
    delegated powers of, 344, 370–71
    demographics, 381
    employment in, 129, 370, 376–77, *377,* 380
    environmental policy and, 368, 371
    executive departments, 371, 383
    functions of, 367–71
    independent agencies, 346, 371, 373, 380, 436
    innovation and, 369–70
    international comparisons, *372*
    judicial review and, 389, 410
    law enforcement by, 369

military and, 373–74, 478
organization of, 371, 373–74, *375*, 378, 380
party machines and, 380
political parties and, 229, 380–81
principal-agent problem, 371
privatization and, 383
public opinion on, *379*
rule-making, 242, 245, 344, 355, 368–69, 398
size of, 346, 354, *372*, 381–83, *382*
solicitor general and, 414
Supreme Court and, 410
bureaucratic control, 383–91
agency location and, 385
budget process and, 384–85, 387
challenges of, 383–84, 390–91
citizen oversight, 389–90
Congress and, 385–89, 390
Consumer Financial Protection Board case study, 387–89
Executive Office of the President and, 384
federal courts and, 389
inspectors general and, 387
policy czars and, 385
presidency and, 383–85, 387–89, 391
reorganization and, 391
whistleblowers and, 389
Bureau of Indian Affairs, 139
Burwell v. Hobby Lobby Stores, 97
Bush, George H. W., 344, 422–23
Bush, George W., and administration
ballots and, 267
business interests and, 381
education and, 83, 446
election of 2000 and, 231, 232, 267, 275
executive orders and, 356
federal government power and, 83
foreign policy and, 468, 472, 474
inherent powers and, 344, 345
Iraq War and, 344
judicial review and, 410–11
micro-targeting and, 275
policy czars and, 385
public opinion and, 163
public-opinion polls and, 175
regulatory review and, 355
Republican Party and, 231
September 11, 2001, terrorist attacks and, 340, 354, 472
Supreme Court appointments and, 423
tax policy and, 166, 204, 434
unitary executive theory and, 342
veto and, 340
Bush, Maggie, 264–65

Bush Doctrine, 468, 472   foreign policy based on the idea that the United States should take preemptive action against threats to its national security

business interests
See also employment; financial industry; wealthy Americans, influence of
American Revolution and, 31–32
Articles of Confederation and, 35
bureaucracy and, 385
bureaucratic law enforcement and, 369
Citizens United v. Federal Election Commission and, 98
congressional decision-making and, 322
congressional elections and, 302–3
congressional oversight of, 325
conservatism and, 154
coronavirus stimulus legislation and, 371, 428–29
corporate taxes, 431, 434
Defense Production Act and, 33
federalism and, 72
foreign policy and, 478
Founding and, 36–37, 39
government regulation and, 72–73, 441
interest groups for, 233–34, 239, 245
lobbying by, 233–34, 242, *242*, 246, 322
media ownership, 185, 188, 191, 202, 207–8
media profit motives, 185, 187, 190, 204
PACs and, 272
political appointees and, 381, 384
political parties and, 219, 226, 228, 229, 230–31, 279
trade associations, 233, 272
trade policy and, 470
transgender discrimination and, 134
busing, 128–29
Byrd, Robert, 303

C
Cabinet, 346, 346, 348, 349, 371, *378*, 381   the secretaries, or chief administrators, of the major departments of the federal government; Cabinet secretaries are appointed by the president with the consent of the Senate

Calhoun, John C., 77
California
Asian/Pacific Islander Americans, 138
environmental policy, 369

California (*continued*)
    government regulation, 76
    Latino/a Americans, 136, 261
    policy diffusion and, 78–79
    school segregation/desegregation, 136
    welfare reform, 79
campaign advertising, 189, 273, 274, 275
campaign consultants, 270
campaign finance
    campaign timing and, 269
    candidate recruitment and, 216
    Citizens United v. Federal Election Commission, 98, 274
    congressional elections and, 270, 300, 303
    dark money, 273
    freedom of speech and, 98, 252, 273, 422
    government regulation of, 272, 273
    importance of, 269
    incumbency and, 270, 303
    lobbying and, 241
    political parties and, 216, 218, 272
    public-opinion polls and, 176
    public policy and, 168
    reform proposals, 422
    socioeconomic status and, 250–52, *251*
    sources of, 272–73
    Super PACs, 218, 273, 274, 303

campaigns, 270 efforts by political candidates and their supporters to win the backing of donors, political activists, and voters in their quest for political office
    See also campaign advertising; campaign finance; congressional elections; elections; presidential elections

campaign spending. *See* campaign finance
campaign strategy, 273–77
campaign volunteering, 253–54
candidates, 216, 273, 278
Cantwell v. Connecticut, 95
capitalism, 18, 70
capital punishment, 111
Carender, Keli, 212–13, *213*
Carter, Jimmy, 385, 438
casework (constituency service), 299, 300, 302, 303
casino gambling, 139

categorical grants, 74, *75* congressional grants given to states and localities on the condition that expenditures be limited to a problem or group specified by law

Catholicism, 14
    See also religion
caucuses (congressional), 309

caucuses (political), 309 congressional grants given to states and localities on the condition that expenditures be limited to a problem or group specified by law
    See also primary elections and caucuses

CBS, 185, 191
cell phones, 108, 193, 195
census, 12, 304, 339
Centers for Disease Control and Prevention (CDC), 365–66, 367, 368, 374, 390, 448
Central Intelligence Agency (CIA), 336, 465, 476, 478
certiorari. *See* writs of certiorari
"Charlotte bathroom bill," *83*, 134
charter schools, 447

checks and balances, 39, 42, 45, *46,* **50–51, 92, 152, 342, 359–60, 402** mechanisms through which each branch of government is able to participate in and influence the activities of the other branches; major examples include the presidential veto power over congressional legislation, the power of the Senate to approve presidential appointments, and judicial review of congressional enactments

Chicago, Burlington, and Quincy R.R. v. Chicago, 95
Chicago Tribune, 190

chief justice, 404 justice on the Supreme Court who presides over the Court's public sessions and whose official title is "chief justice of the United States"

child poverty, 457
Children's Defense Fund, 457
China, 12, 137–38, 465–66, 470, 486, 487–88
Chinese Exclusion Act (1882), 12, 138
Christianity. *See* religion
Chu, Helen Y., 364, *365*
citizen groups, 235

citizen journalism, 189, 195 news reported and distributed by citizens, rather than by professional journalists and for-profit news organizations

citizenship, 9, 9–10 informed and active membership in a political community

ClearChannel Communications, 208

clicktivism, 258

climate change, *10*, 488–89

Clinton, Bill, and administration, 28–29, 350, 352, 354, 355, 381

Clinton, Hillary
  campaign finance and, 272
  congressional investigations and, 325
  divisions within Democratic Party and, 220
  electoral college and, 269, 272
  email controversy, 204, 311, 325
  as first spouse, 350
  gender gap and, 261
  media sensationalism and, 185
  public-opinion polls and, 174–75, *175*
  Russian election interference and, 196, 487
  social media and, 353
  superdelegates and, 268
  voter demographics and, 261

closed primaries, 263   primary elections in which voters can participate in the nomination of candidates but only of the party in which they are enrolled for a period of time prior to primary day

closed rules (gag rules), 315, 318   provisions by the House Rules Committee limiting or prohibiting the introduction of amendments during debate

cloture, 316   a rule or process in a legislative body aimed at ending debate on a given bill; in the U.S. Senate, 60 senators (three-fifths) must agree in order to impose a time limit and end debate

CNN, 185, 187, 191

Code of Federal Regulations, 355

coercion, power of, 64, 66

Cold War, 466–67, *467,* **467**   the period of struggle between the United States and the former Soviet Union lasting from the late 1940s to about 1990

collective goods, 235   benefits sought by groups that are broadly available and cannot be denied to nonmembers

collective security, 482

college education. *See* higher education

college speech codes, 99

colonial America, 31–33, 121, 183
  See also Founding

Colorado, 79

Comey, James, 204, 325

comity (privilege and immunities) clause, 43–44, 67

commander in chief, 336, 344–45   the role of the president as commander of the national military and the state National Guard units (when called into service)

Commerce, Department of, 374

commerce. *See* economic policy; trade policy

commerce clause, 71–72, 72, 73, 77–78   Article I, Section 8, of the Constitution, which delegates to Congress the power "to regulate commerce with foreign nations, and among the several States and with the Indian tribes"; this clause was interpreted by the Supreme Court in favor of national power over the economy

commercial speech, 100–101

committee markup, 313, 315   the session in which a congressional committee rewrites legislation to incorporate changes discussed during hearings on a bill

Common Core State Standards, 446

Communications Decency Act (CDA), 104

Community Oriented Policing Services (COPS), 80

concurrent powers, 66   authority possessed by both state and national governments, such as the power to levy taxes

concurring opinions, 419   written opinions by judges agreeing with the majority opinion but giving different reasons for their decisions

confederations, 34   systems of government in which states retain sovereign authority except for the powers expressly delegated to the national government

conference committees, 311, 317, 319   joint committees created to work out a compromise on House and Senate versions of a piece of legislation

conferences, 309   gatherings of House Republicans every two years to elect their House leaders; Democrats call their gatherings "caucuses"

confidence in government. *See* trust/distrust in government

Congress
See also budget process; congressional
committee system; congressional
elections; congressional
representation; coronavirus stimulus
legislation; lawmaking; lobbying;
redistricting; stimulus legislation
advice and consent powers of, 326
in Articles of Confederation, 34
Benghazi investigation, 311, 316, 325
bicameral nature of, 39, 293
bureaucracy and, 355, 367, 368, 370–71,
378, 410
bureaucratic control and, 385–89, 390
Cabinet members and, 346
civil rights and, 127
constituency service (casework) and, 299,
300, 302, 303
Constitution on, 41–42, 293
contacting your member, 306–7
court system and, 401–2
decision-making in, 321–24
election of 2020 and, 270, 272, 278, 282–83
executive agreements and, 339, 472
executive delegated powers and, 344
executive power expansion and, 359, 360
federal government power and, 72, 73
foreign policy and, 42, 310, 472, 477–78
House vs. Senate, 41, 293–94, 294, 323
impeachment powers, 326–27, 339, 350, 389
importance of, 290–92, 291
inaction of, 291–92
inherent powers and, 345
intelligence agencies and, 476, 478
interest group influence strategies, 240
iron triangles and, 243, 243
judicial review and, 407–8
limitations on federal courts and, 423
national security policy and, 472
oversight powers of, 310, 325, 342, 381,
386–87
party leadership in, 308–9, 318–19, 320, 323
party polarization and, 280, 311–12,
322–23, 324
pork barreling, 303
powers of, 41–42
presidential orders and, 358
Russian election interference investigations,
324, 325, 339
single-member districts, 215
social media and, 299
staff system, 312–13
symbolic legislation and, 303

unemployment insurance and, 443
unitary executive theory on, 342
war powers, 344–45, 472–73, 477
Congressional Budget and Impoundment
Control Act (1974), 313, 319–20
Congressional Budget Office (CBO), 387, 435
congressional committee system, 309–12
conference committees, 311, 317, 319
foreign policy and, 477–78
iron triangles and, 243, 243
joint committees, 311
lawmaking and, 313, 315
lobbying and, 241
oversight and, 310, 325, 386
select committees, 311, 325
standing committees, 310, 477
congressional elections
campaign finance and, 270, 300, 303
candidates in, 300, 302–3
incumbency and, 300, 302–3, 302
midterm elections
party polarization and, 325
redistricting and, 305
symbolic legislation and, 303
voters in, 301
"winner take all" system and, 215–16
congressional representation, 293–99
See also descriptive representation
Great Compromise, 37
House vs. Senate, 293–94, 294
influence of wealthy Americans and, 168
ratification debates and, 47–48
substantive, 48, 296–97
Three-Fifths Compromise, 38, 38
trustee vs. delegate, 294–95
Congressional Research Service (CRS), 312, 387
consent of the governed, 8, 41, 123
conservatism
See also political ideology; Republican Party
federalism and, 83, 86–87
media and, 192
religion and, 162
Supreme Court and, 280, 405, 406, 422–23
Tea Party movement, 212–14, 213, 231

conservatives, 154   today this term refers to
those who generally support the social and
economic status quo and are suspicious of
efforts to introduce new political formulas
and economic arrangements; conservatives
believe that a large and powerful government
poses a threat to citizens' freedom
See also conservatism

misinformation and, 60, 281
Muslim ban and, 463–64
political knowledge and, 167
political parties and, 224
public health and, 167, 282
social policy and, 428–29, *429*
state of emergency declarations, 3–4
task force for, 385
trust/distrust in government and, 24
trust/distrust in media and, 200
unemployment and, 428
unemployment insurance and, 368, 443
coronavirus stimulus legislation, *440*
bureaucracy and, 368, 371
congressional decision-making and, 324
election of 2020 and, 281
government role in economy and, 439
importance of Congress and, 290
social policy and, 428–29, *429*
corporate interests. *See* business interests
corporate taxes, 431, 434
corruption, 184, 195, 245–46

cost-of-living adjustments (COLAs), 442
changes made to the level of benefits of a
government program based on the rate of
inflation

Council of Chief State School Officers, 446
counsel, right to, *95*, 110–11
Court of Appeals for the Federal Circuit, 402
Court of Federal Claims, 401
Court of International Trade, 401

courts of appeals, 400, *401,* **403, 414** courts
that hear appeals of trial court decisions

coverture, 122
COVID-19 pandemic. *See* coronavirus pandemic
criminal justice system
See also due process of law; federal courts
comity clause and, 67
due process of law, 93, *95,* 107–11, *110,*
136, 402
felon voting rights, 118–20, *119,* 132
Miranda rule, *95,* 109, *110*
political ideologies on, 154

criminal law, *397,* **397** the branch of law that
regulates the conduct of individuals, defines
crimes, and specifies punishment for
proscribed conduct

cruel and unusual punishment, *95,* 111
Cruz, Ted, 219, 479
Cuban Americans, 222, 479, *479*

cultural identities. *See* demographics
cyberattacks, 465–66, 478, 487

D
DACA (Deferred Action for Childhood
Arrivals), 137, *295,* 421, *421*
See also DREAM Act
dark money (501(c)(4) committees), 273
Dawes Act (1887), 139
death penalty, 111
debates, political, 216, 218
Declaration of Independence, 17, 18, 33, 55
Declaration of Sentiments and Resolutions, 122

de facto, 125 literally, "by fact"; refers to
practices that occur even when there is no
legal enforcement, such as school segregation
in much of the United States today

de facto segregation, 125,127

defendant, 398 the one against whom a
complaint is brought in a criminal or civil case

Defense, Department of (DoD), 346, 369–70,
373, 475–76, 478
defense industry, *243,* 281, 465, 478
See also military
Defense of Marriage Act (DOMA) (1996),
28–29, 67
Defense Production Act (DPA) (1950),
332–34, *333*
Deferred Action for Childhood Arrivals
(DACA), 137
See also DREAM Act
deficit spending, 439
DeJonge v. Oregon, 95

de jure, 125 literally, "by law"; refers to
legally enforced practices, such as school
segregation in the South before the 1960s

DeLay, Tom, 246

delegate (role), 294–95, *294* a representative
who votes according to the preferences of
his or her constituency

delegated powers, 344, 355 constitutional
powers that are assigned to one governmental
agency but are exercised by another agency
with the express permission of the first

delegates (convention), 267, 268 representatives
who vote according to the preferences of
their constituencies
See also national conventions

democracy, 7 a system of rule that permits citizens to play a significant part in the governmental process, usually through the election of key public officials

deregulation, 230–31, 281, 438 a policy of reducing or eliminating regulatory restraints on the conduct of individuals or private institutions

descriptive representation (Congress), 295 a type of representation in which representatives have the same racial, gender, ethnic, religious, or educational backgrounds as their constituents; it is based on the principle that if two individuals are similar in background, character, interests, and perspectives, then one can correctly represent the other's views

deterrence, 466–67, 467 an effort to prevent hostile action by promising to retaliate forcefully against an attacker

Development, Relief, and Education Act for Alien Minors (DREAM Act), 137, *137*, 421, *421*
See also DACA

devolution, 77, 78–79, 78 policy to remove a program from one level of government by delegating it or passing it down to a lower level of government, such as from the national government to the state and local governments

DeVos, Betsy, 447
Dewey, John, 183–84
Dewey, Thomas, *175*
Dial, Hank, 290–91
diffusion, 78–79

digital citizens, 193 daily internet users with broadband (high-speed) home internet access and the technology and literacy skills to go online for employment, news, politics, entertainment, commerce, and other activities

digital divide, 193 the gap in access to the internet among demographic groups based on education, income, age, geographic location, and race/ethnicity

digital news, 192–97, 200
See also misinformation in media
advertising and, 188
benefits of, 195–96
citizen journalism and, 189, 195
concerns about, 189, 196–97, 200
digital political participation and, 256
evaluating, 198–99, *199*
government regulation and, 208
growth of digital media and, 187–89, *190*, 192
internet access and, *186*, 193
journalism/journalists and, 188, 189, 190
media ownership and, 188
misinformation and, 196–97
native, 189, 190
news aggregators and, 193
newspapers and, 189–91
party polarization and, 197, 200
political knowledge and, 9–10, 166, 195–96, 197, 200
radio and, 192
on social media, 188–89, 193–94, *194*, 196–97
streaming video, 192–93

digital political participation, 193, 256, 258, 274, 353 activities designed to influence

politics using the internet, including visiting a candidate's website, organizing events online, and signing an online petition

digital social networks, 256, 258, 276

diplomacy, 373, 468, 472, 474, 476, 478, 480 the representation of a government to other governments

direct-action politics, *10*
See also protest

direct democracy, 8 a system of rule that permits citizens to vote directly on laws and policies

directives, presidential, 358
Director of National Intelligence (DNI), 391, 476
Disability Rights Education and Defense Fund, 140
disabled Americans, 79, *79*, 139–40, 266, 443, 448
discretionary spending, 440

discrimination, 121 the use of any unreasonable and unjust criterion of exclusion
See also racial discrimination
gender and, 127, 132, *133*, 134, *135*
sexual orientation and, 115, 140

Disney, 187

dissenting opinions, 419 decisions written by justices in the minority in a particular case, in which a justice wishes to express his or her reasoning in the case

district courts, 400, *401*, 403
District of Columbia v. Heller, 105–6
diversity. *See* demographics
DNA testing, 108
Dodd-Frank Wall Street Reform and Consumer Protection Act (2010), 322, 388
Doha Amendment, 488
DOMA (Defense of Marriage Act) (1996), 28–29, 67
Donnelly, Glynis, 290

double jeopardy, 93–94, *95*, 109, 135 the Fifth Amendment right providing that a person cannot be tried twice for the same crime

Douglas, William O., 112
DREAM Act (Development, Relief, and Education Act for Alien Minors), 137, *137*, 421, *421*
See also DACA

Dred Scott v. Sanford, 121–22
drug testing, 108

dual federalism, 70–71, 70, *71*, 73, *75*   the
system of government that prevailed in the
United States from 1789 to 1937 in which
most fundamental governmental powers
were shared between the federal and state
governments

**due process of law, 93, *95*, 107–11, 107, *110*,
135, 402**   the right of every individual
against arbitrary action by national or state
governments

E

early America, 11, 215, 226, 255
early voting, *267*, 282
Earned Income Tax Credit (EITC), 452, 454
East India Company, 32
eBay, 188
economic conditions
    See also Great Depression; Great Recession;
        unemployment
    media priming and, 205
    voter decisions and, 205, 278, 279,
        286, 438
economic inequality
    See also socioeconomic status
    agreement on, 226
    digital divide and, 193
    education and, 447
    Founding and, 162
    growth of, 16, *16*
    housing policy and, 450–51
    minimum wage and, *20*
    political culture and, 20–21
    political knowledge and, 166
    populism and, 223
    public opinion and, 162
    race and, 451, 452, 455, 456–57
    tax policy and, 166
economic policy, 431–41
    See also coronavirus stimulus legislation;
        government spending; stimulus
        legislation; tax policy; trade policy
    agreement on, 226
    Articles of Confederation and, 34, 39
    bureaucracy and, 374
    Constitution and, 39, 431
    consumer protection and, 322, 387–89,
        388, 438, 448
    election of 2020 and, 282
    federal government power and, 21, 70, 73–74

federalism and, 70
federal subsidies, 434–35, 449
foreign policy and, 469–70
Founding and, 37
government role in economy and, 438–41
Great Recession and, 434, 451
Keynesian, 439, 440
minimum wage, *20*, 82, 168, 435, 441
monetary policies, 435–37
political parties and, 223
regulation, 437–38, 441
voter decisions and, 277
voter turnout and, 260
economic sanctions, 482, 487
economic status. *See* socioeconomic status
education
    See also school segregation/desegregation;
        socioeconomic status
    affirmative action and, 141–42
    bureaucracy and, 386
    charter schools, 447
    coronavirus pandemic and, 463–64
    equality of opportunity and, 152, 446
    federal government power and, 83
    first spouse and, 350
    freedom of speech and, 99, 100, *101*
    gender discrimination in, *133*, 134
    Latino/a Americans and, 136
    organized labor and, *234*
    political participation and, 258, 260, *285*
    political socialization and, 156, 157–58
    school shootings, 148–49
    "separate but equal" rule and, 124
    separation of church and state and, 96, *96*
    social composition of Congress and, 296
    social policy and, 83, 445–47
    undocumented immigrants and, 14, 136
    vouchers, 447
Education, Department of, 134, 386
Education Act (1972), Title IX of, 134, 136
EEOC (Equal Employment Opportunity
    Commission), 129, 134
Eighteenth Amendment, 52
Eighth Amendment, 111
Eisenhower, Dwight, and administration, *128*,
    230, 337

**elastic clause (necessary and proper clause),
42, 50, 64, 72**   the concluding paragraph
of Article I, Section 8, of the Constitution
(also known as the "necessary and proper
clause"), which provides Congress with the
authority to make all laws "necessary and
proper" to carry out its enumerated powers

elections (*continued*)
    media priming and, 205
    media sensationalism and, 185, 187
    micro-targeting, 275–76
    political participation and, *285*
    political parties and, 216, 218, 220
    public-opinion polls and, 169, 174–75,
        175, 176
    reform proposals, 258, 266, 267, *267*,
        269, 308
    rules for, 215–16
    streaming video and, 192–93
    voter mobilization, 258, 273–74, *275*,
        276–77, 286

electoral college, 269   the presidential
   electors from each state who meet after the
   general election to cast ballots for president
   and vice president

    campaign finance and, 272
    campaign strategy and, 274
    creation of, 39–40, 43
    election of 2016 and, 258, 269, 272
    election of 2020 and, 269, *285*
    reform/elimination proposals, 258, 269
    voter turnout and, 255
Elementary and Secondary Education Act
      (1965), 446
elite pluralism, 239
elites. *See* wealthy Americans, influence of
Ellis Island, *11*
Ellsberg, Daniel, 205
Emancipation Proclamation, 358

eminent domain, 93, *95,* **112**   the right of
   government to take private property for
   public use

employment
    See also economic policy; organized labor;
        unemployment
    in bureaucracy, 129, 370, 376–77, *377*, 380
    drug testing and, 108
    gender discrimination in, *133*
    government regulation and, 368, 438
    health care and, 448
    minimum wage, *20*, 82, 168, 435, 438, 441
    New Deal and, *73*
    racial discrimination in, 129, 219
    sexual harassment and, 134, 136
    sexual orientation discrimination in, 115, 140
    state-local tensions and, 82
    tax expenditures and, 444
    transgender discrimination in, 134, 355

Energy, Department of, 478
energy policy, 244, 465
entitlements. *See* contributory programs
environmental policy
    bureaucracy and, 368, 371
    election of 2020 and, 281
    executive orders and, 356
    federal government power and, 75, 76
    federalism and, 82
    foreign policy and, 479, 488–89
    government regulation and, 281, 368–69,
        369, 438, 448
    interest groups and, 479
    protest and, *10*, 479
    public opinion on, 168
    regulatory review and, 355
    veto and, 340
Environmental Protection Agency (EPA),
      368–69, *369*, 370, 438, 448
EpiPens, 386–87
Equal Employment Opportunity Commission
      (EEOC), 129, 134
equality, 5, 18, 20–21
    See also equality of opportunity

equality of opportunity, 18, 20, 151, 444
   a widely shared American ideal that all
   people should have the freedom to use
   whatever talents and wealth they have to
   reach their fullest potential
   See also economic inequality

    bureaucracy and, 370
    education and, 152, 446
    political ideologies on, 155
    as political value, 152
    social policy and, 445

equal protection clause, 121, 124, 136, 142
   provision of the Fourteenth Amendment
   guaranteeing citizens "the equal protection
   of the laws." This clause has been the basis
   for the civil rights of African Americans,
   women, and other groups

equal time rule, 208   the requirement that
   broadcasters provide candidates for the
   same political office equal opportunities to
   communicate their messages to the public

Escobedo v. Illinois, 95
Espionage Act (1917), 98

establishment clause, 94–96, *94,* **96**   the First
   Amendment clause that says "Congress shall
   make no law respecting an establishment

of religion"; this constitutional provision means that a "wall of separation" exists between church and state

ethnicity, 161
   See also immigrants; Latino/a Americans; race
Europe, immigrants from, 11–12, 14
European Americans. *See* White Americans
evangelicals, 162, 223, 262, 478–79
Everson v. Board of Education, 95
Every Student Succeeds Act (2015), 83, 446
excessive fines, *95*, 111
excise taxes, 431

exclusionary rule, 107–8, 107   the ability of courts to exclude evidence obtained in violation of the Fourth Amendment

executive agreements, 338, 472, 477
   agreements, made between the president and another country, that have the force of treaties but do not require the Senate's "advice and consent"

executive branch
   See also bureaucracy; executive power expansion; presidency
   Cabinet, 346, 348, 349, 371, *378*, 381
   congressional oversight of, 342, 381, 386–87
   delegated powers of, 344
   foreign policy and, 474–76
   iron triangles and, 243, *243*
   lobbying and, 242, 245
   national security policy and, 474–76
   unitary executive theory and, 342

executive departments, 371, 383   the 15 departments in the executive branch headed by Cabinet secretaries and constituting the majority of the federal bureaucracy

Executive Office of the President (EOP), 348, 352–53, 354–55, 359, 371, 384   the permanent agencies that perform defined management tasks for the president; created in 1939, the EOP includes the OMB, the Council of Economic Advisers (CEA), the NSC, and other agencies
   See also executive branch

executive orders, 356, *357*, 358, *358*   rules or regulations issued by the president that have the effect and formal status of legislation
   See also specific policy issues, e.g. immigration policy

executive power expansion, 352–60
   administrative strategy, 344, 354–59, *357*
   checks and balances and, 342, 359–60, 402
   civil rights and, 127–28
   Congress and, 359, 360
   judicial review and, 410–11
   national security policy and, 472
   political appointees and, 384
   public appeals and, 352–54
   unitary executive theory and, 342

executive privilege, 339   the claim that confidential communications between a president and close advisers should not be revealed without the consent of the president

expressed powers, 42, 64, 336   specific powers granted by the Constitution to Congress (Article I, Section 8) and to the president (Article II)

   Bill of Rights and, 46, 92
   of federal government, 42, 46, 63, 64, 72, 92
   of presidency, 336–40, *341*
extraordinary renditions, 345

F
Facebook
   See also social media
   advertising and, 189, 260
   congressional oversight and, *99*, 181–82, 325
   elections and, 189, 260
   evaluating posts, *199*
   hate speech and, *99*, 100
   misinformation on, 165, 181–82, 189, 196
   news on, 188, 193, 194
   political socialization and, 157
   public opinion and, 163
   Russian election interference and, 196, 487
   user demographics, 194, *194*
   voter mobilization and, 260, 276
fact-checking, 165, 185, 189, 194, 198–99, *199*
FactCheck.org, 196
Fair Housing Act (1968), 131
Fair Housing Amendments Act (1988), 131
fairness doctrine, 208

fake news, 196   false stories intended to be read as factual news that are circulated to benefit one candidate or party over another or to generate ad revenue

   birther conspiracies and, *197*
   concerns about, 196–97

Federal Meat Inspection Act (1906), 437

Federal Register, 355, 368, 438

Federal Regulation of Lobbying Act (1946), 241

Federal Reserve System (Fed), 374, 388, 435–37, *436,* **436** a system of 12 Federal Reserve banks that facilitates exchanges of cash, checks, and credit; regulates member banks; and uses monetary policies to fight inflation and deflation

federal subsidies, 434–35, 449

Federal Trade Commission, 100, 437

Federal Vacancies Reform Act (FVRA) (1998), 381

felon voting rights, 118–19, *119,* 132

FEMA (Federal Emergency Management Agency), 367

fentanyl. *See* opioid crisis

Fifteenth Amendment, *53,* **122, 123** one of three Civil War amendments; it guaranteed voting rights for African American men

Fifth Amendment, 93, *95,* 108–9, *110,* 112, 135

Fight for $15 campaign (2012), *20*

fighting words, 99 speech that directly incites damaging conduct

filibuster, 315–16, 316, 319, 320, 404 a tactic used by members of the Senate to prevent action on legislation they oppose by continuously holding the floor and speaking until the majority backs down; once given the floor, senators have unlimited time to speak, and it requires a vote of three-fifths of the Senate to end a filibuster

filter bubbles, 197, 220

financial crisis and recession (2008). *See* Great Recession

financial industry, 322, 388–89, *388,* 437–38

"fire alarm oversight," 386–87, 386 episodic, as-needed congressional hearings on bureaucratic agency operations, usually prompted by media attention or advocacy group complaints

First Amendment, 94–104
See also freedom of speech
establishment clause, 94–96, *96*
federal government and, 93
freedom of religion in, 94–97, *95*
freedom of the press, 93, *95,* 102, *103,* 104, 152, 183

free exercise clause, 97
lobbying and, 241
pornography and obscenity and, 104
protest and, 101, 253
selective incorporation and, 93, *95*
text of, 94, 97

First Continental Congress, 33

first spouse, 350

fiscal policy, 431–32, 431, 434–35 the government's use of taxing, monetary, and spending powers to manipulate the economy
See also stimulus legislation; tax policy

501(c)(4) committees (dark money), 273 politically active nonprofits; under federal law, these nonprofits can spend unlimited amounts on political campaigns and not disclose their donors as long as their activities are not coordinated with the candidate campaigns and political activities are not their primary purpose

FiveThirtyEight, 173, *173*

527 committees (Super PACs), 218, 273, 274, 303 nonprofit independent political action committees that may raise unlimited sums of money from corporations, unions, and individuals but are not permitted to contribute to or coordinate directly with parties or candidates

flag burning, 101

flawed democracy, 15

Florida
election of 2000 and, 267
felon voting rights and, 118–20, *119*
health care, 455

Florida Rights Restoration Coalition (FRRC), 118, *119*

Floyd, George, killing of, 126, 160, 253, 281, 337

Flynn, Michael, 325

Food and Drug Administration (FDA), 61, 62, 367, 374, 385, 386, 437

food stamps. *See* Supplemental Nutrition Assistance Program

Ford, Gerald, 337, 348–49

Foreign Intelligence Surveillance Act (FISA) (1978), 476–77

foreign policy, 462–89
See also national security policy; trade policy
arbitration and, 484
Articles of Confederation and, 34–35

free riders, 235, 245   those who enjoy the benefits of collective goods but did not participate in acquiring or providing them

free trade, 470
French and Indian War, 31
fugitive slave clause, 71

full faith and credit clause, 66–67, 66   provision from Article IV, Section 1, of the Constitution requiring that the states normally honor the public acts and judicial decisions that take place in another state

Fulton, Robert, 72
fundraising. *See* campaign finance

G

gag rules (closed rules), 315, 318
gambling, 139
Gannett corporation, 187
Garcia, Chuy, *295*
Gardner, Cory, 283
Garland, Merrick, 395, 396, 405

gatekeeping, 202–3, 202   a process by which information and news are filtered to the public by the media; for example, a reporter choosing which sources to include in a story

Gates, Rick, 325
gay rights movement, 140, 141, 244
   See also LGBTQ Americans
Geithner, Timothy, *388*
gender
   See also demographics; transgender
      Americans
   cruel and unusual punishment and, 111
   discrimination based on, 127, 132, *133*, 134, *135*
   political parties and, 221, 223, 261
   public opinion and, 161–62
   social composition of Congress and, 296, *297*, *298*
   social media use and, *194*
   vice presidency and, 278, *349*
   voter demographics and, 161, 221, 223, 261

gender gap, 161, 223, 261   a distinctive pattern of voting behavior reflecting the differences in views between women and men

general elections, 263   regularly scheduled elections involving most districts in the nation or state, in which voters select officeholders; in the United States, general elections for national office and most state and local offices are held on the first Tuesday after the first Monday in November in evennumbered years (every four years for presidential elections)

general revenue sharing, 78   the process by which one unit of government yields a portion of its tax income to another unit of government, according to an established formula; revenue sharing typically involves the national government providing money to state governments

generational differences, 162–63
   See also age
Generation Z, 162
   See also regional differences
Georgia, 114, 278, 282

gerrymandering, 305, 308, 324   the apportionment of voters in districts in such a way as to give unfair advantage to one racial or ethnic group or political party

Gibbons v. Ogden, 72
GI Bill (1944), 447
Gideon v. Wainwright, 95, 110
gig economy, 443
Gilded Age, 16
Gingrich, Newt, 311, 323
Ginsburg, Ruth Bader, 280, 396, 405, 406
Gitlow v. New York, 95
Google, 188, 189, 193
Google News, 193
Gore, Al, 267, 381
Gorsuch, Neil, 115, 316, 395, 396, 404, 405, *406*

government, 5–9, 5   institutions and procedures through which a territory and its people are ruled

   Americans' view of, 4, 5, 21, 24
   corruption, 184, 195, 245–46
   dependence on, 5, 6, 21, 24
   forms of, 5, 7, 15, *15*
   international comparisons, 7, 49, *49*
   limited, 5, 7, 17, 50–51, 50
   trust/distrust in, 5, 24, *164*
Government Accountability Office (GAO), 312, 374, 387

government corporations, 373   government agencies that perform market-oriented public services and raise revenues to fund their activities

government employment. *See* bureaucracy
government regulation
    See also specific laws and agencies, e.g.
      Occupational Safety and Health
      Administration
    bureaucratic rule-making and, 368–69
    business interests and, 72–73, 441
    of campaign finance, 272, 273
    consumer protection, 344, 387–89, *388*,
      438, 448
    deregulation, 230–31, 280, 438
    economic, 437–38, 441
    election of 2020 and, 280, 281
    employment and, 368, 438
    environmental policy and, 281, 368–69,
      369, 438, 448
    federalism and, 72–73, 75–76
    financial industry and, 322, 388–89,
      437–38
    interest groups and, 385, 390–91
    liberty and, 18
    of lobbying, 241, 245–46
    of media, 102, 104, 185, 187, 197,
      207–8
    political parties and, 219, 229, 230–31
    regulatory review, 355
    surveillance and, 476–77
government spending, 434–35
    See also budget process; welfare state
    congressional decision-making and, 324
    devolution and, 78
    discretionary, 440
    government role in economy and, 439
    military, 280, 468, *469*, 478
    political parties and, 440
GPS monitoring, 108
Graham, Lindsey, 316

grand juries, 108–9, 108   juries that
    determine whether sufficient evidence is
    available to justify a trial; grand juries do
    not rule on the accused's guilt or innocence

grants-in-aid, 74, *75*, 78, 79, 80, 127–28
    programs through which Congress provides
    money to state and local governments on
    the condition that the funds be employed
    for purposes defined by the federal
    government

grassroots campaigns, 273–74, *273*, 276–77
    political campaigns that operate at
    the local level, often using face-toface
    communication to generate interest and
    momentum by citizens

Great Compromise, 37   the agreement
    reached at the Constitutional Convention of
    1787 that gave each state an equal number
    of senators regardless of its population
    but linked representation in the House of
    Representatives to population

Great Depression
    See also New Deal
    economic policy and, 438–39
    federal government power and, 21, 73
    federalism and, 73
    laissez-faire capitalism and, 438–39
    political parties and, 229–30, 277
    social policy and, *442*
    socioeconomic status and, 16
Great Recession (2008)
    age differences and, 224
    bureaucracy and, 391
    Consumer Financial Protection Board
      and, 387–88
    economic policy and, 434, 451
    election of 2008 and, 278
    federal government power and, 21, 70
    mortgage lending and, 451
Great Writ. *See* habeas corpus
Green New Deal, 279, 282
Green Party, 155
green technologies
Green-Yates, Kimberly, 2
Griswold v. Connecticut, 112, 422
Grodzins, Morton, 74
group politics. *See* interest groups
Gruber, Justin, 148–49, *149*
Grutter v. Bollinger, 142
gun control
    See also gun rights
    advocacy groups, 236–37, *237*
    agreement on, 226
    executive orders and, 356
    mass shootings and, *105*, 107
    public opinion on, 107, 148–50, 157
    Second Amendment and, 107
    state laws, 105, *106*
    states' rights and, 77–78
gun rights
    See also gun control
    interest groups and, 322, 324
    public opinion on, 107, 148–50,
      149
    Second Amendment and, *95*, 104–6
    state laws, 105–6, *106*
    Supreme Court on, 105–6
gun violence, *105*, 107, 148–49, 157

H

habeas corpus, 92, 335, 402   a court order demanding that an individual in custody be brought into court and shown the cause for detention

Hague v. Committee for Industrial Organization, 101
Hamdi v. Rumsfeld, 410
Hamilton, Alexander
  on Bill of Rights, 91–92
  on Congress, 41, 477
  on executive branch, 42
  on monetary policies, 435
  on political parties, 215
  ratification debates and, 47, 50
Hamilton v. Regents of the University of California, 95
Hanage, William, 365
Hannity, Sean, 192
hard news, 185
Harris, Kamala, 278, 280, *286, 349*
Harrison, Benjamin, 228
Harrison, William Henry, 349
Hatch Act (1939), 370
hate speech, 99–100, *99*
Health, Education, and Welfare, Department of, 141, 386
Health and Human Services, Department of (HHS), 2–3, 370–71, 374, 386, 387
health care
  See also Affordable Care Act; Medicaid
  agreement on, 226
  business interests and, 234
  congressional oversight and, 386–87
  election of 2020 and, 281, 282
  government role in economy and, 440
  Medicare, 440, 443, 448, 452
  party polarization and, 279
  presidential agenda setting power and, 340
  social policy and, 447–50, *449, 450*
  undocumented immigrants and, 14, 136
  uninsured, *449, 450*
  voter decisions and, 277
Hearst Communications, 187
Help Americans Vote Act (HAVA) (2003), 267
Henry, Patrick, 47
Hernandez v. Texas, 136
hidden partisans, 220
higher education
  affirmative action and, 141–42
  civil rights movement and, 260
  freedom of speech and, 99
  gender discrimination in, 134

"separate but equal" rule and, 124
  sexual harassment and, 134, 136
  social policy and, 447
Higher Education Act, 447
Hispanic Americans. *See* Latino/a Americans
Hobby Lobby case, 97
Holder, Eric, 339, 345
holds (Senate), 316
Holmes, Oliver Wendell, 97, 100
Homeland Security, Department of (DHS), 80, 83, 137, 344, 374, 386, 391
homelessness, 18
homeownership
  See also mortgage lending
  racial discrimination and, 127, 131, 136
  segregation/desegregation and, 451
  tax policy and, 452

home rule, 67, 70   power delegated by the state to a local unit of government to manage its own affairs

Hoover, Herbert, 73, 229, 438
House Committee on Foreign Affairs, 477
House Intelligence Committee, 478
House of Representatives
  See also Congress
  apportionment for, 14, 304–5, *304*
  Bill of Rights and, 92
  bureaucratic control and, 390
  Constitutional amendment process and, 51
  Constitution on, 41, 313, 319
  election of 2020 and, 278, 281, 282–83
  foreign policy and, 477–78
  Great Compromise and, 37
  impeachment and, 280, 326, 339, 389
  lawmaking and, 313, 315, 318–19
  majority rule, minority rights and, 21
  party discipline in, 323
  party leadership in, 308–9, 318–19, 320, 323
  presidential succession and, 349
  vs. Senate, 41, 293–94, *294*, 323
House Rules Committee, 310, 315
House Select Committee on Benghazi, 311
House Ways and Means Committee, 310
housing
  homeownership, 127, 131, 136, 451, 452
  mortgage lending, 127, 131, 451
  racial discrimination and, 127, 131, 136, 451
  segregation/desegregation and, 131, 136, 451
  social policy and, 450–51
Housing and Urban Development, Department of (HUD), 131
Hull, Cordell, 474

human rights in foreign policy, 470–71, 479, 482
Hunter, Noelle, 299
Hupp, Suzanna, 148, *149*
Hurricane Katrina, 367

I

ideological groups, 235
"I Have a Dream" (King), 126
iHeartMedia, 208
immigrants
  See also demographics; immigration;
    immigration policy
  age and, 14
  citizenship, 12, 154, 161
  civil rights of, 136–37, *137*
  undocumented, 12, 14, 136–37, *137*, 161
  in U.S. population, 11–12, 13–14, *13*, 14
  voter turnout, 260–61
  voting rights, 255
immigration
  See also immigrants; immigration policy
  anxieties about, 12, 17
  history of, 11–12, *11*
immigration policy
  DREAM Act, 137, *137*, 421, *421*
  election of 2016 and, 137
  election of 2020 and, 281
  executive orders and, 356
  federalism and, 80
  history of, 12
  political ideologies on, 154
  protest and, *137*, *421*
  public opinion on, 161
  regulatory review and, 355
  Secure Communities program, 80
  state of emergency declarations and, 340
  Supreme Court on, 14, 136, 137
  voter demographics and, 260, 261

impeachment, 326–27, 326, *327*   the formal
  charge by the House of Representatives
  that a government official has committed
  "Treason, Bribery, or other high Crimes and
  Misdemeanors"
  See also Trump impeachment

implementation, 355, 368   the efforts of
  departments and agencies to translate laws
  into specific bureaucratic rules and actions

implied powers, 64, 72, 341–42, 341, 345
  powers derived from the necessary and
  proper clause of Article I, Section 8, of
  the Constitution; such powers are not
  specifically expressed but are implied

through the expansive interpretation of
  delegated powers

income inequality. *See* economic inequality
incumbency
  campaign finance and, 270, 303
  congressional elections and, 300, 302–3, *302*
  economic conditions and, 278, 279, 438
  redistricting and, 305

incumbent, 270, 300   a candidate running
  for re-election to a position that he or she
  already holds
  See also incumbency

independent agencies, 346, 371, 373, 380, 436

independent regulatory commissions, 373
  government agencies outside the executive
  department usually headed by commissioners

independents, 220, *221*, 224, 284

indexing, 442   periodic process of adjusting
  social benefits or wages to account for
  increases in the cost of living

Indiana, 131
Indian Removal Act (1830), 139
Indian Self-Determination and Education
    Assistance Act, 139
industry interests. *See* business interests

inflation, 431, 438, 441, 442, 444   a consistent
  increase in the general level of prices

informational benefits, 238   special
  newsletters, periodicals, training programs,
  conferences, and other information provided
  to members of groups to entice others to join

information literacy, 200
infrastructure, 435

inherent powers, 344–46, 344   powers
  claimed by a president that are not expressed
  in the Constitution but are inferred from it

in-kind benefits, 444   noncash goods and
  services provided to needy individuals and
  families by the federal government

innovation, 369–70

inspectors general (IGs), 387   independent
  audit organizations located in most federal
  agencies

Instagram, 165, 188, 193
  See also social media

instant organization, 276
institutional presidency, 346–50, *347*
intelligence agencies, 336, 348, 465,
      476–77, 478
Intercept, The, 188

interest groups, 214, 232–46, 232
    individuals who organize to influence the
    government's programs and policies

    ambivalence about, 9
    bureaucracy and, 385
    congressional decision-making and,
        321–22, 324
    effectiveness of, 244–45
    environmental policy and, 479
    federal courts and, 244
    foreign policy and, 478–79, *479*
    government regulation and, 385, 390–91
    House vs. Senate and, 293–94
    iron triangles and, 242–43, *243*
    legislative scorecards, 322
    lobbying expenditures, 245
    for older Americans, 235, 245, 452
    selective benefits, 235, 238–39, *238*,
        245
    strategy overview, 240–49, *240*
    Supreme Court and, 416
    symbolic legislation and, 303
    types of, 232–35
    unrepresented interests, 239, 455, 457
intergovernmental cooperation. *See* cooperative
    federalism

intergovernmental relations, 63   the processes
    by which the three levels of American
    government (national, state, local) negotiate
    and compromise over policy responsibility

Interior, Department of the, 374
Internal Revenue Service (IRS), 359, 374
international comparisons
    bureaucracy, *372*
    Cabinet, 346
    democracy, 49, *49*
    election rules, 215–16, *217*, 263, 266
    federal courts, 409, *409*
    federalism, 63, 65, *65*
    foreign economic aid, *473*
    forms of government, 7
    freedom of the press, *103*
    gender equality, *135*
    internet, *186*
    legislative representation, *298*
    media regulation, 185, 207

political culture, 152
political parties, 215–16, *217*
presidency, *343*
tax policy, *433*
trust/distrust in government, *164*
voter turnout, *257*
International Court of Justice, 484

International Monetary Fund (IMF), 481
    an institution established in 1944 that
    provides loans and facilitates international
    monetary exchange

international monetary structure, 481
international peacekeeping efforts, 480
internet
    See also digital news; social media
    access to, *186*, 193, *207*
    Congressional representation and,
        299
    content regulation, 102, 104, 207
    creation of, 369–70
    international comparisons, *186*
    national security policy and, 465–66
    net neutrality and, *207*
    political participation and, 193, 256, 258,
        274, 353
    privacy and, 152, *186*
    public-opinion polls on, 171
    Tea Party movement and, 212
interracial marriage, 66, 131–32, *131*,
    141
interstate commerce, 72–73, *128*, 437
Interstate Commerce Act (1887), 437
Interstate Commerce Commission (ICC),
    128, 437
investigative hearings, 310, 325
investment, 438
Iowa, 268
Iran, 468, 472, 474, 478–79, 487
Iraq War, 277, 344, 354, 468, 483, 484

iron triangles, 242–43, 242, *243*   stable,
    cooperative relationships that often develop
    among a congressional committee, an
    administrative agency, and one or more
    supportive interest groups; not all of
    these relationships are triangular, but iron
    triangles are the most typical

IRS (Internal Revenue Service), 359, 374

isolationism, 466   avoidance of involvement
    in the affairs of other nations

Israel, 303, 478–79, 487

issue networks, 244, 413   loose networks of elected leaders, public officials, activists, and interest groups drawn together by specific policy issues

Iye, Mohamed, 462–63, *463*

J

Jackson, Andrew, 226, 228, 423, 436
Jackson, Henry M., 302–3
Jackson, Robert H., 419
Janus v. AFSCME, 394–95, *395, 417*
Japan, 466
Japanese American internment, 138–39, *138*
Jay, John, 47
Jefferson, Thomas
    on civil liberties, 90
    Declaration of Independence and, 33
    on freedom of religion, 96
    judicial review and, 407
    on monetary policies, 435–36
    political parties and, 226
    slavery and, 55
Jeffersonian Republicans (Antifederalists),
    47–48, **47**, *48*, 50–51, 64, 92, 226
Jewish Americans, 14, 223, 261–62, 303,
    478–79
    See also religion
Jim Crow era
    See also civil rights movement
    end of Reconstruction and, 123
    federalism and, 74, 77
    grants-in-aid and, 74
    political parties, 228
    voting restrictions, 256, 260, 419

Jim Crow laws, 123   laws enacted by southern states following Reconstruction that discriminated against African Americans
    See also Jim Crow era; segregation/ desegregation

job discrimination. *See* employment
Johnson, Andrew, 337
Johnson, Lyndon B., and administration, *128*,
    141, 230, 356
Johnson v. McIntosh, 139
Joint Chiefs of Staff, 374, 476

joint committees, 311   legislative committees formed of members of both the House and Senate

Jones, Doug, 283

journalism/journalists
    See also digital news; media
    adversarial, 206–7
    citizen journalism, 189, 195
    digital news and, 188, 189, 190
    influence of, 202
    traditional media and, 184–85

judicial activism, 422   judicial philosophy that posits that the Court should go beyond the words of the Constitution or a statute to consider the broader societal implications of its decisions

judicial branch, 43, 45
    See also federal courts; Supreme Court

judicial restraint, 421   judicial philosophy whose adherents refuse to go beyond the clear words of the Constitution in interpreting the document's meaning

judicial review, 43, 45, 407–8, 407, 410–11   the power of the courts to review actions of the legislative and executive branches and, if necessary, declare them invalid or unconstitutional; the Supreme Court asserted this power in *Marbury v. Madison* (1803)

judicial scrutiny, 97–98, 125, 141
Judiciary Act (1789), 408
Jungle, The (Sinclair), 437

jurisdiction, 400–401, 400, 411–12   the sphere of a court's power and authority

jury trial, right to, 94, *95*
Justice, Department of, 127–28, 129, 134

K

Kagan, Elena, 405, *406*
Kavanaugh, Brett, 316, 396, 405, 406, *406*
Kennedy, Anthony, 396, 406
Kennedy, John F., Jr., and administration, *128*,
    230, 352
Kerry, John, 474
Keynes, John Maynard, 439

Keynesians, 439, 440   followers of the economic theories of John Maynard Keynes, who argued that the government can stimulate the economy by increasing public spending or by cutting taxes

Keystone XL pipeline, 340
Kim Jong-un, *338*, 353, 468

King, Martin Luther, Jr., 126, 303
Korean War, 332, 344, 467, 484
Ku Klux Klan, 228
Kurds, 468
Kyoto Protocol, 488

L

labor relations, 438
 See also organized labor

laissez-faire capitalism, 18, 438–39, 438, 439
 an economic system in which the means of
 production and distribution are privately
 owned and operated for profit with minimal
 or no government interference

Land Ordinance (1785), 35
language minorities, 129, 139
Lanham Act (1946), 89
Lanza, Michael, 3
La Raza Unida, 136
Lasswell, Harold, 8
Latino/a Americans
 See also demographics; race; racial
   discrimination; voter demographics
 apportionment and, 304–5
 civil rights of, 136–37
 Congress and, *295,* 296, *297*
 economic inequality and, 452, 455, 457
 foreign policy and, 479, *479*
 health care and, 455
 political parties and, 222
 poverty and, 455–56, 457
 public opinion and, 161
 in U.S. population, 11, 12, 14, 161, 259,
   260, 305
 voter turnout, 259, 260–61
 voting rights of, 136
law. *See* federal courts; law enforcement;
   lawmaking; Supreme Court; *specific
   laws, e.g. Clean Air Act*
law clerks, 416
law enforcement
 See also criminal justice system
 civil rights movement and, *203*
 election of 2020 and, 196–97, 282
 executive orders and, 356
 Floyd murder and, 126, 160, 253, 281, 337
 judicial review and, 410
 Miranda rights, *95,* 109, *110*
 racial discrimination and, 126–27, 158,
   160–61
 reform proposals, 161, 196–97
 Secure Communities program, 80

lawmaking, 313–20
 See also budget process
 committee deliberation, 313, 315
 conference committees and, 311, 317, 319
 debate, 315–17
 federal courts and, 411
 interest groups and, 322
 new order, 313, 317–20
 overview, *314*
 presidency and, 317, 339–40
 voting, 316–17
Lawrence v. Texas, 114–15, 140
Lawson, April, 22–23
leadership PACs, 272
League of Conservation Voters, 322
League of United Latin American Citizens
   (LULAC), 136
League of Women Voters, 264–65
Lee, Richard Henry, 47
legal system, 397–402
 See also federal courts; judicial branch
legislative branch. *See* Congress
legislative hearings, 310

legislative initiatives, 339–40, 353   the
 president's inherent power to bring a
 legislative agenda before Congress

legislative scorecards, 322
"Letter from Birmingham Jail" (King), *128*
LGBTQ Americans
 See also same-sex marriage; sexual
   orientation
 civil rights, 114–15, 140–41, 421
 discrimination against, 115, 140

libel, 102, 104   a written statement made
 in "reckless disregard of the truth" that is
 considered damaging to a victim because it
 is "malicious, scandalous, and defamatory"

liberal governments, 7

liberals, 153–54, 153, 202, 279   today this
 term refers to those who generally support
 social and political reform, governmental
 intervention in the economy, more
 economic equality, expansion of federal
 social services, and greater concern for
 consumers and the environment
 See also political ideology

libertarians, 154–55, 154   those who
 emphasize freedom and believe in voluntary
 association with small government

liberty, 5, 7, 9, 17–18, *17*, 151–52, *151*, *152*
freedom from governmental control

Liberty Displaying the Arts and Sciences, 38
Library of Congress, 387
Libya, 345
   See also Benghazi investigation
Limbaugh, Rush, 192

limited government, 5, 7, 17, 50–51, *50*
a principle of constitutional government; a
government whose powers are defined and
limited by a constitution

Lincoln, Abraham, 228, 335, *335*, 358
linked fate, 158, 161
literacy tests, 129, 255, 260
   Little Rock school desegregation (1957),
      126, 128, 337, *337*
Livingston, Robert, 33

lobbying, 241–44, *241*   a strategy by which
organized interests seek to influence the
passage of legislation by exerting direct
pressure on government officials

   by business interests, 233–34, 242, *242*,
      246, 322
   by citizen groups, 235
   congressional decision-making and, 322
   costs of, 245
   government regulation of, 241, 245–76
local governments
   bureaucracy and, 382
   federalism and, 67, 70, 82, *83*
   number of, *67*
   political participation and, 68–69, *81*
   state-local tensions, 80, 82, *83*
   state power over, 67, 70
Locke, John, *8*
Louisiana, 123–24
Loving v. Virginia, 66, 131–32, *131*, 141
Lucy, Autherine, *128*

M
Madison, James, 37, 38, 47, 50–51, 215, 407
mail-in voting, 131, 282, *284*, 283–84

majority leader, 309, 318   the elected leader
of the majority party in the House of
Representatives or in the Senate; in the House,
the majority leader is subordinate in the party
hierarchy to the Speaker of the House

majority-minority districts, 308   electoral
districts, such as congressional districts,

in which the majority of the constituents
belong to racial or ethnic minorities

majority rule, minority rights, 21   the
democratic principle that a government
follows the preferences of the majority
of voters but protects the interests of the
minority

Malkin, Michelle, 212
Malloy v. Hogan, 95
Manafort, Paul, 325
manifest destiny, 466
Mapp v. Ohio, 95, 107–8
Mar-a-Lago, 242
Marbury v. Madison, 389, 407
March on Washington (1963), 126
marijuana, 80, *82*, 226
marketplace of ideas, 97
market power, 437
Markey, Edward, 291
marriage. *See* interracial marriage; same-sex
      marriage
Marshall, John, 42, 72, 407, 423
Marucci, Anthony, 376–77
Maryland v. King, 108
Massachusetts, 79
mass incarceration, 132
mass media. *See* media; social media
mass shootings, *105,* 107, 148–49, 157
Matal v. Tam, 88–90, *89*

material benefits, 238–39, *238*   special
goods, services, or money provided to
members of groups to entice others to join

McCain, John, 175
McClatchy corporation, 187
McConnell, Mitch, 299
*McCreary County v. American Civil Liberties
      Union of Kentucky,* 96
McCulloch v. Maryland, 72
*McCutcheon et al. v. Federal Election
      Commission,* 422
McDonald v. Chicago, 95, 106
McKinley, William, 229
McSally, Martha, 283
Meade, Desmond, 118–19, *119,* 132

means testing, 443   a procedure by which
potential beneficiaries of a social assistance
program establish their eligibility by
demonstrating a genuine need for the
assistance

media, 180–211, 183   print and digital forms of communication, including television, newspapers, radio, and the internet, intended to convey information to large audiences
See also digital news; fake news; internet; misinformation in media; social media

adversarial journalism, 206–7
advertising and, 185, 187, 188, 189, 190, 274
agenda setting by, 202–4
alarm vs. patrol modes, 203
campaign strategy and, 274–75
civil rights movement and, 126, 202, *203*
congressional elections and, 302
congressional oversight and, 386–87
evaluating, 198–99, *199*
framing by, 204
freedom of the press and, 183
government regulation of, 102, 104, 185, 187, 197, 207–8
importance to democracy, 182, 183, 206–7
influence of, 200, 202–5
journalism/journalists and, 184–85, 188, 189, 190, 202
leaks, 205, 206
net neutrality, *207*
newspapers, 189–91
news sources, 182, 187–88
ownership of, 185, 187, 188, 191, 202, 207–8
party identification and, 220
political ideology and, 200, 202
political participation and, 183–84, 256, 258
politicians' use of, 202
priming by, 204–5
profit motives in, 185, 187, 189, 204
public broadcasting, 185, 192
public opinion and, 151, 184
public policy and, 184, 202–3, 204
radio, 163, *163*, 185, 192, 206, 207, 352
recent transformation of, 187–89
roles of, 183–84, *184*, 195
sensationalism in, 185, 187, 203
streaming video, 192–93
television, 104, 191–92, 202, 207, 216, 218, 274
trust/distrust in, 200

media monopolies, 187, 207–8   ownership and control of the media by a few large corporations

Medicaid, 74, 374, 443, 444, 448, 449, 455   a federally and statefinanced, state-operated program providing medical services to low-income people

medical care. *See* health care
medical marijuana, 80, *82*

Medicare, 374, 440, 443, 448, 452   a form of national health insurance for the elderly and the disabled

memoranda, presidential, 358
men
    See also gender
    capital punishment and, 111
    economic inequality and, 451
    Republican Party and, 261
    voting rights, 20, *53*, 123, 253, 254, 256

merit system, 370, 380   a product of civil service reform, in which appointees to positions in public bureaucracies must objectively be deemed qualified for those positions

Mexican Americans, 136, 161, 222
    See also Latino/a Americans
Mexico, 14, 136, 137
    See also immigration policy
Michigan, 82
Microsoft, 188
micro-targeting, 275–76
middle/upper classes, 452, 454

midterm elections, 262   congressional elections that do not coincide with a presidential election; also called off-year elections
    See also congressional elections

military
    bureaucracy and, 373–74, 478
    civil rights and, *128*, 281, 337, *337*
    Congress and, 478
    defense industry, 465, 478
    Department of Defense and, 475–76
    deterrence and, 467
    innovation and, 369–70
    political parties and, 221
    presidential powers, 336–37, *337*, 344–45
    Reconstruction and, 123
    spending on, 281, 468, *469*, 478
    as tool for foreign policy, 482–84, *483*
    transgender Americans in, 134

militias, 105

Millennials, 155, 162, 224

See also age; young Americans; youth vote

minimum wage, *20*, 82, 168, 435, 438, 441

Minnesota, 78, 79

minorities. *See* race; *specific groups, e.g. Latino/a Americans*

minority leader, 309   the elected leader of the minority party in the House or Senate

Miranda, Ernesto, 109

Miranda rule, *95*, **109,** *110*   the requirement, articulated by the Supreme Court in Miranda v. Arizona, that persons under arrest must be informed prior to police interrogation of their rights to remain silent and to have the benefit of legal counsel

Miranda v. Arizona, 95, 109

misinformation in media, 165, 194, 196–97, 281, 353, *353*

See also fake news

mobilization, 276   the process by which large numbers of people are organized for a political activity

See also voter mobilization

Moms Demand Action for Gun Sense in America, 236–37, *237*

monetary policies, 374, 435–37, 435, *436*   efforts to regulate the economy through the manipulation of the supply of money and credit; America's most powerful institution in this area of monetary policy is the Federal Reserve Board

money, influence on politics of. *See* business interests; wealthy Americans, influence of

monopolies, 187, 207–8, 437   single firms in a market that control all the goods and services of that market; absence of competition

Monroe, James, 466

Monroe Doctrine, 466

Montgomery Bus Boycott, 126

Montreal Protocol, 488

Moonves, Les, 185

mootness, 412   a criterion used by courts to screen cases that no longer require resolution

Morel, Domingo, 68–69

Mormons, 14

mortgage lending, 127, 131, 451

Mosqueda, Teresa, 251

Mott, Lucretia, 122

MSNBC, 191, 197

Mueller, Robert, 196, 206, 324, 325, 339

multiple referral, 318–19, 318   the practice of referring a bill to more than one committee for consideration

multiracial people, 12

Mulvaney, Mick, 389

Murakami, Pat, 250–51

Murdoch, Rupert, 202

Muslim Americans, 14

See also religion

Muslim ban, 137, 345, *408*, 411, 462–64, *463*

mutually assured destruction (MAD), 467

N

NAACP (National Association for the Advancement of Colored People), 124, 125, 244, 260, 416

Nader, Ralph, 232

NAFTA (North American Free Trade Agreement), 470

NASA (National Aeronautics and Space Administration), *373*

National Association of Manufacturers

national conventions, 268

national debt, 434   the total amount of money the government has borrowed

National Defense Authorization Act (2019), 359

National Defense Education Act (1958), 446, 447

National Emergencies Act (1976), 345–46

National Federation of Independent Business, 233, 322

national government. *See* federal government; federalism

National Governors Association, 446

National Institutes of Health (NIH), 374, 448

National Origins quota system, 12

National Public Radio (NPR), 185, 192

National Restaurant Association

National Rifle Association (NRA), 233, 322, 324

National Right to Life Committee, 114, 322

national security adviser, 348, 474

National Security Agency (NSA), 336, 345, 476–77

National Security Council (NSC), 336, 348, 474 a presidential foreign policy advisory council composed of the president, the vice president, the secretary of state, the secretary of defense, and other officials invited by the president

national security policy, 465–68, *469*
See also foreign policy; military
bureaucracy and, 373–74
Department of Defense and, 475–76
executive branch and, 474
federal government power and, 83
foreign military assistance, 481
freedom of speech and, 98
intelligence agencies and, 336, 348, 465, 476–77, 478
military spending and, 280, 468, *469*, 478
national unity, 33, 43–44, 51, 63, 67, 278, 287

nation-states, 468 political entities consisting of a people with some common cultural experience (nation) who also share a common political authority (state), recognized by other sovereignties (nation-states)

Native Americans, 11, 12, 89–90, 139, 423
See also demographics; voter demographics
native digital news, 189, 190
NATO (North Atlantic Treaty Organization), 464, 482, 486
natural disasters, 354, 367, 471
Navarro, Peter, 333, *333*
NBC, 191
Near v. Minnesota, 95, 102

necessary and proper clause (elastic clause), 42, 50, **64,** 72 Article I, Section 8, of the Constitution, which provides Congress with the authority to make all laws "necessary and proper" to carry out its expressed powers

negative ads, 274
net neutrality, *207*
New Deal
federal government power and, 21, 70, 73–74, 230
government role in economy and, 439
grants-in-aid, 74
health care and, 448
housing policy and, 451
political parties and, 223, 230, 279
socioeconomic status and, 16
Supreme Court and, 420
Works Progress Administration, *73*

New Federalism, 78 attempts by Presidents Nixon and Reagan to return power to the states through block grants

New Hampshire, 268
Newhouse, Neil, 172–73

New Jersey Plan, 37 a framework for the Constitution, introduced by William Paterson, that called for equal state representation in the national legislature regardless of population

news aggregators, 193 applications or feeds that collect web content such as news headlines, blogs, podcasts, online videos, and more in one location for easy viewing

news media. *See* digital news; media
newspapers, 189–91, 192
New York Times, 188, 190, 191, 205, 206
New York Times Co. v. Sullivan, 102
New York Times Co. v. United States (Pentagon Papers case), 102
9/11. *See* September 11, 2001, terrorist attacks
Nineteenth Amendment, *53*, 123, 256
Nixon, Richard, and administration
See also Watergate scandal
devolution and, 78
pardon, 337
political parties and, *229*, 230
regulatory review and, 355
resignation, 348–49
southern strategy, *229*, 230
Vietnam War and, 202
No Child Left Behind Act (NCLB) (2001), 83, 446
nomination, 267–68
See also primary elections and caucuses

noncontributory programs, 443–44, *443, 445* social programs that provide assistance to people on the basis of demonstrated need rather than any contribution they have made

non-state actors, 465 groups other than nation-states that attempt to play a role in the international system; terrorist groups are one type of non-state actor

nonworking poor, 455
North American Free Trade Agreement (NAFTA), 470
North Atlantic Treaty Organization (NATO), 464, 482, 486

open primaries, 263 primary elections in which the voter can wait until the day of the primary to choose which party to enroll in to select candidates for the general election

open rule, 315 provision by the House Rules Committee that permits floor debate and the addition of new amendments to a bill

Operation Fast and Furious, 340
Operation Warp Speed, 281

opinions, 418–19, 418 written explanations of the Supreme Court's decisions in particular cases

opioid crisis, 290–92

oral argument, 418 the stage in the Supreme Court procedure in which attorneys for both sides appear before the Court to present their positions and answer questions posed by the justices

Oregon, 266, 337
organized labor, 73, 221, 234, *234*, 394–95

original jurisdiction, 400–401, 400, 403 the authority to initially consider a case; distinguished from appellate jurisdiction, which is the authority to hear appeals from a lower court's decision

OSHA (Occupational Safety and Health Administration), 368, 374, 378, 438
outsourcing. *See* privatization

oversight, 310, 325, 386–87, 386 the effort by Congress, through hearings, investigations, and other techniques, to exercise control over the activities of executive agencies

P
PACs (political action committees), 233, 272
Palko v. Connecticut, 93–94, 109
Papadopoulos, George, 325
pardons, 337
Paris Climate Accord (2015), 479, 488–89
Parkland school shooting (2018), 107, 148–49
Parks, Rosa, 126

partisanship, 215 identification with or support of a particular party or cause
See also party identification

party activists, 220, 279–80 partisans who contribute time, energy, and effort to support their party and its candidates

party discipline, 322–23, *323*

party identification, 220, *221*, 277 an individual voter's psychological ties to one party or another

party machines, 380

party organization, 216, *218* the formal structure of a political party, including its leadership, election committees, active members, and paid staff

party platforms, 268
party polarization, 224, 226
    budget process and, 320
    Congress and, 280, 311–12, 322–23, 324
    coronavirus pandemic and, 281
    digital news and, 197, 200
    economic policy and, 439
    election of 2020 and, 279–80, *279*, 284
    gerrymandering and, 324
    increase in, 219
    party activists and, 279
    party discipline and, 322–23
    personal nature of, 224
    political knowledge and, 166
    public opinion and, 162, 166
    public policy and, 218–19, 224, 226
    respectful debate and, 22
    Supreme Court appointments and, 395–96, 404, 405–6
party systems, 226, *227*, 228–31

party unity votes, 322, *323* roll-call votes in the House or Senate in which at least 50 percent of the members of one party take a particular position and are opposed by at least 50 percent of the members of the other party

Paterson, William, 37
Patient Protection and Affordable Care Act. *See* Affordable Care Act
pattern-of-cases strategy, 416
Paul, Rand, 154–55, 219
Paycheck Protection Program (2020), 371
    See also coronavirus stimulus legislation
peacekeeping efforts, 480
Pearl Harbor attack (1941), 466
Pell Grants, 447

Pence, Mike, 280, 385

Pendleton Civil Service Reform Act (1883), 380

penny press, 192 cheap, tabloid-style newspaper produced in the nineteenth century, when mass production of inexpensive newspapers first became possible due to the steam-powered printing press; a penny press newspaper cost one cent compared with other papers, which cost more than five cents

Pentagon Papers, 102, 205, 206

Perot, H. Ross, 231

Persian Gulf War, 344

pharmaceutical industry, 281, 385, 386

ping-ponging, 319

plaintiff, 397–98, 397 the individual or organization that brings a complaint in court

Planned Parenthood of Southeastern Pennsylvania v. Casey, 114

platforms, 268 party documents, written at national conventions, that contain party philosophy, principles, and positions on issues

plea bargains, 400 negotiated agreements in criminal cases in which a defendant agrees to plead guilty in return for the state's agreement to reduce the severity of the criminal charge or prison sentence the defendant is facing

Plessy v. Ferguson, 123–24, *124*

pluralism, 9, 239 the theory that all interests are and should be free to compete for influence in the government; the outcome of this competition is compromise and moderation

plurality systems, 215–16 systems in which, to win a seat in the parliament or other representative body, a candidate need only receive the most votes in the election, not necessarily a majority of the votes cast

Plyler v. Doe, 14

pocket veto, 317, 340, 360 a presidential veto that is automatically triggered if the president does not act on a given piece of legislation passed during the final 10 days of a legislative session

podcasting, 192

polarization. *See* party polarization

police behavior. *See* law enforcement

"police patrol" oversight, 386–87, 386 regular or even preemptive congressional hearings on bureaucratic agency operations

police power, 64, 66, *66* power reserved to the state government to regulate the health, safety, and morals of its citizens

policy czars, 385

policy feedback, 168

policy issues. *See* public policy

political action committees (PACs), 233, 272 private groups that raise and distribute funds for use in election campaigns

political appointees, 380–81, 380, 384, 474 the presidentially appointed layer of the bureaucracy on top of the civil service

political culture, 17–18, 17, 20–21 broadly shared values, beliefs, and attitudes about how the government should function; American political culture emphasizes the values of liberty, equality, and democracy

    Americans' views of government, 4, 5, 21, 24

    democracy and, 21

    equality, 18, 20–21

    international comparisons, 152

    liberty, 5, 9, 17–18, 151–52

political efficacy, 10 the belief that one can influence government and politics

political equality, 20 the right to participate in politics equally, based on the principle of "one person, one vote"
    See also civil rights; voting rights

political ideology, 151 a cohesive set of beliefs that forms a general philosophy about the role of government
    See also conservatives; party polarization

    media and, 200, 202

    political parties and, 221, 323

    public opinion and, 152–56, *155*

    social groups and, 162

    Supreme Court and, 422–23

political knowledge, 9–10, 9 information about the formal institutions of government, political actors, and political issues

    digital news and, 9–10, 166, 195–96, 197, 200

    limits of, 9–10

    media profit motive and, 185

    public opinion and, 165–67

social media and, 165, 166, 182, 193, 195, 197, 200

political parties, 212–32, *215* organized groups that attempt to influence the government by electing their members to important government offices

political power, 8 influence over a government's leadership, organization, or policies

political socialization, 156–58, 156, *157*, 220 the induction of individuals into the political culture; learning the underlying beliefs and values on which the political system is based

politics, 5 conflict over the leadership, structure, and policies of governments

popular sovereignty, 21 principle of democracy in which political authority rests ultimately in the hands of the people

pork barreling, 303 appropriations made by legislative bodies for local projects that are often not needed but that are created so that local representatives can win reelection in their home districts

precedents, 398, 418, 420 prior cases whose principles are used by judges as the basis for their decision in a present case

preemption, 76, 82 the principle that allows the national government to override state or local actions in certain policy areas; in foreign policy, the willingness to strike first in order to prevent an enemy attack

presidency, 332–63
    See also executive power expansion; presidential elections; *specific presidents, e.g. Obama, Barack, and administration*
    agency location and, 382
    approval ratings, *351*, 354
    broadcast media and, 163, *163*
    budget process and, 340, 348, 354–55, 435
    bureaucratic control and, 383–85, 387–89, 391
    Constitution on, 42–43, 335–36, 339–40, 341–42, 345, 360
    death in office, 349
    Defense Production Act and, 332–34
    executive agreements, 326, 338, 472, 477
    executive orders, 356, *357*, 358, *358*
    expressed powers of, 336–40, *341*
    foreign policy and, 42, 326, 338, *338*, 345, 472, 477, 480
    head of state role, 336, 350
    implied powers, 64, 72, 341–42, 345
    inherent powers, 344–46
    inspectors general and, 387
    institutional structure, 346–50, *347*, *378*
    international comparisons, *343*
    lawmaking and, 317, 339–40
    legislative initiatives, 339–40, 353
    lobbying and, 242
    media agenda setting and, 202
    policy czars and, 385
    political parties and, 349–50
    powers of, 42–43
    social media and, 163, 165, 194, 353, *353*
    take care clause and, 335, 342, 383
    term limits, 360
    transition into office, 381
    unitary executive theory, 342
    vesting clause, 335, 342
    veto power, 42, 45, 317, 340, *341*, 358
presidential appointments
    bureaucracy and, 381

bureaucratic control and, 384, 385
Cabinet, 346, 381
checks and balances and, 45
expressed powers and, 339
federal judges, 404, 423
Federal Reserve Board, 436
filibuster and, 316
recess, 360, 389, 411
Supreme Court, 280, 316, 395–96, 404, 405–6, *405*, *406*, 422–23
presidential elections, 267–69
    See also elections; electoral college; *specific elections, e.g.* election of 2016
    media agenda setting and, 203–4
    national party conventions, 268
    primary elections and caucuses, 263, 267–68, 280
    social media and, 189, 258
    steps in process, *271*
    vice presidency and, 348, *349*
    voter mobilization, 276–77
Presidential Succession Act (1947), 349
press, freedom of the, 93, *95*, 102, *103*, 104, 152, 183
Pressley, Ayanna, 219

preventive war, 466, 468, 472 a policy of striking first when a nation fears that a foreign foe is contemplating hostile action

primary elections, 263 elections held to select a party's candidate for the general election *See also* primary elections and caucuses

primary elections and caucuses
    election of 2020, *225*, 280
    media agenda setting and, 203–4
    national conventions and, 268
    open vs. closed primaries, 263
    party organizations and, 216
    political participation and, *24*
    public-opinion polls and, 176, 268
    timing of, 267–68
    voter mobilization and, 276
    voter turnout, *225*

priming (media), 204–5, 204 the process of making some criteria more important than others when evaluating a politician, problem, or issue

principal-agent problem, 371 a conflict in priorities between an actor and the representative authorized to act on the actor's behalf

prior restraint, 102   an effort by a governmental agency to block the publication of material it deems libelous or harmful in some other way; censorship; in the United States, the courts forbid prior restraint except under the most extraordinary circumstances

privacy, right to, *50*, 112, *113*, 114–15, 152, *186*, 422
private property, 18, 55, 64, 112

privatization, 383, 478   the process by which a formerly public service becomes a service provided by a private company but paid for by the government

privileges and immunities clause (comity clause), 43–44, 67   provision, from Article IV, Section 2, of the Constitution, that a state cannot discriminate against someone from another state or give its own residents special privileges

probability sample (simple random sample), 169–70, *169*
probable cause, 109
proclamations, presidential, 358
professional associations, 235
progressive caucus (Democratic Party), 219–20, 279, 280, 282
Progressive movement, 8, 231, 263

progressive taxation, 153, 432, 434   taxation that hits upper-income brackets more heavily

Prohibition, 52
property, private, 18, 55, 64, 112
proportional representation, 215–16, *217*
PROTECT Act, 104

protest, 253   participation that involves assembling crowds to confront a government or other official organization
See also Black Lives Matter; racial injustice protests (2020)

civil rights movement and, 126
electoral college and, 258
environmental policy and, *10*, 479
First Amendment and, 101, 253
immigration policy and, *137*, *421*
minimum wage and, *20*
net neutrality and, *207*
as political value, 152
racial injustice protests (2020), 158, 160–61, 196, 253, 281, 337

right to privacy and, *50*
Tea Party movement, 212–14, *213*, 231
third parties and, 231
Vietnam War and, *128*, 256
women's suffrage movement, 123, 256
Protestantism, 14
See also evangelicals; religion
public accommodations, 127
See also segregation/desegregation
public broadcasting, 185, 192
Public Broadcasting Service (PBS), 185
"public forum" assemblies, 101

public goods, 5, *6*   goods or services that are provided by the government because they either are not supplied by the market or are not supplied in sufficient quantities

public health, 167, 281, 282, 447–48
See also consumer protection; environmental policy
public housing, 450–51
public interest groups, 235

public opinion, 148–79, 151   citizens' attitudes about political issues, leaders, institutions, and events
See also public-opinion polls
on bureaucracy, *379*
on environmental policy, 168
expression of, *159*
on government regulation, 441
government responsiveness to, 167–68, *167*
on gun rights/gun control, 107, 148–50, 157
influence of wealthy Americans and, 168
legislative branch and, 41
media and, 151, 184
on minimum wage, 168, 441
political ideology and, 152–56, *155*
political knowledge and, 165–67
political leaders and, 163, *163*, 166
political parties and, 162
political socialization and, 156–58
political values and, 151–52, *153*
presidential approval ratings, *351*, 354
public policy and, 167–68
respectful debate and, 22–23
social groups and, 158, 160–63, *160*
social media and, 163, 182
on tax policy, 440

public-opinion polls, 169–76, 169 scientific
instruments for measuring public opinion

debates and, 218
evaluating, 172–73
inaccuracy in, 174–76, *175*
methods for, 169–71
primary elections and caucuses and,
176, 268

public policy a law, rule, statute, or edict
that expresses the government's goals and
provides for rewards and punishments to
promote those goals' attainment
See also lobbying; *specific policy issues, e.g.*
environmental policy

agreement on, 224, 226
campaign finance and, 168
congressional staff agencies and, 313, 315
election of 2020 and, 280–81
elections and, 277–78
federal courts and, 244
federalism and, 83
foreign policy and, 465
interest groups and, 232, 235
iron triangles and, 242–43, *243*
issue networks and, 244
media and, 184, 202–3, 204
party polarization and, 218–19, 224, 226
policy czars, 385
public opinion and, 167–68
representation and, 299
voter demographics and, 260, 261
public-sector unions, 234, 394–95

purposive benefits, 239 selective benefits
of group membership that emphasize the
purpose and accomplishments of the group

push polls, 175 a polling technique in which
the questions are designed to shape the
respondent's opinion

Putin, Vladimir, 468, 472, 475, *475*, 486
Puzder, Andrew, 384

Q

quota system for immigration, 12

R

race
See also demographics; voter demographics;
specific groups, e.g. African Americans
death penalty and, 111

economic inequality and, 451, 452, 455,
456–57
gerrymandering and, 308
political parties and, 222, *222*, 231
public opinion and, 158, 160–61, *160*
redistricting and, 308
social composition of Congress and, 260,
295, 296, *297*
social media use and, *194*
unemployment and, 456
in U.S. population, 11, 12–14
vice presidency and, 278, *349*
voter turnout and, 259–60
Race to the Top, 447
racial discrimination
See also Black Lives Matter; civil rights
movement; Jim Crow era; racial
injustice protests (2020); school
segregation/desegregation;
segregation/desegregation; voter
suppression
Asian Americans and, 138–39
cruel and unusual punishment and, 111
economic inequality and, 456–57
in employment, 129, 219
in housing, 127, 131, 136, 451
law enforcement and, 126–27, 158,
160–61
pattern-of-cases strategy and, 416
political participation and, 260
in public accommodations, 127
public opinion and, 158, 160–61
Reconstruction and, 77, 123, 402
reparations for, 279
racial injustice protests (2020), 253
election of 2020 and, 281
federal military force and, 281, 337
misinformation and, 196
public opinion and, 158, 160–61
radio, 163, *163*, 185, 192, 206, 207, 352
railroad system, 437
Ramos v. Louisiana, 95
Randolph, Edmund, 37

random digit dialing, 170 a polling method
in which respondents are selected at random
from a list of 10-digit telephone numbers,
with every effort made to avoid bias in the
construction of the sample

Reagan, Ronald, and administration
deregulation and, 230–31, 438
devolution and, 78

evangelicals and, 262
government role in economy and, 439
political socialization and, 157
Republican Party and, 230–31
Supreme Court appointments and, 422
tax policy and, 434
RealClearPolitics.com, 169, 173, 193
recess appointments, 360, 389, 411
Reconstruction, 8, 77, 123, 402
Reddit, 193, 258

redistribution, 432, 442   a policy whose
objective is to tax or spend in such a way as
to reduce the disparities of wealth between
the lowest and the highest income brackets

redistricting, 14, *305*, 305, 308, 324   the
process of redrawing election districts and
redistributing legislative representatives; this
happens every 10 years, to reflect shifts in
population or in response to legal challenges
in existing districts

redlining, 127, 451
red mirage/blue shift, 282
Reed, Stanley, 419

referendum, 8   the practice of referring a
proposed law passed by a legislature to
the vote of the electorate for approval or
rejection

Reform Party, 231
refugees, 137, 483
Regents of the University of California v. Bakke,
142
regional differences, 14, 162, 223–24, 269,
304–5, *485*
See also urban/rural divisions; voter
demographics

regressive taxation, 434   taxation that hits
lower-income brackets more heavily

regular concurrences, 419

regulated federalism, 75–76, 75   a form
of federalism in which Congress imposes
legislation on states and localities, requiring
them to meet national standards

regulation. *See* government regulation

regulatory capture, 390–91, 390   a form
of government failure in which regulatory
agencies become too sympathetic to interests
or businesses they are supposed to regulate

regulatory review, 355
Rehabilitation Act (1973), 139–40
Rehnquist, William, 422
Reid, Harry, 316
religion
See also voter demographics
civil rights movement and, 260, 261
evangelicals, 162, 223, 262, 478–79
freedom of, 94–97, *95*
immigration and, 14, 137
political parties and, 162, 223, 262
public opinion and, 162
Republican Party and, 162, 223, 230, 262
in U.S. population, 14
voter turnout and, 261–62
Religious Freedom Restoration Act (RFRA), 97
Reno v. American Civil Liberties Union, 104
reparations, 279
representation. *See* congressional representation;
descriptive representation

representative democracy (republic), 8
a system of government in which the populace
selects representatives, who play a significant
role in governmental decision-making

Republican National Committee (RNC), 216,
218
Republican Party
See also conservatives; political ideology;
political parties; *specific presidents, e.g.
Bush, George W., and administration*
Benghazi investigation and, 311, 316, 325
budget process and, 319, 320
campaign finance and, 98
congressional committee system and,
311–12
Consumer Financial Protection Board and,
388, 389
demographics and, 123, 162, 221, 223,
224, 230, 261, 262
devolution and, 78
divisions within, 219
economic policy and, 439, 440
election of 2020 results and, 282–83
environmental policy and, 488
evangelicals and, 162, 223, 262
evolution of, 228, 229
felon voting rights and, 132
filibuster and, 316
formation of, 228
gerrymandering and, 305
government regulation and, 76

Republican Party (*continued*)
  health care and, 321, 349–50, 449–50
  House conference, 309
  lawmaking and, 316
  minimum wage and, 441
  party discipline and, 323
  party identification, 220, *221*
  policy and, 219, 223
  policy issues and, 282
  race and, 221, 222
  Reconstruction and, 8, 123
  redistricting and, 305, 308
  religion and, 162, 223, 230, 262
  social issues and, 223, 230
  southern strategy, *229*, 230
  Supreme Court appointments and, 395,
    404, 405–6
  tax policy and, 167
  Tea Party movement and, 213–14, 231
  voter ID laws and, 131
  voter mobilization and, 276
  voting by mail and, 131, 282, 283–84
  White Americans and, 230, 259, 260
republics. *See* representative democracy
research, 369–70
reservations, 139

reserved powers, 64   powers, derived from the
  Tenth Amendment to the Constitution, that
  are not specifically delegated to the national
  government or denied to the states

respectful debate, 22–23
restrictive covenants, 127, 136, 451
Revolutionary War. *See* American Revolution
Rice, Condoleezza, 474

right of rebuttal, 208   a Federal
  Communications Commission regulation
  giving individuals the right to have the
  opportunity to respond to personal attacks
  made on a radio or television broadcast

right to bear arms. *See* gun rights

right to privacy, *50*, **112,** *113*, **114–15,** *116*,
  152, *186*, **422**   the right to be left alone,
  which has been interpreted by the Supreme
  Court to entail individual access to birth
  control and abortions

Riley v. California, 108, 410
Rio Treaty (1947), 482
Roberts, John, Jr., 100, 405, *406*, 420–21
Roberts, Owen, 420

Robinson v. California, 95
robocalls, 276
Roe v. Wade, 113, 114, 244, 412, 422
rogue states, 468

roll-call vote, 322   votes in which each
  legislator's yes or no vote is recorded as
  the clerk calls the names of the members
  alphabetically

rolling panel surveys, 175
Romney, Mitt, 174, 260, 327
Roosevelt, Eleanor, 350
Roosevelt, Franklin Delano, and administration
  See also New Deal
  bureaucracy and, 384
  fireside chats, 163, *163*, 206, 352
  first spouse and, 350
  inherent powers and, 344
  Japanese American internment and, 138–39
  legislative agenda setting power and, 340
  policy czars and, 385
  political parties and, 230, 277
  public appeals, 352
  State Department and, 474
  Supreme Court and, 420
  World War II and, 466
Roosevelt, Theodore, 206, 352, 468
Rubio, Marco, 479, *479*
Russia
  See also Russian election interference (2016)
  cyberattacks and, 465–66, 487
  formation of, 467
  NATO and, 482
  U.S. foreign policy and, 468, 472, 475, *475*,
    486–87
Russian election interference (2016)
  adversarial journalism and, 206
  congressional decision-making and, 324
  fake news and, 165, 196
  foreign policy and, 487
  hacking and, 267
  investigations of, 196, 206, 324, 325, 339
  Trump administration and, 206, 325,
    339, 468

S
Salwell, Eric, 302

same-day registration, 266   the option in
  some states to register on the day of the
  election, at the polling place, rather than in
  advance of the election

same-sex marriage

Defense of Marriage Act and, 28–29, 67
federalism and, 67
interest groups and, 244
Obergefell v. Hodges, 28–30, *29*, 67, 140–41, 244
party polarization and, 279

samples, 169–71, 169   small groups selected by researchers to represent the most important characteristics of entire populations

sampling error (margin of error), 170–71, 170   polling error that arises based on the small size of the sample

San Bernardino, California terrorism incident (2015), *50*
sanctuary cities, 80
Sanders, Bernie, 155, 220, 258, 268, 272, 280
Santelli, Rick, 213
Sasse, Benjamin, 219
Saudi Arabia, 487
savings-and-loan crisis (1980s), 391
Scalia, Antonin, 106, 395, 406, 418
Schattschneider, E. E., 239
Schenk, Maarten, 181
school prayer, 96, *96*
schools. *See* education; school segregation/ desegregation; school shootings
school segregation/desegregation
Asian Americans and, 138
Brown v. Board of Education, 124–25, 126, *128*, 141, 244
busing and, 128–29
Civil Rights Act (1964) and, 127–29
civil rights movement and, 125–26, *126, 128*
de jure vs. de facto, 125
federal military force and, *128*, 337, *337*
Latino/a Americans and, 136
southern resistance to, 125, 126, *126*
school shootings, 148–49
Scott, Dred, 121–22
Scott, Shaun, *251*
scrutiny, levels of, 97–98, 125, 141
searches and seizures, *95*, 107–8, 112, 410
Seattle Democracy Voucher Program, 250–52, *251*
Second Amendment, *95*, 104–7, *105, 106*, 148–50
Second Continental Congress, 33–34
Second Founding, 34–36
See also Constitutional Convention

Secret Service, 374
Secure Communities program, 80
Securities and Exchange Commission (SEC), 374, 378, 437–38
segregation/desegregation
See also Jim Crow era; school segregation/ desegregation
de jure vs. de facto, 125, 127
housing policy and, 131, 136, 451
interstate commerce and, *128*
ongoing, 260
political values and, 152
public accomodations and, 127
"separate but equal" rule and, 123–24, *124*

select committees, 311, 325   (usually) temporary legislative committees set up to highlight or investigate a particular issue or address an issue not within the jurisdiction of existing committees

selection bias, 169, 174–75, 174   polling error that arises when the sample is not representative of the population being studied, which creates errors in overrepresenting or underrepresenting some opinions

selective benefits, 235, 238–39, *238*, 245

selective incorporation, 93–94, 94, 95, 109, 111   the process by which different protections in the Bill of Rights were incorporated into the Fourteenth Amendment, thus guaranteeing citizens protection from state as well as national governments

self-incrimination clause, 109, *110*
Senate
advice and consent powers of, 326
Constitutional amendment process and, 51
Constitution on, 41
election of 2020 and, 278, 281, 282–83
federal court appointments and, 423
filibuster, 315–16, 319, 320, 404
foreign policy and, 42, 310, 472, 477–78
Great Compromise and, 37
vs. House of Representatives, 41, 293–94, *294*, 323
impeachment and, 205, 280, 326–27, 340, 350
party leadership in, 309, 318–19, 320
presidential appointments and, 45, 346, 360, 380, 381, 384
presidential succession and, 349
recess appointments and, 360, 411

socialists, 155 those who generally believe in social ownership, strong government, free markets, and a reduction in economic inequality

social liberalism, 153

social media, 193 web- and mobile-based technologies that are used to turn communication into interactive dialogue among organizations, communities, and individuals; social media technologies take on many different forms, including text, blogs, podcasts, photographs, streaming video, Facebook, and Twitter
See also misinformation in media

advertising and, 189
citizen journalism and, 195
Congress and, 299
congressional oversight and, 99, 181–82, 325
digital social networks and, 256, 258, 276
elections and, 189, 258, 260, 275, 353, *353*
fake news on, 180–82, *181*, 189, 196–97, *201*
hate speech on, *99*, 100
news on, 188–89, 193–94, *194*, 196–97
party identification and, 220
political knowledge and, 165, 166, 182, 193, 195, 197, 200
political participation and, 256, 258
political socialization and, 157
politicians' use of, 163, 194
presidency and, 163, 165, 194, 353, *353*
public opinion and, 163, 182
Russian election interference and, 165, 196
user demographics, 193–94, *194*
voter mobilization and, 258, 260, 275, 276
social policy, 428–30
constituencies for, 451–52, 454–57
contributory programs, 442–43, 452
coronavirus pandemic and, 428–29, *429*
deserving/undeserving concept and, 454, 455
education and, 83, 445–47
equality of opportunity and, 445
grants-in-aid and, 74, 80
Great Depression and, *442*
health care and, 447–50, *449*, *450*
housing and, 450–51
noncontributory programs, 443–44, *445*
political ideologies on, 154, 155
public health and, 447–48
state variations in, *445*
tax expenditures (shadow welfare state), 444, 451
welfare reform, 78, 79, 444, 455

Social Security, 431, 434, 440, 442–43, 442, 452 a contributory welfare program into which working Americans contribute a percentage of their wages and from which they receive cash benefits after retirement or if they become disabled

Social Security Act (1935), 442, 443, 457
Social Security Disability Insurance (SSDI), 443

socioeconomic status, 258 status in society based on level of education, income, and occupational prestige
See also demographics; economic inequality; poverty; voter demographics; wealthy Americans, influence of

campaign finance and, 250–52, *251*
colonial America, 31
education policy and, 447
political parties and, 221, 223
public opinion and, 162–63
social composition of Congress and, 296
social media use and, *194*
unrepresented interests and, 239
in U.S. population, 16
voter turnout and, 258, 260, 263
voting rights based on, 7, 20, 253
sociological representation. *See* descriptive representation
sodomy laws, 140
soft money, 272
soft news, 185
soft power, 470, 484

solicitor general, 414, 416 the top government lawyer in all cases before the Supreme Court where the government is a party

solidary benefits, 239 selective benefits of group membership that emphasize friendship, networking, and consciousnessraising

sophomore surge, 300
Sotomayor, Sonia, 405, *406*
sound bites, 191, 195
South
See also civil rights movement; regional differences
African American political participation, 130
economy of, 121
Jim Crow era, 74, 77, 123, 228, 256, 260, 419

South (*continued*)

    political parties and, 224, 226, 228, 229, *229*, 230

    states' rights and, 74, 77

    Three-Fifths Compromise and, 38–39, *38*

South Carolina, 280

Southeast Asia Treaty Organization (SEATO), 482

Southern Manifesto, 77

southern strategy, *229*, 230

Soviet Union

    Cold War and, 466–67

    collapse of, 467, 482

Speaker of the House, 309, 318 the chief presiding officer of the House of Representatives; the Speaker is the most important party and House leader and can influence the legislative agenda, the fate of individual pieces of legislatoinand members' positions within the House

special concurrences, 419

"speech plus," 101 speech accompanied by conduct such as sit-ins, picketing, and demonstrations; protection of this form of speech under the First Amendment is conditional, and restrictions imposed by state or local authorities are acceptable if properly balanced by considerations of public order

Spencer, Craig, 332–33

spoils system, 380

staff agencies, 312 legislative support agencies responsible for policy analysis

staff system (Congress), 312–13

Stamp Act (1765), 31

standing, 412 the right of an individual or organization to initiate a court case, on the basis of having a substantial stake in the outcome

standing committees, 310, 477 permanent committees with the power to propose and write legislation that covers particular subjects, such as finance or agriculture

Stanton, Elizabeth Cady, 122

stare decisis, 398

starving the beast, 440

State Children's Health Insurance Program (SCHIP), 449

State Department, 373, 474–75, 478

state of emergency declarations, 3–4, 340, 345

State of the Union address, 339–40

states

    See also battleground (swing) states and districts; federalism

    abortion and, *113*, 114

    in Articles of Confederation, 34

    ballot measures, 8

    Bill of Rights and, 93–94

    bureaucracies of, 382

    capital punishment provisions, 111

    Congressional representation, 37

    Constitutional amendment process and, 51

    coronavirus pandemic and, 281

    devolution and, 78–79

    education policy and, 445, 446

    electoral laws, 130–31, 260, 262–63, 266

    expressed powers and, 42

    federal military force and, 337

    grand juries and, 109

    gun control and, 77–78, 105, *106*

    health care and, 449

    Jim Crow era and, 75, 77

    judicial appointments, *415*

    judicial review and, 408, 410

    LGBTQ rights and, 114–15

    local governments and, 67

    obligations among, 66–67

    powers under federalism, 64, 66, *66*, 70

    professional associations and, 235

    reciprocity among, 43

    state-local tensions, 80, 82, *83*

    state of emergency declarations and, 3–4

    supremacy clause and, 44, 408, 410

    Supreme Court and, 43, 93–94

    unfunded mandates and, 79, 446

    voting rights and, *130*

    welfare programs and, 444, *445*

states' rights, 74, 77–78, 77 the principle that the states should oppose the increasing authority of the national government; this principle was most popular in the period before the Civil War

Steering and Policy Committee, 309

Stevens, John Paul, 104, 106

Stewart, Potter, 104

Steyer, Tom, 273

stimulus legislation, 21

    See also coronavirus stimulus legislation

stock market. *See* investment

Stone, Harlan F., 419

Stonewall riots (1969), 140
Strategic National Stockpile, 2–3, 4, 365–66
streaming video, 192–93
strict construction, 421

strict scrutiny, 97–98, 125, 141   a test used by
the Supreme Court in racial discrimination
cases and other cases involving civil liberties
and civil rights that places the burden of
proof on the government rather than on the
challengers to show that the law in question
is constitutional

student debt, 447, *453*
student speech, 99, 100, *101*

subsidies, 434–35, 434, 449   government
grantsof cash or other valuable
commodities, such as land, to an individual
or an organization; used to promote
activities desired by the government,
reward political support, or buy off political
opposition

**substantive representation, 48, 296–97,
296,** *297*   a type of representation in which
a representative is held accountable to a
constituency if he or she fails to represent
that constituency properly; this is incentive
for the representative to provide good
representation when his or her personal
background, views, and interests differ from
those of his or her constituency

suburban areas, 131, 221–22

suffrage, 254   the right to vote; also called *franchise*
See also voting rights; women's suffrage

Sugar Act (1764), 31
superdelegates, 268

**Super PACs (527 committees), 218, 273,
274, 303**   nonprofit independent political
action committees that may raise unlimited
sums of money from corporations, unions,
and individuals but are not permitted to
contribute to or coordinate directly with
parties or candidates

**Supplemental Nutrition Assistance Program
(SNAP), 444, 448, 454–55,** *454,* **646**   the
largest antipoverty program, which provides
recipients with a debit card for food at most
grocery stores; formerly known as food stamps

Supplemental Security Income (SSI), 443

supply-side economics, 440   an economic
theory that posits that reducing the marginal
rate of taxation will create a productive
economy by promoting levels of work
and investment that would otherwise be
discouraged by higher taxes

supremacy clause, 44, 50, 64, 408, 410
Article VI of the Constitution, which states
that laws passed by the national government
and all treaties are the supreme law of the
land and superior to all laws adopted by any
state or any subdivision

Supreme Court
See also specific cases, e.g. Dred Scott v. Sanford
on abortion, 113, 114, 244, 412, 421, 422,
423
access to, 411–14
on affirmative action, 142, 420, 423
on Affordable Care Act, 97, 407, 420, 422, 449
anti-terrorism and, 410–11
appeals to, 401
appointments to, 280, 316, 395–96, 404,
405–6, *405, 406,* 422
on Bill of Rights, 93–94
bureaucracy and, 410
on bureaucratic control, 389
on campaign finance, 98, 272, 274
caseload, 403
cases filed in, **413**
chief justice, 404
on comity clause, 67
on commerce clause, 71–72, 77–78
on commercial speech, 100–101
Constitution on, 43, 403
on cruel and unusual punishment, 111
on double jeopardy, 109
on drug testing, 108
on education, 447
on eminent domain, 93
on employment discrimination, 129
on executive privilege, 339
federal government power and, 72–73, 77–78
on freedom of religion, 96, 97
on freedom of speech, 89–90, 97–98, 99,
100–101
on freedom of the press, 102, 104, 205
on gender discrimination, 132, 134
on gun rights/gun control, 77–78, 105–6
on immigration policy, 14, 136, 137
influences on, 420–23
on inherent powers, 345
interest groups and, 416

Supreme Court (*continued*)
   interpretation of the Constitution,
      421–22, 423
   on interracial marriage, 66, 131, 132, 141
   on Japanese American internment, 138
   judicial restraint/activism, 421–22
   judicial review and, 43, 45, 389, 407–8,
      410–11
   jurisdiction of, 400–401, 403, 408, 410,
      411–12
   law clerks and, 416
   on law enforcement, 410
   on LGBTQ rights, 114–15, 140–41
   on medical marijuana, 80
   on Miranda rule, *95*, 109
   on Muslim ban, 345, 411, 463
   on New Deal, 420
   on obscenity, 104
   on organized labor, 73, 394–95
   on presidential orders, 358
   procedures, 416, *417*, 418–19
   racial discrimination and, 77, 126, 422
   on recess appointments, 360, 411
   on redistricting, 308
   on right to counsel, 110–11
   on right to privacy, 112, 113, 114–15
   on school segregation/desegregation,
      124–25, 126, 128–29, *128*, 141, 244
   on searches and seizures, 107–8, 112, 410
   on selective incorporation, 93–94, *95*, 111
   "separate but equal" rule and, 123–24
   on sexual harassment, 134
   size of, 404, 420, 423
   on slavery, 121–22
   solicitor general and, 414, 416
   on tribal sovereignty, 139
   on voting rights, 130, 131

supreme courts (general), 400 the highest
  courts in particular states or in the United
  States; these courts primarily serve an
  appellate function
  See also Supreme Court

surveillance, *50*, 83, 345, 476–77
surveys. *See* public-opinion polls
swing states and districts. *See* battleground
    (swing) states and districts
symbolic legislation, 303
Syria, 468, 472, 482, 486

T
take care clause, 335, 342, 383
takings clause, 112

talk radio, 192, 197
TANF (Temporary Assistance for Needy
    Families), 444, *445*, 455, 457

tariffs, 431, 470, 488 taxes on imported
goods
  See also trade policy

Tax Cuts and Jobs Act (2017), 454
tax expenditures (shadow welfare state), 444,
    451
tax policy, 431–32
   Affordable Care Act and, 359
   agreement on, 226
   American Revolution and, 31, 32–33
   congressional standing committees on, 310
   election of 2020 and, 280, 281
   excise taxes, 431
   goals of, 432, 434
   government role in economy and, 439–40
   influence of wealthy Americans and, 168,
      281, 434
   international comparisons, *433*
   lawmaking and, 318, 319
   media and, 204
   middle/upper classes and, 452, 454
   political ideologies on, 153
   political knowledge and, 167
   preemption and, 76
   presidential agenda setting power and, 340
   progressive vs. regressive taxation, 432
   shadow welfare state (tax expenditures),
      444, 451
   Super PACs and, 218
   tax expenditures, 444, 451
   Tea Party movement and
   trust/distrust in government and, 24
   types of tax, *432*
   voter demographics and, 260
Tea Act (1773), 32–33
Tea Party movement, 212–14, *213*, 231
Telecommunications Act (1996), 104, 187, 207–8
television, 104, 191–92, 202, 207, 216, 218, 274
Temporary Assistance for Needy Families
    (TANF), 444, *445*, 455, 457
Tenth Amendment, 42, 64, 77–78, 92
terrorism, *50*, 465, 467–68
   See also anti-terrorism; September 11, 2001,
      terrorist attacks
Texas
   abortion laws, 114
   capital punishment, 111
   environmental policy, 82
   health care, 455

segregation, 124, 136
welfare reform, 79
Third Amendment, 94, 112

third parties, 231–32, 231, *232*   parties that organize to compete against the two major American political parties

Thirteenth Amendment, 70, 122   one of three Civil War amendments; it abolished slavery

Thomas, Clarence, 405, *406*, 418

Three-Fifths Compromise, 38–39, 39   the agreement reached at the Constitutional Convention of 1787 that stipulated that for purposes of the apportionment of congressional seats only three-fifths of slaves would be counted

Tillerson, Rex, 474
Timbs v. Indiana, 95, 111
Title IX (Education Act of 1972), 134, 136
Tlaib, Rashida, 219
tolerance. *See* party polarization
torts cases, 398
torture. *See* anti-terrorism

totalitarian governments, 7   a system of rule in which the government recognizes no formal limits on its power and seeks to absorb or eliminate other social institutions that might challenge it

trade associations, 234, 235, 272
trade policy, 468–69
    arbitration and, 484
    current issues, 487–88
    divisions within Republican Party and, 219
    free trade and, 469
    intellectual property and, 486
    interest groups and, 478
    political ideologies on, 154
    regional differences, *485*
traditional media
    See also broadcast media
    journalism and, 184–85
    newspapers, 189–91, 192
    ownership of, 185, 187, 189
traditional system, 70, *71*
transgender Americans, 82, *83,* 115, 134, 355, 421
    See also LGBTQ Americans
Trans-Pacific Partnership Agreement (TPP), 488

transportation. *See* infrastructure
Transportation, Department of, 374, 386
Transportation Security Administration, 386
Treasury, Department of, 374
treaties, 42, 326, 472
Treaty of Guadalupe Hidalgo (1848), 136

trial court, 400   the first court to hear a criminal or civil case

tribal reservations, 139
Truman, Harry S., and administration, *175,* 344
Trump, Donald, and administration
    See also coronavirus pandemic; Russian election interference (2016); Trump administration foreign policy; Trump impeachment
    abortion and, 113
    adversarial journalism and, 206
    approval ratings, *351, 354*
    battleground states and, 282
    budget process and, 340
    bureaucracy and, 381–82
    bureaucratic control and, 387
    business interests and, 381
    campaign finance and, 272
    census and, 339
    Consumer Financial Protection Board and, 389
    debates and, 218
    Democratic Party and, 231
    divisions within Republican Party and, 219
    electoral college and, 258, 272
    environmental policy and, 355, 368–69, *369,* 479, 488–89
    evangelicals and, 262
    executive orders and, 356
    executive privilege and, 339
    fake news accusations by, 102, 200
    filibuster and, 316
    free media and, 275
    gender gap and, 161, 223
    government regulation and, 76, 438
    gun control and, 149
    health care and, 280–81, 321, 359
    immigration policy, 80, 137, 219, 261, 280, 355
    integrity and, 278
    Latino/a Americans and, 261
    lobbying and, 242, *242*
    media framing and, 204
    misinformation and, 60, 165, 194, 196–97, 281, *353*

unemployment insurance, 368, 443
UN Framework Convention on Climate
       Change, 488

unfunded mandates, 79, 446 laws or
   regulations requiring a state or local
   government to perform certain actions
   without providing funding for fulfilling
   the requirement

UN General Assembly, 480
Unified Combatant Commands, 374
unions. *See* organized labor
unitary executive theory, 342

unitary systems, 63, 65, *65* centralized
   government systems in which lower levels of
   government have little power independent
   of the national government

United Nations (UN), 480–81, *480* an
   organization of nations founded in 1945 to
   be a channel for negotiation and a means of
   settling international disputes peaceably

**United States–Mexico–Canada Agreement
   (USMCA), 470** trade treaty between
   the United States, Canada, and Mexico to
   lower and eliminate tariffs among the three
   countries

United States v. Jones, 108
United States v. Lopez, 77–78
United States v. Nixon, 339
*United States v. Playboy Entertainment
       Group,* 104
United States v. Wong Kim Ark, 138
universities. *See* higher education
UN Security Council, 480–81
upper classes. *See* middle/upper classes; wealthy
       Americans, influence of
urbanization, 14
   See also urban/rural divisions
urban/rural divisions
   monetary policy and, 435–36
   party polarization and, 162
   political parties and, 221, 323
   redistricting and, 17, 305
   regional differences and, 223, 224
USAJobs, 376, *377*
USA PATRIOT Act (2001), 83
U.S. Chamber of Commerce, 233
U.S. Foreign Service, 474
U.S. Patent and Trademark Office, 89
U.S. Public Health Service, 448

V
values (beliefs), 5, 7, 151–52, 151, *153* basic
   principles that shape a person's opinions
   about political issues and events
   See also political culture

Van Orden v. Perry, 96
venue shopping, 83
vesting clause, 335, 342
Veteran Affairs, Department of, 367, 390
Veterans Health Administration (VHA), 390

veto, 42, 45, 317, 340, *341,* **358, 500** the
   president's constitutional power to turn
   down acts of Congress; a presidential veto
   may be overridden by a two-thirds vote of
   each house of Congress

vice presidency, 278, 280, 348–49, *349*
Vietnam War
   adversarial journalism and, 206
   Cold War and, 467
   Democratic Party and, 230
   freedom of the press and, 102
   media and, 202
   media leaks and, 205, 206
   political repercussions of, 484
   protest and, *128,* 256
   voting rights and, 256

Virginia Plan, 37 framework for the
   Constitution, introduced by Edmund
   Randolph, that called for representation in the
   national legislature based on the population
   of each state

Volkswagen, 369
voter demographics
   economic policy and, 260
   election of 2012, 260
   election of 2016, 222, 224, 258, 259, 260,
       261, 262
   election of 2018, *19,* 222, 259, 260, 261
   election of 2020, 161, 222, *222,* 223, 224,
       259, 260, 261, 280, 284–86
   political parties and, 123, 162, 220,
       221–24, *222,* 230, 231, 261, 262
   public policy and, 260, 261
   turnout and, *19,* 258–62
voter fraud, 131
voter ID laws, 130, 266
voter mobilization, 258, 273–74, *275,*
       276–77, 286
voter registration, 252, *262,* 263, 264, *265,* 266
voter suppression, 119–20, 130–31, 136, 266

voter turnout
See also voter mobilization; youth vote
campaign finance and, 251
demographics and, *19*, 258–62
early America, 255
election of 2014, *19*
election of 2016, 260
election of 2018, *19*
election of 2020, 282, 286
international comparisons, *257*
primary elections and caucuses, *225*
state electoral laws and, 262–63, 266
trends in, *255*
welfare programs and, 452
voting
See also voter mobilization; voter
suppression; voting rights
early, *267*, 282
how to register and vote, 264–65, *265*
ranked choice
state electoral laws, 130–31, 262–63,
266
voter decisions, 277–78
voter ID laws, 130–31, 266
voter registration, 252, *262*, 263, 264,
265, 266
voter suppression, 119–20, 130–31,
136, 266
voting by mail, 131, 282, *284*,
283–84
voting rights, 254–56
See also African American voting rights;
women's suffrage
age and, 256, *262*
felons, 118–19, *119*, 132
immigrants, 255
language minorities, 129, 139
Latino/a Americans, 136
original restrictions on, 7, 20, 254–55
political parties and, 229
as political value, 152
young Americans, *53*
Voting Rights Act (VRA) (1965), 256,
262
Democratic Party and, 230
impact of, 130, *130*
1970 and 1975 amendments, 139
on preclearance, 130
protest and, *128*
provisions of, 129
redistricting and, 308
vouchers, 447, 451
VRA. *See* Voting Rights Act

W
Wagner-Steagall National Housing Act (1937), 450
Wallace, George, *128*
Wall Street Journal, 188, 190, 205
war, declaration of, 344–45, 472–73, 477
War of 1812, 226
war on drugs, 132
War on Poverty, 74, *128*
War Powers Resolution (1973), 345, 477
Warren, Earl, 109, 404, 422
Warren, Elizabeth, 280, 388–89, *388*
Washington, George, 36, 215, 371, 466
Washington Post, 188, 189, 191, 196, 205, 206
Washington Redskins football team, 89–90
Washington State, 127, 302–3
watchdog role of the media, 184, *184*, 195
Watergate scandal (1972), 206, 311, 339, 348–49
Watts, Shannon, 236–37
wealth inequality. *See* economic inequality
wealthy Americans, influence of
See also business interests
American Revolution and, 31–32
campaign finance and, 98, 250, 273
*Citizens United v. Federal Election
Commission* and, 98
congressional representation and, 168
Founding and, 7, 35, 36–37, 39
Gilded Age and, 16
interest groups and, 239
public opinion and, 168
tax policy and, 168, 281, 434
web surfing, 195–96

welfare state, 441–44, 441, *445* the collection
of policies a nation has to promote and
protect the economic and social well-being
of its citizens
See also social policy

bureaucracy and, 374
contributory programs, 442–43, 452
election of 2020 and, 281
noncontributory programs, 443–44, *445*
public opinion on, 171
state variations in, 444, *445*
tax expenditures, 444, 451
welfare reform, 78, 79, 444, 455
West Virginia, 303
*West Virginia State Board of Education v.
Barnette,* 97
westward expansion, 33, 35
WhatsApp, 188
Wheeler-Howard Law (1934), 139
Whig Party, 228

whip, 309 a party member in the House or Senate responsible for coordinating the party's legislative strategy, building support for key issues, and counting votes

Whistleblower Protection Act (1989), 389

whistleblowers, 195, 205, 389 federal employees who report wrongdoing in federal agencies

White Americans
    See also race
    citizenship, 12
    economic inequality and, 451, 457
    evangelicals, 162, 262
    immigration and, 12
    political parties and, 221, 222, 223
    poverty and, 456, 457
    public opinion and, 158, *160*
    redistricting and, 308
    Republican Party and, 230, 259, 260
    in U.S. population, 11–12
    voter turnout, 260, 261
    voting rights, 7, 20, *53*, 253
White House Communications Office, 352–53
Whitehouse.gov, 353

White House staff, 347 analysts and advisers to the president, each of whom is often given the title "special assistant"

Whitmar, Bill, 60–61
Wilson, James, 38
Wilson, Woodrow, and administration, 123, 206, 352, 466
"winner take all" systems, 215–16, 269
women
    See also gender; women's rights movement; women's suffrage
    Democratic Party and, 223
    discrimination against, 127, 132, *133*, 134, *135*
    economic global equality, *135*
    in electoral office, *133*, 223, 296, *297*, *298*
    poverty and, 457
    sexual harassment and, 134, 136
women's rights movement, 122, 244
women's suffrage
    denial of, 121, 123
    Nineteenth Amendment and, *53*, 123, 256
    Progressive movement and, 8
    protest and, 123, 256
    separate sphere and, 121

Woods, C. Shonda, 428, 429
working poor, 454–55
workplace. *See* employment
Works Progress Administration (WPA), *73*
World Bank, 481

World Trade Organization (WTO), 470 international organization promoting free trade that grew out of the General Agreement on Tariffs and Trade

World War I, 98, 466, 481
World War II
    bureaucracy and, 383
    foreign policy and, 466–67
    immigration policy and, 12, 138
    inherent powers and, 344, 345
    international monetary structure and, 481
    Japanese American internment, 138–39, *138*
WPA (Works Progress Administration), *73*
writ of appeal, 414
writ of certification, 414

writs of certiorari, 412–14, 412, 416 a decision of at least four of the nine Supreme Court justices to review a decision of a lower court; certiorari is Latin, meaning "to make more certain"

writs of habeas corpus. *See* habeas corpus

Y
young Americans
    See also age; youth vote
    digital news and, 192
    political participation, *19*, *24*, 193, 259
    political parties and, 220, 221, 224
    public opinion and, 162–63
    social media use, *194*
    in U.S. population, 14
    voting rights, *53*
youth vote
    election of 2016, 224, 259
    election of 2018, *19*
    election of 2020, 284–86
    social media and, 193
    voter registration and, 263, 266
    voting by mail and, 131
YouTube, 188, 189, 194, *194*, 256

Z
Zelensky, Volodymyr, 205, 475
    See also Ukraine scandal
Zuckerberg, Mark, *99*, 181, 189

Voter Registration Information

State	Registration Deadline before Election	Early Voting Permitted?	Identification Required to Vote?*	More Information
Alabama	15 days	No	Photo ID required	alabamavotes.gov
Alaska	30 days	Yes	ID requested; photo not required	elections.alaska.gov
Arizona	20 days**	Yes	ID required; photo not required	azsos.gov/elections
Arkansas	30 days	Yes	Photo ID required	sos.arkansas.gov
California	15 days; Election-Day registration permitted	Yes	No	sos.ca.gov
Colorado	8 days by mail or online; no in-person deadline	Yes (all voting by mail)	ID requested; photo not required	sos.state.co.us
Connecticut	7 days by mail or online; no in-person deadline	No	ID required; photo not required	portal.ct.gov/sots
Delaware	Fourth Saturday prior to election	No	ID requested; photo not required	elections.delaware.gov
District of Columbia	21 days by mail or online; no in-person deadline	Yes	No	dcboee.org
Florida	28 days**	Yes	Photo ID requested	dos.myflorida.com/elections
Georgia	28 days	Yes	Photo ID required	sos.ga.gov
Hawaii	30 days; no in-person deadline	Yes (all voting by mail)	Photo ID requested	hawaii.gov/elections
Idaho	25 days; Election-Day registration permitted	Yes	Photo ID requested	idahovotes.gov
Illinois	28 days by mail; 16 days online; no in-person deadline	Yes	No	elections.il.gov
Indiana	29 days	Yes	Photo ID required	in.gov/sos/elections
Iowa	10 days; Election-Day registration permitted	Yes	Photo ID required	sos.iowa.gov
Kansas	21 days	Yes	Photo ID required	kssos.org
Kentucky	29 days	Yes	Photo ID required	elect.ky.gov
Louisiana	30 days; 20 days online	Yes	Photo ID required	sos.la.gov
Maine	15 days by mail**; no in-person deadline	Yes	No	maine.gov/sos
Maryland	21 days	Yes	No	elections.state.md.us
Massachusetts	10 days**	No	Photo ID requested	sec.state.ma.us
Michigan	15 days online or by mail; no in-person deadline	No	Photo ID required	michigan.gov/sos
Minnesota	21 days; Election-Day registration permitted	Yes	No	mnvotes.org
Mississippi	30 days	No	Photo ID required	sos.ms.gov
Missouri	Fourth Wednesday prior to election	No	ID requested; photo not required	sos.mo.gov
Montana	37 days by mail**; no in-person deadline	Yes	ID requested; photo not required	sos.mt.gov
Nebraska	Third Friday prior to election by mail; second Friday prior to election in person; 10 days online	Yes	No	sos.nebraska.gov
Nevada	28 days by mail; 21 days in person; 19 days online	Yes	No	nvsos.gov
New Hampshire	6–13 days before the election, varies by county; Election-Day registration permitted	No	ID requested; photo not required	sos.nh.gov